Ubuntu

22.04
LTS
Desktop

Applications
and
Administration

To Marylou and George

Ubuntu 22.04 LTS Desktop: Applications and Administration

Richard Petersen

Surfing Turtle Press

Alameda, CA

www.surfingturtlepress.com

Please send inquiries to: editor@surfingturtlepress.com

ISBN-13   978-1-949857-25-2

Preface

This book covers the Ubuntu 22.04 LTS (Jammy Jellyfish) release, focusing on applications and administrative tools. The emphasis here is on what users will face when using Ubuntu, covering topics like installation, applications, software management, the Ubuntu desktops (GNOME, MATE, and KDE), shell commands, network connections, and system administration tasks. Ubuntu 22.04 LTS introduces several new features, as well as numerous smaller modifications. It is a long-term support release. The Ubuntu desktop, which uses GNOME, is examined in detail, along with Snap and APT package management.

The Ubuntu desktop uses a Dock and an Activities overview to manage access to applications and devices. In addition, Ubuntu 22.04 LTS desktop is based on GNOME 42, with several desktop configuration tools and the Settings dialog. In addition, features such as workspaces, extensions, and the GNOME Files file manager, are covered. The Kubuntu desktop, which uses KDE, provides a different interface using plasma containers to support panels, menus, activities, configuration tools, and widgets. Ubuntu MATE is based on the traditional GNOME 2 desktop, buy with alternative menus, panel layouts, and a dock.

Part 1 focuses on getting started, covering Ubuntu information and resources, using Ubuntu Live USB/DVD drives, installing and setting up Ubuntu, upgrading Ubuntu, basic use of the desktop interface, and connecting to wired and wireless networks. Repositories and their use are covered in detail, along with the Snap system for managing Snap packages. Ubuntu Snap package management with Ubuntu Software, the **snap** command, the Snap Store are examined, as well as APT package management with Gnome Software, the Synaptic Package Manager, and the **apt** and **apt-get** commands.

Part 2 focuses in on office, multimedia, mail, Internet, and social media applications such as the Evolution and Thunderbird email applications, the Videos media player, the Rhythmbox music player, and the LibreOffice office suite. The section includes coverage of the PulseAudio sound interface, Firefox Web browser, and VoIP applications like Skype.

Part 3 covers the Ubuntu, Kubuntu, Ubuntu MATE, Xubuntu, and Lubuntu desktops. as well as the BASH shell. The Ubuntu desktop with the GNOME desktop features a Dock, Activities overview, Applications overview, and system area menu. The Kubuntu desktop is examined which is based on the KDE desktop with features such as widgets, activities, panels, menus, desktop effects, and the Discover software manager. Ubuntu MATE provides an the traditional GNOME 2 panels, but with alternative menus and panel layouts. It also provides a dock. All the desktops are different, but all access and install software from the Ubuntu APT software repositories and the Ubuntu Snap Store. All are also official Ubuntu Flavours, different desktops but the same compatible software, most of which can run on any of the flavours. The BASH shell interface is also explored, with its command editing, folder navigation, and file operations.

Part 4 deals with administration topics, first discussing system tools like the GNOME system monitor, the Disk Usage Analyzer, Seahorse, and Disk Utility. Then a detailed chapter on Ubuntu system administration tools is presented, covering tasks such as managing users and file systems, Bluetooth setup, network folder sharing, backups, and printing. The network connections chapter covers a variety of network tasks, including manual configuration of wired and wireless connections, and firewalls (the Gufw and FirewallD).

Overview

Part 3: Desktops

Part 4: Administration

Contents

Part 1: Getting Started

Part 2: Applications

Part 3: Desktops

10. Ubuntu MATE...371

Part 4: Administration

13. System Tools 485

15. Network Connections...565

Part 1: Getting Started

Introduction
Installation
Usage Basics
Managing Software

ubuntu

1. Ubuntu 22.04 LTS Introduction

Ubuntu Releases

Ubuntu 22.04 LTS

Ubuntu Release

Ubuntu Flavours

Ubuntu Live DVD and USB

Ubuntu Software

Ubuntu Help and Documentation

Open Source Software

History of Linux and UNIX

Ubuntu Linux is currently one of the most popular end-user Linux distributions (**https://ubuntu.com**). Ubuntu Linux is managed by the Ubuntu foundation, which is sponsored by Canonical, Ltd (**https://canonical.com**), a commercial organization that supports and promotes open source projects. Ubuntu is based on Debian Linux, one of the oldest Linux distributions, which is dedicated to incorporating cutting-edge developments and features (**https://www.debian.org**). Mark Shuttleworth, a South African and Debian Linux developer, initiated the Ubuntu project. Debian Linux is primarily a Linux development project, trying out new features. Ubuntu provides a Debian-based Linux distribution that is stable, reliable, and easy to use.

Ubuntu is designed as a Linux operating system that can be used easily by everyone. The name Ubuntu means "humanity to others." As the Ubuntu project describes it: "Ubuntu is an African word meaning 'Humanity to others", or "I am what I am because of who we all are." The Ubuntu distribution brings the spirit of Ubuntu to the software world."

The official Ubuntu philosophy lists the following principles.

1.   Every computer user should have the freedom to download, run, copy, distribute study, share, change, and improve their software for any purpose, without paying licensing fees.

2.   Every computer user should be able to use their software in the language of their choice.

3.   Every computer user should be given every opportunity to use software, even if they work under a disability.

The emphasis on language reflects Ubuntu's international scope. It is meant to be a global distribution that does not focus on any single market. Language support has been integrated into Linux in general by its internationalization projects, denoted by the term i18n.

Making software available to all users involves both full accessibility supports for users with disabilities as well as seamless integration of software access using online repositories, making massive amounts of software available to all users at the touch of a button. Ubuntu also makes full use of Linux's automatic device detection ability, greatly simplifying installation as well as access to removable devices and attached storage.

Ubuntu aims to provide a fully supported and reliable, open source and free, easy to use and modify, Linux operating system. Ubuntu makes the following promises about its distribution.

Ubuntu will always be free of charge, including enterprise releases and security updates.

Ubuntu comes with full commercial support from Canonical and hundreds of companies around the world.

Ubuntu includes the very best translations and accessibility infrastructure that the free software community has to offer.

Ubuntu DVDs contain only free software applications; we encourage you to use free and open source software, improve it and pass it on (Ubuntu repositories contain some proprietary software like vendor graphics drivers that is also free).

Ubuntu 22.04 LTS

Ubuntu 22.04 LTS introduces several new features, as well as numerous smaller modifications. It is a long-term support release based on the Linux 5.0 kernel. The Ubuntu repositories support several major desktops, including the Ubuntu Desktop (GNOME), Kubuntu (KDE), and Ubuntu MATE. You can think of Ubuntu as a multi-desktop system, where the same repositories support different desktops. The Ubuntu Desktop features the GNOME user interface with a Dock, dash, and system area menu. Referred to as simply the Ubuntu desktop, GNOME is the default desktop (see Figure 1-1). It is based on GNOME 4.2.

Figure 1-1: Ubuntu 22.04 LTS Ubuntu Desktop

For documentation check:

```
https://help.ubuntu.com/
```

Check the Ubuntu Release Notes for an explanation of changes.

```
https://wiki.ubuntu.com/JammyJellyfish/ReleaseNotes
```

For basic tutorials of Ubuntu tasks such as installation and setting up Samba, see the Ubuntu tutorials site.

```
https://ubuntu.com/tutorials/
```

Ubuntu 22.04 LTS also features a minimal install. Only the Web browser and a few utilities are installed, instead of a full set of applications (see Figure 1-2). There is no Utilities application folder in the applications overview. You can choose the minimal installation options during the Installation processes on the "Updates and other software" screen. Under the heading "What apps would you like to start with?", there are two options: Normal Installation and Minimal Installation. The Normal Installation option is selected by default. For minimal, choose the Minimal Installation option.

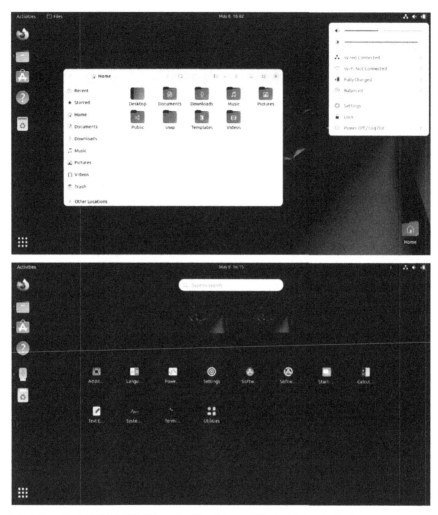

Figure 1-2: Ubuntu 22.04 LTS Ubuntu Desktop, Minimal Installation

Ubuntu 22.04 LTS Key Changes

Several key changes have been made for the 22.04 LTS release.

During installation from a USB/DVD Ubuntu session (Try Ubuntu option) you have the option to create a recovery key you can use to unlock an encrypted system, should you forget your security key. Be sure to copy to recovery key from your install system to a USB or remote file system before you end your USB/DVD session.

On the System Settings Appearance dialog you can configure your desktop appearance, your desktop icons, and configure the dock. For the desktop, you can choose from several accent colors, as well as the light and dark themes. Light is the default. You can adjust the size and positions of icons. The dock can be positioned on any side, its icon sizes adjusted, and the dock size adjusted to the number of its icons. You can choose not to display unmounted and network volumes.

The system status area menu has a power mode selection: Power Saver, Balanced, and Performance.

Faster and smoother desktop performance due to underlying bug fixes and efficiency modifications.

Ubuntu uses GNOME 42, which implements dynamic triple buffering when needed by your display.

Ubuntu retains several applications from GNOME 41, such as Gedit and GNOME terminal.

Ubuntu Settings has a Multi-tasking dialog where you can configure various features such as the Activities Hot Corner, the Workspace Selector, screen edges, and workspaces on multiple monitors.

Ubuntu now provides a hot corner capability which you can configure to quickly access the Activities overview. Simply move your mouse to the upper right corner of the screen.

Ubuntu has a new workspace selector that is accessible from both the Activities overview and the Applications overview. It can be fixed or dynamic. The workspace switcher displays a thumbnail bar at the top of the screen for easy switching.

Kubuntu has replaced the Kickstart menu used in previous releases with three alternative main menus: the Application Launcher (the default), the Application menu, and the Applications Dashboard.

Kubuntu provides three alternative task manager for the panel: the new Icon-only Task Manager, the older Task Manager, and Window List. Kubuntu also features three activity switchers for both the desktop and the panel: Activities, Activities Pager, and Activities Bar.

Ubuntu MATE features the Plank dock applet that provides a dock on the edge of your screen for managing applications and open windows. The Plank dock can be added to any Ubuntu MATE desktop layout.

Ubuntu MATE supports various panel layouts using the Brisk, Classic, and Compact menus.

Ubuntu MATE has several color accent themes to choose from.

Ubuntu MATE no longer supports Login Preferences configuration.

Ubuntu Studio is now based on Kubuntu, instead of Xubuntu.

GNOME Documents has been deprecated.

Firefox is now only available from the Snap repository. It is no longer on the Apt repositories. You cannot install it with the **apt** command.

Snap remains the primary package manager for Ubuntu. It uses the snapd daemon to install, update, and run Snap installed applications. Since Ubuntu 20.04, the snap-store application has been modified to have nearly the same interface as the previous GNOME-based Ubuntu

Software. Though they have the same name, same icon, and function almost the same, they are actually different packages (the snap-store package is installed, but the GNOME Software package is not, **gnome-software**). The Ubuntu Software (snap-store version) installs Snap packages by default, though it can also manage Apt (DEB) packages. To install the APT version, select the APT repository version (deb) from the Ubuntu Software's Source menu. Ubuntu Software cannot manage Flathub packages. If you want to install from the Flathub repository, you should install the original GNOME Software software manager, available on the APT repository as **gnome-software**.

Ubuntu Releases

Ubuntu provides both long-term and short-term support releases. Long-term support releases (LTS), such as Ubuntu 22.04, are released every two years. Short-term releases, such as Ubuntu 21.04, are provided every six months between the LTS versions. They are designed to make available the latest applications and support for the newest hardware. Each has its own nickname, like Jammy Jellyfish for the 22.04 LTS release. The long-term support releases are supported for three years for desktops and five years for servers, whereas short-term support releases are supported for 18 months. In addition, Canonical provides limited commercial support for companies that purchase it.

Installing Ubuntu is easy to do. A core set of applications are installed, and you can add to them as you wish. Following installation, additional software can be downloaded from online repositories. There are only a few install screens, which move quickly through default partitioning, user setup, and time settings. Hardware components such as graphics cards and network connections are configured and detected automatically. With Ubuntu Software (installed by default), you can find and install additional software with the click of a button.

The Ubuntu distribution of Linux is available online at numerous sites. Ubuntu maintains its own site for the desktop edition at **https://ubuntu.com/desktop** You can download the current release of Ubuntu Linux from **https://ubuntu.com/download/desktop**.

Ubuntu Flavours

Ubuntu supports several desktops, known as flavours, each designed for a distinct group of users or functions. Flavours install different collections of software such as the Xfce (Xubuntu) or MATE desktops, the KDE desktop (Kubuntu), servers, educational software, and multimedia applications. Table 1-2 lists the websites where you can download ISO images for these flavours. ISO images can be downloaded directly or by using a BitTorrent application like Transmission. Metalink downloads are also supported which make effective use of mirrors. If you have already downloaded a pre-release ISO image, like a beta version, you can use zsync to download just the final changes, greatly reducing download times.

The Ubuntu Desktop edition provides desktop functionality for end users. The Ubuntu Desktop release provides a Live USB/DVD using the GNOME desktop. Most users would install this version. You can download the Ubuntu Desktop from the Download page, which you can access from the Ubuntu site (**https://ubuntu.com**) by clicking on the Download menu and choosing Desktop. The page address is:

```
https://ubuntu.com/download/desktop
```

For upgrade instructions, click on the "Software Updater" link in the "From an older version" section.

`https://ubuntu.com/tutorial/tutorial-upgrading-ubuntu-desktop`

Ubuntu Flavor	Description
Ubuntu Desktop	Live USB/DVD and Install with the GNOME interface, **https://ubuntu.com/download/desktop**.
Ubuntu Server	Install server software (no desktop), **https://ubuntu.com/download/server**
Kubuntu	Live USB/DVD and Install using the KDE desktop, instead of GNOME, **https://www.kubuntu.org**. Add to Ubuntu desktop with the **kubuntu-desktop** metapackage.
Ubuntu MATE	Uses the MATE desktop, **https://ubuntu-mate.org.** Add to Ubuntu desktop with the **ubuntu-mate-desktop** metapackage.
Xubuntu	Uses the Xfce desktop instead of GNOME, **http://xubuntu.org**. Useful for laptops.
Lubuntu	Lightweight version of Ubuntu based on the LXDE desktop, **https://lubuntu.me/**
Ubuntu Studio	Ubuntu desktop with multimedia and graphics production applications, **https://ubuntustudio.org**. Add to Ubuntu desktop with the **ubuntustudio-desktop** metapackage
Ubuntu Kylin	Ubuntu Desktop for Chinese users
Ubuntu Budgie	The Budgie desktop based on the Ubuntu desktop, **https://ubuntubudgie.org**

Table 1-1: Ubuntu Flavours

To open the Alternative Download page, click on the "Alternative downloads and torrents" link below the Download button.

`https://ubuntu.com/download/alternative-downloads`

The Alternative Downloads page provides information on BitTorrent files for downloading the Ubuntu 22.04 LTS DVD release.

Those who want to run Ubuntu as a server, to provide an Internet service such as a website, would use the Ubuntu Server edition. The Server edition provides only a simple command line interface; it does not install the desktop. It is designed primarily to run servers. Keep in mind that you could install the desktop first, and later download server software from the Ubuntu repositories, running them from a system that also has a desktop, though there are overhead costs for a server running a desktop. You do not have to install the Server edition to install and run servers. You can download the Server edition from the Ubuntu Server download page, which you can access from the Ubuntu site (**https://ubuntu.com**). The page address is:

`https://ubuntu.com/download/server`

URL	Internet Site
https://ubuntu.com/download/	Primary download site for Desktop and Server DVDs
http://releases.ubuntu.com/jammy/	Download site for Desktop DVD and Server CDs, including alternate install methods like torrent, zsync, and metalink.
http://cdimages.ubuntu.com/releases/jammy/release/	Download site for Ubuntu DVDs for Apple powerpc, arm, and IBM z systems.
http://cdimages.ubuntu.com/	Download site for all Ubuntu flavors, including Kubuntu, Ubuntu MATE, Ubuntu Cinnamon, Xubuntu, and Ubuntu Studio. Check also their respective websites.

Table 1-2: Ubuntu DVD ISO Image locations

The releases site provides a DVD download page with download files for BitTorrent, zsync, and metalink, as well as a direct download link.

```
http://releases.ubuntu.com/jammy/
```

Apple powerpc, ARM, and IBM z compatible Ubuntu Desktop DVDs can also be downloaded from cdimages site:

```
http://cdimages.ubuntu.com/releases/jammy/release/
```

Ubuntu Flavours have the same Ubuntu packages but use either a different desktop or a specialized collection of software for certain groups of users. Kubuntu uses the KDE desktop instead of GNOME. Xubuntu is a stripped down and highly efficient desktop using the Xfce desktop, ideal for low power use on laptops and smaller computer. Edubuntu provides educational software that can be used with a specialized Edubuntu server, providing educational software on a school network. Ubuntu Studio provides a collection of multimedia and image production software. Lubuntu is based on the LXDE desktop, providing a very lightweight version of Ubuntu. Ubuntu MATE uses the MATE desktop. Ubuntu Kylin is the Ubuntu Desktop for Chinese users. Table 1-2 lists websites where you can download ISO images for the various flavors.

You can download flavours from their respective websites, or from **http://releases.ubuntu.com**. The links for their sites are available at:

```
https://ubuntu.com/download/flavours
```

The versions featuring different desktops are listed here.

https://www.kubuntu.org   KDE desktop version

https://ubuntu-mate.org   MATE desktop version

https://xubuntu.org   Xfce desktop version

https://lubuntu.me/   LXDE desktop version

https://ubuntubudgie.org/   Budgie desktop version

You can find out more about flavours at: **https://ubuntu.com/download/flavours**, which you can access from the Ubuntu site (**https://ubuntu.com**). Click the Download menu, choosing Ubuntu Flavours. Links to their websites are provided on the Ubuntu flavours page, where you can then download their live/install DVDs. All these flavors can be downloaded from their respective websites, as well as from:

```
http://releases.ubuntu.com/
```

The **http://releases.ubuntu.com** and **http://cdimages.ubuntu.com** sites hold both BitTorrent and full image files for the flavours they provide. The **http://releases.ubuntu.com** site also provides downloads from multiple mirrors and zsync files for synchronizing downloads. Keep in mind that most of these flavours are released as Live USB/DVD discs, 64 bit versions.

Ubuntu Live USB/DVD

The Ubuntu Desktop USB/DVD can operate as a Live session (the Server edition does not), so you can run Ubuntu from any DVD or USB drive. New users can also use the Live-USB/DVD to try out Ubuntu to see if they like it. The Ubuntu Desktop USB/DVD will run as a Live session automatically using Ubuntu as the desktop. To create a Live USB, you install the Ubuntu Desktop ISO image to a USB drive using a USB creator application such as Startup Disk Creator on Ubuntu or the Fedora Media Writer on Windows or MAC systems.

The Desktop Live USB/DVD provided by Ubuntu includes a basic collection of software packages. You will have a fully operational Ubuntu desktop (see Figure 1-3). You have the full set of administrative tools, with which you can add users, change configuration settings, and even add software, while the Live session is running. When you shut down, the configuration information is lost, including any software you have added. Files and data can be written to removable devices like USB drives, DVD write discs, and network drives, letting you save your data during a Live session.

When you start up the Ubuntu Desktop USB/DVD, the startup screen is displayed, with the "Try Ubuntu" option selected. This option starts up a Live session, and will start automatically after a few seconds. The Live USB/DVD desktop is then displayed (see Figure 1-2) and you are logged in as the **ubuntu** user. The Dock on the left side displays icons for a Web browser (Firefox), Thunderbird mailer, Rhythmbox music player, LibreOffice writer, Ubuntu Software, and Ubuntu desktop help. The desktop shows icons for the home folder (ubuntu), the trash, and an Install Ubuntu icon. On the top bar to the right is the System Status area menu with entries for network connections, which you can configure for wireless access, as well as a power button for shutting down your system.

You can save files to your home folder, but they are temporary and disappear at the end of the session. Copy them to a DVD, USB drive, another removable device, or to a network file system (if you have network access) to save them.

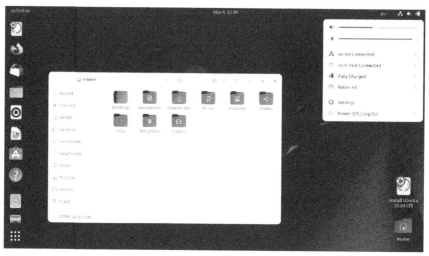

Figure 1-3: Ubuntu Live USB/DVD

All the Live USB/DVDs also function as install discs for Ubuntu, providing a collection of software, and installing an Ubuntu operating system that can be expanded and updated from Ubuntu online repositories. An Install icon lets you install Ubuntu on your computer, performing a standard installation to your hard drive. From the Live session desktop, double-click the Install Ubuntu icon on the desktop to start the installation.

Ubuntu Live USB drive

On Ubuntu, you can use the USB Startup Disk Creator utility to install any Ubuntu disc image on a USB drive. The USB Live/install drive is generated using the DVD image that you first have to download. Check the Ubuntu tutorial on create a Live USB drive.

`https://ubuntu.com/tutorial/tutorial-create-a-usb-stick-on-ubuntu`

Note: Alternatively, you could download and use the Fedora Media Writer to create the USB drive. The Fedora Media Writer can be installed on Windows and Mac operating systems. If you do not already have an Ubuntu system, you could use the Fedora Media Writer to create your Ubuntu USB drives on Windows or Mac. If you access the Fedora download site from a Windows system, the download button downloads the Fedora Media Writer for Windows, **https://getfedora.org/en/workstation/download/**.

Click "Startup Disk Creator" icon on the Applications overview to open the Make Startup Disk window with an entry at the top to select an ISO image and an entry below to select the USB drive to use. Click the Other button to locate a specific disk image to use. Then click the "Make Startup Disk" button to install the ISO on the USB drive.

The "Make Startup Disk" operation will not erase any data already on your USB drive. You can still access it, even Windows data. The Ubuntu Live OS will coexist with your current data, occupying available free space.

To boot from the Live USB, be sure your computer (BIOS) is configured to boot from the USB drive. The Live USB drive will then start up just like the Live DVD, displaying the install screen with options to try Ubuntu or install it.

When you create the Live USB drive, you have the option to specify writable memory. This will allow you to save files to your USB drive as part of the Ubuntu Live operating system. You can save files to your Document or Pictures directory and then access them later. You can also create new users, and give those users administrative permission, just as you would on a normally installed OS. With the Settings User Accounts tool, you could even have the new user be the automatic login, instead of the **ubuntu** user. In effect, the Ubuntu Live USB drive becomes a portable Ubuntu OS. Even with these changes, the Ubuntu Live USB remains the equivalent of a Live DVD, just one that you can write to. There is no GRUB boot loader. You still use the install start up screen. In addition, you cannot update the kernel.

If you want a truly portable Ubuntu OS, just perform a standard installation to a USB drive, instead of to a hard drive. You will have to create a new clean partition on the USB drive to install to. You would either reduce the size of the current partition, preserving data, or simply delete it, opening up the entire drive for use by the new Ubuntu OS.

Ubuntu Software

All Linux software for Ubuntu is currently available from online repositories. You can download applications for desktops, Internet servers, office suites, and programming packages, among others. Software packages are distributed primarily through the official Ubuntu repository. Downloads and updates are handled automatically by your desktop software manager and updater. Many popular applications are included in separate sections of the repository. During installation, your system is configured to access Ubuntu repositories. You can update to the latest software from the Ubuntu repository using the software updater.

A complete listing of software packages for the Ubuntu distribution, along with a search capability is located at:

```
https://packages.ubuntu.com
```

In addition, you could download from third-party sources software that is in the form of compressed archives or in DEB packages. DEB packages are archived using the Debian Package Manager and have the extension **.deb**. Compressed archives have an extension such as **.tar.gz**. You also can download the source version and compile it directly on your system. This has become a simple process, almost as simple as installing the compiled DEB versions.

There are two software management systems supported and used by Ubuntu 22.04, the older APT (Advanced Package Tool) software management system that uses DEB packages, and the newer Snap system that uses snap packages. Snap is the new package format that will replace the deb package management system on Ubuntu. The packages are called **snaps**. With Snap, the software files for an application are not installed in global folders. They are installed in one separate location, and any dependent software and libraries are included as part of the snap package.

Due to licensing restrictions, multimedia support for popular operations like MP3, DVD, and DivX are included with Ubuntu in a separate section of the repository called multiverse. Ubuntu includes on its restricted repository NVIDIA and AMD vendor graphics drivers. Ubuntu also provides as part of its standard installation, the generic X.org drivers that will enable your graphics cards to work.

All software packages in the Ubuntu repositories are accessible directly with Ubuntu Software and the Synaptic Package Manager, which provide easy software installation, removal, and searching. Ubuntu Software is an implementation of GNOME Software. Ubuntu Software will support both APT and Snap packages, but gives priority to Snap packages. Your install USB/DVD, though, installs software mostly from the APT repositories.

Ubuntu Help and Documentation

A great deal of help and documentation is available online for Ubuntu, ranging from detailed install procedures to beginner questions (see Table 1-3). The documentation for Ubuntu 22.04 LTS is located at **https://help.ubuntu.com/**. The Firefox Web browser start page displays links for two major help sites: Ubuntu documentation at **https://help.ubuntu.com** and Ubuntu Community at **https://help.ubuntu.com/community**. Check the Ubuntu tutorials site (**https://ubuntu.com/tutorials/**) for basic tutorials on different Ubuntu tasks Tutorials for Ubuntu topics and tasks, such as running the Live USB/DVD, setting up Samba, Install the Ubuntu desktop, and configuring the Apache Web server.

Site	Description
https://help.ubuntu.com/	Help pages and install documentation
https://packages.ubuntu.com	Ubuntu software package list and search
https://ubuntuforums.org	Ubuntu forums
https://askubuntu.com	Ask Ubuntu Q&A site for users and developers (community based)
https://ubuntu.com/tutorials/	Tutorials for Ubuntu topics and tasks
http://fridge.ubuntu.com	News and developments
http://planet.ubuntu.com	Member and developer blogs
https://ubuntu.com/blog	Latest Ubuntu news
http://www.tldp.org	Linux Documentation Project website
https://help.ubuntu.com/community	Community Documentation
https://lists.ubuntu.com	Ubuntu mailing lists

Table 1-3: Ubuntu help and documentation

For detailed online support, check the Ubuntu forums at **https://ubuntuforums.org**. In addition, there are blog and news sites as well as the standard Linux documentation. Ubuntu Community features Ubuntu documentation, support, blogs, and news. A Contribute section links to sites where you can contribute for development, artwork, documentation, and support. The Ask Ubuntu site is a question and answer site based on community support, which provides answers to many common questions (**https://askubuntu.com**). For mailing lists, check **https://lists.ubuntu.com**. There are lists for categories like Ubuntu announcements, community support for specific flavors, and development for areas like the desktop, servers, or mobile implementation.

help.ubuntu.com

Ubuntu-specific documentation is available at **https://help.ubuntu.com**. Here, on listed links, you can find specific documentation for different releases. Always check the release help page first for documentation, though it may be sparse and cover mainly changed areas. For 22.04 LTS the Documentation section provides the Ubuntu Desktop Guide (Desktop), the Ubuntu Server Guide, and the Ubuntu Installation Guide (per architecture). The Ubuntu Desktop Guide covers the GNOME interfaces and is the same guide installed with your desktop, accessible as Help (Applications overview).

```
https://help.ubuntu.com/stable/ubuntu-help/index.html
```

One of the more helpful pages is the Community Help page, **https://help.ubuntu.com/community**. Here you will find detailed documentation on the installation of all Ubuntu releases, using the desktop, installing software, and configuring devices. Always check the page for your Ubuntu release first. The page includes these main sections:

Installation: Link to Install page with sections on desktop, server, and alternate installations.

Hardware: Sections on managing hardware. Links to pages on drives and partitions, input devices, wireless configuration, printers, sound, and video.

Further Topics: Links to pages on system administration, security, and troubleshooting, servers, networking, and software development.

Ubuntu Flavours: Links to documentation on different Ubuntu versions such as Lubuntu and Kubuntu.

ubuntuforums.org

Ubuntu forums provide detailed online support and discussion for users (**https://ubuntuforums.org**). A "New to Ubuntu" forum provides an area where new users can obtain answers to questions. Sticky threads include both quick and complete guides to installation for the current Ubuntu release. You can use the search feature to find discussions on your topic of interest. The main support categories section covers specific support areas like networking, multimedia, laptops, security, and 64-bit support.

The Other Community Discussions and Support forums cover ongoing work such as virtualization, art and design, gaming, education and science, Wine, assistive technology, and the Ubuntu cloud. Here you will also find community announcements and news.

The Community Discussions forums is where you talk about anything else. The Ubuntu Forums site also provides a gallery page for posted screenshots as well as RSS feeds for specific forums.

Ubuntu news and blog sites

Several news and blog sites are accessible from the News page at
https://wiki.ubuntu.com/Home.

http://fridge.ubuntu.com The Fridge site lists the latest news and developments for
Ubuntu. It features the Weekly newsletter, latest announcements, and upcoming events.

http://planet.ubuntu.com Ubuntu blog for members and developers

https://ubuntu.com/blog Ubuntu news

Linux documentation

The Linux Documentation Project (LDP) has developed a complete set of Linux manuals.
The documentation is available at the LDP home site at **http://www.tldp.org**. The Linux
documentation for your installed software will be available in your **/usr/share/doc** directory.

Open Source Software

Linux is developed as a cooperative Open Source effort over the Internet, so no company
or institution controls Linux. Software developed for Linux reflects this background. Development
often takes place when Linux users decide to work together on a project. Most Linux software is
developed as Open Source software. The source code for an application is freely distributed along
with the application. Programmers can make their own contributions to a software package's
development, modifying and correcting the source code. As an open source operating system, the
Linux source code is included in all its distributions and is freely available. Many major software
development efforts are also open source projects, as are the KDE and GNOME desktops along
with most of their applications. You can find more information about the Open Source movement
at **https://opensource.org**.

Open source software is protected by public licenses that prevent commercial companies
from taking control of open source software by adding modifications of their own, copyrighting
those changes, and selling the software as their own product. The most popular public license is the
GNU General Public License (GPL) provided by the Free Software Foundation. Linux is
distributed under this license. The GNU General Public License retains the copyright, freely
licensing the software with the requirement that the software and any modifications made to it are
always freely available. Other public licenses have been created to support the demands of different
kinds of open source projects. The GNU Lesser General Public License (LGPL) lets commercial
applications use GNU licensed software libraries. The Qt Public License (QPL) lets open source
developers use the Qt libraries essential to the KDE desktop. You can find a complete listing at
https://opensource.org.

Linux is currently copyrighted under a GNU public license provided by the Free Software
Foundation (see **http://www.gnu.org/**). GNU software is distributed free, provided it is freely
distributed to others. GNU software has proved both reliable and effective. Many of the popular
Linux utilities, such as C compilers, shells, and editors, are GNU software applications. In addition,
many open source software projects are licensed under the GNU General Public License (GPL).
Most of these applications are available on the Ubuntu software repositories. Chapter 4 describes in
detail the process of accessing these repositories to download and install software applications from
them on your system.

Under the terms of the GNU General Public License, the original author retains the copyright, although anyone can modify the software and redistribute it, provided the source code is included, made public, and provided free. In addition, no restriction exists on selling the software or giving it away free. One distributor could charge for the software, while another could provide it free of charge. Major software companies are also providing Linux versions of their most popular applications (you can use Wine, the Windows compatibility layer, to run many Microsoft applications on Linux, directly).

Linux

Linux is a fast, stable, and open source operating system for PCs and workstations that features professional-level Internet services, extensive development tools, fully functional graphical user interfaces (GUIs), and a massive number of applications ranging from office suites to multimedia applications. Linux was developed in the early 1990s by Linus Torvalds, along with other programmers around the world. As an operating system, Linux performs many of the same functions as UNIX, Macintosh, and Windows. However, Linux is distinguished by its power and flexibility, along with being freely available. Most PC operating systems, such as Windows, began their development within the confines of small, restricted personal computers, which have become more versatile and powerful machines. Such operating systems are constantly being upgraded to keep up with the ever-changing capabilities of PC hardware. Linux, on the other hand, was developed in a different context. Linux is a PC version of the UNIX operating system that has been used for decades on mainframes and is currently the system of choice for network servers and workstations.

Technically, Linux consists of the operating system program referred to as the kernel, which is the part originally developed by Linus Torvalds. However, it has always been distributed with a large number of software applications, ranging from network servers and security programs to office applications and development tools. Linux has evolved as part of the open source software movement, in which independent programmers joined to provide free quality software to any user. Linux has become the premier platform for open source software, much of it developed by the Free Software Foundation's GNU project. Most of these applications are also available on the Ubuntu repository, providing packages that are Debian compliant.

Linux operating system capabilities include powerful networking features, including support for Internet, intranets, and Windows networking. As a norm, Linux distributions include fast, efficient, and stable Internet servers, such as the Web, FTP, and DNS servers, along with proxy, news, and mail servers. Linux has everything you need to set up, support, and maintain a fully functional network.

Linux is distributed freely under a GNU General Public License (GPL) as specified by the Free Software Foundation, making it available to anyone who wants to use it. GNU (which stands for "GNU's Not Unix") is a project initiated and managed by the Free Software Foundation to provide free software to users, programmers, and developers. Linux is copyrighted, not public domain. The GNU General Public License is designed to ensure that Linux remains free and, at the same time, standardized. Linux is technically the operating system kernel, the core operations, and only one official Linux kernel exists. Its power and stability have made Linux an operating system of choice as a network server.

Originally designed specifically for Intel-based personal computers, Linux started out as a personal project of computer science student Linus Torvalds at the University of Helsinki. At that time, students were making use of a program called Minix, which highlighted different UNIX features. Minix was created by Professor Andrew Tanenbaum and widely distributed over the Internet to students around the world. Torvalds's intention was to create an effective PC version of UNIX for Minix users. It was named Linux, and in 1991, Torvalds released version 0.11. Linux was widely distributed over the Internet, and in the following years, other programmers refined and added to it, incorporating most of the applications and features found in standard UNIX systems. All the major window managers have been ported to Linux. Linux has all the networking tools, such as FTP file transfer support, Web browsers, and the whole range of network services such as email, the domain name service, and dynamic host configuration, along with FTP, Web, and print servers. It also has a full set of program development utilities, such as C++ compilers and debuggers. Given all its features, the Linux operating system remains small, stable, and fast.

Linux development is overseen by The Linux Foundation (**https://www.linuxfoundation.org**), which is a merger of The Free Standards Group and Open Source Development Labs (OSDL). This is the group with which Linux Torvalds works to develop new Linux versions. Linux kernels are released at **https://www.kernel.org/**.

ubuntu

2. Installing Ubuntu

Install Discs

Installation Overview

Installation with the Ubuntu Desktop DVD

Recovery

Re-Installing the Boot Loader

Installing Ubuntu Linux is a very simple procedure, using just a few screens with default entries for easy installation. A pre-selected collection of software is installed. Most of your devices, like your display and network connection, are detected automatically. The most difficult part would be a manual partitioning of the hard drive, but you can use automatic partitioning for fresh installs, as is usually the case.

See the Ubuntu documentation for a detailed reference on the Ubuntu installer, as well as details for PC, PowerPC, and ARM.

`https://help.ubuntu.com/20.04/installation-guide/index.html`

Install Discs

In most cases, installation is performed using an Ubuntu Desktop USB/DVD that will install the Ubuntu desktop, along with a pre-selected set of software packages for multimedia players, office applications, and games. The Ubuntu Desktop USB/DVD is also designed to run from a USB drive or DVD disc, while providing the option to install Ubuntu on your hard drive. You can download the ISO disc image from the Ubuntu download site. The Ubuntu Desktop USB/DVD has only a 64-bit version.

`https://ubuntu.com/download/desktop`

You can also download the Ubuntu ISO images for both the desktop and server from:

`https://releases.ubuntu.com/jammy`

Ubuntu releases	Description
Ubuntu Desktop Live/Install USB/DVD	Primary Ubuntu release, Ubuntu desktop, can be burned to either DVD disc or USB drive.
Ubuntu Server CD	Server-only installation, no desktop, command line interface
Ubuntu Cloud	Cloud based install for OpenStack

Table 2-1: Ubuntu releases

Ubuntu tailors its installs by providing different install ISO images for different releases and versions (see Table 2-1). These include the Desktop ISO image, the Server ISO image designed for servers, and the Mac ISO image for Apple desktops.

Desktop DVD Run as a Live DVD or install Ubuntu Linux with the Ubuntu desktop and a standard set of applications.

Desktop USB Run as Live USB or install Ubuntu Linux with the Ubuntu desktop and a standard set of applications, uses the Ubuntu Desktop DVD ISO image installed on a USB drive.

Server install USB/CD   Install Ubuntu with a standard set of servers; this uses the command line interface (no desktop). Can use either a DVD or USB disk.

Using BitTorrent: Transmission

Most current Linux and Windows systems support BitTorrent for downloading. BitTorrent provides an efficient, safe, and fast method for downloading large files. Various BitTorrent clients are available, including one from the original BitTorrent developer. Transmission is the preferred BitTorrent client for Ubuntu 22.04 LTS. BitTorrent relies on making multiple connections that can use up bandwidth quickly. The BitTorrent files for all versions (Desktop and Server) can be found at the primary download sites, along with direct downloads:

```
http://releases.ubuntu.com/22.04
```

Metalinks

Metalinks are XML files that work like mirror lists, allowing download clients to easily choose a fast mirror and perform a more controlled download. You would need to use a download client that supports metalinks, like KGet, **gget**, or **aria2**. For more information about using metalink with Ubuntu, see:

```
https://wiki.ubuntu.com/MetalinkIsoDownloads
```

For general information see.

```
https://en.wikipedia.org/wiki/Metalink
```

A metalink file will have the extension **.metalink**. Metalink files for the Ubuntu releases are available at:

```
http://releases.ubuntu.com/22.04/
```

Zsync

Ubuntu also provides zsync downloads for its Ubuntu ISO images. The **zsync** program operates like **rsync**, but with very little overhead. It is designed for distributing a single file to many locations. In effect, you are synchronizing your copy to the original. The zsync program is designed to download just those parts of the original file that the downloaded copy needs. It uses a **.zsync** file that has the name of the ISO image you want to download. You can download **.zsync** files for Ubuntu ISO images from the **http://releases.ubuntu.com/jammy/** download page.

The **zsync** program is useful for users who have already download a pre-release version of an Ubuntu ISO image, such as the beta version. You would rename the beta image file to that of the new release, and then perform a zsync operation on it using the appropriate **.zsync** file provided by the Ubuntu download page. Only those parts of the final version that differ from the beta version would be downloaded, greatly reducing the actual amount of data downloaded.

You can install **zsync** using the Synaptic Package Manager. For more information, see the zsync Man page and the Zsync site: **http://zsync.moria.org.uk/**. For information on how to use zsync with Ubuntu, see:

```
https://ubuntu-tutorials.com/2009/10/29/use-zsync-to-update-existing-iso-images/
```

Installing Multiple-Boot Systems

The GRUB boot loader already supports multiple booting. Should you have both Ubuntu and Windows systems installed on your hard disks. GRUB will let you choose to boot either the Ubuntu system or a Windows system. During installation, GRUB will automatically detect any other operating systems installed on your computer and configure your boot loader menu to let you access them. You do not have to perform any configuration yourself.

If you want a Windows system installed on your computer, you should install it first. Windows would overwrite the boot loader installed by a previous Ubuntu system, cutting off access to the Linux system. If you installed Windows after having installed Ubuntu, you will need to re-install the Ubuntu GRUB boot loader. See the section at the end of this Chapter on re-installing the boot loader. There are several ways you can do it, most very simple.

If you have already installed Windows on your hard drive and configured it to take up the entire hard drive, you can select the "Install alongside" option during installation to free up space and set up Ubuntu partitions.

Tip: You can also use the Ubuntu Live USB/DVD to start up Ubuntu and perform any necessary hard disk partitioning using GParted.

Hardware Requirements

Most hardware today meets the requirements for running Ubuntu. Ubuntu can be installed on a wide variety of systems, ranging from the very weak to the very powerful. The install procedure will detect most of your hardware automatically. You will only need to specify your keyboard, though a default is automatically detected for you. Check the Ubuntu installation guide's chapter on System Requirements for details.

```
https://help.ubuntu.com/20.04/installation-guide/
```

You can also check the Ubuntu System Requirements page at **http://help.ubuntu.com** for details:

```
https://help.ubuntu.com/community/Installation/SystemRequirements
```

Installation Overview

Installing Ubuntu involves several processes, beginning with creating Linux partitions, then loading the Ubuntu software, selecting a time zone, and creating new user accounts. The installation program used for Ubuntu is a screen-based program that takes you through all these processes, step-by-step, as one continuous procedure. You can use either your mouse or the keyboard to make selections. When you finish with a screen, click the Continue button at the bottom to move to the next screen. If you need to move back to the previous screen, click Back. You can also press TAB, the arrow keys, SPACEBAR, and ENTER keys to make selections.

Installation is a straightforward process. A graphical installation is easy to use, providing full mouse support.

Most systems today already meet hardware requirements and have automatic connections to the Internet.

They also support booting a DVD-ROM disc or USB drive, though this support may have to be explicitly configured in the system BIOS.

If you are installing on a blank hard drive or on a drive with free space, or if you are performing a simple update that uses the same partitions, installing Ubuntu is a simple process. Ubuntu also features an automatic partitioning function that will perform the partitioning for you.

A preconfigured set of packages are installed, so you will not even have to select packages.

For a quick installation, you can simply start up the installation process by placing your DVD disc in the DVD drive, or attaching your USB disk, and starting up your system. To boot from the the USB disk, you may have to temporarily select the boot disk (F12 at start up on many computers). Graphical installation is a simple matter of following the instructions in each window as you progress. Installation follows a few easy stages:

1. **Welcome**   A default language is chosen for you, like English, so you can usually just click Continue.

2. **Keyboard Layout**   A default is chosen for you; you can usually just click Continue.

3. **Updates and other software**   On the "Updates and other software" screen you can choose a normal installation that includes a collection of popular applications, or you can choose a minimal install that install just the operating system with supporting tools and the web browser. You can also opt to install updates during installation and certain third party software.

4. **Installation type**   For automatic partitioning you have different options, depending on what other operating systems may have been installed on your hard drive. For drives that have other operating systems installed, you can install alongside them or, if Ubuntu 20.04 or 21.10 is installed, choose to upgrade, or choose to erase the entire disk. In all cases, you can also choose to partition your disk manually instead (the "Something else" option). As soon as you click the "Install Now' button, formatting and installation begins.

5. **Installation type: partitioner**   Used for manual partitioning only, in which you set up partitions yourself. Otherwise, this is skipped.

6. **Where are you? Time Zone**   Use the map to choose your time zone or select your city from the drop-down menu.

7. **Who are you?**   Set up a username and hostname for your computer, as well as a password for that user. You can also choose to log in automatically.

After the installation completes, you are asked to restart your system. You will then be asked to remove your USB/DVD disk.

Installation with the Ubuntu Desktop USB/DVD

The Ubuntu Desktop DVD/USB is designed for running Ubuntu from the DVD/USB (Live DVD/USB) and installing Ubuntu. You can first start up Ubuntu, and then initiate an installation, or install directly. Attach your Ubuntu USB drive or place the Ubuntu DVD disc in the DVD drive before you start your computer. Be sure that your computer is configured to boot from the USB drive or from the DVD drive. If you are using a DVD, most computers are already set up to boot first from the DVD drive. To boot from the USB drive, you may have to either temporarily select the boot disk (F12 at start up on many computers), or configure your BIOS to boot from the USB drive. After you start your computer, the installation program starts up.

On most screens, a Continue button is displayed on the lower-right corner of an installation dialog. Once finished with a screen, click Continue to move on. In some cases, you will be able to click a Back button to return to a previous screen. As each screen appears in the installation, default entries will be selected, usually by the auto-probing capability of the installation program. If these entries are correct, you can click Continue to accept them and go on to the next screen.

You have two ways to begin the install. You can start the installation directly or you can first start up the Ubuntu Live session. The Advantage to the Live session is that you will be able to configure your Network access and any other devices you have. Most users will not need to perform any configuration. In this case, you could perform a direct install, instead of starting the live session. With a direct install, the System Status Area menu, located at the top-right of the screen, is available, but it only allows you to choose the Wi-Fi connections. You cannot perform any network configuration.

The Live session is a fully functional Ubuntu system. Configuration options are listed in the System Status Area menu (top right side) (see Figure 2-1). If your computer has a wired connection, it will be already be configured for you and the Wired entry will show that you are connected. For a Wi-Fi connection you will have to choose a connection to use. Click the Wi-Fi entry to expand to a menu showing and entry for "Select Network", which you can click to display a dialog showing all available Wi-Fi networks near you. Choose the one you want to use. Should you have to perform more detailed network configurations, choose the "Wired Settings" or "Wi-Fi Settings" entries the respective expanded menus. To perform other configurations, open the Settings dialog, by clicking the Setting entry near the bottom of the System Status Area menu.

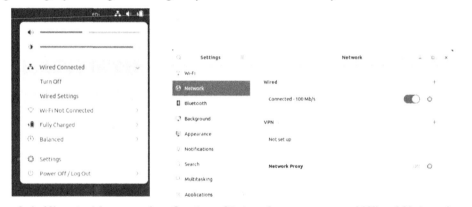

Figure 2-1: Ubuntu Live session System Status Area menu and Wired Network configuration

Welcome and Language

When the Ubuntu Desktop USB/DVD first boots, a text screen first appears with the following options.

```
Ubuntu
Ubuntu (safe graphics)
OEM install (for manufacturers)
Boot from next volume
UEFI Firmware Settings
```

An asterisk appears before the selected entry. Use the up and down arrows to move between entries, and press ENTER to choose one. The UEFI Firmware Settings entry starts up your computer's BIOS settings.

The " Ubuntu" and "Ubuntu (safe graphics)" entry starts an automatic disk checking process, which you can cancel by pressing **Ctrl-c**. As the system starts up, the Ubuntu logo is displayed along with your computer's logo.

Once started, a Welcome screen (see Figure 2-2) is displayed with buttons for two options, Try Ubuntu and Install Ubuntu. The Install Ubuntu entry installs directly, displaying a Welcome screen and letting you choose your language.

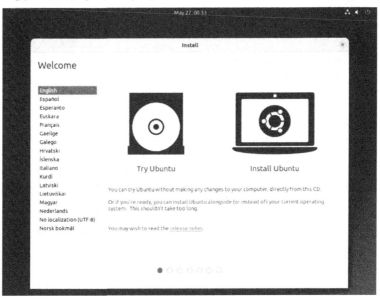

Figure 2-2: Install Welcome screen for Ubuntu Desktop USB/DVD

The "Try Ubuntu" button will start Ubuntu as a Live session. Even if you just opt to try Ubuntu, you can still perform an installation from the Live USB/DVD. To install, click the "Install Ubuntu" icon on the desktop or on the dock (the Ubuntu icon at the top) (see Figure 2-3). The Install window opens to the Welcome screen for choosing your language.

On the Welcome screen, select the language you want from the list on the left. A default language will already be selected, usually English. Click the Continue button to start up the installation.

Figure 2-3: Live USB/DVD (Desktop) with Install icon

Keyboard Layout

You are then asked to select a keyboard layout, "Keyboard layout." Keyboard entries are selected first by location in the left scroll box, and then by type on the right scroll box. A default is already selected, such as English (US) (see Figure 2-4). If the selection is not correct, you can choose another keyboard, first by location in the left scroll box, and then by type on the right scroll box.

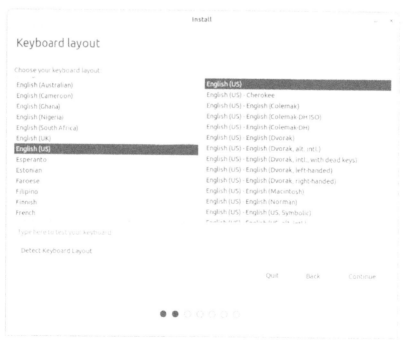

Figure 2-4: Keyboard Layout

To test your keyboard, click on the text box at the bottom of the screen and press keys, "Type here to test your keyboard."

The "Detect Keyboard Layout" button tries to detect the keyboard using your input. A series of dialogs opens, prompting you to press keys and asking you if certain keys are present on your keyboard. When the dialogs finish, the detected keyboard is then selected in the "Keyboard layout" scroll boxes.

Click the Continue button to continue.

Minimal Install, Updates, and Third Party Software

The "Updates and other software" dialog lets you choose a normal or minimal installation (see Figure 2-5). You can also choose to download current updates while installing, using the latest packages, and avoiding an extensive update after the install. This can take longer, though. You can also install third party applications and codecs (non-open source). If you have an Nvidia graphics card, you should check the "Install third-party software for graphics and Wi-Fi hardware and additional media formats" option. This option will detect your Nvidia card and download and install the appropriate proprietary Nvidia driver.

Click the Continue button to continue.

Your system detects your hardware, providing any configuration specifications that may be required.

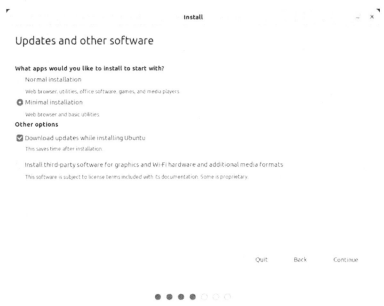

Figure 2-5: Updates and Other Software

Installation type

You are now asked to designate the Linux partitions and hard disk configurations you want to use on your hard drives. Ubuntu provides automatic partitioning that covers most situations, like using a blank or new hard drive and overwriting old partitions on a hard drive. Ubuntu can even repartition a system with an operating system that uses all of the hard drive, but with unused space within it. In this case, the install procedure reduces the space used by the original operating system and installs Ubuntu on the new free space. A default partition layout sets up a root partition of type **ext4** (Linux native) for the kernel and applications (the swap partition has been replaced by a swap file in the root folder).

Alternatively, you can configure your hard disk manually (the "Something else" option). Ubuntu provides a simple partitioning tool you can use to set up Linux partitions.

For multiple-boot systems using Windows, Ubuntu automatically detects the Windows system.

No partitions will be changed or formatted until you click the "Install Now" button. You can opt out of the installation until then, and your original partitions will remain untouched.

Warning: The "Erase disk and install Ubuntu" option will wipe out any existing partitions on the selected hard drive. If you want to preserve any partitions on that drive, like Windows or other Linux partitions, always choose a different option such as "Install Ubuntu alongside ..." or "Something else".

You are given choices, depending on the state of the hard disk you choose. A hard disk could be blank, have an older Ubuntu operating system on it, or have a different operating system, such as Windows, already installed. If an operating system is already installed, it may take up the entire disk or may only use part of the disk, with the remainder available for the Ubuntu installation.

Tip: Some existing Linux systems may use several Linux partitions. Some of these may be used for just the system software, such as the boot and root partitions. These can be formatted. Others may have extensive user files, such as a /home partition that normally holds user home folders and all the files they have created. You should *not* format such partitions.

No detected operating systems

If no operating systems are detected on the hard drive, which is the case with a drive with only data files or a blank hard drive, you are given several choices: to use the entire disk with advanced options: to use LVM instead of standard partitions, encrypt the entire disk, or use the ZFS file system. Alternatively you can specify partitions manually (Something else) (see Figure 2-6). Encryption and LVM are options that you can choose in addition to the "Erase disk and install Ubuntu option." They have square buttons. The message displayed on the Installation type dialog is:

"This computer currently has no detected operating systems. What would you like to do?"

You are given two choices.

```
Erase disk and install Ubuntu
Something else
```

If you choose to install "Erase disk and install Ubuntu", your hard drive is automatically partitioned creating a primary partition for your entire file system (a root file system).

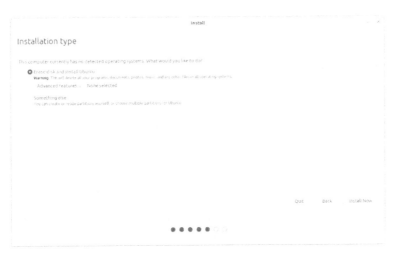

Figure 2-6: No detected operating systems

Advanced Features: LVM, Encryption, and ZFS

Should you want to use LVM, ZFS for your partitions, or disk encryption, click the "Erase disk and install Ubuntu" entry to activate the "Advanced features" button. Then click the "Advanced features" button to open a dialog showing options for LVM, ZFS, and Encryption (see Figure 2-7).

Figure 2-7: LVM install option

There is a None option in case you decided not use LVM or ZFS. Once you have made your selection click the OK button. The Installation type screen will then show your selection, next to the "Advanced features" button. For LVM it will display "LVM selected" (see Figure 2-8).

Figure 2-8: LVM selection

ZFS will perform automatic snapshots of your system, letting you restore your system to a previous state. It will add a History entry to your Grub boot menu that you can use to restore your system to a selected state. Both LVM and ZFS are covered in more detail in Chapter 13.

With the "Use LVM with the new Ubuntu installation" option, LVM partitions are set up using physical and logical volumes, which can be added to and replaced easily. An LVM physical volume is set up, which contains two LVM logical volumes, one for the swap space and one for the root (see Figure 2-8). After you have installed your system, you can manage your LVM partitions using the LVM commands (see Chapter 13). The default LVM partitions are shown here with **pvscan** (physical volumes), **vgscan** (volume group), and **lvscan** (logical volume) operations. There is one volume group, **vgubuntu**, with two logical volumes, **root** and **swap_1**. The physical LVM partition is named **lvm2**. Two physical partitions are created on your system, an EFI boot partition and the LVM physical partition.

```
$ sudo pvscan
  PV /dev/mapper/sda2   VG vgubuntu         lvm2 [<464.54 GiB / 0    free]
  Total: 1 [<464.54 GiB] / in use: 1 [<464.54 GiB] / in no VG: 0 [0    ]
$ sudo vgscan
  Found volume group "vgubuntu" using metadata type lvm2
$ sudo lvscan
  ACTIVE            '/dev/vgubuntu/root' [463.58 GiB] inherit
  ACTIVE            '/dev/vgubuntu/swap_1' [980.00 MiB] inherit
```

Encrypt the disk

The "Encrypt the new Ubuntu installation for security" option on the "Advanced Features" dialog lets you encrypt your entire system with a password (see Figure 2-9) .

Figure 2-9: LVM with encryption

You cannot access your system without that password. The encryption option will destroy any existing partitions if there are any, creating new partitions. Your hard drive will then have only your new Ubuntu system on it. On the "Choose a security key" screen that follows you are prompted to enter a security key (password), along with the option to overwrite empty space (see Figure 2-10).

You also have the option to create a recovery key that you can use to unlock your disk, should you forget or lose your security key. The recovery key is saved on the USB/DVD installation session in memory at the **/home/Ubuntu** folder in a file named **recovery.key**. The key is a password consisting of 48 text numbers. Be sure to make a copy of the recovery key before you end the installation, saving it to a USB drive, to another system, or just open the **recovery.key** file and copy the key by hand. Otherwise you will lose it when you end the installation process. Should you want to save the **recovery.key** file, you have to have started the install process from a Live USB/DVD session. Choose "Try Ubuntu" instead of "Install Ubuntu" when you first start up the Live USB/DVD. Otherwise you will not be able to save the **recovery.key** file. If you have chosen "Install Ubuntu" the only way to save the recovery key it is open the **recovery.key** file and write down the numbers in it.

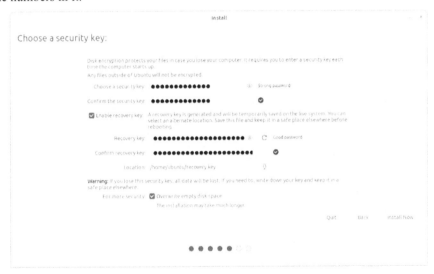

Figure 2-10: Security key for encrypted system

After installation, whenever you start up your system, you are prompted to enter that security key (see Figure 2-11).

Figure 2-11: Security key login

Detected Ubuntu operating system

If you have another Ubuntu operating system on your disk, you will have the option to erase the Ubuntu system and replace it with Ubuntu 22.04 LTS. If the installed Ubuntu system is version 19.10, then you are also given the option to upgrade your system, preserving your personal files and installed software. You are also given the option to erase the installed operating system, and install the new system.

If the current system has enough unused space, you are also given an install alongside option, resizing the disk to free up space, and installing 22.04 LTS in added partitions on the free space. This will keep your original Linux system, as well as install the new one.

The message displayed on the Installation type dialog is something like this:

"This computer currently has Ubuntu 21.10 on it. What would you like to do?"

You are given three choices. The Upgrade Ubuntu option is selected by default.

If you choose to Erase Ubuntu 21.10 and reinstall, you can also choose the options to encrypt the drive and to use LVM partitions.

```
Upgrade Ubuntu 21.10 to Ubuntu 22.04
Erase Ubuntu 21.10 and reinstall
Something else
```

On systems that also have Windows installed alongside Ubuntu, you are given the same options, but with an added option to erase everything including your Windows system. You are warned that both Windows and Ubuntu are installed on your system. Should you choose to erase Ubuntu and reinstall (the first entry), your Windows system will be preserved.

Detected other operating systems with free space

If you have another operating system on your disk that has been allocated use of part of the disk, you will have an option beginning with "Install Ubuntu alongside" with the name of the installed operating system listed. Keep in mind that LVM installations, like Fedora Linux, are not detected. To preserve an LVM installation you should choose the "Something else" option and enter the disk configuration manually.

In this example, you are given three choices. Should you choose to Replace, then the disk encryption and LVM options become active. However, with the Replace option, your Windows system will be overwritten and erased.

```
Install Ubuntu alongside Microsoft Windows
Replace Microsoft Windows with Ubuntu
Something else
```

Detected another operating system using entire disk (resize)

If you have another operating system on your disk that has been allocated use of the entire disk, you will have an option beginning with "Install Ubuntu alongside" with the name of the installed operating system listed. This option is selected initially. This option is designed for use on hard disks with no unallocated free space but with a large amount of unused space on an existing partition. This is the case for a system where a partition has already been allocated the entire disk. This option will perform a resize of the existing partition, reducing that partition, preserving the data on it, and then creating an Ubuntu partition on that free space. Be warned that this could be a very time-consuming operation. If the original operating system was used heavily, the disk could be fragmented, with files stored all over the hard disk. In this case, the files have to be moved to one area of the hard disk, freeing up continuous space on the remaining area. If the original operating system was used very lightly, then there may be unused continuous space already on the hard drive. In this case, re-partitioning would be quick.

On the "Install alongside" dialog two partitions are displayed, the original showing the new size it will have after the resize, and the new partition for Ubuntu 22.04 LTS formed from the unused space. The size is automatically determined. You can adjust the size if you want by clicking on the space between the partitions to display a space icon, which you can drag left, or right to change the proportional sizes of the partitions.

Upon clicking the Install Now button, a dialog will prompt you with the warning that the resize cannot be undone, and that it may take a long time. Click Continue to perform the resize, or click Go Back to return to the "Installation type" screen. The time it will take depends on the amount of fragmentation on the disk.

Something else

All install situations will include a "Something else" option to let you partition the hard drive manually. The "Something else" option starts up the partitioner, which will let you create, edit, and delete partitions. You can set your own size and type for your partitions. Use this option to preserve or reuse any existing partitions. When you have finished making your changes, click the Install Now button to continue. At this point, your partitions are changed and software is installed, while you continue with the remaining install configuration for time zone and user login.

The partitioner screen displays the partitions on your current hard disk, and lists options for creating your Linux partitions. A graphical bar at the top shows the current state of your hard disk, showing any existing partitions, if any, along with their sizes and labels.

A Boot Loader section at the bottom of the screen provides a drop-down menu of hard drives where you can install the boot loader (see Figure 2-16). Your first hard drive is selected by default. If you have several hard drives on your system, you can choose the one on which to install the boot loader. Systems with only one hard drive, such as laptops, have only one hard drive entry.

The partitioner interface lists any existing partitions (see Figure 2-18). The graphical bar at the top will show the partition on your selected hard drive. The depiction changes as you add, delete, or edit your partitions. Each partition device name and label will be displayed. Unused space will be labeled as free space.

Each hard disk is labeled by its device name, such as **sda** for the first Serial ATA device. Underneath the hard disk graphics bar are labels for the partitions and free space available, along with the partition type and size. The partitions are identified by their colors. At the bottom of the screen are actions you can perform on partitions and free space. To the right are the "New partition table" and Revert buttons for the entire disk. To the left are add, delete, and edit buttons for partitions (+, -, and Change). Your current hard disks and their partitions are listed in the main scrollable pane, with headings for Device, Type, Mount point, Format, Size, and Used space, as well as the name of an operation system (System) installed on the partition, should there be one.

Creating new partitions on a blank hard drive manually

To create partitions on a blank hard drive manually, choose "Something else" (see Figure 2-12). The partitioner interface starts up with the "Installation type" screen, listing any existing partitions (see Figure 2-13). For a blank hard drive, the hard drive only is listed in the main pane.

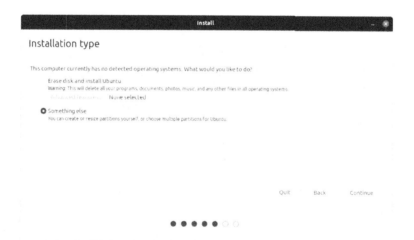

Figure 2-12: Something Else (manual partitioning)

For a new blank hard drive, you first create the partition table by clicking the New Partition Table button (see Figure 2-13). This displays a warning that it will erase any data on the drive. Click Continue (see Figure 2-14). The warning dialog is there in case you accidentally click the New Partition Table button on a drive that has partitions you want to preserve. In this case, you can click Go Back and no new partition table is created.

Figure 2-13: Manually partitioning a new hard drive

Figure 2-14: Create a new partition table on a blank hard drive

Figure 2-15: Select free space on a blank hard drive

Once the new partition table is set up, the free space entry appears and a graphical bar at the top shows the free space (see Figure 2-15). If your system already has an operating system installed that takes up only part of the disk, you do not need to create a new partition table. Your free space is already listed.

For Ubuntu Linux, you will have to create at least one partition, a Linux root partition, where your system will be installed. If your computer also supports EFI boot, as most do, you will also have to add a boot partition of type EFI System Partition. You can create other partitions if you wish. The swap partition is no longer needed. A swap file is used instead (**/swapfile**). You can, though, if you want, still set up and use a swap partition. To create a new partition, select the free space entry for the hard disk and click the + button. This opens a Create Partition dialog where you can choose the file system type (Use as) and the size of your partition (see Figure 2-16). Do this for each partition. The EFI and swap partitions have no mount point. You only set the size.

Figure 2-16: Create a new boot partition

The Create Partition dialog displays entries for the partition type (Primary or Logical), the size in megabytes, the location (beginning or end), the file system type (Use as), and the Mount point. For the partition type, the "Do not use" partition entry is initially selected. Choose a partition type from the drop-down menu. Select "Ext4 journaling file system" for the root partition and choose Boot for the boot partition.

For the root partition, from the Mount point drop down menu choose the mount point /, which is the root directory (see Figure 2-17). This is where your system will be installed. The size of the partition is specified in megabytes. It will be set to the remaining space. If you want to also set up additional partitions, such as a partition for the **/home** folder, reduce the size to allow space for those partitions.

Figure 2-17: Create a new root partition

Figure 2-18: Manual partitions

If you make a mistake, you can edit a partition by selecting it and clicking the Change button. This opens an Edit partitions window where you can make changes. You can also delete a partition, returning its space to free space, and then create a new one. Select the partition and click the - button (delete). The partition is not actually deleted at this point. No changes are made at all until you start installing Ubuntu. The "Revert" button is always available to undo all the possible changes you specified so far, and start over from the original state of the hard disk.

When you have finished setting up your partitions, you will see entries for them displayed. The graphical bar at the top will show their size and location (see Figure 2-18). Click the "Install Now" button to perform the partitioning, formatting, and installation.

Where Are You?

On the "Where are you?" screen, you can set the time zone by using a map to specify your location (see Figure 2-19). The Time Zone tool uses a map feature that displays the entire earth, with sections for each time zone. Click on your general location, and the entire time zone for your part of the world will be highlighted in green. The major city closest to your location will be labeled with its current time. The selected city will appear in the text box located below the map. You can also select your time zone entering the city in the text box. As you type in the city name, a pop-up menu appears showing progressively limited choices. The corresponding time zone will be highlighted on the map. Click the Continue button to continue.

Figure 2-19: Where Are You, Time zone

Who Are You?

On the Who are you? screen you enter your name, your user login name, and password (see Figure 2-20). When you enter your name, a username will be generated for you using your first name, and a computer name will be entered using your first name and your computer's make and model name. You can change these names if you want. The name for the computer is the computer's network host name. The user you are creating will have administrative access, allowing you to change your system configuration, add new users and printers, and install new software. When you enter your password a Strength notice is displayed indicating whether it is too short, weak, fair, or good. For a good password include numbers and uppercase characters.

Figure 2-20: Who are you?

At the bottom of the screen, you have the options: "Log in automatically" and "Require my password to log in." Choose the "Log in automatically" option to have your system login to your account when you start up, instead of stopping at the login screen. The "Require my password to log in" entry provides a standard login screen.

Install Progress

Your installation continues with a slide show of Ubuntu 22.04 LTS features such as Web browsers, social services, Ubuntu Software, and photo editing. You can click on the arrow tabs at either end to move through the slide show manually (see Figure 2-21).

A progress bar at the bottom of the dialog shows the progress of the install process. You can click an expansion arrow next to the progress bar to open a small terminal section that displays the install operations as they occur.

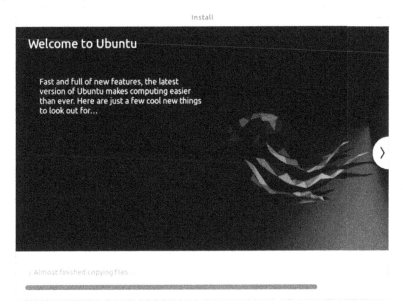

Figure 2-21: Install progress slide show

Once finished, the Installation Complete dialog appears (see Figure 2-22). Click the Restart Now button to restart and reboot to the new installation. If you installed from the Live USB/DVD session, the Continue Testing button lets you return to that session, if you want.

A message will appear prompting you to remove the USB/DVD disk, and then press ENTER.

Figure 2-22: Installation completed

Tip: Pressing ESC from the graphics menu places you at the boot prompt for text mode install.

After starting Ubuntu for the first time, you will be prompted to install the updates that were downloaded during the installation process.

Upgrading

You can upgrade a current Ubuntu system to the next release using the APT package manager or the Ubuntu Desktop USB/DVD. Upgrading is a simple matter of updating software to the new release versions, along with updating your GRUB configuration. Check the following site for upgrade details:

```
https://help.ubuntu.com/community/DiscoUpgrades
```

You can only upgrade to Ubuntu 22.04 LTS from Ubuntu 21.10 or from 20.04. Be sure you have first performed any needed updates for your Ubuntu system. It must be completely up to date before you perform an upgrade to Ubuntu 22.04.

You cannot upgrade from Ubuntu 19.10, or earlier to 22.04 directly. To upgrade from an earlier release other than 21.10 or 20.04, first, upgrade sequentially up to one of those.

Upgrade over a network from Ubuntu 20.04 and 21.10

To upgrade your system using your Internet connection, you can use Software Updater. The upgrade will be performed by downloading the latest package versions from the Ubuntu repository, directly. When a new release becomes available, Software Updater will display a message notifying you of the new release (provided it is configured to do so).

Be sure to first enable distribution notification for long term support versions. On the Ubuntu Software Updater dialog, click the Settings button on the lower left to open the Software & Updates dialog at the Updates tab. On the last menu "Notify me of a new Ubuntu version," choose the "For any new versions" for Ubuntu 21.10, and "For long-term support versions" for Ubuntu 20.04.

An Upgrade button will be displayed next to the message should you decide to upgrade your system to that release (see Figure 2-23). If you want to stay with your installed release, for now, you just click the OK button. Should you want to upgrade to the new release, in this case, Ubuntu 22.04 LTS, you click the Upgrade button to start the upgrade. A Welcome dialog is displayed with links for information about the release. Click the Upgrade button on this dialog to begin the upgrade. Be sure first to update all your current software. An upgrade should be performed from the most recent versions of your current release's software packages.

Figure 2-23: Upgrade message

You can also start the software updater directly for the distribution upgrade by entering the following on a command line (the **-d** option performs a distribution upgrade). Use either a terminal window or press Alt-F2 to open a Run Application window.

```
sudo update-manager -d
```

A Distribution Upgrade dialog opens showing the progress of the upgrade. The upgrade procedure will first prepare the upgrade, detecting the collection of software packages that have to be downloaded. A dialog will notify you of software packages for which support has ended (older deprecated software). Then a dialog will then open asking if you want to start the upgrade, displaying both a Cancel and Start Upgrade button. You can still cancel the upgrade at this time and nothing will be changed on your system (click the Cancel button). To continue with the Upgrade, click the Start Upgrade button.

The Distribution Upgrade dialog is again displayed (see Figure 2-24). Packages are downloaded (Getting new packages), and then installed on your system (Installing the upgrades). The download process can take some time depending on the speed of your Internet connection.

Distribution Upgrade

Upgrading Ubuntu to version 22.04

> Preparing to upgrade
> Setting new software channels
> Getting new packages
> Installing the upgrades
> Cleaning up
> Restarting the computer

Checking for installed snaps

> Terminal

Figure 2-24: Distribution Upgrade dialog

If the download is taking too long, you can click the Cancel button and run the upgrade later. A dialog is displayed telling you that the download will continue later from where it left off.

To start the upgrade again, first start Software Updater, click the Upgrade button, and proceed through the initial steps again, though this time will be much faster (Release notes, Preparing to upgrade, Setting new software channels). The Getting new packages stage will continue with next package.

Depending on the packages you are upgrading, you may have to enter configuration information through the terminal interface. Click the terminal arrow to open the terminal interface and respond to any prompts that may occur.

Once the upgrade is completed, a completion message is displayed. Reboot to start your system with the new release and its kernel.

Upgrading to a new release with apt-get

You can also use the **apt-get** command in a terminal window or on a command line interface to upgrade your system. To upgrade to an entirely new release, use the **dist-upgrade** option. A **dist-upgrade** would install a new release, preserving your original configuration and data. This option will also remove obsolete software packages.

```
sudo apt-get update
sudo apt-get dist-upgrade
```

Recovery, rescue, and boot loader re-install

Ubuntu provides the means to start up systems that have failed for some reason. A system that may boot but fails to start up, can be started in a recovery mode, already set up for you as an entry on your boot loader menu.

Recovery Mode (Advanced Options menu)

If for some reason your system is not able to start up, it may be due to conflicting configurations, libraries, or applications. On the GRUB menu first, choose the "Advanced options for Ubuntu" to open the advanced options menu(see Figure 2-25). Then select the recovery mode entry, the Ubuntu kernel entry with the (recovery mode) label attached to the end. This starts up a menu where you can use the arrow and ENTER keys to select from several recovery options (see Figure 2-26). These include resume, clean, dpkg, grub, network, and root. Short descriptions for each item are displayed on the menu.

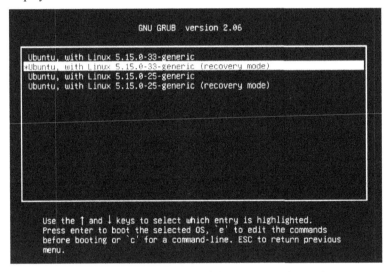

Figure 2-25: Grub advanced options menu with recovery kernels

```
Recovery Menu (filesystem state: read-only)
        resume          Resume normal boot
        clean           Try to make free space
        dpkg            Repair broken packages
        fsck            Check all file systems
        grub            Update grub bootloader
        network         Enable networking
        root            Drop to root shell prompt
        system-summary  System summary


                        <Ok>
```

Figure 2-26: Recovery options

The root option starts up Ubuntu as the root user with a command line shell prompt. In this case, you can boot your Linux system in a recovery mode and then edit configuration files with a text editor such as Vi, remove the suspect libraries, or reinstall damaged software with **apt-get**.

The resume entry will start up Ubuntu normally to your desktop.

The **grub** entry will update the grub boot loader. With GRUB2 your hard drive is re-scanned, detecting your installed operating systems and Ubuntu kernels, and implementing any GRUB configuration changes you may have made without updating GRUB.

To rescue a broken system, choose the **root** entry. Your broken system will be mounted and made accessible with a command line interface. You can then use command line operations and editors to fix configuration files.

Re-Installing the Boot Loader

If you have a multiple-boot system, that runs both Windows and Linux on the same machine, you may run into a situation where you have to reinstall your GRUB boot loader. This problem occurs if your Windows system completely crashes beyond repair and you have to install a new version of Windows, if you added Windows to your machine after having installed Linux, or if you upgraded to a new version of Windows. A Windows installation will automatically overwrite your boot loader.

You can reinstall your boot loader manually, using your Ubuntu Desktop USB/DVD live session. The procedure is more complicated, as you have to mount your Ubuntu system. On the Ubuntu Desktop USB/DVD Live session, you can use GParted to find out what partition your Ubuntu system uses. In a terminal window, create a directory on which to mount the system.

```
sudo mkdir myubuntu
```

Then mount it, making sure you have the correct file system type and partition name (usually **/dev/sda5** on dual boot systems).

```
sudo mount -t ext4 /dev/sda5 myubuntu
```

Then use **grub-install** and the device name of your first partition to install the boot loader, with the **--root-directory** option to specify the directory where you mounted your Ubuntu file system. The **--root-directory** option requires a full path name, which for the Ubuntu Desktop USB/DVD would be **/home/ubuntu** for the home directory. Using the **myubuntu** directory for this example, the full path name of the Ubuntu file system would be **/home/ubuntu/myubuntu**. You would then enter the following **grub-install** command.

```
sudo grub-install --root-directory=/home/ubuntu/myubuntu /dev/sda
```

This will re-install your current GRUB boot loader. You can then reboot, and the GRUB boot loader will start up.

3. Usage Basics: Login, Desktop, Network, and Help

Accessing your Ubuntu System

Display Manager

Ubuntu GNOME

Network Connections: wired and wireless

GNOME Settings

Help Resources (Ubuntu Desktop Guide)

Command Line Interface

Terminal Window

Using Linux has become an almost intuitive process, with easy-to-use interfaces, featuring graphical logins and desktops. Even the standard Linux command line interface is user-friendly with editable commands, history lists, and cursor-based tools. To start using Ubuntu, you have to know how to access your system and, once you are on the system, how to execute commands and run applications. Access is supported through a graphical login.

Linux is noted for providing easy access to extensive help documentation. It is easy to obtain information quickly about any Linux command and utility while logged into the system. You can access an online manual that describes each command, or obtain help that provides explanations that are more detailed. Your desktop provides help systems with easy access to desktop, system, and application help files.

Accessing Your Ubuntu System

You access your Ubuntu system using the GRUB bootloader to first start Ubuntu, and then use the display manager to log in to your account. From the desktop System Status Area menu (top right) you can shut down, restart, or suspend your system. It is also possible to access Ubuntu using a command line interface only, bypassing the desktop interface and its required graphical support.

GRUB Boot Loader

When your system starts, the GRUB boot loader will quickly select your default operating system and start up its login screen. If you have just installed Ubuntu, the default operating system will be Ubuntu.

If you have installed more than one operating system, the GRUB menu is displayed for several seconds at startup, before loading the default operating system automatically. To display the GRUB menu should you have only your Ubuntu system installed, press the SHIFT key at start up. Once displayed, press the ESC key to have GRUB wait until you have made a selection. Your GRUB menu is displayed as shown in Figure 3-1. The Advanced options entry allows you to start Ubuntu in recovery mode or choose a previously installed kernel to use.

The GRUB menu lists Ubuntu along with any other operating systems installed on your hard drive, such as Windows or other versions of Linux. Use the arrow keys to move to the entry you want and press ENTER

For graphical installations, some displays may have difficulty running the graphical startup display. If you have this problem, you can edit your Linux GRUB entry and remove the **splash** term at the end of the **linux** line. Press the **e** key to edit a GRUB entry (see Figure 3-2).

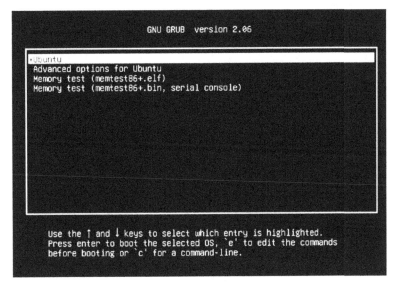

Figure 3-1: Ubuntu GRUB menu

To change a particular line, use the up/down arrow keys to move to the line. You can use the left/right arrow keys to move along the line. The Backspace key will delete characters and typing will insert characters. The editing changes are temporary. Permanent changes can only be made by directly editing the GRUB configuration **/etc/default/grub** file, and then running the following command:

```
sudo update-grub
```

```
                         GNU GRUB  version 2.06

 ┌──────────────────────────────────────────────────────────────────┐
 │ setparams 'Ubuntu'                                                 │
 │                                                                    │
 │         recordfail                                                 │
 │         load_video                                                 │
 │         gfxmode $linux_gfx_mode                                    │
 │         insmod gzio                                                │
 │         if [ x$grub_platform = xxen ]; then insmod xzio; insmod lzopio; \│
 │ fi                                                                 │
 │         insmod part_gpt                                            │
 │         insmod ext2                                                │
 │         search --no-floppy --fs-uuid --set=root 632494cb-45bc-4f08-9f3f-\│
 │ c495ae5cec90                                                       │
 │         linux       /boot/vmlinuz-5.15.0-33-generic root=UUID=632494cb-\│
 │ 45bc-4f08-9f3f-c495ae5cec90 ro  quiet splash $vt_handoff          │
 │         initrd       /boot/initrd.img-5.15.0-33-generic          ↓│
 └──────────────────────────────────────────────────────────────────┘

      Minimum Emacs-like screen editing is supported. TAB lists
      completions. Press Ctrl-x or F10 to boot, Ctrl-c or F2 for a
      command-line or ESC to discard edits and return to the GRUB
      menu.
```

Figure 3-2: Editing a GRUB menu item

When your Ubuntu operating system starts up, an Ubuntu logo appears during the startup. You can press the ESC key to see the startup messages instead. Ubuntu uses Plymouth with its kernel modesetting ability to display a startup animation. The Plymouth Ubuntu logo theme is used by default.

The GNOME Display Manager: GDM

The graphical login interface displays a list of usernames. When you click a username, a login screen replaces the listing of users, displaying the selected user and a text box in which you then enter your password. Upon pressing Enter, you log in and your desktop starts up.

Graphical logins are handled by the GNOME Display Manager (GDM). The GDM manages the login interface, in addition to authenticating a user password and username, and then starts up a selected desktop. From the GDM, you can shift to the command-line interface with Ctrl+Alt+F2, and then shift back to the GDM with Ctrl+Alt+F1. The keys F2 through F6 provide different command-line terminals, as in Ctrl+Alt+F3 for the third command-line terminal.

When the GDM starts up, it shows a listing of users (see Figure 3-3). A System Status Area menu at the top right of the screen displays entries for sound adjustment, screen brightness (for laptops), network wired and wireless (if supported) status, and the battery status (if a laptop). Click the "Power Off/Log Out entry to expand the menu to show Suspend and Power Off items. The Power Off entry displays the Power Off dialog with options to Power Off and Restart.

Figure 3-3: The GDM user listing

At the top center of the screen is the date (day of the week) and time. Clicking on the time displays the calendar with the full date specified, and the notifications menu if allowed.

Next to the System Status Area icons is an accessibility button, which displays a menu of switches that let you turn on accessibility tools and such features as the onscreen keyboard, enhanced contrast, and the screen magnifier.

To log in, click a username from the list of users. You are then prompted to enter the user's password (see Figure 3-4). A login screen replaces the user list, showing the username you selected and a Password text box in which you can enter the user's password. By default, the password you enter is hidden. Should you want to display the text of your password, you can click the eye button located to the right in the password text box. Click the eye button again to hide the password. Once you enter the password, press Enter. Your desktop starts up.

If the name of a user you want to log in as is not listed, click the "Not listed?" entry at the end of the list, to open a text box, which prompts you first for a username, and then a password.

On the login screen, there is a session button (gear icon) located at the right bottom corner. You can click this button to display a menu listing other installed desktops or the same desktop using a different display server. When you installed the Ubuntu desktop, two display servers were installed, X11 and Wayland. On the session menu you can choose Ubuntu (the Wayland display server and the default) or "Ubuntu on X.org", which uses the older X.org display server.

The session menu will also show other installed desktops you could use instead of Ubuntu (GNOME). Though GNOME is the primary desktop for Ubuntu, it is possible to install and use other desktops, known as Ubuntu Flavors, such as Kubuntu (Plasma, KDE), Xubuntu (Xfc), and Ubuntu MATE (MATE). These are available on the Ubuntu repository (see Figure 3-5).

Ubuntu now uses the systemd login manager, logind, to manage logins and sessions, replacing consolekit, which is no longer supported. You can configure login manager options with the **/etc/systemd/logind.conf** file. You can set options such as the number of terminals, the idle action, and hardware key operations, such as the power key. Check the **logind.conf** man page for details.

Figure 3-4: GDM login

Figure 3-5: GDM Session menu

The System Status Area

Once logged in, the System Status Area button is displayed on the right side of the top bar of the desktop (see Figure 3-6). The button will display emblems for network, sound, and power. Clicking the button displays the System Status Area menu, with items for sound, brightness, wired and wireless connections, Bluetooth, the battery, GNOME Settings, the lock screen, and a "Power Off/Log Out" submenu for shutting down or logging out. The sound and brightness items feature sliding bars with which you can adjust the volume and brightness. The Wired, Wi-Fi, Bluetooth, Battery, and Power Off/Log Out entries expand to submenus with added entries.

Figure 3-6: System Status Area menu

You can also set the power profile from the System Status Area menu (see Figure 3-7). You can choose from three profile modes: Balanced, Power Saver, and Performance. The profile mode entry on the menu is the name of the currently selected profile. Profile modes are useful for laptops running on batteries, and may only show the Balanced and Power Saver modes. Balanced is the default and balances power use and performance. Performance gives priority to CPU performance. Power Saver reduces performance to save power, especially for display (GPU) operations. Click on the profile modes entry (the name of the currently active profile mode) to expand it to a submenu where you can choose the profile mode you want.

Figure 3-7: System Status Area menu power profile modes

On systems that are not laptops, there will be no brightness slider or Battery entry on the System Status Area menu. If the system also has no wireless device, the Wi-Fi entry will also be missing.

Lock Screen

You can choose to lock your screen and suspend your system by click the Lock entry on the System Status Area menu. To start up again, press the spacebar and the Lock Screen dialog appears (see Figure 3-8). Your user login screen is then displayed with a password text box. Enter your password to start up your desktop session again. Like the login screen, the password you enter is hidden. Should you want to display the text of your password, you can click the eye button located to the right in the password text box. Click the eye button again to hide the password. The background for the lock screen is a blurred version of your desktop background.

Figure 3-8: Lock Screen

Logging Out and Switching Users

If you want to exit your desktop and return to the GDM login screen, or switch to a different user, you click the "Power Off/Log Out" entry in the System Status Area menu to expand to a menu with entries for Switch User, Log Out, Suspend, and Power Off (see Figure 3-9). If you have only one user configured for your system, then the Switch User entry does not appear.

⏻ Power Off / Log Out ﹀

Suspend

Restart...

Power Off...

Power Off

The system will power off automatically in 60 seconds.

Log Out

Switch User...

Cancel   Power Off

Figure 3-9: GNOME Log Out menu entry

Click the Log Out entry to display a dialog that shows buttons for Cancel and Log Out (see Figure 3-10). Then click the Log Out button to log out of your account, exiting GNOME and returning to the login screen, where you can log in again as a different user or shut down the system. A countdown will commence in the dialog, showing how much time you have left before it performs the logout automatically.

Log Out Richard Petersen

Richard Petersen will be logged out automatically in 60 seconds.

Cancel   Log Out

Figure 3-10: Log Out dialog

The Switch User entry switches out from the current user and runs the GDM to display a list of users you can log in as. Click the name to open a password prompt and display a session button. You can then log in as that user. The sessions of users already logged will continue with the same open windows and applications that were running when the user switched off. You can switch back and forth between logged-in users, with all users retaining their session from where they left off. When you switch off from a user, that user's running programs will continue in the background.

Poweroff

From the login screen, you can poweroff (shut down) the system using the System Status Area menu on either the login screen or the desktop. Click the "Power Off/Log Out" entry to expand to a list of menu items, which include a "Power Off" entry. Clicking this entry displays a Power Off dialog with options to restart or power off (see Figure 3-11). A countdown will commence in the dialog, showing how much time you have left before it performs the shutdown automatically. You can also simply press the power button on your computer to display the Power Off dialog.

⏻ Power Off / Log Out ▾

    Log Out

    Switch User...

    Suspend

    Power Off...

Power Off

The system will power off automatically in 60 seconds.

| Cancel | Restart | Power Off |

Figure 3-11: Power Off and Restart dialog

Should your display freeze or become corrupted, one safe way to shut down and restart is to press a command line interface key (like CTRL-ALT-F2) to revert to the command line interface, and then press CTRL-ALT-DEL to restart. You can also log in on the command line interface (terminal) and then enter the **sudo poweroff** command.

On the desktop, you can also shut down your system from a terminal window, using the **poweroff** command with the **sudo** command. You will be prompted to enter your password.

```
sudo poweroff
```

To perform a reboot from a terminal window, you can use the **reboot** command.

```
sudo reboot
```

Accessing Linux from the Command Line Interface

You can access the command-line interface by pressing CTRL-ALT-F2 at any time (CTRL-ALT-F1 returns to the graphics interface, login screen). For the command line interface, you are initially given a login prompt. The login prompt is preceded by the hostname you gave your system. In this example, the hostname is **richard-desktop**. When you finish using Linux, you log out with the **logout** command. Linux then displays the same login prompt, waiting for you or another user to log in again. This is the equivalent of the login window provided by the GDM display manager. You can then log in to another account.

Once you log in as a user, you can enter and execute commands. To log in, enter your username and your password. If you make a mistake, you can erase characters with the **backspace** key. In the next example, the user enters the username **richard** and is then prompted to enter the password:

```
Ubuntu 22.04 LTS richard-desktop tty3

richard-desktop login: richard
Password:
```

When you type in your password, it does not appear on the screen. This is to protect your password from being seen by others. If you enter either the username or the password incorrectly, the system will respond with the error message "Login incorrect" and will ask for your username again, starting the login process over. You can then re-enter your username and password.

Once you enter your username and password, you are logged in to the system and the command line prompt is displayed, waiting for you to enter a command. The command line prompt is a dollar sign (**$**). On Ubuntu, your prompt is preceded by the hostname and the folder you are in. The home folder is indicated by a tilde (~).

```
richard@richard-desktop:~$
richard@richard-desktop:~$ cd Pictures
richard@richard-desktop:~/Pictures$
```

To end your session, issue the **logout** or **exit** command. This returns you to the login prompt, and Linux waits for another user to log in.

```
richard@richard-desktop:~$ logout
```

To shut down your system from the command line, you can use the **poweroff** command with the **sudo** command. You will be prompted to enter your password.

```
sudo poweroff
```

To perform a reboot from the terminal window, you can use the **reboot** command.

```
sudo reboot
```

If you want a time delay on the shutdown, you would use the **shutdown** command with **-h** and the time options with administrative access (**sudo** command). This command will log you out and shut down the system after 5 minutes.

```
richard@richard-desktop:~$ sudo shutdown -h +5
```

The Ubuntu Desktop

The Ubuntu 22.04 LTS desktop uses the Ubuntu GNOME interface. Ubuntu uses the Ubuntu Yaru theme for its interface with the Ubuntu screen background, and menu icons as its default (see Figure 3-12). You can change themes using the GNOME Tweaks Appearance tab's. The Yaru theme places the window control buttons (close, maximize, and minimize buttons) on the right side of a window title bar, as shown here. There are three window buttons: an x for close, a dash (-) for minimize, and a square for maximize. The close button is highlighted in orange.

window buttons

Ubuntu GNOME

Ubuntu 22.04 LTS uses the GNOME desktop. It provides easy-to-use overviews and menus, along with a flexible file manager and desktop. GNOME is based on the gnome-shell, which is a compositing window manager.

The Ubuntu desktop displays a top bar, through which you access your applications, windows, and settings. Clicking the System Status Area button at the right side of the top bar displays the status user area menu, from which you can access the system setting dialog, lock the screen, and shut down (Power Off) the system (see Figure 3-11). The dock is a bar on the left side with icons for your favorite applications. Initially, there are icons for the Firefox web browser, Thunderbird mail, Files (the GNOME file manager), Rhythmbox music application, LibreOffice Writer, Ubuntu Software, GNOME help, and the Applications overview, as depicted in Figure 3-11. The last icon opens an Applications overview that you can use to start other applications. To open an application from the dock, click its icon or right-click on the icon and choose New Window from the pop-up menu. You can remove any of the dock icons except the Applications overview icon by right-clicking on the icon and choosing "Remove from Favorites." Running applications will also be shown in the dock, which you can make part of your Favorites if you want. The Ubuntu dock is a GNOME extension implemented by Ubuntu and is a modified version of the GNOME Dock to Dash extension, which places a GNOME dash on the desktop.

Figure 3-12: The Ubuntu GNOME desktop

You can also access applications and windows by using the Activities overview mode. Click the Activities button at the left side of the top bar (or press the Super (Windows) key). The overview mode consists of a dash (dock) listing your favorites and running applications, workspaces, and windows (see Figure 3-13). Large thumbnails of open windows are displayed on the windows overview (the desktop area). You can use the Search box at the top to locate an application quickly. Partially hidden thumbnails of your desktop workspaces are displayed on the right side. Initially, there are two. Moving your mouse to the right side displays the workspace thumbnails.

Figure 3-13: Activities overview

You can manually leave the overview at any time by pressing the ESC key, pressing the Super key (Windows key), or by clicking a window thumbnail.

The dash is a bar on the left side of the overview with icons for your favorite applications. Initially. It operates the same as the Ubuntu dock, from which it was derived. as on the dock, the last icon opens an Applications overview that you can use to start other applications. To open an application from the dash, click its icon or right-click on the icon and choose New Window from the pop-up menu. You can also click and drag the icon to the windows overview or to a workspace thumbnail on the right side.

You can access windows from the windows overview, which is displayed when you start Activities. The windows overview displays thumbnails of all your open windows. When you pass your mouse over a window thumbnail, a close box appears, at the upper-right corner, with which you can close the window. You can also move the window on the desktop and to another workspace.

To move a window on the desktop, click and drag its title bar. To maximize a window, double-click its title bar or drag it to the top bar. To return to normal, double-click the title bar again or drag it away from the top bar. To close a window, click its close box (upper right). To minimize a window, click its minimize button. To maximize a minimized window, click its icon in the dock.

The Ubuntu desktop also supports corresponding keyboard operations for desktop tasks, see Table 3-1.

Keypress	Action
SHIFT	Move a file or folder, default
CTRL	Copy a file or folder
CTRL-SHIFT	Create a link for a file or folder
F2	Rename selected file or folder
CTRL-ALT-Arrow (right, left, up, down)	Move to a different desktop
CTRL-w	Close current window
ALT-spacebar	Open window menu for window operations
ALT-F2	Open Run command box
ALT-F1	Open Applications menu
Ctrl-F	Find file

Table 3-1: Window and File Manager Keyboard shortcuts

Clicking the Applications icon on the dash or dock (bottom icon) opens the Applications overview listings all your installed applications (see Figure 2-14). Click an application icon to start its applications. You can also right-click and choose the New Window entry on the pop-up menu. There is an application folder called Utilities on the applications overview. Utilities lists several tools, such as archive manager, backup tool, log viewer, font manager, system monitor, terminal window, and, when installed, GNOME Tweaks.

Applications Overview with workspace selector

Figure 3-14: Applications Overview

GNOME File Manager

You can access your home folder from the Files icon on the dash. A file manager window opens, showing your Home folder (see Figure 3-15). Your Home folder will already have default folders created for commonly used files. These include Documents, Downloads, Music, Pictures, and Videos. Your office applications will automatically save files to the Documents folder by default. Image and photo applications place image files in the Pictures folder. The Desktop folder will hold all files and folders saved to your desktop. When you download a file, it is placed in the Downloads folder.

The file manager window displays several components, including a header bar, which combines the title bar and toolbar, and a sidebar. When you open a new folder, the same window is used to display it, and you can use the forward and back arrows to move through previously opened folders. The header bar displays navigation folder buttons that show your current folder and its parent folders. You can click a parent folder to move to it. The GNOME file manager also supports tabs. You can open several folders in the same file manager window.

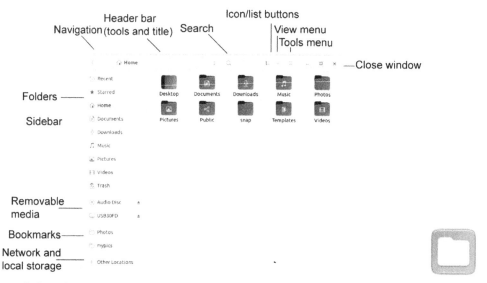

Figure 3-15: File manager for the Home folder

There are three menus on the file manager header bar, the folder menu on the navigation button for the current folder, the view menu (down-arrow button) and tools menu (menu button), both on the right side of the header bar (see Figure 3-16). The view menu provides zoom buttons for enlarging or reducing the size of the folder icons and sort options for your files and folders, as well as a Reload option to update the display. The tools menu shows file manager tools with buttons to add a new folder, tab, or bookmark, show hidden files, display the sidebar, and access file manager preferences. On the navigation section of the header bar, the folder button for the displayed (current) folder will have a folder menu as indicated by the down-arrow emblem, which lets you create a new folder, add the folder to your folder bookmarks, select all folders and files in the folder, open the Properties dialog for this folder, and open the folder in a terminal window. Click the folder button to display the menu.

Figure 3-16: File manager folder, view, and tools menus

GNOME Customization with Tweak Tool: Themes, Icons, Fonts, and Startup Applications

You can perform common desktop customizations using the GNOME Tweak Tool. Areas to customize include fonts, themes, startup applications, workspaces, window behavior, and the time display. You can access Tweak Tool from the Applications overview | Utilities. The GNOME Tweak Tool has tabs for Appearance, Extensions, Fonts, Keyboard and Mouse, Startup Applications, Top Bar, Window Titlebars, Windows, and Workspaces (see Figure 3-17). GNOME Tweaks is not installed by default. Use Ubuntu Software to install it.

The Appearance tab lets you set the theme for your sound, icons, and cursor. Ubuntu uses the Yaru theme. Traditionally, GNOME uses the Adwaita Theme with its light and dark variants. As you add other desktops, such as MATE, the available themes increase. There would be many window themes and icons to choose from.

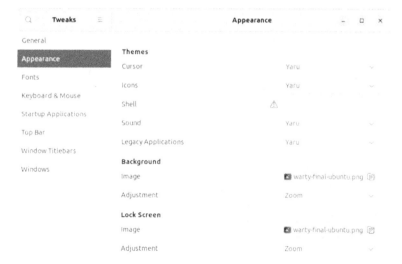

Figure 3-17: GNOME Tweak Tool - Appearance tab (themes)

Desktop fonts for window titles, interface (application or dialog text), documents, and monospace (terminal windows or code) can be changed in the Fonts tab (see Figure 3-18) . You can adjust the size of the font or change the font style. Clicking the font name opens a "Pick a Font" dialog from which you can choose a different font. The quality of text display can be further adjusted with Hinting and Antialiasing options. To simply increase or decrease the size of all fonts on your desktop interface, you can adjust the Scaling Factor.

Figure 3-18: GNOME Tweak Tool - Fonts tab

At times, there may be certain applications that you want started up when you log in, such as the Gedit text editor, the Firefox web browser, or the Videos movie player. On the Startup Applications tab, you can choose the applications to start up (see Figure 3-19). Click the plus (+) button to open an applications dialog from which you can choose an application. Once added, you can later remove the application by clicking its Remove button.

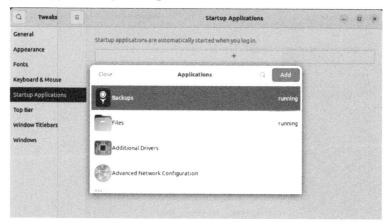

Figure 3-19: GNOME Tweak Tool - Startup Applications tab

Network Connections

Network connections will be set up for you by Network Manager, which will detect your network connections automatically, both wired and wireless. Network Manager provides status information for your connection and allows you to switch easily from one configured connection to another, as needed. For initial configuration, it detects as much information as possible about the new connection.

Network Manager is user specific. Wired connections will be started automatically. For wireless connections, when a user logs in, Network Manager selects the connection preferred by that user. From a menu of detected wireless networks, the user can select a wireless connection to use.

Network Manager displays active network connections in the System Status Area: Wired for the wired connection and Wi-Fi for a wireless connection. Each entry will indicate its status, as connected or disconnected. The Network Manager icon for these entries will vary according to the connection status: solid for an active connection and empty for a disconnected connection (see Figure 3-20). On wired systems that have no wireless devices, there is no Wi-Fi network entry in the System Status Area menu.

Figure 3-20: System Status Area Network Connections

Network Manager Wired Connections

For computers connected to a wired network, such as an Ethernet connection, Network Manager automatically detects and establishes the network connection. Most networks use DHCP to provide such network information as an IP address and DNS server. With this kind of connection, Network Manager can connect automatically to your network whenever you start your system.

Network Manager Wireless Connections

With multiple wireless access points for Internet connections, a system could have several network connections to choose from. This is particularly true for notebook computers that access different wireless connections at different locations. Instead of manually configuring a new connection each time one is encountered, the Network Manager tool can configure and select a connection to use automatically. Click the Wired entry in the System Status Area to expand the menu to show entries from which to connect or disconnect to wired networking, and open the GNOME Network Settings dialog at the Wired tab (Wired Settings).

Network Manager will scan for wireless connections, checking for Extended Service Set Identifiers (ESSIDs). If an ESSID identifies a previously used connection, it is selected. If several are found, the recently used one is chosen. If only new connections are available, Network Manager waits for the user to choose one.

Click the Wi-Fi entry in the System Status Area to expand the menu to show entries from which to select a network, turn off wireless networking, and open the GNOME Network Settings dialog at the Wi-Fi tab (Wi-Fi Settings). Click the Select Network item to open a dialog that shows a list of all available wireless connections (see Figure 3-21). Entries display the name of the wireless network and a wave graph showing the strength of its signal. To connect to a network, click its entry, then click the Connect button, to activate the connection. If this is the first time you are trying to connect to that network, you will be prompted to enter the password or encryption key (see Figure 3-22).

Figure 3-21: Network Manager connections menu - wireless

Figure 3-22: Network Manager wireless authentication

You can turn off wireless by clicking the Turn Off entry in the expanded Wi-Fi section of the System Status Area (see Figure 3-23). When turned off, the entry label changes to Turn On. To reactivate your wireless connection, click the Turn On entry.

Figure 3-23: Network Manager wireless on and off

Configuring Network Connections with GNOME Settings

On the GNOME Settings dialog there is a Wi-Fi tab for wireless configuration and a Network tab for wired, VPN, and proxy configurations. Choose Wi-Fi Settings from the expanded Wi-Fi entries in the System Status Area, or click the Wi-Fi tab in the Settings dialog, to open the Wi-Fi tab (see Figure 3-24). On the Wi-Fi tab, an Airplane Mode switch and a list of visible wireless connections are listed. The currently active connection will have a checkmark next to its name. On the right side of the titlebar is a switch for turning wireless on and off. A menu to the right of the switch list entries for connections to hidden networks, turning on your computer's Wi-Fi hotspot capability, and listing previously accessed Wi-Fi Networks (Known Wi-Fi Networks). The "Known Wi-Fi Networks" entry opens a dialog listing your previously accessed Wi-Fi networks, which you can choose to edit or delete (Forget button).

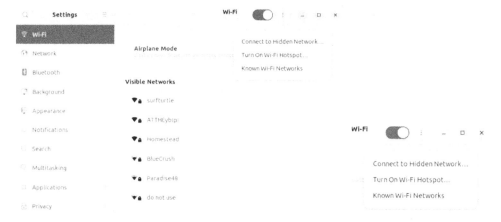

Figure 3-24: Settings Network wireless connections

Your current active connection will have a checkmark next to it and a gear button to the right. Click the gear button to display a dialog with tabs for managing the connection. The Details tab provides information about the connection (see Figure 3-25). The Security, Identity, IPv4, and IPv6 tabs let you perform a detailed configuration of your connection, as described in Chapter 15. The settings are fixed to automatic by default. Should you make any changes, click the Apply button to have them take effect. The Details tab has options both for connecting automatically and for providing availability to other users. These are set by default. Should you not want to connect to the wireless network automatically, be sure to uncheck this option. To remove a network's connection information, click the Forget Connection button on the Details tab.

Figure 3-25: Settings Network wireless connection - Details tab

For a wired connection, click the Wired Settings entry from the expanded Wired entries in the System Status Area, or click the Network tab on GNOME Settings. This will display lists of Wired and VPN connections, as well as an entry for the Network Proxy. The Wired list shows your current wired connections with on and off switched for each. A plus button at the top right of the Wired list lets you add more wired connections. Next to a connection's switch a gear button is displayed (see Figure 3-26). Clicking the gear button opens a configuration dialog for that connection with tabs for Details, Identity, IPv4, IPv6, and Security (see Chapter 15).

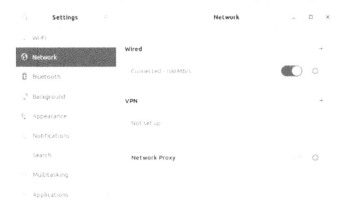

Figure 3-26: Settings Network wired connection

Clicking on the Network proxy gear button opens a Network Proxy dialog menu with Disabled, Manual, and Automatic options (see Figure 3-27). The Manual option lets you enter address and port information. For the Automatic option, you enter a configuration address.

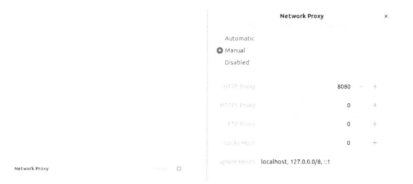

Figure 3-27: Network proxy settings (Settings Network)

To add a vpn connection, click the plus (+) button to the right of the VPN title to open the Add Vpn dialog listing the supported VPN protocols. You can add more (see Chapter 15). Once a protocol is selected, an appropriate configuration dialog for your VPN network is displayed.

Settings

You can configure desktop settings and perform most administrative tasks using the GNOME configuration tools (see Table 3-2) listed in the GNOME Settings dialog, accessible from the System Status Area dialog as the Settings entry. It displays tabs for different desktop and system configurations (see Figure 3-28). There are two subheadings for Applications and Privacy. Tabs for devices such as keyboards, displays, and printers, are located in the middle of the list. Tabs for administration such as users, system information, date and time, and universal access are located at the bottom of the list.

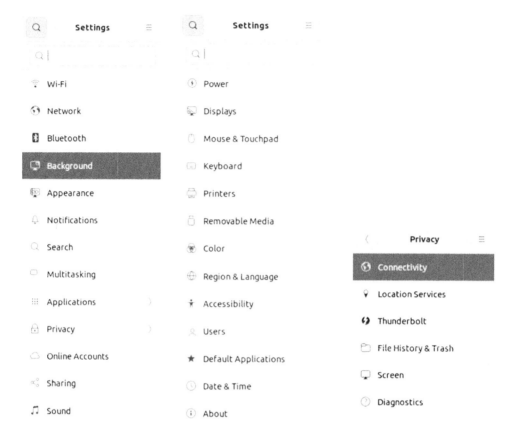

Figure 3-28: GNOME Settings

Setting	Description
About	Sets the hostname of your computer, displays hardware and operating system information
Accessibility	Enables universal access features for the display, keyboard, and mouse
Appearance	Style (light, dark, and color accents), desktop icon, and dock configuration.
Applications	Opens a dialog where you can set permissions for applications such as file types and notifications
Background	Sets desktop background
Bluetooth	Sets Bluetooth detection and configuration
Color	Sets the color profile for a device

Date & Time	Sets the date, time, and time zone
Default Applications	Default applications for types of files
Displays	Changes your screen resolution, refresh rate, and screen orientation for your connected displays
Keyboard Shortcuts	Configures shortcut keys
Mobile Network	Configure a Wireless/Wan cellular device, if detected.
Mouse & Touchpad	Sets mouse and touchpad configuration
Multitasking	Turn on hot corner, screen edge window resizing, dynamic or fixed workspaces, show workspaces on all displays, and application switching on workspaces and monitors.
Network	Lets you turn wired networks on or off. Allows access to an available wired network. Also specifies proxy configuration, if needed.
Notifications	Turns on notifications for different applications
Online Accounts	Configures online accounts for use by e-mail and browser applications
Power	Sets the power saving options and lists battery levels.
Printers	Configure printers and access print queues
Privacy	Turns on privacy features with tabs for Connectivity, Location Services, Thunderbolt, File History & Trash, Screen Lock, and Diagnostics.
Region & Language	Chooses a language, format, input source, and keyboard layout
Removable Media	Default applications for removeable media
Sharing	Turns on sharing for media, remote login, and screen access
Sound	Configures system levels, output and input sound devices, and sound effects.
Search	Specifies the resources and locations searched by the GNOME activities overview search box
Users	Manages users and add new ones
Wi-Fi	Lets you configure and manage wireless networks.

Table 3-2: Settings

About (System Information)

The About dialog shows system information, displaying your hardware specifications (memory, CPU, graphics card chip, and disk capacity), the hostname (Device name), and operating system information such as OS type (64- or 32-bit system), OS name (the Ubuntu version), the GNOME version in use, and the selected Windowing system (X11 or Wayland) (see Figure 3-29). You can change the hostname if you wish. Click on the Device Name entry to open a Rename Device dialog where you can change the hostname. Clicking on the Software Updates entry opens the Software & Updates dialog where you can configure updates (see Chapter 4).

Figure 3-29: About

Accessibility (Universal Access)

The Accessibility dialog in Settings lets you configure alternative access to your interface for your keyboard and mouse actions. Four sections set the display (Seeing), sound (Hearing), typing, and point-and-click features. Seeing lets you adjust the contrast and text size, and whether to allow zooming or use of screen reader (see Figure 3-30). Hearing uses visual cues for alert sounds. Typing enables the screen keyboard with repeat keys and cursor blinking options. Click on Typing Assist to enable features such as sticky keys, slow keys, and bounce keys. Pointing and Clicking lets you use the keyboard for mouse operations, adjust the double-click delay, and implement hover clicks (Click Assist).

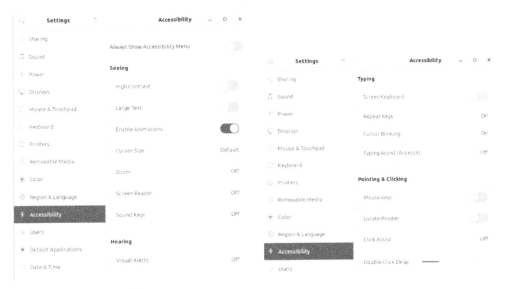

Figure 3-30: Accessibility

Appearance

The Appearance dialog lets you set options for the desktop style, icons, and the dock (see Figure 3-31). The Style section lets you choose either a light or dark theme (Light is the default). You can also choose an accent color from the Color buttons. In the Desktop Icons section you can choose the size, position of new icons on the screen (Bottom Right is the default), and whether to show your personal folder (home folder). The dock section lets you set the size of the dock icons, auto-hide the dock, reduce the size of the dock to just the icons on it, and, for systems with multiple displays, whether to show it on all of them. You can also configure the dock to include unmounted and network file systems, as well as the trash ("Configure dock behavior" option).

Figure 3-31: Appearance

Application Permissions

With GNOME Settings you can configure permissions for resources for your installed applications. For a selected application, you can set permissions for resources such as notifications, sound, disk space, desktop search, as well as the file types and links that an application can open. Resources are arranged according to integration (notification and search), default handlers (file types), and usage (disk usage). The Integration section will usually list a notification entry with a switch to turn notifications on or off. If the application is supported by desktop search, there will also be a Search entry with a switch you can use to turn off desktop searches for this application. The default handlers are organized into categories by type, such as image files, audio files, text files, and other files. The categories are expandable trees you can click on to display the file types. Expanding a category shows the file types and an Unset button next to each type that you can use to unset the type, denying access by the application to that file type (see Figure 3-32). Some applications, such as Videos and Firefox, will have a large number of handlers (see Figure 3-33). Expanding a Links category displays the various links for that application such as FTP links and Web links.

Clicking on the Applications entry on the GNOME Settings opens a dialog listing your applications in a sidebar. Selecting an application displays a dialog to the right with the resources for that application listed according to Integration, Default Handlers, and Usage. Sections are only shown if there are resources available for that application. Many applications will only have an Integration section with a Notification entry.

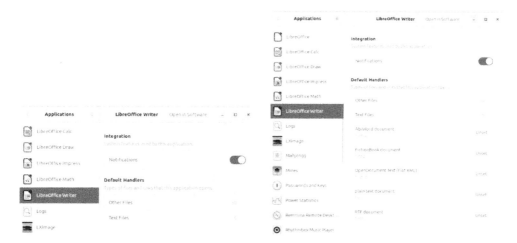

Figure 3-32: Applications Permissions - Settings

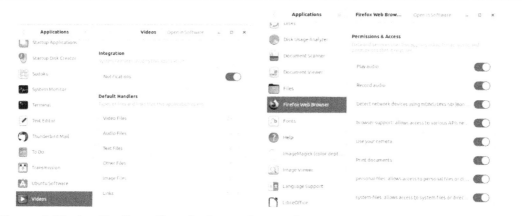

Figure 3-33: Applications Permissions - Categories

Background

With the Background dialog, you can set your background for the desktop. You can access the Background dialog from the Settings dialog (see Figure 3-34). The current background is shown and icons of installed backgrounds are displayed. Click on an image to make it your current background. The background on your display is updated immediately. The background image you choose for your desktop also becomes the background image of the login screen. A blurred version of the new background image becomes the background for the lock screen.

To add your own image, click the Add Picture button in the Settings titlebar to open a dialog listing the images in your Pictures folder (see Figure 3-35). You can select images from other folders. Once you make your selection, click the Open button at the upper right. You then return to the main Background dialog, showing your new background. An x is displayed on the icons of the images you add, allowing you to remove the image.

Figure 3-34: Background

Figure 3-35: Select Background

Install the **gnome-backgrounds** package to add a collection of GNOME backgrounds. They will appear automatically in the Settings Background dialog. You can download more GNOME backgrounds (wallpapers) from **https://www.gnome-look.org/**.

Color Profiles (GNOME Color Manager)

You can manage the color for different devices by using color profiles specified with the Color dialog accessible from Settings. The Color dialog lists devices for which you can set color profiles. Click a device to display buttons at the bottom of the screen for Add profile and Calibrate. Your monitor will have a profile set up automatically. Click the Add Profile button to open a dialog with an Automatic Profiles menu from which you can choose a color profile. Click the Add button to add the profile. Available profiles include Adobe RGB, sRGB, and Kodak ProPhoto RGB. You can also import a profile from an ICC profile file of your own.

When you click on a profile entry, its Profiles are listed (see Figure 3-36). Click on a profile to display buttons to Set for all users, Remove profile, and View details. Click the View details button for the color profile information.

Figure 3-36: Color management dialog

Date & Time

The Date & Time calendar and menu are located on the top bar at the center (see Figure 3-37). The dialog displays the current time and day of the week but can be modified to display 24-hour or AM/PM time. The calendar shows the current date, but you can move to different months and years using the month scroll arrows at the top of the calendar.

Figure 3-37: Date & Time dialog

You can further adjust the top bar time display using the GNOME Tweak Tool's Top Bar tab (see Figure 3-38). In the Clock section, there are options to show the date, weekday, and seconds. For the Calendar, you can show week numbers.

Figure 3-38: GNOME Tweak Tool - Top Bar (clock options)

Date & Time options are set using the Date & Time tab in Settings. The Date & Time tab lets you set the time zone and time. Both are configured for automatic settings using Internet time servers (see Figure 3-39). The time zone or the time and date can be set manually by turning off the Automatic switches. Once turned off, the Date & Time and the Time Zone entries become active.

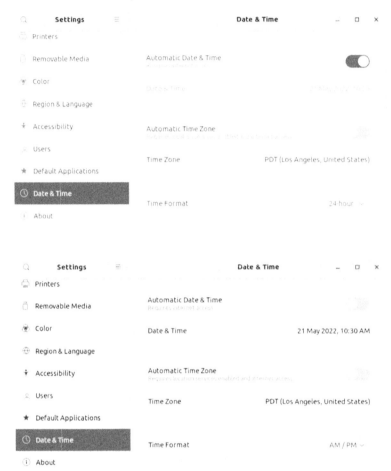

Figure 3-39: Date & Time Settings dialog with automatic settings turned on (top) and off (bottom)

The Date & Time entry opens a dialog with settings for the hour, minutes, day, and year, with a menu for the month (see Figure 3-40). You can use the plus (+) and minus (-) buttons to sequentially change the values.

Figure 3-40: Date & Time manual settings

Clicking the Time Zone entry opens a dialog with a map of the time zones and the current one selected (see Figure 3-41). Click a new time zone to change the zone.

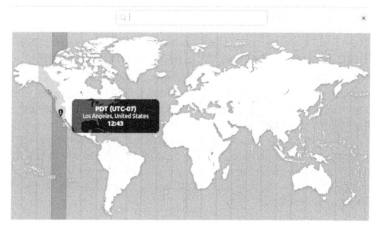

Figure 3-41: Time Zone dialog

You can also set the system time manually using the **date** command. The **date** command has several options for adjusting both displaying and setting the date and time. Check the date man page for a detailed list, **man date**. You can set the time with the **--set** option and a string specifying the date. You use human readable terms for the time string, such as Mon or Monday for the day and Jul or July for the month. Hour, minute, and second can be represented by numbers separated by colons. The following sets the date to July 9, 8:15 AM 2022.

```
sudo date --set='Monday July 9 08:15 2022'
```

To just set the time you would enter something like:

```
sudo date --set='12:15:43'
```

Default Applications

The Default Applications tab lets you set default applications for basic types of files: Web, Mail, Calendar, Music, Video, and Photos (see Figure 3-42). Use the drop-down menus to choose installed alternatives, such as Evolution instead of Thunderbird for Mail or Shotwell instead of Image Viewer for Photos.

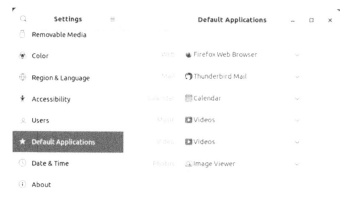

Figure 3-42: Default Applications

Displays (Resolution, Rotation, Scaling, and Night Light)

The display drivers for Linux used on Ubuntu support user-level resolution and orientation changes. Any user can specify a resolution or orientation, without affecting the settings of other users. The Settings Displays dialog provides a simple interface for setting rotation, resolution, and selecting added monitors, allowing for cloned or extended displays across several connected monitors. Menus let you configure the orientation, resolution, and refresh rate (see Figure 3-43). Should you make changes, an Apply button will appear in the titlebar which you can click. For changes to resolution, the new resolution is displayed with a dialog asking if you want to keep the new display settings. The Revert Settings button returns to the previous resolution and the Keep Changes button keeps the new one.

The display server supports scaling using the Scale entry on the Display dialog. To enable scaling, turn on the switch for Fractional Scaling to display the Scale option with a list of possible scales. A Scale entry is displayed showing buttons for possible scale percentages (see Figure 3-44).

Should you have multiple displays connected to your system, tabs are displayed on the Displays dialog for Join Display, Mirror, and Single Display. Should you only want to use one display, click on the Single Display tab (see Figure 3-45). On the Join Display tab you can choose the primary display. There are tabs for configuring each of your displays. You can also choose to have a display adjusted for TV using the "Adjust for TV" switch. Should you want to mirror your display instead, showing the same screen on a different display, you can click on the Mirror tab and then configure the mirror display.

Whenever you click on a tab you are changing the display configuration (joined, mirrored, or single), and an Apply button will appear on the right side of the Display dialog header. Clicking that Apply button changes to that configuration. The Apply button also appears if you make any configuration changes.

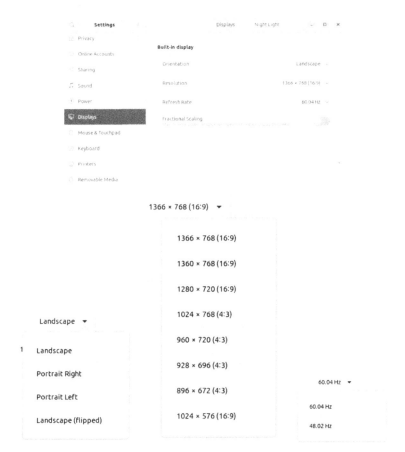

Figure 3-43: Displays

Two display servers are available for Ubuntu, X.org and Wayland. The newer Wayland display server is the default, except for systems using the Nvidia proprietary video driver. You can find out more about Wayland at **https://wayland.freedesktop.org/**. You can still use the older X.org displays server. You can find out more about X.org at **https://www.x.org/wiki**. On the login screen you can choose whether to use the Wayland display server, the Ubuntu entry, or the X.org display server, the "Ubuntu on X.org entry. Click the gear icon at the bottom right of the login screen to display these display server options (see Figure 3-5).

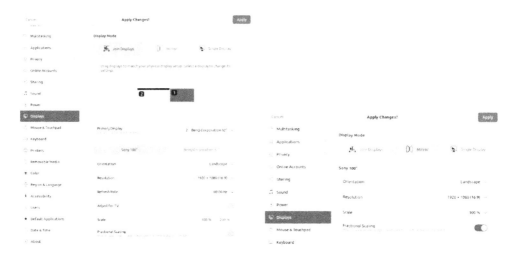

Figure 3-44: Displays - scaling and multiple displays (join and mirror)

The Night Light feature lets you adjust the color temperature of your display to show a warmer image (see Figure 3-45). A warmer color temperature at night helps to reduces eye strain. Click the Night Light tab on the Settings titlebar to display the Night Light dialog. The Night Light switch lets you turn the Night light on or off. Use the items in the Schedule menu to choose an automatic or manual schedule. The Sunset to Sunrise entry operates from 8 PM to 6 AM. The Manual entry lets you set your own time period. A slider bar at the bottom of the dialog lets you adjust color temperature.

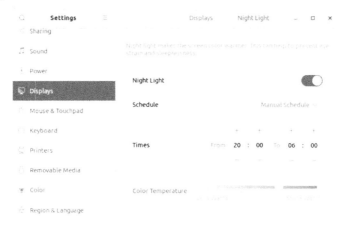

Figure 3-45: Displays - Night Light

Keyboard and Language

The Settings Keyboard Shortcuts dialog shows tabs for shortcuts (see Figure 3-46). You can assign keys to perform such tasks as starting the web browser or moving a window. The plus button at the bottom of the screen lets you create custom shortcuts. The Reset All button at the top left of the dialog resets the shortcuts to their default value. Click on an entry to set the shortcut.

When the Set Shortcut dialog appears, type the keys for the shortcut, usually three. The keys appear on the next dialog with a Set button in the upper right corner. The changed entry then appears on the Keyboard Shortcuts dialog with a delete button you can click to remove your shortcut setting. The plus button opens an Add Custom Shortcut dialog where you enter the name and command before setting the shortcut. To perform a search on the shortcuts, click the find button to open a find text box at the top of the Keyboard Shortcuts dialog.

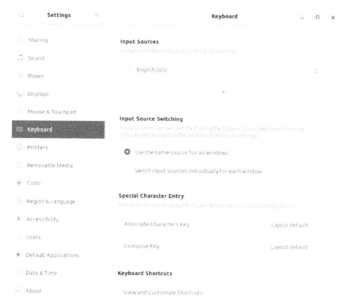

Figure 3-46: Keyboard Shortcuts

The Region & Language Settings dialog lets you set the input source for the keyboard (see Figure 3-47). The current input language source is listed and selected. Click the plus (+) button to open a dialog listing other language sources, which you can add. Click the Eye button to see the keyboard layout of your currently selected input source. The configuration button by the Input Sources heading opens an input source options dialog where you can choose whether to allow different sources for each window. Keyboard shortcuts for selecting sources are listed.

To install additional languages, click on the "Manage Installed Languages" button to open the Language Support dialog with tabs for Language and Regional Formats. On the Language tab click the Install/Remove Languages button to open the Installed Languages dialog. Click the checkbox of the language you want to add, and then click the Apply button. To remove a language, you would click the checkbox to uncheck it.

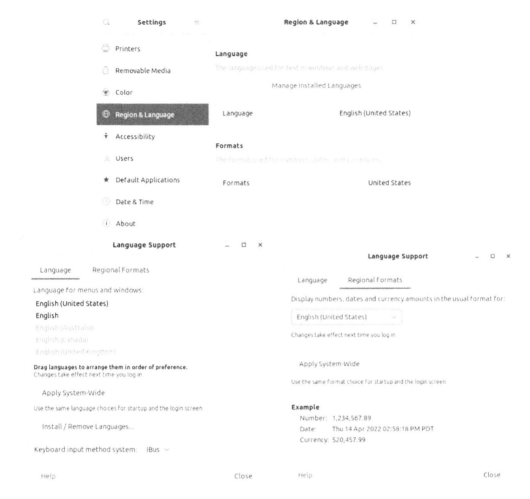

Figure 3-47: Region & Language with Input Sources

Mouse and Touchpad

The Mouse & Touchpad dialog is the primary tool for configuring your mouse and touchpad (see Figure 3-48). Mouse preferences allow you to choose the mouse's speed, hand orientation, and double-click times. A "Test Your Settings" button in the Settings titlebar lets you check clicks, double-clicks, and scrolling. For laptops, you can configure your touchpad, enabling touchpad clicks and disabling them when typing. You can turn the touchpad on or off.

The GNOME Tweak Tool's Keyboard and Mouse tab has options to enable a middle-click paste for the mouse, to show the location of the pointer on the screen, and specify an acceleration profile for mouse movement (default, flat, and adaptive).

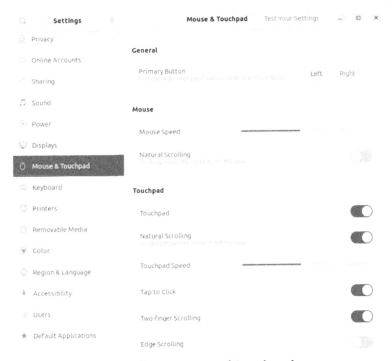

Figure 3-48: GNOME system tools - mouse and touchpad

Multitasking

Multitasking lets you set various desktop components and features (see Figure 3-49). In the General section you can turn on the Hot Corner function, which will open the Activities overview whenever you move your mouse to the upper right corner of the screen. The Active Screen Edges option lets you resize a window by moving it to the top, right, or left side of the screen.

In the Workspace section you can choose whether to use dynamic or fixed workspaces. If you choose fixed, you can set the number of workspaces.

In the Multi-Monitor section, for systems with multiple displays, you can choose whether to show your workspaces on just your primary display, or on all displays.

In the Application Switching section, when using the Meta-Tab keys to switch applications, you can choose to limit application switching to just the current workspace or to applications on other workspaces. Should you have multiple monitors, you can limit switching to just the monitor you are on.

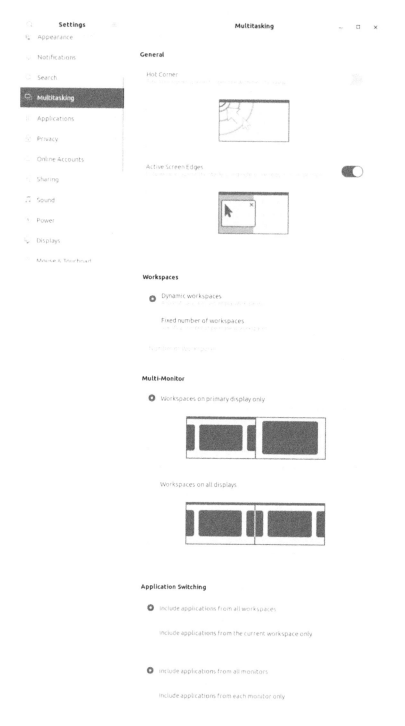

Figure 3-49: Multitasking

Notifications

The Notifications dialog lets you configure notifications for different applications (see Figure 3-50). You also have the options to show pop-up banners at the top of the screen or show notices on the lock screen. The Do Not Disturb option is turned off by default, allowing the display of pop-up banners at the top of the screen, as is done when you insert removable media (USB drives). You can also set the Do Not Disturb option on the desktop notifications section of the clock/calendar on the desktop top bar.

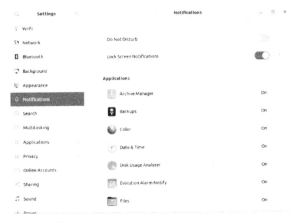

Figure 3-50: Notifications dialog

A listing of supported applications for notifications is displayed. Click an application to display a dialog from which you can turn notifications for the application on or off, as well as set options such as sound alerts, pop-up notifications, and lock screen notification (see Figure 3-51).

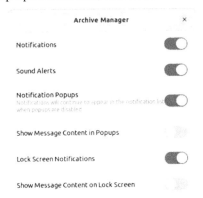

Figure 3-51: Notification settings for an application

Online Accounts

You can configure your online accounts using the Online Accounts dialog in Settings. Instead of separately configuring mail and chat clients, you can set up access once, using online accounts. Click on an entry to start the sign-in procedure. You are prompted to sign in using your email and password. Access is provided to Google, Facebook, Flickr, Microsoft, Microsoft Exchange, Nextcloud, Foursquare, and Pocket. Once access is granted, you will see an entry for service. Clicking on the service shows the different kinds of applications that it can be used for such as mail, calendar, contacts, chat, and documents (see Figure 3-52). Switches that you can use to turn access on and off are provided.

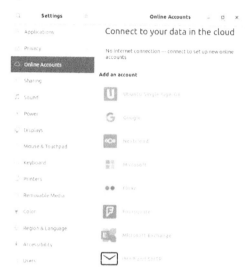

Figure 3-52: Online Accounts

Power Management

For laptops and systems with remote battery devices such as mice, a power icon is displayed in the System Status Area (right side of the top bar). The System Status Area menu shows the current strength of the battery, as shown here. The entry expands to show a Power Settings entry, which you can use to open the Settings Power dialog.

The Power profile mode entry on the System Status Area menu shows your current power mode. Expanding it lets you choose from the power mode profiles available: Balanced, Power Saver, and Performance. Some laptops may only have two settings: Balanced and Power Saver.

The GNOME Power manager is configured with the Settings Power dialog (see Figure 3-53). The dialog is organized into four sections: Battery, Devices, Power Modes, Power Saving Options, and Suspend & Power Button. On laptops, the Battery section shows the battery charge. The Devices section shows the strength of any remote devices, such as a wireless mouse. The Power Mode lets you choose between the three power profile modes: Balanced, Power Saver, and Performance. In the Power Saving Options section, you can set power saving features for your monitor. When inactive for a period of time, you can choose to turn off the screen, as well as dim it whenever it is inactive. You can turn on the automatic suspend for when a system remains inactive and, for laptops, suspend when the battery reaches a specified percentage. In the Suspend & Power Button section, you can configure your computer's power button to power off (the default), suspend, or do nothing. For laptops, you can choose to show the battery percentage.

Using the GNOME Tweak Tool's General tab, you have the option to suspend when the laptop lid is closed.

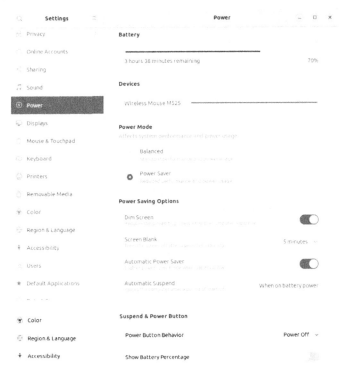

Figure 3-53: GNOME Power manager

To see how your laptop or desktop is performing with power, you can use Power statistics. This is accessible from the Applications Overview as Power Statistics. The Power Statistics window will display a sidebar listing your different power devices (see Figure 3-54). A right pane will show tabs with power use information for a selected device. The Laptop battery device will display three tabs: Details, History, and Statistics. The History tab will show your recent use, with graph options (Graph type menu) for Time to empty (time left), Time to full (recharging), Charge, and Rate. The Statistics tab can show charge and discharge graphs.

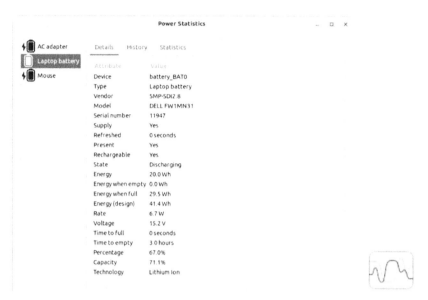

Figure 3-54: GNOME Power Statistics

powertop and tuned

For more refined power management you can use the **powertop** and tuned tools. The **powertop** tool runs in a terminal window as the administrative user. It will detect and display information about the use of the CPU by running applications and connected devices. Recommendations are listed on how to configure the power usage. To display a listing of the **powertop** results including recommendations, add the **-d** option.

```
sudo powertop -d
```

For automatic tuning of hard disk and network devices you can use tuned (**tuned**, **tune-gtk**, and **tuned-utils** packages). The tuned daemon monitors your system and tunes the settings dynamically. You can use tuned's **diskdevstat** and **netdevstat** tools to monitor your hard disk and network devices.

Privacy

The Privacy dialog allows you to turn privacy features, such as the screen lock, managing history logs, and the purging of trash and temporary files, on or off (see Figure 3-55). Clicking on the Privacy tab in Settings opens a set of tabs for Connectivity, Location Services, Thunderbolt, File History & Trash, Screen Lock, and Diagnostics. The Connectivity tab turns on connectivity checking for you network connections. It is on by default. The Location Services tab allows your geographical location to be determined. It is turned off by default (switch is on the Settings/Privacy titlebar). Thunderbolt displays the Thunderbolt security level if Thunderbolt is supported on your system. Diagnostics lets you choose whether to send error reports to Canonical, and if so, to do it automatically or manually.

Figure 3-55: Privacy

Clicking the Screen Lock entry opens the Screen Lock configuration dialog, from which you can turn automatic screen lock on or off, lock the screen on a suspension, set it to turn on after a period of idle time, and allow or deny notifications on the Screen Lock screen (see Figure 3-56). Automatic Screen Lock is turned on by default, which activates the Automatic Screen Lock Delay where you choose the time delay for locking the screen.

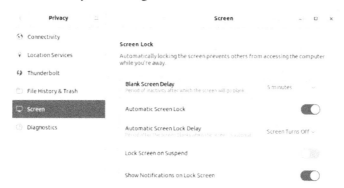

Figure 3-56: Privacy - Screen Lock configuration

Click the File History & Trash tab to open a dialog from which you can turn usage history on or off and set how long to keep it. The entry also has a button that allows you to clear recent history (see Figure 3-57). You can also configure the behavior of your trash folder, with options to automatically empty trash and remove temporary files. You can also set a time limit for deleting files in the trash. These options are turned off by default. There are also buttons that allow you to empty trash and delete temporary files immediately.

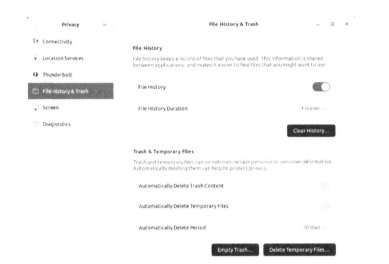

Figure 3-57: Privacy - File History, Trash, and Temporary files management

Removable Devices and Media

Ubuntu supports removable devices and media, such as digital cameras, USB drives, card readers, and USB printers. These devices arc handled automatically with device interfaces set up for them when needed. Removable storage devices and media will appear in the file manager sidebar and on the Ubuntu dock. For example, when you connect a USB drive to your system, it will be detected and can be displayed as a storage device with its own file system by the file manager. An icon for it is also displayed on the Ubuntu dock, which you can click to open a file manager window for it.

Removable devices and media, such as USB drives and DVD/CD discs, can be ejected using Eject buttons on the file manager sidebar. The sidebar lists all your storage devices, including removable media. Removable devices and media will have an Eject button to the right. Just click the Eject button, and the media is ejected or unmounted. You can also right-click the device entry in the file manager sidebar or on icon for the device on the Ubuntu dock and, from a pop-up menu, choose the Eject entry. Be sure always to click the Eject button for device entry before removing a drive, such as a USB drive or removable disk drive. Removing the drive before clicking eject can result in incomplete write operations on the disk.

The Settings Removable Media tab lets you specify default actions for CD Audio, DVD Video, Music Player, Photos, and Software media (see Figure 3-58 You can select from drop-down menus the application to use for the different media. These menus also include options for Ask What To Do, Do Nothing, and Open Folder. The Open Folder option will open a window displaying the files on the disc. A button labeled "Other Media" opens a dialog that lets you set up an association for less used media such as Blu-Ray discs and Audio DVD. Initially, the Ask What To Do option is set for all entries. Possible options derived from installed applications are listed for the appropriate media, such as Rhythmbox for CD Audio discs and Videos (Totem) for DVD-Video. Photos can be opened with the Shotwell photo manager.

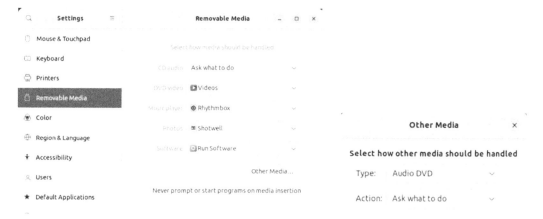

Figure 3-58: Removable Media defaults

When you insert removable media, such as a CD audio disc, its associated application is automatically started, unless you change that preference. If you want to turn off this feature for a particular kind of media, you can select the Do Nothing entry. If you want to be prompted for options, use the Ask What To Do entry. Then, when you insert a disc, a dialog with a menu for possible actions is displayed. From this menu, you can select another application or select the Do Nothing or Open Folder options.

You can turn the automatic startup off for all media by checking the box labeled "Never prompt or start programs on media insertion," at the bottom of the Removable Media tab.

Sharing

On the Sharing dialog, you can allow access to your desktop by another computer and select folders to share over a network (see Figure 3-59). A switch lets you turn all sharing on or off. You can also choose to share your desktop and media folders, as well as what network device to use if you have more than one.

Figure 3-59: Sharing

The Remote Desktop entry enables remote desktop access, allowing your system to be accessed by other computers using a remote sharing protocol such as Remote Desktop Protocol (RDP) or the older Virtual Network Computing (VNC). Ubuntu recommends using RDP. Clicking on the Remote Desktop entry opens the Remote Desktop dialog where you can turn on remote desktop access, use the VNC protocol if you wish (RDP is the default), set up connection information (device name and address), and authentication (user name and password) (see Figure 3-60).

The Media Sharing entry lets you specify what folders to share over a network and the connection to use. Your Music, Videos, and Pictures folders are already selected. Click the plus button to open a "Choose a Folder" dialog to select more. To remove a folder, click the x button to its right.

Should you want to access another desktop remotely would use the Remmina Remote Desktop Client, accessible from the Applications Overview as Remmina.

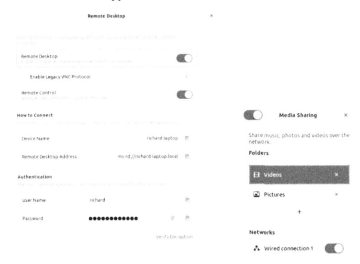

Figure 3-60: Sharing - Screen and Media access by other users

File Manager Search

The file manager provides a search tool, with similar features. You can access the file manager search from any file manager window by clicking the Search button on the toolbar (Looking glass on the right side) to open a Search box. Enter the pattern to search and press ENTER. The results are displayed (see Figure 3-61). Click the menu button to the right (down arrow) to add file-type (What) and date (When) search parameters, or to search file text or just the file name. Selecting the When entry opens a dialog where you can specify the recency of the document's last use or modification, by day, week, month, or year. A calendar button to the right of the text box for the date opens a calendar to let you choose a specific date. The What entry displays a menu with different file categories such as music, Documents, folders, picture, and PDF.

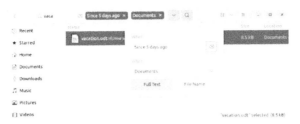

Figure 3-61: Gnome File Manager Search

Accessing File Systems and Devices

When you attach an external storage device such as a USB or CD/DVD-ROM drive, it will be mounted automatically, and you will be prompted to open it in a file manager window. Be sure to unmount (Eject) a drive before removing it, so that data will be written.

Your file systems and removable media appear as entries in the file manager sidebar (see Figure 3-62). External devices such as USB drives are mounted automatically and have Eject buttons next to their entries. Internal hard drive partitions, such as Windows file systems, are not mounted automatically. Double-click the hard drive partition entry to mount them. An Eject button then appears next to the hard drive entry. You are also prompted to open the drive's file system in a new file manager window.

Figure 3-62: Devices sidebar in the file manager window and icons on the desktop

Removable media also appears on the Ubuntu dock as an icon. Click on it to open it in a file manager window. Right-click on the icon to display options, such as Eject, and New Window.

File systems on removable media will also appear automatically as entries directly on your desktop notifications dialog (see Figure 3-63). A dialog briefly appears that lets you open the media in a file window.

Figure 3-63: Removable Devices message tray menu with hard drives mounted

If you have already configured associated applications for video and audio DVD/CDs, or disks with images, sound, or video files, the disk will be opened with the appropriate application, such as Shotwell for images, Rhythmbox for audio, and Videos for DVD/video. If you have not yet configured these associations, you will be prompted to specify which application you want to open it with.

To see network resources, click the Other Locations entry in the file manager sidebar. This network window will list your connected network Linux computers. Opening these networks displays the shares they provide, such as shared folders that you can have access to. Drag-and-drop operations are supported for all shared folders, letting you copy files and folders between a shared folder on another computer with a folder on your system. Opening a network resource may require you to login to access the resource. Currently, because of the transition from SMBv1 to SMBv3, browsing for Windows shares (Samba) does not work. You have to access a specific Windows share directly using its host name and folder name (see Chapter 15).

Accessing Archives from GNOME: Archive Manager

Ubuntu supports the access of archives directly from GNOME using Archive Manager. You can select the archive file, then right-click and select Archive Mounter to open the archive. The archive contents are listed by Archive Manager. You can extract or display the contents.

You can also use Archive Manager to open CD/DVD disk ISO image files as archives. You can then browse and extract the contents of the CD/DVD. Right-click on a ISO disk image file (**.iso** extension) and select "Open with Other Application" and then choose "Archive Manager" on the Select Application dialog. The ISO image file is opened as an archive in Archive Manager.

Mounting ISO Disk Image files: Disk Image Mounter

You can use the GNOME Disk Utility's Disk Image Mounter to mount any ISO disk image file as a file system, accessible with the file manager. Right-click on the ISO image file (**.iso** extension) and select "Open with Other Application" and then choose "Disk Image Mounter" on the Select Application dialog. The ISO image is then mounted as a file system and a notification is displayed with an Open with Files entry you can click to open the image file with a file manager window. An entry for it will also appear on the file manager sidebar, and as an icon on the Ubuntu dock. It will be read-only. The ISO image will also appear in the Other Locations folder as an attached file system. To unmount the disk image, click the eject button on a file manager sidebar, or right-click on the sidebar entry or the image file's Ubuntu dock icon, and then choose Unmount.

File Manager CD/DVD Creator interface

Using the GNOME file manager to burn data to a DVD or CD is a simple matter of dragging files to an open blank CD or DVD. When you insert a blank DVD/CD disc, a file manager window will open for it with "Blank DVD Disc" as its folder name. To burn files, just drag them to that window. The files are immediately written to the disc (see Figure 3-64). Eject it as you would any disc. You can insert the disk later and add more files if you want.

Figure 3-64: File manager window, writing to blank DVD disc

ISO Image File Writing with Disk Utility and Brasero

The GNOME Disk Utility supports burning ISO images to either a USB drive or a DVD drive. Right-click on the ISO image file and choose "Open with Other Application." Then select "Disk Image Writer" on the Select Application dialog. If "Disk Image Writer" is already the default application for ISO image files, you can just double-click the ISO image file in a file manager window. The GNOME Disks utility will then open and display a Restore Disk image dialog with the destination set to None. Use the Destination menu to carefully select the USB drive or DVD drive you want to write the image to (see Figure 3-65), Then click the Start Restoring button. You are then asked to confirm the write operation. Click Restore to have Disk Utility write the image to the drive.

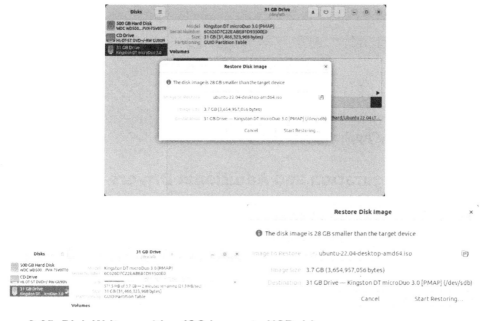

Figure 3-65: Disk Writer, writing ISO image to USB drive.

You can also still use the older Brasero CD/DVD burner to write an ISO image file to a DVD disc (not a USB drive). Brasero is not installed by default and is no longer supported by Ubuntu (Universe repository). Once installed you can selected it as one of the options on the Select Application dialog (right-click on the ISO file and choose Open with Other Application). This opens the Image Burning Setup dialog, which prompts you to burn the image. Be sure first to insert a blank CD or DVD into your CD/DVD burner (see Figure 3-66).

Figure 3-66: Brasero, writing ISO image to USB drive.

Startup Applications Preferences

On the Startup Applications Preferences dialog, you can select additional programs you want started automatically (accessible from the Applications overview as Startup Applications). Some are selected automatically (see Figure 3-67). Uncheck an entry if you no longer want it to start up automatically. To add an application not listed, click the Add button and enter the application name and program (use Browse to select a program, usually in **/usr/bin**).

Figure 3-67: Startup Applications Preferences

Display Configuration and Additional Drivers

The graphics interface for your desktop display is implemented by the X Window System. The version used on Ubuntu is X.org (**x.org**). X.org provides its own drivers for various graphics cards and monitors. You can find out more about X.org at **https://www.x.org/wiki/**.

Your display is detected automatically, configuring both your graphics card and monitor. Normally you should not need to perform any configuration yourself. However, if you have a graphics card that uses Graphics processors from a major Graphics vendor like NVIDIA, you have the option of using their driver, instead of the open source X drivers installed with Ubuntu. Some graphics cards may work better with the vendor driver, and provide access to more of the card's features. The open source AMD driver is **xserver-xorg-video-amdgpu** for newer cards and

xserver-xorg-video-radeon for older ones. The open source NVidia driver is **xserver-xorg-video-nouveau**.

Should your system require an Nvidia proprietary driver, the appropriate driver for you detected graphics card will be installed and enabled during installation, if you checked the "Install third-party software for graphics and Wi-Fi hardware and additional media formats" option on the "Updates and other software" install screen.

You can also manually select a proprietary drivers to use. Open the Software & Updates application (Applications overview) and click on the Additional Drivers tab to list available drivers (see Figure 3-68). Select the driver entry you want and then click on the Apply Changes button to use download and install the driver. The drivers are part of the restricted repository, supported by the vendor but not by Ubuntu. They are not open source, but proprietary.

Once installed, an examination of the Additional Drivers tab on Software & Updates will show the selected driver in use. Should you want to use the original driver, click the Revert button. The open source Xorg driver will be automatically selected and used. For NVIDIA cards, the Nouveau open source drivers are used, which provides some acceleration support. You can switch to another driver by selecting it and clicking the Apply Changes button.

Figure 3-68: Hardware Drivers: Software & Updates, Additional Drivers tab

When you install a new kernel, compatible kernel drivers for your proprietary graphics driver are generated automatically for you by the DKMS (Dynamic Kernel Module Support) utility.

The graphic vendors also have their own Linux-based configuration tools, which are installed with the driver. The NVIDIA configuration tool is in the **nvidia-settings** package. Once installed, you will see NVIDIA Server Settings in the Applications overview. This interface provides NVIDIA vendor access to many of the features of NVIDIA graphics cards like color corrections, video brightness and contrast, and thermal monitoring. You can also set the screen resolution and color depth.

For AMD you would use the open source drivers, Xorg amdgpu, radeon, or ati. For AMD video cards with GCN 1.2 capability and above (series 300 and above), it is recommended that you use the amdgpu AMD open source driver, **xserver-xorg-video-amdgpu**.

If you have problems with the vendor driver, you can always switch back to the original (Revert button). Your original Xorg open source driver will be used instead. The change-over will be automatic.

If the problem is more severe, with the display not working, you can use the GRUB menu on startup to select the recovery kernel. Your system will be started without the vendor graphics driver. You can use the "drop to shell" to enter the command line mode. From there you can use **apt** command-line APT tool to remove the graphics driver. The NVIDIA drivers have the prefix **nvidia**. In the following example, the asterisk will match on all the **nvidia** packages.

```
sudo apt remove nvidia*
```

Help Resources

A great deal of support documentation is already installed on your system and is accessible from online sources. Table 1-3 lists Help tools and resources accessible on your Ubuntu Linux system. Both the GNOME and KDE desktops feature Help systems that use a browser-like interface to display help files.

If you need to ask a question, you can access the Ubuntu help support at **https://answers.launchpad.net**. and at **https://askubuntu.com**. Here you can submit your question, and check answered questions about Ubuntu.

Ubuntu Desktop Guide

To access the Ubuntu Desktop Guide, click the Help icon (question mark) on the Ubuntu dock or on the applications overview's Utilities application folder. The Guide displays several links covering Ubuntu topics (see Figure 3-69). Topics covered include the desktop, networking, drivers, video, and system settings.

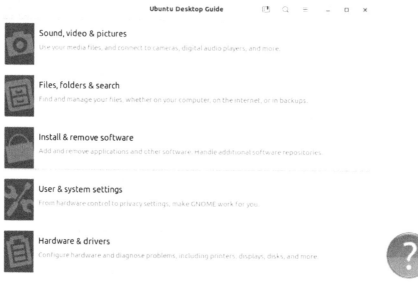

Figure 3-69: Ubuntu Desktop Guide

You can use the right and left arrows to move through the previous documentation you displayed. You can also search for topics. Click on the search button on the right side of the toolbar to open a search box. As you enter a search term possible results are displayed. You can also add bookmarks for documents and search results by clicking the Bookmarks button on the right side of the toolbar to open the bookmark menu with an "Add Bookmark" button. You can also quickly access a bookmarked page from the bookmark menu (Bookmark button).

The pages are organized more like frequently asked questions documents, with more detailed headings designed to provide a clearer understanding of what the document is about (see Figure 3-70). The Sound, video, and pictures link opens a page with entries like "Why won't DVDs play" and "I can't play the songs I bought."

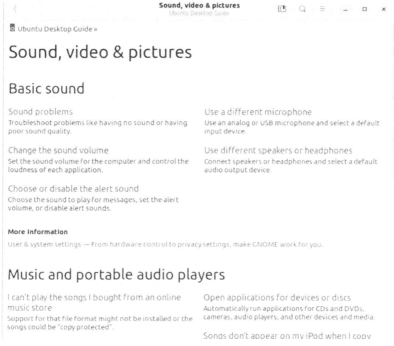

Figure 3-70: Ubuntu Desktop Guide topics

Help documents will include helpful links (see Figure 3-71). At the bottom of most pages, a More Information section will have links for more detailed information.

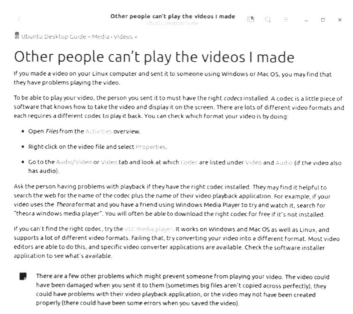

Figure 3-71: Ubuntu Desktop Guide page

If you want to see the application help documents available, choose All Help from the Help menu on the right side of its toolbar. You will see application manuals installed applications such as the Shotwell, Synaptic package manager, Videos movie player, and Rhythmbox (see Figure 3-72).

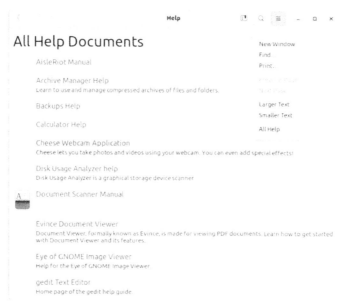

Figure 3-72: Ubuntu Help, All Documents

Context-Sensitive Help

Desktops such as GNOME and KDE, along with applications, provide context-sensitive help. Each KDE and GNOME application features detailed manuals that are displayed using their respective Help browsers. In addition, system administrative tools feature detailed explanations for each task.

Application Documentation

On your system, the **/usr/share/doc** folder contains documentation files installed by each application. Within each folder, you can usually find HOW-TO, README, and INSTALL documents for that application.

The Man Pages

You can access the Man pages, which are manuals for Linux commands available either from the command line interface, using the **man** command. In a terminal window, enter **man** along with the command on which you want information. The following example asks for information on the **ls** command:

```
$ man ls
```

Pressing the SPACEBAR key advances, you to the next page. Pressing the **b** key moves you back a page. When you finish, press the **q** key to quit the Man utility and return to the command line. You activate a search by pressing either the slash (/) or question mark (?) keys. The / key searches forward and the ? key searches backward. When you press the / key, a line opens at the bottom of your screen, where you can enter a text to search for. Press ENTER to activate the search. You can repeat the same search by pressing the **n** key. You need not re-enter the pattern.

The Info Pages

Documentation for GNU applications, such as the gcc compiler and the Emacs editor, also exist as info pages accessible from the GNOME and KDE Help Centers. You can also access this documentation by entering the command **info** in a terminal window. This brings up a special screen listing different GNU applications. The info interface has its own set of commands. You can learn more about it by entering **info info** at the command prompt. Typing **m** opens a line at the bottom of the screen where you can enter the first few letters of the application. Pressing ENTER brings up the info file on that application.

Terminal Window

The Terminal window allows you to enter Linux commands on a command line. It is installed by default, and is accessible from the Applications overview as Terminal. Its package name is **gnome-terminal** and it is a GNOME 4.1 application retained in Ubuntu 20.04, instead of the GNOME 4.2 GNOME Console application, which is intended as a replacement for the older GNOME terminal application.

It also provides you with a shell interface for using shell commands instead of your desktop. The command line is editable, allowing you to use the backspace key to erase characters on the line. Pressing a key will insert that character. You can use the left and right arrow keys to move anywhere on the line, and then press keys to insert characters, or use backspace to delete characters (see Figure 3-73). Folders, files, and executable files are color-coded: white for files (black if background is white), blue for folders, green for executable files, and aqua for links. Shared folders are displayed with a green background.

You can have several terminal windows open at the same time. Any terminal window's application menu on the top bar will list all the open terminal windows in the Open Windows section. You can use this list to quickly move to another terminal window. Use the Quit entry to close all your open terminal windows at once. The terminal window application menu on the top bar will also let you open a new terminal window and open the Preferences dialog. Also, on the Ubuntu dock, you can right-click on the terminal icon to list all your open terminal windows and use that list to move to a different one or to close a terminal. The Ubuntu dock menu's Quit entry will close all your open terminal windows.

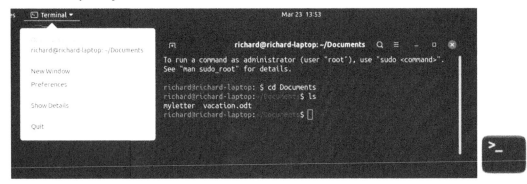

Figure 3-73: Terminal Window

The terminal window menu lets you open a new terminal window and lock the current window to a read only status (see Figure 3-74). Use the Full Screen entry of expand the window and the scaling buttons at the top of the menu to increase or decrease the font size. The Preferences entry opens the terminal window Preferences dialog where you can configure your terminal windows. The Advanced sub-menu lets you reset and clear the window, erasing previously displayed commands. You can also change the size of the terminal window from a set of listed sizes.

Figure 3-74: Terminal Window menu

The terminal window will remember the previous commands you entered. Use the up and down arrows to have those commands displayed in turn on the command line. Press the ENTER key to re-execute the currently displayed command. You can even edit a previous command before running it, allowing you to execute a modified version of a previous command. This can be helpful if you need to re-execute a complex command with a different argument, or if you mistyped a complex command and want to correct it without having to re-type the entire command. The terminal window will display all your previous interactions and commands for that session. Use the scrollbar to see any previous commands you ran and their displayed results.

To quickly locate either a previous command or message in the terminal window you can use the the search dialog (see Figure 3-75). Click on the search button (looking glass button) located on the right side of the terminal window's titlebar. This open a search dialog with options for case, words, regular expressions, and wrap around.

Figure 3-75: Terminal Window Search dialog

You can open as many terminal windows as you want, each working in its own shell. Instead of opening a separate window for each new shell, you can open several shells in the same window, using tabs. Use the keys **Shift-Ctrl-t** or click the Tab button on the left side of the terminal window's titlebar (plus symbol) to open a new tab. A tab toolbar opens at the top of the terminal window with the folder name and a close button for each added tab. Each tab runs a separate shell, letting you enter different commands in each (see Figure 3-76). You can right-click on the tab's folder name to display a pop-up menu with options to move to the next or previous tab, close the tab, or detach the tab to a new terminal window. You can move to any tab by clicking on a tab's folder name, selecting its name from the Tabs menu, or pressing the **Ctrl-PageUp** and **Ctrl-PageDown** keys to move through the tabs sequentially. The Tabs menu is the down arrow on the right side of the terminal window and to the right of the tab names. It is displayed if multiple tabs are open.

The terminal window also supports desktop cut/copy and paste operations. You can copy a line from a Web page and then paste it to the terminal window by pressing **Shift-Ctrl-v**. The command will appear and then you can press ENTER to execute the command. This is useful for command line operations displayed on an instructional Web page. Instead of typing in a complex command yourself, just select and copy from the Web page directly, and then paste to the Terminal window. You can also perform any edits on the command, if needed, before executing it. Also, should you want to copy a command on the terminal window, select the text with your mouse and then use **Shift-Ctrl-c** keys to copy the command. You can select part of a line or multiple lines, as long as they are shown on the terminal window.

Figure 3-76: Terminal Window with tabs showing tabs menu

You can customize terminal windows using profiles. A default profile is set up already. To customize your terminal window, select Preferences from the terminal window menu or the Terminal applications menu on the top bar. This opens a window for setting your default profile options with option categories on the sidebar for Global and Profiles. In the Profiles section there will be an "Unnamed" profile, the default. Click on the down menu button to the right to open a menu with the options to copy (clone) the profile or change the name. To add another profile, click on the plus button to the right of the "Profiles" heading to open a dialog to create a new profile. For profiles you create you have the added options to delete them and or to set one as the default. A selected profile displays tabs for Text, Colors, Scrolling, Command, and Compatibility (see Figure 3-77). On the Text tab, you can select the default size of a terminal window in text rows and columns, as well as the font, spacing, and cursor shape.

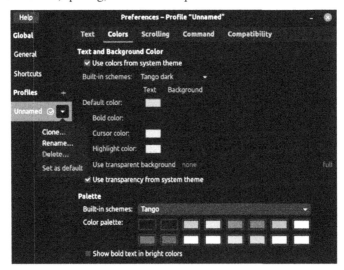

Figure 3-77: Terminal Window Profile configuration

Your terminal window will be set up to use a white background with dark text. To change this, you can edit the profile to change the background and text colors on the Colors tab. De-select the "Use colors from system theme" entry. This enables the "Built-in schemes" menu from which you can select a "Black on white" display. Other color combinations are also listed, such as "Black on light yellow" and "Green on black." The Custom option lets you choose your own text and background colors. The colors on your open terminal window will change according to your selection, allowing you to see how the color choices will look. For a transparent background, choose the "Use transparent background" entry and then set the amount of shading (none is completely transparent and full shows no transparency).

The Scrolling tab specifies the number of command lines your terminal history will keep, as well as other scroll options such as whether to display the scrollbar. These are the lines you can move back through and select to re-execute. You can de-select the Limit scrollback option to set this to unlimited to keep all the commands.

To later edit a particular profile, select Preferences from the terminal window menu to open the Preferences window, and then click on the one you want in the Profiles section.

GNOME Console: GNOME 4.2

As a beta release you can install the new GNOME terminal application released for GNOME 4.2, GNOME console (see Figure 3-78). Its package name is **gnome-console,** and you can install it from the APT repository.

```
sudo apt install gnome-console
```

GNOME Console is accessible from the Applications overview as Console. It provides a basic terminal window with a search function and tab support. Its menu lets you choose a light or dark theme, or to use the system theme. It also has zoom functions and supports keyboard shortcuts as well as search operations. It has no preferences to set.

Figure 3-78: GNOME Console

Command Line Interface

When using the command line interface, you are given a simple prompt at which you type in a command. Even when you are using a desktop like GNOME, you sometimes need to execute commands on a command line. You can do so in a terminal window, which is accessed from the Applications overview. You can keep the terminal window icon on the Dock by right-clicking on it and choosing "Add to Favorites"

Linux commands make extensive use of options and arguments. Be careful to place your arguments and options in their correct order on the command line. The format for a Linux command is the command name followed by options, and then by arguments, as shown here:

```
$ command-name options arguments
```

An option is a one-letter code preceded by one or two hyphens, which modifies the type of action the command takes. Options and arguments may or may not be optional, depending on the command. For example, the **ls** command can take an option, **-s**. The **ls** command displays a listing of files in your folder, and the **-s** option adds the size of each file in blocks. You enter the command and its option on the command line as follows.

```
$ ls -s
```

If you are uncertain what format and options a command uses, you can check the command syntax quickly by displaying its man page. Most commands have a man page. Just enter the **man** command with the command name as an argument.

An argument is data the command may need to execute its task. In many cases, this is a filename. An argument is entered as a word on the command line that appears after any options. For example, to display the contents of a file, you can use the **more** or **less** commands with the file's name as its argument. The **less** or **more** command used with the filename **mydata** would be entered on the command line as follows.

```
$ less mydata
```

The command line is actually a buffer of text you can edit. Before you press ENTER to execute the command, you can edit the command on the command line. The editing capabilities provide a way to correct mistakes you may make when typing a command and its options. The **Backspace** key lets you erase the character you just typed (the one to the left of the cursor) and the **Del** key lets you erase the character the cursor is on. With this character-erasing capability, you can backspace over the entire line if you want, erasing what you entered. **Ctrl-u** erases the whole command line and lets you start over again at the prompt.

You can use the **Up Arrow** key to redisplay your last executed command. You can then re-execute that command, or you can edit it and execute the modified command. This is helpful when you have to repeat certain operations, such as editing the same file. It is also helpful when you have already executed a command you entered incorrectly.

4. Installing and Updating Software: Snap and APT

Ubuntu software distribution is implemented using the online Ubuntu software repositories, which contain an extensive collection of Ubuntu-compliant software. With the integration of repository access into your Linux system, you can think of that software as an easily installed extension of your current collection. You can add software to your system by accessing software repositories that support Debian packages (DEB) and the Advanced Package Tool (APT), or the newer Snap packages known as **snaps** and the Snap package manager. Software is packaged into DEB or Snap software package files. These files are, in turn, installed and managed by APT or Snap. Ubuntu Software provides an easy-to-use front end for installing software with just a click, accessible from Ubuntu Software dock icon and from the Applications overview. Ubuntu Software is the snap-store application that has been modified with an interface similar to the the GNOME Software application used in previous Ubuntu releases. It supports both Snap and APT (DEB) packages, giving priority to Snap packages.

You can also download source code versions of applications, then compile, and install them on your system. Where this process once was complex, it has been streamlined significantly with the use of configure scripts. Most current source code, including GNU software, is distributed with a configure script, which automatically detects your system configuration and creates a binary file that is compatible with your system.

You can download Linux software from many online sources directly, but it is always advised that you use the Ubuntu prepared package versions if available. Most software for GNOME and KDE have corresponding Ubuntu-compliant packages in the Ubuntu Universe and Multiverse sections. Several proprietary versions of popular software packages, such as Skype, are freely available as Snap packages.

Installing Software Packages: APT and Snap

Installing software is an administrative function performed by a user with administrative access. During the Ubuntu installation, only some of the many applications and utilities available for users on Linux were installed on your system. On Ubuntu, you can install or remove software from your system with Ubuntu Software, the Synaptic Package Manager, or the **snap**, **apt** and **apt-get** commands. Alternatively, you could install software as separate DEB files, or by downloading and compiling its source code.

Ubuntu supports two packages management systems, Snap and DEB (Debian package format). For the older DEB formatted packages, the underlying software management tool is APT. Snap packages (**snaps**) have a different format from DEB, and cannot be managed by APT. Instead they are managed by the Snap package manager, which uses the **snapd** daemon to install, update, and run snap applications. Snap is a completely different package management system, though Snap packages can be installed alongside APT packages, and accessed seamlessly on the Ubuntu desktop.

APT (Advanced Package Tool) is the older tool for installing packages, and is still used for most applications. When you install a DEB package with Ubuntu Software or with the Synaptic Package Manager, APT will be invoked and will select and download the package automatically from the appropriate online APT managed repository. This will include the entire Ubuntu online repository, including the main, universe, multiverse, and restricted sections.

A DEB software package includes all the files needed for a software application. A Linux software application often consists of several files that must be installed in different folders. The application program itself is placed in a system folder such as **/usr/bin**, online manual files go in another folder, and library files go in yet another folder. When you select an application for installation, APT will install any additional dependent (required) packages. APT also will install all recommended packages by default. Many software applications have additional features that rely on recommended packages.

Snap is the new package format that will replace the DEB package management system on Ubuntu. As noted, the packages are called **snaps**. With the DEB format, as with other Linux pack formats like RPM, the component software files for a software application are installed directly to global system folders such as **/lib**, **/etc**, and **/usr/bin**. In effect, such a package has access to your entire system during installation, posing security risks. In addition, a DEB software package usually has several dependent packages, which also have to be installed. These can be extensive. Under this system, shared libraries, used by different applications can be a problem for developers, as changes in software may have to wait for supporting changes in the shared libraries.

With Snap, the software files for an application are no longer installed in global folders. They are installed in one separate folder, and any dependent software and shared libraries are included as part of the snap package. In effect, there are no longer any dependencies, and libraries are no longer shared. This makes for more secure and faster updates, though a larger set of installed files. The installation process no longer needs access to your entire system. The entire application is isolated in one location. The problem of a failed update due to broken dependencies is no longer an issue. Applications that used to make use of the same shared library, will now have their own copies of that library. Developers that used to have to wait for changes to be made to a shared library, can now directly just change their own copy.

Keep in mind, that your Ubuntu install USB/DVD will currently install primarily APT supported software applications, even for those that have corresponding Snap packages. The Ubuntu Software software manager, however, is a modified version of the snap-store application, and gives priority to Snap packages. It will also display and manage a corresponding APT/DEB version of an application, should there be one. Keep in mind that the Synaptic Package Manager and the **apt** command only manage the APT versions of software applications. For example, there are both APT and Snap packages for Inkscape. The **apt install** command installs the APT version of Inkscape, whereas Ubuntu Software would install the Snap version. Should you install both, you will then have two versions of Inkscape on your system.

Should you want to also use the older GNOME Software version of Ubuntu Software, you can can install it as GNOME Software. This older version of Ubuntu Software manages APT supported packages. However, you can install the GNOME Software snap plugin to let it also manage Snap packages (gnome-software-plugin-snap). Should you also want to use Flatpak, there is also a GNOME Software Flatpak plugin (gnome-software-plugin-flatpak).

Software Package Types

Ubuntu uses both Snap (snaps) and Debian-compliant software packages (DEB). Snap packages have the extension **.snap** and DEB packages have a **.deb** extension. Other packages, such as those in the form of source code that you need to compile, may come in a variety of compressed archives. These commonly have the extension **.tar.gz**, **.tgz**, or **.tar.bz2**. Packages with the **.rpm** extension are Red Hat Package software packages used on Red Hat, Fedora, SuSE and other Linux distributions that use RPM packages. They are not compatible directly with Ubuntu. You can use the **alien** utility to convert most RPM packages to DEB packages that you can then install on

Ubuntu. Table 4-1 lists several common file extensions that you will find for the great variety of Linux software packages available. You can download any Ubuntu-compliant DEB package as well as the original source code package, as single files, directly from **http://packages.ubuntu.com**.

Extension	File
.deb	A Debian/Ubuntu Linux package
.gz	A **gzip**-compressed file (use **gunzip** to decompress)
.bz2	A **bzip2**-compressed file (use **bunzip2** to decompress; also use the **j** option with **tar**, as in **xvjf**)
.tar	A tar archive file (use **tar** with **xvf** to extract)
.tar.gz	A **gzip**-compressed **tar** archive file (use **gunzip** to decompress and **tar** to extract; use the **z** option with **tar**, as in **xvzf**, to both decompress and extract in one step)
.tar.bz2	A **bzip2**-compressed **tar** archive file (extract with **tar -xvzj**)
.tz	A **tar** archive file compressed with the **compress** command
.Z	A file compressed with the **compress** command (use the **decompress** command to decompress)
.bin	A self-extracting software file
.rpm	A software package created with the Red Hat Software Package Manager, used on Fedora, Red Hat, Centos, and SuSE distributions
.snap	A snap package, replacement for .deb

Table 4-1: Linux Software Package File Extensions

Ubuntu Package Management Software

Software packages can be managed and installed using different package management software tools. The Ubuntu Software package manager (snap-store) supports both Snap (snaps) and APT (DEB). The **snap** command supports only Snap packages (**snaps**), and all the other package managers support APT. The Software Updater application supports both Snap and APT packages.

APT (Advanced Package Tool) performs the actual software management operations for all applications installed from an APT repository. The Synaptic Package Manager, **dpkg**, **apt**, and **apt-get** are all front-ends for APT, repository files at **/var/cache/apt**. Ubuntu Software, though, is also a front-end for Snap and the Snap Store, though it can also manage APT packages.

Snap Snap is the alternative and eventual replacement for APT. Snap packages are downloaded and installed from the Snap Store using the **snapd** daemon. A snap package, in addition to an application, installs a copy of supporting libraries and configuration files, all located in a separate folder in the **/snap** folder, with user data located in a home folder's **snap** folder. They are not installed on the system globally as APT does. Snap packages and applications are also run and updated by the **snapd** daemon. Each update to a snap package, has, in turn, a separate revision folder, each with a copy of supporting libraries and configuration files. Updates are easy to perform and require no system-wide updating of supporting libraries. You can easily switch from one revision to another. Ubuntu Software, and the **snap** command are front-ends for Snap and the Snap Store. Ubuntu Software is a modified version of the **snap-store** application, which manages Snap packages. Ubuntu Software can, however, also install and manage DEB packages from APT repositories, though priority is given to Snap packages.

Snap and APT package managers

Ubuntu Software is the primary desktop interface for locating and installing Ubuntu software. Ubuntu Software is an implementation of the snap-store application. Ubuntu Software can manage both snap packages (Snap) and DEB packages (APT). In Ubuntu Software, snap packages are given priority.

Software updater is the Ubuntu graphical front end for updating installed software. It updates APT supported packages and, also, invokes the **snapd** daemon to update snap packages from the Snap Store.

GNOME Software is the is the older version of Ubuntu Software that is based on the GNOME Software application. The basic install supports the APT repositories only (DEB packages). But you can install a Gnome Software plugin for snap packages, letting you use it to manage snap packages. You can also install a Flatpak plugin to manage Flatpak packages.

Snap only package managers

snap is the command line command for managing snap packages (Snap). Packages are installed at **/snap**, with user data in the home folder's **snap** folder.

APT only package managers

Synaptic Package Manager is a Graphical front end for managing DEB packages on APT repositories. It does not support Snap.

Discover Package Manager is the KDE software manager based on Ubuntu Software and is a graphical front end for APT.

Muon Package Manager is an older KDE software manager similar to the Synaptic Package Manager and is a graphical front end for APT.

tasksel is a command-line cursor-based tool for selecting package groups and particular servers (front-end for APT). You can run it in a terminal window on a desktop (**sudo tasksel**). Use arrow keys to move to an entry, the spacebar to select, the tab key to move to the OK button. Press ENTER on the OK button to perform your installs.

apt is the primary command line tool for APT, and is used to install, update, and remove software. It is based on **apt-get** and does not have as many options. It uses the APT database, **/var/lib/apt** with repository information at **/var/cache/apt**

apt-get is the older command line tool for APT to install, update, and remove software. It has more options than **apt**. It uses the APT database, **/var/lib/apt** with repository information at **/var/cache/apt**

dpkg is the older command line tool used to install, update, remove, and query DEB software packages. It uses its own database, **/var/lib/dpkg**, Repository files are kept at **/var/cache/apt**, the same as APT.

aptitude is a cursor based front end for **dpkg** and **apt-get**, which uses its own database, **/var/lib/aptitude**.

Snaps Packages

Snaps are designed to provide a universal and independent software repository whose packages will run on any Linux distribution or, even, versions of a Linux distribution. A snap package can be downloaded and installed on any distribution, including Ubuntu, Fedora, Debian, Centos, Linux Mint, and openSUSE. A snap package can also run on any version of that distribution. The same snap package will also run on different Linux releases of a distribution, such as Ubuntu 20.04 and 22.04. Software developers can simply maintain the one snap package, instead of several for different distributions. This design make it much easier for commercial software companies to provide Linux clients of their proprietary applications. Currently these include Skype, Zoom, and Slack. Such a structure makes updating a simple and fast procedure. Updates are performed automatically within six hours of a revision by the developer by the **snapd** server on your system. You can update manually if you wish or set a different update schedule.

The Snap system is maintained and supported by Ubuntu. An alternative system, called Flatpaks (**https://www.flatpak.org/**), is an independent project with a similar design.

Check the Snapcraft documentation and tutorials at:

```
https://snapcraft.io/docs
https://snapcraft.io/tutorials
```

It is important to keep in mind the difference between a snap package and a snap application. Some snap packages install several applications. Most install only one. There are snap commands that work on packages, such as **install** and **disable**. But there are others that work only on snap applications, such as the **run** command. The Skype package installs only the Skype application, and the name for the package and application are the same. Whereas the Nextcloud service installs several applications, each with a different name such as **nextcloud.apache** for the web server. So for Skype, you can manage both the package and application with the just the name **skype**. But for nextcloud you use the name **nextcloud** to manage the package, but the name of particular nextcloud application to run the application.

```
snap enable nextcloud
snap run nextcloud.apache
```

Managing Snap: Ubuntu Software and the snap command

Ubuntu Software has a Snap backend that integrates snap packages and allows you to install and remove them. The Synaptic Package Manager and the **apt** command do not support snap packages. The easiest way to find and install snap packages is to use Ubuntu Software, which is a modified version of the snap-store application. On Ubuntu Software, for snap packages, the Source entry in the Details section will be **snapcraft.io**, the location of the Snap Store (see Figure 4-1). Also, a Channel button is shown on the Ubuntu Software titlebar that lists various Snap tracks (**snapcraft.io**) with their risk levels. Ubuntu Software supports packages both from the Snap Store (**snapcraft.io**) and APT repositories. Many packages, such as those part of the GNOME desktop like Gedit, will have as their source the Ubuntu main, multiverse, or universe repositories. However, there could be corresponding Snap and Deb packages, as is the case with Inkscape. Should you install the Inkscape snap package you are installing from the Snap Store (**snapcraft.io**), whereas if you install the Inkscape DEB package you are installing a separate application from the APT Universe repository.

Figure 4-1: Ubuntu Software - Snap Package

Alternatively, you can simply use the **snap** command in a terminal window to install and manage snap packages (see Table 4-2). To find a Snap package, use the **snap find** command with the search term (see Figure 4-2).

```
snap find skype
```

You can also search on a search term. The following example searches for FTP clients and servers, and for Web servers.

```
snap find ftp
snap find "web server"
```

Without the search term, a list of popular snap packages is displayed.

```
snap find
```

Snaps are further organized into sections such as entertainment, games, and productivity. You can see the available sections with the **find --section** command.

```
snap find --section
```

To see available games you would enter the section name preceded by the = sign, as in **--section=games**.

```
snap find --section=games
```

To install a package, use the **snap** command with the **install** option. The following installs the skype snap package.

```
sudo snap install skype
```

Once installed, the snap applications installed by the package will appear on the Applications overview, just as any other application.

Use the **remove** command to remove a package completely from your system.

```
sudo snap remove skype
```

Command	Description
find *pattern*	Search for available snap packages. Without a search term, a list of popular packages is displayed.
find --section	List the available snap package categories (sections)
find --section=*section-name*	List the snap packages in a section
refresh	Manually update packages, installing new revisions of installed packages if available. Snaps are automatically updated every six hours by default.
install *snap-package*	Install a snap package
remove	Remove a a snap package completely
revert [*revision-number*]	Revert to a previous installed revision of a snap. Without a revision number the previous installed revision is used.
disable *snap-package*	Disable a snap without uninstalling it. The installed snap remains on your system, but is unavailable to users. Will disable all snap applications installed by the package.
enable *snap-package*	Enable a disabled snap, making it available to users again. Will enable all snap applications installed by the package
list	List your installed snap packages
list --all	List all your snap packages along with the revisions for each package, which will also display the revision number of revision
list --all *snap-package*	List all the revisions for a snap package, which will also display the revision number for each
connections	List interfaces with their plugs and slots
interface	List available interfaces with a description of each
install channel=*risk-level*	Install a snap package revision from a specified risk-level (**stable**, **candidate**, **beta**, and **edge**)
info *snap-package*	Display detailed information for an installed snap package, including all revisions
connect *plug slot*	Manually connect a snap application (plug) to a system resource (slot)
get	List configuration options for a package you can set if there are any
set	Change configuration options for a package if there are any
unset	Set configuration options to nothing for a package if there are any
run *snap-application*	Run a snap application

Table 4-2: snap commands

Figure 4-2: Listing of popular available snaps: find

With Snap, you have the option of simply disabling a package, instead of removing it completely. The Snap package remains installed, but is unavailable to any users. Use the **disable** command to disable a package. You can enable a disabled package with the **enable** command. Keep in mind that if the package installed several applications, all those applications are disabled by the **disable** command. The **enable** command will enable all of them.

```
sudo snap disable skype
sudo snap enable skype
```

Use the **refresh** command to update your snap packages.

```
sudo snap refresh skype
```

To see a list of snap packages already installed, use the **list** command (see Figure 4-3).

```
snap list
```

Figure 4-3: Listing of installed snaps: list

To display detailed information about a particular snap package, you use the **info** command.

```
snap info skype
```

Snap applications are stored as revisions in the **/snap** folder under the package name. Each revision has its own folder, which includes the application executables, as well as all configuration and system support files. In effect, each revision of a Snap application has its own **/etc**, **/usr**, **/bin**, **/lib**, and **/var** folder. A link to the application program currently enabled is held in the **/snap/bin** folder. User data for a Snap application is held in a **snap** folder in your home folder. Systemd support for Snap is provided by the systemd **snapd.service** and **snapd.socket** files.

Should you want to create a snap package, you can use **snapcraft**, which you can install with Ubuntu Software or the **snap install --classic** command .

Snap Channels: tracks and risk levels

Snap packages are managed by channels which organize a package into tracks and risk levels. Developers may also add a branch category for short-term versions of an applications. You will see track and risk-levels listed as possible channel selections in Ubuntu Software for a Snap package.

```
track/risk-level
```

The track indicates the revision of a package installed. By default this is **latest**. The risk level indicates the reliability of the software. There are four risk levels: **stable**, **candidate**, **beta**, and **edge**. The **stable** risk level is for reliable software considered ready for mass distribution. The **candidate** risk level is for a version of the application being readied for release but still being tested. The **beta** risk level is for beta versions of applications that may incorporate new features but is considered unstable. The **edge** risk level is for versions that are still under development with ongoing changes that may not always run.

Packages are installed with the latest risk level by default.

```
snap install
```

Should you want to use a different risk level, you can specify it with the appropriate risk level track: --**stable**, --**candidate**, --**beta**, and --**edge**. You can also use the --**channel** option.

```
snap install --candidate
snap install --channel=candidate
```

You can later change the risk level tracked using the **switch** command. This only changes the tracking. It does not install the version for that track. To do that you would have to run the **refresh** command.

```
snap switch --candidate
```

To both perform a switch to a different track and install the version of the applications from that track, you can run the **refresh** command directly.

```
snap refresh --channel=candidate
```

On Ubuntu Software, when you display the application page for a Snap package, a Channels menu is displayed on the right side of the titlebar. Clicking this menu lets you choose from the available versions for this snap package on different channels, usually stable, beta, and edge (see Figure 4-4). Each version will list the URL, channel, and version. The URL is **snapcraft.io** for the Ubuntu Snap Store. The channel will list the track and risk level, usually **latest/stable** or **latest/beta**. The version shows the version of the software package. The **stable** and

candidate risk levels usually have the same version, where the **beta** risk level will be different. Some applications will have tracks for special releases, such as the **esr/stable** channel for Firefox's Extended Support Release (**esr**).

Mozilla Firefox web browser

Figure 4-4: Ubuntu Software - Snap Tracks and Risk Levels

Snap Confinement

Most snap packages are run using a strict confinement mode, running in isolation with only minimal access to system resources such as networks, system folders, and processes. Some snap packages are allowed to run in the classic mode, if officially approved, letting them access system resources just as a traditional DEB package can. These packages can only be installed with the **--classic** option. For a package to obtain classic status, it must be carefully examined by Snapcraft for security and stability issues. There is also a **devmode** reserved for developers. To see the confinement mode for a package use the **snap info** command with the **--verbose** option. The **snap list** command, which lists all your snap packages, will also display each package's confinement mode.

```
snap info --verbose inkscape
```

Access to system resources by a package is setup up by interfaces, which are determined by the developer and implemented when the package is installed. Interfaces usually allow access to resources such as devices. This often includes your home folder, pulseaudio, network access, system files, and the display server (wayland or X11). A snap package can only access your system through these interfaces. Interfaces consist of plugs and slots. The plug is the package or process that needs the interface (the consumer), and the plug is the service that supports it (the provider). The **snap connections** command will list the interfaces for a package.

```
snap connections inkscape
```

The **snap connections** command with no package as an argument, will list all the packages (plugs) along with the interfaces and slots they use.

```
snap connections
```

A sample of the list is shown here.

```
Interface             Plug                              Slot                  Notes
appstream-metadata    snap-store:appstream-metadata    :appstream-metadata   -
audio-playback        chromium:audio-playback          :audio-playback       -
audio-record          chromium:audio-record            :audio-record         -
avahi-observe         firefox:avahi-observe            :avahi-observe        -
browser-support       chromium:browser-sandbox         :browser-support      -
browser-support       firefox:browser-sandbox          :browser-support      -
camera                chromium:camera                  :camera               -
camera                firefox:camera                   :camera               -
gsettings             chromium:gsettings               :gsettings            -
gsettings             firefox:gsettings                :gsettings            -
gsettings             inkscape:gsettings               :gsettings            -
gsettings             snap-store:gsettings             :gsettings            -
home                  chromium:home                    :home                 -
home                  firefox:home                     :home                 -
home                  gwenview:home                    :home                 -
home                  inkscape:home                    :home                 -
network               chromium:network                 :network              -
network               firefox:network                  :network              -
network               gwenview:network                 :network              -
network               snap-store:network               :network              -
opengl                chromium:opengl                  :opengl               -
opengl                firefox:opengl                   :opengl               -
opengl                gwenview:opengl                  :opengl               -
pulseaudio            firefox:pulseaudio               :pulseaudio           -
pulseaudio            gwenview:pulseaudio              :pulseaudio           -
wayland               firefox:wayland                  :wayland              -
wayland               inkscape:wayland                 :wayland              -
wayland               snap-store:wayland               :wayland              -
x11                   chromium:x11                     :x11                  -
x11                   firefox:x11                      :x11                  -
x11                   gwenview:x11                     :x11                  -
x11                   inkscape:x11                     :x11                  -
x11                   snap-store:x11                   :x11                  -
```

The **snap interface** command lists all your interfaces on your system with a description of each.

```
snap interface
```

A sample of the interface list is shown here.

```
Name                         Summary
audio-playback               allows audio playback via supporting services
audio-record                 allows audio recording via supporting services
avahi-observe                allows discovery on a local network via the mDNS/DNS-SD
camera                       allows access to all cameras
hardware-observe             allows reading information about system hardware
home                         allows access to non-hidden files in the home directory
network                      allows access to the network
opengl                       allows access to OpenGL stack
password-manager-service     allows access to common password manager services
personal-files               allows access to personal files or directories
physical-memory-observe      allows read access to all physical memory
pulseaudio                   allows operating or interacting with pulseaudio service
snapd-control                allows communicating with snapd
system-files                 allows access to system files or directories
system-observe               allows observing all processes and drivers
wayland                      allows access to compositors supporting wayland
x11                          allows interacting with or running as an X11 server
```

To see the slots and plugs used for an interface, use the **snap interface** command with the name of that interface. The following command lists all the plugs and slots for the network interface.

```
richard@richard-laptop:~$ snap interface network
name:    network
summary: allows access to the network
plugs:
  - chromium
  - digikam
  - dragon
  - firefox
  - gwenview
  - snap-store
slots:
  - snapd
```

You can use the **connect** and **disconnect** commands to manually connect or disconnect an interface for a package. They take as their arguments the plug and slot, with the plug preceded by the package name and a colon. As noted, interfaces for packages are normally set up for you and activated when a package is installed. The following connects the Gwenview image manager to your home folder.

```
sudo snap connect gwenview:home :home
```

Not all interfaces available to a package may be activated when you install it. You can also turn activated interfaces off, denying access for that package to the resource. On Ubuntu Software you can easily manage the interfaces for a package by clicking on the Permissions button on that application's page. In Figure 4-5, the Gwenview application is not allowed to read and write to removeable media, whereas it is allowed access to your network and home folder, as well as to your sound device and display acceleration server (OpenGL).

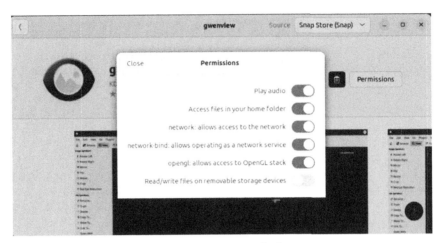

Figure 4-5: Snap package permissions - Ubuntu Software

You can also check the connections (permissions) allowed using the connections command with the package name, showing the slots and plugs for that package. The following show the Gwenview interfaces. The plug for removable media has no slot, showing that it is disconnected. This permission is not allowed.

```
richard@richard-laptop:~$ snap connections gwenview
Interface              Plug                        Slot                             Notes
dbus                   –                           gwenview:session-dbus-interface  –
desktop                gwenview:desktop            :desktop                         –
desktop-legacy         gwenview:desktop-legacy     :desktop-legacy                  –
home                   gwenview:home               :home                            –
network                gwenview:network            :network                         –
network-bind           gwenview:network-bind       :network-bind                    –
opengl                 gwenview:opengl             :opengl                          –
pulseaudio             gwenview:pulseaudio         :pulseaudio                      –
removable-media        gwenview:removable-media    –                                –
unity7                 gwenview:unity7             :unity7                          –
x11                    gwenview:x11                :x11                             –
```

Snap Revisions: revert

Snaps are installed as revisions. For any given application, you may have several revisions of an application installed. Each revision is able to run as the application. Priority is given to the the current revision, the most recently installed. But you could easily decide to run a previous revision instead. This could happen if a new revision is installed that becomes unstable, or if the changes made to the software have deprecated capabilities you normally use. Major changes to an application are released as a version, which is also considered a revision. Though you could have several revisions for a given version, for most less complex applications you will usually have just the one revision per version.

Whereas a **list** command will display your installed snaps, adding the **--all** option will also display all the revisions of each snap. This operation will display the name, version, revision, tracking, publisher, and notes for each revision.

```
richard@richard-laptop:~$ snap list --all
Name            Version            Rev   Tracking          Publisher      Notes
chromium        81.0.4044.129      1135  latest/stable     canonical✓     disabled
chromium        81.0.4044.138      1143  latest/stable     canonical✓     –
digikam         6.4.0              6     latest/beta       sergiusens     –
dragon          19.04.2            27    latest/stable     kde✓           –
firefox         76.0.1-1           359   latest/stable     mozilla✓       –
gwenview        22.04.0            48    latest/stable     kde✓           –
sensors-unity   18.02              202   latest/stable     paroj          –
skype           8.59.0.77          123   latest/stable     skype✓         disabled,classic
skype           8.60.0.76          128   latest/stable     skype✓         classic
snap-store      3.36.0-80-g208fd61 454   latest/stable/… canonical✓     –
snap-store      3.36.0-74-ga164ec9 433   latest/stable/… canonical✓     disabled
snapd           2.44.3             7264  latest/stable     canonical✓     snapd
spectacle       19.04.3            25    latest/stable     kde✓           –
```

Instead of listing all the snaps, you could just list the revisions for a particular snap.

```
richard@richard-laptop:~$ snap list --all skype
Name    Version    Rev   Tracking        Publisher   Notes
skype   8.59.0.77  123   latest/stable   skype✓      disabled,classic
skype   8.60.0.76  128   latest/stable   skype✓      classic
```

The revision number is unique. You could have several revisions with the same version number, but the revision number is the unique identifier for that install. Previous revision can be run using their revision number.

Only one revision of an application can be enabled. This is the one that Snap will run. All other revision of that application are disabled, as shown in the Notes field of the **list --all** output.

You can enable a previous revision, disabling the current one, and thereby letting Snap run it. You do this with the **revert** command and the number of the revision you want to enable. The following example reverts Skype to revision 123.

```
sudo snap revert skype 123
```

If you just want to enable the previous revision, you can leave out the number.

```
sudo snap revert skype
```

If you decide, after reverting to a previous revision, that you want to return to using the latest revision, run the **revert** command with the revision number of the latest revision.

```
sudo snap revert skype 128
```

You could also just run the **refresh** command on that snap. The latest revision is automatically enabled.

```
sudo snap refresh skype
```

Keep in mind, that if a new update of a snap is later released, the automatic **refresh** operation, will update the snap to that new revision.

Snap Package Configuration

Some Snap package, such as those for services, may have configuration options you can manage using the **snap get**, **snap set**, and **snap unset** commands. The **snap get** command list configuration options for a snap and their current setting. The **snap set** command can change an option, and the **snap unset** command removes a value. Some Snap packages, such as servers, have options that can be set when the application is started. Each revision will have a configuration that will be applied when that revision is run. Using the **revert** command you could change from using one revision of a server to another, each running separate configurations.

In addition, all snap applications have supporting environment variables. Environment variables will show folders that the snap can access, as well as application information such as the revision and version number. You can see the environment variable for an application by first starting that application's shell with the **run --shell** command.

```
sudo snap run --shell skype
```

Keep in mind that sometimes the package name may not be the same as the application name. A package could install several applications, as is the case with the nextcloud package. To access the Nextcloud web server you would use its application name, **nextcloud.apache**.

```
sudo snap run --shell nextcloud.apache
```

You can then use the shell **env** command to list your environment variables, filtering the output with **grep** and the SNAP pattern to show just the snap related ones.

```
env | grep SNAP
```

The environment variables for the current enabled revision is listed. The folder variables will show the folder of that revision. The SNAP_COMMON and SNAP_USER_DATA variables show the location of the folders that your application can write to.

To leave the shell enter the **exit** command.

Snap and systemd

Snap is managed by the **snapd** daemon, which runs several services. The service files for these are located in the **/lib/systemd/system** folder. Applications installed by a Snap package have access to the application configured by **systemd** using **.mount** files located in the **/etc/systemd/system** folder. The mount file will begin with the term **snap** and have the application name and its revision number. Each revision will have a separate mount file. The mount file for Skype revision 128 is **snap-skype-128.mount**.

/etc/systemd/system/snap-skype-128.mount

```
[Unit]
Description=Mount unit for skype, revision 128
Before=snapd.service

[Mount]
What=/var/lib/snapd/snaps/skype_128.snap
Where=/snap/skype/128
Type=squashfs
Options=nodev,ro,x-gdu.hide
LazyUnmount=yes
```

```
[Install]
WantedBy=multi-user.target
```

The file shows the revision number and the location of the revision.

```
Where=/snap/skype/128
```

Snap and Services

Services installed as snap packages can be managed by **systemctl** commands such as **systemctl start** and **systemctl stop** to start and stop a service. In addition, some snap packaged services will also provide configuration options you can manage using the snap **get**, **set**, and **unset** commands. There are few services currently available as snap packages. For most services like the FTP and Web servers, you would still use APT.

Services installed as snap packages have their systemd service files installed in the **/etc/systemd/system** folder, not in **/lib/systemd/system** as APT services are. All snap installed services are managed through the **snapd** server. The **snapd** server, in turn, has service files for **snapd** in the **/lib/system/system** folder. Furthermore, all the snap installed services have their service files begin with the term **snap**, as in **snap.nextcloud.apache.service** for the Nextcloud web server (part of the **nextcloud** snap package). You can then use **systemctl** commands to manage the service.

```
systemctl status snap.nextcloud.apache
sudo system restart snap.nextcloud.apache
```

The format of the service file is much the same as other systemd service files, except that execution operation are run by the **snap run** command. The service also requires supporting snap systemd operations such as the **snap-nextcloud** mount and **snapd.apparmor.service**.

/etc/systemd/system/snap.nextcloud.apache.service

```
[Unit]
# Auto-generated, DO NOT EDIT
Description=Service for snap application nextcloud.apache
Requires=snap-nextcloud-20498.mount
Wants=network.target
After=snap-nextcloud-20498.mount network.target snapd.apparmor.service
X-Snappy=yes

[Service]
EnvironmentFile=-/etc/environment
ExecStart=/usr/bin/snap run nextcloud.apache
SyslogIdentifier=nextcloud.apache
Restart=always
WorkingDirectory=/var/snap/nextcloud/20498
ExecStop=/usr/bin/snap run --command=stop nextcloud.apache
TimeoutStopSec=30
Type=simple

[Install]
WantedBy=multi-user.target
```

Ubuntu Software for Snap

To perform simple installation and removal of software, you can use Ubuntu Software, which is the primary supported package manager for Ubuntu (see Figure 4-6). Ubuntu Software is now a modified version of the the **snap-store** application, which manages snap packages. Ubuntu Software is designed to be the centralized utility for managing your software. Ubuntu Software performs a variety of different software tasks, including installation, removal, updating of software.

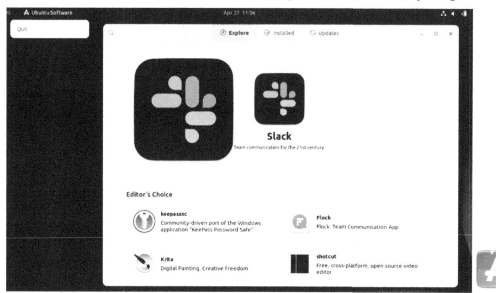

Figure 4-6: Ubuntu Software

To use the Ubuntu Software, click the Ubuntu Software icon on the dock or on the Applications overview. A window opens with three tabs at the top for Explore, Installed, and Updates. You can install applications from the Explore tab, which displays, a collection of category buttons, a list of editor picks, and recent releases (see Figure 4-6) (see Figure 4-7).

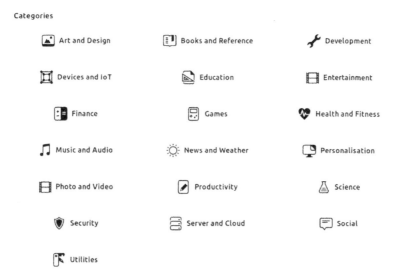

Figure 4-7: Ubuntu Software Categories

The category buttons include Photo and Video, Art and Design, Games, News and Weather, Music and Audio, Productivity, and Science. Click on any category button to open a dialog with icons for applications in that category. Categories will allow you to further filter the selection a Sort menu, which lets you sort items by name or rating (Figure 4-8). The software in each category is listed as icons. Packages already installed have a checkmark on a packet emblem displayed in the upper right corner of the package icon.

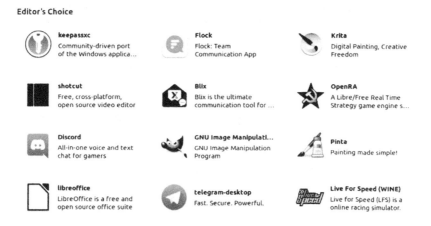

Figure 4-8: Ubuntu Software category with Sort menu

To search for a package, click the search button on the left side of the Explore tab's title bar to open a search text box. Enter part of the name or a term to describe the package (see Figure

4-9). Results are listed, showing an icon, name, and description. Click on an entry to open its description page where you can perform possible actions such as install, remove, or launch.

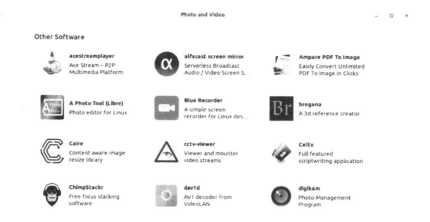

Figure 4-9: Ubuntu Software, using the search box

The software's description page provides a brief description of the software and a link to its related website (see Figure 4-10). Uninstalled software displays an Install button below the software's name, and installed software shows a Remove button. To the right of the name is a star rating with the number of reviews.

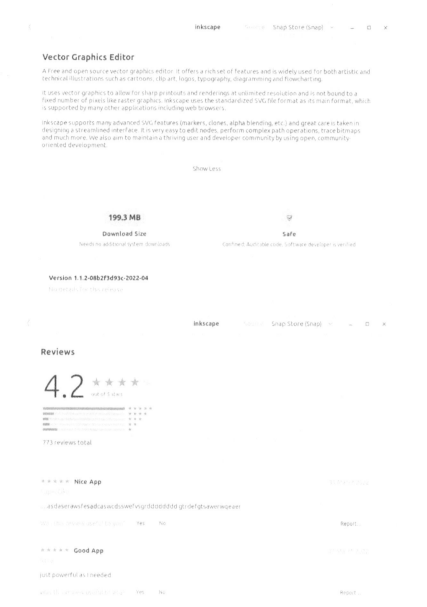

Figure 4-10: Ubuntu Software, software descriptor page

If the package is installed from the Snap Store (**snapcraft.io**), you can choose from different channels including stable, candidate, beta, and edge. Channels are selected from the Channel menu on the right side of the titlebar (see Figure 4-11).

Figure 4-11: Ubuntu Software, Snap Store (snapcraft.io) snap package channels

Click the Install button to install the software. As the software is installed, an Installing progress bar appears (see Figure 4-12). When complete, a Remove button is displayed below the name, which you can use to uninstall the software.

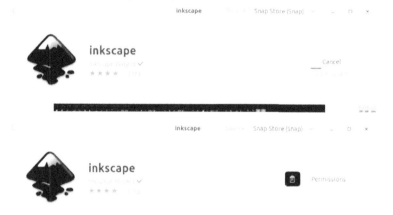

Figure 4-12: Ubuntu Software, installing software

For snapcraft packages, once installed, a Permissions button is displayed next to the Remove button. Click this button to display permissions for the application such as access to the home folder and access to removable devices (see Figure 4-13). Snap packages are isolated from your system resources such as your home folder and the Settings configuration dialogs (gsettings). They must have permission to access them. Several basic permissions will be set by default when the package is installed. Others you will have to set.

Figure 4-13: Ubuntu Software, Snapcraft snap package permissions

The Installed tab lists your installed software (see Figure 4-14). To remove an application, click its Remove button.

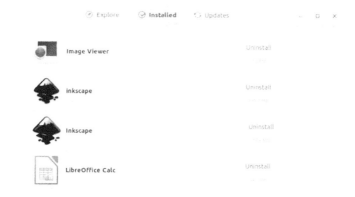

Figure 4-14: Ubuntu Software, installed tab

APT: Deb Package Management

As noted previously, Ubuntu also uses Debian packages (DEB) and the Advanced Package Tool (APT) to manage them. Ubuntu Software manages both Snap and APT package systems, whereas the Synaptic Package Manager is a front-end for APT and only manages DEB packages. The command-line tools for managing DEB packages with APT are **apt** and **apt-get**.

Ubuntu APT Repositories

For Ubuntu, its APT-based software repository is organized into sections, depending on how the software is supported. Software supported directly is located in the main Ubuntu repository section. Other Linux software that is most likely compatible is placed in the Universe repository section. Many software applications, particularly multimedia applications, have potential licensing conflicts. Such applications are placed in the Multiverse repository section, which is not maintained directly by Ubuntu. Many of the popular multimedia drivers and applications, such as video and digital music, support can be obtained from the Ubuntu Multiverse sections using the same simple

APT commands you use for Ubuntu-supported software. Software from the Multiverse and Universe sections are supported by package managers like Ubuntu Software and the Synaptic Package Manager, and can be installed just as easily as Ubuntu main section software. Some drivers are entirely proprietary and supplied directly by vendors. This is the case with the NVIDIA vendor-provided drivers. These drivers are placed in a restricted section, noting that there is no open source support.

Four main components or sections make up the Ubuntu APT repository: main, restricted, universe, and multiverse. These components are described in detail at:

```
https://help.ubuntu.com/community/Repositories/Ubuntu
```

To see a listing of all packages in the Ubuntu APT repository see:

```
https://packages.ubuntu.com
```

To see available repositories and their sections, see the Ubuntu Software and Other Software tabs on Software & Updates, which is accessible from the Applications overview.

APT Repository Components

The following repository components are included in the Ubuntu APT repository:

main: Officially supported Ubuntu software (canonical), such as the GStreamer Good plug-in.

restricted: Software commonly used and required for many applications, but not open source or freely licensed. Because they are not open source, they are not guaranteed to work.

universe: All open source Linux software not directly supported by Ubuntu such as GStreamer Bad plug-ins.

multiverse: Linux software that does not meet licensing requirements and is not considered essential. It is not guaranteed to work. For example, the GStreamer ugly package is in this repository. Check **https://ubuntu.com/licensing**.

APT Repositories

In addition to the Ubuntu APT repository, Ubuntu maintains several other APT repositories used primarily for maintenance and support for existing packages. The updates repository holds updated packages for a release. The security updates repository contains critical security package updates every system will need.

Ubuntu repository: Collection of Ubuntu-compliant software packages for releases organized into main, universe, multiverse, and restricted sections.

Updates: Updates for packages in the main repository, including main, restricted, universe, and multiverse sections.

Backports: Software under development for the next Ubuntu release, but packaged for use in the current one. Not guaranteed or fully tested. Backports access is now enabled by default.

Security updates: Critical security fixes for Ubuntu repository software.

Partners: Third party proprietary software tested to work on Ubuntu. You need to enable access manually using the Software & Updates's Other Software tab.

The Backports repository provides un-finalized or development versions for new and current software. They are not guaranteed to work, but may provide needed features.

Note: Though it is possible to add the Debian Linux distribution repository, it is not advisable. Packages are designed for specific distributions. Combining them can lead to irresolvable conflicts.

APT Ubuntu Repository Configuration file: sources.list and sources.list.d

Ubuntu APT repository configuration is managed by APT using configuration files in the **/etc/apt** directory. The **/etc/apt/sources.list** file holds repository entries. The main, restricted, and universe sections are enabled by default. An entry consists of a single line with the following format:

```
format   URI   release   section
```

The format is normally **deb**, for Debian package format. The URI (universal resource identifier) provides the location of the repository, such as an FTP or Web URL. The release name is the official name of a particular Ubuntu distribution like jammy and bionic. Ubuntu 22.04 LTS has the name **jammy**. The section can be one or more terms that identify a section in that release's repository. There can be more than one term used to specify a section, like **restricted** to specify the restricted section in the Ubuntu APT repository. The Multiverse and Universe sections are referenced as **universe** and **multiverse**. You can also list individual packages if you want. The entry for the Jammy main, restricted, and universe sections is shown here.

```
deb http://us.archive.ubuntu.com/ubuntu/ jammy main restricted universe
```

The update repository for a section is referenced by the **-updates** suffix, as in **jammy-updates**.

```
deb https://us.archive.ubuntu.com/ubuntu/ jammy-updates  main restricted universe
```

The security repository for a section is referenced with the suffix **-security**, as **jammy-security**. Security repositories are provided for each of these repositories.

```
deb http://security.ubuntu.com/ubuntu jammy-security main restricted universe
# deb-src http://security.ubuntu.com/ubuntu jammy-security main restricted
# deb-src http://security.ubuntu.com/ubuntu jammy-security universe
deb http://security.ubuntu.com/ubuntu jammy-security multiverse
# deb-src http://security.ubuntu.com/ubuntu jammy-security multiverse
```

Comments begin with a # character. You can add comments of your own if you wish. Placing a # character before a repository entry will effectively disable it, turning the entry into just a comment that is ignored.

Corresponding source code repositories will use a **deb-src** format. They are disabled by default and so are commented out using the #.

```
# deb-src http://us.archive.ubuntu.com/ubuntu/ jammy main restricted
# deb-src http://us.archive.ubuntu.com/ubuntu/ jammy universe
```

The Universe repository is enabled along with the main and restricted repositories. There are commented lines to enable it separately if you want. If you do so, be sure to remove it from the main and restricted line.

```
# deb http://us.archive.ubuntu.com/ubuntu/ jammy universe
# deb-src http://us.archive.ubuntu.com/ubuntu/ jammy universe
# deb http://us.archive.ubuntu.com/ubuntu/ jammy-updates universe
# deb-src http://us.archive.ubuntu.com/ubuntu/ jammy-updates universe
```

The Multiverse repository should already be enabled along with its update repository.

```
deb http://us.archive.ubuntu.com/ubuntu/ jammy multiverse
# deb-src http://us.archive.ubuntu.com/ubuntu/ jammy multiverse
deb http://us.archive.ubuntu.com/ubuntu/ jammy-updates multiverse
# deb-src http://us.archive.ubuntu.com/ubuntu/ jammy-updates multiverse
```

The Backports repository is enabled by default. Backports holds applications being developed for future Ubuntu releases and are, as yet, untested.

```
deb http://us.archive.ubuntu.com/ubuntu/ jammy-backports main restricted
multiverse universe
# deb-src http://us.archive.ubuntu.com/ubuntu/ jammy-backports main restricted
universe multiverse
```

Entries are also included for the Canonical Partner repository. If you have enabled the Canonical Partner repository, it will be uncommented, otherwise it will be commented.

```
deb http://archive.canonical.com/ubuntu jammy partner
# deb-src http://archive.canonical.com/ubuntu jammy partner
```

Most entries, including third-party entries for Ubuntu partner, can be managed using Software & Updates. Entries can also be managed by editing the **sources.list** file with the following command.

```
sudo gedit /etc/apt/sources.list
```

Remove the # at the beginning of the line to activate a repository such as partner.

```
# deb http://archive.canonical.com/ubuntu/ jammy partner
```

New APT repositories can be added using the Software & Updates's Other Software tab. You can, though, simply add the repository entries directly. To do this, you do not have to edit the **/etc/apt/sources.list** file. Editing such an important file always includes the risk of incorrectly changing the entries. Instead, new repository entries can be placed in a text file in the **/etc/apt/sources.list.d** folder, which APT will read as if part of the **sources.list** file.

APT Software Repositories managed with Software & Updates

You can manage your APT repositories with the Software & Updates dialog, allowing you to enable or disable repository sections, as well as add new entries. This dialog edits the **/etc/apt/sources.list** file directly. You can access Software & Updates from the Applications overview. You can also access it on the Synaptic Package Manager from the Settings menu as the Repositories entry. The Software & Updates dialog displays seven tabs: Ubuntu Software, Other Software, Updates, Authentication, Additional Drivers, Developer Options, and Livepatch (see Figure 4-15).

Figure 4-15: Software & Updates Ubuntu Software repository sections

The Ubuntu Software tab lists all the Ubuntu APT repository section entries. These include the main repository, universe, restricted, and multiverse, as well as source code. Those that are enabled will be checked. Initially, all of them, except the source code, will be enabled. You can enable or disable a repository section by checking or un-checking its entry. You can select the repository server to use from the "Download from" drop-down menu.

On the Other Software tab, you can add repositories for third-party APT software (see Figure 4-16). The repository for Ubuntu partners will already be listed, but not checked. Check that entry if you want access to software from the Partners repository such as the Adobe Flash plugin. To add a third-party repository manually, click the Add button. This opens a dialog where you are prompted to enter the complete APT entry, starting with the deb format, followed by the URL, release, and sections or packages. For a Personal Package Archives (PPA) APT repository, such as those maintained by the Wine project, you would just enter the ppa: entry. This is the line as it will appear in the **/etc/apt/sources.list** file. Once entered, click the Add Source button.

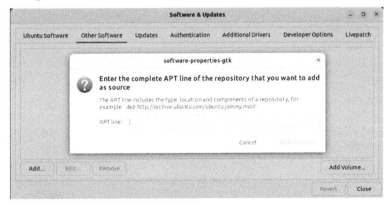

Figure 4-16: Software & Updates Other Software configuration

The Authentication tab shows the repository software signature keys that are installed on your system (see Figure 4-17). Ubuntu requires a signature key for any package that it installs. Signature keys for all the Ubuntu repositories are installed and are listed on this tab.

Most other third party or customized APT repositories will provide a signature key file for you to download and import. You can add such keys manually from the Authentication tab. Click the "Import Key File" button to open a file browser where you can select the downloaded key file. This procedure is the same as the **apt-key add** operation. Both add keys that APT then uses to verify DEB software packages downloaded from repositories before it installs them.

Figure 4-17: Software & Updates Authentication, package signature keys

On the Developer Options tab, you can click the Pre-released software (jammy-proposed) option to choose to receive development updates (see Figure 4-18). These are for testing and may introduce instability.

Figure 4-18: Software & Updates Developer Options

After you have made changes and click the Close button. If you made any repository changes (Ubuntu Software and Other Software tabs) such as adding or disabling a repository, the Software & Updates tool will notify you that your software package information is out of date, displaying a Reload button. Click the Reload button to make the new repositories or components available on your package managers like Ubuntu Software and the Synaptic Package Manager. You also can reload your repository configuration by running the **apt update** command or clicking the Reload button on the Synaptic Package Manager.

Ubuntu Software for APT packages

Though Ubuntu Software gives priority to Snap packages, you can also use it to also manage APT packages (see Figure 4-19).

Figure 4-19: Ubuntu Software, APT (DEB) package

The application page for an APT managed package will list an APT repository as its source (see Figure 4-20), such as ubuntu-jammy-universe for the Universe section of the Ubuntu APT repository. As the package is managed by the APT system, there is no Channels menu in the titlebar as there is for Snap packages.

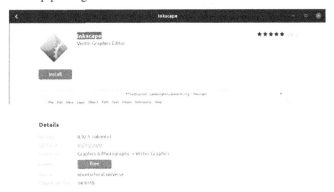

Figure 4-20: Ubuntu Software, APT (DEB) package application page

If an application has both APT and Snap versions available, and you install both, you can run either of them from the Applications Overview (see Figure 4-21).

Figure 4-21: Ubuntu Software, APT and Snap package versions

GNOME Software

You can install the original GNOME Software application using either the Synaptic Package Manager or the **apt** command. You cannot install it from Ubuntu Software. Keep in mind that Ubuntu Software is a customized version of GNOME Software for the Snap store. So Ubuntu Software already shows GNOME Software as installed, along with the Snap store. You can install GNOME Software as the **gnome-software** package using the Synaptic Package Manager or the **apt install** command.

```
sudo apt install gnome-software
```

Once installed, you can use it to manage Apt packages, and, if you have installed support for it, Flathub packages. The icon for it is labeled Software on the applications overview (see Figure 4-22). GNOME Software also has GNOME Other Categories section for GNOME addons, organized into four categories on the main page: codecs, fonts, drivers, and input sources (see Figure 4-23). Categories have a fully functional Show menu with a complete listing of sub-categories.

The GNOME Software Snap plugin is already installed and allows GNOME Software to manage Snap packages. Like Ubuntu Software (snap-store), for snap packages it will display a menu on the right side of the titlebar of snap channels to install. On GNOME Software the Snap menu is labeled "Ubuntu."

Figure 4-22: GNOME Software

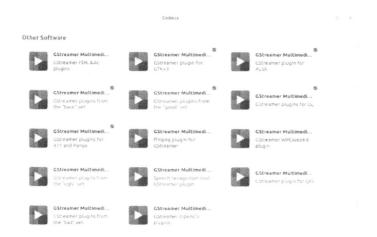

Figure 4-23: GNOME Software Addons for codecs

Synaptic Package Manager: APT only

The Synaptic Package Manager has been replaced by Ubuntu Software as the primary package manager. It is not installed by default. Synaptic is no longer supported by Ubuntu, though support is still provided by the Ubuntu community. Packages are listed by name and include supporting packages like libraries and system critical packages. Once installed, you can access the Synaptic Package Manager on the Applications overview.

```
sudo apt install synaptic
```

The Synaptic Package Manager is a front-end for the APT system and can only access APT repositories. It cannot manage Snap packages. Some packages are available both as Snap and APT packages. Should you install such a snap package using Ubuntu Software and then, again, using the Synaptic Package Manager, you would have two installations of the the same software application, one managed by APT and the other by Snap.

Many APT software packages will not be available from Ubuntu Software. But you can install them using the Synaptic Package Manager or the **apt** command. Many servers, such as the Vsftpd FTP server and Apache Web server, and desktops, such as Kubuntu and Xfce, are not listed by Ubuntu Software, as well as many applications in Universe and Multiverse. You will have to use the Synaptic Packages Manager or the **apt** command to install them.

The Synaptic Package Manager displays three panes: a side pane for listing software categories and buttons, a top pane for listing software packages, and a bottom pane for displaying a selected package's description. When a package is selected, the description pane also displays a Get Screenshot button. Clicking this button will download and display an image of the application if there is one. Click the Get Changelog button to display a window listing the application changes.

Buttons at the lower left of the Synaptic Package Manager window provide options for organizing and refining the list of packages shown (see Figure 4-24). Five options are available: Sections, Status, Origin, Custom Filters, Search results, and Architecture. The dialog pane above the buttons changes depending on which option you choose. Clicking the Sections button will list section categories for your software such as Graphics, Communications, and Development. The

Status button will list options for installed and not installed software. The Origin button shows entries for different repositories and their sections, as well as those locally installed (manual or disc based installations). Custom filters lets you choose a filter to use for listing packages. You can create your own filter and use it to display selected packages. Search results will list your current and previous searches, letting you move from one to the other.

Figure 4-24: Synaptic Package Manager

The Sections option is selected by default (see Figure 4-25). You can choose to list all packages, or refine your listing using categories provided in the pane. The All entry in this pane will list all available packages. Packages are organized into categories such as Cross Platform, Communications, and Editors. Each category is, in turn, subdivided by multiverse, universe, and restricted software.

Figure 4-25: Synaptic Package Manager: Sections

To perform a search, you use the Search tool. Click the Search button on the toolbar to open a Search dialog with a text box where you can enter search terms. A pop-up menu lets you specify what features of a package to search such as the "Description and Name" feature. You can search other package features like the Name, the maintainer name (Maintainer), the package version (Version), packages it may depend on (Dependencies), or associated packages (Provided Packages). A list of searches will be displayed in Search Results. You can move back and forth between search results by clicking on the search entries in this listing.

Status entries further refine installed software as manual or as upgradeable (see Figure 4-26). Local software consists of packages you download and install manually.

Figure 4-26: Synaptic Package Manager: Status

With the Origin options, Ubuntu-compliant repositories may further refine access according to multiverse, universe, and restricted software. A main section selects Ubuntu-supported software. The Architecture options let you select software compatible with a specified architecture, such as 64-bit or 32-bit.

Properties

To find out information about a package, select the package and click the Properties button. This opens a window with Common, Dependencies, Installed Files, Versions, and Description tabs (see Figure 4-24). The Common tab provides section, versions, and maintainer information. The Installed Files tab show you exactly what files are installed, which is useful for finding the exact location, and names for configuration files, as well as commands. The Description tab displays detailed information about the software. The Dependencies tab shows all dependent software packages needed by this software, usually libraries.

Installing packages

Before installing software, you should press the Reload button to load the most recent package lists from the active repositories

To install a package, single click on its empty checkbox or right-click on its name to display a pop-up menu and select the Mark for installation entry. Should any dependent packages exist, a dialog opens listing those packages. Click the Mark button in the dialog to mark those packages for installation. The package entry's checkbox will then be marked in the Synaptic Package Manager window.

Once you have selected the packages you want to install, click the Apply button on the toolbar to begin the installation process. A Summary dialog opens showing all the packages to be installed. You have the option to download the package files only. The number of packages to be installed is listed, along with the size of the download and the amount of disk space used. Click the Apply button on the Summary dialog to download and install the packages. A download window will then appear showing the progress of your package installations. You can choose to show the progress of individual packages, which opens a terminal window listing each package as it is downloaded and installed.

Once downloaded, the dialog name changes to Installing Software. You can choose to have the dialog close automatically when finished. Sometimes installation requires user input to configure the software. You will be prompted to enter the information if necessary.

When you right-click a package name, you also see options for Mark Suggested for Installation or Mark Recommended for Installation. These will mark applications that can enhance your selected software, though they are not essential. If there are no suggested or recommended packages for that application, then these entries will be grayed out.

Certain software, like desktops or office suites that require a significant number of packages, can be selected all at once using metapackages. A metapackage has configuration files that select, download, and configure the range of packages needed for such complex software. For example, the **kubuntu-desktop** meta package will install the entire Kubuntu desktop (Sections | Meta Packages (universe)).

Removing packages

To remove a package, first, locate it. Then right-click it and select the "Mark package for removal" entry. This will leave configuration files untouched. Alternatively, you can mark a package for complete removal, which will also remove any configuration files, "Mark for Complete Removal." Dependent packages will not be removed.

Once you have marked packages for removal, click the Apply button. A summary dialog displays the packages that will be removed. Click Apply to remove them.

The Synaptic Package Manager may not remove dependent packages, especially shared libraries that might be used by other applications. This means that your system could have installed packages that are never being used.

Search filters

You can further refine your search for packages by creating search filters. Select the Settings | Filters menu entry to open the Filters window. The Filters window shows two panes, a filter list on the left, and three tabs on the right: Status, Section, and Properties. To create a new filter, click the New button located just below the filter listing. Click the New Filter 1 entry in the filter list on the left pane. On the Status tab, you can refine your search criteria according to a package's status. You can search only uninstalled packages, include installed packages, include or exclude packages marked for removal, or search or those that are new in the repository. Initially, all criteria are selected. Uncheck those you do not want included in your search. The Section tab lets you include or exclude different repository sections like games, documentation, or administration. If you are looking for a game, you could choose to include just the game section, excluding everything else. On the Properties tab, you can specify patterns to search on package information such as package names, using Boolean operators to refine your search criteria. Package search criteria are entered using the two pop-up menus and the text box at the bottom of the tab, along with AND or OR Boolean operators.

Note: For KDE you can use the Discover Software Center and the Muon package manager to install and update packages (see Chapter 9).

Ubuntu Software for separate DEB packages

You can also use Ubuntu Software to perform an installation of a single DEB software package. Usually, these packages are downloaded directly from a website and have few or no dependent packages. When you right-click on a deb package, you should see the entry "Open With Software Install." Choose this entry to open Ubuntu Software, listing the package name, description, details (version number, size, and source), and an Install button.

Source code files

You can install source code files using **apt-get** (not **apt**). Specify the **source** operation with the package name. Packages will be downloaded and extracted.

```
sudo apt-get source mplayer
```

The **--download** option lets you just download the source package without extracting it. The **--compile** option will download, extract, compile, and package the source code into a Debian binary package, ready for installation.

With the **source** operation, no dependent packages will be downloaded. If a software packages requires any dependent packages to run, you would have to download and compile those. To obtain needed dependent files, you use the **build-dep** option. All your dependent files will be located and downloaded for you automatically.

```
sudo apt-get build-dep mplayer
```

Installing from source code requires that supporting development libraries and source code header files be installed. You can do this separately for each major development platform like GNOME, KDE, or the kernel. Alternatively, you can run the APT meta-package **build-essential** for all the Ubuntu development packages. You will have to do this only once.

```
sudo apt-get install build-essential
```

DEB Software Packages

A Debian package will automatically resolve dependencies, installing any other needed packages instead of simply reporting their absence. Packages are named with the software name, the version number, and the **.deb** extension. Check **https://www.debian.org/doc** for more information. The package filename format is as follows:

the package name

version number

distribution label and build number. Packages created specifically for Ubuntu have the ubuntu label here. Attached to it is the build number, the number of times the package was built for Ubuntu.

architecture   The type of system on which the package runs, like i386 for Intel 32-bit x86 systems, or amd64 for both Intel and AMD 64-bit systems, x86_64.

package format. This is always **deb**

For example, the package name for 3dchess is 3dchess, with a version and build number 0.8.1-21, and an amd64 architecture for a 64-bit system.

```
3dchess_0.8.1-21_amd64.deb
```

The following package has an Ubuntu label, a package specifically created for Ubuntu that is not the same as the original Debian version (**dfsg**). The version and build number is 2:4.15.5 The architecture is amd64 for a 64-bit system.

```
samba_2:4.15.5+dfsg-0ubuntu5_amd64.deb
```

Managing software with apt and apt-get

APT is designed to work with repositories, and will handle any dependencies for you. It uses **dpkg** to install and remove individual packages, but can also determine what dependent packages need to be installed, as well as query and download packages from repositories. Several popular tools for APT let you manage your software easily, like the Synaptic Package Manager, Ubuntu (GNOME) Software, and aptitude. Ubuntu Software and the Synaptic Package Manager rely on a desktop interface like GNOME. If you are using the command line interface, you can use **apt** or **apt-get** to manage packages. Using the **apt** or **apt-get** commands on the command line you can install, update, and remove packages. Check the **apt** and **apt-get** man page for a detailed listing of **apt-get** commands (see Table 4-3). The **apt** command is a new version of **apt-get** with fewer options. For example, the **apt-get** command has the **check** option to check for broken dependencies. Older systems may want to continue using **apt-get**, especially the command is used in customized system scripts. For basic operations, such as upgrading, installing, or removing packages, you could use **apt** instead.

```
apt-get command   package
```

```
apt command   package
```

The **apt** and **apt-get** commands usually take two arguments: the command to perform and the name of the package. Other APT package tools follow the same format. The command is a term such as **install** for installing packages or **remove** to uninstall a package. You only need to specify the software name, not the package's full filename. APT will determine that. To install the MPlayer package you would use:

```
sudo apt install mplayer
```

To make sure that **apt** or **apt-get** has current repository information, use the **update** command.

```
sudo apt update
```

To remove packages, you use the **remove** command.

```
sudo apt remove mplayer
```

Command	Description
update	Download and resynchronize the package listing of available and updated packages for APT supported repositories. APT repositories updated are those specified in **/etc/apt/sources.list**
upgrade	Update packages, install new versions of installed packages if available.
install	Install a specific package, using its package name, not full package filename.
remove	Remove a software package from your system.
source	Download and extract a source code package
check	Check for broken dependencies (**apt-get** command)
clean	Removes the downloaded packages held in the repository cache on your system. Used to free up disk space (**apt-get** command)

Table 4-3: apt-get commands

You can use the **-s** option to check the remove or install first, especially to check whether any dependency problems exist. For remove operations, you can use **-s** to find out first what dependent packages will also be removed.

```
sudo apt-get remove -s mplayer
```

The **apt-get** and **apt** commands can be helpful if your X Windows System server ever fails (your display driver). For example, if you installed a restricted vendor display driver, and then your desktop fails to start, you can start up in the recovery mode, start the root shell, and use **apt** or **apt-get** to remove the restricted display driver. Your former X open source display drivers would be restored automatically. The following would remove the NVIDIA restricted display driver.

```
sudo apt-get remove nvidia*
```

A complete log of all install, remove, and update operations are kept in the **/var/log/dpkg.log** file. You can consult this file to find out exactly what files were installed or removed.

Configuration for APT is held in the **/etc/apt** folder. Here the **sources.list** file lists the distribution repositories from where packages are installed. Source lists for additional third-party repositories are kept in the /**etc/apt/sources.list.d** folder. GPG (GNU Privacy Guard) database files hold validation keys for those repositories. Specific options for **apt-get** are can be found in an **/etc/apt/apt.conf** file or in various files located in the **/etc/apt/apt.conf.d** folder.

Updating packages (Upgrading) with apt

The **apt** tool also lets you update your entire system at once. The terms **update** and **upgrade** are used differently from other software tools. In **apt**, the **update** command just updates your package listing, checking for packages that may need to install newer versions, but not installing those versions. Technically, it updates the package list that APT uses to determine what packages need to be updated. The term **upgrade** is used to denote the actual update of a software package. A new version is downloaded and installed. What is referred to as updating by **apt**, other package managers refer to as obtaining the list of software packages to be updated (the reload operation). In **apt**, upgrading is what other package managers refer to as performing updates.

Note: The terms **update** and **upgrade** can be confusing when used with **apt**. The update operation updates the Apt package list only, whereas an upgrade actually downloads and installs updated packages.

Upgrading is a simple matter of using the **upgrade** command. With no package specified, using **apt-get** with the **upgrade** command will update your entire system. Add the **-u** option to list packages as they are updated. First, make sure your repository information (package list) is up to date with the **update** command, then issue the **upgrade** command.

```
sudo apt update
sudo apt -u upgrade
```

Command Line Search and Information: dpkg-query and apt-cache tools

The **dpkg-query** command lets you list detailed information about your packages. It operates on the command line (terminal window). Use **dpkg-query** with the **-l** option to list all your packages.

```
dpkg-query -l
```

The **dpkg** command can operate as a front end for **dpkg-query**, detecting its options to perform the appropriate task. The preceding command could also be run as:

```
dpkg -l
```

Listing a particular package requires and exact match on the package name unless you use pattern matching operators. The following command lists the **samba** package.

```
dpkg-query -l samba
```

A pattern matching operator, such as *, placed after a pattern will display any packages beginning with the specified pattern. The pattern with its operators needs to be placed in single quotation marks to prevent an attempt by the shell to use the pattern to match on filenames in your current folder. The following example finds all packages beginning with the pattern "samba". This would include packages with names such as **samba-client** and **samba-common**.

```
dpkg-query -l 'samba*'
```

You can further refine the results by using **grep** to perform an additional search. The following operation first outputs all packages beginning with **samba**, and from those results, the **grep** operations lists only those with the pattern "common" in their name, such as **samba-common**.

```
dpkg -l  'samba*' | grep 'common'
```

Use the **-L** option to list the files that a package has installed.

```
dpkg-query -L samba
```

To see the status information about a package, including its dependencies and configuration files, use the **-s** option. Fields will include Status, Section, Architecture, Version, Depends (dependent packages), Suggests, Conflicts (conflicting packages), and Conffiles (configuration files).

```
dpkg-query -s samba
```

The status information will also provide suggested dependencies. These are packages not installed, but likely to be used. For the samba package, the **chrony** time server package is suggested.

```
dpkg-query -s  samba | grep Suggests
```

Use the **-S** option to determine to which package a particular file belongs to.

```
dpkg-query -S  filename
```

You can also obtain information with the **apt-cache** tool. Use the search command with **apt-cache** to perform a search.

```
apt-cache search samba
```

To find dependencies for a particular package, use the **depends** command.

```
apt-cache depends samba
```

To display the package information, use the **show** command.

```
apt-cache show samba
```

Note: If you have installed Aptitude software manager, you can use the aptitude command with the search and show options to find and display information about packages.

Managing non-repository packages with dpkg

You can use **dpkg** to install a software package you have already downloaded directly, instead of with an APT enabled software tools like **apt-get**, Ubuntu Software, or the Synaptic Package Manager. In this case, you are not installing from a repository. Instead, you have manually downloaded the package file from a Web or FTP site to a folder on your system. Such a situation would be rare, reserved for software not available on the Ubuntu repository or any APT enabled repository. Keep in mind that most software is already on your Ubuntu or APT enabled repositories. Check there first for the software package before performing a direct download and installing with **dpkg**. The **dpkg** configuration files are located in the **/etc/dpkg** folder. Configuration is held in the **dpkg.cfg** file. See the **dpkg** man page for a detailed listing of options.

One situation, for which you would use **dpkg**, is for packages you have built yourself, like packages you created when converting a package in another format to a Debian package (DEB). This is the case when converting an RPM package (Red Hat Package Manager) to a Debian package format.

For **dpkg**, you use the **-i** option to install a package and **-r** to remove it.

```
sudo dpkg -i package.deb
```

The major failing for **dpkg** is that it provides no dependency support. It will inform you of needed dependencies, but you will have to install them separately. **dpkg** installs only the specified package. It is useful for packages that have no dependencies.

You use the **-I** option to obtain package information directly from the DEB package file.

```
sudo dpkg -I package.deb
```

To remove a package, you use the **-r** option with the package software name. You do not need version or extension information like **.386** or **.deb**. With **dpkg**, when removing a package with dependencies, you first have to remove all its dependencies manually. You will not be able to uninstall the package until you do this. Configuration files are not removed.

```
sudo dpkg -r packagename
```

If you install a package that requires dependencies, and then fail to install these dependencies, your install database will be marked as having broken packages. In this case, APT will not allow new packages to be installed until the broken packages are fixed. You can enter the **apt-get** command with the **-f** and install options to fix all broken packages at once.

```
sudo apt-get -f install
```

Using packages with other software formats

You can convert software packages in other software formats into DEB packages that can then be installed on Ubuntu. To do this you use the **alien** tool, which can convert several different kinds of formats such as RPM and even TGZ (**.tgz**). You use the **--to-deb** option to convert to a DEB package format that Ubuntu can then install. The **--scripts** option attempts also to convert any pre or post install configuration scripts.

```
alien --scripts --to-deb package.rpm
```

Once you have generated the **.deb** package, you can use **dpkg** to install it.

Updating Ubuntu

New updates are continually being prepared for particular software packages as well as system components. These are posted as updates you can download from software repositories and install on your system. These include new versions of applications, servers, and the kernel. Such updates may range from single software packages to whole components. When updates become available, a message appears on your desktop.

Updating Snaps

Snap packages (snaps) are updated automatically by the **snapd** daemon, four times a day (every six hours) . You can manually update your snaps with the **snap refresh** command. You can to this for an individual package or for all snaps.

```
sudo snap refresh
sudo snap refresh skype
```

See the Snapcraft update documentation for more details.

```
https://snapcraft.io/docs/keeping-snaps-up-to-date
```

With the **--time** option you can check the time of the last update and when the next one will take place.

```
snap refresh --time
```

To see the list of packages updated with the last refresh, use the **snap changes** command.

```
snap changes
```

The listing will show the number of the package change ID (ID), its status (Status), the time of its revision (Spawn), when it was available (Ready), and a short description of the update including the name of the application affected (Summary).

```
richard@richard-laptop:~$ snap changes
ID   Status  Spawn                Ready                Summary
33   Done    today at 11:37 PDT   today at 11:38 PDT   Auto-refresh snap "skype"
```

To see the changes performed for a particular software package update use the **snap change** command with the change ID of the update.

```
richard@richard-laptop:~$ snap change 33
Status   Spawn                Ready                Summary
Done     today at 11:37 PDT   today at 11:37 PDT   Ensure prerequisites for "skype"
are available
Done     today at 11:37 PDT   today at 11:37 PDT   Download snap "skype" (128) from
channel "latest/stable"
Done     today at 11:37 PDT   today at 11:37 PDT   Fetch and check assertions for
snap "skype" (128)
Done     today at 11:37 PDT   today at 11:37 PDT   Mount snap "skype" (128)
Done     today at 11:37 PDT   today at 11:37 PDT   Run pre-refresh hook of "skype"
snap if present
Done     today at 11:37 PDT   today at 11:37 PDT   Stop snap "skype" services
Done     today at 11:37 PDT   today at 11:37 PDT   Remove aliases for snap "skype"
Done     today at 11:37 PDT   today at 11:37 PDT   Make current revision for snap
"skype" unavailable
Done     today at 11:37 PDT   today at 11:37 PDT   Copy snap "skype" data
Done     today at 11:37 PDT   today at 11:37 PDT   Setup snap "skype" (128) security
profiles
Done     today at 11:37 PDT   today at 11:37 PDT   Make snap "skype" (128) available
to the system
Done     today at 11:37 PDT   today at 11:37 PDT   Automatically connect eligible
plugs and slots of snap "skype"
Done     today at 11:37 PDT   today at 11:38 PDT   Set automatic aliases for snap
"skype"
Done     today at 11:37 PDT   today at 11:38 PDT   Setup snap "skype" aliases
Done     today at 11:37 PDT   today at 11:38 PDT   Run post-refresh hook of "skype"
snap if present
Done     today at 11:37 PDT   today at 11:38 PDT   Start snap "skype" (128) services
Done     today at 11:37 PDT   today at 11:38 PDT   Clean up "skype" (128) install
Done     today at 11:37 PDT   today at 11:38 PDT   Run configure hook of "skype"
snap if present
Done     today at 11:37 PDT   today at 11:38 PDT   Run health check of "skype" snap
```

You can configure snap updates by adjusting the time, suspending updates, and setting a limit on how many package revisions you want to keep. Use the **snap set system** command with various options to configure snap updates. The **refresh.timer** option lets you specify times for updates and how many you want performed. The time is specified by the Snap timer string format (**https://snapcraft.io/docs/timer-string-format**). Use the dash to indicate a range. The following first entry updates only on Monday and Friday. The second entry updates Tuesday through Thursday.

```
sudo snap set system refresh.timer=mon,fri
sudo snap set system refresh.timer=tue-thu
```

Use the **refresh.hold** option to delay updates to a specified time. The **time-metered** option pauses updates, and the **refresh.retrain** option sets the number of stored revisions. The default is 3, and the maximum allowed is 20.

```
sudo snap set system refresh.retrain=4
```

Updating Ubuntu APT software with Software Updater

Updating your APT software on your Ubuntu system is a simple procedure, using Software Updater, which provides a graphical update interface for APT. The Software Updater icon appears on the Dock when updates are available. The Software Updater then displays a simple dialog that shows the amount to be downloaded with "Remind Me Later" and "Install Now" buttons (see Figure 4-27). The Settings button opens the Software & Update dialog to the Updates dialog where you can configure updates (see Figure 4-32). You can also manually update by starting the Software Updater from the Applications overview.

Software Updater will also invoke the **snapd** daemon to update your Snap packages. It does not update them directly. The Software Updater interface only explicitly manages APT packages.

Figure 4-27: Software Updater with selected packages

To see actual packages to be updated, click the "Details of updates" arrow. Packages are organized into application categories such as Ubuntu base for the Ubuntu desktop and Linux OS packages, Firefox for Firefox updates, and LibreOffice for office updates. You can expand these to individual packages. The checkboxes for each entry lets you de-select any particular packages you do not want to update (see Figure 4-28). All the APT-compatible repositories that are configured on your system will be checked for updates.

Figure 4-28: Details of updates

To see a detailed description of a particular update, select the update and then click the "Technical description" arrow (see Figure 4-29). Two tabs are displayed: Changes and Description. The Changes tab lists detailed update information, and Description provides information about the software.

Click the Install Now button to start updating. The packages will be downloaded from their appropriate repository. Once downloaded, the packages are updated.

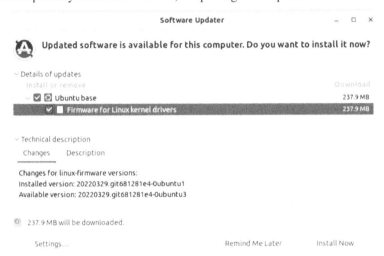

Figure 4-29: Details of updates, Technical description

When downloading and installing, a dialog appears showing the download and install progress (see Figure 4-30). You can choose to show progress for individual files. A window will open up that lists each file and its progress. Once downloaded, the updates are installed. Click the Details arrow to see install messages for particular software packages.

Figure 4-30: Downloading updates

When the update completes, Software updater will display a message saying that your system is up-to-date. If a critical package was installed such as a new kernel, you will be prompted to restart your system. You can restart now or later (see Figure 4-31).

Figure 4-31: Downloaded updates

You can configure Software Updater using the dconf editor. The Software Updater keys are located at apps | update-manager. There are keys to auto-close the install window, check for distribution upgrades, show details and versions, and set the window dimensions.

Configuring Updates with Software & Updates

The Updates tab in Software & Updates lets you configure how updates are managed (see Figure 4-32). Snap packages are updated automatically, which is a feature the Snap system. You do not configure their updates. For packages that are are not installed by Snap, which includes many of the Ubuntu main, universe, and multiverse packages, you can configure updates. Keep in mind that the options listed on this tab have no effect on Snap updates.

Figure 4-32: Software & Updates Update configuration

From the menu labeled "For other packages, subscribe to:" you can choose All updates, security and recommended updates, and security updates only (jammy-security). The "All updates" entry is already selected. Your system is already configured to check for updates automatically on a daily basis. For packages not installed by Snap, you can opt not to check for updates by choosing never from the "Automatically check for updates" menu. You also have options for how security updates are handled. You can download and install any security updates automatically, without confirmation. You can download them and install them later. Or you can just be notified of available security updates, and then choose to install them when you want. For all other updates you can adjust when you want to be notified of updates (immediately, weekly, or every two weeks). On this tab, you also can choose what Ubuntu releases to be notified of: the long term support (LTS) releases only, all releases, or none.

The Livepatch tab lets you use the Canonical Livepatch service, which allows you to install security updates that do not require a restart immediately (see Figure 4-33). You will need a Canonical account to use it. When turned on, you can click on the Livepatch menu on the top bar to see the current status and access the Livepatch settings directly.

Figure 4-33: Software & Updates Livepatch

Flatpak

Flatpak is an open source alternative to Snap. A Flatpak package installs its own set of supporting libraries that can be kept up to date without affecting those on your system. In effect, Flatpak packages run inside their own environment, separate from your system. These include popular applications such as VLC, Spotify, Bookworm, Krita, Steam, and Blender. These applications are downloaded from the Flathub repository. The applications are available from the flathub repository. Some applications, such as Bookworm, are only available as Flatpak packages.

With the GNOME Software Flatpak plugin (**gnome-software-plugin-flatpak**), you can also manage Flatpak packages. You will have to install the plugin. You can install the plugin from the GNOME Software page on Software, or from a terminal window with a shell command.

For a terminal window use the following.

```
sudo apt install gnome-software-plugin-flatpak
```

You will also have to add the **flathub** repository.

```
flatpak remote-add flathub https://flathub.org/repo/flathub.flatpakrepo
```

Restart your system to load the repository.

For Flatpak packages, GNOME Software will list the **dl.flathub.org** site as the source on the application description page. Should there also be an APT version of an application available, a Flathub menu is displayed on the right side of the titlebar showing the Flatpak application and the DEB (APT) application (see Figure 4-34). Choose the one you want to install. Should GNOME Software be configured to support Snap, APT, and Flatpak, applications available on all of them, such as FireFox, will list separate entries for for each.

Figure 4-34: GNOME Software Flatpak

Installing and Running Windows Software on Linux: Wine

Wine is a Windows compatibility layer that will allow you to run many Windows applications natively on Linux. The actual Windows operating system is not required. Windows applications will run as if they were Linux applications, able to access the entire Linux file system and use Linux-connected devices. Applications that are heavily driver-dependent, like graphic intensive games, may not run. Others that do not rely on any specialized drivers, may run very well, including Photoshop and Microsoft Office. For some applications, you may also need to copy over specific Windows dynamic link libraries (DLLs) from a working Windows system to your Wine Windows system32 or system folder.

You can install Wine on your system with Ubuntu Software or the Synaptic Package Manager. The **ttf-mscorefonts-installer** for the Microsoft core fonts will also be installed. You will be prompted to accept the Microsoft end user agreement for using those fonts.

Wine should work on both **.exe** and **.msi** files. You may have to make them executable by checking the file's Properties dialog Permissions tab's Execute checkbox. If an **.msi** file cannot be run, you may have to use the **msiexec** command with the **/a** option.

```
msiexec /a winprogram.msi
```

The Wine applications include Wine configuration (**winecfg**), the Wine software uninstaller, and Wine file browser, as well as Winetricks and notepad. The Winetricks application can be run directly on you Ubuntu desktop and provides an easy way to install compatible Windows applications.

For many windows applications, including **winecfg**, you will need to install the Wine Geckos package. You can download it directly from the WineHQ website at **https://wiki.winehq.org/Gecko**. Once installed you can use the **wine msiexec** command to install it.

```
wine msiexec wine-gecko-2.47.1-x86_64
```

To set up Wine, start the Wine Configuration tool (enter the **sudo winecfg** command in a terminal window) to open a window with tabs for Applications, Libraries (DLL selection), Audio (sound drivers), Drives, Desktop Integration, and Graphics. On the Applications tab, you can select the version of Windows an application is designed for. The Drives tab lists your detected partitions, as well as your Windows-emulated drives, such as drive C. The C: drive is actually just a folder, **.wine/drive_c**, not a partition of a fixed size. Your actual Linux file system will be listed as the Z drive.

```
sudo winecfg
```

Once configured, Wine will set up a **.wine** folder on the user's home folder (the folder is hidden, enable Show Hidden Files in the file manager View menu to display it). Within that folder will be the **drive_c** folder, which functions as the C: drive that holds your Windows system files and program files in the Windows and Program File subfolders. The System and System32 directories are located in the Windows folder. This is where you would place any needed DLL files. The Program Files folder holds your installed Windows programs, just as they would be installed on a Windows Program Files folder.

You can open a terminal window and run the **wine** command with a Windows application as an argument.

```
$ wine winprogram
```

The following starts the MS Paint application on your Ubuntu desktop using Wine.

```
wine mspaint
```

To run the Windows explorer file manager for your Wine Window files, enter the following.

```
wine explorer
```

The command for the Wine task manager is **taskmgr** and for the registry editor it is **regedit**. The Wine task manager lets you search for and run installed applications.

```
wine taskmgr
wine regedit
```

An easy way to install and manage Window applications on Wine is to use Winetricks. You can start Winetricks directly from the Ubuntu applications overview. A "What do you want to do" dialog lets you choose different task such as install an application or game. To install an application, click the "Install an application" entry and then click the OK button to display a list of possible compatible Windows applications. Some you can download and install directly. A few require an application DVD or CD. Some will require a manual download. Once installed you can then return to the wineprefix dialog. The "Select the default wineprefix" option lets you perform system tasks such as running **winecfg**, the explorer file manager, and install fonts. When Wine installs a Windows application, it may display several install messages. You can turn this off by choosing "Enable silent install" on the "What do you want to do" dialog. The term wineprefix in the Winetricks titebar refers to the folder Wine is installed on.

Alternatively, you can use the commercial Windows compatibility layer called Crossover Office. This is a commercial product tested to run certain applications like Microsoft Office. Check **https://www.codeweavers.com** for more details. Crossover Office is based on Wine, which CodeWeavers supports directly.

Part 2: Applications

Office Suites, Editors, and E-mail
Multimedia and Graphics
Internet Applications

5. Office Suites, Editors, and E-mail

LibreOffice

Calligra

GNOME Office Applications

Running Microsoft Office on Linux

Document Viewers (PostScript, PDF, and DVI)

E-book readers

GNOME Notes, Clocks, and Weather

Editors

Database Management Systems

Mail Clients: Evolution, Thunderbird, Kmail

Command Line Mail Clients

Newsreaders

Several office suites are now available for Ubuntu (see Table 5-1). These include professional-level word processors, presentation managers, drawing tools, and spreadsheets. The freely available versions are described in this chapter. LibreOffice is currently the primary office suite supported by Ubuntu. Calligra is an office suite designed for use with KDE. CodeWeavers CrossOver Office provides reliable support for running Microsoft Office Windows applications directly on Linux, integrating them with KDE and GNOME. You can also download the Apache OpenOffice suite (originally, Oracle/StarOffice).

Web Site	Description
https://www.libreoffice.org	LibreOffice open source office suite
https://calligra.org	Calligra Suite, for KDE
https://www.codeweavers.com	CrossOver Office (MICROSOFT Office support)
https://www.openoffice.org	Apache OpenOffice
https://www.scribus.net	Scribus desktop publishing tool

Table 5-1: Linux Office Suites

Several database management systems are also available for Linux, which include high-powered, commercial-level database management systems, such as Oracle and IBM's DB2. Most of the database management systems available for Linux are designed to support large relational databases. Ubuntu includes both MySQL and PostgreSQL open source databases in its distribution, which can support smaller databases. Various database management systems available to run under Linux are listed in Table 5-8 later in this chapter.

Linux also provides several text editors that range from simple text editors for simple notes to editors with more complex features such as spell-checkers, buffers, or complex pattern matching. All generate character text files and can be used to edit any Linux text files. Text editors are often used in system administration tasks to change or add entries in Linux configuration files found in the /**etc** folder or a user's initialization or application configuration files located in a user's home folder (dot files). You can also use a text editor to work on source code files for any of the programming languages or shell program scripts.

Ubuntu also supports several E-book readers. Some such as Calibre and FBReader run natively on Linux. Some of the Window versions of E-book readers such as Adobe Digital Editions run under Wine (the Windows compatibility layer for Linux).

LibreOffice

LibreOffice is a fully integrated suite of office applications developed as an open source project and freely distributed to all. It is the primary office suite for Ubuntu. LibreOffice applications are accessible from the Applications overview. There is also a default dock item for LibreOffice Writer. LibreOffice is the open source and freely available office suite derived originally from OpenOffice. LibreOffice is supported by the Document Foundation, which was established after Oracle's acquisition of Sun, the main developer for Open Office. LibreOffice is now the primary open source office software for Linux. Oracle retains control of all the original OpenOffice software and does not cooperate with any LibreOffice development. LibreOffice has replaced OpenOffice as the default Office software for most Linux distributions.

LibreOffice includes word processing, spreadsheet, presentation, and drawing applications (see Table 5-2). Versions of LibreOffice exist for Linux, Windows, and Mac OS. You can obtain information such as online manuals and FAQs as well as current versions from the LibreOffice website at **https://www.libreoffice.org**. The LibreOffice suite of applications is installed as part of the Ubuntu Desktop installation. Ubuntu 2.0.04 installs LibreOffice 7.3. Check its release notes for more information.

```
https://wiki.documentfoundation.org/ReleaseNotes/7.3
```

Application	Description
Calc (Spreadsheet)	LibreOffice spreadsheet
Draw (Drawing)	LibreOffice drawing application
Writer (Word Processing)	LibreOffice word processor
Math (Formula)	LibreOffice mathematical formula composer
Impress (Presentation)	LibreOffice presentation manager
Base (Database)	Database front end for accessing and managing a variety of different databases.

Table 5-2: LibreOffice Applications

Figure 5-1: LibreOffice Writer word processor

LibreOffice is an integrated suite of applications. You can open the writer, spreadsheet, or presentation application directly. The LibreOffice Writer word processor supports standard word processing features, such as cut and paste, spell-checker, and text formatting, as well as paragraph styles (see Figure 5-1). Context menus let you format text easily. Wizards (Letter, Web page, Fax, and Agenda) let you generate different kinds of documents quickly. You can embed objects within documents, such as using Draw to create figures that you can then drag-and-drop to the Writer document. LibreOffice Writer is compatible with earlier versions of Microsoft Word. It will read and convert Word documents to LibreOffice Writer document, preserving most features including contents, tables, and indexes. Writer documents also can be saved as Word documents.

LibreOffice provides access to many database files. File types supported include ODBC (Open Database Connectivity), JDBC (Java), MySQL, PostgreSQL, and MDB (Microsoft Access) database files. You can also create your own simple databases. Check the LibreOffice Features | Base page (**https://www.libreoffice.org/discover/base/**) for detailed information on drivers and supported databases.

LibreOffice Calc is a professional-level spreadsheet. With LibreOffice Math, you can create formulas that you can embed in a text document. With the presentation manager (Libre Office Impress), you can create images for presentations, such as circles, rectangles, and connecting elements like arrows, as well as vector-based illustrations. Impress supports advanced features such as morphing objects, grouping objects, and defining gradients. LibreOffice Draw is a sophisticated drawing tool that includes 3-D modeling tools. You can create simple or complex images, including animation text aligned on curves. LibreOffice also includes a printer setup tool with which you can select printers, fonts, paper sizes, and page formats.

Scribus is a desktop publishing tool, **https://www.scribus.net**. Scribus is available from the Universe repository.

Calligra

Calligra is an integrated office suite for the K Desktop Environment (KDE) consisting of several office applications, including a word processor, a spreadsheet, and graphics applications. You can download and install it from the Universe repository, using Ubuntu Software, the Synaptic Package Manager (Ubuntu desktop), or the Discover Package Manager (Kubuntu). Calligra allows components from any one application to be used in another, letting you embed a spreadsheet from Calligra Sheets or diagrams from Karbon in a Calligra Words document. It also uses the open document format (ODF) for its files, providing cross-application standardization. There is also a Windows version available. You can obtain more information about Calligra from **https://calligra.org**.

Currently, Calligra includes Calligra Sheets, Calligra Flow, Calligra Words, Karbon, Krita, Plan, Calligra Stage, and Kexi (see Table 5-3). The contact application, Kontact, has been spun off as a separate project. Kontact is an integrated contact application including Kmail, Korganizer, Kaddressbook, and Knotes. Calligra Sheets is a spreadsheet, Calligra Stage is a presentation application, Karbon is a vector graphics program, and Calligra Words is a publisher-like word processor. Krita is a paint and image editor. Kexi provides database integration with Calligra applications, currently supporting PostgreSQL and MySQL.

Application	Description
Stage	Presentation application
Words	Word processor (desktop publisher)
Sheets	Spreadsheet
Karbon	Vector graphics program
Kexi	Database integration
Plan	Project management and planning
Krita	Paint and image manipulation program
Kontact (separate project)	Contact application including mail, address book, and organizer

Table 5-3: Calligra Applications

Calligra Sheets is the spreadsheet application, which incorporates the basic operations found in most spreadsheets, with formulas similar to those used in MS Excel. You can also embed charts, pictures, or formulas using Krita and Karbon. With Calligra Stage, you can create presentations consisting of text and graphics modeled using different fonts, orientations, and attributes such as colors. Karbon is a vector-based graphics program, much like Adobe Illustrator and LibreOffice Draw. It supports the standard graphic operations such as rotating, scaling, and aligning objects. Calligra Words can best be described as a desktop publisher, with many of the features found in publishing applications. Although it is a fully functional word processor, Calligra Words sets up text in frames that are placed on the page like objects. Frames, like objects in a drawing program, can be moved, resized, and reoriented. You can organize frames into a frame set, having text flow from one to the other.

GNOME Office Applications

There are several GNOME office applications available including AbiWord, Gnumeric, Evince, and Evolution. GNOME office applications are part of Ubuntu and can be downloaded with Ubuntu Software. A current listing of common GNOME office applications is shown in Table 5-4. All implement the support for embedding components, ensuring drag-and-drop capability throughout the GNOME interface.

AbiWord is an open source word processor that aims to be a complete cross-platform solution, running on Mac, Unix, and Windows, as well as Linux. It is part of a set of desktop productivity applications being developed by the AbiSource project (**https://www.abisource.com**).

Gnumeric is a professional-level GNOME spreadsheet meant to replace commercial spreadsheets. Gnumeric supports standard spreadsheet features, including auto filling and cell formatting, and an extensive number of formats. Gnumeric also supports plug-ins, making it possible to extend and customize its abilities.

Dia is a drawing program designed to create diagrams, such as database, circuit object, flow chart, and network diagrams. You can create elements along with lines and arcs, with different types of endpoints such as arrows or diamonds. Data can be saved in XML format, making it transportable to other applications.

GnuCash (**http://www.gnucash.org**) is a personal finance application for managing accounts, stocks, and expenses.

Application	Description
AbiWord	Cross-platform word processor
Gnumeric	Spreadsheet
Evince	Document Viewer
Evolution	Integrated email, calendar, and personal organizer
Dia	Diagram and flow chart editor
GnuCash	Personal finance manager
Glom	Database front end for PostgreSQL database
glabels	Label Designer

Table 5-4: Office Applications for GNOME

Running Microsoft Office on Linux: Wine and CrossOver

One of the concerns for new Linux users is what kind of access they will have to their Microsoft Office files, particularly Word files. The Linux operating system and many applications for it are designed to provide seamless access to Microsoft Office files. The major Linux Office suites, including Calligra, LibreOffice, and Oracle Open Office, all read and manage Microsoft Office files. In addition, these office suites are fast approaching the same level of features and support for office tasks as found in Microsoft Office.

Note: You can, of course, use your browser to run the Microsoft Office Online version, which runs from a remote Microsoft cloud site.

Wine (Windows Compatibility Layer) allows you to run many Windows applications directly, using a supporting virtual windows API. See the Wine website for a list of supported applications, **https://www.winehq.org**, AppDB tab. Well-written applications may run directly from Wine. Sometimes you will have to have a working Windows system from which you can copy system DLLs needed by particular applications. You can also import Windows fonts by directly copying them to the Wine font folder. Each user can install and run their own version of Wine with its own simulated C: partition on which Windows applications are installed. The simulated drive is installed as **drive_c** in your **.wine** folder. The **.wine** folder is a hidden folder. It is not normally displayed with the ls command or the GNOME file manager (Show Hidden Files). You can also use any of your Linux folders for your Windows application data files instead of your simulated C: drive. These are referenced by Windows applications as the **z:** drive.

In a terminal window, using the wine command with an install program will automatically install that Windows application on the simulated C: drive. The following example installs Microsoft Office. Though there may be difficulties with the latest Microsoft Office versions and with the 64-bit versions, Office 2002, 2007, 2010, and 2013 32bit versions should work fine (see **https://www.winehq.org**, AppDB tab, search for Office Suites). Applications are rated platinum, gold, silver, bronze, and garbage. Several of the Microsoft Office suites are gold or platinum.

When you insert the Microsoft Office CD, it will be mounted to the **/media**/*username* folder using the disk label as its folder name. Check the **/media** folder under the user's name to see what the actual name is. You then run the **setup.exe** program for Office with wine. Depending on the version of Office you have, there may be further subfolders for the actual Office **sctup.exe** program. The following example assumes that the label for Office is OFFICE and that the **setup.exe** program for Office is on the top-level folder of that CD.

```
$ wine /media/richard/OFFICE/setup.exe
```

The install program will start up and you will be prompted to enter your product key. Be sure to use only uppercase as you type. Once installed, choose Applications | Wine | Programs | Microsoft Office, and then choose the application name to start up. The application should start up normally. The application is referenced by Wine on the user's simulated **c:** drive.

The Windows My Documents folder is set up by Wine to be the user's Ubuntu Documents folder. There you will find any files saved to My Documents.

Wine is constantly being updated to accommodate the latest versions of Windows applications. However, for some applications you may need to copy DLL files from a working Windows system to the Wine Windows folder, **.wine/drive_c/windows**, usually to the **system** or **system32** folders. Though effective, Wine support will not be as stable as Crossover.

CrossOver Office is a commercial product that lets you install and run most Microsoft Office applications. CrossOver Office was developed by CodeWeavers, which also supports Windows web browser plug-ins as well as several popular Windows applications like Adobe Photoshop. CrossOver features both standard and professional versions, providing reliable application support. You can find out more about CrossOver Office at **https://www.codeweavers.com**.

CrossOver can be installed either for private multi-user mode or managed multi-user mode. In private multi-user mode, each user installs Windows software, such as full versions of Office. In managed multi-user mode, the Windows software is installed once and all users share it. Once the software is installed, you will see a Windows Applications menu on the main menu, from which you can start your installed Windows software. The applications will run within a Linux window, but they will appear just as if they were running in Windows.

Also, with VMware, you can run Windows under Linux, allowing you to run Windows applications, including Microsoft Office, on your Linux system. For more information, check the VMware website at **https://www.vmware.com**.

Another option, for users with high-powered computers that support virtualization, is to install the Windows OS on a virtual machine using the Virtual Machine Manager or Boxes. You could then install and run Windows on the virtual machine and install Microsoft Office on it.

Document Viewers, and DVI)

Though located under Applications overview, PostScript, PDF, DVI, and E-book viewers are more commonly used with Office applications (see Table 5-5). You can install these viewers with Ubuntu Software. Evince (PostScript, PDF and Okular can display both PostScript (**.ps**) and PDF (**.pdf**) files.

Evince is the default document viewer for GNOME. It is started automatically whenever you double-click a PDF file on the GNOME desktop. Okular is the default document viewer for KDE. Okular, and Evince are PDF viewers. Atril is the MATE desktop document viewer. They include many of the standard Adobe reader features such as zoom, two-page display, and full-screen mode.

All these viewers have the ability to print documents. To generate PDF documents you can use LibreOffice Writer or the Scribus desktop publisher (**https://www.scribus.net**).

Viewer	Description
Evince	Document Viewer for PostScript, DVI, and PDF files
Okular	KDE5 tool for displaying PDF, DVI, and postscript files
Scribus	Desktop publisher for generating PDF documents
Simple Scan	GNOME Scanner interface for scanners
Atril	MATE Document Viewer for PostScript, DVI, and PDF files

Table 5-5: PostScript, PDF, and DVI viewers

Linux also supports a professional-level typesetting tool, called TeX, commonly used to compose complex mathematical formulas. TeX generates a DVI document that can be displayed by

DVI viewers, several of which are available for Linux. DVI files generated by the TeX document application can be viewed by Evince and Okular.

Note: To scan documents directly, you can use Simple Scan which you can save as jpeg, png, or PDF files.

E-book Readers: FBReader, Foliate, and Calibre

To read E-books on Ubuntu, you can use Calibre, FBReader, and Foliate (see Table 5-6). FBReader is an open source reader that can read non-DRM E-books, including mobipocket, html, chm, EPUB, text, and rtf. The toolbar holds operations that move you through the text and configure your reader, adding books and setting interface preferences (see Figure 5-2). To see your selection of books click the Library Tree icon on the left. You can organize text by author or tag. On the Options window, the Library tab lets you choose where your books are stored. You also can search for public domain books.

Foliate is a GNOME E-book reader. Install with Ubuntu Software and be sure that its permissions are set to allow local and network access, as well as desktop Settings access. From the Foliate menu you can set formats such as fonts and margins. You can choose from several themes, setting different shadings. Additional options for layout and text be set in the Advanced menu. The Preferences dialog lets you configure paging, footer notices, and selection actions. You can also choose to open to the last opened file automatically.

Note: Also available is the beta version of FBReader 2.0, which include the capability of linking to ebooks on your Google drive and purchasing books.

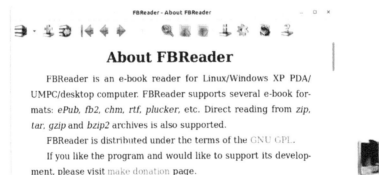

Figure 5-2: FBReader E-book reader

Calibre reads PDF, EPUB, Lit (Microsoft), and Mobipocket E-books. Calibre functions as a library for accessing and managing your E-books (see Figure 5-3). Calibre also can convert many document files and E-books to the EPUB format, the open source standard used by Apple (iPad) and Barnes and Noble (Nook). It can take as conversion input text, HTML, TRF, and ODT (LibreOffice), as well as E-books.

Figure 5-3: Calibre E-book reader, organizer, and converter

Viewer	Description
Calibre	E-book reader and library, also converts various inputs to EPUB E-books.
E-book reader	FBReader E-book reader
Foliate	GNOME E-book reader

Table 5-6: E-book Readers

GNOME Notes (bijiben)

The GNOME Notes application lets you create and organize simple notes on your desktop. Install using the **bijiben** package. The Notes window lists your new and recent notes, showing the note title and the first few lines of text (see Figure 5-4). In the header bar, the search button opens a search box that lets you search for notes. The list button lets you switch between icon and list views. The check button lets you delete or organize your notes. A checkbox is displayed at the right lower corner of the note icons. Clicking on that checkbox opens a taskbar at the bottom with buttons to delete the note, add it to a collection (notebooks), or email it. There is also a color button you can use the background color.

Figure 5-4: GNOME Notes

To create a new note, click on the New button on the header bar to open a new text. The first line is the title of your note (see Figure 5-5). Press the ENTER key to move to the next line. A button at the top right opens a dialog that lets you choose the color for a note. The task menu (menu button) provides undo/redo functions, deletion, and email options. You can also add the note to a notebook. You can use notebooks to organize your notes. To delete a note, click on the checkmark button to display a checkbox next to each note. Check the ones you want to delete and click the Done button.

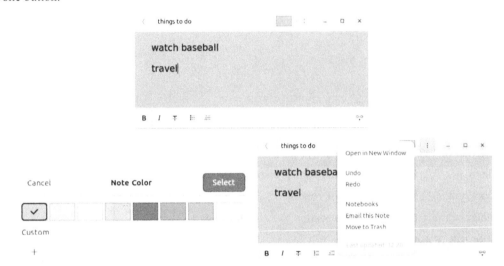

Figure 5-5: GNOME Notes, editing notes

Note: You can also use the Gnome To Do application to create and manage to-do lists.

GNOME Clocks and Weather

Two helpful tools are the clocks and weather applications. Clocks has four tabs: World, Alarm, Stopwatch, and Timer. The World tab displays the current time at any city and at your current location (see Figure 5-6). Click the plus button to open a dialog where you can add a city. To remove a city, click the button button the right of an entry. The Alarm tab works as an alarm clock. The Stopwatch tab operates a stopwatch, letting you mark laps. The timer counts down in time. You set the start amount.

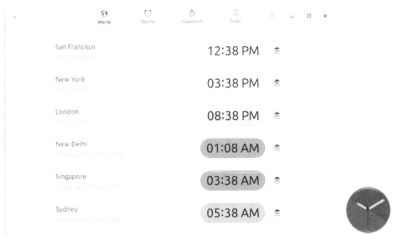

Figure 5-6: GNOME Clocks: World tab

The GNOME weather tool lets you display the weather in any city. Ubuntu 22.04 retains the GNOME 41 version of GNOME weather. If you want, you can download the GNOME 42 version of weather from the Flatpak repository. Click the Places button to open a dialog where you can enter the name of a city. A partial entry is matched on, giving you a listing of possible cities. Clicking on a city displays a full image of the weather for that city, with the temperature and forecast for the next several hours, and a sidebar with the forecast for the next five days (see Figure 5-7). The Today and Tomorrow buttons show to the current weather and tomorrow's weather. The current time is displayed in the upper right corner. A reload button on the right side of the header bar lets you refresh the weather display.

Figure 5-7: GNOME Weather: city with forecast

The Places dialog shows a list of previous cities you have viewed with the temperature and weather icons. If Automatic location is turned on, the weather at your current location is also listed (first entry).

GNOME Characters and Fonts

The GNOME Characters utility lets you copy a color character image to use in a document. You can choose from several categories (see Figure 5-8). These characters are open source emojis. You can access GNOME Characters form the applications overview Utilities application folder as Characters. Click on the character you want to display. A dialog prompts you to copy the character to the copy the character to the clipboard. In your text editor, you can then paste it as an inline character. The characters include images, as well as math symbols, punctuation, and currencies.

Figure 5-8: GNOME Characters

Fonts provides a simple listing of your installed fonts, showing the font style (see Figure 5-9). You can access Fonts from the applications overview's Utilities application folder. Click on a font image to display examples of the font and an info button at the top right on the title bar, which you can click to display information about the font, including style, type, version, and copyright.

Figure 5-9: Fonts

GNOME Calendar

GNOME Calendar lets you manage a calendar, specifying events (see Figure 5-10). Events can be imported from Web sources. To add an event, click on a date to open a dialog where you can enter the event name and select a calendar. Click the Edit Details button to display a dialog for setting the time, duration, location, and any notes. Personal and Birthday calendars are already set up. Click the calendar button at the right side of the title bar to open a dialog to let you add new calendars.

Figure 5-10: GNOME Calendar

Editors

The Ubuntu desktop supports powerful text editors with full mouse support, scroll bars, and menus. These include basic text editors, such as Gedit and Kate, as well as word processors, such as LibreOffice Word, and Calligra Words. Ubuntu also provides the cursor-based editors Nano, Vim, and Emacs. Nano is a cursor-based editor with an easy-to-use interface supporting menus and mouse selection (if run from a terminal window). Vim is an enhanced version of the Vi text editor used on the Unix system. These editors use simple, cursor-based operations to give you a full-screen format. Table 5-7 lists several desktop editors for Linux. Vi and Emacs have powerful editing features that have been refined over the years. Emacs, in particular, is extensible to a full development environment for programming new applications. Later versions of Emacs and Vim, such as GNU Emacs, XEmacs, and Gvim provide support for mouse, menu, and window operations.

GNOME Text Editors: Gedit and Text Editor

For Ubuntu 20.04, Gedit remain the default text editor (GNOME 4.1). You can install the new Gnome Text Editor, if you wish (GNOME 4.2).

GNOME Gedit (GNOME 4.1)

The Gedit editor is a basic text editor for the GNOME desktop. It is an application from of the GNOME 4.1 release which Ubuntu retained as the default editor for Ubuntu 22.04. Gedit provides full mouse support, implementing standard desktop operations, such as cut and paste to move text, and click and drag to select and move/copy text (see Figure 5-11). It supports standard text editing operations such as Find and Replace. The editor is accessible from the Applications overview as Text Editor. You can use Gedit to create and modify your text files, including configuration files. Gedit also provides more advanced features such as print preview and configurable levels of undo/redo operations, and it can read data from pipes. To configure Gedit, select Preferences from the menu to open the Preferences dialog with tabs for View, Editor, Font & Colors, and Plugins. On the Views tab you can configure options such as text wrapping, highlighting, and what features to display such as line numbers and the statusbar. On the Editor tab you can set tab stops and file saving, including autosave. On the Font & Colors tab you can select the font and color scheme. Clicking on the font entry opens the "Pick the editor font" dialog, where you can select the font and the size.

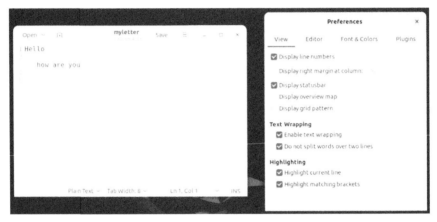

Figure 5-11: GNOME Gedit

Gedit features plug-ins that provide added functionality, including spell checking, document statistics, and sorting. Install **gedit-plugins** for more plugins such as word completion and color schemes. To activate a plugin, select on the Preferences Plugins tab. Plugins are accessible from the Gedit menu and its Tools submenu.

GNOME Text Editor (GNOME 4.2)

GNOME Text Editor is the new replacement text editor included in the GNOME 4.2 release (see Figure 5-12). It is not installed by default. You can install it from either the Snap or Apt repositories. The name of the application is **gnome-text-editor**.

```
sudo apt install gnome-text-editor
sudo snap install gnome-text-editor
```

Text Editor is accessible from the Applications Overview as Text Editor (see Figure. It supports tabs. From the menu you can choose the light or dark style, or to use the system theme. It also supports find and replace, printing, and keyboard shortcuts. From the configuration menu you can activate features such as line numbers, right margin, automatic indentation, tabs, text wrapping, and spell check. The document type entry lets you choose a document a programming or scripting type such as C++ or Python.

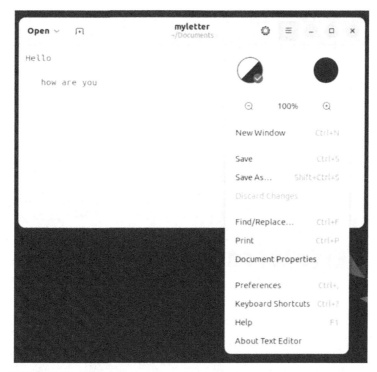

Figure 5-12: GNOME Text Editor

The Preferences dialog lets you select a style and font, set the right margin, and to set display features such as an overview map (pages), highlighting the current line, and a grid pattern on the text.

Application	Description
Kate	Text and program editor
Calligra Words	Desktop publisher, part of Calligra Suite
Text Editor	GNOME text editor
Gedit	GNOME legacy text editor
AbiWord	Word processor
OpenWriter	LibreOffice word processor that can edit text files
nano	Easy to use screen-based editor, installed by default
GNU Emacs	Emacs editor with X Window System support
XEmacs	X Window System version of Emacs editor
gvim	Vim version with X Window System support

Table 5-7: Desktop Editors

The nano text editor

The nano editor is a simple screen-based editor that lets you visually edit your file, using arrow and page keys to move around the file. You use control keys to perform actions. **Ctrl-x** will exit and prompt you to save the file, **Ctrl-o** will save it. **Ctrl-k** will cut the current line.

You start nano with the **nano** command entered in a terminal window or on the command line interface. To edit a configuration file, you will need administrative access. Figure 5-13 shows the nano editor being used to edit the GRUB configuration file, **/etc/default/grub**.

```
sudo nano /etc/default/grub
```

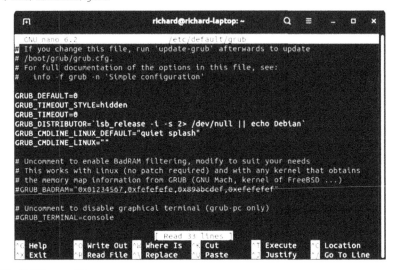

Figure 5-13: Editing with nano

KDE Editor: Kate

The KDE editor Kate provides full mouse support, implementing standard GUI operations, such as cut and paste to move text, and click and drag to select and move/copy text. The editor is accessible from the Applications | Utilities menu on the KDE desktop, and from the Applications overview on the Ubuntu desktop. Kate is an advanced editor, with such features as spell checking, font selection, and highlighting. Most commands can be selected using menus. A toolbar of icons for common operations is displayed across the top of the Kate window. A sidebar displays panels for a file list. Kate also supports multiple views of a document, letting you display segments in their own windows, vertically or horizontally. You can also open several documents at the same time, moving among them with the file list. Kate is designed to be a program editor for editing software programming/development-related source code files. Kate can format the syntax for different programming languages, such as C, Perl, Java, and XML.

The Emacs Editor

Emacs can best be described as a working environment featuring an editor, a mailer, a newsreader, and a Lisp interpreter. The editor is tailored for program development, enabling you to format source code according to the programming language you use. Many versions of Emacs are currently available for use on Unix and Linux systems. The versions usually included with Linux distributions are either GNU Emacs or XEmacs. GNU Emacs is X Window System capable, enabling GUI features such as menus, scroll bars, and mouse-based editing operations. You can find out more information about Emacs at **https://www.gnu.org/software/emacs/**, and for XEmacs at its website, **http://www.xemacs.org**.

The Emacs editor operates much like a standard word processor. The keys on your keyboard represent input characters. Commands are implemented with special keys, such as control (CTRL) keys and alternate (ALT) keys. There is no special input mode, as in Vi. You type in your text, and if you need to execute an editing command, such as moving the cursor or saving text, you use a CTRL key. You invoke the Emacs editor with the command **emacs**. You can enter the name of the file you want to edit, and if the file does not exist, it is created. In the next example, the user prepares to edit the file **mydata** with Emacs:

```
$ emacs mydata
```

The GNU Emacs editor supports basic desktop editing operations such as selection of text with click-and-drag mouse operations, cut/copy/paste, and a scroll bar for moving through text. The Mode line and Echo areas are displayed at the bottom of the window, where you can enter keyboard commands.

The Vi Editor: Vim and Gvim

The Vim editor is an enhanced version of the Vi editor. It includes all the commands and features of the Vi editor. Vi, which stands for *visual,* remains one of the most widely used editors in Linux. On Ubuntu, a basic version of Vi, called **vim-tiny**, is installed as part of the basic installation. For the full version, install the Vim package from Ubuntu Software or the Synaptic Package Manager.

Keyboard-based editors like Vim and Emacs use a keyboard for two different operations: to specify editing commands and to receive character input. Used for editing commands, certain keys perform deletions, some execute changes, and others perform cursor movement. Used for character input, keys represent characters that can be entered into the file being edited. Usually, these two different functions are divided among different keys on the keyboard. Alphabetic keys are reserved for character input, while function keys and control keys specify editing commands, such as deleting text or moving the cursor. Such editors can rely on the existence of an extended keyboard that includes function and control keys.

Editors in Unix were designed originally to assume a minimal keyboard with alphanumeric characters and some control characters, as well as the ESC and ENTER keys. Instead of dividing the command and input functions among different keys, the Vi editor has three separate modes of operation for the keyboard: command and input modes, and a line editing mode. In command mode, all the keys on the keyboard become editing commands; in the input mode, the keys on the keyboard become input characters. Some of the editing commands, such as **a** or **i**, enter the input mode. On typing **i**, you leave the command mode and enter the input mode. Each key now represents a character to be input to the text. Pressing ESC automatically returns you to the command mode, and the keys once again become editor commands. As you edit text, you are constantly moving from the command mode to the input mode and back again. With Vim, you can use the **Ctrl-o** command to jump quickly to the command mode and enter a command, and then automatically return to the input mode. Table 5-8 lists a basic set of Vi commands to get you started.

Although you can create, save, close, and quit files with the Vi editor, the commands for each are not similar. Saving and quitting a file involves the use of special line editing commands, whereas closing a file is a Vi editing command. Creation of a file is usually specified on the same shell command line that invokes the Vi editor. To edit a file, type **vi** or **vim** and the name of a file on the shell command line. If a file by that name does not exist, the system creates it. In effect, entering the name of a file that does not yet exist instructs the Vi editor to create that file. The following command invokes the Vi editor, working on the file **booklist**. If **booklist** does not yet exist, the Vi editor creates it.

```
$ vim booklist
```

Command	Description
h	Moves the cursor left one character.
l	Moves the cursor right one character.
k	Moves the cursor up one line.
j	Moves the cursor down one line.
CTRL-F	Moves forward by a screen of text; the next screen of text is displayed.
CTRL-B	Moves backward by a screen of text; the previous screen of text is displayed.
Input	*(All input commands place the user in input; the user leaves input with* ESC.*)*
a	Enters input after the cursor.
i	Enters input before the cursor.
o	Enters input below the line the cursor is on; inserts a new empty line below the one the cursor is currently on.
Text Selection (Vim)	
v	Visual mode; move the cursor to expand selected text by character. Once selected, press key to execute action: **c** change, **d** delete, **y** copy, **:** line-editing command, **J** join lines, **U** uppercase, **u** lowercase.
V	Visual mode; move the cursor to expand selected text by line.
Delete	
x	Deletes the character the cursor is on.
dd	Deletes the line the cursor is on.
Change	*(Except for the replace command, r, all change commands place the user into input after deleting text.)*
cw	Deletes the word the cursor is on and places the user into the input mode.
r	Replaces the character the cursor is on. After pressing **r**, the user enters the replacement character. The change is made without entering input; the user remains in the Vi command mode.

R	First places into input mode, and then overwrites character by character. Appears as an overwrite mode on the screen but actually is in input mode.
Move	Moves text by first deleting it, moving the cursor to the desired place of insertion, and then pressing the **p** command. (When text is deleted, it is automatically held in a special buffer.)
p	Inserts deleted or copied text after the character or line the cursor is on.
P	Inserts deleted or copied text before the character or line the cursor is on.
dw p	Deletes a word, and then moves it to the place you indicate with the cursor (press **p** to insert the word *after* the word the cursor is on).
yy or Y p	Copies the line the cursor is on.
Search	The two search commands open up a line at the bottom of the screen and enable the user to enter a pattern to be searched for; press ENTER after typing in the pattern.
/*pattern*	Searches forward in the text for a pattern.
?*pattern*	Searches backward in the text for a pattern.
n	Repeats the previous search, whether it was forward or backward.
Line Editing Commands	**Effect**
w	Saves file.
q	Quits editor; **q!** quits without saving.

Table 5-8: Vi Editor Commands

After executing the **vim** command, you enter Vi's command mode. Each key becomes a Vi editing command, and the screen becomes a window onto the text file. Text is displayed screen by screen. The first screen of text is displayed, and the cursor is positioned in the upper-left corner. With a newly created file, there is no text to display. When you first enter the Vi editor, you are in the command mode. To add text, you need to enter the input mode. In the command mode, **a** is the editor command for appending text. Pressing this key places you in the input mode. Now the keyboard operates like a typewriter, and you can input text to the file. If you press ENTER, you merely start a new line of text. With Vim, you can use the arrow keys to move from one part of the entered text to another and work on different parts of the text. After entering text, you can leave the input mode and return to the command mode by pressing ESC. Once finished with the editing session, you exit Vi by typing two capital Zs, ZZ. Hold down the SHIFT key and press **Z** twice. This sequence first saves the file and then exits the Vi editor, returning you to the Linux shell. To save a file while editing, you use the line editing command **w**, which writes a file to the disk; **w** is equivalent to the Save command found in other word processors. You first type a colon to access the line editing mode, and then type **w** and press ENTER, **:w.**

You can use the **:q** command to quit an editing session. Unlike the **ZZ** command, the **:q** command does not perform any save operation before it quits. In this respect, it has one major constraint. If any modifications have been made to your file since the last save operation, the **:q** command will fail and you will not leave the editor. You can override this restriction by placing a **!** qualifier after the **:q** command. The command **:q!** will quit the Vi editor without saving any modifications made to the file in that session since the last save (the combination **:wq** is the same as ZZ).

To obtain online help, enter the **:help** command. This is a line editing command. Type a colon, enter the word **help** on the line that opens at the bottom of the screen, and then press ENTER. You can add the name of a specific command after the word **help**. Pressing the **F1** key also brings up online help.

As an alternative to using Vim in a command line interface, you can use gvim, which provides X Window System–based menus for basic file, editing, and window operations. Gvim can be installed from Ubuntu Software. On the Synaptic Package Manager, the package is called the **vim-gui-common** package, which includes several links to Gvim such as **evim**, **gview**, and **gex** (open Ex line editor). To use Gvim, you can enter the **gvim** command at a terminal prompt. The standard Vi interface is shown, but with several menu buttons displayed across the top along with a toolbar with buttons for common commands like search and file saves. All the standard Vi commands work just as described previously. However, you can use your mouse to select items on these menus. You can open and close a file, or open several files using split windows or different windows. The editing menu enables you to cut, copy, and paste text, as well as undo or redo operations. In the editing mode, you can select text with your mouse with a click-and-drag operation, or use the Editing menu to cut or copy and then paste the selected text. Text entry, however, is still performed using the **a**, **i**, or **o** command to enter the input mode. Searches and replacements are supported through a dialog window. There are also buttons on the toolbar for finding next and previous instances. You can also split the view into different windows to display parts of the same file or different files. Use the **:split** command to open a window, and use **:hide** to close the current one. Use **Ctrl-w** with the up and down arrow keys to move between them. On Gvim, you use entries in the Windows menu to manage windows. Configuration preferences can be placed in the user's **.vimrc** file.

Database Management Systems

Several database systems are provided for Ubuntu, including LibreOffice Base, MySQL, SQLite, and PostgreSQL. Ubuntu continues to provide the original MySQL database. In addition, commercial SQL database software is also compatible with Ubuntu. Table 5-9 lists database management systems currently available for Linux. SQLite is a simple and fast database server requiring no configuration and implementing the database on a single disk file. For small embedded databases you can use Berkeley DB (db4). In addition, Ubuntu also supports document-based non-SQL databases such as MongoDB. MongoDB is a document-based database that can be quickly searched.

SQL Databases (RDBMS)

SQL databases are relational database management systems (RDBMSs) designed for extensive database management tasks. Many of the major SQL databases now have Linux versions, including Oracle and IBM. These are commercial and professional database management systems. Linux has proved itself capable of supporting complex and demanding database management tasks. In addition, many free SQL databases are available for Linux that offer much the same functionality. Several commercial databases also provide free personal versions.

System	Site
LibreOffice	LibreOffice database (Ubuntu repository): **https://www.libreoffice.org/discover/base/**
PostgreSQL	The PostgreSQL database (Ubuntu repository): **https://www.postgresql.org/**
MySQL	MySQL database (Ubuntu repository): **https://www.mysql.com/**
SQLite	Simple SQL database: **https://www.sqlite.org/index.html**
MongoDB	Document-based database: **https://www.mongodb.com/**
MariaDB	MariaDB database, based on MySQL: **https://mariadb.org/**

Table 5-9: Database Management Systems for Linux

LibreOffice Base

LibreOffice provides a basic database application, LibreOffice Base that can access many database files. You can set up and operate a simple database, as well as access and manage files from other database applications. When you start up LibreOffice Base, you will be prompted either to start a new database or connect to an existing one. File types supported include ODBC (Open Database Connectivity), JDBC (Java), MySQL, PostgreSQL, and MDB (Microsoft Access) database files (install the **unixodbc** and **libmysql-java** packages). You can also create your own simple databases. Check the LibreOffice Base page (**https://www.libreoffice.org/discover/base/**) for detailed information on drivers and supported databases.

PostgreSQL

PostgreSQL is based on the POSTURES database management system, though it uses SQL as its query language. POSTGRESQL is a next-generation research prototype developed at the University of California, Berkeley. Linux versions of PostgreSQL are included in most distributions, including the Red Hat, Fedora, Debian, and Ubuntu. You can find more information on it from the PostgreSQL website at **https://www.postgresql.org**. PostgreSQL is an open source project, developed under the GPL license.

MySQL

MySQL, included with Ubuntu, is a true multi-user, multithreaded SQL database server, supported by MySQL AB. MySQL is an open source product available free under the GPL license. You can obtain current information on it from its website, **https://www.mysql.com**. The site includes detailed documentation, including manuals and FAQs. Currently, MySQL is owned by Oracle.

MariaDB

MariaDB is a fully open source derivative of MySQL, developed after MySQL was acquired by Oracle. It is designed to be fully compatible with MySQL databases. Like MySQL, MariaDB is structured on a client/server model with a server daemon filling requests from client programs. MariaDB is designed for speed, reliability, and ease of use. It is meant to be a fast database management system for large databases and, at the same time, a reliable one, suitable for intensive use. To create databases, you use the standard SQL language. Packages to install are **mariadb-client** and **mariadb-server**.

E-Mail Clients

You can send and receive email messages in a variety of ways, depending on the type of mail client you use. Although all email utilities perform the same basic tasks of receiving and sending messages, they tend to use different interfaces. Some mail clients are designed to operate on a specific desktop interface such as KDE and GNOME. Several older mail clients use a screen-based interface and can be started only from the command line. For Web-based Internet mail services, such as Gmail and Yahoo, you use a Web browser instead of a mail client to access mail accounts provided by those services. Table 5-10 lists several popular Linux mail clients. Mail is transported to and from destinations using mail transport agents like Sendmail, Exim, and Postfix. To send mail over the Internet, Simple Mail Transport Protocol (SMTP) is used.

Mail Client	Description
Kontact	Includes the K Desktop mail client, KMail; integrated mail, address book, and scheduler (KMail, KAddressbook, KOrganizer)
Evolution	Email client, **https://wiki.gnome.org/Apps/Evolution**
Thunderbird	Mozilla mail client and newsreader
Sylpheed	Gtk mail and news client
Claws-mail	Extended version of sylpheed Email client
Mutt	Screen-based mail client
bsd-mailx	Original Unix-based command line mail client
unity mail	GNOME email notification
gnubiff	Email checker and notification tool
newmail	email notification

Table 5-10: Linux Mail Clients

Thunderbird

Thunderbird is a full-featured stand-alone email client provided by the Mozilla project (**https://www.mozilla.org**). It is installed by default along with LibreOffice. Thunderbird is designed to be easy to use, highly customizable, and heavily secure. It features advanced intelligent spam filtering, as well as security features like encryption, digital signatures, and S/MIME. To protect against viruses, email attachments can be examined without being run. Thunderbird supports both Internet Message Access Protocol (IMAP) and the Post Office Protocol (POP). It also functions as a newsreader and features a built-in RSS reader. Thunderbird also supports the use of the Lightweight Directory Access Protocol (LDAP) for address books. Thunderbird is an extensible application, allowing customized modules to be added to enhance its abilities. You can download extensions such as dictionary search and contact sidebars from the website. GPG encryption can be supported with the **enigmail** extension (Ubuntu main repository).

Thunderbird is installed by default. You can access it from the dock. It provides better integration with popular online mail services like Gmail, saved searches, and customized tags for selected messages. You can access Thunderbird from the dock and the Applications overview.

The Thunderbird interface uses a standard three-pane format, with a side pane for listing mail accounts and their mailboxes (see Figure 5-14). The top pane is the message list pane and the bottom pane shows a selected message's text. Commands can be run using the toolbar, menus, or keyboard shortcuts. You can even change the appearance using different themes. Thunderbird also supports HTML mail, displaying Web components like URLs in mail messages.

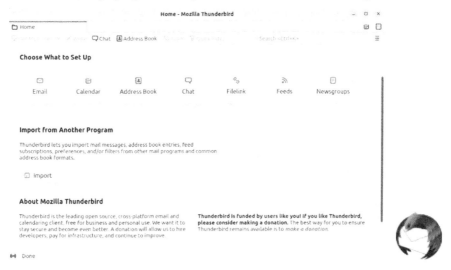

Figure 5-14: Thunderbird Email client

The message list pane shows several fields by which you can sort your messages. Some use just symbols like the Threads, Attachments, and Read icons. Clicking Threads will gather the messages into respective threads with replies grouped together. The last icon in the message list fields is a pop-up menu that lets you choose which fields to display. Thunderbird provides a variety of quick display filters, such as displaying only messages from people included in your address book and display messages with attached files. Search and sorting capabilities also include filters that can match selected patterns in any field, including subject, date, or the message body. To compose a message, click the Write button to open the Write window. The Security button lets you digitally sign and encrypt a message.

When you first start up Thunderbird, The Mail Account Setup dialog opens, which prompts you to create an email account. You can add more email accounts or modify current ones by selecting Account Settings from the Preferences menu (Preferences | Account Settings). The first page of the Mail Account Setup dialogs prompts you to enter your name, email address, and password. Thunderbird then attempts to detect and configure your email account automatically. Popular email services such as Gmail (Google) and Yahoo will be detected and their incoming and outgoing mail servers configured automatically. If the username entry is wrong you can click the Username Edit button to edit it. For more email configuration options, you can click the Manual Setup button. You can also just choose to abandon the email setup by clicking the Start Over link. If the settings are correct, click the Create Account button to create the account. The account will be accessed. If the account detection fails, you will be prompted to enter the username and password, along with the names of the incoming and outgoing mail servers for that account. For a more detailed configuration, click the Manual Setup button where you can specify the security protocol like SSL/TSL.

To edit an email account, select the Preferences | Account Settings menu entry. In the Account Settings window, you will see an entry for your mail account, with tabs for Server Settings, Copies & Folders, Composition & Addressing, Offline & Disk Space, Synchronization & Storage, Return Receipt, and Security. The Server Settings tab has entries for your server name, port, username, and connection and task configurations such as downloading new messages automatically. The Security tab opens the Certificate Manager, where you can select security certificates to use to digitally sign or encrypt messages.

Thunderbird provides an address book where you can enter complete contact information, including email addresses, street addresses, phone numbers, and notes. Select Address Book from the Tools submenu to open the Address Book window (Tools | Address Book). There are three panes: one for the address books available; another listing the address entries with field entries like name, email, and organization; and one for displaying address information. You can sort the entries by these fields. Clicking an entry will display the address information, including email address, street addresses, and phone. Only fields with values are displayed. To create a new entry in an address book, click New Contact to open a window with tabs for Contact, Private, Work, Other, Chat, and Photo. To create mailing lists from the address book entries, you click the New List button, specify the name of the list, and enter the email addresses.

Once you have set up your address book, you can use its addresses when creating mail messages. On the Write window, when you start to enter an email address in the To text box, the address will auto-complete to the corresponding address in your address book. Alternatively, you can open the address book and drag-and-drop addresses to an address box in the message window.

A user's email messages, addresses, and configuration information are kept in files located in the **.thunderbird** folder within the user's home folder. Backing up this information is as simple as making a copy of that folder. Messages for the different mailboxes are kept in a **Mail** subfolder. If you are migrating to a new system, you can copy the folder from the older system. To back up the mail for any mail account, just copy the **Mail** subfolder for that account. Though the default address books, **abook.mab** and **history.mab**, can be interchangeably copied, non-default address books need to be exported to an LDIF format and then imported to the new Thunderbird application. It is advisable to export your address books regularly to LDAP Data Interchange Format (LDIF) files as backups.

Evolution

Evolution is the primary mail client for the GNOME desktop. Though designed for GNOME, it will work equally well on KDE. Evolution is an integrated mail client, calendar, and address book. It supports numerous protocols (SMTP, POP, and IMAP). With Evolution, you can create multiple mail accounts on different servers, including those that use different protocols such as POP or IMAP. You can also decrypt Pretty Good Privacy (PGP) or GNU Privacy Guard (GPG) encrypted messages. Messages are indexed for easy searching. As an added feature, you can display Web calendars within evolution. See the Evolution website for resources and documentation links.

```
https://wiki.gnome.org/Apps/Evolution
```

The Evolution mailer provides a simple desktop interface, with a toolbar for commonly used commands and a sidebar for shortcuts. A set of buttons on the lower left allows you to access other operations, such as the calendar and contacts. The main screen is divided into two panes, one for listing the mail headers and the other for displaying the currently selected message (see Figure 5-15. You can click any header label to sort your headers by that category. Evolution also supports the use of virtual folders that can be created by the user to hold mail that meets specified criteria. Incoming mail can be automatically distributed to a virtual folder.

With evolution, you can also create search folders to organize access to your messages. A search folder is not an actual folder. It simply collects links to messages based on certain search criteria. Using search folders, you can quickly display messages on a topic, or subject, or from a specific user. In effect, it performs an automatic search on messages as they arrive. To set up a search folder, select Search Folders in the Edit menu (Edit | Search Folders) and click Add to open the Add Rule dialog. Here you can add criteria for searches and the folders to search. You can also right-click a message header that meets criteria you want searched and select Create Rule from Message, and then select one of the Search Rule entries.

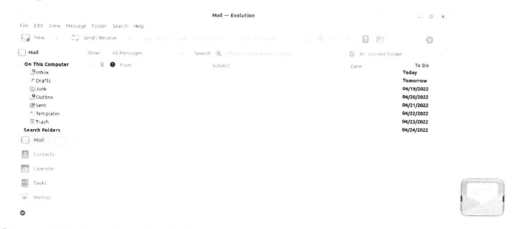

Figure 5-15: Evolution Email client

To configure Evolution, select Preferences from the Edit menu (Edit | Preferences). On the Evolution Preferences window, a sidebar shows icons for mail accounts, contacts, mail preferences, composition preference, calendar and tasks, and certificates. The Mail accounts tab displays a list of current accounts. An Add button lets you add new accounts, and the Edit button allows you to change current accounts. When editing an account, the Account Editor displays tabs for Identity, Receiving email (your incoming mail server), sending email (outgoing mail server), and security (encryption and digital signatures) among others. Mail Preferences lets you configure how Evolution displays and manages messages. The Mail Preferences Automatic Contacts tab is where you can specify whether the addresses of mail you have replied to should be added automatically to the Evolution Contacts list. Composer Preferences lets you set up composition features like signatures, formatting, and spell-checking. Calendar and Tasks lets you configure your calendar, specifying a type zone, work days, display options, and publishing.

Numerous plugins are available to extend Evolution's capabilities. Most are installed and enabled for you automatically, including the SpamAssassin plug-in for handling junk mail. To manage your plug-ins, select the Plugins entry in the Edit menu (Edit | Plugin) to open the Plugin Manager, with plug-ins listed in a left scroll window and configuration tabs located for a selected plug-in on the right side.

Evolution also supports filters. You can use filters to direct some messages automatically to certain folders, instead of having all incoming messages placed in the inbox folder. To create a filter, you can select the Message Filters entry in the Edit menu (Edit | Message Filters) and click Add to open the Add Rule window. You can also right-click the header of a message whose heading meets your criteria, like a subject or sender, and select Create Rule from Message and select a Filter entry for sender, subject, or recipient. On the Add Rule window, you can add other criteria and specify the action to take, like moving the message to a particular folder. You can also add other actions, like assigning a score, changing the color, copying the message, or deleting it.

A user's email messages, addresses, and configuration information are kept in files located in the **.evolution** folder within the user's home folder. Backing up this information is as simple as making a copy of that folder. Messages for the different mailboxes are kept in a **mail** subfolder. If you are migrating to a new system, you can just copy the folder from the older system. To back up the mail for any given mail account, just copy the **mail** subfolder for that account. You can also backup the address book, calendar, memos, and tasks subfolders.

Figure 5-16: Evolution Calendar

Evolution also supports contact operations like calendars, contact lists, and memos. On the left side pane, the bottom section displays buttons for these different functions: Mail, Contacts, Calendars, Tasks, and Memos. To see and manage your contacts, click the Contacts button on the left sidebar. The Calendar displays a browsable calendar on the left pane to move easily to a specific date (see Figure 5-16). The right pane shows a daily calendar page by the hour with sections for tasks and memos. You can set up several calendars, which you can access at the top of the right pane. A personal calendar is set up for you already. To add a new calendar, select Calendar from the New menu to open a New Calendar dialog where you can choose the type and name.

Note: Other GNOME mail clients include sylpheed and Claws-mail (both are on the Ubuntu Universe repository). Sylpheed is a mail and news client with an interface similar to Windows mail clients. Claws-mail is an extended version of Sylpheed with many additional features (**https://www.claws-mail.org/**).

The KDE Mail Client: KMail

The KDE mail client, KMail, provides a full-featured desktop interface for composing, sending, and receiving email messages. KMail is part of the KDE Personal Information Management suite (KDE-PIM) which also includes an address book (KAddressBook), an organizer and scheduler (KOrganizer), and a note writer (KNotes). All these components are also directly integrated on the desktop into Kontact. You can start up KMail directly or as part of the Kontact applications (Mail). KMail is installed as part of the KDE desktop, but you can also install it separately with the Synaptic Package Manager.

The KMail window displays three panes for folders, headers, and messages. The lower-left pane displays your mail folders: an inbox folder for received mail, an outbox folder for mail you have composed but have not sent yet, and a sent-mail folder for messages you have previously sent. You can create your own mail folders and save selected messages in them. You can designate certain folders as favorite folders and have them listed in the Favorite Folders pane (right-click on the Favorite Folders pane and select Add Favorite Folder to choose a folder).

Command Line Mail Clients

Several mail clients use a simple command line interface. They can be run without any other kind of support, such as the X Window System, desktops, or cursor support. They are simple and easy to use but include an extensive set of features and options. Two of the more widely used mail clients of this type are Mail and Mutt. Mail is the mailx mail client that was developed for UNIX. It is considered a default mail client that can be found on all UNIX and Linux systems. Mutt is a cursor-based client that can be run from the command line.

Mutt

Mutt has an easy-to-use cursor-based interface with an extensive set of features. You can find more information about Mutt from the Mutt website, **http://www.mutt.org**. The Mutt manual is located in the **/usr/doc** folder under Mutt. To use Mutt, enter the **mutt** command in a terminal window or on the command line.

Mail

What is known now as the Mail utility was originally created for BSD Unix and called, simply, mail. Later versions of Unix System V adopted the BSD mail utility and renamed it mailx. Now, it is simply referred to as Mail. Mail functions as a default mail client on most Unix and

Linux systems. It is not installed by default on Ubuntu. Install the **bsd-mailx** package with the Synaptic Package Manager or the **apt** command.

To send a message with Mail, type `mail` on the command line along with the address of the person to whom you are sending the message. Press ENTER and you are prompted for a subject. Enter the subject of the message and press ENTER again. At this point, you are placed in input mode. Anything you type is considered the contents of the message. Pressing ENTER adds a new line to the text. When you finish typing your message, press CTRL-D on a line of its own to end the message. You will then be prompted to enter a user to whom to send a carbon copy of the message (cc). If you do not want to send a carbon copy, just press ENTER. You will then see EOT (end-of-transmission) displayed after you press CTRL-D

You can send a message to several users at the same time by listing those users' addresses as arguments on the command line following the `mail` command. In the next example, the user sends the same message to both **chris** and **aleina**.

```
$ mail chris aleina
```

To receive mail, you first enter the `mail` command and press ENTER. This invokes a Mail shell with its own prompt and mail commands. A list of message headers is displayed. Header information is arranged into fields beginning with the status of the message and the message number. The status of a message is indicated by a single uppercase letter, usually N for new or U for unread. A message number, used for easy reference to your messages, follows the status field. The next field is the address of the sender, followed by the date and time the message was received, and then the number of lines and characters in the message. The last field contains the subject the sender gave for the message. After the headers, the Mail shell displays its prompt, an ampersand (&). At the Mail prompt, you enter commands that operate on the messages. An example of a Mail header and prompt follows:

```
$ mail
Mail version 8.2 01/15/2001. Type ? for help.
"/var/spool/mail/larisa": 3 messages 1 new 2 unread
 1 chris@turtle.mytrek. Thu Jun 7 14:17 22/554 "trip"
>U 2 aleina@turtle.mytrek Thu Jun 7 14:18 22/525 "party"
 U 3 dylan@turtle.mytrek. Thu Jun 7 14:18 22/528 "newsletter"
& q
```

Mail references messages either through a message list or through the current message marker (>). The greater-than sign (>) is placed before a message considered the current message. The current message is referenced by default when no message number is included with a Mail command. You can also reference messages using a message list consisting of several message numbers.

You use the **R** and **r** commands to reply to a message you have received. The **R** command entered with a message number generates a header for sending a message and then places you into input mode to type the message. The **q** command quits Mail. When you quit, messages you have already read are placed in a file called **mbox** in your home folder. Instead of saving messages in the **mbox** file, you can use the **s** command to save a message explicitly to a file of your choice. Mail has its own initialization file, called **.mailrc**, which is executed each time Mail is invoked, either for sending or receiving messages. Within it, you can define Mail options and create Mail aliases.

Notifications of Received Mail

As your mail messages are received, they are automatically placed in your mailbox file, but you are not automatically notified when you receive a message. You can use a mail client to retrieve any new messages, or you can use a mail monitor tool to tell you when new mail has arrived in your inbox. Several mail notification tools are also available, such as **gnubiff**, **unity-mail**, **gnome-shell-mailnag**, **evolution-plugins**, and **birdtray** (Thunderbird notifications). The **gnubiff** tool will notify you of any POP3 or IMAP mail arrivals.

For command line interfaces, you can use the biff utility, which notifies you immediately when a message is received. biff automatically displays the header and beginning lines of messages as they are received. To turn on biff, you enter `biff y` on the command line. To turn it off, you enter `biff n`. To find out if biff is turned on, enter `biff` alone.

Accessing Mail on Remote Mail Servers

Most new mail clients are equipped to access mail accounts on remote servers. Mail clients, such as Evolution, KMail, Sylpheed, and Thunderbird, enable you to set up a mailbox for such an account and access a mail server to check for and download received mail. You must specify what protocol a mail server uses. This is usually either the Post Office Protocol (POP) or the IMAP protocol (IMAP). Using a mail server address, you can access your account with your username and password.

For email clients such as **mail** and **mutt** that do not provide mail server access, you can use Fetchmail to have mail from those accounts sent directly to the inbox maintained by your Linux system for your Linux account. All your mail, whether from other users on your Linux system or from remote mail accounts, will appear in your local inbox. Fetchmail checks for mail on remote mail servers and downloads it to your local inbox, where it appears as newly received mail. Enter **fetchmail** on the command line with the mail server address and any needed options. The mail protocol is indicated with the **-p** option and the mail server type, usually POP3. If your email username is different from your Linux login name, you use the **-u** option and the email name. Once you execute the **fetchmail** command, you are prompted for a password. The syntax for the **fetchmail** command for a POP3 mail server follows:

```
fetchmail -p POP3 -u username mail-server
```

You will see messages telling you if mail is there and, if so, how many messages are being downloaded. You can then use a mail client to read the messages from your inbox. You can run Fetchmail in daemon mode to have it check automatically for mail. You have to include an option specifying the interval in seconds for checking mail.

```
fetchmail -d 1200
```

To have fetchmail run automatically you can set the START DAEMON option to yes in the **/etc/default/fetchmail** file. Edit the file with the **sudo gedit** command.

You can specify options such as the server type, username, and password in a **.fetchmailrc** file in your home folder. You can also include entries for other mail servers and accounts you may have. Once Fetchmail is configured, you can enter **fetchmail** with no arguments; it will read entries from your **.fetchmailrc** file. You can also make entries directly in the **.fetchmailrc** file. An entry in the **.fetchmailrc** file for a particular mail account consists of several fields and their values: poll, protocol, username, and password. The poll field refers to the mail server name. You can also specify your password, instead of having to enter it each time Fetchmail accesses the mail server.

Mailing Lists

Users on mailing lists automatically receive messages and articles sent to the lists. Mailing lists work much like a mail alias, broadcasting messages to all users on the list. Mailing lists were designed to serve specialized groups of people. Numerous mailing lists, as well as other subjects, are available for Linux. By convention, to subscribe to a list, you send a request to the mailing list address with a **-request** term added to its username. For example, to subscribe to **gnome-list@gnome.org**, you send a request to **gnome-list-request@gnome.org**.

You can use the Mailman application to manage your mailing lists automatically. Mailman is the GNU mailing list manager, included with Ubuntu (**http://www.list.org**).

MIME: /etc/mime.types

MIME (Multipurpose Internet Mail Extensions) is used to enable mail clients to send and receive multimedia files and files using different character sets such as those for different languages. Multimedia files can be images, sound clips, or even video. Mail clients that support MIME can send binary files automatically as attachments to messages. MIME-capable mail clients maintain a file called **mailcap** that maps different types of MIME messages to applications on your system that can view or display them. For example, an image file will be mapped to an application that can display images. Your mail clients can then run that program to display the image message. A sound file will be mapped to an application that can play sound files. Most mail clients have MIME capabilities built in and use their own version of the **mailcap** file. Others use a program called metamail that adds MIME support. MIME is used not only in mail clients. Both the KDE and GNOME file managers use MIME to map a file to a particular application so that you can launch the application directly from the file.

Applications are associated with binary files by means of the **mailcap** and **mime.types** files. The **mime.types** file defines different MIME types, associating a MIME type with a certain application. The **mailcap** file then associates each MIME type with a specified application. Your system maintains its own MIME types file, usually **/etc/mime.types**.

Entries in the MIME types file associate a MIME type and possible subtype of an application with a set of possible file extensions used for files that run on a given kind of application. The MIME type is usually further qualified by a subtype, separated from the major type by a slash. For example, a MIME type image can have several subtypes such as jpeg, gif, or tiff. A sample MIME type entry defining a MIME type for JPEG files are shown here. The MIME type is image/jpeg, and the list of possible file extensions is "jpeg jpg jpe":

```
image/jpeg        jpeg jpg jpe
```

The applications specified will depend on those available on your particular system. The application is specified as part of the application type. In many cases, X Window System–based programs are specified. Comments are indicated with a **#**. The following entries associate **odt** files with the LibreOffice writer and **qtl** files with the QuickTime player.

```
application/vnd.oasis.opendocument.text    odt
application/x-quicktimeplayer              qtl
```

Though you can create your own MIME types, a standard set already is in use. The types text, image, audio, video, application, multipart, and message, along with their subtypes, have already been defined for your system. You will find that commonly used file extensions such as **.tif** and **.jpg** for TIFF and JPEG image files are already associated with a MIME type and an application. Though you can easily change the associated application, it is best to keep the MIME types already installed. The current official MIME types are listed at the IANA website (**https://www.iana.org/assignments/media-types/media-types.xhtml**) under the name Media Types, provided as part of their Assignment Services.

S/MIME and OpenPGP/MIME are authentication protocols for signing and encrypting mail messages. S/MIME was originally developed by the RSA Data Security. OpenPGP is an open standard based on the PGP/MIME protocol developed by the PGP (Pretty Good Privacy) group. Clients like Evolution can use OpenPGP/MIME to authenticate messages.

Usenet News

Usenet is an open mail system on which users post messages that include news, discussions, and opinions. It operates like a mailbox to which any user on your Linux system can read or send messages. Users' messages are incorporated into Usenet files, which are distributed to any system signed up to receive them. Certain Usenet sites perform organizational and distribution operations for Usenet, receiving messages from other sites and organizing them into Usenet files, which are then broadcast to many other sites. Such sites are called backbone sites, and they operate like publishers, receiving articles and organizing them into different groups.

To access Usenet news, you need access to a news server, which receives the daily Usenet newsfeeds and makes them accessible to other systems. Your network may have a system that operates as a news server. There are also many commercial servers you can access for a fee. To read Usenet articles, you use a newsreader, a client program that connects to a news server and accesses the articles. On the Internet and in TCP/IP networks, news servers communicate with newsreaders using the Network News Transfer Protocol (NNTP) and are often referred to as NNTP news servers. You can also create your own news server on your Linux system to run a local Usenet news service or to download and maintain the full set of Usenet articles. News transport agent applications can be set up to create such a server.

Usenet files were originally designed to function like journals. Messages contained in the files are referred to as articles. A user could write an article, post it in Usenet, and have it immediately distributed to other systems. Usenet files themselves were organized as journal publications. Because journals are designed to address specific groups, Usenet files are organized according to groups called newsgroups. When a user posts an article, it is assigned to a specific newsgroup. You can also create articles of your own, which you can then add to a newsgroup for others to read. Linux has newsgroups on various topics. Some are for discussion, and others are sources of information about recent developments. On some, you can ask for help for specific problems. A selection of some of the popular Linux newsgroups is provided here:

Newsgroup	Topic
comp.os.linux.announce	Announcements of Linux developments
comp.os.linux.admin	System administration questions

comp.os.linux.misc	Special questions and issues
comp.os.linux.setup	Installation problems
comp.os.linux.help	Questions and answers for particular problems
linux.help	Obtain help for Linux problems

Newsreaders

You read Usenet articles with a newsreader, such as Pan and tin, which enable you to select a specific newsgroup and then read the articles in it. A newsreader operates like a user interface, letting you browse through and select available articles for reading, saving, or printing. Most newsreaders employ a retrieval feature called threads that pulls together articles on the same discussion or topic. Several popular newsreaders are listed in Table 5-11.

Most newsreaders can read Usenet news provided on remote news servers that use the NNTP protocol. Desktop newsreaders, such as Pan, have you specify the Internet address for the remote news server in their own configuration settings. Shell-based newsreaders such as **tin**, obtain the news server's Internet address from the NNTPSERVER shell variable, configured in the **.profile** file.

```
NNTPSERVER=news.domain.com
export NNTPSERVER
```

Newsreader	Description
Pan	GNOME Desktop newsreader
Thunderbird	Mail client with newsreader capabilities (X based)
Sylpheed	GNOME Windows-like newsreader
Slrn	Newsreader (cursor based)
Emacs	Emacs editor, mail client, and newsreader (cursor based)
tin	Newsreader (command line interface)
trn4	Newsreader (command line interface)
SABnzbd+	Binary only NZB based news grabber

Table 5-11: Linux Newsreaders

Binary Newsreaders and Grabbers

A binary newsreader can convert text messages to binary equivalents, like those found in **alt.binaries** newsgroups. There are some news grabbers, applications designed only to download binaries. The binaries are normally encoded with RAR compression, which have an **.rar** extension. To decode them you first have to install the **unrar-free** (free version) or **unrar** packages (proprietary version). The **ubuntu-restricted-extras** package will install the **unrar** proprietary version for you. Binaries normally consist of several **rar** archive files, some of which may be incomplete. To repair them you can use Par2 recovery program. Install the **par2** or **parchive** package. A binary should have its own set of par2 files also listed on the news server that you can download and use to repair any incomplete **rar** files. The principle works much the same as RAID arrays using parity information to reconstruct damaged data.

The SABnzbd+ nzb grabber application works using NZB files to locate and download binaries. You first have to obtain the NZB file to use. But if you can obtain an NZB file, then NZB is by far the easiest to use. It works through you Web browser. Simply add an NZB file. Configuration is detailed letting you specify folders, server, notifications, and download scheduling.

slrn

The **slrn** newsreader is cursor-based. Commands are displayed across the top of the screen and can be executed using the listed keys. Different types of screens exist for the newsgroup list, article list, and article content, each with its own set of commands. An initial screen lists your subscribed newsgroups with commands for posting, listing, and subscribing to your newsgroups. When you start slrn for the first time, you may have to create a **.jnewsrc** file in your home folder. Use the following command: **slrn -f .jnewsrc -create**. Also, you will have to set the **NNTPSERVER** variable in your **.profile** file and make sure it is exported.

The slrn newsreader features a utility called **slrnpull** that you can use to download articles in specified newsgroups automatically. This allows you to view your selected newsgroups offline. The slrnpull utility was designed as a simple single-user version of Leafnode; it will access a news server and download its designated newsgroups, making them available through slrn whenever the user chooses to examine them. Newsgroup articles are downloaded to the **SLRNPULL_ROOT** folder. On Ubuntu, this is **/var/spool/slrnpull**. The selected newsgroups to be downloaded are entered in the **slrnpull.conf** configuration file placed in the **SLRNPULL_ROOT** folder. In this file, you can specify how many articles to download for each group and when they should expire. To use **slrn** with **slrnpull**, you will have to configure the **.slrnrc** file to reference the **slrnpull** folders where newsgroup files are kept.

News Transport Agents

Usenet news is provided over the Internet as a daily newsfeed of articles and postings for thousands of newsgroups. This newsfeed is sent to sites that can then provide access to the news for other systems through newsreaders. These sites operate as news servers. The newsreaders used to access them are their clients. The news server software called news transport agents, provide newsreaders with news, enabling you to read newsgroups and post articles. For Linux, several popular news transport agents are INN, Leafnode, Papercut, and sn. Both Papercut and Leafnode are small and simple, and useful for small networks. INN is more powerful and complex, designed with large systems in mind (see **https://www.isc.org/** for more details).

Daily news feeds on Usenet are often large and consume much of a news server's resources in both time and memory. For this reason, you may not want to set up your own Linux system to receive such newsfeeds. If you are operating in a network of Linux systems, you can designate one of them as the news server and install the news transport agent on it to receive and manage the Usenet newsfeeds. Users on other systems on your network can then access that news server with their own newsreaders. If your network already has a news server, you need not install a news transport agent at all. You only have to use your newsreaders to access that server remotely.

You can also use news transport agents to run local versions of news for only the users on your system or your local network. To do this, install INN, Leafnode, or Papercut configure them just to manage local newsgroups. Users on your system could then post articles and read local news.

6. Graphics and Multimedia

Graphics Applications

Multimedia

Music Applications

Video Applications

Sound Configuration with PulseAudio

Ubuntu includes a wide range of graphics and multimedia applications, including simple image viewers such as the Eye of GNOME, sophisticated image manipulation programs like GIMP, music, music players such as Rhythmbox, and video players like Videos. Several helpful Linux multimedia sites are listed in Table 6-1. There is strong support for graphics and multimedia tasks from image management, video and DVD, to sound and music editing (see Tables 6-1, 6-4 and 6-5). Most are available on Ubuntu's multiverse and universe repositories. In addition, the Ubuntu Studio project has collected popular multimedia development software into several collections for audio, video, and graphics.

Projects and Sites	Description
Advanced Linux Sound Architecture (ALSA)	The Advanced Linux Sound Architecture (ALSA) project for current sound drivers: **www.alsaproject.org**
Open Sound System	Open Sound System, drives for older devices: **www.opensound.com**
PulseAudio	PulseAudio sound interface, now the default for Ubuntu. **https://www.freedesktop.org/wiki/Software/PulseAudio/**
Phoronix	Site for the latest news and reviews of Linux hardware compatibility, including graphics cards. **https://www.phoronix.com**
Ubuntu Studio	Ubuntu Studio multimedia development applications and desktop, audio, video, and graphics collection installed from ubuntustudio meta packages, Meta Packages (universe) **https://ubuntustudio.org**

Table 6-1: Linux and Ubuntu Multimedia Sites

Support for many popular multimedia operations, specifically MP3, DVD, and DivX, are not included on the Ubuntu Desktop USB/DVD because of licensing and other restrictions. To play MP3, DVD, or DivX files, you will have to download and install support packages manually. For Ubuntu, precompiled packages for many popular media applications and libraries, such as VideoLan, Celluloid, and XviD, as well as MP3 and DVD video support, are available on the Ubuntu multiverse and universe repositories.

Graphics Applications

The GNOME and KDE desktops support an impressive number of graphics applications, including image viewers, screen grabbers, photo managers, image editors, and paint tools. Table 6-2 lists some popular graphics tools for Linux.

Tools	Description
Shotwell	GNOME digital camera application and image and video library manager (**https://wiki.gnome.org/Apps/Shotwell**)
Photos	GNOME photo viewer and organizer
Cheese	GNOME Webcam application for taking pictures and videos
ubuntustudio-graphics	Ubuntu Studio meta package (Meta Packages (universe)), includes a collection of graphics applications. Use Synaptic Package Manager.
Digikam	Digital photo management tool, works with both GNOME and KDE (**https://www.digikam.org/**)
KDE	
Gwenview	Image browser and viewer (default for KDE)
ShowFoto	Simple image viewer, works with digiKam
Spectacle	Screen grabber
KolourPaint	Paint program
Krita	Image editor (**https://krita.org/en/**)
GNOME	
Eye of Gnome	GNOME Image Viewer (eog package)
GIMP	GNU Image Manipulation Program (**https://www.gimp.org/**)
Inkscape	GNOME Vector graphics application (**https://inkscape.org/en/**)
gpaint	GNOME paint program
Blender	3d modeling, rendering, and animation
LibreOffice Draw	LibreOffice Draw program
X Window System	
Xpaint	Paint program
Xfig	Drawing program
ImageMagick	Image format conversion and editing tool

Table 6-2: Graphics Tools for Linux

Photo Management: Shotwell, Photos, and Cheese

Shotwell provides an easy and powerful way to manage, display, and import, and publish your photos and images (**https://wiki.gnome.org/Apps/Shotwell**). It is the default photo manager for Ubuntu 22.04 LTS. See the Shotwell user manual for full details (Help | Contents menu and at **http://yorba.org/shotwell/help/**). Shotwell is accessible as the Shotwell Photo Manager from the Applications overview. Shotwell also supports video files.

You can import folders from cameras or folders (see Figure 6-1). Your Pictures folder is the default library folder, whose photos are imported automatically. Adding an image file to the

Pictures folder also imports it to Shotwell. Photo thumbnails are displayed in the main right pane. The View menu lets you control the thumbnail display, allowing you to sort photos, zoom, show photo filenames (Titles), or select by rating or event. You can adjust the size of the displayed thumbnails using a slider bar in the toolbar located at the bottom right of the Shotwell window. The small figure button to the left of the slider reduces thumbnails to their smallest size, and the large figure button to the right of the slider expands them to the largest size.

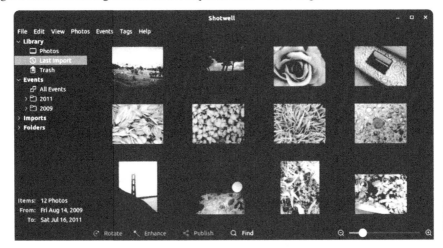

Figure 6-1: Shotwell Photo Management

To see a full-screen slide show of the photos, choose the Slideshow entry in the View menu. The slide show starts automatically. During the slideshow, moving your mouse to the center bottom of the screen displays slideshow controls for pausing and stepping through photos. The Settings button opens a dialog where you can set the display time. To end the slide show and return to the desktop, click the full-screen button. The slideshow buttons are shown here.

Photos are organized automatically by the time they were taken. Dates are listed under the Events entry in the left sidebar, arranged by year, month, and date. To name a photo, right-click on it and choose Edit Title to open a dialog where you can enter the name. You can also tag photos placing them in groups, making them easier to access. To tag a photo, right-click it and choose Add Tags to open a dialog where you can enter a tag name. The tag will show up as a label for the photo. You can access photos by tags using the Tags entries in the left sidebar. For each photo, you can also set a rating indicated by five stars or less.

To search for photos, click the Find button to open a search bar, which displays a text box for entering the search pattern. Buttons to the left let you refine the search by image type, photos or videos, flagged files, and ratings.

You can perform complex edits either within the Shotwell window or in full screen. To edit a photo within the Shotwell window, double-click its image to display the edit toolbar, which hold Rotate, Crop, Straighten, Red-eye, Adjust, and Enhance buttons. For full-screen edits, select the photo and then choose View | Fullscreen (F11) to open the photo in the Shotwell photo editor (see Figure 6-2). Move your mouse to the bottom of the screen to display edit toolbar (Rotate,

Crop, Straighten, Red-eye, Adjust, and Enhance buttons). You can also zoom in or out from the photo using the slider bar. The Crop button opens an adjustable border, with a menu for choosing the display proportions you may want such as HD video or postcard. The Adjust button opens a dialog for refined changes such as exposure, saturation, tint, temperature, shadows, and highlights. Edits are stored in a Shotwell database; they are not made to the original photo. To revert to the original photo, right-click and choose "Revert to Original" or choose that entry from the Photos menu.

Figure 6-2: Shotwell Photo Editing

Note: You can also set Shotwell display features using the dconf editor's Shotwell keys located at org | yorba | shotwell.

DigiKam (**https://www.digiKam.org**) is a KDE photo manager with many of the same features as Shotwell. DigiKam is accessible from the Applications overview. A side panel allows easy access by album, date, tags, or previous searches (see Figure 6-3). The program also provides image-editing capabilities, with numerous effects. The digiKam configuration (Settings menu) provides extensive options, including image editing, digital camera support, and interface configuration.

Figure 6-3: digiKam Photo Manager

Tip: The Windows version of Photoshop is supported by Wine. You can install Photoshop CS on Ubuntu using Wine. Once started, Photoshop will operate like any Linux desktop application.

Cheese is a Webcam picture-taking and video-recording tool (**https://wiki.gnome.org/Apps/Cheese**). You can snap pictures from your Webcam and apply simple effects. Click the Photo button to manage photos and the Video button to record video (located to the left). Icons of photos and video will appear on the bottom panel, which you can select for effects or removal. The effects tab will show effects that can be turned on or off for the current image. To save a photo, right click on its icon on the lower panel and select Save As from the pop-up menu.

GNOME Photos is a simple image viewer and organizer for the images in your Pictures folder. GNOME Photos has three tabs: Photos, Albums, and Favorites (see Figure 6-4). It opens to the Photos tab. You can also click on the search button at the right side of the menu bar to open a search box at the top of the window to search for photos. A pop-up menu to the right of the search box lets you limit searches by favorites, albums, title, or author.

Click on a photo to open it, and then use arrow buttons to display the next or previous ones (see Figure 6-5). A task menu at the top right lets you open the photo with Shotwell, print it, set it as the background of your desktop, or display it on another device. The Properties dialog displays detailed information about the image and lets you give it a name. Click the back arrow on the menu bar to return to the main dialog. To choose several photos to work on, click on the checkmark button at the top right. Check boxes appear on the lower right corner of each image (see Figure 6-6). A menu at the top center lets you choose all or deselect all images. If you check a single image, a toolbar appears at the bottom, which lets you print the image, check its properties, add it to an album, delete it, or tag it as a Favorite. If you check several photos, the toolbar only lets you add them to an album, delete them, or mark them as favorites.

Figure 6-4: GNOME Photos

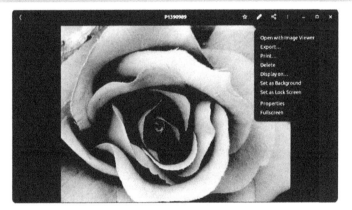

Figure 6-5: GNOME Photos: image display

When you open a photo, you can also tag it as a favorite by clicking on the star button in the lower right corner. Favorite images show a star emblem in the lower right corner of the image. Click on the Favorites tab to show only the favorite images. To remove an image from favorites, click its star to open the photo and then click the Favorites button in the photo's menu bar. Photos can be organized into albums, which are displayed on the Albums tab. When you add a photo to an album, you are prompted to choose an existing album, or create a new one.

Figure 6-6: GNOME Photos selection

GNOME Graphics Applications

GNOME features several powerful and easy-to-use graphics applications. The Eye of GNOME is the GNOME image viewer. It is installed by default and is accessible as "Image Viewer" on the Applications overview's Utilities application folder. The image viewer provides basic image display operations such as enlargement, full-screen display, rotation, and slide shows (see Figure 6-7). The image Gallery (icon list of images at the bottom of the screen), the Statusbar (bottom bar with size and position of selected photo), and Side Pane (properties of a selected image) are configured for display from entries in the Show submenu. Most preferences can be set using the preferences dialog (Preferences entry in the menu). User interface preferences, such as trash confirmations and the gallery position, can be set using the dconf editor's eog keys at org | gnome | eog | ui.

Figure 6-7: Image Viewer (Eye of Gnome)

The gThumb application is an image viewer and browser that lets you browse images using thumbnailsand organize them into catalogs for easy reference.

Figure 6-8: GIMP

GIMP is the GNU Image Manipulation Program, a sophisticated image application much like Adobe Photoshop (see Figure 6-8). You can use GIMP for such tasks as photo retouching, image composition, and image authoring. It supports features such as layers, channels, blends, and gradients. GIMP makes effective use of the GTK+ widget set. GIMP is accessible as the GIMP Image Editor. You can find out more about GIMP from its website at **https://www.gimp.org**. GIMP is freely distributed under the GNU Public License. You can install GIMP from Ubuntu Software.

Inkscape is a vector graphics application for SVG (Scalable Vector Graphics) images (see Figure 6-9). Inkscape is accessible as Inkscape Image Editor on the Applications overview. It features abilities similar to professional level vector graphics. The SVG format allows easy generation of images for Web use as well as complex art. Though its native format is SVG, it can also export to the Portable Network Graphics (PNG) format. It features layers and easy object creation, including stars and spirals. A color bar lets you quickly change color fills. You can install Inkscape from Ubuntu Software.

Figure 6-9: Inkscape

KDE Graphics Applications

The KDE desktop features the same variety of graphics applications found on the GNOME desktop. Many are available from the Ubuntu main repository. Most do not require a full installation of the KDE desktop. The Spectacle program is a simple screen grabber for KDE. Gwenview is an easy-to-use image browser and viewer supporting slide shows and numerous image formats. It is the default viewer for KDE, but can also be used on GNOME (see Figure 6-10). Gwenview can share photos with social networking sites directly. KolourPaint is a basic paint program with brushes, shapes, and color effects. Krita is the Calligra professional image paint and editing application, with a wide range of features such as the ability to create web images and modify photographs. You can install them on the Ubuntu desktop with Ubuntu Software or the Synaptic Package Manager.

Figure 6-10: Gwenview

X Window System Graphic Programs

X Window System–based applications run directly on the underlying X Window System. These applications tend to be simpler, lacking the desktop functionality found in GNOME or KDE applications. Most are available on the Ubuntu Universe repository. Xpaint is a simple paint program that allows you to load graphics or photographs and then create shapes, add text and colors, and use brush tools with various sizes and colors. Xfig is a drawing program. ImageMagick lets you convert images from one format to another. You can install them with Ubuntu Software or the Synaptic Package Manager.

Multimedia

Many applications are available for both video and sound, including sound editors, MP3 players, and video players (see Tables 6-5 and 6-6). Linux sound applications include mixers, digital audio tools, CD audio players, MP3 players, and network audio support. To use restricted formats such as commercial DVD video and Blu-Ray see the following site.

```
https://help.ubuntu.com/community/RestrictedFormats
```

Note: For games, Ubuntu 22.04 installs by default the **gamemode** daemon, which temporarily optimizes a games uses of system resources such as the CPU.

Multimedia support

A listing of popular multimedia codecs available is shown in Table 6-3. Of particular interest may be the liba52, faad2, and lame codecs for sound decoding, as well as the xvidcore, x264, libdvdcss, vaapi, and libdvbpsi for video decoding.

Figure 6-11: Ubuntu codec wizard selection

Ubuntu provides a codec wizard that automatically detects whenever you need to install a new multimedia codec. If you try to run a media file for which you do not have the proper codec, the codec wizard will appear, listing the codecs you need to download and install. Often there are several choices (see Figure 6-11). The codec wizard will select and install these packages for you, simplifying the process of installing the various multimedia codecs available for Linux.

To install support for most of the commonly used codecs, you can install the Ubuntu restricted packages, **ubuntu-restricted-addons** and **ubuntu-restricted-extras**, which are available from the Synaptic Package Manager (Meta Packages (multiverse) section, ubuntu-restricted-extras and ubuntu-restricted-addons). These packages are meta packages that will download a collection of other packages that provide support for DVD, MP3, MPEG4, DivX, and AC3, as well as Flash (non-free). The **ubuntu-restricted-addons** package will install the GStreamer ugly package, ffmpeg Chromium codecs and ffmpeg gstreamer plugin, as well as the Gstreamer Video

Acceleration API packages (**gstreamer1.0-vaapi**). The **ubuntu-restricted-extras** package will install the Microsoft font collection (**ttf-mscorefonts**), RAR archive extraction (**unrar**), and additional ffmpeg audio codecs (**libavcodec-extra**) .

```
ubuntu-restricted-addons
ubuntu-restricted-extras
```

Package	Description
liba52	HDTV audio (ATSC A/52, AC3)
faad	MPEG2/ 4 AAC audio decoding, high quality (faad2)
faac	MPEG2/ 4 AAC sound encoding and decoding
ffmpeg	Play, record, convert, stream audio and video. Includes digital streaming server, conversion tool, and media player.
libavcodec-extra	FFmpeg libraries, includes encoders and additional formats
gstreamer1.0-libav	ffmpeg plug-in for GStreamer
gstreamer-plugins-bad	Not fully reliable codecs and tools for GStreamer, some with possible licensing issues
gstreamer-plugins-ugly	Reliable video and audio codecs for GStreamer that may have licensing issues
gstreamer1.0-vaapi	The Gstreamer Video Acceleration API packages.
lame	MP3 playback capability
libdvbpsi	MPEG TS stream (DVB and PSI) decoding and encoding capability, VideoLAN project
libdvdcss (libdvd-pkg)	DVD commercial decryption, install and configure the **libdvd-pkg** package.
libmad0	MPEG1 audio decoding
libmpeg2	MPEG video audio decoding (MPEG1/2 audio and video, AC3, IFO, and VOB)
libquicktime2	QuickTime playback
mpeg2dec	MPEG2 and MPEG1 playback
x264	H264/AVC encoding (high definition media)
libxvidcore4	OpenDivx codec (DivX and Xvid playback)
libsmpeg	Smpeg MPEG 1 video and audio decoder
libxine2-all-plugins	Added video/ audio playback plugins for Xine

Table 6-3: Multimedia third-party codecs

For the Kubuntu desktop, you would also install the KDE version (install with the Synaptic Package Manager or the Discover Package Manager).

```
kubuntu-restricted-addons
kubuntu-restricted-extras
```

GStreamer

Many GNOME-based applications make use of GStreamer, a streaming media framework based on graphs and filters (**https://gstreamer.freedesktop.org/**). Using a plug-in structure, GStreamer applications can accommodate a wide variety of media types. For example, the Videos (Totem) video player uses GStreamer to play DVDs, VCDs, and MPEG media, Rhythmbox and Clementine provide integrated music management, and Sound Juicer is an audio CD player.

GStreamer Plug-ins: the Good, the Bad, and the Ugly

Many GNOME multimedia applications like Videos use GStreamer to provide multimedia support. To use such features as DVD-Video and MP3, you have to install GStreamer extra plugins. You can find more information about GStreamer and its supporting packages at **https://gstreamer.freedesktop.org/**.

GStreamer has four different support packages called the base, the good, the bad, and the ugly. The base package is a set of useful and reliable plug-ins. These are in the Ubuntu main repository. The good package is a set of supported and tested plug-ins that meets all licensing requirements. This is also part of the Ubuntu main repository. The bad package is a set of unsupported plug-ins whose performance is not guaranteed and may crash, but still meet licensing requirements. The ugly package contains plug-ins that work fine, but may not meet licensing requirements, like DVD support. The codec wizard will automatically detect the codec you will need to use for your GStreamer application.

The base   Reliable commonly used plug-ins

The good   Reliable additional and useful plug-ins

The ugly   Reliable but not fully licensed plug-ins (DVD/MP3 support)

The bad   Possibly unreliable but useful plug-ins (possible crashes)

Another plug-in for GStreamer that you may want include is **ffmpeg** for Matroska (mkv) and OGG support (**gstreamer1.0-libav** package). The Gstreamer Video Acceleration API packages (**gstreamer1.0-vaapi**) provides hardware video acceleration for gstreamer applications, **https://01.org/linuxmedia/vaapi**.

GStreamer MP3 Compatibility: iPod

Ubuntu provides support for your iPod and iPod Touch from your desktop directly. For your iPod and other MP3 devices to work with GNOME applications like Rhythmbox, you are prompted to install MP3 support for GStreamer the first time you use them (**gstreamer-plugins-ugly** package). MP3 support is not installed initially because of licensing issues.

The **libgpod** library allows player applications like Rhythmbox and Clementine to play songs from your iPod. To synchronize, import, or extract data from your iPod, you can use iPod management software such as **gtkpod** (Universe). For the iPhone, you can use **ifuse**.

Music Applications

Many music applications are currently available for GNOME, including sound editors, MP3 players, and audio players (see Table 6-4). You can use Rhythmbox, GNOME Music, and

Sound Juicer to play music from different sources, and the GNOME Sound Recorder to record sound sources. Several applications are also available for KDE, including the media players Clementine and Juk, and a mixer (KMix).

GNOME includes music applications like the Sound Juicer (Audio CD Extractor), GNOME Music, and Rhythmbox. Rhythmbox is the default sound multimedia player, supporting music files, radio streams, video, and podcasts (see Figure 6-12). When you open Rhythmbox, the indicator sound menu on the top panel displays options for Rhythmbox to play or stop playing, and to move to the next or previous audio source, such as a song or radio station.

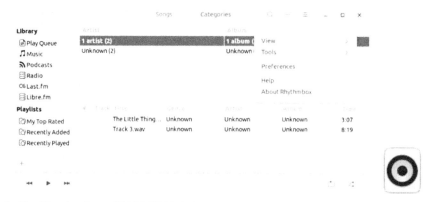

Figure 6-12: Rhythmbox GNOME Multimedia Player

Application	Description
Rhythmbox	Music management (GStreamer), default Music player with iPod support
Clementine	Multimedia audio player based on Amarok (KDE)
Elisa	KDE music player
Sound Juicer	GNOME CD audio ripper (GStreamer)
GNOME Music	GNOME Music player
Audacious	Multimedia player
JuK (Kmix)	KDE5 Music player (jukebox) for managing music collections
Goobox	CD player and ripper
Sound Recorder	GNOME Sound recorder
XMMS2	CD player
ubuntustudio-audio	Ubuntu Studio meta package (Meta Packages (universe)), includes a collection of audio applications. Use Synaptic Package Manager
QMidiRoute	MIDI event router and filter (universe)

Table 6-4: Music players, editors, and rippers

KDE music applications include Elisa, Clementine and Juk. Elisa is a basic music player for KDE with browsing and playlist support (see Figure 6-13). The Clementine music player is based on Amarok and will play on the GNOME desktop. It includes access to Internet sources, local music files, and local devices like Audio CDs. JuK (Music Jukebox) is the KDE music player for managing music collections.

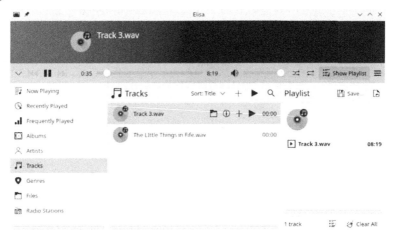

Figure 6-13: Elisa KDE Multimedia Player

GNOME Music is the GNOME Music player with tabs for Albums, Artists, Songs, and Playlists (see Figure 6-14). GNOME Music accesses sound files in your Music folder. On the Songs tab, you can click on a file to play it. A toolbar opens at the bottom with buttons to control the playback. The button to the right opens a menu with shuffle and repeat options. At the top, click on the Search button to search the list of sound files. To add files to the playlist, click on the check button to displays checkbox next to each sound file, which you can check and then click the "Add to Playlist" button.

Figure 6-14: GNOME Music

Due to licensing and patent issues, Ubuntu does not install MP3 support by default. MP3 playback capability has been removed from multimedia players like Rhythmbox. The Ubuntu codec wizard will prompt you to install MP3 support when you first try to play an MP3 file, usually the Gstreamer package. As an alternative to MP3, you can use Ogg Vorbis compression for music files.

CD/DVD Burners

Several CD/DVD ripper and writer programs can be used for CD music and MP3 writing (burners and rippers). These include Sound Juicer, Brasero, and K3b (See Table 6-5). GNOME features the CD audio ripper Sound Juicer and Goobox. For burning DVD/CD music and data discs, you can still use the Brasero CD/DVD burner and for KDE you can use K3b.

Brasero, K3b, ogmrip, and dvdauthor can all be used to create DVD-Video discs. All use mkisofs, cdrecord, and cdda2wav DVD/CD writing programs installed as part of your desktop. OGMrip can rip and encode DVD video. DVD-Video and CD music rippers may require addition codecs installed, for which the codec wizard will prompt you.

Application	Description
Brasero	Full service CD/DVD burner, for music, video, and data discs (no longer supported)
Sound Juicer (Audio CD Extractor)	GNOME music player and CD burner and ripper (Ubuntu Software)
Goobox	GNOME CD player and ripper (Ubuntu Software)
ogmrip	DVD ripping and encoding with DivX support
K3b	KDE CD writing interface
dvdauthor	Tools for creating DVDs

Table 6-5: CD/DVD Burners

Video Applications

Several projects provide TV, video, DivX, DVD, and DVB support for Ubuntu (see Table 6-6). Aside from GStreamer applications, there are also several third-party multimedia applications you may want, also available on the Ubuntu repositories, such as MPlayer and vlc.

Video and DVD Players

Most current DVD and media players are provided on the Ubuntu repositories. The default video player is GNOME Videos, whose interface has undergone a major change. The main dialog displays two tabs: Videos and Channels (see Figure 6-15)The Videos tab lists videos on your system and for those at specific sites on the Internet. Click the plus button at the left side of the header bar to display a menu for adding local or Web videos. For a Web video, you enter the video's Web address.

Figure 6-15: GNOME Videos: Videos tab

To Play a video, click on it (see Figure 6-16). For full-screen viewing, click the expand icon on the right side of the header bar. Move the mouse toward the bottom of the dialog to display viewing controls, including pause/play, repeat, sound volume, and skipping to the next or previous video. Click the back button (left side of the header bar) to return to the video listing.

Figure 6-16: GNOME Videos, playing a video

To play several videos in sequence click on the check icon at the right side of the header bar to display checkboxes at the corner of each video icon. Click the checkboxes of the videos you want to see, and then click the Play button on the lower left corner of the dialog. To randomize the sequence, click the Shuffle button instead.

To remove a video, click the check icon at the right side of the header bar to display checkboxes at the corner of each video icon. Click the checkboxes of the videos you want to remove and then click the Delete button on the lower right corner of the dialog. The Channels tab list streaming services.

Clicking on the search icon opens a text box for searching for videos (see Figure 6-17). The resource searched is shown on the right side of the text box. Clicking on the resource name displays a menu with possible resources you can search, including your local system, DLNA connection, YouTube, bookmarks, and supported streaming services.

Figure 6-17: GNOME Videos Search

Projects and Players	Sites
Videos	video and DVD player for GNOME using GStreamer, includes plugins for DVB, YouTube, and MythTV. It is based on the original GNOME Totem video player
Celluloid	GTK+ frontend for the MPV video player (**https://github.com/celluloid-player/celluloid**)
Dragon Player	Dragon Player video and DVD player for KDE
VLC Media Player (vlc)	Network multimedia streaming. **www.videolan.org**
MPlayer	MPlayer DVD/multimedia player **www.mplayerhq.hu**
MythTV	Home media center with DVD, DVR, and TV capabilities **https://www.mythtv.org**
tvtime	TV viewer, **http://tvtime.sourceforge.net**
XviD	Open Source DivX, **https://www.xvid.com/**
ubuntustudio-video	Ubuntu Studio meta package (Meta Packages (universe)), includes a collection of video applications. Use Synaptic Package Manager.
Kaffeine	An older KDE media player, including HDTV, DVB, DVD, CD, and network streams (Universe repository, install with Synaptic or Discover)
PiTiVi	Video editor
Shotcut	Video editor

Table 6-6: Video and DVD Projects and Applications

Several popular video players available for Ubuntu are listed here:

Dragon Player is a KDE multimedia player, installed with KDE desktop but will play on the GNOME Ubuntu desktop For the KDE players like Dragon Player, be sure to install the **kubuntu-restricted-extras** and **kubuntu-restricted-addons** packages.

MPlayer is one of the most popular and capable multimedia/DVD players in use. It is a cross-platform open source alternative to RealPlayer and Windows Media Player (**www.mplayerhq.hu**). MPlayer uses an extensive set of supporting libraries and applications like **lirc**, **lame**, **lzo**, and **aalib**, which are also available on the Ubuntu repository. If you have trouble displaying video, be sure to check the preferences for different video devices and select one that works best (**mplayer** package, Universe repository). Install with Ubuntu Software or the Synaptic Package Manager.s

mpv is an open source video player based on Mplayer and supports an extensive selection of codecs and formats. Run the Applications Overview or from a terminal window with the **mpv** command. Install with Ubuntu Software or the Synaptic Package Manager.

Videos is the GNOME Video player that uses GStreamer (see Figure 6-14), labeled with the name Videos. To expand Videos capabilities, you need to install added GStreamer plug-ins, as discussed previously. The codec wizard will prompt you to install any needed media codecs and plugins. You can use the **dconf** editor to modify default settings (org.gnome.Totem) (**totem** package, Ubuntu main repository). Though the name of the application is Videos, the package name is still totem.

The **VideoLAN** project (**http://www.videolan.org**) offers network streaming support for most media formats, including MPEG-4 and MPEG-2 (see Figure 6-18). It includes a multimedia player, VLC, which can work on any kind of system (**vlc** package, Universe repository). VLC supports high-def hardware decoding. Install from Ubuntu Software or the Synaptic Package Manager.

Celluloid is a GTK+ frontend for the MPV video player (**https://github.com/celluloid-player/celluloid**) (see Figure 6-19). It provides a basic interface with standard controls and playlist. You can also select video, audio, and subtitle tracks. It is the default video player for Ubuntu MATE.

Xine is a multipurpose video engine and for Linux/Unix systems that can play video, DVD, and audio discs. Many applications like Videos and Kaffeine use Xine support to playback DVD Video. See **http://xinehq.de** for more information. (**xine** support packages, universe repository). For the Xine user interface, install the **xine-ui** package with the Synaptic Package Manager.

Kaffeine is an older KDE multimedia player (video and dvb) (**kaffeine** package, Ubuntu Universe repository, install from Ubuntu Software or the Synaptic Package Manager).

Figure 6-18: VLC Video Player (VideoLAN)

Figure 6-19: Celluloid on Ubuntu

Videos Plugins

The Videos movie player uses plugins to add capabilities like a subtitle downloader. Select Preferences from the Videos top bar menu to open the Preferences dialog. On the General tab click on the Plugins button to open the Configure Plugins window (see Figure 6-20).

Figure 6-20: Videos (Totem) Movie Player plugins

DVD Video support

Unencrypted DVD Video support is provided by three packages available on the Ubuntu repository: **gstreamer-plugins-ugly**, **libdvdnav4**, and **libdvdread7**. These packages are available on the Ubuntu repository and can be installed with Synaptic Package Manager. With the **libdvdnav4** library, these players feature full DVD menu support. The **libdvdread7** library provides basic DVD interface support, such as reading IFO files.

None of the DVD-Video applications will initially play commercial DVD-Video discs. That requires Content Scrambling System (CSS) decryption for commercial DVDs, which is provided by the **libdvdcss** package. This package is not available on the primary Ubuntu repositories. It is only available on the third-party **download.videolan.org** repository. The packages on **videolan.org** are fully compatible with Ubuntu, but the packages, due to licensing restrictions, are not considered part of the official Ubuntu or Linux software collections.

The **libdvdcss** library works around CSS decryption by treating the DVD as a block device, allowing you to use any of the DVD players to play commercial DVDs. It also provides region-free access. See the following page for complete details.

```
https://help.ubuntu.com/community/RestrictedFormats/PlayingDVDs
```

The easiest way to install the **libdvdcss** package is to use the **libdvd-pkg** package, which is provided on the Ubuntu repository, multiverse. This package will compile the libdvdcss library, prompting you for the automatic upgrades option. You can install it either from the Synaptic Package Manager or with the **apt** command and then run the **dpkg-reconfigure** command on it. When it installs, it will also install the C++ compiler (**g++** and **gcc**) along with development tools and libraries, if you have not done so already.

```
sudo apt install libdvd-pkg
sudo dpkg-reconfigure libdvd-pkg
```

Alternatively, you can directly download the source code with your Web browser from the VideoLan site.

```
http://download.videolan.org/pub/libdvdcss/
```

PiTiVi and Shotcut Video editors

The PiTiVi Video editor is an open source application that lets you edit your videos. It is accessible from the Applications overview. Check the PiTiVi website for more details (**http://www.pitivi.org**). You can download a quick-start manual from the Documentation page. Pitivi is a GStreamer application and can work with any video file supported by an installed GStreamer plugin, including the GStreamer Ugly plugin.

Figure 6-21: Pitivi video editor

The PiTiVi window shows a Clip Library pane on the left, and video playback for a selected video clip on the right (see Figure 6-21). To run a video clip, right click on its icon and select Play Clip. To add a video file to the library, click the Import clips button on the toolbar. You can also drag-and-drop files directly to the Clip Library. The timeline at the bottom of the window displays the video and audio streams for the video clip you are editing, using a rule to shows your position. To edit a video, drag its icon from the Clip Library to the timeline. To trim a video, you pass the mouse over the timeline video and audio streams. Trimming handles will appear that you can use to shorten the video. PiTiVi features ripple editing and rolling editing, splitting, and transitions.

Shotcut is a another open-source video editor that supports numerous video formats (see Figure 6-22) .

Figure 6-22: Shotcut video editor

TV Players

The following TV players are provided on Ubuntu repositories:

TV player **tvtime** works with many common video capture cards, relying on drivers developed for TV tuner chips on those cards like the Conexant chips. It can only display a TV image. It has no recording or file playback capabilities. Check **http://tvtime.sourceforge.net** for more information.

MythTV is a popular video recording and playback application on Linux systems.

Kaffeine is a popular KDE video recording and playback application on Linux systems. It can also play ATSC over the air digital broadcasts.

DVB and HDTV support

For DVB and HDTV reception, you can use most DVB cards as well as many HDTV cards. The DVB kernel driver is loaded automatically. You can use the **lsmod** command to see if your DVB module is loaded.

Be sure you have installed the restricted add-ons and extras packages (**kubuntu-restricted-extras**, **kubuntu-restricted-addons**, **ubuntu-restricted-extras**, and **ubuntu-restricted-addons**), which provide support for appropriate decoders like mpeg2, FFmpeg, and A52 (ac3) (**liba52**, **libxine2-ffmpeg**, **gstreamer1.0-libav**, and **libdvbpsi**). You can use the Synaptic Package Manager to install them.

For DVB broadcasts, some DVB-capable players and tools like Kaffeine , as well as vdr, will tune and record DVB broadcasts in t, s, and c formats. Some applications, like Kaffeine, can scan DVB channels directly. Others may require that you first generate a **channels.conf** file. You can do this with the **w_scan** command (**w-scan** package). Then copy the generated **channels.conf** file to the appropriate applications folder. Channel scans can be output in vdr, Kaffeine, and Xine formats for use with those applications as well as others like Mplayer and MythTV. The **w_scan** command can also generate **channel.conf** entries for ATSC channels (HDTV), though not all applications can tune ATSC channels (Kaffeine can tune HDTV as well as scan for HDTV channels). You can also use the **dvbscan** tool (**dvb-apps** package) for scanning your channels and the **azap** tool for accessing the signal directly. This tool makes use of channel frequencies kept in the **/usr/share/dvb** folder. There are files for ATSC broadcast as well as cable.

Kaffeine DVB and ATSC tuning

The Kaffeine KDE media player can scan for both DVB and ATSC channels. You will need to have a DVB or ATSC tuner installed on your system. On Kaffeine, from the Television menu choose Configure Television, and on the device tab choose the source such as ATSC. Then from the Television menu, select Channels to open a Channel dialog. Your tuner device is selected on the Search on menu. Click on the Start scan button to begin scanning. Detected channels are listed on the "Scan results" scroll box. Select the ones you want and click Add Selected to place them in the Channels scroll box. Be sure to add the channel you want to watch on the Channel list.

You can use Kaffeine to both tune and record both DVB and ATSC HDTV channels. Kaffeine records an HDTV file as an **m2t** HDV MPEG-2 file, the High Definition Video (HDV) format used for high definition camcorders. The **m2t** files that Kaffeine generates can be played back by most video players, including Videos, Dragon Player, and vlc. To schedule a recording on Kaffeine, click the Television tab or click Digital TV from the Start tab. From the Television menu choose Recording Schedule or click the calendar button in the lower left corner to open the Recording Schedule dialog. Click the New button to open a Schedule Entry dialog where you can name the program, select the channel, set the time and duration, and choose to repeat daily or weekly.

Xvid (DivX) and Matroska (mkv) on Linux

MPEG-4 compressed files provide DVD-quality video with relatively small file sizes. They have become popular for distributing high-quality video files over the Internet. When you first try to play an MPEG-4, the codec wizard will prompt you to install the needed codec packages to play it. Many multimedia applications like VLC already support MPEG-4 files.

MPEG-4 files using the Matroska wrapper, also known by their file extension **mkv**, can be played on most video players including the VideoLan vlc player, Videos, Dragon Player, and Kaffeine. You will need HDTV codecs, like MPEG4 AAC sound codec, installed to play the high definition **mkv** file files. If needed, the codec wizard will prompt you to install them. For the KDE players be sure to install the **kubuntu-restricted-extras** and **kubuntu-restricted-addons** packages. To manage and create MKV files you can use MakeMKV, MkvToolNix (**mkvtoolnix-gui** package). Install with Ubuntu Software.

You use the open source version of DivX known as Xvid to play DivX video (**libxvidcore4** package, Universe repository, install with the Synaptic Package Manager). Most DivX files can be run using XviD. XviD is an entirely independent open source project, but it is compatible with DivX files. You can also download the XviD source code from **https://www.xvid.com/**.

Ubuntu Studio

Ubuntu Studio features Linux software for multimedia production, including sound, music, video, and graphics applications. You can install Ubuntu Studio as its own installation (see Chapter 11) or as an added desktop on your Ubuntu desktop install.

You can download the Ubuntu Studio install USB/DVD from **https://ubuntustudio.org**. This is a USB/DVD that installs using the text install utility. Use the arrow keys and tabs to move the cursor, the spacebar to choose, and ENTER key to select. The install procedure is the same for the desktop. Use the arrow keys and spacebar to select entries. Select them all for the entire collection.

To add Ubuntu Studio to your current desktop, use the Synaptic Package Manager and find the Meta Package (universe) section. There you will find the **ubuntustudio-desktop** Meta package, which will install the complete Ubuntu Studio desktop. You also install the Ubuntu Studio software collections including **ubuntustudio-audio, ubuntustudio-graphics**, and **ubuntustudio-video**. Ubuntu studio uses its own Ubuntu Studio desktop theme with its own icons, Applications menu categories, and background image.

Sound Settings

Your sound cards are detected automatically for you when you start up your system, by ALSA, which is invoked by udev when your system starts up. Removable devices, like USB sound devices, are also detected. See Table 6-7 for a listing of sound device and interface tools.

In addition to hardware drivers, sound systems also use sound interfaces to direct encoded sound streams from an application to the hardware drivers and devices. Ubuntu uses the PulseAudio server for its sound interface. PulseAudio aims to combine and consolidate all sound interfaces into a simple, flexible, and powerful server. The ALSA hardware drivers are still used, but the application interface is handled by PulseAudio. Pulse audio is installed as the default set up for Ubuntu.

PulseAudio is cross-platform sound server, allowing you to modify the sound level for different audio streams separately. See **https://www.freedesktop.org/wiki/Software/PulseAudio/** for documentation and help. PulseAudio offers complete control over all your sound streams, letting you combine sound devices and direct the stream anywhere on your network. PulseAudio is not confined to a single system. It is network capable, letting you direct sound from one PC to another.

As an alternative, you can use the command-line ALSA control tool, **alsamixer** (**alsamixergui** is the desktop version). This will display all connections and allow you to use a keyboard command to select (arrow keys), mute (m key), or set sound levels (Page Up and Down). Press the ESC key to exit. The **amixer** command lets you perform the same tasks for different sound connections from the command line. To actually play and record from the command-line, you can use the **play** and **rec** commands. They are installed as part of the **alsa-utils** package.

Note: Sound devices on Linux are supported by hardware sound drivers. With the Ubuntu kernel, hardware support is implemented by the Advanced Linux Sound Architecture (ALSA) system. You can find more about ALSA at **https://alsa-project.org/**.

Sound tool	Description
alsamixer	ALSA sound connection configuration and volume tool
amixer	ALSA command for sound connection configuration
Sound Settings	GNOME Sound Settings, used to select and configure your sound interface
PulseAudio	PulseAudio sound interface, the default sound interface for Ubuntu. **https://www.freedesktop.org/wiki/Software/PulseAudio/**
PulseAudio Volume Control	PulseAudio Volume Control, controls stream input, output, and playback, **pavucontrol** package
PulseAudio Volume Meter	Volume Meter, displays active sound levels
PulseAudio Preferences	Options for network access and virtual output

Table 6-7: Sound device and interface tools

Volume Control

Volume control for different applications is displayed on the application's dialog as the speaker icon. You can click it to change your application's output sound volume using a sliding bar. The sliding sound bar on the system status area menu also lets you set the sound volume, as shown here.

To perform volume control for specific devices like a microphone, you use the GNOME Settings Sound dialog.

Sound: PulseAudio

You configure sound devices and set the volume for input, output, and the system using the GNOME Settings Sound dialog. The Sound dialog has been combined into one dialog with five sections: System Volume, Volume Levels, Output, Input, and the Alert Sound (see Figure 6-23). System Volume lets you set the output volume for all applications and devices, including your speakers. To turn off the sound, click the speaker button on the right side of the volume slider. This will set the volume to zero. The button is a toggle. To turn on the sound again, click the speaker button. This will return sound levels to their previous settings. This section includes an Over-Amplification option that lets you raise volume over 100 percent, which may be useful for low powered speakers.

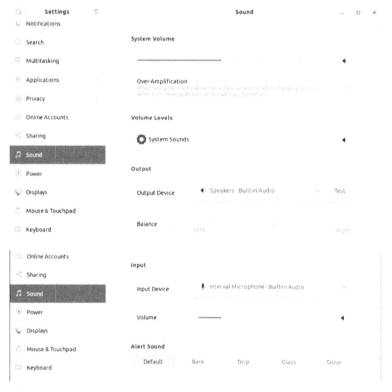

Figure 6-23: Sound

Volume Level has a System Sounds sliding bar that sets the volume for system sounds such as alert sounds. To turn off system sound, click the speaker button on the right side of the System Sounds volume slider. This will set the volume to zero. To turn the system sounds back on, simply click the speaker button again, returning the sound levels to their previous settings.

On the Output section, you can configure balance settings for a selected output device. If you have more than one device, it will be listed in the Output Device menu. Choose the one you want to configure. The available settings will change according to the device selected. For a simple Analog Stereo Output, there is only a single balance setting.

On the Input section, you set the input volume for an input device such as a microphone. When speaking or recording, the input level is displayed. If you have more than one input device, they will be listed in the Input Device menu. Choose the one you want to configure. To turn off the microphone, click the speaker button on the right side of the volume slider. This will set the volume to zero. To turn the microphone back on, click the speaker button again to return to the previous settings.

The Alert section lets you select an alert sound, such as Drip or Sonar. Use the Volume Levels System Sound to set the volume for your sound alerts.

Sound devices that support multiple interfaces like analog surround sound 7.1 and digital SPDIF output, may have an extensive list of interface combinations in the Output Device menu. The Output section will then display configuration settings for the selected device. With Analog Surround 7.1 Output selected, the Output section will show settings for Balance, Fade, and Subwoofer. Configuring digital output for SPDIF (digital) connectors is a simple matter of selecting the digital output entry on the Output Device menu.

PulseAudio applications

For additional configuration abilities, you can also install the PulseAudio applications. They begin with the prefix **pa** in the package name. PulseAudio applications are accessible from the Applications overview.

PulseAudio Volume Control, **pavucontrol**

PulseAudio Volume Meter, **pavumeter**

PulseAudio Preferences, **paprefs**

You can use the PulseAudio Volume Control application (**pavucontrol**) to set the sound levels for different playback applications and sound devices (choose PulseAudio Volume Control on the Applications overview). The PulseAudio Volume Control applications will show tabs for Playback, Recording, Output Devices, Input Devices, and Configuration. The Playback tab shows all the applications currently using PulseAudio. You can adjust the volume for each application separately. You can use the Output tab panel to set the volume control at the source and select different output devices, such as Headphones. The volume for input and recording devices are set on the Recording and Input Devices tabs. The Configuration tab lets you choose different device profiles, such as selecting Digital output or Surround Sound.

You can also use the PulseAudio Volume control to direct different applications (streams) to different outputs (devices). For example, you could have two sound sources running, one for video and another for music. The video could be directed through one device to headphones, and the music through another device to speakers, or even to another PC. To redirect an application to a different device, right-click its name in the Playback tab. A pop-up menu will list the available devices and let you select the one you want to use.

The PulseAudio Volume Meter application will show the actual volume of your devices.

To configure network access, you use the PulseAudio Preferences application (**paref**). Here you can permit network access, configure the PulseAudio network server, and enable multicast and simultaneous output. Simultaneous output creates a virtual output device to the same hardware device. This lets you channel two sources onto the same output. With PulseAudio

Volume Control, you could then channel playback streams to the same output device, but using a virtual device as the output for one. This lets you change the output volume for each stream independently. You could have music and voice directed to the same hardware device, using a virtual device for music and the standard device for voice. You can then reduce the music stream, or raise the voice stream.

In addition, there are PulseAudio command-line tools available as shown in Table 6-8. Install the **pulseaudio-utils** package.

Sound tool	Description
pacat	Play, record, and configure a raw audio stream
pacmd	Generates a shell for entering configuration commands
pactl	Control a PulseAudio server, changing input and output sources and providing information about the server.
padsp	PulseAudio wrapper for OSS sound applications
pamon	Link to pacat
paplay	Playback audio. The -d option specifies the output device, the -s option specifies the server, and the --volume option sets the volume (link to pacat)
parec	Record and audio stream (link to pacat)
parecord	Record and audio stream (link to pacat)
pasuspender	Suspend a PulseAudio server
pax11publish	Access PulseAudio server credentials

Table 6-8: PulseAudio commands (command-line)

7. Internet Applications

Web Browsers: Firefox, GNOME Web, Chromium, Links

Web-Apps: GNOME

BitTorrent: Transmission

Java for Linux

Network File Transfer: FTP

FTP Clients

Online Accounts

Instant Messenger

VoIP: Skype

GNOME Maps

Ubuntu provides powerful Web and FTP clients for accessing the Internet. Some of these applications are installed automatically and are ready to use when you first start up your Ubuntu system. Ubuntu also includes full Java development support, letting you run and construct Java applets. Web and FTP clients connect to sites that run servers, using Web pages and FTP files to provide services to users.

On your Ubuntu system, you can choose from several Web browsers, including Firefox, Web (Epiphany), Chromium, and Links. Firefox, Chromium, and Web are desktop browsers that provide full picture, sound, and video display capabilities. The Links browser is a line-mode browser that displays only lines of text.

Web browsers and FTP clients are commonly used to conduct secure transactions, such as logging into remote sites, ordering items, or transferring files. Such operations are currently secured by encryption methods provided by the Transport Layer Security (TLS) and its older Secure Sockets Layer (SSL) protocols. If you use a browser for secure transactions, it should be TLS/SSL enabled. Most browsers include TLS/SSL support. Ubuntu distributions include SSL (OpenSSL) as part of a standard installation.

URL Addresses

An Internet resource is accessed using a Universal Resource Locator (URL). A URL is composed of three elements: the transfer protocol, the hostname, and the pathname. The transfer protocol and the hostname are separated by a colon and two slashes, **://**. The pathname begins with a single slash:

```
transfer-protocol://host-name/path-name
```

The transfer protocol is usually HTTP (Hypertext Transfer Protocol), indicating a Web page. Other possible values for transfer protocols are **ftp** and **file**. As their names suggest, **ftp** initiates FTP sessions, whereas **file** displays a local file on your own system, such as a text or HTML file. The hostname is the computer on which a particular website is located. You can think of this as the address of the website. By convention, many hostnames begin with **www**, though not necessarily. In the next example, the URL locates a Web page called **guides.html** on the **http://tldp.org** website:

```
http://tldp.org/guides.html
```

If you do not want to access a particular Web page, you can leave the file reference out, and then you access the website's home page automatically. To access a website directly, use its hostname. If no home page is specified for a website, the file **index.html** in the top folder is used as the home page. In the next example, the user brings up the GNOME home page:

```
https://www.gnome.org/
```

Most Web sites use the protocol (Hypertext Transfer Protocol Secure), as shown in the previous example. This protocol uses Transport Layer Security (TLS) encryption for security. For these sites you use the **https://** designation as show in the previous example. TLS is based on the older Secure Sockets Layer (SSL) security.

The resource file's extension indicates the type of action to be taken on it. A picture has a **.gif** or **.jpeg** extension and is converted for display. A sound file has an **.au** or **.wav** extension and is played. The following URL references a **.gif** file. Instead of displaying a Web page, your browser invokes a graphics viewer to display the picture.

Note: You can install the Adobe version of the Flash plug-in for Linux with the Synaptic Package Manager (adobe-flashplugin). Be sure the Partners repository is enabled.

Web Browsers

Popular browsers for Ubuntu include Firefox (Mozilla), Chromium (Google), Epiphany, and Links (see Table 7-1). Firefox is the default Web browser used on most Linux distributions, including Ubuntu. Web is the GNOME Web browser (formerly known as Epiphany). Chromium is the open source version of the Google Web browser. Links, Lynx, and ELinks are text based browsers with no graphics capabilities, but in every other respect, they are fully functional Web browsers.

Web Site	Description
Firefox	The Mozilla project Firefox Web browser, Ubuntu desktop default browser **https://www.mozilla.org**
Web	GNOME Web browser (formerly called Epiphany) **https://wiki.gnome.org/Apps/Web**
Chromium	Open source version of Google Chrome Web browser **http://www.chromium.org**
lynx	Text-based command-line Web browser (Ubuntu supported)
Links and Links2	Text-based command-line Web browser (Ubuntu supported), Link2 also provides a graphical interface.
elinks	Text-based command-line Web browser **http://elinks.or.cz**

Table 7-1: Web browsers

The Firefox Web Browser

The Mozilla project is an open source project based on the original Netscape browser code that provides a development framework for web-based applications, primarily the web browser and e-mail client. The Mozilla project site is **https://www.mozilla.org**, and the site commonly used for plug-in and extension development is **https://www.mozdev.org**. You can also sign up for a Firefox account which can then make your bookmarks available to the Firefox browsers on all your devices. So you can save a bookmark on one of your Firefox browsers, and have it available on the Firefox browsers on all your devices.

Ubuntu uses Firefox as its primary browser (see Figure 7-1). Firefox is installed by default with icons on the dock and the Applications overview. Firefox is no longer available on the Apt (DEB) repositories. It is now installed and maintained from the the Snap repository.

When opened, Firefox displays the first tab. Firefox is designed to display tabs, each of which can display a complete Web page, including the Firefox toolbar and sidebar. The tab title is shown at the top, and next to it is a plus button (+) you can click to add a new tab. You can also press Ctrl+t. You can easily switch from one page to another by click its tab. You can re-arrange tabs by clicking and holding on a tab title and moving it to the right or left.

Within a tab, a navigation toolbar is displayed at the top, with an address bar (text box) for entering a URL address and a series of navigation buttons for accessing web pages. On the left side of the toolbar are the Next and Previous buttons for paging through previously accessed web pages, followed by a cancel button for loading a page (X) which becomes a refresh button when the page is fully displayed.

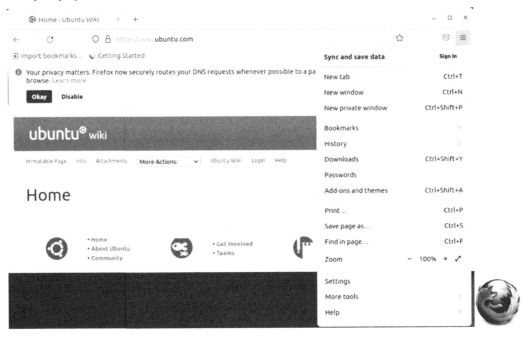

Figure 7-1: Firefox Web Browser

When you enter a web page name in the address bar, Firefox performs a dynamic search on previously accessed pages and displays the pages in a drop-down menu, which you can choose from. Within the address bar to the right are buttons for recent history (down arrow), page actions (…),and marking the page as a bookmark (star). The page actions button displays a menu for tasks such as bookmarking the page, saving to the pocket, and emailing the link.

Firefox provides a search bar (text box) for searching the Web, selected sites, or particular items. To the right of the address bar are buttons for saving to Pocket and the Firefox menu. The menu displays entries for accessing your bookmarks, history, and downloads, .

To add a bookmark for a page, click the bookmark button on the right side of the address bar (the star button). This displays an New Bookmark dialog with a pop-up menus for folders and tags. The Folder menu is set to the Other Bookmarks folder by default. You can also select the Bookmarks Toolbar or the Bookmarks Menu. The Bookmark Toolbar displays bookmark buttons at the top of the browser.

To search a current page for certain text, enter Ctrl+f. This opens a search toolbar at the bottom of Firefox from which you can enter a search term. You have search options to highlight found entries or to match character case. The Next and Previous buttons let you move to the next found pattern.

When you download a file using Firefox, the download is managed by the Download Manager. You can download several files at once. Progress is displayed download button on the toolbar, which you can click to see your downloads. You can cancel a download at any time or just pause a download, resuming it later.

Selecting History on the history/bookmarks menu (accessible from the toolbar) displays the History menu, showing a list of your recently accessed Web pages from which you can select one to view. You can also see recently closed tabs and Firefox windows. To clear your recent history, chose the "Clear Recent History" entry. The "Show All History" option opens the Library dialog as the history entry, letting you edit, access, bookmark, or remove previous pages.

The Firefox menu (right-side of the window) lets you perform Web page tasks such as zooming, opening new windows, printing and saving a page, and performing searches on a page. There are also administrative options such as Settings (preferences), Add-ons, and the Library. The Library dialog lets you manage all your history and bookmarks. On Preferences you can set your privacy and search options, as well as setting your home page, language, fonts, download location (see Figure 7-2). On the Search tab you can choose your default search engine, which includes Google, Bing, Amazon, DuckDuckGo, Twitter, Wikipedia, and eBay.

Figure 7-2: Firefox Settings

The Add-ons entry on the menu opens the Add-ons window with tabs for Get Add-ons, Extensions, Themes, and Plugins (see Figure 7-3). Click the one you want to open a brief description and display the Add to Firefox button, which you click to open a download and install dialog. The Extensions tab lists installed Extensions with buttons for Preferences, Disable, and Uninstall for each. On the Plugins tab, you can disable or enable embedded applications, such as iTunes, QuickTime, and Skype. The Themes tab lets you choose a theme.

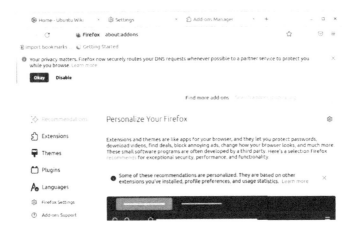

Figure 7-3: Firefox Add-ons Management

Firefox also supports profiles. You can set up different Firefox configurations, each with preferences and bookmarks. This is useful for computers like laptops that connect to different networks or are used for different purposes. You can select and create profiles by starting up the profile manager. Enter the **firefox** command in a terminal window with the -P option.

```
firefox -P
```

A default profile is already set up. You can create a new profile, which runs the profile wizard to prompt you for the profile name and folder to use. Select a profile to use and click Start Firefox. The last profile you used will be used again the next time you start Firefox. You have the option to prompt for the profile to use at startup, otherwise run the **firefox -P** command again to change your profile.

GNOME Web (Epiphany)

GNOME Web, formerly known as Epiphany, is a GNOME web browser with a simple interface designed to be fast (see Figure 7-4). You can find out more about Epiphany at **https://wiki.gnome.org/Apps/Web**. Web works well as a simple browser with a clean interface. It is also integrated with the desktop, featuring a download applet that will continue after closing Web. Web also supports tabbed panels for multiple web site access. Its menu (click the menu button at the top right) lists options such as New Window, New Incognito Window, the import and export of bookmarks, History, and Preferences, as well as page-specific operations such as tabs, print, save, zooming, and find. You can install GNOME Web using Ubuntu Software (search under "Gnome Web") or with the Synaptic Package Manager or the **apt** command (**epiphany-browser** package). Once installed, you can access it as Web.

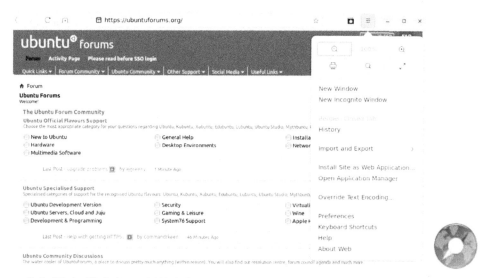

Figure 7-4: Web (Epiphany) Web browser

Chromium

Google's Chromium web browser (**https://www.chromium.org**) provides easy and very secure access to the Web with full Google integration. You can install it using Ubuntu Software (Snap repository). You can access Chromium from the Applications overview as Chromium Web Browser. You are first prompted to enter your Google account e-mail and password so that your online preferences and bookmarks can be used, but you can pass.

On Chromium, primacy is afforded to tabs. At the top of the Chromium window are your tabs for open web pages, with a square image button at the end of the tabs for opening a new tab (see Figure 7-3). Chromium features a simple toolbar with navigation buttons and a bookmark button (star icon). To close a tab, click the close button to the right of the tab title.

To the right of the URL box, a menu button displays a drop-down menu for menu items for browser operations such as new tabs, print, zoom, history, bookmarks, and downloads. To configure Chromium, select Settings from this menu to open the Chromium Settings tab. Here you can set your home page, default search service, and themes. Click the Advanced on the sidebar to expand the Settings dialog to let you manage passwords, languages, downloads, printing, and accessibility.

When you open a new tab, a thumbnail listing of recently closed and most visited sites is displayed, as well as bookmarked sites. Clicking a thumbnail moves you to that site.

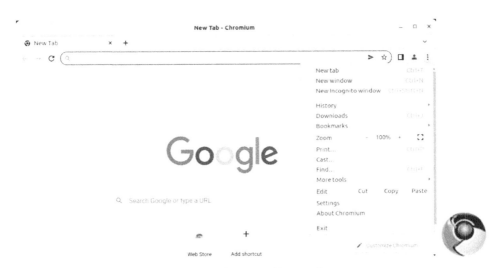

Figure 7-5: Chromium Web Browser (Google Chrome)

Links, Lynx, and ELinks: Line-Mode Browsers

Linux features line-mode browsers such as Links, Lynx, and ELinks, which you can use from a command line interface. You can install Links with Ubuntu Software, and Lynx and Elinks from the Synaptic Package Manager. On these browsers, a Web page is displayed as text only. A text page can contain links to other Internet resources but does not display graphics, video, or sound. Except for the display limitations, Links, Lynx, and Elinks are fully functional Web browsers. You can also use them to download files or access local pages. All information on the Web is still accessible to you. Because they do not require as much overhead as desktop-based browsers, they can operate much faster, quickly displaying Web page text. To start the Lynx browser, use the `lynx` command, and to start Links use the **links** command. Use the ESC key to display the menu. The Links2 application (**links2**) also provides a graphical interface you can access from the desktop. ELinks includes features such as frame, form, and table support. It also supports SSL secure encryption. To start ELinks, enter the **elinks** command in a terminal window. You can find out more about elinks at **http://elinks.or.cz**.

Java for Linux

To develop Java applications, use Java tools, and run many Java products, you use the Java 2 Software Development Kit (SDK) and the Java Runtime Environment (JRE). The SDK is a superset of the JRE, adding development tools like compilers and debuggers. Together with other technologies like the Java API, they make up the Java Platform, Standard Edition.

Oracle has open sourced Java as the OpenJDK project and supports and distributes Linux versions. The JRE subset can be installed as OpenJRE. They are directly supported by Ubuntu as packages on the main Ubuntu repository. You can install them with the Synaptic Package Manager or the **apt** command. The **openjdk-11-jre** package installs the Java runtime environment, and **openjdk-11-jdk** installs both the JRE and the Java development tools. Java packages and applications are listed in Table 7-2.

Application	Description
Java Development Kit, OpenJDK	An open source Java development environment with a compiler, interpreters, debugger, and more (include the JRE), **http://openjdk.java.net**. Included on the Ubuntu main repository **openjdk-11-jdk**
Java Runtime Environment, OpenJRE	An open source Java runtime environment, including the Java virtual machine, included on the Ubuntu main repository, **openjdk-11-jre**. **http://openjdk.java.net**
Java Platform Standard Edition (JSE)	Complete Java collection, including JRE, JDK, and API, **http://www.oracle.com/technetwork/java/javase/downloads/index.html**

Table 7-2: Java Packages and Java Web Applications

BitTorrent Clients (transmission)

GNOME and KDE provide effective BitTorrent clients. With BitTorrent, you can download large files quickly in a shared distributed download operation where several users participate in downloading different parts of a file, sending their parts of the download to other participants, known as peers. Instead of everyone trying to access a few central servers, all peers participating in the BitTorrent operation become sources for the file being downloaded. Certain peers function as seeders, those who have already downloaded the file, but continue to send parts to those who need them.

Ubuntu installs the GNOME BitTorrent client, Transmission, accessible from the Applications overview. For Kubuntu, you can use the Ktorrent BitTorrent client. To perform a BitTorrent download you need the BitTorrent file for the file you want to download. The BitTorrent file for the Ubuntu Desktop USB/DVD iso image is **ubuntu-22.04-desktop-amd64.iso.torrent**. You can download the file from the **https://ubuntu.com/download/alternative-downloads** site. When you double-click the file it will open it directly with Transmission.

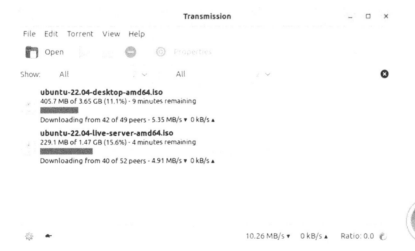

Figure 7-6: Transmission BitTorrent client

Transmission can handle several torrents at once. On the toolbar are buttons for starting, pausing, and remove a download. The Open button can be used to load a BitTorrent file (**.torrent**), setting up a download. You also can drag-and-drop a torrent file to the Transmission window. When you first open a torrent file, the Torrent Options window opens where you can specify the destination folder and the priority. The option to start the download automatically is selected by default. Figure 7-6 shows the Transmission window with two BitTorrent operations set up, both of which are active. A progress bar shows how much of the file has been downloaded.

You could set up Transmission to manage several BitTorrent operations, of which only a few may be active, others paused, and still others that have finished but continue to function as seeders. From the first Show menu, you can select All, Active, Downloading, Seeding, Paused, and Finished torrents. You can also choose those verifying and those that have errors. From the second menu, you can choose Trackers.

To remove a torrent, right-click on it and select Remove. Choose Delete Files and Remove to remove what you have downloaded so far.

To see more information about a torrent, select it and then click the Properties button (see Figure 7-7). This opens a Properties window with tabs for Information, Peers, Tracker, Files, and Options. On the Information tab, the Activity section shows statistics like the progress, times, and errors, and the Details section shows the origin, comment, and locations of the download folder. Peers show all the peers participating in the download. Tracker displays the location of the tracker, the server that manages the torrent operation. Files shows the progress of the file download (a torrent could download more than one file). The Options tab lets you set bandwidth and connection parameters, limiting the download or upload, and the number of peers.

Figure 7-7: Transmission BitTorrent client properties

FTP Clients

With File Transfer Protocol (FTP) clients, you can connect to a corresponding FTP site and download files from it. These sites feature anonymous logins that let any user access their files. Basic FTP client capabilities are incorporated into the Files (GNOME), Dolphin (KDE), and Caja

(MATE) file managers. You can use a file manager window to access an FTP site and drag files to local folders to download them. Effective FTP clients are also now incorporated into most Web browsers, making Web browsers the primary downloading tool. Firefox, in particular, has strong FTP download capabilities.

Although file managers and Web browsers provide effective access to public (anonymous login) sites, to access private sites, you may need a stand-alone FTP client like curl, wget, Filezilla, gFTP, lftp, or **ftp**. These clients let you enter usernames and passwords with which you can access a private FTP site. The stand-alone clients are also useful for large downloads from public FTP sites, especially those with little or no Web display support. Popular Linux FTP clients are listed in Table 7-4.

Network File Transfer: FTP

With File Transfer Protocol (FTP) clients, you can transfer extremely large files directly from one site to another (see Table 7-3). FTP can handle both text and binary files. FTP performs a remote login to another account on another system connected to you on a network. Once logged into that other system, you can transfer files to and from it. To log in, you need to know the login name and password for the account on the remote system. Many sites on the Internet allow public access using FTP. Such sites serve as depositories for large files anyone can access and download. These sites are often referred to as FTP sites, and in many cases, their Internet addresses begin with the term ftp, such as **ftp.gnome.org**. These public sites allow anonymous FTP login from any user. You can then transfer files from that site to your own system.

FTP Clients	Description
Caja	MATE file manager
Dolphin	KDE file manager
Files	GNOME file manager (nautilus)
gFTP	GNOME FTP client, **gftp** package
ftp	Command line FTP client
lftp	Command line FTP client capable of multiple connections
curl	Internet transfer client (FTP and HTTP)
Filezilla	Linux version of the open source Filezilla ftp client (Universe repository)

Table 7-3: Linux FTP Clients

Several FTP protocols are available for accessing sites that support them. The original FTP protocol is used for most anonymous sites. FTP transmissions can also be encrypted using SSH2, the SFTP protocol. More secure connections may use FTPS for TLS/SSL encryption. Some sites support a simplified version of FTP called File Service Protocol, FSP. FTP clients may support different protocols like gFTP for FSP and Filezilla for TLS/SSL. Most clients support both FTP and SSH2.

Web Browser–Based FTP

You can access an FTP site and download files from it with any Web browser. Browsers are useful for locating individual files, though not for downloading a large set of files. A Web browser is effective for checking out an FTP site to see what files are listed there. When you access an FTP site with a Web browser, the entire list of files in a folder is listed as a Web page. You can move to a subfolder by clicking its entry. You can easily browse through an FTP site to download files. To download a file, click the download link. This will start the transfer operation, opening a dialog for selecting your local folder and the name for the file. The default name is the same as on the remote system. On many browsers, you can manage your downloads with a download manager, which will let you cancel a download operation in progress or remove other downloads requested. The manager will show the time remaining, the speed, and the amount transferred for the current download.

GNOME Desktop FTP: Connect to Server

The easiest way to download files from an FTP site is to use the built-in FTP capabilities of the GNOME file manager, GNOME Files. On GNOME, the desktop file manager has a built-in FTP capability much like the KDE file manager. The FTP operation has been seamlessly integrated into standard desktop file operations. Downloading files from an FTP site is as simple as dragging files from one folder window to another, where one of the folders happens to be located on a remote FTP site. Use the GNOME file manager (GNOME Files) to access a remote FTP site, listing files in the remote folder, just as local files are (see Figure 7-8). In a file manager's Location bar (**Ctrl-l**), enter the FTP site's URL using the prefix **ftp://** and press ENTER. A dialog opens prompting you to specify how you want to connect. You can connect anonymously for a public FTP site, or connect as a user supplying your username and password (private site). You can also choose to remember the password.

Figure 7-8: GNOME FTP access with the file manager

Folders on the FTP site will be displayed, and you can drag files to a local folder to download them. You can navigate through the folders as you would with any file manager folder, opening folders or returning to the parent folder. To download a file, just drag it from the FTP window to a local folder window. To upload a file, drag it from your local folder to the window for the open FTP folder. Your file will be uploaded to that FTP site (if you have permission to do so). You can also delete files on the site's folders if allowed.

You can also use the Connect to Server bar in the file manager (see Figure 7-9) to connect, which remembers your previous FTP connections. To access the Connect to Server bar, click on the "Other Locations" entry in any file manager sidebar. The Connect to server bar is displayed at the bottom of the file manager window. It shows a text box for the server address, a menu button to display previous addresses, and a Connect button. Enter the server address. The address is remembered and added to the previous servers list. Then click the Connect button. A dialog opens letting you specify an Anonymous login or to enter a username and password. Click the Connect button to access the site.

Figure 7-9: GNOME FTP access with Connect to Server and the file manager

The top folder of the remote FTP site will be displayed in a file manager window. Use the file manager to progress through the remote FTP site's folder tree until you find the file you want. Then, open another window for the local folder to which you want the remote files copied. In the window showing the FTP files, select those you want to download. Then click and drag those files to the window for the local folder. As files are downloaded, a dialog appears showing the progress.

The file manager window's sidebar will list an entry for the FTP site accessed. An eject button is shown to the right of the FTP site's name. To disconnect from the site, click this button. The FTP entry will disappear along with the FTP sites icons and file listings.

Filezilla

Filezilla is an open source FTP client originally implemented on Windows systems (**https://filezilla-project.org/**). Use the Synaptic Package Manager or Ubuntu Software to install it. Once installed, you can access it from the Applications overview. The interface displays a left and right pane for local and remote folders. You can navigate through folder trees, with the files of a selected folder displayed below. To download a file, right-click on a file in the Remote site pane (right) and select Download. To upload, right-click on the file in the Local site pane (left) and select Upload. Text boxes at the top let you specify the host, username, password, and port. A Quick connect menu will connect to a preconfigured site.

To configure a remote site connection, use the Site Manager (File | Site Manager). In the Site Manager window, click on the New Site button to create a new site connection. Four configuration tabs become active: General, Advanced, Transfer settings, and Charset. On the General tab, you can specify the host, user, password, and account. The server type menu lets you specify a particular FTP protocol like SFTP for SSH encrypted transmissions or FTPS for TLS/SSL encryption.

gFTP

The gFTP program is an older GNOME FTP client designed to let you make standard FTP file transfers. The package name for gFTP is **gftp**, and it is located in the Universe repository. You can install it from Ubuntu Software or the Synaptic Package Manager.

The gFTP window consists of several panes. The top-left pane lists files in your local folder, and the top-right pane lists your remote folder. Subfolders have folder icons preceding their names. The parent folder can be referenced by the double period entry (**..**) with an up arrow at the top of each list. Double-click a folder entry to access it. The pathnames for all folders are displayed in boxes above each pane. A drop down menu to the far right lets you specify the FTP protocol to use such as FTP for a standard transmission, SSH2 for SSH encrypted connections, and FSP for File Service Protocol transmissions. Two buttons between the panes are used for transferring files. The left arrow button, <-, downloads selected files in the remote folder, and the right arrow button, ->, uploads files from the local folder. Menus across the top of the window can be used to manage your transfers.

wget

The wget tool lets you access Web and FTP sites for particular folders and files. Folders can be recursively downloaded, letting you copy an entire website. The **wget** command takes as its option the URL for the file or folder you want. Helpful options include **-q** for quiet, **-r** for recursive (folders), **-b** to download in the background, and **-c** to continue downloading an interrupted file. One drawback is that your URL reference can be very complex. You have to know the URL already. You cannot interactively locate an item as you would with an FTP client. The following would download the Ubuntu Install DVD in the background.

```
wget -b ftp://releases.ubuntu.com/jammy/ubuntu-22.04-desktop-amd64.iso
```

curl

The **curl** Internet client operates much like **wget**, but with much more flexibility. With curl, you can specify multiple URLs on its command line. You can also use braces to specify multiple matching URLs, like different websites with the same domain name. You can list the different website host names within braces, followed by their domain name (or vice versa). You can also use brackets to specify a range of multiple items. This can be very useful for downloading archived files that have the same root name with varying extensions. **curl** can download using any protocol, and will try to intelligently guess the protocol to use if none is provided. Check the **curl** man page for more information.

ftp

The **ftp** client uses a command line interface, and it has an extensive set of commands and options you can use to manage your FTP transfers. It is the original FTP client used on Unix and Linux systems. See the **ftp** man page for more details. Alternatively, you can use **sftp** for more secure access. The **sftp** client has the same commands as **ftp** but provides SSH (Secure SHell) encryption.

You start the **ftp** client by entering the command **ftp** at a shell prompt. If you want to connect to a specific site, you can include the name of that site on the command line after the **ftp** keyword. Otherwise, you need to connect to the remote system with the ftp command **open**. You are then prompted for the name of the remote system with the prompt "(to)". When you enter the remote system name, ftp connects you to the system and then prompts you for a login name. After entering the login name, you are prompted for the password. In the next example, the user connects to the remote system **garnet**, and logs in to the **robert** account:

```
$ ftp
ftp> open
(to) garnet
Connected to garnet.berkeley.edu.
220 garnet.berkeley.edu FTP server ready.
Name (garnet.berkeley.edu:root): robert
password required
Password:
user robert logged in
ftp>
```

Once logged in, you can execute Linux commands on either the remote system or your local system. You execute a command on your local system in ftp by preceding the command with an exclamation point. Any Linux commands without an exclamation point are executed on the remote system. One exception exists to this rule. Whereas you can change folders on the remote system with the **cd** command, to change folders on your local system, you need to use a special ftp command called **lcd** (local **cd**). In the next example, the first command lists files in the remote system, while the second command lists files in the local system:

```
ftp> ls
ftp> !ls
```

The ftp program provides a basic set of commands for managing files and folders on your remote site, provided you have the permission to do so. You can use **mkdir** to create a remote folder, and **rmdir** to remove one. Use the **delete** command to erase a remote file. With the **rename** command, you can change the names of files. You close your connection to a system with the **close** command. You can then open another connection if you want. To end the ftp session, use the **quit** or **bye** command.

```
ftp> close
ftp> bye
Good-bye
$
```

To transfer files to and from the remote system, use the **get** and **put** commands. The **get** command receives files from the remote system to your local system, and the **put** command sends files from your local system to the remote system. In a sense, your local system gets files from the remote folder and puts files to the remote remote folder. In the next example, the file **weather** is sent from the local system to the remote system using the **put** command:

```
ftp> put weather
PORT command successful.
ASCII data connection
ASCII Transfer complete.
ftp>
```

lftp

The **lftp** program is an enhanced FTP client with advanced features such as the abilities to download mirror sites and to run several FTP operations in the background at the same time. You can install it with the Synaptic Package Manager.

It uses a command set similar to that for the ftp client. You use **get** and **mget** commands to download files, with the **-o** option to specify local locations for them. Use **lcd** and **cd** to change local and remote folders.

When you connect to a site, you can queue commands with the **queue** command, setting up a list of FTP operations to perform. With this feature, you could queue several download operations to a site. The queue can be reordered and entries deleted if you wish. You can also connect to several sites and set up a queue for each one. The **mirror** command lets you maintain a local version of a mirror site. You can download an entire site or just update newer files, as well as remove files no longer present on the mirror.

You can tailor **lftp** with options set in the **.lftprc** file. System-wide settings are placed in the **/etc/lftp.conf** file. Here, you can set features like the prompt to use and your anonymous password. The **.lftp** folder holds support files for command history, logs, bookmarks, and startup commands. The **lftp** program also supports the **.netrc** file, checking it for login information.

Social Networking

Ubuntu provides integrated social networking support for broadcasting, IM (Instant Messenger), and VoIP (Voice over Internet). User can communicate directly with other users on your network (see Table 7-1). Most of these applications are not supported by Ubuntu and are not installed by default. You can install them from Ubuntu Software or the Synaptic Package Manager.

Instant Messenger

Instant messenger (IM) clients allow users on the same IM service to communicate across the Internet (see Table 7-4). Currently, some of the major IM services are AIM (AOL), Microsoft Network (MSN), Yahoo, ICQ, and Jabber. Some use an XML protocol called XMPP, Extensible Messaging and Presence Protocol.

Note: A beta version of Slack is available from Snap. Slack is collaboration software featuring instant messaging and shared files for groups (teams). Slack is proprietary software.

Empathy

Empathy is the GNOME messaging application. Empathy is based on the Telepathy framework., which is designed to provide IM support to any application that wants an IM capability. All major IM services are supported, including Google Talk, AIM, Salut, zephyr, Jabber (XMPP), ICQ, and Yahoo. You can install Empathy with Ubuntu Software or the Synaptic Package Manager.

Clients	Description
Skype	VoIP application (Partner repository)
empathy	GNOME instant messenger
Pidgin	Older instant messenger client used in previous releases and still available.
Jabber	Jabber IM (XMPP)
Finch	Command line cursor-based IM client
Konversation	KDE IRC client

Table 7-4: Instant Messenger, Talk, and VoIP Clients

Empathy is accessible from the Applications overview. Click the Accounts entry in the Empathy menu to open the Online Account dialog, letting you add new accounts for Empathy. Click the plus button to add a new account. Choose the Empathy entry in the drop down menu labeled "Show accounts that integrate with" to show instant messaging services such as AIM, Yahoo, Jabber, and Facebook. A drop down menu on the Contact List window lets you select your status, like Available, Busy, Away, Invisible, or Offline. You can specify a custom message for a particular status.

Pidgin

Pidgin is an older IM client that works with most IM protocols. It is still available on the Universe repository, and can be installed with Ubuntu Software or the Synaptic Package Manager. Pidgin will be accessible from the Applications overview. Pidgin will open a Buddy List window with menus for Buddies, Accounts, Tools, and Help. Use the Buddies menu to send a message or join a chat. The Accounts menu lets you configure and add accounts. The Tools menu provides configuration features, such as preferences, plugin selection, privacy options, and sound.

The first time you start Pidgin, the Add Account window is displayed with Basic, Advanced, and Proxy tabs for setting up an account. Later you can edit the account by selecting it in the Accounts window (Accounts | Manage) and clicking the Modify button. Pidgin is not supported by Online Accounts.

To create a new account, select Manage Accounts from the Accounts menu (Accounts | Manage). This opens the Accounts dialog, which lists your current accounts. Click the Add button to open the Add Account dialog with a Basic, Advanced, and Proxy tabs. On the Basic panel, you choose the protocol from a pop-up menu that shows items such as AIM, Bonjour, Yahoo, and IRC, and then enter the appropriate account information. You can also select a buddy icon to use for the account. On the Advanced tab, you specify the server and network connection settings. Many protocols will have a server entered already.

To configure your setup, select Preferences from the Tools menu (Tools | Preferences) to open the Preferences dialog where you can set options for logging, sounds, themes, and the interface display. You can find out more about Pidgin at **http://pidgin.im**. Pidgin is a GNOME front end that used the libpurple library for actual IM tasks (formerly libgaim). The libpurple library is used by many different IM applications.

VoIP Applications

Ubuntu provides the popular VoIP applications Skype, which is proprietary (available on Ubuntu Software, Snap repository).

Skype

Skype is part of the Snap repository. You can install Skype using Ubuntu Software. Once installed, you can access Skype from the Applications overview. The interface is similar to the Windows version (see Figure 7-10). A Skype panel icon will appear on the panel, once you start Skype. You can use it to access Skype throughout your session. Click to open Skype and right-click to display a menu from which you can change your status and sign out. The panel icon changes according to your status.

Also, the **pidgin-sipe** package provides a Skype plugin, which will let you use Ubuntu applications like Pidgin, Finch, and Empathy to operate through Skype connections.

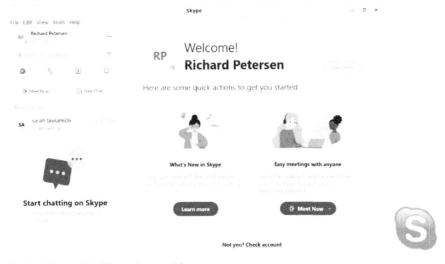

Figure 7-10: Skype VoIP and panel icon

GNOME Maps

GNOME Maps is a GNOME map utility that provides both street and satellite maps. It can also detect your current location (see Figure 7-11). From the task menu at the left, you can choose a street or satellite view. Use the zoom buttons, also at the left, or mouse scroll button to zoom in and out. To search for a location, enter the name in the search box, and options will be listed. To see your current location, click the Geolocation button to the left. To trace routes click the route planner button to the right to open a dialog where you can enter the source and destination locations.

Figure 7-11: GNOME Map

Part 3: Desktops

Ubuntu Desktop
Kubuntu
Ubuntu MATE
Ubuntu Flavors
The Shell

8. Ubuntu Desktop

Ubuntu GNOME

Favorites/Dock

System Status Area

Activities

Applications Overview

Windows

Workspaces

The GNOME Files File Manager

The Ubuntu 22.04 desktop is based on GNOME. As discussed in Chapter 3, check the Ubuntu Desktop Guide for a help and documentation. The Ubuntu GNOME desktop uses the GNOME Files file manager, as well as GNOME desktop configuration tools (see Chapter 3).

GNOME

The GNU Network Object Model Environment, also known as GNOME, is a powerful and easy-to-use environment consisting primarily of a panel, a desktop, and a set of desktop tools with which program interfaces can be constructed. GNOME is designed to provide a flexible platform for the development of powerful applications. Currently, GNOME is supported by several distributions and is the primary interface for the Ubuntu Desktop. GNOME is free and released under the GNU Public License. GTK+ is the widget set used for GNOME applications. The GTK+ widget set is entirely free under the Lesser General Public License (LGPL). The LGPL enables developers to use the widget set with proprietary software, as well as free software (the GPL is restricted to free software).

For detailed documentation, check the GNOME documentation site at **https://help.gnome.org**. Documentation is organized by users, administrators, and developers. "GNOME Help" provides a complete tutorial on desktop use. For administrators, the "GNOME System Administration Guide" details how administrators can manage user desktops. Table 8-1 offers a listing of useful GNOME sites.

Web Site	Description
https://www.gnome.org	Official GNOME website
https://help.gnome.org	GNOME documentation website for users, administrators, and developers
https://wiki.gnome.org/Personalization	Desktop themes and background art
https://wiki.gnome.org/Apps	GNOME software applications, applets, and tools
https://developer.gnome.org/	GNOME developer's site

Table 8-1: GNOME Resources

GNOME releases new versions on a frequent schedule. The Ubuntu Desktop uses GNOME 4.2, with some applications retained from from GNOME 4.1. The Settings About tab will tell you what version of GNOME you are using. Key changes with GNOME 4.0, 4.1, and 4.2 are described in detail at the following:

```
https://help.gnome.org/misc/release-notes/40.0/
https://release.gnome.org/41/
https://release.gnome.org/42/
```

The Ubuntu GNOME Desktop

GNOME is based on the gnome-shell, which is a compositing window manager (see Figure 8-1). The key components of the gnome-shell are a top bar, an Activities overview, the Ubuntu Dock, clock and calendar, and a notifications feature. The top bar has a dialog for the date and time (calendar) with notifications, and a status area menu for sound volume, network connections, power information, and user tasks such as accessing settings and logging out. The

Activities overview lets you quickly access favorite applications, locate applications, select windows, and change workspaces. The notification system notifies you of recent events, such as updates and recently attached devices. To the right of the Activities button is the Applications menu, which is a menu for the currently selected open application, such as the Files menu for a file manager window. The menu will provide a list of all windows open with that application, and some application menus will also have entries for application tasks.

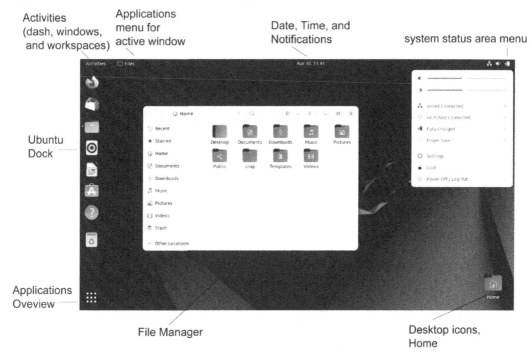

Figure 8-1: GNOME Desktop

You can configure desktop settings and perform most administrative tasks using the GNOME configuration tools (see Table 8-1) listed in the GNOME Settings dialog, accessible from the System Status Area menu (see Figure 8-25). Most use the GNOME 4 configuration and administrative tools such as Background, Lock Screen, Users, and Power. In addition, the GNOME Tweaks application lets you customize your desktop, windows, the top bar, selecting desktop fonts, and changing the appearance (themes and backgrounds).

Top Bar

The screen displays a top bar, through which you access your applications, windows, and such system properties as sound and networking. Clicking the System Status Area button (network, sound, power, and down arrow emblems) at the right of the top bar displays the System Status Area menu with options to set the sound level, screen brightness (laptop), wired and wireless connections, Bluetooth, and to logout, shut down, or lock the screen (see Figure 8-1). The center of the top bar has a button to display your clock and calendar, which will also display your notifications. To the left is the Activities button, which displays thumbnails of your open windows.

The System Status Area

Once logged in, the System Status Area is displayed on the right side of the top bar (see Figure 8-2). The area will include status icons for features such as sound and power. The System Status Area button shows network, sound, power, and down arrow emblems. Clicking the button displays the System Status Area menu, with items for sound, brightness, wired and wireless connections, Bluetooth status, and the battery. It also has entries for opening GNOME Settings, activating the lock screen, power mode profiles, and shutting down or rebooting the system. The sound and brightness items feature sliding bars with which you can adjust the volume and brightness. The Wired, Wi-Fi, Bluetooth, Battery and Power Off/Log Out entries expand to submenus with added entries.

Figure 8-2: System Status Area menu

On systems that are not laptops, there will be no brightness slider or Battery entry on the System Status Area menu. If the system also has no wireless device, the Wi-Fi entry will also be missing. A system of this kind will only have a sound slider and a user entry.

To log out, you click the "Power Off / Log Out" entry to expand the menu to show Log Out, Switch User, Suspend, and Power Off entries. The Log Out returns you to the login screen, where you can log in as another user. The Switch User entry is not shown unless your system has more than one user configured. To switch to another user, click the Switch User entry to display the login screen. You can then log in as another user. When you log out or choose Switch User, you can then select the original user. When you log back in, your session is restored.

Desktop menu and Desktop folder

Right-clicking anywhere on the desktop background displays the desktop menu with entries for the Desktop folder and the access to commonly used GNOME Settings dialogs (see Figure 8-3). You can use this menu to create a new folder directly on the desktop, as well as open the Desktop folder with the file manager or a terminal window. Items you place on the the desktop are located in your home folder's Desktop folder. Adding a file or folder directly to your Desktop folder displays it on your desktop. The "Change Background" entry open GNOME Settings at the

Background dialog where you can choose a new background, and the "Display Settings" entry opens GNOME Settings at the Displays dialog where you can configure your monitor. The Settings entry open GNOME Settings.

Figure 8-3: GNOME Desktop Menu

Should you create a folder on the desktop using the desktop menu, the folder is displayed on the desktop (see Figure 8-4). Its location is your home folder's Desktop folder. You can right-click on a folder on the desktop to display a menu with tasks you can perform on that folder, as shown here.

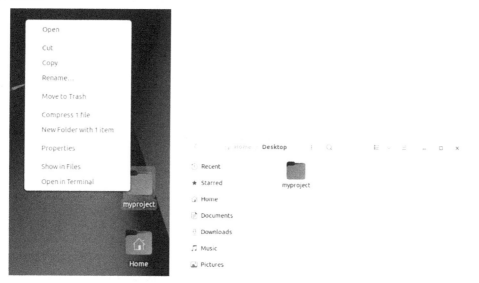

Figure 8-4: GNOME Desktop folder

Activities Overview

To access applications and windows, you use the Activities overview mode. Click the Activities button at the left side of the top bar or press the Super (Windows) key. The Activities overview mode consists of a dash/dock listing your favorite and running applications, thumbnails of open windows, and workspace thumbnails (see Figure 8-5). You can use the search box at the top center to locate applications and files.

Figure 8-5: GNOME Activities Overview

Another way to quickly access the Activities overview is to enable the hot corner option in the Settings Multitasking tab (see Figure 8-6). Instead of clicking on the Activities button, just move your mouse to that upper left corner. The Activities overview is then displayed.

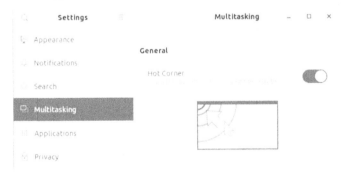

Figure 8-6: GNOME Settings Multitasking tab Hot Corner option

Partially hidden thumbnail of your adjacent desktops workspace are displayed on either side, to the right and left of you current workspace. Ubuntu is initially configured for dynamic, not fixed, workspaces. It shows only your current workspace and an empty one to the right. When you first use another empty workspace, it becomes activated, with another empty one generated to its right. Moving your mouse to the right side moves you to the adjacent workspace, making it your current workspace. To move a window from your current workspace to an adjacent workspace, click and drag it to the right or left side of the screen showing part of the adjacent workspace.

The first time you move to the empty adjacent workspace on the right, that workspace becomes activated and you now have multiple workspaces. Whenever you have multiple workspaces, a workspace selector is displayed at the top of the screen showing thumbnails of your workspaces (see Figure 8-7). You can use the workspace selector to move directly from one workspace to another, as well as move windows displayed in the thumbnails from to another workspace. To move to another workspace, just click on the workspace want. To move a window, click and drag it to another workspace thumbnail.

You can configure your workspaces to be fixed instead of dynamic, setting up a limited number of workspaces. In this case, the workspace thumbnail list is always displayed, letting you move to whatever workspace you want with just a click. Fixed and dynamic workspaces are configured in the the Settings Multitasking tab in the Workspaces section.

You can manually leave the Activities overview mode at any time by pressing the ESC key, the Super key, or clicking the activities button on the top bar.

Figure 8-7: GNOME Activities Overview with workspace selector (multiple workspaces)

Ubuntu Dock and GNOME Dash

The Ubuntu dock is a bar on the left side of the desktop with icons for your favorite applications (see Figure 8-8). It is displayed on the desktop and Activities and Applications overviews. The Ubuntu dock is a GNOME extension implemented by Ubuntu and is a modified version of the GNOME Dock to Dash extension, which places the GNOME dash on the desktop. Both the Ubuntu Dock and the GNOME Dash look the same and operate in the same way, and both are referred to as the Ubuntu dock. Initially, there are icons for the Firefox web browser, Thunderbird mail, Files (the GNOME file manager), Rhythmbox music application, LibreOffice

Writer, Ubuntu Software, GNOME help, the Trash folder, and the Applications overview. To open an application from the dock, click its icon, or right-click and choose New Window from the pop-up menu. On the Activities overview click-and-drag the icon to the windows thumbnail area or to a workspace thumbnail at the top. Clicking on the dock icon for an application with an open window, brings that window to the forefront. If you want, you can change this action to a minimize operation instead. In that case clicking the icon would minimize the open window. To do so you have to change the default action using **gsettings** or the the **deconf** editor. The setting to change is org.gnome.shell.extensions.dash-to-dock's click action option.

```
gsettings set org.gnome.shell.extensions.dash-to-dock click-action 'minimize'
```

Favorites are always displayed on the dock. When you run other applications, they are also placed on the dock during the time they are running. To add a running application to the dock as a favorite, right-click the icon on the dock and choose Add to Favorites. You can later remove an application as a favorite by choosing Remove from Favorites. You can also add any application to the dock from the Applications overview, by clicking-and-dragging its icon to the dock, or by right-clicking the icon and choosing Add to Favorites from the menu (see Figure 8-8).

Should you want to disable the dock, no longer showing it, you can do so by switching off the Ubuntu Dock entry in the Extensions application. The GNOME dock on the Activities and application overview will remain, as this is integral to the GNOME desktop.

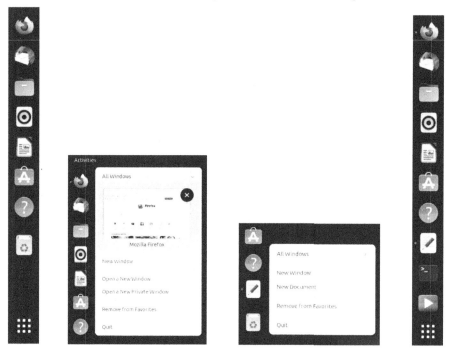

Figure 8-8: Dock/Dash with favorites and running applications

You can configure the Ubuntu dock using the Settings Appearance tab's Dock section (see Figure 8-9). Here you can adjust the size of the icons, the location of the dock on the screen (left, right, bottom), and whether to hide the dock when not in use (Auto-hide). The "Configure dock behavior" entry opens a dialog with options to include unmounted and network file systems, and whether to show the trash.

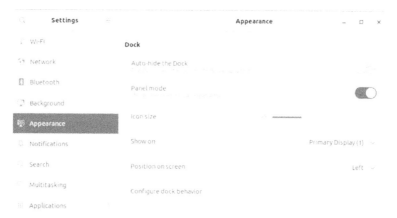

Figure 8-9: Dock Configuration on Settings Appearance

Window Thumbnails

You access windows using the window thumbnails on the Activities overview. Thumbnails are displayed of all your open windows (see Figure 8-10). To select a window, move your mouse over the window's thumbnail. The selected window also shows an x (close) button at the top right of the window's thumbnail, which you can use to close the window directly. To access the window, move your mouse over it and click. This displays the window, exiting the overview and returning to the desktop.

Figure 8-10: Window thumbnails

The windows displayed are those for the current workspace. To see windows for another workspace, you can use the scroll button on your mouse to scroll through workspaces, as well as use the Ctrl-Alt left and right arrow keys. To move to just the next or previous workspace you can click on the part of the workspace displayed on the left and right sides of the screen. As you move to a different workspace, the windows on that workspace are displayed (see Figure 8-11). You can also move windows or applications directly to an adjoining workspace by clicking and dragging it to the right and left side of the screen, which then switches you to the adjoining workspace. Your window is now placed on that workspace.

As noted previously, whenever you have multiple workspaces, a workspace selector is displayed at the top of the screen showing thumbnails of your workspaces. You can use the workspace selector to move directly from one workspace to another, as well as move windows displayed in the thumbnails to other workspaces. To move a window from one workspace to another, click and drag it to another workspace thumbnail in the workspace selector.

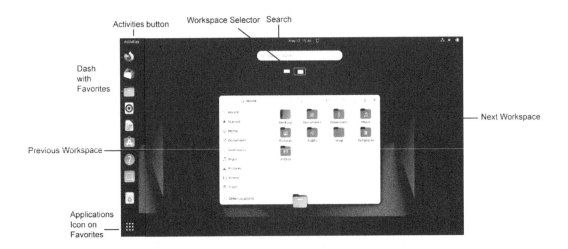

Activities Overview with workspace selector

Figure 8-11: Workspace thumbnails with workspace selector

Applications Overview

Clicking the Applications icon (last icon, grid button) on the dash opens the Applications overview, from which you can locate and open applications. Icons for installed applications are displayed (see Figure 8-12). The Frequent button at the bottom of the overview lets you see only your most frequently used applications. Click the All button to see them all. A pager consisting of buttons, on the right side, lets you move quickly through the list of applications. You can move anywhere to a page in the list using the buttons. There is a special application folder called Utilities. Clicking on its icon opens another, smaller overview, showing system tool applications, such as Tweak Tool and Backups. Click an application icon to open it and exit the overview. Should you return to the overview mode, you will see its window in the overview. The super key (Windows key) with the **a** key (super+a) will switch automatically from the desktop to the Applications overview. Continuing to press it, switches between the applications overview and the window thumbnails.

The top of the Applications overview shows the workspace selector that contains thumbnails of your workspaces. You can switch to another workspace directly by clicking its thumbnail.

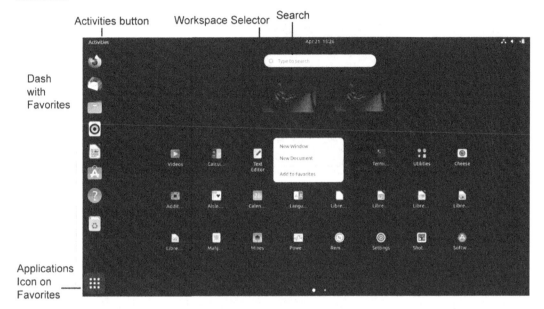

Applications Overview with workspace selector

Figure 8-12: Applications overview

To add an application as a favorite on the dock, you can simply drag its icon from the Applications overview to the dock directly.

Overview Application Folders

You can organize the overview icons into application folders, much in the same way as your phone. Decide on two icons you want to group into a folder, and then drag one icon on top of the other. A new application folder is automatically created for them, placing both within the new application folder. You can then add more icons to the folder.

The name given to the folder will be based on the category of the icon you dragged the other icon to. Clicking on the folder open a dialog displaying the icons and an edit button on the top left. Click on the edit button to change the folder's name.

To remove an icon from a folder, open the folder and drag the icon outside the folder dialog. Removing all the icons from the folder will also remove the folder.

In Figure 8-13, the LibreOffice Calc icon is dragged to the LibreOffice Draw icon, creating a new application folder that is named Graphics. This folder is then opened and its name edited and changed to LibreOffice (see Figure 8-14). The LibreOffice Writer and LibreOffice Impress icons are then added to the new LibreOffice application folder (see Figure 8-15).

Figure 8-13: Creating Overview Application Folders

Figure 8-14: Changing Overview Application Folder Names

Figure 8-15: Adding Icons to an Overview Application Folder

You can make as many application folders as you want. In Figure 8-16, a Game folder is created by dragging the Mahjongg icon to the Mines icon. The new application folder is automatically created and given the default name Games, as Mines is a game. AisleRiot and Sudoku are then added to it.

Figure 8-16: Overview Application Folders

Activities Search

The Activities search will search applications and files. Should you know the name of the application you want, you can simply start typing, and the matching results are displayed (see Figure 8-17). Your search term is entered in the search box as you type. The results dynamically narrow the more you type. The first application is selected automatically. If this is the one you want, just press ENTER to start it. Results will also show Settings tools as well as folders and files files.

The search box for the Activities overview can be configured from the Settings Search tab (see Figure 8-18). Here, you can turn search on or off and specify which applications are to support searches. By default, these include Calendar, the Files file manager, Passwords and Keys, and terminal. You can also configure search permissions for applications using the Settings Application dialogs. Other GNOME applications are added automatically when installed such as GNOME Notes, Photos, Documents, and Weather. You can change the priority of the applications searched by moving them up or down in the list.

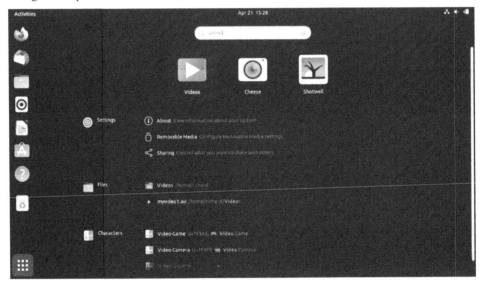

Figure 8-17: Activities - search box

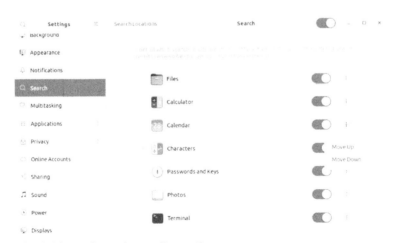

Figure 8-18: Activities - Search configuration

Managing Windows

You can select the color accents of your windows using the Settings Appearance tab(see Figure 8-19). In the Style section, you can choose either a light or dark theme (Light is the default). You can also choose an accent color from the Color buttons. Clicking on an button changes the colors for your desktop immediately.

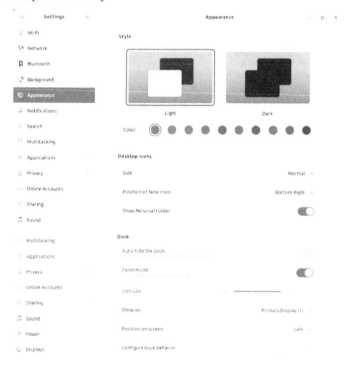

Figure 8-19: Window colors, Settings | Appearance

The title bar and the toolbar for GNOME windows have been combined into a single header bar, as shown in the following for the file manager.

The minimize and maximize buttons are shown on the right side of the header bar by default. The display of these buttons can be configured by the Tweak Tool's Window Titlebars tab. The maximize operations can also be carried out by a dragging operation or by double-clicking the header bar. To maximize a window, double-click its header bar or drag the header bar to the top edge of the screen. To return a window to its normal size, drag the title away from the top edge of the screen. You can also use a window's menu entries to maximize or minimize it. Right-click the header bar or press Alt+spacebar to display the window menu. The option to resize an application window by dragging to the top, right, or left edge is set in the Settings Multitasking tab as Active Screen Edges (see Figure 8-20). Turning this option off no longer resizes the window when you move it to the top, right, or left edge of the screen.

Note: The Active Screen Edges function for the left and right edge does not work for Files file manager (the top edge does work).

Figure 8-20: Settings Multitasking Active Screen Edges option

Open application windows also have an Applications menu on the left side of the top bar (see Figure 8-21). For applications that can support multiple open windows such as the file manager and Web browsers, the Open Windows list in this menu will show all the open windows for that application. You can use it to move quickly to another of the application's windows. Such applications will also have an "Open in a New Window" entry for new application windows. Some applications will also list tasks in this menu such as Rythmbox's Play and Next operations and Firefox's Open a New Private Window. This menu will always have a Quit entry (see Figure 8-21). Be warned that this menu's Quit entry will close all the open windows for this application, not just the active one.

Figure 8-21: Window with Applications menu

For favorite applications on the dock, a corresponding application menu is also provided. Right-click on the dock icon to display this menu, which will show an "All windows" entry, a "New window" entry, "Remove from Favorites", and a Quit entry. Also any task for that application will also be listed such as "Open a New Private Window" for Firefox. The menu will also show a Quit entry. If multiple windows are open for an application, the Quit entry will also show the number of windows it will close, such as "Quit 3 windows."

Clicking on the "All windows" entry displays a submenu show thumbnails for all the open windows for that application (see Figure 8-22). Move through the list to select a window you want to either switch to or close. A close button appears on the currently selected thumbnail.

Figure 8-22: Favorites window thumbnails

To minimize an open window so that it no longer displays on the desktop, click the minimize button on the header bar or right-click the header bar to display the window menu and choose minimize. This will hide the window. You can then display the window later, using the window's thumbnails on the activities overview (Activities button). If the application for a minimized window is shown on the dock, you can display that minimized window again by using that dock icon's menu "All windows" entry. Right-click on the dock icon and click on the "All windows" entry to display all the open windows. Find the minimized one you want, and then click on it to re-display that window. If a minimized window is one of several windows open for a given application, such as one of several file manager windows, you can use the Open Windows list in the applications menu (top bar) to find the minimized window and select it to display it. First you will have to click on any of that application's displayed windows so that you can access the application menu for that application on the top bar.

To close a window, click its close box or right-click on its titlebar and choose "Close" from the menu. You can also choose the Quit entry in the application menu on the top bar, though, if you have multiple windows open for that application, this Quit entry will close all of them.

To tile a window, click-and-drag its header bar to the left or right edge of the screen. When your mouse reaches the edge of the screen, the window is tiled to take up that half of the screen (see Figure 8-23). You can do the same with another window for the other edge, showing two windows side by side. Tiling currently does not work for the file manager windows.

Figure 8-23: Window Tiling

To resize a window, move the mouse to the edge or corner or the window until it changes to an edge or corner mouse, then click-and-drag.

The scrollbar to the right also features fine scrolling. When scrolling through a large number of items, you can fine scroll to slow the scrolling when you reach a point to search. To activate fine scrolling, click and hold the scrollbar handle, or press the Shift key while scrolling.

You can use the Window Switcher on the desktop to search open windows. Press the Alt+Tab keys to display an icon bar of open windows on the current workspace (see Figure 8-24). While holding down the Alt key, press the Tab key to move through the list of windows. Instead of continuing to press the Tab keys to move through the list of windows, you can use the forward and back arrow keys while holding the Alt key down. To move through the applications directly use the Super key (Windows key) and the Tab key, Super-Tab. Open windows are grouped by application and displayed as a list below the selected application. This is helpful if you have many windows open that use a many of the same applications. For those applications with multiple open windows, press the tilde (~) key (above the Tab key) to move through a list of the open windows.

Figure 8-24: Window Switcher (Alt+Tab)

On the GNOME Tweak Tool's Windows tab, you can configure certain windows' actions and components. Attached Modal Dialogs will attach a dialog that an application opens to the application's window (see Figure 8-25). You can use the switch to turn this feature off, allowing you to move a modal dialog away from the application window. The Window Titlebar tab lets you configure actions on the title bar, such as double-click to maximize and secondary-click to display the menu (see Figure 8-26). There are also switches to display the Maximize and Minimize buttons on the title bar, and buttons to position them on the right or left side.

Figure 8-25: GNOME Tweak Tool, Windows configuration

Figure 8-26: GNOME Tweak Tool, Window Titlebars configuration

Workspaces

You can organize your windows into different workspaces. Workspaces are accessed using the Workspace selector in either the Activities or Applications overview. Workspaces can be either dynamic or fixed. As installed, Ubuntu is configured to use dynamic workspaces. You can use the Settings Multitasking tab to change workspaces from dynamic to fixed, letting you specify a fixed number of workspaces (see Figure 8-27).

Figure 8-27: GNOME Settings Multitasking tab Dynamic and Fixed workspaces

With dynamic workspaces, any empty workspaces (those without open windows) are automatically removed. A new empty workspace is always generated to the right of the last workspace. If you are using only one workspace, that workspace will have an one empty workspace to the right. With fixed workspaces you can have empty workspaces (see Figure 8-28). The Activities overview with dynamic and fixed workspaces is shown in Figure 8-29.

Figure 8-28: Workspaces, dynamic and fixed.

Figure 8-29: Workspaces on the activities overview, dynamic and fixed

Should you be using multiple monitors, on the Settings Multitasking tab you can specify whether the workspaces should be on the primary display or on all displays (see Figure 8-30).

Figure 8-30: GNOME Settings Multitasking - workspaces on multiple monitors

You can choose which workspace to use with the workspace selector. This is an thumbnail bar at the top of the Activities and Applications overviews. To move to a workspace click on its thumbnail in the workspace selector (see Figure 8-31). You can also use Ctrl+Alt with the right and left arrow keys to move to the next or previous workspaces. For dynamic workspaces, if you use only one workspace, then the workspace selector is not shown. If you start using another workspace, the workspace selector is then displayed. For fixed workspaces, the workspace selector is always shown, displaying thumbnails for all you workspaces, even the empty ones.

Figure 8-31: Workspace selector on the Applications overview - dynamic and fixed

The workspace selector appears differently in the Activities and Application overviews. On the Application overview it appears as large thumbnails, and on the Activities overview it appears and small thumbnails (see Figure 8-32). Even though the thumbnails on the Activities overview are small, you can still move open windows between the thumbnails, changing their workspace.

Figure 8-32: Workspace selector on the Applications and Activities overviews

The Activities overview provides yet another way to move to another workspace. Other workspaces are partially shown on the left or right of the screen. Click on one to move to that workspace, showing it on the Activities window.

You can also move an open window in a workspace to another workspace using the workspace selector. The workspace thumbnails in the workspace selector show thumbnails of your open windows in that workspace. You can click and drag a window thumbnail to any other workspace thumbnail in the selector, moving the window to that workspace.

You can also move a window using the window's menu and choose Move to Workspace Down or Move to Workspace Up.

On the Activities overview, you can move an open window to an adjacent workspace by clicking and dragging it to the part of the adjacent workspace showing on either side of the screen. You can also use Ctrl+Alt+Shift and the up or down arrow keys to move the window to the next workspace. Continue pressing the arrow to move it further should you have several workspaces.

Notifications and Message dialog

Notifications, such as software updates and removable device activation, are displayed in the message area on the left side of the clock/calendar dialog (see Figure 8-33). Click on the clock/calendar button on the center of the top panel to display your messages. You can also press the super key with the **m** key to display your messages. The dialog has a "Do not Disturb" switch at the bottom, which you can flip to turn off notification pop-ups such as those for newly attached drives. Notifications will still be listed in the clock/calendar dialog. A Clear button lets you delete all the displayed notifications.

When you first attach a removable device such as a USB drive or DVD, a pop-up notification is displayed asking you what you want to do, such as open it with the file manager.

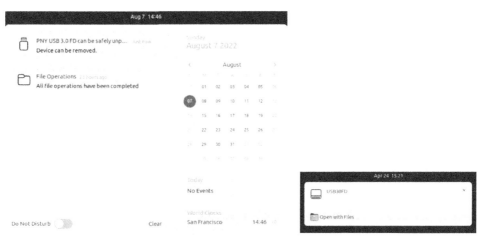

Figure 8-33: Notifications

Desktop Customization with Tweak Tool: Themes, Icons, Fonts, and Startup Applications

You can perform common desktop customizations using the GNOME Tweak Tool. Areas to customize include the desktop icons, fonts, themes, startup applications, workspaces, window behavior, and the time display. You can access Tweak Tool from the Applications overview Utilities application folder. The GNOME Tweak Tool has tabs for Appearance, Fonts, Keyboard and Mouse, Startup Applications, Top Bar, Window Titlebars, and Windows (see Figure 8-34).

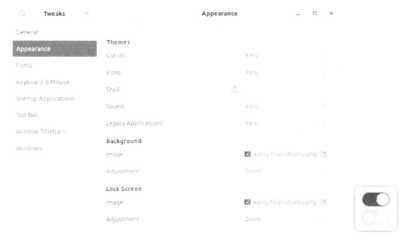

Figure 8-34: GNOME Tweak Tool - Appearance tab (themes)

The General tab lets can suspend the system when the laptop lid is closed.

The Appearance tab lets you set the theme for your windows, icons, and cursor. Ubuntu uses the Yaru theme as its default. GNOME traditionally uses the Adwaita Theme, with its light and dark variant.

Desktop fonts for window titles, interface (application or dialog text), documents, and monospace (terminal windows or code) can be changed in the Fonts tab. You can adjust the size of the font or change the font style. Clicking the font name opens a "Pick a Font" dialog from which you can choose a different font. The quality of text display can be further adjusted with Hinting and Antialiasing options. To simply increase or decrease the size of all fonts on your desktop interface, you can adjust the Scaling Factor.

At times, there may be certain applications that you want started up when you log in, such as the Gedit text editor, the Firefox web browser, or the Videos movie player. On the Startup Applications tab, you can choose the applications to start up. Click the plus (+) button to open an applications dialog from which you can choose an application to start up. Once added, you can later remove the application by clicking its Remove button.

Desktop Customization with Extensions

Extensions function much as applets did in GNOME 2. They are third-party programs that enhance or modify the GNOME desktop. You can use the Extensions application to manage your extensions. It is not installed by default. You can install it with Ubuntu Software (Utilities category). Extensions will fully manage your extensions, letting you turn off the Ubuntu built-in extension like Desktop Icons or Ubuntu Dock (unlike Tweak Tool). You can open Extensions from the application overview. It displays a dialog showing your Built-in extensions, with switches to the right for turning them on or off (see Figure 8-35). Switching the Ubuntu Dock extension off will disable the Ubuntu Dock and no longer display it, though the GNOME dock is still shown on the activities overview and application overview as this is an integral part of the GNOME desktop. Switching off the Ubuntu Icons extension no longer displays the icons on your desktop.

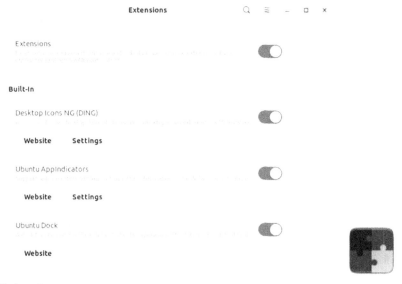

Figure 8-35: Extensions

If an extension can be configured, it will display a Settings button below its name, as is the case with the Desktop Icons extension. Clicking on the Settings button open a dialog with options for the extension (see Figure 8-36). For the Desktop extension you can add the trash, network drives, and external drives such as USB drives to the desktop. You can set the size of the icons (standard, tiny, small, and large) as well as select which corner you of the screen you want them displayed. You can also choose to display hidden files and use dark text for icon names.

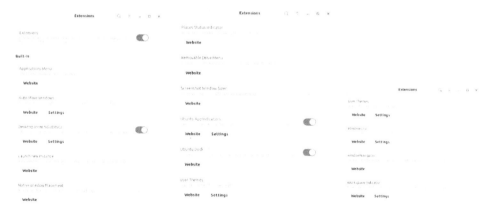

Figure 8-36: Extension Configuration

You can also use Extensions to manage any additional extensions you installed with **gnome-shell-extensions** (see Figure 8-37). You can install it in a terminal window with the **apt install** command. These extensions function much as applets did in GNOME 2. They are third-party programs that enhance or modify the GNOME desktop, such as a window list, workspace indicator, a removable drive menu, and an applications menu. Extensions appear on the top bar or, in the case of the window list, in an added bottom bar.

Figure 8-37: Extensions with added GNOME shell extensions

There is a switch on the at the top of the Extension dialog labeled Extensions that you can use to turn off all extensions. This does not apply to the three Ubuntu built-in extensions, but will work on the added GNOME shell extensions.

Desktop Customization: manually placing application launchers on the Desktop

To place an application launcher directly on desktop, as you could with older versions of GNOME, you would copy the application's launcher file to your Desktop folder, and then make that copy launchable. The launcher files for applications are located in the **/usr/share/applications** folder and have the extension **.desktop**. You can open this folder using your file manager and clicking the Other Locations entry in the sidebar, and then clicking on the Computer icon. Access the **/usr/share/applications** folder (see Figure 8-38). Then open another file manager window and click the Desktop entry in the sidebar. Find the application launcher you want to copy in the Applications folder, and then click and drag it, while holding the **Ctrl** key, to the Desktop folder. The launcher file will appear on your desktop as a file. Right-click it and select the "Allow Launching" entry (see Figure 8-39). The launcher file will be displayed as its application icon on the desktop, which you can double-click to start that application.

![Figure 8-38 image]

Figure 8-38: Accessing and copying application launchers

Figure 8-39: Application Launchers on the Desktop

GNOME Desktop Help

The GNOME Help browser provides a browser-like interface for displaying the GNOME Desktop Help and documentation for various GNOME applications, such as System Monitor, Software Updater, Rhythmbox, and Gedit. You can access it from the dock (question mark icon) or from the Applications overview Utilities application folder (see Figure 8-40). It features a toolbar that enables you to move through the list of previously viewed documents. You can even bookmark specific items. You can search for topics using the search box, with results displayed in the drop-down menu. Initially, the Ubuntu Desktop Help manual is displayed. To see other help pages and manuals, choose All Help from the menu next to the close box (see Figure 8-41).

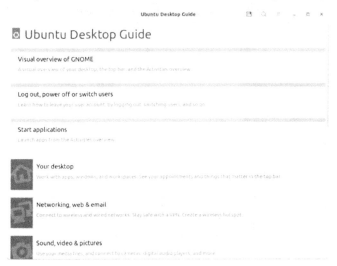

Figure 8-40: GNOME Help browser

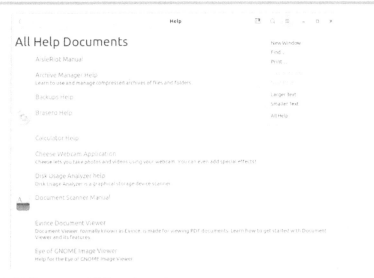

Figure 8-41: GNOME Help - All Documents

The GNOME Files File Manager

The GNOME file manager supports the standard features for copying, removing, and deleting items as well as setting permissions and displaying items. The name used for the file manager is Files, but the actual program name is still nautilus. When you select a file manager window, a Files menu appears as the Applications menu on the top bar to the left (see Figure 8-42). The Files menu lists your open folder windows, which you can use to quickly access those windows. It also has has an entry for opening a new file manager window (see Table 8-2).

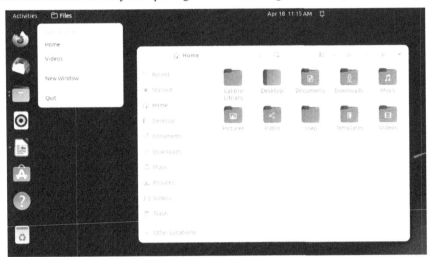

Figure 8-42: File manager with Files applications menu

Menu Item	Description
open windows list	Entries for file manager windows, folders you have opened and display in separate file manager windows.
New Window	Open a new file manager window
Quit	Close the file manager

Table 8-2: File Manager GNOME Menu (top bar)

Home Folder Subfolders

GNOME uses the Common User Directory Structure (xdg-user-dirs at **http://freedesktop.org**) to set up subfolders in the user home folder (directory). Folders include Documents, Music, Pictures, Downloads, and Videos. These localized user folders are used as defaults by many desktop applications. Users can change their folder names or place them within each other using the GNOME file browser. For example, Music can be moved into Videos or Documents into Pictures. Local configuration is held in the **.config/user-dirs.dirs** file. System-wide defaults are set up in the **/etc/xdg/user-dirs.defaults** file. You can edit the local configuration using a text editor and change the folders for the current ones.

File Manager Windows

When you click the Files icon on the dock, a file manager window opens showing your home folder. The file manager window displays several components, including a toolbar and a sidebar (see Figure 8-43). The sidebar displays folder, device, bookmark, and network items showing your removable file systems and the default home folders. You can choose to display or hide the sidebar toolbar by selecting the Show Sidebar entry in the Tools menu. The main pane (to the right) displays the icons or lists files and subfolders in the current folder.

When you select a file, a status section at the bottom right of the window displays the name of the file and its size. Selecting several files displays the number of files selected and their total size. When you select a folder, a status section shows the name of the folder and the number of items in the folder. Selecting several folders displays the number of folders selected and the total number of folders and files in them.

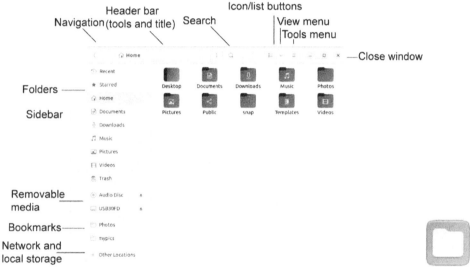

Figure 8-43: File manager with sidebar

When you open a new folder, the same window is used to display it, and you can use the forward and back arrows to move through previously opened folders (top left). As you open subfolders, the main toolbar displays buttons for your current folder and its parent folders, as shown here:

You can click a folder button to move to it directly. You can also display a location URL text box instead of buttons, from which you can enter the location of a folder, either on your system or on a remote one. Press Ctrl+l to display the text box. Press the ESC key to revert back to the folder location buttons.

The button for the current folder displays a menu button (three vertical dots) which you can click to display the folder menu for the current folder (see Figure 8-44). The menu shows common folder tasks such as creating a new folder, bookmarking the folder, and selecting all items in the folder. The Restore Missing Files entry can restore files from a backup archive. The Properties entry displays the folders Properties dialog, showing folder information, permissions, and the folder sharing dialog for this folder. You can also open the folder in a terminal window, which is useful for running shell commands on the folder files and subfolders or running shell scripts from that folder (see Figure 8-45).

Figure 8-44: File manager folder menu

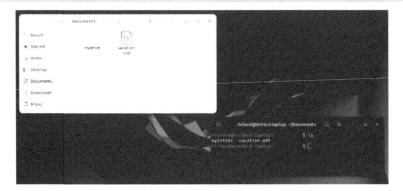

Figure 8-45: File manager folder menu - Open in Terminal

You can right-click anywhere on the empty space on the main pane of a file manager window to display a pop-up menu with entries to create a new folder, select all icons in the folder, open the current folder in a terminal window with a command line prompt, and open the file manager properties dialog. A right-click on the icon for any of the subfolders in the current folder displays a folder menu for operations on that subfolder.

When you create a folder, a New Folder dialog is displayed with a text box where you enter the name of the new folder (see Figure 8-46).

Figure 8-46: File manager New Folder

Menu Item	Description
New Folder	Creates a new subfolder in the current folder
Add to Bookmarks	Bookmark this folder and display an entry for it on the sidebar
Paste	Pastes files that you have copied or cut, letting you move or copy files between folders, or make duplicates
Select All	Select all files and folders in the current folder
Properties	Opens the Properties dialog for the folder
Restore Missing Files	Restore missing files from backups
Open in Terminal	Open a terminal window at the current folder

Table 8-3: File Manager Folder Menu

File Manager Sidebar

The file manager sidebar shows file system locations that you can access such as folders, devices, bookmarks, and network folders (See Figure 8-47). The Recent folder holds links to your recently used files. Selecting the Other Locations entry opens a folder with a Computer icon which you can open to place you at the top of the file system, letting you move to any accessible part of it. Should you bookmark a folder (Add to Bookmarks entry in the folder menu), the bookmark will appear on the sidebar. To remove or rename a bookmark, right-click its entry on the sidebar and choose Remove or Rename from the pop-up menu. The bookmark's name changes, but not the original folder name.

You can also mark a file or folder as a favorite and have them displayed in the Starred folder. Right-click on the file and choose Star from the pop-up menu. To see your favorites, click the Starred entry on the sidebar.

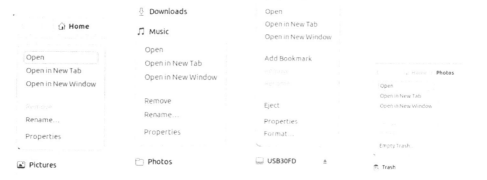

Figure 8-47: File manager sidebar menus

Tabs

The GNOME file manager supports tabs with which you can open several folders in the same file manager window. To open a tab, click the tab button on the Tools menu (see Figure 8-43) or press Ctrl+t. You can use the Tabs buttons to move from one tab to another, or to rearrange tabs.

You can also use the Ctrl+PageUp and Ctrl+PageDown keys to move from one tab to another. Use the Shift+Ctrl+PageUp and Shift+Ctrl+PageDown keys to rearrange the tabs. To close a tab, click its close (x) button on the right side of the tab (see Figure 8-48), or press Ctrl+w. Tabs are detachable. You can drag a tab out to open a separate window.

Figure 8-48: File manager window with tabs

Displaying and Managing Files and Folders

You can view a folder's contents as icons or as a detailed list, which you can choose by clicking the icon/list button between the search and view menu buttons on the right side of the toolbar as shown here. This button toggles between icon and list views.

Use the Ctrl key to change views quickly: Ctrl+1 for Icons and Ctrl+2 for list. The List view provides the name, size, date, and favorite status. Buttons are displayed for each field across the top of the main pane. You can use these buttons to sort the list according to that field. For example, to sort the files by date, click the Modified button; to sort by size, click Size. Click again to alternate between ascending and descending order. Certain types of file icons display previews of their contents. For example, the icons for image files display a thumbnail of the image.

To the right of the list/icon button is a button for the View menu (down-arrow). The Views menu has entries for managing and sorting your file manager icons (see Table 8-4) (see Figure 8-49). The sort entries allow you to sort your icons by name (A-Z and Z-A), size, type, and modification date. You can also reverse the order by name and modification date. At the top of the menu is a zoom bar, with zoom in and zoom out buttons, showing the zoom percentage between them. The zoom in button (+ button) enlarges your view of the window, making icons bigger. The zoom out button (- button) reduces your view, making them smaller. You can also use the Ctrl++ and Ctrl+- keys to zoom in and out. The Reload button refreshes the display, updating any changes. You may need to do this for folders connected to remote sites, where changes have been made on the remote site, but may not show up on your folder.

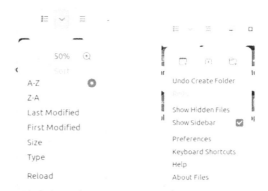

Figure 8-49: File manager View and Tools menus

Menu Item	Description
Zoom In button	Enlarge icon size
Zoom Out button	Reduce icon size
Undo	Undo the previous operation
Redo	Redo an undo operation
A-Z	Sort in alphabetic order
Z-A	Sort in reverse alphabetic order
Last Modified	Sort by last modified date
First Modified	Sort by recent modified date
Size	Sort by file size
Type	Sort by file type
Reload	Refreshes file and folder list

Table 8-4: File Manager View Menu

To the right of the View menu is a button for the Tools menu (lines icon) (see Table 8-5). The Tools menu has toolbars for managing folders and files, as well as entries for configuring the file manager display. The top bar of the Tools menu has buttons to access the home folder, create a new file manager tab, and to create a new folder. An edit toolbar lets you cut, copy, and paste selected files and folders instead of using mouse drag operations. There are entries for selecting all items in the folder, showing hidden files, and showing the sidebar. The Keyboard Shortcuts entry displays the list of available shortcut keys, organized by function such as open operations, tabs, navigation, view operations, and edit tasks such as renaming, editing, and copying files.

The Preferences entry opens the Files Preferences dialog where you can configure your file manager interface by view, behavior, columns listed (list view), and search and preview (thumbnail) options.

Menu Item	Description
New Folder button	Creates a new subfolder in the current folder
Bookmark button	Creates bookmark for current folder
Tab button	Creates a new tab
Edit toolbar	Shows buttons for cut, copy, and paste folders and files
Select All	Select all items in the current folder
Show Hidden Files	Shows administrative dot files
Sidebar	Toggle display of the sidebar on an off
Preferences	Open the Files Preferences dialog
Keyboard Shortcuts	Display a dialog listing keyboard shortcuts
Help	Open GNOME desktop help
About Files	Display the about dialog for Files, showing the version and a link to its Web site.

Table 8-5: File Manager Tools Menu

Navigating in the File Manager

The file manager operates similarly to a web browser, using the same window to display opened folders. It maintains a list of previously viewed folders, and you can move back and forth through that list using the toolbar buttons. The left arrow button moves you to the previously displayed folder, and the right arrow button moves you to the next displayed folder. Use the sidebar to access your storage devices (USB, DVD/CD, and attached hard drives), as well as mounted network folders. You can also access your home folders, trash, and recent files. As noted, the Computer icon on the Other Locations folder opens your root (top) system folder.

To open a subfolder, you can double-click its icon or right-click the icon and select Open from the menu (see Table 8-6). To open the folder in a new tab, select Open in New Tab.

You can open any folder or file system listed in the sidebar by clicking it. You can also right-click an entry to display a menu with entries to Open in a New Tab and Open in a New Window (see Table 8-7). The menu for the Trash entry lets you empty the trash. You can also remove and rename the bookmarks.

Entries for removable devices in the sidebar, such as USB drives, also have eject buttons and a menu item for Eject. Internal hard drives have an Unmount option instead.

Menu Item	Description
Open	Opens the file with its associated application. Folders are opened in the file manager. Associated applications are listed.
Open in New Tab	Opens a folder in a new tab in the same window
Open in New Window	Opens a folder in a new file manager window
Open With Other Application	Selects an application with which to open this file. An Open With dialog lists the possible applications
Cut, Copy	Cuts or copies the selected file
Copy To	Copies a file to another folder
Move To	Moves a file to another folder
Rename (F2)	Renames the file
Move To Trash	Moves a file to the Trash folder, where you can later delete it
Send to	E-mails the file
Compress	Archives the file with zip, tar.xz, or 7z formats
Star	Mark the file for folder as a favorite to be displayed by clicking the Starred entry in the sidebar
Properties	Displays the Properties dialog
Open in Terminal	Open a folder in a terminal window
Local Network Share	Open the sharing dialog for a folder

Table 8-6: The File and Folder Pop-up Menu

Menu Item	Description
Open	Opens the file with its associated application. Folders are opened in the file manager. Associated applications are listed.
Open in a New Tab	Opens a folder in a new tab in the same window
Open in a New Window	Opens a folder in a separate window, accessible from the toolbar with a right-click
Remove	Removes the bookmark from the sidebar
Rename	Renames the bookmark
Properties	Open the folder's properties dialog

Table 8-7: The File Manager Sidebar Pop-up Menu

Managing Files and Folders

As a GNOME-compliant file manager, Files supports desktop drag-and-drop operations for copying and moving files. To move a file or folder, drag-and-drop from one folder to another.

The move operation is the default drag-and-drop operation in GNOME. To copy a file to a new location, press the Ctrl key as you drag-and-drop.

You can also perform remove, rename, and copy operations on a file by right-clicking its icon and selecting the action you want from the pop-up menu that appears (see Table 8-5). For example, to remove an item, right-click it and select the Move To Trash entry from the menu. This places it in the Trash folder, where you can later delete it.

Renaming Files

To rename a file, you can either right-click the file's icon and select the Rename entry from the pop-up menu or click its icon and press the F2 function key. A dialog is displayed with the current name in a small text box (see Figure 8-50). You can overwrite the old one or edit the current name by clicking a position in the name to insert text, as well as by using the Backspace key to delete characters. When renaming a file, be sure to click the Rename button once you have entered the new name. You can also rename a file by entering a new name in its Properties dialog box (Basic tab).

Figure 8-50: File manager Rename dialog

You can also change several filenames at once by selecting the files and then right-clicking and choosing Rename. A dialog opens listing the selected files and a text box for specifying the new names (see Figure 8-51). You can add to the name (Rename using a template) or choose the "Find and replace text" option to change a common part of the names. For the template option, clicking the Add button lets you choose from a list of possible automatic number formats to add. The template is displayed in brackets in the text box. The Original File Name entry adds the original file name specifier to the text box, should you remove it. Once you have selected a template, an Automatic Number Order menu is displayed with options for sorting the renamed files (ascending, descending, first or last modified.

Figure 8-51: File manager - Renaming several files at once - template

The "Find and replace text" option lets you replace a common part of the names (see Figure 8-52). This could even be the file type if you wish. The selected parts of the files to be change will be highlighted. Should you want to undo the changes, press Ctrl-Z in the file manager window.

Figure 8-52: File manager - Renaming several files at once - Find and Replace

Compress and Archive Files

You can also compress and archive files and folders (see Figure 8-53). Select the files or folders to compress and archive, right-click and choose the Compress option. A Create Archive dialog opens where you can specify the name of the compressed archive and the archive format. Choose the format of the archive from the list below the name (zip, tar, and 7z).

Figure 8-53: File manager - Compress and Archive dialogs

Copying Files

To copy a file to a new location, press the Ctrl key as you drag-and-drop. When copying a large file or many files, an icon is displayed on the titlebar to the right showing a circle chart and the progress of the copy operation (see Figure 8-54). Clicking on the icon displays a menu showing the progress of the copy operation, with an x to the right you can click to cancel the copy. When the copy process for a file is completed, the x becomes a checkmark. When the entire copy process is completed for all files, the icon shows a full circle.

Figure 8-54: File manager - Copying files

Grouping Files

You can select a group of files and folders by clicking the first item and then holding down the Shift key while clicking the last item, or by clicking and dragging the mouse across items you want to select. To select separated items, hold the Ctrl key down as you click the individual icons. If you want to select all the items in the folder, choose the Select All entry from the Tools menu (Tools | Select All), or choose Ctrl+a. You can then copy, move, or delete several files at once.

Opening Applications and Files MIME Types

You can start any application in the file manager by double-clicking either the application or a data file used for that application. If you want to open the file with a specific application, you can right-click the file and select one of the Open With entries. One or more Open With entries will be displayed for default and possible applications, such as Open With Text Editor for a text file. If the application you want is not listed, you can select Open With Other Application to access a list of available applications.

To change or set the default application to use for a certain type of file, you open a file's Properties dialog and select the Open With tab. Here, you can choose the default application to use for that kind of file. Possible applications will be listed, organized as the default, recommended, and other categories. Click the one you want, and click the "Set as default" button. Once you choose the default, it will appear in the Open With list for this file.

The Recommended Applications list is the the list of applications shown in the Open With Other Application's Select Application dialog. If you want to add an application to this dialog, click the entry for that application in the Other Applications section and then click the Add button at the bottom of the Open With tab. The application will be moved to the Recommended Applications list. If there is an application on the Open With tab's Recommended Applications list that you do not want listed, right-click it and choose Forget association. It will no longer be listed in the Open With Other Application's Select Application dialog.

File and Folder Properties

In a file's Properties dialog, you can view detailed information on a file and set options and permissions (see Figure 8-55). Right-click on the file and choose Properties from the menu. A file's Properties dialog has three tabs: Basic, Permissions, and Open With. Folders will have an additional Local Network Share tab, instead of an Open With tab. The Basic tab shows detailed information, such as type, size, location, accessed, and date modified. The type is a MIME type, indicating the type of application associated with it. The file's icon is displayed at the top, with a text box showing the file's name. You can edit the filename in the Name text box. If you want to change the icon image used for the file or folder, click the icon image (next to the name) to open a Select Custom Icon dialog and browse for the one you want. The **/usr/share/pixmaps** folder holds the set of common used images, although you can select your own images (click the Other Locations | Computer entry to locate the **pixmaps** folder). In the **pixmaps** folder, click an image file to see its icon displayed in the right pane. Double-click to change the icon image.

Figure 8-55: File properties

The Permissions tab for files shows the read, write, and execute permissions for owner, group, and others, as set for this file. You can change any of the permissions here, provided the file belongs to you. You configure access for the owner, the group, and others, using drop-down menus. You can set owner permissions as Read Only or Read and Write. For group and others, you can also set the None option, denying access. Clicking the group name displays a menu listing different groups, allowing you to select one to change the file's group. If you want to execute the file as an application, you check the "Allow executing file as program" entry. This has the effect of setting the execute permission.

The Open With tab for files lists all the applications associated with this kind of file. You can select the one you want to use as the default. This can be useful for media files, for which you may prefer a specific player for a file or a particular image viewer for pictures.

Certain kind of files will have additional tabs, providing information about the file. For example, an audio file will have an Audio tab listing the type of audio file and any other information, such as a song title or the compression method used. An image file will have an Image tab listing the resolution and type of image. A video file will contain an Audio/Video tab showing the type of video file, along with compression and resolution information.

The Permissions tab for folders operates much the same way, with Access menus for Owner, Group, and Others. The Access menu controls access to the folder with options for None, List files only, Access files, and Create and delete Files. These correspond to the read and execute permissions given to folders. To set the permissions for all the files in the folder accordingly (not just the folder), click the "Change Permissions for Enclosed Files" button to open a dialog where you can specify the owner, group, and others permissions for files and folders in the folder.

File Manager Preferences

You can set preferences for your file manager in the Preferences dialog, accessible by selecting the Preferences item in any file manager window's Tools menu to open the Preferences dialog (see Figure 8-56). The Preferences dialog has four sections: General, Optional Context Menu Actions, Performance, and Icon View Captions. In the General section you can choose to sort folders separately before files and whether to open items with a double-click (the default) or a single click. You can also choose to have the list view display an expandable tree, showing files and subfolders within an expanded folder.

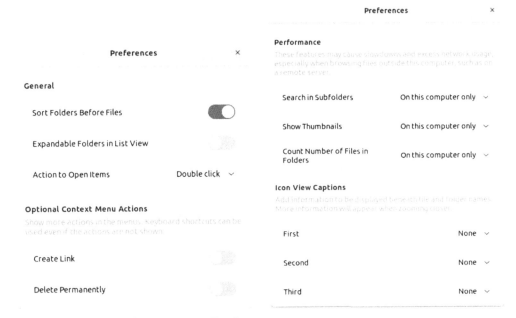

Figure 8-56: GNOME file manager Preferences

For the Context Menu you can add entries to the context menu for a file or folder (right-click) to create a link (Create Link) and delete a file or folder permanently (Delete Permanently), instead of sending it to the trash.

In the Performance section, you can choose whether to limit searches to your local computer, to display as a file's icon as a thumbnail of that file's content, and whether to show the number of files in a folder on the file manager window.

In the Icon Views Captions section, you can choose what information you want displayed in an icon caption, such as the size or modification date. You can choose up to three items to display.

File Manager Search

Two primary search tools are available for your GNOME desktop: the GNOME dash search and the GNOME file manager search. With GNOME file manager, you enter a pattern to search. You can further refine your search by specifying dates and file types. Click the Search button (looking glass icon) on the toolbar to open a Search box. Enter the pattern to search, then press Enter. The results are displayed (see Figure 8-57). Click the menu button to the right to add file-type (What) and date (When) search parameters, or to search file text or just the file name. Selecting the When entry opens a dialog where you can specify the recency of the document's last use or modification, by day, week, month, or year. A calendar button to the right of the text box for the date opens a calendar to let you choose a specific date. The What entry displays a menu with different file categories such as music, Documents, folders, picture, and PDF.

Figure 8-57: GNOME file manager search

9. Kubuntu (KDE Plasma)

The KDE Plasma Desktop

Application Menus

Plasma

Widgets

Activities

Desktop Effects

KDE File Manager: Dolphin

Discover Package Manager

KDE System Settings

Plasma is the desktop developed and distributed by KDE (the K Desktop Environment). It is often referred to as simply the KDE desktop. Plasma includes the standard desktop features, such as a window manager and a file manager, as well as an extensive set of applications that cover most Linux tasks. The KDE Plasma version of Ubuntu is called Kubuntu and is available as a separate desktop USB/DVD, and as the **kubuntu-desktop** meta-package on the APT repository (Synaptic Package Manager or **apt** command). The KDE Plasma desktop is developed and distributed by the KDE Project. KDE is open source software provided under a GNU Public License and is available free of charge along with its source code. KDE development is managed by the KDE Core Team.

The KDE software development and distribution is organized into three projects: Plasma, Gear (formerly Applications), and Frameworks. KDE Gear provide numerous applications written specifically for KDE Plasma that are accessible from the desktop. These include editors, photo and image applications, sound and video players, and office applications. Some applications have the letter *K* as part of their name, for example, Kate. On a system administration level, KDE provides several tools for managing your system, such as the Discover Software Manager, and the KDEsystem monitor. KDE applications also feature a built-in Help application. The current KDE Gear release is 21.12. See **https://apps.kde.org//** Applications tab for a list and descriptions of current applications.

KDE Frameworks provides support libraries designed to work with the Qt libraries that KDE Plasma and Applications depend on. Frameworks is designed to be cross-platform, enabling any KDE Application to run on systems that support the Qt libraries. Frameworks can be used as a basis for any custom operating system, such as Lubuntu. KDE Framework packages have the prefix **kf5**, such as the **kf5-filesystem** that provides support for the KDE filesystem. Development for Plasma, Frameworks, and Applications proceed at different paces. The KDE Frameworks version used in Kubuntu 22.04 Plasma Desktop is 5.92, whereas the KDE Plasma version is 5.24.

Web Site	Description
`https://www.kde.org`	KDE website
`https://www.kubuntu.org`	Kubuntu site
`https://www.kde.org/applications/`	KDE Applications website
`https://www.qt.io/`	Site for the Qt company
`https://store.kde.org`	KDE desktop themes
`https://mail.kde.org/mailman/listinfo/`	KDE mailing lists
`https://www.kde.org/plasma-desktop`	KDE Plasma desktop website
`https://docs.kde.org`	KDE documentation site

Table 9-1: KDE Web Sites

KDE, initiated by Matthias Ettrich in October 1996, is designed to run on any Unix implementation, including Linux, Solaris, HP-UX, and FreeBSD. The official KDE website is **https://www.kde.org**, which provides news updates, download links, and documentation. Detailed documentation for the KDE desktop and its applications is available at **https://docs.kde.org**. Several KDE mailing lists are available for users and developers, including announcements, administration, and other topics. Development support and documentation can be obtained at the KDE Techbase site at **https://techbase.kde.org**. Most applications are available on the Ubuntu repositories and can be installed directly from Discover Software and the Synaptic Package Manager. Various KDE websites are listed in Table 9-1. KDE uses as its library of GUI tools the Qt library, currently developed and supported by the QT company, owned by Digia (**https://www.qt.io**). It provides the Qt libraries as Open Source software that is freely distributable, though a commercial license is also available.

KDE Plasma 5 and Kubuntu 22.04 LTS

The KDE Plasma 5 release is a major reworking of the KDE desktop. KDE Plasma 5.24.4 is included with the Kubuntu 22.04 LTS distribution. Check the Kubuntu and KDE sites for detailed information on KDE 5.

```
https://www.kde.org/announcements/plasma5.0/
```

For features added with KDE Plasma 5.24, check:

```
https://kde.org/announcements/plasma/5/5.24.0/
```

KDE development is organized into a plasma, frameworks, and applications releases. The plasma release covers the desktop interface (the Plasma desktop shell), and the applications release covers KDE applications. Plasma has containments and plasmoids (also called widgets). Plasmoids operate similar to applets, small applications running on the desktop or panel. Plasmoids operate within containments. On KDE 5, there are two Plasma containments, the panel and the desktop. In this sense, the desktop and the panel are features of an underlying Plasma operation. They are not separate programs. Each has their own set of plasmoids. Kubuntu also supports Activities, multiple plasma desktop containments, each with their own set of active plasmoids (widgets) and open windows.

The Kubuntu edition of Ubuntu installs KDE as the primary desktop from the Kubuntu install disc. Kubuntu 22.04 LTS officially supports and installs KDE Plasma 5.24. The latest features included with Kubuntu 22.04 LTS are discussed at:

```
https://kubuntu.org/news/kubuntu-22-04-lts-released/
```

Kubuntu 22.04 LTS also usesKDE Gear 21.12 updates, check:

```
https://kde.org/announcements/gear/21.12.0/
```

Installing Kubuntu

You can download the Kubuntu Desktop discs from the Kubuntu site at:

```
http://www.kubuntu.org/
```

You can obtain the ISO image for Kubuntu from:

```
https://kubuntu.org/getkubuntu/
```

If you are installing Kubuntu from the Kubuntu USB/DVD, you will follow the same steps as those used for the Ubuntu Desktop USB/DVD: language, keyboard, partition (Disk Setup), time zone, user and host name (User Info). Installation will begin as soon as you choose the partition configuration. The artwork will be different, but the tasks will be the same. The "Installation type" screen (partitioning) shows lets you choose Guided or Manual partitioning. For guided you can choose the default, LVM, or encrypted LVM.

You can also add Kubuntu as a desktop to an Ubuntu desktop installation. KDE includes numerous packages. Instead of trying to install each one, you should install KDE using its meta packages on the Synaptic Package Manager, **kubuntu-desktop**. You will be prompted to keep the GDM display manager for logins, though you can change to SDDM, the Simple Desktop Display Manager. Once installed, KDE will then become an option you can select from the Sessions menu on the Login screen as "Plasma."

Note: Kubuntu has its own restricted packages, kubuntu-restricted-extras and kubuntu-restricted-addons, for multimedia codecs.

Kubuntu 22.04 Key Changes

Kubuntu 22.04 has several key changes to its Plasma desktop.

Kubuntu has replaced the Kickstart menu used in previous releases with three alternative main menus: the Application Launcher (the default), the Application menu, and the Applications Dashboard. You can easily switch between them (right-click on the menu icon in the panel and choose "Show Alternatives"). The Application Launcher is the new advanced menu, whereas the Application menu is a simplified menu, and the Dashboard is the same as the Dashboard available in previous releases.

Kubuntu provides three alternative task manager for the panel which you can switch between (right-click on the task manager in the panel and choose "Show Alternatives"). They are the Icon-only Task Manager, the Task Manager, and the Window List. The Icon-only Task Manager is a new task manager, managing open windows with application icons, whereas the Task Manager is the older task manger that uses buttons to manage each open window separately. The Window list is the older window list panel application which provides a simple list of open windows.

Kubuntu features three activity switchers for both the desktop and the panel. You can easily switch between them by right-clicking on the activity switcher icon and choosing "Show Alternatives" to display a menu listing them. The three activity switchers are: Activities, Activities Pager, and Activities Bar. Activities open the Activities Manager which you can then use the switch between activities. The Activities Pager and Activities Bar let you switch to a different activity directly.

SDDM

Kubuntu uses the Simple Desktop Display Manager (SDDM) to manage logins. A login greeter is displayed at the center of the screen where you can select a user icon and enter a password (see Figure 9-1). A user list of user icons is shown that you can choose from. Sleep, Restart, Shut Down, and Other buttons are displayed below the login button. Use the Other button to login as a user not displayed in the user list. Click the "Virtual Keyboard" link in the lower left corner to display a virtual keyboard.

Figure 9-1: SDDM Display Manager, login screen

Upon choosing a user icon and entering the password, press ENTER or clicking the login button (right arrow symbol) at the right end of the password text box. Your KDE session then starts up.

If you have more than one desktop installed on your system, such as MATE or LXDE, then a Desktop Sessions menu appears in the bottom left of the screen (see Figure 9-2). Click on it to display available desktops you can choose. The name for KDE is "Plasma", which is displayed as one of the menu items. You can use it to return to using the KDE desktop.

Figure 9-2: SDDM Display Manager, Desktop Session menu

You can change the theme of the login greeter using the Login Screen (SDDM) tab in the Startup and Shutdown dialog (System Settings | Startup and Shutdown in the Workspace section). The theme section lists available themes. Currently, only Breeze is listed. To change the background image, click on a theme to display it in the Customize section to the right. Then click on the Background icon and choose the "Load from file" option from the pop-up menu. On the Advanced tab, you can choose the default user, the desktop for your session, and whether to automatically log in. You can also manually configure SDDM using the **/etc/sddm.conf** file, which lists your default user and desktop (Session).

The Plasma Desktop

One of KDE's aims is to provide users with a consistent integrated desktop (see Figure 9-3). Plasma provides its own window manager (KWM), file manager (Dolphin), program manager, and desktop and panel (Plasma). You can run any X Window System or Wayland compliant application, such as Firefox, in Plasma, as well as any GNOME application. Kubuntu still uses the X.org server as its default. Though you can choose to try the Wayland server, it is not supported.

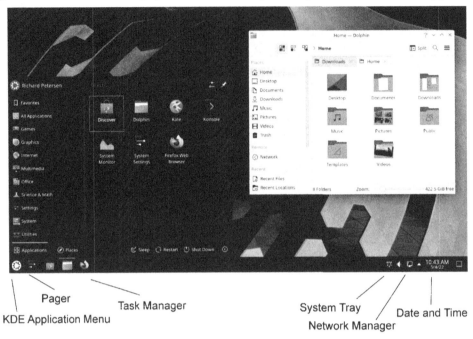

Figure 9-3: The KDE desktop

In turn, you can also run any KDE application, including the Dolphin file manager in GNOME. The Plasma 5 desktop features the Plasma desktop shell with new panel, menu, widgets, and activities. Keyboard shortcuts are provided for many desktop operations, as well as plasmoid (widget) tasks (see Table 9-2).

Table 9-2: Desktop, Plasma, and KWin Keyboard Shortcuts

To configure your desktop, you use the System Settings dialog (Favorites | System Settings), which lists tabs for dialogs such as Global Theme, Font, Icons, Application Style, Workspace behavior, Search, Window Management, Driver Manager, and Bluetooth. Workspace Theme lets you choose desktop, cursor, and splash themes. Workspace behavior is where you can set desktop effects and virtual desktops. Windows Management controls window display features like window switchers and title bar actions.

The desktop supports drag-and-drop and copy-and-paste operations. With the copy-and-paste operation, you can copy text from one application to another. You can even copy and paste from a Konsole terminal window.

Keys	Description
Alt-F1	Application menu
Alt-F2	KRunner, command execution, entry can be any search string for a relevant operation, including bookmarks and contacts, not just applications.
up/down arrows	Move among entries in menus, including Application and menus
left/right arrows	Move to submenus menus, including Application and Quick Access submenus menus
ENTER	Select a menu entry, including a Application or QuickAccess
PageUp, PageDown	Scroll up fast
Alt-F4	Close current window
Alt-F3	Window menu for current window
Ctrl-Alt -F6	Command Line Interface
Ctrl-Alt -F8	Return to desktop from command line interface
Ctrl-r	Remove a selected widget
Ctrl-s	Open a selected widget configuration's settings
Ctrl-a	Open the Add Widgets window to add a widget to the desktop
Ctrl-l	Lock your widgets to prevent removal, adding new ones or changing settings
Alt-Tab	Cover Switch or Box Switch for open windows
Ctrl-F8	Desktop Grid
Ctrl-F9	Present Windows Current Desktop
Ctrl-F10	Present Windows All Desktops
Ctrl-F11	Desktop Cube for switching desktops

The KDE Help Center

The KDE Help Center provides a browser-like interface for accessing and displaying both KDE Help files and Linux Man and info files (see Figure 9-4). The same documentation is available at **https://docs.kde.org**. You can start the Help Center from the Applications menu, the Help entry. The Help window displays a sidebar that holds two tabs, one listing contents and one providing a glossary. The main pane displays the currently selected document. A help tree on the contents tab in the sidebar lets you choose the kind of Help documents you want to access. Here you can choose KDE fundamentals (overview of the KDE desktop), the Plasma Manual (KDE manual pages), info documents (Browse info Pages), or application manuals (Application Manuals). Online Help provides links to KDE websites such as the KDE user forum and the KDE tech base sites. Click the "Table of Contents" button on the toolbar to open a listing of all KDE help documents, which you can browse through and click on to open.

A navigation toolbar enables you to move through previously viewed documents. KDE Help documents contain links you can click to access other documents. The Back and Forward buttons move you through the list of previously viewed documents. The KDE Help system provides an effective search tool for searching for patterns in a Help document. Click the Find button on the toolbar or choose the Find entry from the Edit menu, to open a search box at the bottom of the Help window where you can enter a pattern to search on the current open help document. The Options menu lets you refine your search with regular expressions, case sensitive queries, and whole words-only matches.

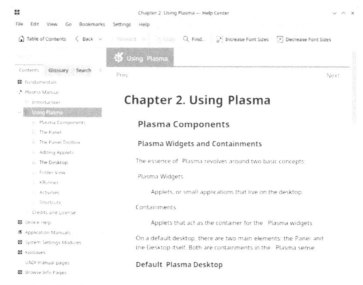

Figure 9-4: KDE Help Center

Desktop Menu and Display Configuration

Right-clicking anywhere on the desktop background displays the desktop menu with options to configure the desktop and display, sort icons on your desktop, add widgets and panels, open the activity switcher, enter edit mode for the desktop and panel, lock the screen, and open the logout dialog (Leave) (see Figure 9-5) .

Figure 9-5: Desktop Menu

Should you want to configure your display settings, choose Configure Display Settings from the desktop menu to open the System Settings Display and Monitor dialog (see Figure 9-6). The dialog has four tabs: Display Configuration, Compositor, Gamma, and Night color. On the Display Configuration tab you can set the resolution, orientation, and refresh rate, as well as the scale. On the Gamma tab you can set the gamma, and color saturations (red, green, and blue). On the Night Color tab you can set the night color temperature and the activation time.

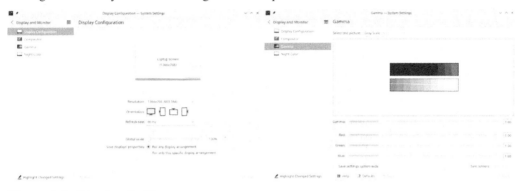

Figure 9-6: Display Settings

Edit Mode

In Edit Mode, you can modify widgets on both the desktop and panel. On the panel you can move and remove widgets (see Figure 9-7). On the desktop, you can hover your mouse over a widget to display its sidebar, allowing you to move, configure, or remove the widget. You can enter edit mode either from the desktop menu or from the panel menu, Enter Edit Mode. In edit mode a button bar at the top of the screen has buttons to open the System Settings dialogs for the desktop and wallpaper, the global theme selection, and the display settings. You can also open the Widgets dialog where you can add widgets to the desktop.

Figure 9-7: Edit Mode

Desktop Backgrounds (Wallpaper)

The background (wallpaper) is set from the desktop menu directly. Right-click on the desktop to display the desktop menu and then select Configure Desktop and Wallpaper to open the Desktop Settings dialog (see Figure 9-8).

Figure 9-8: Desktop Settings, wallpaper

You can also select Desktop Settings from the activities menu in the upper left corner of the desktop. The background is called wallpaper in KDE and can be changed in the Wallpaper tab. You can select other wallpapers from the wallpaper icons listed or select your own image by clicking the Open button.

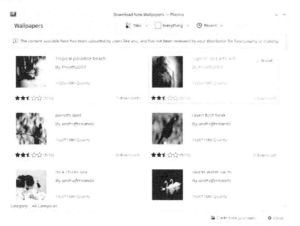

Figure 9-9: Desktop Settings, Get New Wallpapers

You can add more wallpaper by clicking the "Get New Wallpaper" button to open a "Wallpapers" dialog, which lists and downloads wallpaper posted on the **https://store.kde.org** site (see Figure 9-9). Each wallpaper entry shows an image, description, and rating. Buttons on the header bar of the dialog let you view the entries in details (list) or icon mode. You can use menus at the bottom of the dialog to refine the wallpaper listing by category), installed, newest, rating, and popularity (most downloads). Pass your mouse over the icon of the wallpaper you want to display Install and Details buttons. Click the Install button to download the wallpaper and add it to your Desktop Setting's Wallpaper tab. The wallpaper is downloaded and the Install button changes to Uninstall. To remove a wallpaper, you can select installed wallpapers to find the entry quickly. You can also search by pattern for a wallpaper.

Themes

For your desktop, you can also select a variety of different themes, icons, and window decorations. A theme changes the entire look and feel of your desktop, affecting the appearance of desktop elements, such as scrollbars, buttons, and icons. Themes and window decorations are provided for workspaces. Access the System Settings dialog from any of the Application menus' Settings submenu. On the System Settings dialog, click the Global Theme entry in the "Appearance" section. The Global Theme tab lets you choose overall look and feel, cursor themes, and a splash screen (startup) themes. The Plasma Style dialog lists plasma style themes. Click the Get New Global Themes button to open a Global Themes dialog, listing desktop themes from **https://store.kde.org** (see Figure 9-10). Pass your mouse over the theme you want, to display the Install button. Click the theme's Install button to download and install the theme.

For window decorations, you use the Application Style dialog, Window Decorations tab, where you can select window decoration themes. Click the Get New Window Decorations button to download new decorations. Icons styles are chosen using the Icons tab where you can choose the icon set to use, and even download new sets (Get New Icons).

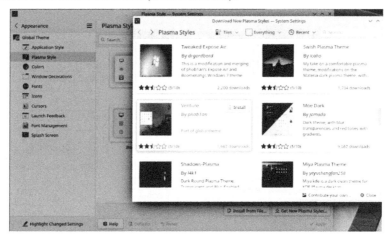

Figure 9-10: System Settings | Global Theme | Get New Themes

Leave KDE

You can right-click anywhere on the desktop and select the Leave entry from the pop-up menu, to open a leave dialog with the Log Out button selected (see Figure 9-11). Buttons to the left let you choose between the sleep, restart, and shutdown operations.

Figure 9-11: Log Out dialog

If you just want to lock your desktop, you can select the Lock entry from the desktop pop-up menu, and your screen saver will appear. To access a locked desktop, click on the screen and a box appears prompting you for your login password. When you enter the password, your desktop re-appears.

To shut down your system, you use the KDE Applications menus. KDE now uses the Application menus as its main menu, accessible by clicking on the KDE icon on the left side of the panel. The Application menus replace the older Kickoff menus used in previous releases. You use an Application menu to leave the KDE desktop. There are three Application menus you can use: Application Launcher, Application Menu, and Application Dashboard. The leave options are displayed differently on each Application menu.

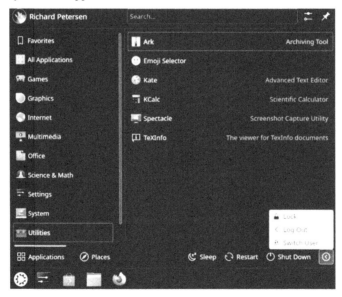

Figure 9-12: Application Launcher leave buttons

For the Application Launcher (the default), there are there are Sleep, Restart, Shut Down, and leave buttons on the lower right of the Application Launcher dialog (see Figure 9-12). The leave button has a left-arrow image. Clicking on the leave button displays a menu for Lock, Log Out, and Switch User.

If you are using the Application Menu, click the Power Session entry on the KDE Application Menu (see Figure 9-13) to display a submenu with entries to lock, log out, switch user, sleep, restart, and shut down.

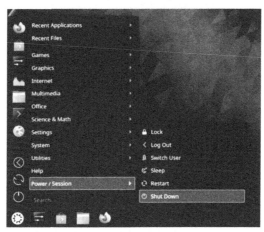

Figure 9-13: Application Menu Power/Session menu

If you are using the Application Dashboard for your main menu, instead of the Application Launcher, you can click the logout, shut down, and restart buttons on the lower left. For a complete selection choose the Power/Session category on the right (see Figure 9-14) .

Figure 9-14: Application Dashboard Power/Session

The Shut Down entry will display the Leave dialog with the Shut Down button selected (see Figure 9-15). The Log Out option displays the same dialog with the Log Out button selected. The Switch User option displays a dialog showing a user list to choose from. Should the user you want not be listed, you can click the Other button at the bottom of the list to open a dialog where you can enter the username along with the password. Click the List Users button at the bottom to return to the user list.

Figure 9-15: Shut Down dialog

The Main Menu - Application Menus

The KDE main menu is now provided by the Application Menus, of which there are three: Application Launcher, Application Menu, and Application Dashboard. They replace the older Kickoff menu, which is no longer used. You can switch between the three by right-clicking on the KDE main menu icon on the left side of the panel and choosing Show Alternatives from the pop-up menu (see Figure 9-16). This displays the list of the Application menus, with the one in use highlighted. Click on the one you want to use and click the Switch button shown below the list.

Figure 9-16: Application menu alternatives

Application Launcher

The Application Launcher is the default used for the main menu (see Figure 9-17). The sidebar has tabs for displaying either Application categories or Places, which includes locations of frequently used applications. Click the button at the bottom of the sidebar for the one you want. Initially the Applications tab is displayed. On the bottom right are the sleep, restart, and shut down buttons along with a leave button for a pop-up menu listing lock, logout, and switch user. The top bar of the dialog shows the user icon, the user name, a search box for searching for applications and locations, an Application Launcher configuration button, and a toggle pin to let you keep the menu open. Clicking on the user icon opens the System Settings User dialog at that user's entry, where you can make user configuration changes.

Figure 9-17: Application Launcher

The Applications tab on the sidebar lists entries for common categories such as Office, Multimedia, and Graphics (see Figure 9-18). Icons for applications in a selected category are shown on the right side. Click on an application icon to start it. The Favorites category lists commonly used applications. The All Applications entry lists all your applications organized under alphabetic headings (see Figure 9-15). In addition to the software categories, there are three administration categories: Settings, System, and Utilities. Settings holds the System Settings icon for configuring your desktop. System has administration tools such as the Discover software manager, the Konsole terminal window, the KSystemLog log manager, and the System Monitor. The Utilities entry list helpful system tools such as the Ark archiver, Kate text editor, the Spectacle screenshot tool, and the Kcalc calculator.

Figure 9-18: Application Launcher Applications

The Places tab on the sidebar lists entries for Computer, History, and Frequently used (see Figure 9-19). The Computer entry displays items in sections: Applications, Places, Remote, Recent, and Searched For. The Applications section lists a few helpful system tools such as the Discover software manager and the System Settings desktop configuration tool. The Places section lists all your default home folders such as Documents and Pictures. The Remote section has an entry for Network, which opens a file manager folder with icons for all your network devices and shares

(Bluetooth and Samba). The Recent and Searched For section have entries for open a file manager window at the Recent or Searched For tabs.

Figure 9-19: Application Launcher Places

To configure the Application Launcher click on the configure button at the top right to open the Application Launcher Settings dialog (see Figure 9-20). Here you can choose an icon to use for the Application Launcher on the panel. You can choose whether to display favorite and application icons in a list or a grid. The "Configure enabled search plugins" button opens the System Settings Search dialog where you can select and configured search plugins.

Figure 9-20: Application Launcher Settings

You can choose to show buttons for either the session, power, or power and session (see Figure 9-21). Power is the default and shows Sleep, Restart, and Shut Down buttons with a leave menu. Session shows only Lock, Logout, and Switch User buttons along with a power button in place of the leave menu. Power and Session displays buttons for all options: Lock, Log Out, Switch User, Sleep, Restart, and Shut Down.

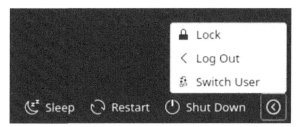

Figure 9-21: Application Launcher Power and Session buttons

Application Menu

The Application Menu implements a traditional menu, with a main menu listing categories, each with submenus for application (see Figure 9-22). There are categories such as System for system configuration dialogs and Utilities for system tools. Office lists the LibreOffice applications, and Graphics the KDE graphic applications. Recently accessed applications are listed under Recent Applications, and recent files used are under Recent files. The Power/Session category lists exit operations such as Shut Down and Log Out. A sidebar shows icons for common applications such as Firefox, the Discover software manager, System Settings, System Monitor, Dolphin file manager, the Konsole terminal window, and the Kate text editor. There are also buttons for Log Out, Reset, and Shut Down. A search box at the bottom of the menu lets you search for applications. Dialogs open with headings for Applications and for System Settings, listing match found for the search pattern.

Figure 9-22: Application Menu

To configure the Application Menu, right-click on the main menu icon on the panel and choose "Configure Application Menu" to open the Application Menu Settings dialog (see Figure 9-23). You can choose to show applications by their name or description, or both. The behavior of the menus can be adjusted to list alphabetically and remove any subcategories in the submenus. You can choose where to show the Recent applications, Recent files, or Recent contacts categories.

Recent can be defined as either recently used or often used. Search can be expanded to include bookmarks, files, and emails. Search results can be listed at the bottom or top.

Figure 9-23: Application Menu Settings

Application Dashboard

The Applications Dashboard displays menu entries on a full-screen dashboard, showing sections for applications, favorites, logout/shutdown options, and categories (see Figure 9-24). Press the Esc key to leave the dashboard without making a selection. You can add an application to the Favorites section by right-clicking on the application's icon and selecting Add to Favorites. To remove an application from the Favorites section, right-click on it and select Remove from Favorites. The Applications section shows categories to the right. and the icons for a selected category to the left. There are also categories for recent applications and documents. The Power/Session category lists the complete set of leave options, including lock, sleep, and switch user. The All Applications category lists all your applications under alphabetic headings (see Figure 9-25).

Figure 9-24: Application Dashboard

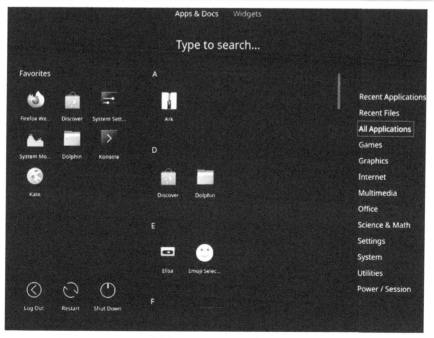

Figure 9-25: Application Dashboard - All Applications

To configure the Application Dashboard, right-click on the main menu icon on the panel and choose "Configure Application Dashboard" to open the Application Dashboard Settings dialog (see Figure 9-26. You can choose to show applications by their name or description, or both. The behavior of the menus can be adjusted to list alphabetically. You can choose where to show the Recent applications, Recent files, or Recent contacts categories. Recent can be defined as either recently used or often used. Search can be expanded to include bookmarks, files, and emails.

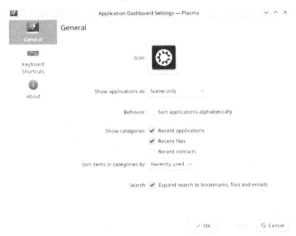

Figure 9-26: Application Dashboard Settings

KRunner

For fast access to applications, bookmarks, contacts, and other desktop items, you can use KRunner. The KRunner widget operates as a search tool for applications and other items such as bookmarks. To find an application, enter a search pattern and a listing of matching applications is displayed. Click on an application entry to start the application. You can also place an icon (application launcher) for an entry on the desktop by simply clicking and dragging its entry from the list to the desktop. For applications where you know the name, part of the name, or just its basic topic, KRunner is a fast way to access the application. To start KRunner, press Alt-F2, Alt-space, or right-click on the desktop to display the desktop menu and select "Show KRunner." Enter the pattern for the application you want to search for and press enter. The pattern "software" or "package" would display an entry for Discover Software. Entering the pattern "office" displays entries for all the LibreOffice applications, as well as additional office applications you can install (see Figure 9-27).

Clicking the settings button at the left opens the Configure Search dialog, which lists plugins for searching applications, widgets, and bookmarks, as well as providing capabilities such a running shell commands, opening files, and spell checking. The Clear History button deletes earlier search results. You can also configure KRunner search using System Settings | Search | KRunner (Workspace section).

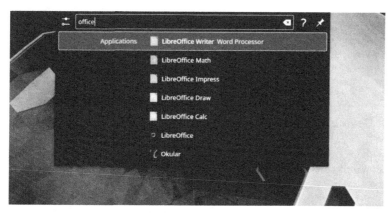

Figure 9-27: KRunner application search

Removable Devices: Device Notifier

Installed on the system tray to the right is the Device Notifier. Removable devices are not displayed as icons on your desktop. Instead, to open the devices, you use the Device Notifier. Click on the Device Notifier icon in the panel to open its dialog (see Figure 9-28). The device is unmounted initially with an mount button displayed. Click on this button to mount the device. An eject button is then displayed which you can later use to unmount and eject the device. Clicking on the eject button for a DVD/CD disc will physically eject it. For a USB drive, the drive will be unmounted and prepared for removal. You can then safely remove the USB drive. The Device Notifier is displayed on the system tray only if at least one removable device is attached.

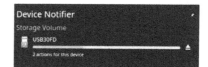

Figure 9-28: Device Notifier

The first time you attach a device to your system, it is not mounted. To open a device, click on its entry in the Device Notifier to display a menu of the actions you can use to open the device, such as the file manager or image viewer applications (see Figure 9-29). Click on the action you want to open the device with. The next time you attach a devices, it will be mounted automatically.

Figure 9-29: Device Notifier menu and its panel icon

Removable media are also displayed on the File manager window's side pane. You can choose to eject removable media from the file manager instead of from the Device Notifier by right-clicking on the removable media entry, and select "Safely remove" from the popup menu.

KDE Network Connections: Network Manager

On KDE, the Network Manager plasma widget provides panel access for Network Manager. This is the same Network Manager application but adapted to the KDE interface. The widget icon image changes for wireless only and wired connections. Clicking on the widget icon in the panel opens a dialog listing your current available wireless and wired connections. When you pass the mouse over an active connection, a Disconnect button appears (see Figure 9-30). For entries not connected, Connect buttons are displayed. Clicking on a connected entry opens tabs for Speed and Details (see Figure 9-31). Networks you have connected to are listed in the Active connections section and the Available connections section list networks you have not connected to. These will include available Wi-Fi networks. To connect to a Wi-Fi network, click on the network's Connect button to open a textbox where you enter the passcode. The connected Wi-Fi network is then listed as an active connection.

Figure 9-30: Network Manager connections and panel icons:

Figure 9-31: KDE Network Manager connection information - speed and details:

The toolbar at the top of the network plasma widget has buttons for wireless and airplane mode connections (shown below). Checkboxes next to each connection icon show if it is enabled. Clicking on the checkbox for a connection will enable or disable the connection. Disabled connections have an empty checkbox and a red icon.

You can use the "Connection editor" to configure your established connections. Either click the settings button on the right side of the toolbar at the top of the network dialog or right-click on the network dialog to display a menu where you can choose "Configure Network Connections." The Connection editor then opens, which lists your connections (see Figure 9-32). Select a connection in the sidebar with tabs for General, Wired, Security, and IPv tabs for a wired or wireless connections as described in Chapter 15. To add a new connection manually, click the Add button at the bottom of the sidebar to display a dialog listing different connection types.

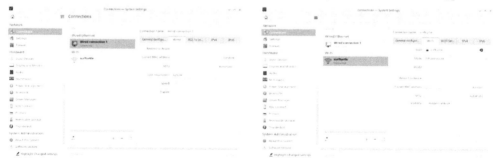

Figure 9-32: KDE connection editor and KDE Network Manager

Desktop Widgets (Plasmoids)

The KDE desktop features the Plasma desktop that supports plasmoids. Plasmoids are integrated into the desktop on the same level as windows and icons. Just as a desktop can display windows, it can also display plasmoids. Plasmoids can take on desktop operations, running essential operations, even replacing, to a limited extent, the need for file manager windows. The name for plasmoids used on the desktop is widgets. The tools and commands on the desktop that manage plasmoids, refer to them as widgets. For that reason, they will be referred to as widgets.

Managing desktop widgets

When you either long click (click and hold for several seconds) your mouse on a widget its sidebar is displayed with buttons for rotating, configure, and removing the widget (see Figure 9-18), as well as a grid for resizing the widget. Click and drag buttons on the grid to change the widget size. Clicking the configure button opens that widget's settings dialog (see Figure 9-33). You can also display the sidebar by entering Edit Mode by selecting Enter Edit Mode from the desktop or panel menus and then hovering your mouse over the widget.

To move a widget, long click on it to display its sidebar and while holding the click, drag the icon to the position you want. In Edit Mode, you can hover over the widget to display the sidebar and then click and drag the widget.

Figure 9-33: Clock Widget with task sidebar and configuration dialog

To add a widget to the desktop, right-click anywhere on the desktop and select Add Widgets from the pop-up menu. This opens the Widgets dialog at the left side of the desktop that lists widgets you can add (see Figure 9-34). Clicking on the Categories button (top-right) opens a pop-up menu with different widget categories like Date and Time, Online Services, and Graphics. Double-click or drag a widget to the desktop to add it to the desktop. You can enter a pattern to search for a widget using the search box located at the top of the dialog.

Figure 9-34: Adding a widget - Widgets dialog

To remove a widget, long click on the widget to display its toolbar, and then click on the red Remove button (trash icon) at the bottom of the toolbar. In Edit Mode, you can hover over the widget to display the sidebar and then click its remove button. When you remove a widget, a notification message is displayed with an Undo button, as shown here. Clicking on the Undo button will restore the widget.

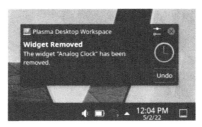

Figure 9-35 shows the folder, digital clock, notes, calculator, and cpu monitor widgets. The desktop folder widget is just a folder widget set initially to the desktop folder.

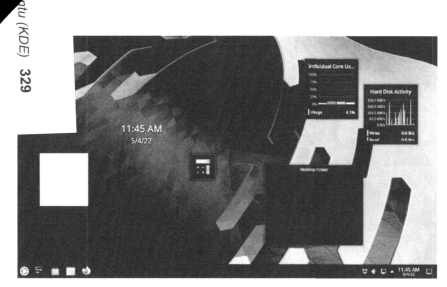

Figure 9-35: Folder, Calculator, Digital clock, CPU Load monitor, and Notes widgets:

Folder and Icon Widgets

You can place access to any folders on the desktop by simply dragging their icons from a file manager window to the desktop (see Figure 9-36). A small menu will appear that includes options for the Icon and Folder widgets. The Folder option sets up a Folder widget for the folder showing icons for subfolders and files. The Icon entry creates an Icon widget.

Figure 9-36: Folder and Icon widgets:

For any Folder widget, you can use that widget's settings dialog to change the folder it references. A Folder widget has options for showing the desktop folder, a folder on your Places list, or a specific folder. You can also specify a title. You can easily create a Folder widget for your home folder.

Activities

KDE is designed to support multiple activities. Activities are different plasma containments, each with its set of widgets. An activity is not the same as virtual desktop. Virtual desktops affect space, displaying additional desktops. An activity has its own set of widgets (widgets) and windows, displaying a different set of widgets and windows for each activity. In effect, each activity has a different desktop and set of virtual desktops. Technically, each activity is a Plasma containment that has its own collection of widgets and windows. You can switch to a different activity (containment) and display a different collection of widgets and windows on your desktop.

An activity is often tailored for a certain task. You could have one activity for office work, another for news, and yet another for media. Each activity could have its own set of appropriate widgets, like clock, calculator, notes, and folder widgets for an office activity. A media activity might have a Media Player widget and media applications open.

Multiple activities are managed using the Activities Manager, which is accessed through the Activities entry on the desktop menu or the Activities widget, which you can install on the panel or desktop (see Figure 9-37).

Figure 9-37: Activities menu entry and the Activities widget

Files and folders can be attached to an activity, displaying them only on that activity. Right-click on the folder or file icon in the File Manager, and choose the Activities submenu to choose an activity. Windows are set by default to display on the activity they are opened on. The window switcher is configured to work only on the current activity. The setting is configured in the Window Management dialog (Workspace section of the System settings dialog). On the Task Switcher tab, the 'Filter windows by" section has Activities checked and "Current activity" selected.

To add an activity, click the "Show Activities Switcher" entry in the desktop menu The Activities Manager is displayed listing your activities on the left side of the screen (see Figure 9-38). A default activity icon for your desktop will already be displayed. Click the "Create activity" button (plus button) at the bottom of the Activities Manager to add a new activity. A "Create a new activity" window opens with entries for the name and description (see Figure 9-39). Click on the Icon image to open a dialog where you can choose an icon for your activity. You can choose not to track usage and to set up a keyboard shortcut for the activity. Click the Create button to add the new activity. An activity entry then appears on the Activities Manager. To switch to another activity, click its icon in the Activities Manager.

Figure 9-38: Activities Manager

Moving the mouse over an activity icon displays Configure and Stop buttons. The Configure button opens the "Activity settings" dialog for that activity, which is the same as the create dialog, with Name, description, and icon settings. The Stop button deactivates the activity and places it at the bottom of the Activity Manager under the "Stopped activities" heading. To start a stopped activity, simply click its icon in the "Stopped activities" list.

To remove an activity, first stop it, then move your mouse over the activity icon in the Stopped activities section (see Figure 9-40). A remove button (trash icon) appears to the right of the activity entry. Click it to remove the activity. You are prompted to confirm the deletion.

Figure 9-39: Create an activity

To add widgets to an activity, first, click the activity to make it the current activity, and then click the Add Widgets button to display the Widgets dialog. Widgets you add are placed in the current activity.

To switch from one activity to another, first, display the Activities Manager by choosing "Show Activities Switcher" from the desktop menu (right-click on desktop) or the Activities button on the panel (if installed). Then click on the activity icon you want. The new Activity becomes your desktop (see Figure 9-41). To change to another activity, open the Activities Manager again, and click the activity icon you want. Your original desktop is the first icon (Default).

Figure 9-40: stop Activity icons

Figure 9-41: Activity Manager and screen of selected activity

Activities Widgets for the Desktop and Panel

To move easily between activities, you can add the Activity widgets to either the desktop or to the panel. Both desktop and panel Activity widgets appear and operate the same with the same configuration dialogs. There are three desktop and panel widgets: the Activities button, the Activities pager, and the Activities bar (see Figure 9-42) ."

Figure 9-42: Activity Widgets for Desktop and Panel

The Activity button is a simple button that appears on the desktop or panel that will display the Activities Switcher when clicked (see Figure 9-43). You can configure the button to show either a generic image or the name of the current Activity.

Figure 9-43: Activity button for desktop and panel

The Activity Pager operate like the workspace pager. Each activities is a square on the pager that you can click to move to that Activity (see Figure 9-44). The Activities Pager Settings dialog has a general and Keyboard shortcuts tab for configuring the pager. You can configure the pager to show the activity number or name. You could show the bare desktop upon clicking the current activity is you want. You can choose between a horizontal, vertical, or the default square layouts for the pager. You can also choose to show the outlines of open windows on the activities.

Figure 9-44: Activity Pager for the desktop and panel

The Activity bar displays buttons for each activity. Click on one to move to a different activity (see Figure 9-45). The current activity has a blue line above. There is no configuration dialog for the activity bar.

Figure 9-45: Activity Bar for desktop and panel

The desktop activity widgets only appear on the activity they were created on, whereas the panel activity widgets appear on the panel for on each activity.

Should you right click on either a desktop or panel activity widget, a menu will display an entry for Show Alternatives (see Figure 9-46). This will display a menu showing the three Activity widgets. Selecting a different activity widget displays that widget in place of the current one. The other widgets do not have to be be first installed.

Figure 9-46: Activity Widget alternatives selection

KDE Windows

A KDE window has the same functionality you find in other window managers and desktops. You can re-size the window by clicking and dragging any of its corners or sides. A click-and-drag operation on a side extends the window in that dimension, whereas a corner extends both height and width at the same time. Within the window, menus, icons, and toolbars for the particular application are displayed.

The top of the window has a title bar showing the name of the window, the program name in the case of applications, and the current folder name for the file manager windows. The active window has the title bar highlighted. To move the window, click the title bar and drag it where you want. Right-clicking the window title bar displays a pop-up menu with entries for window operations, such as minimize, maximize, and moving the window to a different desktop or activity.

The More Actions submenu includes closing or resizing the window, the shade option to roll up the window to the title bar, and full screen.

You can configure the appearance and operation of a window by selecting "Configure Window Manager" from the More Actions submenu in the Window menu (right-click the title bar). Here you can set appearance (Window Decoration), button and key operations (Window Actions), the focus policy, such as a mouse-click on the window or just passing the mouse over it (Window Focus Behavior), and how the window is displayed when moving it (Window Movement). All these features can be configured also using the System Setting's Window Behavior tool in the Workspace section.

To the right of the title bar are three small buttons for minimizing, maximizing, or closing the window (down, up, and x symbols). You can switch to a window at any time by clicking its task manager button. You can also maximize a window by dragging it to the top edge of the screen.

From the keyboard, you can use the ALT-TAB key combination to display a list of current open windows. Holding down the ALT key and sequentially pressing TAB moves you through the list.

A window can be displayed as a tile on one-half of the screen. Another tile can be set up for a different window on the other side of the screen, allowing you to display two windows side by side on the full screen (see Figure 9-47). You can tile a window by dragging it to the side of the screen (over the side edge to the middle of the window). A tile outline will appear. Add a second tile by moving a window to the other side edge. You can add more windows to a tile by moving them to that edge. Clicking on a window's task manager button will display it on its tile.

The same process works for corners. You can tile a window to a corner by moving it to that corner. You can then have four tiled windows open at each corner. You could even have several windows open on the same corner, displaying the one you want by clicking its task manager button.

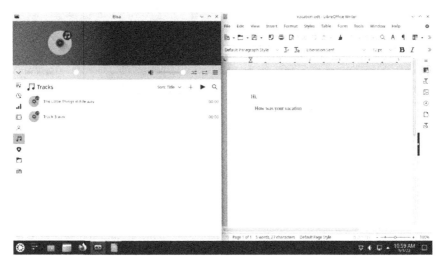

Figure 9-47: Window tiles

Task Managers

KDE proves three different task managers that you can use to manage your open windows: the Icon-only Task Manager (the default), Task Manager, and Window list. The Icon-only Task Manager is a new task manager with enhanced capabilities. Task Manager is the older version used in previous KDE releases, along with Window list. The Icon-only Task Manager is the default, but you can choose one of the other options by right-clicking on an empty space on the panel and selecting "Show Alternatives" to display the Alternative Widgets dialog (see Figure 9-48). Click on the one you want and then click on Switch.

Figure 9-48: Choosing a task manager from panel menu

Both the Icon-only Task Manager and the Task Manager show the same menus when you right-click on an application or widget icon on the panel. The menus applications display a menu with common window operations such as move to a different desktop or selecting which activities it is to be shown on (see Figure 9-49). A More submenu displays standard window operations such as move, resize, minimize, maximize. Application specific operations are shown at the top of the menu such as the "Open a New Private Window" for Firefox, and a Places section for the home folders such as Documents and Music.

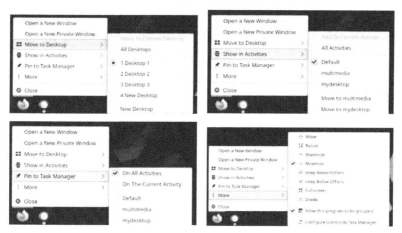

Figure 9-49: Application panel menus

Application specific operations are shown at the top of the menu such as the "Open a New Private Window" for Firefox, and, for the Dolphin file manager, a Places section for the home folders such as Documents and Music (see Figure 9-50). The Dolphin file manager menu also features a "6 More Places" submenu that expands to include all the home folder bookmarks such as Pictures, Videos, and Trash, as well as submenus for Remote (Network), Recent (Recent Files and Recent Locations), and Search For folders (Documents, Images, Audio, and Video). Multimedia applications will show media controls such as play, pause, and stop.

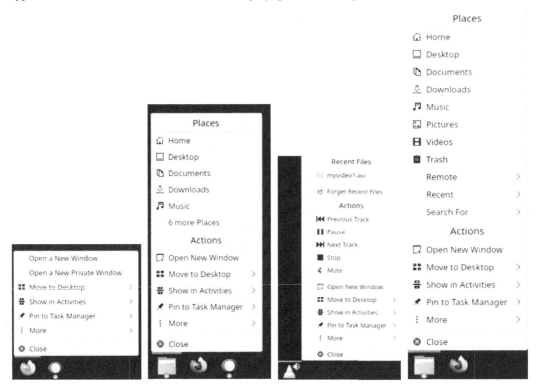

Figure 9-50: Application panel menus Application section

Icon-only Task Manager

The Icon-only Task Manager is the new task manager used for the KDE desktop. It reduces all the open windows that an application has open to a single application icon (see Figure 9-51). Should you have several file manager windows open, these are referenced by a single file manager application icon in the panel. If you were to have several web browser windows open, there would only be a single web browser icon on the panel that you would use to reference them.

Figure 9-51: Icon-only Task Manager, application icons

Passing your mouse over an Icon-only Task Manager application icon automatically displays a thumbnail bar above the icon showing thumbnails of all the application's open windows (see Figure 9-52). The thumbnails of those windows currently displayed on the desktop will show contents of those displayed window. Those windows that are minimized will only show the application's icon. To select or to maximize a minimized window, click on its thumbnail.

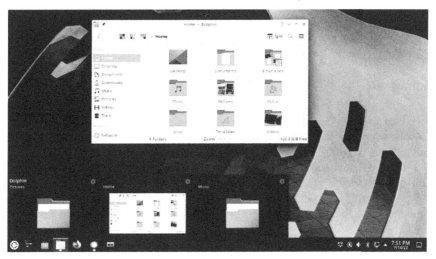

Figure 9-52: Icon-only Task Manager, application thumbnails for open windows

Should you then move your mouse over the thumbnail of a minimized window, the window it references is shown as it would appear maximized on your desktop (see Figure 9-53). Clicking on on it maximizes the window. This is how you maximize a window that has been minimized on the Icon-only Task Manager. When you minimize a window, it disappears from the desktop. There will be an application icon on the panel for the the application that the window was using. To maximize the window again, pass your mouse over its application icon on the panel to display the thumbnail bar of all the windows open with that application. Click on the one you want to maximize.

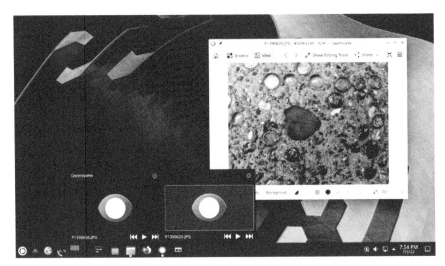

Figure 9-53: Icon-only Task Manager, maximizing a minimized window using thumbnails

The Icon-only Task Manager reduces the task manager to a small list of application icons. To maximize a minimized window, it would help to keep in mind the application it was using, though, by passing your mouse over all the application icons in the task manager, you can quickly display the thumbnails of all your open windows, one application at a time.

Task Manager

Task Manager is similar to the traditional task manager used in previous releases. Icons are displayed for application added to the panel and have no open windows, ones that are not running. When an application opens a window, its application icon disappears and is replaced by a button for that open window. Each open window, whether for the same application or a different one, has a button. When you close all the open windows for an application, if the application has been added to the panel, its application icon is again displayed on the panel, otherwise it disappears. Figure 9-54 shows the Task Manager panel application icons (applications added to the panel) with no open windows, and then with buttons for open windows for the Dolphin file manager and Firefox web browser.

Figure 9-54: Task Manager panel applications with unopened and opened windows

The task manager shows buttons for the different programs you are running or windows you have open (see Figure 9-55). This is essentially a docking mechanism that lets you change to a window or application by clicking its button. When you minimize a window, it is reduced to its task manager button. You can then restore the window by clicking its task manager button. A live thumbnail of a window on the task manager is displayed as your mouse passes over its task manager button, showing its name, desktop, and image. Music and video players will show basic multimedia controls, such as pause, stop, and play on the thumbnail. All thumbnails will feature a red close button (x) in the upper right corner that you can use to close the window.

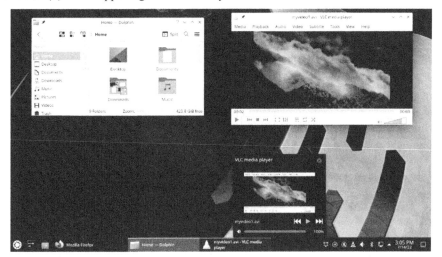

Figure 9-55: Task Manager

Window List

Window List is a stripped down version of the task manager, displaying a menu of opened windows you can select to access. The entire task manager is reduced to a single window list icon. Clicking on the icon displays the menu of open windows, with a description of the content opened (see Figure 9-56). Both displayed and minimized windows are listed. Click on an entry to access it.

Figure 9-56: Window List

Applications

You can start an application in KDE in several ways. If an entry for it is in the Applications menu, you can select that entry to start the application. You can right-click on any application entry in the Applications menu to display a pop-up menu with "Add to Panel (Widgets)", "Add to Desktop", and "Pin to Task Manager" entries. Select one to add a shortcut icon for the application to the desktop, the panel, or the task manager. You can then start an application by double-clicking its desktop icon, or single-clicking its panel or task manager icon.

The applications will appear differently in the Icon-only Task Manager (the default) and the Task Manager (similar to the one used in previous releases). The Icon-only Task Manager only displays the application icons (see Figure 9-57). Applications with open windows have a dot underneath their icons, and passing your mouse over it displays an thumbnail bar showing all the open windows for that application.

Figure 9-57: Icon-only Task Manager Applications

The Task Manger show icons for applications with no open windows. For applications with open windows, it shows buttons for each open window instead of the application icon. In Figure 9-58, the Kate, Memory Usage, and Weather Report applications have been added to the panel as widgets (Add to Panel), appearing as icons next to the Pager widget. The Konsole, LibreOffice Writer, and VLC media player applications have been added to the Task Manager (Pin to Task Manager), appearing just before the Task manager window buttons.

Figure 9-58: Task Manager Applications and opened buttons

An application icon on the desktop is implemented as a desktop widget. Performing a long click on the application icon on the desktop displays a sidebar with the icon for the widget settings. This opens a Settings window that allows you to specify a keyboard shortcut.

You can also run an application by right-clicking on the desktop and selecting the Show KRunner (or press Alt-F2 or Alt-space) which will display the KRunner tool consisting of a box to enter a single command. You need only enter a pattern to search for the application. Results will be displayed in the KRunner window. Choose the one you want.

Virtual Desktops: Pager and Overview

KDE supports virtual desktops, extending the desktop area on which you can work. They function the same as workspaces on GNOME (Ubuntu and MATE). You could have a Web browser running on one desktop and be using a text editor in another. KDE can support up to 16 virtual desktops. To use virtual desktops, you use the Pager widget on your panel or desktop, or the Overview Effect.

Pagers

When a pager is added to the panel, it will have just one desktop. The pager on the panel is not shown if it has only one desktop . This is the case for your initial default panel. The pager is there, but not visible until you add more desktops.

To add desktops to the pager, use the System Settings Workspace Behavior tab's Virtual Desktops configuration tab (System Settings | Workspace Behavior | Virtual Desktops). Once you have added the desktops, the pager will appear on the panel, next to the Applications menu.

To configure the rows, name, and the number of desktop, select the Configure Virtual Desktops entry in the pop-up menu to open the Virtual Desktops dialog, which displays entries for your active desktops (see Figure 9-59). Click the Add button to add a desktop and the Rows button to add the number of rows you want them organized into. To delete a desktop, move the mouse over the desktop entry to display edit and x buttons. Click the x button to delete the desktop. You can change any of the desktop names by moving the mouse over the entry and click the edit button (pencil) and then entering a new name. Click the Apply button to make the changes.

You can also access the Virtual Desktops dialog right-clicking on the Desktop Pager widget and, from the menu, select Configure Virtual Desktops. If you just want to add a desktop, right-click on the Desktop Pager widget and click the Add Virtual Desktop entry.

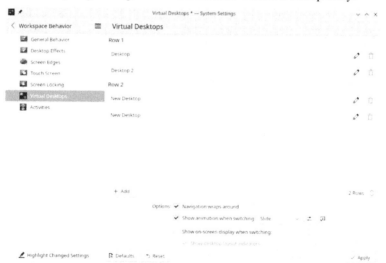

Figure 9-59: Virtual Desktops configuration with System Settings and the Pager widget

You can also add additional pagers to the panel or desktop. On the panel, you can use edit mode (right-click on panel and choose Enter Edit Mode) to move it to the location you want on the panel. The panel and desktop pagers are shown here.

Figure 9-60: Pager Panel and Desktop widgets

The Pager represents your virtual desktops as miniature screens showing small squares for each desktop. It works much like the GNOME Workspace Switcher (see Figure 9-60). To move from one desktop to another, click the square for the destination desktop. The selected desktop will be highlighted. Just passing your mouse over a desktop image on the Pager will open a message displaying the desktop number along with the windows open on that desktop.

If you want to move a window to a different desktop, first open the window's menu by right-clicking the window's title bar. Then select the Move To Desktop entry, which lists the available desktops. Choose the one you want.

You can also configure KDE so that if you move the mouse over the edge of a desktop screen, it automatically moves to the adjoining desktop. You need to imagine the desktops arranged next to each. You enable this feature by enabling the "Switch desktop on edge" feature in the System Settings | Workspace Behavior | Screen Edges tab. This feature will also allow you to move windows over the edge to an adjoining desktop.

To change how the pager displays desktops, right-click on the pager and choose Configure Pager to open the Pager Settings dialog (see Figure 9-61). Here you can configure the pager to display numbers or names for desktops, or show icons of open windows.

Figure 9-61: Pager Widget Settings:

Tip: Use **Ctrl** key in combination with a function key to switch to a specific desktop: for example, **Ctrl-f1** switches to the first desktop and **Ctrl-f3** to the third desktop.

Overview Effect

The Overview effect also accesses and manages your virtual desktops. You can access the Overview effect from your keyboard by pressing the Meta (Windows key) and the **w** key (see Figure 9-62).

Figure 9-62: Overview effect

This displays a screen with a thumbnail bar of your virtual desktops at the top of the screen (see Figure 9-63). Your current desktop is outlined in blue. To move to a different desktop, click on the desktop's thumbnail. The Overview effect closes and you are placed in the selected desktop.

Figure 9-63: Overview effect virtual desktops

Using the thumbnail bar, you can easily add and remove desktops (see Figure 9-64). You can add more desktops by clicking on the large plus button on the right side of the thumbnail bar. Hovering your mouse over a desktop's thumbnail displays a trash icon in its upper right corner that you can click to remove the desktop.

Figure 9-64: Overview effect managing desktops

You can return to the current desktop at any time by clicking anywhere on the screen, which closes the Overview effect.

The Overview effect also shows the windows open on the current desktop. To move a window to a different desktop, drag and drop it to the thumbnail of the desktop you want it moved to. You are also moved to that desktop, still within the Overview effect screen.

Hovering your mouse over a window displays a close box (red x), which you can use to close a window.

The Overview effects screen also provides a Krunner text box you can use to search from and start applications. Once you start an application from Krunner, you return to the current desktop.

The Overview effect is enabled and configured on the System Settings | Workspace behavior | Desktop Effects tab, in the Window Management section (see Figure 65). Click on its configuration button to open the Overview dialog where you can set the key to use to open the Overview effect, the layout mode for the displayed windows (closest or natural), and whether to blur the background. Click the Default button to return to the defaults (Natural layout and Meta-w key).

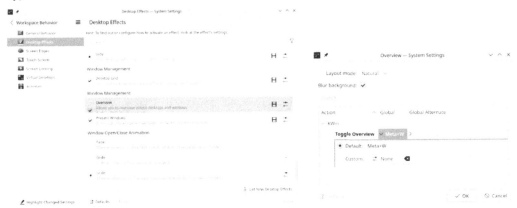

Figure 9-65: Overview effect configuration on System Settings

KDE Panel

The KDE panel, located at the bottom of the screen, provides access to most KDE functions (see Figure 9-66). The panel is a specially configured Plasma containment, just like the desktop. The panel can include icons for menus, folder windows, specific programs, and virtual desktops. These are widgets that are configured for use on the panel. At the left end of the panel is a button for the Application menus.

To add an application to the panel, right-click on its entry in any of the Application menus to open a pop-up menu and select Add to Panel.

As noted in the previous section on task managers, there are three different task managers on for the panel: the new Icon-only Task Manager, Task Manager (similar to the one use in previous releases), and Window List. Both the Icon-only Task Manager and Task Manager look the same when you have no windows open. Figure 9-67 shows the Icon-only task manager with a single window open for the Dolphin file manager as shown by its thumbnail. Figure 9-57 shows the Task Manager with a button for the open Dolphin file manager window.

Figure 9-66: KDE panel with Icon-only Task Manager and open window

Figure 9-67: KDE panel with Task Manager and open window

KDE Panel Widgets

The Plasma panel supports several kinds of Windows and Tasks widgets, including the Task Manager and system tray. To the right of the system tray is the digital clock. To add a widget to the panel, right-click on the panel, or on any panel widget, to open a pop-up menu and select the Add Widgets entry (see Figure 9-68). This opens the Widgets dialog that lists widgets you can add to the panel (see Figure 9-69). A search box at the top of the dialog lets you search for widgets. A drop-down menu to the right of the search box lets you choose different widget categories like Date and Time, Online Services, and Graphics. You add a widget just as you add a desktop widget, click on the widget to want. An icon for the widget is shown on the left side of the panel. In Figure 9-70, the weather report, Kate sessions launcher, and the memory usage widget has been added to the panel. Clicking on a widget displays information the widget provides.

Another way to open the Widgets dialog is to right-click on the panel and choose "Enter Edit Mode" to open the configuration panel, and then click the Add Widgets button on the top left side of the desktop.

Figure 9-68: KDE Add Widgets option on panel

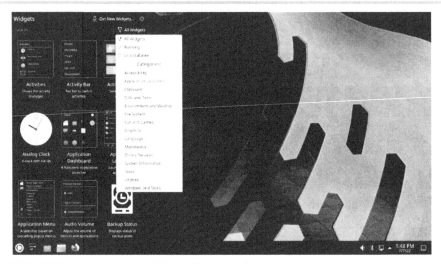

Figure 9-69: KDE Add Widgets dialog for panel

Figure 9-70: Displaying panel widget information

To remove a widget, you have to enter edit mode (right-click on the panel and choose Enter Edit Mode from the menu). In edit mode, when pass your mouse over a widget, a menu is displayed showing a Remove option (see Figure 9-71). You can also right click on the widget to display a menu with a Remove option.

Figure 9-71: Removing a widget from the panel in edit mode

KDE System Tray

The system tray holds widgets for desktop operations like update notifier, the clipboard, Bluetooth, device notifier, sound settings, media player (if a multimedia player is active), and network manager, as shown here.

The pop-up menu (arrow icon) on the right side of the system tray display widgets that are not in use, or not often used (see Figure 9-72). The Battery and Brightness entry displays a dialog to see battery charges and set screen brightness.

Figure 9-72: System Tray

To configure the system tray, right-click on the system tray menu (arrow icon) and choose Configure System Tray to open the system tray to open a configuration dialog at the Entries tab, where you can decide what items to always show, hide until needed, hide always, or disable (see Figure 9-73). The entries are organized into Application Status, Hardware Control, System Services, and Miscellaneous. You can also add keyboard shortcuts for the entry. Click on its keyboard shortcut button to change the button to Input from None, then press the keys you want associated with the entry. The keys will appear on the button. If the keys you chose are already in use, you are notified to choose a different set of keys. When you click the Apply button your changes are made and any additional items you want shown are displayed.

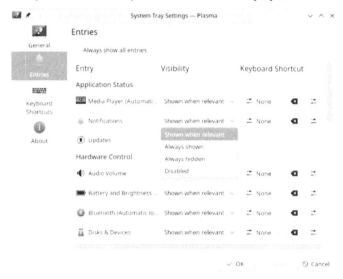

Figure 9-73: KDE panel system tray settings

KDE Panel Configuration

To configure a panel, changing its position, size, and display features, select the Enter Edit Mode entry in the panel menu (right-click on the panel to display the menu). This will open an additional configuration panel with buttons for adding widgets, moving the panel, changing its size, and a More Settings menu for setting visibility and alignment features. Figure 9-74 shows the configuration panel as it will appear on your desktop. Figure 9-75 provides a more detailed description, including the More Settings menu entries.

With the configuration panel activated, you can also move widgets around the panel. Clicking on a widget will overlay a movement icon, letting you then move the widget icon to a different location on the panel.

As you move your mouse over a widget in the panel, a pop-up dialog opens showing the widget's name, a settings button, and a delete button. To remove the widget from the panel, click its delete button.

Figure 9-74: KDE Panel Configuration

The lower part of the configuration panel is used for panel position settings. On the left side is a slider for positioning the panel on the edge of the screen. On the right side are two sliders for the minimum (bottom) and maximum (top) size of the panel.

The top part of the panel has buttons for changing the location and the size of the panel. The Screen Edge button lets you move the panel to another side of the screen (left, right, top, bottom). Just click and drag. The height button lets you change the panel size, larger or smaller. The Add Widgets button will open the Add Widgets dialog, letting you add new widgets to the panel. The Add Spacer button adds a spacer to separate widgets. Right-click on the spacer to set the flexible size option or to remove the spacer.

Figure 9-75: KDE Panel Configuration details and display features

The More Setting menu lets you set Visibility and Alignment features. You can choose an AutoHide setting that will hide the panel until you move the mouse to its location. The "Windows can cover" option lets a window overlap the panel. For smaller panels, you can align to the right, left, or center of the screen edge. The More Settings menu also has an entry to remove the panel. Use this entry to delete a panel you no longer want.

When you are finished with the configuration, click the red x icon the upper right side.

Desktop Effects

Desktop effects can be enabled on the System Settings Desktop Effects tab in the Workspace Behavior dialog in the Workspace section (System Settings | Workspace Behavior). For virtual desktop switching you can choose Slide, Fade, and Scale (see Figure 9-76). The more dramatic effects are found in the Windows Management section. Desktop Effects requires the support of a capable graphics chip (GPU). You may have to install a proprietary graphics driver (System Settings | Driver Manager).

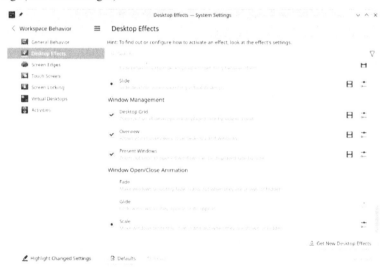

Figure 9-76: Desktop Effects selection

KEY	Operation
ALT-TAB	Cover Switch, Thumbnail, or Breeze for open windows
CTRL-F8	Desktop Grid (use mouse to select a desktop)
CTRL-F9	Present Windows Current Desktop
CTRL-F10	Present Windows All Desktops
CTRL-F11	Desktop Cube (use mouse or arrow keys to move, ESC to exit)

Table 9-3: KWin desktop effects keyboard shortcuts

Several Windows effects are selected by default, depending on whether your graphics card can support them. A check box is filled next to active effects. If there is a dialog icon to the right of the effects entry, it means the effect can be configured. Click on the icon to open its configuration dialog. Figure 9-77 shows the configuration dialog for the Desktop Grid effect. For several effects, you use certain keys to start them. The more commonly used effects are Cover Switch, Desktop Grid, Present Windows, and Desktop Cube. The keys for these effects are listed in Table 9-3.

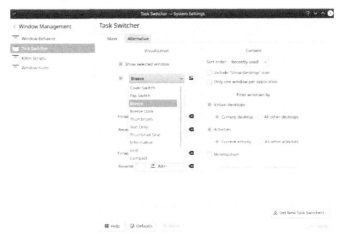

Figure 9-77: Desktop Effects configuration

Window switching using Alt-Tab is controlled on the Window Management dialog's Task Switcher tab, not from Workspace behavior's Desktop Effects tab (see Figure 9-78). In the Visualization section, you can choose the window switching effect you want to use from the drop-down menu. These include Breeze, Thumbnails, Grid, Cover Switch, and Flip Switch, as well as smaller listings such as informative, compact, text icons, and small icons. The Alt-Tab keys implement the effect you have chosen. Continually pressing the Tab key while holding down the Alt key moves you through the windows. Thumbnails displays windows in a boxed dialog (see Figure 9-79, whereas Cover Switch arranges windows stacked to the sides, and Flip Switch arranges the windows to one side. The default is Breeze, which arranges the window images to the left side of the screen (see Figure 9-80).

Figure 9-78: Window Management | Task Switcher

Figure 9-79: Thumbnail Switch - Alt-Tab

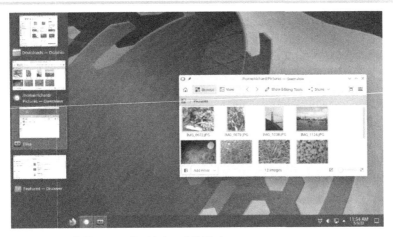

Figure 9-80: Thumbnail Breeze Switch - Alt-Tab

The Present Windows effect displays images of the open windows on your screen with the selected one highlighted (see Figure 9-81). You can use your mouse to select another. This provides an easy way to browse your open windows. You can also use Ctrl-F9 to display windows on your current virtual desktop statically and use the arrow key to move between them. Use Ctrl-F10 to display all your open windows across all your desktops. Press the ESC key to return to the desktop.

Desktop Grid will show a grid of all your virtual desktops (Ctrl-F8), letting you see all your virtual desktops on the screen at once (see Figure 9-82). You can then move windows and open applications between desktops. Clicking on a desktop makes it the current one. The plus and minus keys allow you to add or remove virtual desktops.

Figure 9-81: Present Windows (Windows effects) Ctrl-F9 and Ctrl-f10

Figure 9-82: Desktop Grid - Ctrl-F8

KDE File Manager: Dolphin

Dolphin is KDE's dedicated file manager (see Figure 9-83). A navigation bar shows the current folder either in a browser or edit mode. In the browse mode it shows icons for the path of your current folder, and in the edit mode, it shows the path name in a text-editable box. You can use either to move to different folders and their subfolders. Click to the right of the folder buttons to use the edit mode. Clicking on the checkmark at the end of the editable text box returns you to the browser mode. If you are using the menubar, you can also choose View | Location Bar | Editable Location.

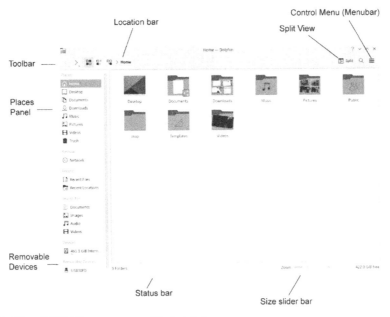

Figure 9-83: The KDE file manager (Dolphin)

The Dolphin menubar has been hidden by default. The menus are displayed when clicking the Control button on the right end of the toolbar (see Figure 9-84). You can redisplay the menubar by choosing "Show Menubar" from the menu (**Ctrl-m**). You can hide the menubar again by choosing Show Menubar from the Settings menu (or pressing **Ctrl-m**).

Figure 9-84: The KDE file manager menus

You can open a file either by double-clicking it or by right-clicking it, and choosing the "Open With" entry to list applications to open it with. If you want to just select the file or folder, just single-click it. A double-click will open the file. If the file is a program, that program starts up.

If it is a data file, such as a text file, the associated application is run using that data file. Clicking a text file displays it with the Kate editor while clicking an image file displays it with the Gwenview image viewer. If Dolphin cannot determine the application to use, it opens a dialog box prompting you to enter the application name. Also, if the application you want is not listed in the "Open With" menu, you can choose "Other Application" to open this same dialog. You can choose from a list of installed applications or search for an application. You can also click the folder button by the search box to use a folder tree to locate the application program you want.

Dolphin can display panels to either side (Dolphin refers to these as panels, though they operate more like stand-alone tabs). The Places panel will show icons for often-used folders like Home, Network, and Trash, as well as removable devices. To add a folder to the Places panel, just drag it there.

The files and folders listed in a folder can be viewed in several different ways using the icons on the left side of the toolbar. If you are using the menubar, you also can choose an option from the View | View Mode submenu. Files and folders can be displayed as icons, a detailed list, and as columns. See Table 9-4 for keyboard shortcuts.

The "Show Additional Information" submenu in the menu lets you display additional information about files such as the size, date, type, and comments (if you are using the menubar, you can choose it on the View menu). Type specific information can also be displayed such as album, track, and duration for audio files, and word and line counts for documents. You can also display the full path, permissions, and group information (Other submenu).

Keys	Description
ALT-LEFT ARROW, ALT-RIGHT ARROW	Backward and Forward in History
ALT-UP ARROW	One folder up
ENTER	Open a file/folder
LEFT/RIGHT/UP/DOWN ARROWS	Move among the icons
PAGE UP, PAGE DOWN	Scroll fast
CTRL-C	Copy selected file to clipboard
CTRL-V	Paste files from clipboard to current folder
CTRL-S	Select files by pattern
CTRL-L	URI text box location bar
CTRL-F	Find files
CTRL-Q	Close window

Table 9-4: KDE File Manager Keyboard Shortcuts

You can display additional panels by selecting them from the Show Panels submenu in the menu (if you are using the menubar, choose it from the View menu). The Information panel displays detailed information about a selected file or folder, and the Folders panel displays a folder tree for the file system. The panels are detachable from the file manager window (see Figure 9-85). Be sure to choose "Unlock Panels" in the Show Panels menu to make them detachable.

Figure 9-85: The KDE file manager with panels

The Places panel makes use of file metadata to provide easy access to files by category and date. The Places panel has five sections: Places, Remote, Recent, Search For, and Devices. The Places section holds your home folder, the Desktop folder, and the trash. The Devices section holds your attached devices, including removable devices. The Recent section lets you display files and folders you access fairly recently (see Figure 9-86). The Search For section lets you displays files of specified types: documents, images, audio files, and videos. The Remote section holds a Network entry that lists your network devices.

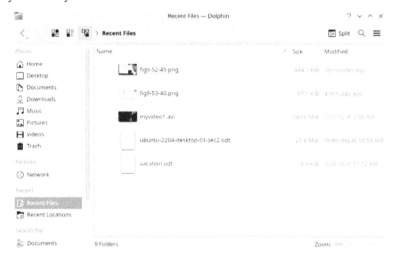

+Figure 9-86: The KDE file manager panel Recent

Dolphin supports split views, where you can open two different folders in the same window. Click the Split button in the toolbar. You can then drag folder and files from one folder to the other (see Figure 9-87).

Figure 9-87: The KDE file manager with split views

Dolphin also supports file sharing with Samba. To share a folder, right-click on the folder icon and choose Properties to open the Properties dialog. Then on the Share tab, you can choose to share the folder with Samba (Microsoft Windows). You can also set permissions for users: Read Only, Full Control, and Deny (See Figure 9-88). For the Everyone entry, you would usually set the permission to Read Only.

Figure 9-88: The KDE file manager share dialog for folders

If the Samba service is not yet installed, this tab will show a button, which you can click to install it. Should it fail to install, open the Konsole terminal window and issue the following command.

```
sudo apt install samba
```

You are then prompted to create a Samba user password, which you use to access shares (see Figure 9-89). You will also have to enter the password of an administrative user to create the Samba password.

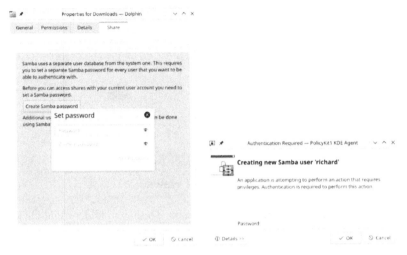

Figure 9-89: The KDE file manager Samba password creation

To configure Dolphin, click Configure Dolphin from the Control menu to open the Dolphin Preferences dialog with tabs for General, Startup, View Modes, Navigation, Context Menu, Trash, and User Feedback (see Figure 9-90). If you are using the menubar, you can select Configure Dolphin from the Settings menu.

Figure 9-90: Dolphin file manager configuration

The General tab has sub-tabs for Behavior, Previews, Confirmations, and Status Bar. The Behavior tab is where you can enable tool tips and show selection markers. Preview lets you choose which type of files to preview. The image, jpeg, and PDF types are already selected. On Confirmations, you can require confirmation prompts for emptying the trash, moving files to the trash, or closing multiple tabs. On the Status tab, you can choose to show the zoom slider and the amount of free storage.

On the Startup tab, you can specify features like the split view and the default folder to start up with. On the View Modes tab, you can set display features for the different display modes (Icons, Details, and Column), like the icon size, font type, and arrangement. The Navigation tab sets features like opening archives as folders. The Context Menu tab is where you specify services to be shown in the context menu such as "open in New Window", Delete, and "Run in Konsole." he Trash tab lets you configure trash settings like deleting items in the trash after a specified time and setting the maximum size of the trash.

Navigating Folders

Within a file manager window, a double-click on a folder icon moves to that folder and displays its file and sub-folder icons. To move back up to the parent folder, you click the back arrow button located on the left end of the navigation toolbar. A double-click on a folder icon moves you down the folder tree, one folder at a time. By clicking the back arrow button, you move up the tree.

The Navigation bar can display either the folder path for the current folder or an location box where you can enter in a pathname. For the folder path, you can click on any displayed folder name to move you quickly to an upper-level folder.

The location box can be opened in editable mode, or in replacement mode. The replacement mode selects the path for you to let you press the delete key to remove it entirely so that you can type in another path.

To use the location box, click to the right of the folder path. The Location box is is opened in edit mode. If you are using the menubar, you can select Show Full Location in the View | Location Bar | Editable location menu item. The navigation bar changes to an editable textbox where you can edit a path name. To change back to the folder path, click the check mark to the right of the text box. You can also press F6 to display the location box in edit mode. To open the location box in replacement mode, you press Ctrl-L. If you are using the menubar, you can choose Show Full Location in the View | Location Bar | Replace location menu item. Both F6 and Ctrl-L will toggle between the folder path and location box.

Like a Web browser, the file manager remembers the previous folder it has displayed. You can use the back and forward arrow buttons to move through this list of prior folders. You can also use several keyboard shortcuts to perform such operations, like Alt-back-arrow to move up a folder, and the arrow keys to move to different icons.

Copy, Move, Delete, Rename, and Link Operations

To perform an operation on a file or folder, you first have to select it by clicking the file's icon or listing. To select more than one file, hold down the CTRL key while you click the files you want. You can also use the keyboard arrow keys to move from one file icon to another.

To copy and move files, you can use the standard drag-and-drop method with your mouse. To copy a file, you locate it by using the file manager. Open another file manager window to the folder to which you want the file copied. Then drag-and-drop the file icon to that window. A pop-up menu appears with selections for Move Here, Copy Here, or Link Here. Choose Copy Here. To move a file to another folder, follow the same procedure, but select Move Here from the pop-up menu. To copy or move a folder, use the same procedure as for files. All the folder's files and subfolders are also copied or moved. Instead of having to select from a pop-up menu, you can use the corresponding keys: **Ctrl** for copy, **Shift** for move, and **Ctrl-Shift** for link.

To rename a file, Click its icon and then click the icon's name or press F2. You can also right-click the icon and select Rename from the pop-up menu. A text box appears around the name and you can enter a new name or edit the current one.

You can delete a file by placing it in the Trash folder to delete later. To place a file in the Trash folder, drag-and-drop it to the Trash icon on the Dolphin Places panel, or right-click the file and choose "Move To Trash" from the pop-up menu. You can later open the Trash folder and delete the files. To delete all the files in the Trash folder, right-click the Trash icon in Dolphin file manager Places panel, and select Empty Trash from the pop-up menu. To restore files in the Trash bin, open the Trash window and right click on the file to restore and select Restore.

Each file or folder has properties associated with it that include permissions, the filename, and its folder. To display the Properties dialog for a given file, right-click the file's icon and select the Properties entry. On the General tab, you see the name of the file displayed. To change the filename, replace the name there with a new one. Permissions are set on the Permissions tab. Here, you can set read, write, and execute permissions for user, group, or other access to the file. The Group entry enables you to change the group for a file. The Checksums tab lets you check the validity of a downloaded file by checking its checksum to make sure it was downloaded correctly. The Details tab show information about the file such as size, modification time, and type.

Search Bar and Filter Bar

The Dolphin search tool provides a simplified search bar for files and folders. KDE also supports a filter bar to search files and folders in the current folder. For quick access to basic categories and recent use you can use the Dolphin file manager Places panel's Recent and Search For entries, as noted previously.

Search Bar

To search for files, click the Find button on the icon bar to open the search bar, which displays a search text box (**Ctrl-f**). The search bar displays a search text box where you enter the pattern of the file or folder you are searching for. Click the red x button to the left to close the find bar, and use the black x button in the text box to clear the search pattern.

Buttons below the search box provide options to qualify the search. The Filename button (the default) searches on the filename. The Content button will search the contents of text files for the pattern. The "From Here" button searches from the current folder, and the "Your files" button searches from the user's home folders (see Figure 9-91). The "More Search Tools" button displays a menu of other search tools you can use.

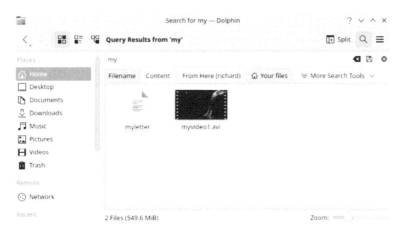

Figure 9-91: The KDE Search Bar

The search results are displayed in the main pane. You can double-click a file to have it open with its appropriate application. Text files are displayed by the Kate text editor, images by Gwenview, and applications are run. When you are finished searching, click the Search close button.

The search operation makes use of the KDE implementation of Baloo desktop search. To configure desktop search, choose System Settings | Workspace | Search | File Search tab. On the File Search tab, you can enable or disable file searching, and choose folders not to search. You can also enable file content indexing.

Filter Bar

For a quick search of the current folder, you can activate the Filter bar by choosing Filter entry on the menu or by pressing **Ctrl-i** (if you are using the menubar, you can choose it from the Tools menu) This opens a Filter search box at the bottom of the window. Enter a pattern, and only those file and folder names containing that pattern are displayed. Click the x button at the right of the Filter box to clear it (see Figure 9-92).

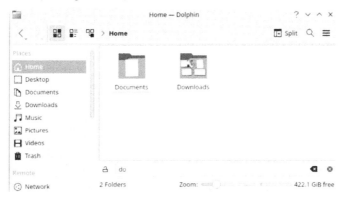

Figure 9-92: The KDE Filter Bar

FTP

Onthe KDE Desktop, the desktop file manager Dolphin has built-in FTP capability. The FTP operation has been seamlessly integrated into standard desktop file operations. Downloading files from an FTP site is as simple as copying files by dragging them from one folder window to another, with one of the folders located on a remote FTP site. To download files from an FTP site, you open a window to access that site, entering the URL for the FTP site in the window's location box. Use the **ftp://** protocol for FTP access. Once connected, open the folder you want, and then open another window for the local folder to which you want the remote files copied. In the window showing the FTP files, select the ones you want to download. Then click-and-drag those files to the window for the local folder. A pop-up menu appears with choices for Copy, Link, or Move. Select Copy. The selected files are then downloaded. Another window opens, showing the download progress and displaying the name of each file in turn, along with a bar indicating the percentage downloaded so far.

KDE Configuration: KDE System Settings

With the Plasma configuration tools, you can configure your desktop and system, changing the way it is displayed and the features it supports. The configuration dialogs are accessed on the System Settings. On Plasma, you can access System Settings from the System Settings entry in the Computer or Favorites menus, or from Applications | Settings | System Settings.

The System Settings window can be displayed either with the icon view or sidebar view. Use the Configure dialog | General tab to choose the view you want. You can access the Configure dialog from the menu on the sidebar view (upper left corner) or the Configure button on the icon view (top toolbar). The sidebar view is the current default (see Figure 9-93).

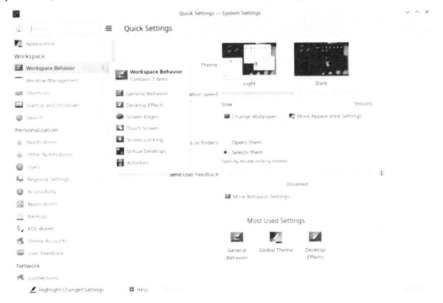

Figure 9-93: Plasma System Settings - Sidebar view

The sidebar organizes settings into several sections (see Figure 94). The Appearance section lets you set the desktop theme, manage fonts, choose icon sets, and select application and window styles (see Figure 9-95). The Workspace section lets you set desktop effects, virtual desktops, window actions, startup applications, and desktop search. The Network section holds icons for configuring networking preferences, Bluetooth connections, and sharing. Personalization lets you perform administrative tasks such as user management, the date and time, notifications, online accounts, and file/application associations. Hardware lets you set the printer configuration, power management, multimedia devices (sound), your display resolution, and to manage drivers.

Note: On KDE, use the System Settings Online Accounts to set up access to your online services, where you can add and configure online accounts such as Google.

Figure 9-94: Plasma System Settings - Sidebar icon list

Figure 9-95: KDE System Settings | Application Style, Widget Style

User management is provided by Kuser, accessible from System Settings | Account Details (Personalization section), User Manager tab (see Figure 9-96) .

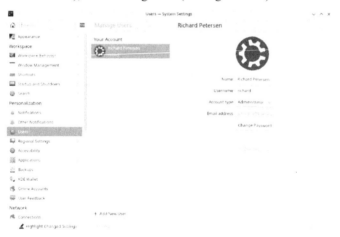

Figure 9-96: KDE System Settings | User Manager

The icon view was the default in previous releases. With the sidebar view, System Settings shows an icon list of setting categories arranged in several sections: Appearance, Workspace, Personalization, Network, Hardware, and System Administration (see Figure 9-97).

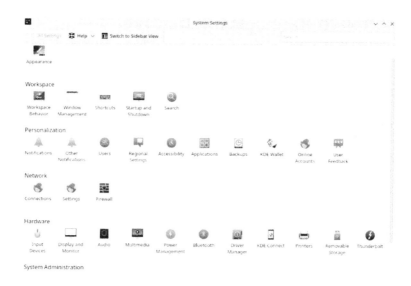

Figure 9-97: Plasma System Settings - Icon view

Click an entry to display a new icon list in the sidebar with configuration entries for that category. Some entries, such as Color and Global Theme, will have no added configuration entries. Selecting an entry shows the configuration settings on the right pane (see Figure 9-98).

Figure 9-98: Plasma System Settings - Icon view

Plasma Software Management: Discover

Discover is Plasma's corresponding application to Ubuntu Software. It uses a simple interface to let you quickly locate and install software. Applications can be easily removed with a click. With Discover, you can also install Plasma (KDE) desktop add-ons, including widgets for the desktop and panel. Discover shows a sidebar on the left and a list of applications to the right (see Figure 9-99). You use the Discover sidebar to locate software packages. Clicking on a package entry expands it to a software description with an Install button (installed packages have a Remove button) (see Figure 9-100). A Sources menu, next to the Install menu, lets you choose whether to install from an APT repository such as ubuntu-jammy-universe, or from the Snap repository.

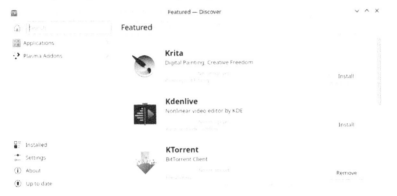

Figure 9-99: Discover Software Manager

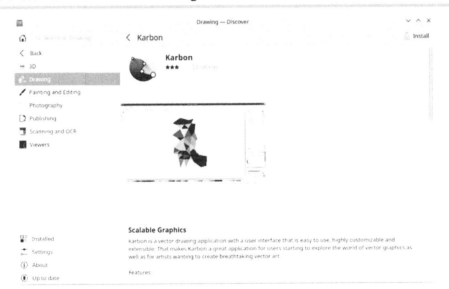

Figure 9-100: Discover Software Manager - Application Description

The Applications entry expands to software categories on the sidebar, which, when selected, will display a list of available and installed packages in the right pane. The Installed entry lists all your installed packages with a Remove button for easy deletion. You can also use the

Search box at the top of the sidebar to locate a package. The Settings entry lists your repositories, which you can enable or disable.

The Plasma Addons entry on the sidebar provides an extensive set of addons to different parts of the Plasma desktop. There are categories for fonts, themes, icons, window effects, window switching, and wallpapers, among others. You use the Plasma Widgets entry to manage your desktop and panel widgets.

The Application Addons entry lists addons for particular applications, such as calendar events for Korganizer.

+

10. Ubuntu MATE

MATE Desktop

Windows

Workspaces

MATE Menu

MATE Panel

Applets

The Caja File Manager

Preferences (desktop configuration)

The MATE desktop is a simplified and easy to use desktop derived from the GNOME 2.4 desktop. MATE's official file manager is Caja. Those familiar with GNOME 2 will find similar features. The Ubuntu MATE desktop use the MATE desktop with Ubuntu software repositories. The MATE version of Ubuntu is called Ubuntu MATE and is available as a separate Desktop USB/DVD, and as the **ubuntu-mate-desktop** meta-package on the APT repository (Synaptic Package Manager or **apt** command). The version of MATE used for 22.04 is MATE 1.26.1. It uses several different applications from Ubuntu, such as the Ayatana Indicator applet, the Arctica Greeter (login screen), the Celluloid video player, and the Webcamoid webcam application. Ubuntu MATE is an official Ubuntu Flavour, supported by Ubuntu. The Ubuntu MATE website is:

```
https://ubuntu-mate.org
```

Ubuntu MATE Help and Documentation: Welcome

The first time you access Ubuntu MATE, the Welcome dialog is displayed (see Figure 10-1), with links for configuration, information, and online sites about Ubuntu MATE (you are initially asked whether to send system information to Ubuntu MATE or not). Be sure to check the Getting Started link, which covers key post-install topics such as updates, drivers, firewalls, backups, and user configuration, as well as customization links to background settings (wallpaper), the control center, and the desktop configuration dialog (MATE Tweak) (see Figure 10-2) . You can redisplay the Welcome dialog anytime from Welcome entry in the Administration menu.

Figure 10-1: Ubuntu MATE Welcome dialog

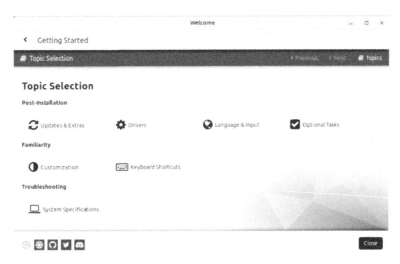

Figure 10-2: Ubuntu MATE Welcome dialog - Getting Started

The Desktop Layout dialog lets you choose from different MATE desktop themes that approximate other popular desktops such as Mutiny for Ubuntu, Redmond for Windows, and Cupertino for the Mac (see Figure 10-3). Familiar is the default, the Ubuntu MATE layout. The Traditional layout is the version used in previous Ubuntu Mate releases, featuring a Classic menu. Contemporary is similar to the Familiar layout, but features an application menu on the top panel. Pantheon features a dock instead of a bottom panel.

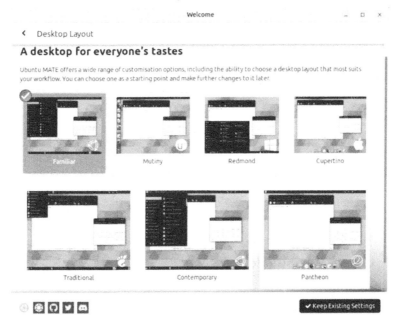

Figure 10-3: Ubuntu MATE Welcome dialog - Desktop Layout

The Browser Selection button lets you choose which browser you want to use with Install buttons for those not installed (see Figure 10-4). Firefox is the default. With the Color Selection dialog you can change both the color of your desktop and the shade (light or dark).

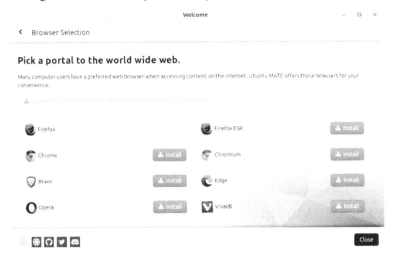

Figure 10-4: Ubuntu MATE Welcome dialog - Browser Selection

The Ubuntu MATE Guide provides detailed documentation on using MATE (see Figure 10-5) . It is accessible from the Accessories menu, Ubuntu MATE Guide entry. The "All Help" option on the menu displays a lists of documentation for applications.

Figure 10-5: Ubuntu MATE Guide

You should also check the online Ubuntu Guide at:

`https://guide.ubuntu-mate.org/`

If provides a detailed description of all the Ubuntu Mate desktop features, with examples.

Software Boutique

Ubuntu MATE also provides a software manager called Software Boutique, which provides the MATE applications available on the Ubuntu repositories (see Figure 10-6) . Use the icon bar at the top to move to different categories, such as Graphics, Office, Sound & Video, and Servers. lick the install button to install a package. Use the Filter menu to reduce the selection by subcategory. Software Boutique access to Ubuntu Snap repositories as well as APT repositories. It has enabled support for Flathub, but has not enabled the repository. You can do so with the following command in a terminal window.

```
flatpak remote-add --if-not-exists flathub
https://flathub.org/repo/flathub.flatpakrepo
```

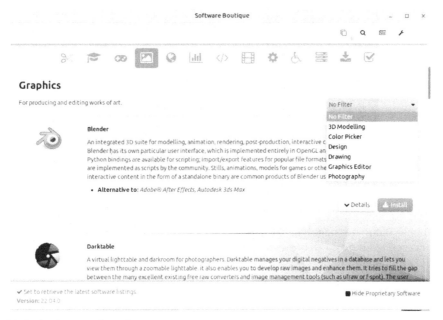

Figure 10-6: Software Boutique

MATE Applications

MATE features several applications. The applications are on the Ubuntu repository and can be installed on Ubuntu, but are promoted to default status on Ubuntu Mate. For example, Ubuntu uses Videos as its primary video player, whereas Ubuntu MATE uses Celluloid. In place of the Ubuntu Cheese web cam, MATE uses Webcamoid. For a text editor, MATE uses Pluma, instead of Gedit. MATE also has versions of system tools and utilities that operate in a similar way to their corresponding Ubuntu versions such as the Engrampa Archive Manager, Software Boutique, Eye of MATE Image Viewer, MATE Dictionary, MATE terminal, and the MATE System Monitor.

Webcamoid is a cross-platform basic webcam picture and video capture (see Figure 10-7) application available for Linux, MACOS, and Windows. It is based on the Qt library used by KDE. A simple dock at the bottom of the Webcamoid window lets you run and configure your webcam. Click the Play button to turn the webcam on or off. There are buttons to configure sources, sound, and effects. When running you can take a photo and record the session. The Preferences dialog lets you add a webcam, enable advanced effects, select video and audio libraries to use, add plugins. The Webcamoid configuration settings are located in your home folder in the **.config/Webcamoid** folder.

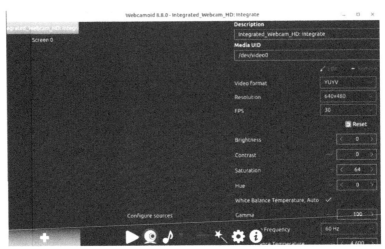

Figure 10-7: Webcamoid webcam application

Webcamoid provides virtual camera support allowing other applications to interface with it. Linux applications are supported, such as Gstreamer and mplayer, as well as commercial application such as Firefox web browser and Skype. See the Webcamoid web site for more details: **https://webcamoid.github.io/**.

Celluloid is a GTK+ frontend for the MPV video player formerly known as GNOME MPV (**https://github.com/celluloid-player/celluloid**). It provides a basic interface with standard controls and playlist (see Figure 10-8). You can also select video, audio, and subtitle tracks. The Preferences dialog has four tabs: Interface, Config Files, Miscellaneous, and Plugins. On the Interface tab you can configure the application with features such as the dark theme, floating controls, and cursor autohide. Config Files lets you load an MPV configuration file containing additional MPV option. A list of available MPV options are described in the MPV manual, **https://mpv.io/manual/stable/#synopsis**. Should you have user scripts for configuration, you can load them on the on Miscellaneous tab. The configuration file for Celluloid is **/etc/mpv/mpv.conf**.

Figure 10-8: Celluloid on MATE

The MATE Desktop

The MATE desktop is designed to be simple, with a two panels and desktop icons (see Figure 10-9). The top panel appears as a long bar across the top of the screen, and holds menus, program launchers, and applet icons. You can display the panel horizontally or vertically, and have it automatically hide to show you a full screen.

Figure 10-9: MATE desktop and panel

On the left side of the top panel is the button for the main menu. With this menu, you can access places and applications. On the right side of the panel is the indicator applet that includes icons for system tools such as Keyboard, Bluetooth, Network Manager, notifications, power, sound volume, the clock, and the system menu. On the bottom panel to the left is the Show Desktop button, which hides your open windows, followed by the Window List applet, which shows buttons for open windows. On the right side is the workspace switcher and the trash.

On the right side of the top panel is the system menu (power button) with entries for opening the Control Center (System Settings), switching users, locking the screen, and performing log out, suspend, and shut down operations (see Figure 10-10). The Lock/Switch Account entry displays the lock screen that has a button for Switch User. This starts the login manager and displays a list of users you can login as. Below the Lock/Switch Account entry on the user switcher menu is a list of favorite users you can directly switch to. There are also entries to access the MATE Desktop User Guide (MATE Help) and the Ubuntu Documentation web site which has a link to the installation guide (Ubuntu Help). The "About this Computer" entry opens the System Monitor at the System tab showing information about your Ubuntu version, your computer hardware, and available disk space.

Figure 10-10: MATE system menu

The remainder of the screen is the desktop, where you can place folders, files, and application launchers. You can use a click-and-drag operation to move a file from one window to another or to the desktop. A drag-and-drop with the CTRL key held down will copy a file. A drag-and-drop operation with both the CTRL and SHIFT keys held down (Ctrl-Shift) creates a link on the desktop to that folder or file. Your home folder is accessed from the Home Folder icon on the desktop. Double clicking it opens a file manager window for your home folder. A right-click anywhere on the desktop displays a desktop menu with which you can align your desktop icons, change the background, and create new folders.

To quit the desktop, you click the system menu the right side of the top panel and select the Shut Down entry. This opens a menu with options to Suspend, Restart, and Shut Down.

Indicator Applet Configuration

MATE uses the Ayatana Indicators applet, a cross-platform compatible version of the Ubuntu Indicators. You can configure the indicator applet (top right panel) with the System Settings Indicator dialog. Open System Settings and click on the Indicators icon in the Look and

Feel section to open the Ayatana Indicators Settings dialog (see Figure 10-11).The dialog has tabs for Session (System Menu), Date and Time, Sound, Power, Messages, Bluetooth, Notifications, and Keyboard. A button at the bottom of each tab lets you enable the indicator on login. On the Sessions tab you can set options for the System Menu such as showing the user name on the panel, removing log out or restart entries, or removing the list of users from the menu.

Figure 10-11: MATE Indicator Applet Configuration - Sessions (System Menu)

For Date and Time you can choose to show the year, month, weekdays, and seconds on the panel, as well as the calendar, calendar week numbers, and events in the menu (see Figure 10-12) .

Figure 10-12: MATE Indicator Applet Configuration - Date and Time

Sound has an option to allow the volume to go above 100%. For Power you can show the percentage left on a battery as well as the time. For Notifications you can choose the maximum number of items to show (see Figure 10-13). You can also choose what applications not to display in the indicator messages menu. The Spotify, Network Manager and MATE Tweak applications are already chosen. To add more, right-click on the cursor in the text box below the list to display a menu of possible applications to choose from. Once chosen, click the Add button.

Figure 10-13: MATE Indicator Applet Configuration - Notifications

MATE Components

From a user's point of view, the desktop interface has four components: the desktop, the panels, the main menu, and the file manager (see Figure 10-14). You have two panels displayed, used for menus, application icons, and managing your windows. When you open a window, a corresponding button for it will be displayed in the lower panel, which you can use to minimize and restore the window.

Figure 10-14: MATE with Brisk Menu and Caja file manager

To start a program, you can select its entry from the main menu. You can also click its application icon in the panel (if one is present) or drag-and-drop data files to its icon. To add an icon for an application to the desktop, right-click on its entry in the main menu and select "Add to desktop". You can also click the Alt-F2 keys to open the Run Applications dialog which lists available applications (see Figure 10-15). A search box at the top of the dialog lets you search for an application. There are options you can select to run in a terminal window, "Run in a terminal", and to select a file to open with the application, "Run with file…".

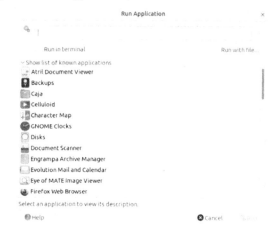

Figure 10-15: Run Application dialog, Alt-F2

You can also quickly access a menu of applications on the desktop with the Alt-F1 keys (see Figure 10-16). Click anywhere on the desktop and press Alt-F2 to display a menu of application categories which expand to submenus of applications when you pass your mouse over them. Click on the application you want to start.

Figure 10-16: Application desktop menu, Alt-F1

Drag-and-Drop Files to the Desktop

Any icon for an item that you drag-and-drop from a file manager window to the desktop also appears on the desktop. However, the default drag-and-drop operation is a move operation. If you select a file in your file manager window and drag it to the desktop, you are actually moving the file from its current folder to the desktop folder, which is located in your home folder and holds all items on the desktop. The desktop folder is named **Desktop**. In the case of dragging folders to the desktop, the entire folder and its subfolders will be moved to the Desktop folder.

To remove an icon from the desktop, you right-click and choose "Move to Trash." If you choose to display the trash icon on the desktop, you can simply drag-and-drop it in the trash.

You can copy a file to your desktop by pressing the Ctrl key and then clicking and dragging it from a file manager window to your desktop. You will see the mouse icon change to hand with a small + symbol, indicating that you are creating a copy, instead of moving the original.

You can also create a link on the desktop to any file. There are two ways to create a link. While holding down the Ctrl and Shift keys, Ctrl-SHIFT, drag the file to where you want the link created. A copy of the icon then appears with a small arrow in the right corner indicating it is a link. You can click this link to start the program, open the file, or open the folder, depending on the type of file to which you linked. Alternatively, first click and drag the file out of the window, and after moving the file but before releasing the mouse button, press the ALT key. This will display a pop-up menu with selections for Move Here, Copy Here, and Link Here. Select the Link Here option to create a link.

The drag-and-drop file operation works on virtual desktops provided by the Workspace Switcher. The Workspace Switcher creates icons for each virtual desktop in the panel, along with task buttons for any applications open on them. The Workspace Switcher is not added by default. You will have to add it to the panel.

MATE Tweak

You can configure desktop and window display settings using the MATE Tweak dialog, which you can access from the Preferences menu, or from the Control Center (see Figure 10-17). The MATE Tweak dialog has three tabs: Desktop, Panel, and Windows. The Desktop tab lets you choose which system icons to display on the desktop. The Computer and Home folder icons are initially selected, along with Mounted volumes for external file systems such as USB drives and DVDs that you insert. You can also choose to display the Computer, Network, and Trash icons. The first option lets you disable this feature, hiding all the desktop icons.

Figure 10-17: MATE Tweak

The Panel tab lets you configure your panel, choosing from a panel layout style, possible features for the panel chosen (Panel Menu Features), and added panel features such as using a dock, displaying a keyboard LED, and choosing the size of icons in the panel.

On Windows tab, you can turn off compositing by changing the window manager. Change the location of the minimize, maximize, and close buttons from the right side of the title bar to the left side. You can also enable or disable window features such as window snapping and animations, as well as select the font you want to use for windows.

Applications on the Desktop

In some cases, you will want to create another way on the desktop to access a file without moving it from its original folder. You can do this either by using an application launcher icon or by creating a link to the original program. Application launcher icons are the components used in menus and panels to display and access applications. To place an application icon on your desktop for an entry in the menus, you can simply drag-and-drop the application entry from the menu to the desktop, or right-click and select "Add to desktop."

For applications that are not on a menu, you can either create an application launcher button or create a direct link for it. To create an application launcher, right-click the desktop background to display the desktop menu, and then select the "Create Launcher" entry. To create a simple link, click-and-drag a program's icon while holding the Ctrl-Shift keys down to the desktop.

The Desktop Menu

You can right-click anywhere on the empty desktop to display the desktop menu that includes entries for common tasks, such as creating an application launcher, creating a new folder, or organizing the icon display (see Figure 10-18). Keep in mind that the Create Folder entry creates a new folder on your desktop, specifically in your Desktop folder (**Desktop**), not your home folder. The entries for this menu are listed in Table 10-1.

Menu Item	Description
Create Folder	Creates a new folder on your desktop, within your DESKTOP folder.
Create Launcher	Creates a new desktop icon for an application.
Create Document	Creates files using installed templates or a simple text file
Revert to Previous Version	Restore files from backup
Open in Terminal	Open Desktop folder in a terminal window
Keep Aligned	Aligns your desktop icons.
Organize Desktop by Name	Arranges your desktop icons.
Lock Icons Position	Fix icons at current positions.
Cut, Copy, Paste	Cuts, copies, or pastes files, letting you move or copy files between folders.
Change Desktop Background	Opens a Background Preferences dialog to let you select a new background for your desktop.

Table 10-1: The GNOME Desktop Menu

Figure 10-18: MATE Desktop Menu

Windows

You can resize a window by clicking any of its sides or corners and dragging. You can move the window with a click-and-drag operation on its title bar. You can also ALT-click and drag anywhere on the window. The upper-right corner of a window shows the Minimize, Maximize, and Close buttons (minus, square, and x buttons). Clicking the Minimize button no longer displays the window on the desktop. A button for it remains on the bottom panel (the Window list applet) that you can click to restore it. The panel button for a window works like a display toggle. If the window is displayed when you click the panel button, it will no longer be shown. If not displayed, it will then be shown. Right-click anywhere on the title bar displays a window menu with entries for window operations (see Figure 10-19). The options include workspace entries to move the window to another workspace (virtual desktop) or make visible on all workspaces, which displays the window no matter to what workspace you move.

Figure 10-19: MATE window and window menu

You can quickly move between windows by pressing the Alt-Tab keys. A window switcher bar opens displaying thumbnails of open windows (see Figure 10-20). Continue pressing the Alt-Tab keys to move through them. To enable thumbnails, be sure that the "Enable software compositing window manager" option is selected on the Windows Preferences dialog's General tab (Preferences | Windows). You also have the option to disable thumbnails for the switcher, displaying only small icons for the open windows.

Figure 10-20: Switching Windows with thumbnails

You can configure window behavior using the Window Preferences dialog's Behavior tab accessible from the Preference menu and the Control Center. You choose features such as to select windows by moving the mouse over them and use the Super key instead of the Alt key to move a window. From a menu, you can choose the action to perform when the title bar is double-clicked. The default is maximize, but other options include to roll up the window and minimize it.

On the Placement tab, you can choose to center new windows and to enable window snapping (side by side tiling).

Window List

The Window List applet on the left side of the bottom panel shows currently opened windows (see Figure 10-21). The Window List arranges opened windows in a series of buttons, one for each window. A window can include applications such as a Web browser or a file manager window displaying a folder. You can move from one displayed window to another by clicking its button. When you minimize a window, you can later restore it by clicking its entry in the Window List. Hovering your mouse over a window button displays a thumbnail of the window, showing you the application opened and its content.

Right clicking a window's Window List button opens a menu that lets you Minimize or Unminimize, Move, Resize, Maximize, or Close the window, and move the window to another workspace. The Minimize operation will reduce the window to its Window List entry. Right clicking the entry will display the menu with an Unminimize option instead of a Minimize one, which you can then use to redisplay the window. The Close entry will close the window, ending its application. There are also entries for moving the window to another workspace.

Figure 10-21: Window List applet

The Window List applet is represented by a small bar at the beginning of the window list applet. To configure the Window List applet, right-click on this area and select the Preferences entry to open the Window List Preferences dialog (see Figure 10-22). Here, you can set features such as whether to group windows on the panel, whether to show all open windows or those from just the current workspace, and which workspace to restore windows to.

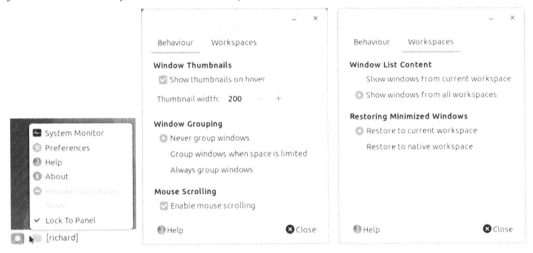

Figure 10-22: Window List Preferences

If you choose to group windows, then common windows are grouped under a button that will expand like a menu, listing each window in that group. For example, all open terminal windows would be grouped under a single button, which when clicked would pop up a list of their buttons. The button shows the number of open windows. You can also choose to group only if there is not enough space on the Window List applet to display a separate button for each window.

Workspace Switcher

The Workspace Switcher applet, located on the right side of the bottom panel, lets you switch to different virtual desktops (see Figure 10-23 You can add the Workspace Switcher to any panel by selecting it from that panel's Add To dialog. The Workspace Switcher shows your entire virtual desktop as separate rectangles listed next to each other. Open windows show up as small rectangles in these squares. You can move any window from one virtual desktop to another by clicking and dragging its image in the Workspace Switcher from one workspace to another.

Figure 10-23: Workspace switcher, one row and two rows

In addition to the Workspace Switcher, you can use the scroll button on your mouse, or the Ctrl-Alt-*arrow* keys to move from one workspace to another. When you use the Ctrl-Alt-arrow keys, the right and left arrows move you through a row, and the up and down keys move you from one row to another. A small workspace bar appears at the center of the screen, highlighting the current workspace and displaying its name (see Figure 10-24).

Figure 10-24: Switching workspaces, Ctrl-Alt-*arrow*

To configure the Workspace Switcher, right-click on the applet to display a menu, and then select Preferences to display the Workspace Switcher Preferences dialog box (see Figure 10-25). Here, you can select the number of workspaces and name them. The default is four. You can also choose the number of rows for the workspace and whether to show their names.

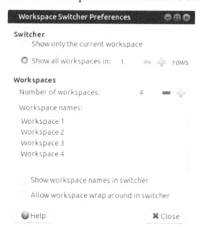

Figure 10-25: Workspace Switcher Preferences

MATE Panel Layouts

Ubuntu MATE provides a variety of panel layouts to choose from. You can choose the panel layout using the Panel tab on the MATE Tweak dialog (Preferences menu) (see Figure 10-26). Available layouts include Familiar (the default), Contemporary, Cupertino, Mutiny, Netbook, Pantheon, Redmond, and Traditional. You can easily choose a layout using the Welcome dialogs (Administration menu) and clicking on the "Desktop Layout" button in the lower right corner to open the "Desktop Layout" dialog, as noted previously in this chapter's "Help and Documentation" section. Also, for a detailed description, check the online MATE Desktop Guide at:

`https://guide.ubuntu-mate.org/#personalization-panel-layouts`

You can activate certain features for a panel, as well as add applets to the panel, and then save it as your own, using the "Save as" button.

The Familiar layout is the default Ubuntu MATE layout with two panels, a top and bottom one. It uses the Brisk menu. The Traditional panel layout also has two panels, but use a Classic menu at the top. The Traditional layout is the one used in previous releases of Ubuntu MATE.

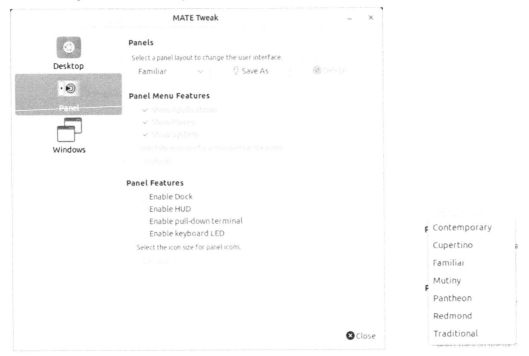

Figure 10-26: MATE Tweaks, Panel tab

The Cupertino, Pantheon, and Mutiny panel layouts all use the MATE Plank dock, which works similar to the dock on the MAC OS. Cupertino and Mutiny use the Brisk menu with a dash layout, whereas most of the others use the Brisk menu.

The Contemporary and Cupertino layouts feature an application menu on the top panel. For the currently active window, that application's menus are displayed on the top panel.

Familiar Layout

The Familiar layout is the default Ubuntu MATE layout, with two panels, top and bottom. It uses the Brisk menu, locate at the left side of the top menu. (see Figure 10-27) .

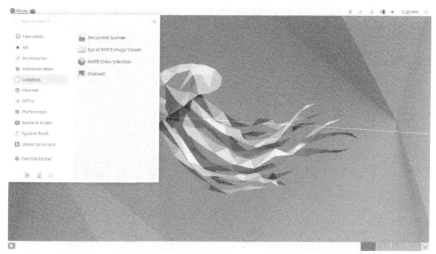

Figure 10-27: Familiar Panel Layout

Traditional Layout

The Traditional layout implements a top and bottom panel, but uses the Classic menu instead of the Brisk menu (see Figure 10-28). The Classic menu is the menu used in previous releases. On the Traditional panel layout you can use the MATE Tweak Panel tab to choose whether to show applications, places, or system menus. You can also set the icon size for icons in the menus.

Figure 10-28: Traditional Panel Layout

Redmond Layout

The Redmond layout uses a standard Brisk menu but only one bottom panel. The Brisk menu is on the left side of the bottom panel (see Figure 10-29).

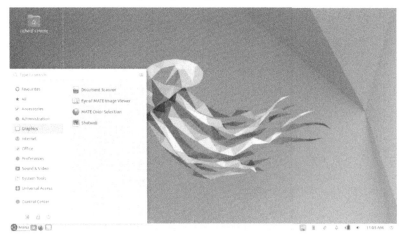

Figure 10-29: Redmond Panel Layout

Cupertino Layout

The Cupertino layout is modeled on the MAC OS and features the MATE Plank dock in place of the bottom panel (see Figure 10-30). The top panel uses the Brisk menu with the dash layout, using the entire screen and icons for menu entries. The top panel also implements an application menu. For the currently active window, its application menus are displayed on the top menu. Clicking on the desktop, displays a Desktop menu for desktop and system settings, a File menu of recently accessed files, and menus for the contents of the Documents, Music, Pictures, and Video folders.

Figure 10-30: Cupertino Panel Layout

Mutiny Layout

The Mutiny layout is also modeled on the MAC OS and features the MATE Plank dock on the left side of the screen (see Figure 10-31). The top panel uses the Brisk menu with the dash layout, using the entire screen and icons for menu entries.

Figure 10-31: Mutiny Panel Layout

Pantheon Layout

The Pantheon layout uses a standard Brisk menu, but features the MATE Plank dock in place of the bottom panel (see Figure 10-32) .

Figure 10-32: Pantheon Panel Layout

Contemporary Layout

The Contemporary layout uses a standard Brisk menu and the two top and bottom panels (see Figure 10-33). The top panel also implements an application menu, like the Cupertino layout.

Figure 10-33: Contemporary Panel Layout

MATE Panel Menus

Several different types of menus are available for Ubuntu MATE. These are incorporated into the different panel layouts. The menus include Brisk menu on the top panel (Familiar, Contemporary, and Pantheon), Brisk menu on the bottom panel (Redmond), Classic and Compact menus (Traditional), and the Brisk menu with dash layout (Mutiny and Cupertino). You can add any of these menus to a panel by using the Add to Panel dialog. The Cupertino and Pantheon layouts will also include the MATE Dock, which operates much like the dock on Apple systems.

You can edit any of the menus using the Main Menu editor, with which you can add and remove applications from the menus, create new menus, and add or remove submenus (see Figure 10-34). You can open the editor by right-clicking on the menu button on the top bar and choosing "Edit Menus" from the pop-up menu. Menus are listed to left and items shown in a selected menu are check marked on the right. Click a checkmark to no longer display an entry.

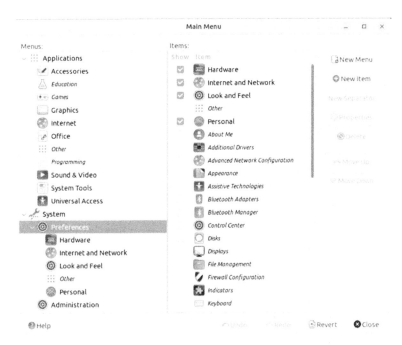

Figure 10-34: Main Menu Editor

Brisk Menu

Ubuntu MATE uses the Brisk menu on the top panel for the Familiar, Contemporary, Cupertino, and Pantheon panel layouts. On the Redmond layout the Brisk menu is placed on the single bottom panel. The Familiar panel layout is the default. Application categories are lists to the left and applications in a selected category are shown on the right (see Figure 10-35). The All category lists all the applications. The Favorites category lists only those application you have selected as your favorites. You can also access the Control Center and Universal Access dialog directly. Buttons at the bottom of the menu let you logout, lock, or shut down (power button) your system. At the top of the menu is a search box where you can search directly for an application. The search is dynamic, reducing the selection of found applications as you add more characters to the search pattern. If you right-click on an application, a menu is displayed with "Pin to favorites menu" and "Pin to desktop" options.

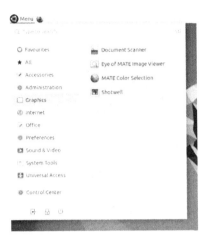

Figure 10-35: Brisk Menu - Applications

On the Redmond panel layout there is only one panel on the bottom edge of the screen. The Brisk menu is located on the left side of the panel (see Figure 10-36).

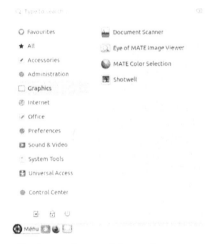

Figure 10-36: Brisk Menu - Redmond panel layout

Brisk Menu with dash layout

The Cupertino and Mutiny panel layouts (MATE-Tweak) use the Brisk Menu with a dash layout. Like GNOME, it displays an overview of icons for applications in different categories. Categories are listed at the top, along with a search box for locating applications (see Figure 10-37).

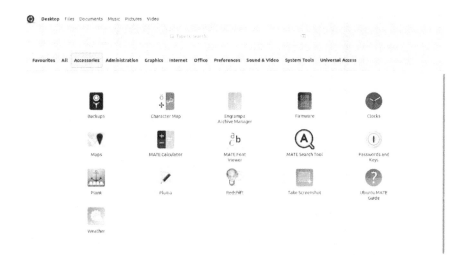

Figure 10-37: Brisk Menu with dash layout, Cupertino panel layout

Classic and Compact Menus

Ubuntu MATE uses the Classic Menu menu on the top panel for the Traditional panel layouts. It was the default panel layout used in previous release of Ubuntu MATE. The Classic Menu is a menubar that has three menus: Applications, Places, and System (See Figure 10-38). From the Applications menu, you can access your installed software applications. They are arranged by category with submenus for Internet, Graphics, Office, Sound & Video, and Accessories. The Places menu lets you access locations such as your home folder and removable devices. On the System menu you can access Administration tools from the Administration submenu, and Preferences dialogs from the Preferences submenu.

Figure 10-38: Classic Menu

The Compact menu combines the Classic menu into one menu, with the System and Places menus as submenus (see Figure 10-39). You can install the Compact menu on any panel using the "Add to Panel" dialog.

Figure 10-39: Compact Menu

Plank Applet (dock)

The Plank applet sets up a dock on the panel for applications. It initially shows a set of default applications (see Figure 10-40). As you open additional applications, icons for them appear on the panel (see Figure 10-41). In this way, the dock operates like the window list. If you minimize an application, you can maximize it again by clicking its icon. When the application closes, the icon disappears. Moving your mouse over an icon in the dock enlarges it and displays the name of the application. To have an application remain on the dock, you can right-click on it to display its menu and choose the "Keep in Dock" entry (see Figure 10-42). In effect, with the icons that remain, you can use the dock as a launcher for favorite applications. The menu also allows you to close added applications and well as perform some basic operations.

Figure 10-40: MATE Plank applet (dock) with default applications

Figure 10-41: MATE Plank on panel layout with additional applications

Figure 10-42: MATE Plank on panel layout docklet menu

You can set up the dock on any of the panel layouts by clicking the "Enable Dock" option in the MATE Tweaks Panel tab's Panel Features section (see Figure 10-43). A dock is set up at the bottom of the screen that operates more like docks in other operating systems. A set of favorite application docklets is already displayed. In the Cupertino, Pantheon, and Mutiny panel layouts, the "Enable Dock" option is selected by default. On the Mutiny panel layout the dock is placed on the left edge of the screen.

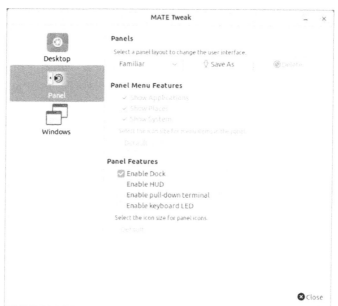

Figure 10-43: MATE Dock enabled on Mate Tweaks

You use the Plank Preferences dialog to configure your dock. It is accessible from the Preferences menu and from the Control Center | Look and Feel section as Plank Preferences. On the Plank Preferences dialog you configure the appearance, behavior, and the selection of default docklets. There are three tab: Appearance, Behavior, and Docklets. The Appearance tab lets you set the position and alignment of the dock, along with its theme (see Figure 10-44). The default theme is Yaru-light. You can position the dock on any edge of the screen: top, bottom, left, or right. The alignment can be at the center (the default), at the left of the start (left side or top), the end (right side or bottom) or fill (expands to entire edge. For fill you can align the docklets to the center, start, or end of the dock. You can also change the size of your icons making them larger or smaller. Icon zoom, where the icons enlarge when you pass your mouse over them, can be turned off. If you have multiple monitors you can choose which one to display the dock on.

Figure 10-44: MATE Plank Preferences - Appearance

       On the Behavior tab you can choose different ways to hide the dock, such as autohide when the dock is not used, or window dodge when a window covers it (see Figure 10-45). If you only want to show icons pinned to the dock, you can turn off the Show Unpinned option. To prevent icons from being removed, you can turn off the Lock Icons option. If you want to show only those icons open on a specific workspace, you can turn on the "Restrict to Workpace" option. Otherwise applications opened on one workspace are also displayed as icons in the docks shown on other workspaces.

Figure 10-45: MATE Plank Preferences - Behavior

       On the Docklets tab you have docklets you can add to your dock (see Figure 10-46) . Shown on this tab are the docklets available for your docks. The Applications docklet manages the application icons add to the dock when you open an application or window. Other docklets you can add include the clock, battery, trash, and CPU monitor. To add one, just drag it to the dock. To remove one, just drag it from the dock. These docklets have no menu with a removal option.

Figure 10-46: MATE Plank Preferences - Docklets

MATE Panel

The panel is the main component of the MATE desktop. Through it, you can start your applications, run applets, and access desktop areas. You can think of the MATE panel as a type of tool you can use on your desktop. You can have several MATE panels displayed on your desktop, each with applets and menus you have placed in them. In this respect, MATE is flexible, enabling you to configure your panels any way you want. The MATE panel works the same as the GNOME 2 panel. You can easily add applets to the panel, along with application launchers.

Ubuntu MATE uses the traditional GNOME 2 top and bottom panels by default, though you can add more. The top panel holds applets for the main menu (MATE Brisk menu), a launcher for the Firefox Web browser, and the indicator applet with several system buttons (see Figure 10-47). The indicator applet display buttons for Bluetooth, Network Manager, networking, the power manager, volume control, the clock, and shutdown.

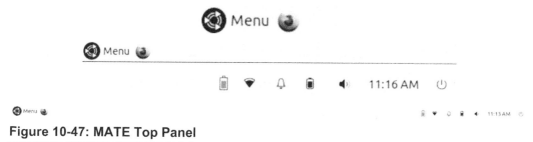

Figure 10-47: MATE Top Panel

The bottom panel has applets for Show Desktop and the window list on the left, and the workspace switcher and the Trash on the right (see Figure 10-48).

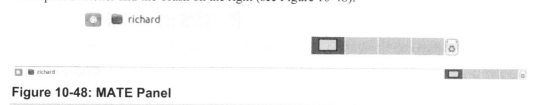

Figure 10-48: MATE Panel

Panel configuration tasks such as adding applications, selecting applets, setting up menus, and creating new panels are handled from the Panel pop-up menu (see Figure 10-49). Just right-click anywhere on the empty space of your panel to display a menu with entries for Properties, New Panel, Add To Panel, Reset Panel, and Delete This Panel, along with Help and About entries. New Panel lets you create other panels; Add To Panel lets you add items to the panel such as application launchers, applets for simple tasks like the Workspace Switcher, and menus like the MATE brisk or classic menus. The Reset Panel entry restores the panel to its desktop default state, removing any changes you made to it such as added applets, applications, or folders. The Properties entry will display a dialog for configuring the features for that panel, like the position of the panel and its hiding capabilities.

To add a new panel, select the New Panel entry in the Panel pop-up menu. A new expanded panel is automatically created and displayed at the top of your screen. You can then use the panel's Properties dialog to set different display and background features.

Figure 10-49: MATE Panel pop-up menu

Panel Properties

To configure individual panels, you use the Panel Properties dialog (see Figure 10-50). To display this dialog, you right-click a panel and select the Properties entry in the pop-up menu. For individual panels, you can set general configuration features and the background. The Panel Properties dialog displays two tabs, General and Background.

Displaying Panels

On the General tab of a panel's Properties dialog, you determine how you want the panel displayed. Here you have options for orientation, size, and whether to expand, auto-hide, or display hide buttons. The Orientation entry lets you select which side of the screen you want the panel placed on. You can then choose whether you want a panel expanded or not. An expanded panel will fill the edges of the screen, whereas a non-expanded panel is sized to the number of items in the panel and shows handles at each end. Expanded panels will remain fixed to the edge of the screen, whereas unexpanded panels can be moved.

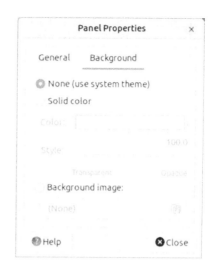

Figure 10-50: MATE Panel Properties

Moving and Hiding Expanded Panels

Expanded panels can be positioned at any edge of your screen. You can move expanded panels from one edge of a screen to another by selecting an edge from the Orientation menu on the Panel Properties General tab. If a panel is already there, the new one will stack on top of the current one. You cannot move unexpanded panels in this way. You can hide expanded panels either automatically or manually. These are features specified in the panel properties General box as the Autohide and "Show hide buttons" options. To automatically hide panels, select the Autohide feature. The panel will be hidden. To display the panel, move your mouse to the edge where the panel is located.

If you want to hide a panel manually, select the "Show hide buttons" option. Two hide buttons showing arrows will be displayed at either end of the panel. You can further choose whether to have these buttons display arrows or not (displaying arrows is the default). You can then hide the panel at any time by clicking either of the hide buttons located on each end of the panel. The arrows show the direction in which the panel will hide.

Unexpanded Panels: Movable and Fixed

Whereas an expanded panel is always located at the edge of the screen, an unexpanded panel is movable. It can be located at the edge of a screen, working like a shrunken version of an expanded panel, or you can move it to any place on your desktop, just as you would an icon.

An unexpanded panel will shrink to the number of its components, showing handles at either end (on the default Ambient-MATE theme for Ubuntu MATE, the handles show up as simply blank areas). You can then move the panel by dragging its handles. To access the panel menu with its properties entry, right-click either of its handles.

To fix an unexpanded panel at its current position, select the "Show hide buttons" option on the General tab of the panel Properties dialog. This will replace the handles with hide buttons and make the panel fixed. Clicking a Hide button will hide the panel to the edge of the screen, just as with expanded panels. If another expanded panel is already located on that edge, the button for a hidden unexpanded panel will be on top of it. The Autohide feature will also work for unexpanded panels placed at the edge of a screen.

If you want to fix an unexpanded panel to the edge of a screen, make sure it is placed at the edge you want, and then set its "Show hide buttons" option.

Panel Background

With a panel's Background tab on its Panel Properties dialog, you can change the panel's background color or image. For a color background, click the "Solid color" option, and then click the Color button to display a color selection window where you can choose a color from a color graph or a list of color boxes, or you can enter its number. Once your color is selected, you can use the Style slide bar to make it more transparent or opaque. To use an image instead of a color, select the "Background image" option and use the browse button to locate the image file you want. For an image, you can also drag and drop an image file from the file manager to the panel. That image then becomes the background image for the panel.

Panel Objects

A panel can contain several different types of objects. These include menus, launchers, applets, drawers, and special objects.

Menus   A panel menu has launchers that are buttons used to start an application or execute a command.

Launchers   You can select any application entry in the main menu and drag it to the panel, creating a launcher for it on the panel.

Applets   An applet is a small application designed to run within the panel. The Workspace Switcher showing the different desktops is an example of an applet.

Drawers   A drawer is an extension of the panel that can be opened or closed. You can think of a drawer as a shrinkable part of the panel. You can add anything to it that you can to a regular panel, including applets, menus, and even other drawers.

Special objects   These are used for special tasks not supported by other panel objects. For example, the Logout and Lock Screen buttons are special objects.

Moving, Removing, and Locking Objects

To move any object within the panel, right-click it and choose the Move entry. You can move it either to a different place on the same panel or to a different panel. For launchers, you can just drag the object directly where you want it to be. To remove an object from the panel, right-click it to display a pop-up menu for it, and then choose the "Remove From Panel" entry. To prevent an object from being moved or removed, you set its lock feature. Right-click the object and select the "Lock To Panel" entry. For a locked object, a checkmark appears before the "Lock to Panel" entry. To later allow it to be moved, you first have to unlock the object, Right-click it and select "Lock to Panel" to remove the checkmark and making the Move entry active.

Adding Objects

To add an object to a panel, select the object from the panel's "Add to Panel" dialog (see Figure 10-51). To display the Add To Panel dialog, right-click on the panel and select the "Add to Panel" entry. The "Add to Panel" dialog displays a lengthy list of common objects, such as the Classic Menu, Log Out, and Clock. For Application applets, you can click on the Applications Launcher entry and click the Add button to list all your installed applications. Launchers can also be added to a panel by just dragging them directly. Launchers include applications, folders, and files. The Custom Application Launcher lets you create a custom launcher, choosing an application or script.

Application Launchers

To add an application that already has an application launcher to a panel is easy. You just drag the application launcher to the panel. This will automatically create a copy of the launcher for use on that panel. Launchers may be menu items or desktop icons. All the entries in the main menu are application launchers. To add an application from the menu, just select it and drag it to the panel. For example, should you use the Pluma text editor frequently and want to add its icon to the panel, click and drag the Pluma menu entry in the Accessories menu to the panel. The Pluma text editor icon will appear in your panel. For any menu item, you can also go to its entry and right-click it, and then select the "Add to panel" entry. An application launcher for that application is then added to the panel.

You can also drag any desktop application icon to a panel to add a copy of it to that panel.

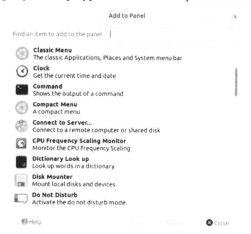

Figure 10-51: MATE Panel "Add to Panel" dialog for panel applets

Also, as previously noted, you can open the "Add to Panel" dialog, and then choose the Application Launcher entry and click the Add button. This will display a dialog with a listing of all the Application menu entries along with Preferences and Administration menus, expandable to their items. Just find the application you want added, select it, and click the Add button.

Adding Drawers

You can also group applications under a Drawer icon. Clicking the Drawer icon displays a list of the different application icons you can then select. To add a drawer to your panel, right-click the panel and select the "Add to panel" entry to display the "Add to Panel" dialog. From that list select the Drawer entry. This will create a drawer on your panel. You can then drag any items from desktop, menus, or windows (folders or launchers) to the drawer icon on the panel to have them listed in the drawer.

You can also add applets and applications to a drawer using the "Add to Drawer" dialog. Right-click on the drawer and choose the "Add to Drawer" entry to open the dialog. Then click the applet you want added to the drawer. To add applications, select the Applications Launcher entry and click Add to list your application menu categories, which are expandable to list applications. You can add an entire menu to the drawer by choosing the application category and clicking the Add button.

Adding Menus

A menu differs from a drawer in that a drawer holds application icons instead of menu entries. You can add application menus to your panel, much as you add drawers. To add an application menu to your panel, open the "Add to Panel" dialog and select the Application Launcher entry, clicking Forward to open the list of Application categories. Select the category you want, and click the Add button. That menu category with all its application items is added to your panel as a menu.

Adding Folders and Files

You can also add files and folders to a panel. For folders, click and drag the folder icon from the file manager window to your panel. Whenever you click this folder button, a file manager window opens, displaying that folder. You can also add folders to any drawer on your panel. To add a file, also drag it directly to the panel. To add a file (except for images, which, instead, change the background of the panel to that image), click and drag the file to the panel or drawer. When you click on the file icon, the file opens with its application.

Adding Applets

Applets are small programs that perform tasks within the panel. To add an applet, right-click the panel and select "Add to Panel" from the pop-up menu. This displays the "Add To Panel" dialog listing common applets along with other types of objects, such as launchers. Select the one you want. For example, to add the clock to your panel, select Clock. Once added, the applet will show up in the panel. If you want to remove an applet, right-click on the applet in the panel and select the "Remove From Panel" entry. To configure an applet, right-click on the applet and select the Preferences entry.

MATE features a number of helpful applets. Some applets monitor your system, such as the Battery Charge Monitor, which checks the battery in laptops, and System Monitor, which shows a graph indicating your current CPU and memory use.

Caja File Manager

The Caja file manager supports the standard features for copying, removing, and deleting items as well as setting permissions and displaying items. The program name for the file manager is **caja**. You can enhance Caja using extensions such as "Open terminal" to open the current folder in a new terminal window, and Engrampa that allows you to create (compress) and extract archives, including epub, arc, and rar files. Several extensions are already installed and enabled by default. They will display entries in appropriate menus. Extensions are enabled on the Extension tab of the File Management Preferences dialog (Edit | Preferences). To add more extension, use the Software Manager to install the caja extension packages. Extension packages have the prefix **caja-**, such as **caja-share**, **caja-dropbox**, and **caja-wallpaper**.

Home Folder Sub-folders and Bookmarks

Like Ubuntu, MATE uses the Common User Directory Structure (xdg-user-dirs at **https://freedesktop.org**) to set up sub-folders in the user home folder. Folders will include **Documents**, **Music**, **Pictures**, **Downloads**, and **Videos**. These localized user folders are used as defaults by many desktop applications. Users can change their folder names or place them within each other using the file browser. For example, Music can be moved into **Documents**, **Documents/Music**. Local configuration is held in the **.config/user-dirs.dirs** file. System-wide defaults are set up in the **/etc/xdg/user-dirs.defaults** file.

The folders are also default bookmarks. You can access a bookmarked folder directly from the Caja window side pane. You can also add your own bookmarks for folders by opening the folder and choosing "Add Bookmark" from the Bookmarks menu. Your folder will appear in the Bookmarks section of the Caja side pane Places menu and on the Bookmarks menu. Use the Edit Bookmarks dialog to remove bookmarks. Here you can remove a bookmark or change is name and location.

File Manager Windows

When you click your home folder icon on the desktop, a file manager window opens showing your home folder. The file manager window displays several components, including a menubar, a main toolbar, and a side pane (see Figure 10-52). The side pane works like the sidebar in the Nautilus (Ubuntu) file manager, but with a menu, like the file manager in GNOME 2. The file manager window's main pane (to the right) displays the icons or listing of files and sub-folders in the opened folder. When you select a file and folder, the status bar at the bottom of the window displays the name of the file or folder selected, and for files the size, and for folders the number of items contained. The status bar also displays the remaining free space on the current file system.

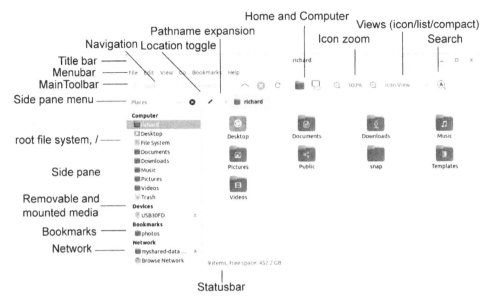

Figure 10-52: Caja file manager with side pane

Note: Caja works as an operational FTP browser. You can use the Connect to Server entry on the File menu to open a "Connect to Server" dialog, where you can enter the address for the FTP site.

When you open a new folder, the same window is used to display it, and you can use the Forward and Back buttons to move through previously opened folders (top left on the main toolbar) (see Figure 10-53). Down triangles to the right of the Back and Forward buttons display menus of previously accessed folders, which you can use to access a previous folder directly. There is also an up arrow to move to the parent folder, and a Home folder button to move directly to your home folder. The Computer button displays the computer window showing your file systems and attached devices. You can also access these operations from the file manager's Go menu (see Table 10-2). In addition there are reload and stop reload buttons to refresh the folder listing, should the list of files or folders change.

Figure 10-53: Caja navigation buttons: back, forward, parent, home, computer

As you open sub-folders, the main toolbar displays buttons for your current folder and its parent folders (see Figure 10-36). You can click on a folder button to move to it directly. Initially, the button shows a path of sub-folders from your home folder. Clicking on the small triangle arrow to the left expands the path to the top level, from the root folder (the hard disk icon).

Menu Item	Description
Open Parent	Move to the parent folder
Back	Move to the previous folder viewed in the file manager window
Forward	Move to the next folder viewed in the file manager window
Paste	Paste files that you have copied or cut, letting you move or copy files between folders, or make duplicates.
Same Location as Other Pane	If you have two panes open on the window, you can make both panes view the same folder
Home Folder	Move to the Home folder
Computer	Move to the Computer folder, showing icons for your devices
Templates	Move to the Templates folder
Trash	Open the trash folder to see deleted files and folders, which can be restored.
Network	Move to the network folder showing connected systems on your network and open remote folders.
Location	Open the location navigation box for entering the path name of a file or folder
Search for Files	Search for files and folders using the file manager window

Table 10-2: File Manager Go Menu

You can also display a location URL text box instead of buttons, where you can enter the location of a folder, either on your system or on a remote system. To display the location text box, press **Ctrl-l**, or from the Go menu select Location, or click the Location toggle (pencil icon) at the beginning of the location path on the main toolbar (see Figure 10-54). These access methods operate as toggles that move you a back and forth from the location text box to the button path.

Figure 10-54: Caja locations: unexpanded, expanded, and location path

The File menu has entries for opening a new tab (Ctrl-t), opening a new file manager window (Ctrl-n), creating a new folder (Shift-Ctrl-n), connecting to a remote FTP server, and displaying the properties of the current folder (Alt-Return). Most have corresponding keys (see Table 10-3) (see Figure 10-50).

Menu Item	Description
New Tab	Creates a new tab.
New Window	Open a new file manager window
Create Folder	Creates a new subfolder in the folder.
Create Document	Creates a text document.
Connect to server	Connect to an FTP server using the file manager
Open in Terminal	Open the current folder in a new terminal window (Open Terminal extension)
Properties	Properties for the current open folder
Empty Trash	Empty the trash folder
Close All Windows	Close all file manage windows
Close	Close the file manager window.
Open With	When a file is selected the Open With item is displayed showing possible applications to open the file with
Open	When a folder is selected the Open item is displayed showing also the "Open in New Tab" and "Open in New Window" items, along with the Open With submenu.

Table 10-3: File Manager File Menu

File Manager Side Pane

The file manager side pane has a menu from which you can choose to display places (Places), the tree view of the file system (Tree), information on the current or selected folder or file (Information), the history of previously opened folders for that login session (History), notes (Notes), and emblems you can place on a file or folder (Emblems).

The default for the side pane is the Places view, which displays sections for Computer, Devices, Bookmarks, and Network items showing your file systems and default home folder sub-folders (see Figure 10-55). You can choose to display or hide the side pane by selecting the "Side Pane" entry in the View menu, or by clicking the close button on the right side of the side pane menu. You can also use F9 to toggle the side pane on and off.

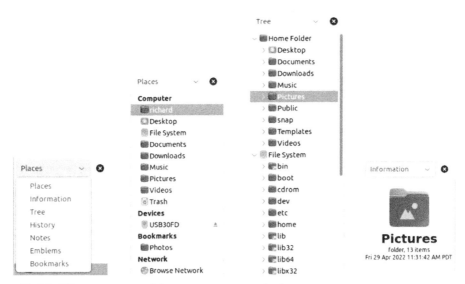

Figure 10-55: File manager side pane menu and views

Selecting the File System entry in the side pane places you at the top of the file system, letting you move to any accessible part of it. In the Computer section, you can search your default folders, such as Documents and Pictures. Should you bookmark a folder (Bookmarks menu, "Add Bookmark" entry (Ctrl-d)), a Bookmark section appears on the side pane with the bookmark. To remove or rename a bookmark, right-click on its entry in the side pane and choose Remove or Rename from the pop-up menu (see Figure 10-56). The bookmark name changes, but not the original folder name.

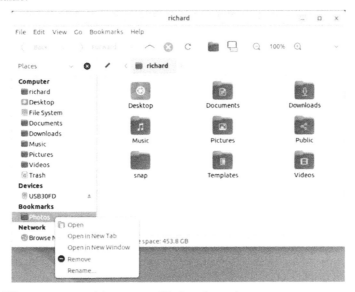

Figure 10-56: File manager side pane with bookmarks menu

Tabs

The Caja file manager supports tabs with which you can open up several folders in the same file manager window. To open a tab, select New Tab from the File menu or press **Ctrl-t**. A tab bar appears with tab icons for each tab, displaying the name of the folder open, and an **x** close button (see Figure 10-57). You can re-arrange tabs by clicking and dragging their tabs to the right or left. You can also use the Ctrl-PageUp and Ctrl-PageDown keys to move from one tab to another. Use the Shift-Ctrl-PageUp and Shift-Ctrl-PageDown keys to rearrange the tabs. To close a tab, click its close **x** button on the right side of the tab.

Figure 10-57: File manager window with tabs

Displaying Files and Folders

You can view a folder's contents as icons, a compact list, or as a detailed list, which you can choose from the menu on the right side of the main toolbar: icon, list, and compact views (see Figure 10-58).

Figure 10-58: File manager file and folder views

Use the control keys to change views quickly: **Ctrl-1** for Icons, **Ctrl-2** for list, and **Ctrl-3** for the compact view. The List view provides the name, size, type, and date. Buttons are displayed for each field across the top of the main pane. You can use these buttons to sort the list according to that field. For example, to sort the files by date, click the Date Modified button; to sort by size, click Size button. Click again to alternate between ascending and descending order.

Certain types of file icons will display previews of their contents. For example, the icons for image files will display a thumbnail of the image. A text file will display in its icon the first few words of its text.

The View menu has entries for managing and arranging your file manager icons (see Table 10-4) (see Figure 10-59). You can choose Icons, List, and Compact views. In the Icon view, the "Arrange items" submenu appears, which provides entries for sorting icons by name, size, type, emblem, extension, and modification date. You can also simply reverse the order, or position icons manually.

Figure 10-59: File manager File, Edit, and View menus

The View | Zoom In entry enlarges your view of the window, making icons bigger, and Zoom Out reduces your view, making them smaller. Normal Size restores icons to the standard size. You can also use the **Ctrl-+** and **Ctrl--** keys to zoom in and out.

File manager tools and menus

From the Edit menu, you can paste files you have cut or copied to move or copy them between folders, or make duplicates (see Table 10-5 and see Figure 10-50). The selection menu items let you select all files and folders, those matching a simple regular expression, and to invert a selection, choosing all those not selected. On the Files menu, the Properties entry opens the folder properties dialog with Basic and Permissions tabs.

In the icon view, you can click anywhere on the empty space on the main pane of a file manager window to display a pop-up menu with entries to create a new folder, arrange icons, zoom icons, and open the folder properties dialog (see Table 10-4).

Navigating in the file manager

The file manager operates similarly to a web browser, using the same window to display opened folders. It maintains a list of previously viewed folders, and you can move back and forth through that list using the toolbar navigation buttons (left side). The Back button with the left arrow moves you to the previously displayed folder, the Forward button with the right arrow moves you to the next previously displayed folder, and the up arrow moves to the parent folder. The home folder icon opens your home folder, and the computer icon (monitor) opens the Computer window, which lists icons for your file systems and removable devices.

Use the side pane's Places view to access your bookmarked folders, storage devices (USB, CD/DVD disc, and attached hard drives), and mounted network folders. On the Computer section of the side pane, you can access your home folders, trash, the file system (root folder). On the Bookmarks section, you can access any additional bookmarks you created. Attached devices are listed in the Devices section, and mounted network folders are listed in the Network section.

Menu Item	Description
Stop	Stop current task
Reload	Refresh file and folder list
Main Toolbar	Displays main toolbar
Side Pane	Displays side pane
Location Bar	Displays location bar
Statusbar	Displays status bar at bottom of folder window
Extra Pane	Display dual panes for file manager window, with separate folders open in each
Reset View to Defaults	Displays files and folders in default view
Show Hidden Files	Show administrative dot files.
Arrange Items: By Name, Size, Type, Modification Date, and Emblems	Arrange files and folder by specified criteria
Organize by Name	Sort icons in Icon view by name
Zoom In	Provides a close-up view of icons, making them appear larger.
Zoom Out	Provides a distant view of icons, making them appear smaller.
Normal Size	Restores view of icons to standard size.
Icons	Displays icons
List	Displays file list with name, size, type, and date. Folders are expandable.
Compact	Displays compact file list using only the name and small icons

Table 10-4: File Manager View Menu

Menu Item	Description
Cut, Copy	Move or copy a file or folder
Paste	Paste files that you have copied or cut, letting you move or copy files between folders, or make duplicates.
Undo, Redo	Undo or Redo a paste operation
Select All	Select all files and folders in this folder
Select Items Matching	Quick search for files using basic pattern matching.
Invert Selection	Select all other files and folders not selected, deselecting the current selection.
Duplicate	Make a copy of a selected file
Make Link	Make a link to a file or folder
Rename	Rename a selected file or folder
Copy to	Copy a file or folder to one of the default bookmarks
Move to	Move a file or folder to one of the default bookmarks
Move To Trash	Move a file for folder to the trash folder for later deletion
Delete	Delete a file or folder immediately.
Compress	Compress selected files and folders to a compressed archive file such as a tar, cpio, or zip file (Engrampa extension).
Backgrounds and Emblems	Choose a background for the file manager windows. Add emblems to any folder or file in the file manager window.
Preferences	The Caja File Manager preferences for your account.

Table 10-5: File Manager Edit Menu

To open a subfolder, you can double-click its icon or right-click the icon and select Open from the menu. You can also open the folder in a new tab or a new window. The Open With submenu lists other possible file managers and applications to open the folder with such as Files (Caja). You can also click on the folder to select it, and then choose Open from the File menu (File | Open). The tab, new window, and Open With items are also listed when a folder is selected. Figure 10-60 shows the File menu with the different Open items for a folder and the Open With submenu for a file. Table 10-3 lists the File menu options.

Figure 10-60: File manager File | Open

Menu Item	Description
Create Folder	Creates a new subfolder in the folder.
Create Document	Creates a text document.
Arrange Items: By Name, Size, Type, Modification Date, and Emblems	Arrange files and folder by specified criteria
Organize by Name	Sort icons in Icon view by name
Open in Terminal	Open a terminal window at that folder (Open terminal extension)
Zoom In	Provides a close-up view of icons, making them appear larger.
Zoom Out	Provides a distant view of icons, making them appear smaller.
Normal Size	Restores view of icons to standard size.
Properties	Opens the Properties dialog for the folder

Table 10-6: File Manager Pop-up Menu

You can open any folder or file system listed in the side pane Places view by clicking on its folder or bookmark. You can also right-click on a bookmark or folder to display a menu with entries to Open, "Open in a New Tab", and "Open in a New Window" (see Table 10-7). The "Open in a New Window" item is an easy way to access devices from the file manager. The menu for the Trash entry lets you empty the trash. For any bookmark, you can also remove and rename the entry. Entries for removable devices in the side pane such as USB drives also have a menu item for Eject. Internal hard drives have an Unmount entry instead.

Menu Item	Description
Open	Opens the file with its associated application. Folders are opened in the file manager. Associated applications are listed.
Open In A New Tab	Opens a folder in a new tab in the same window.
Open In A New Window	Opens a folder in a separate window, accessible from the toolbar, right-click.
Remove	Remove bookmark from the side pane.
Rename	Rename a bookmark.

Table 10-7: The File Manager Side Pane Pop-Up Menu

Caja File Manager Search

From a file manager window, click the Search button on the toolbar (Looking glass at right), or select Go | Search for Files, to open a Search box below the toolbar. Enter the pattern to search and press ENTER or click the looking glass button on the right side of the text box. The results are displayed.

Menus for location and file type will appear in the folder window, with + and - buttons for adding or removing search parameters, including location, file type, tags, modification time, size, and text in the content of the file. Click the plus + button to add more search parameters. The search begins from the folder opened, as specified by the first location parameter. But you can specify another folder to search, using the Location parameter's folder menu listing possible folders. To search multiple folders at once, click the + button to add a Location parameter, and specify the folder to be searched on that Location parameter's folder menu. You can do the same for multiple file types, specifying only files with certain types, as well as for modification times, file sizes, tags, and searched content.

Managing Files and Folders

As a GNOME-compliant file manager, Caja supports desktop drag-and-drop operations for copying and moving files. To move a file or folder, drag-and-drop from one folder to another. The move operation is the default drag-and-drop operation in GNOME. To copy a file to a new location, press the Ctrl key as you drag.

Using a file's pop-up menu

You can also perform remove, rename, and link creation operations on a file by right-clicking its icon and selecting the action you want from the pop-up menu that appears (see Table 10-8). For example, to remove an item, right-click it and select the Move To Trash entry from the pop-up menu. This places it in the Trash folder, where you can later delete it. To create a link, right-click the file and select Make Link from the pop-up menu. This creates a new link file that begins with the term "Link." If you select an archive file, the pop-up menu also displays entries to "Extract Here" and "Extract to" (Engrampa extension).

Menu Item	Description
Open	Opens the file with its associated application. Folders are opened in the file manager. Associated applications are listed.
Open In A New Tab	Opens a folder in a new tab in the same window.
Open In A New Window	Opens a folder in a new window
Open With	Selects an application with which to open the file, or a file manager to use to open a folder.
Cut Copy	Entries to cut and copy the selected file.
Paste into Folder	Paste the selected folder
Make Link	Creates a link to that file in the same folder.
Rename (F2)	Renames the file.
Copy To	Copy a file to the Home Folder, Desktop, or to a folder displayed in another pane in the file manager window.
Move To	Move a file to the Home Folder, Desktop, or to a folder displayed in another pane in the file manager window.
Move To Trash	Moves a file to the Trash folder, where you can later delete it.
Delete	Delete the file or folder permanently
Compress	Archives files (Engrampa extension).
Extract Here Extract To	When an archive is selected, these entries appear (Engrampa extension).
Properties	Displays the Properties dialog.

Table 10-8: The File and Folder Pop-Up Menu

Renaming Files

To rename a file, you can either right-click the file's icon and select the Rename entry from the pop-up menu or click its icon and press the F2 function key. The name of the icon will be bordered, encased in a small text box. You can overwrite the old one, or edit the current name by clicking a position in the name to insert text, as well as use the backspace key to delete characters. You can also rename a file by entering a new name in its Properties dialog box (Basic tab).

Grouping Files

You can select a group of files and folders by clicking the first item and then hold down the SHIFT key while clicking the last item, or by clicking and dragging the mouse across items you want to select. To select separated items, hold the CTRL key down as you click the individual icons. If you want to select all the items in the folder, choose the Select All entry in the Edit menu (Edit | Select All) (**Ctrl-a**). You can then copy, move, or even delete several files at once. To select items that have a certain pattern in their name, choose Select Items Matching from the Edit menu to open a search box where you can enter the pattern (**Ctrl-s**). Use the * character to match partial patterns, as in **let** to match on all filenames with the pattern "let" in them. The pattern **my*** would match on filenames beginning with the "my" pattern, and ***png** would match on all PNG image files.

Opening Applications and Files MIME Types

You can start any application in the file manager by double-clicking either the application itself or a data file used for that application. If you want to open the file with a specific application, you can right-click the file and select one of the Open With entries. One or more Open with entries will be displayed for default and possible application, like "Open with Text Editor" for a text file. If the application you want is not listed, you can select "Open with Other Application" to open a dialog listing available applications.

Folders also have an Open With submenu, listing alternative file managers you can use to open the folder, should they be installed. Applications that work on folders are also listed such as the Shotwell image manager and the Rhythmbox music player.

To change or set the default application to use for a certain type of file, you open a file's Properties dialog and select the Open With tab. Here you can choose the default application to use for that kind of file. Possible applications will be listed with a button next to each entry. The default has its button turned on. Click the button of the one you want to change to the default. Once you choose the default, it will appear in the Open With item for this type of file. If there is an application on the Open With tab you do not want listed in the Open With menu, select it and click the Remove button.

If you want to add an application to the Open With menu, click the "Add" button to open the Add Application dialog, which lists possible applications. Select the one you want and click the Add button. You can use the "Use a custom command" text box to enter a command. The Browse button lets you locate a command.

File and Folder Properties

In a file's Properties dialog, you can view detailed information on a file and set options and permissions (see Figure 10-61). A file's Properties dialog has five tabs: Basic, Emblems, Permissions, Open With, and Notes. Folders do not have an Open With tab. Certain kinds of files will have additional tabs, providing information about the file. For example, an audio file will have an Audio tab listing the type of audio file and any other information like a song title or compression method used. An image file will have an Image tab listing the resolution and type of image. Folders also have an "Access Control List" and "Extended user attributes" tabs that you can use to control user access to a folder.

The Basic tab shows detailed information such as type, size, location, and date modified. The type is a MIME type, indicating the type of application associated with it. The file's icon is displayed at the top with a text box showing the file's name. You can edit the filename in the Name text box, changing that name.

If you want to change the icon image used for the file or folder, click the icon image (next to the name) to open a Select Custom Icon dialog to browse for the one you want. The **/usr/share/pixmaps** folder holds the set of current default images, though you can select your own images (click **pixmaps** entry in the side pane). Click an image file to see its icon displayed in the right pane. Double-click to change the icon image.

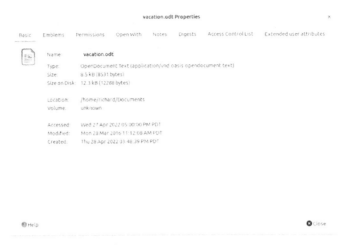

Figure 10-61: File properties on Caja

The Permissions tab for files shows the read, write, and execute permissions for owner, group, and others, as set for this file. You can change any of the permissions here, provided the file belongs to you. You configure access for the owner, the group, and others, using menus. You can set owner permissions as Read Only or Read And Write. For group and others, you can also set the None option, denying access. Clicking on the group name displays a menu listing different groups, allowing you to select one to change the file's group. If you want to execute the file as an application, you check the "Allow executing file as program" entry. This has the effect of setting the execute permission.

The Permissions tab for folders operates much the same way, but it includes two access entries: Folder Access and File Access. The Folder Access entry controls access to the folder with options for None, List Files Only, Access Files, and Create And Delete Files. These correspond to read, write, and execute permissions given to folders. The File Access entry lets you set permissions for all those files in the folder. They are the same as for files: for the owner, Read or Read and Write; for the group and others, the entry adds a None option to deny access. To set the permissions for all the files in the folder accordingly (not just the folder), you click the "Apply Permissions To Enclosed Files" button.

The Open With tab for files lists all the applications associated with this kind of file. You can select the one you want to use as the default. This can be particularly useful for media files, where you may prefer a specific player for a certain file or a particular image viewer for pictures. To add an applications that is not listed, click the Add button to open an "Add Application" dialog listing installed applications you can choose from.

The Notes tab lets you add notes about the file. A note emblem will then appear on the right top corner of the file's icon.

The Digest tab lets you easily perform checksum confirmations on downloaded files. Enter the checksum value into the Check text box. A green checkmark means it is confirmed. You can choose which hash functions to use.

For folders, the Access Control List tab lets you set ACL controls for a folder, specifying those users that can have access to a folder. This will afford you more refined control over access to a folder. In general, only the owner has write access and all other users have read and execute access (Other). Should you also want certain users to also have write access you could do so on this tab, selecting the users from the "Available participants" list. You could also change the current entry for Other, removing read an execute access, and then only allowing certain users to access the folder. To add a user to the "Current participants in ACL" list, select it in the "Available participants" list and click the "Add participant to ACL" button. To remove a user from the "Current participants in ACL" list, select it and click the "Remove participant from ACL" button. If a user is not listed in the "Available participants" list, click "Advanced features" to open a text box where you can search for the user. You can also choose to list system users.

The "Extended user attributes" tab lets you add ACL attributes to a folder. Click the Add button to create an attribute entry where you can enter its name and value. Use the Remove button to remove an attribute.

The Share tab for folders allows you to share folders as network shares. If you have Samba or NFS, these will allow your folders and files to be shared with users on other systems. Be sure to first install the Caja Share package (you can use Software Botique). You have the option to specify whether the shared folder or file will be read-only or allow write access. To allow write access check the "Allow other to create and delete files in this folder" entry. To open access to all users, check the Guest access entry.

Caja Preferences

You can set preferences for your Caja file manager in the Preferences dialog, accessible by selecting the Preferences item in any Caja file manager window's Edit menu (Edit | Preferences). The File Management Preferences dialog has seven tabs: Views, Behavior, Display, List Columns, Preview, Media, and Extensions.

The Views tab allows you to select how files are displayed by default, such as the list, icon, or compact view. You can set default zoom levels for icon, compact, and list views.

Behavior lets you choose how to select files, manage the trash, and handle scripts.

Display lets you choose what added information you want displayed in an icon caption, like the size or date. You can also specify the format of the date.

The List Columns tab lets you choose both the features to display in the list view and the order in which to display them. In addition to the already-selected Name, Size, Date, and Type, you can add features such as permissions, group, MIME type, and owner. For folders you can also display a count the number of items.

The Preview tab lets you choose whether you want small preview content displayed in the icons, like beginning text for text files.

The Media tab lets you choose what applications to run for certain media, such as run the Celluloid media player for DVD videos, or Rhythmbox for audio files.

Extensions lists extensions installed for Caja such as "Open Terminal" which lets you open a folder in a terminal window (Open in Terminal menu item), Engrampa which allows you to create and extract archives directly from the file manager window (Compress menu item), and caja-seahorse that allows you to encrypt files and folders (Encrypt menu item).

Control Center

Both Preference and Administration tools can be accessed either from the MATE menu or from the Control Center (see Figure 10-62). You can access the Control Center at the bottom of the MATE menu. The Control Center opens a window listing the different applications by section: Administration, Hardware, Internet and Network, Look and Feel, and Personal. Icons for the tools are displayed. Single-click on an icon to open it. The Control Center also has a dynamic search capability. A side pane holds a filter search box and links for the groups. As you enter a pattern in the Filter search box, matching applications appear at the right. Commonly used applications can be listed under Common Tasks. If you want an application to be started when your system starts, you can right-click on its icon and choose "Add to Startup Programs" to add it directly to the Startup Applications dialog. Several of the tools are administration applications such as Software Boutique, Users and Groups, and Printers. Others are GNOME preferences used for MATE, such as Appearance, About Me, Screensaver, and Keyboard.

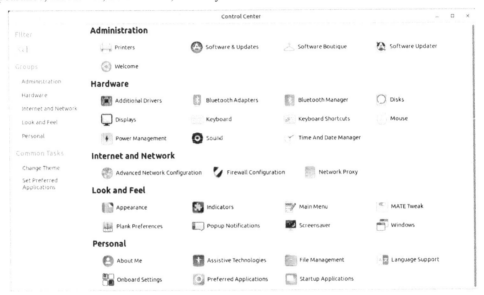

Figure 10-62: GNOME Control Center

MATE Preferences

You can configure different parts of your MATE interface using tools listed in the Preferences menu and from the Control Center. MATE provides several tools for configuring your MATE desktop. The MATE preferences are listed in Table 10-9. On some preferences tools, a Help button displays detailed descriptions and examples. Some of the more important tools are discussed here.

The keyboard shortcuts configuration (Keyboard Shortcuts) lets you map keys to certain tasks, like mapping multimedia keys on a keyboard to media tasks like play and pause. There are tasks for the desktop, multimedia, and window management. With window management, you can also map keys to perform workspace switching. The tasks and keys that are already assigned are listed. To change the keys used for a task, double click its shortcut entry and type the new keys. A task that has no assigned keys is disabled. Click the shortcut entry to enter a key sequence for it. To add a new task, click add to choose the application and a name for it. These are added under the Custom Shortcuts section. Click the new task's shortcut to add a key for it. To disable a shortcut, click the shortcut entry and press the backspace key.

The Windows configuration (Windows) is where you can enable features like window roll-up (Titlebar Action), window movement key, and mouse window selection.

Note: To manage users on Ubuntu Mate you can install the Synaptic Package Manager and then install **gnome-system-tools**, which includes the "Users and Groups" application (**users-admin**) (see Chapter 14). You can then access "Users and Groups" from the Administration menu.

Preferences	Description
About Me	Personal information like image, addresses, and password.
Additional Drivers	Ubuntu Software and Updates Additional Drivers tab for detecting and adding commercial drivers.
Advanced Network Configuration	Network Manager Network Connections editor for managing and adding network devices.
Appearance	Desktop Appearance configuration: Themes, Fonts, Backgrounds, and Visual Effects.
Assistive Technologies	Enables features like accessible login and keyboard screen.
Bluetooth Adapters	Manage and connect Bluetooth devices.
Disks	Opens the GNOME Disks utility.
Displays	Opens the GNOME Monitor Preferences dialog for detecting monitors and setting resolution, with an option to show monitors in the panel.
File Management	File Manager options including media handling applications, icon captions, and the default view (also accessible from file manager window, Edit | Preferences).
Firewall Configuration	Gufw firewall management application for the Ubuntu ufw firewall
Indicators	Configure indicators in the Indicator applet (System Menu, Date, sound, power, and notifications)
Keyboard	Configure your keyboard: selecting options, models, and typing breaks, as well as accessibility features like slow, bounce, and sticky keys.
Keyboard Shortcuts	Configure keys for special tasks, like multimedia operations.
Language Support	Specify a language.
Main Menu	Add or remove categories and menu items for the Applications, Preferences, and System menus.
MATE Tweak	MATE Tweak application for configuring your desktop, panel, and windows.

Mouse	Mouse and touchpad configuration: select hand orientation, speed, and accessibility.
Network Proxy	Specify proxy configuration if needed: manual or automatic
Onboard Settings	Options for the screen based keyboard.
Plank Preferences	Configure the MATE Plank dock
Popup Notifications	Placement and display theme for notifications.
Power Management	The GNOME power manager for configuring display, suspend, and shutdown options.
Preferred Applications	Set default Web browser, mail application, music player, and terminal window.
Screensaver	Select and manage your screen saver, including the activation time.
Sound	Configure sound effects, output volume, sound device options, input volume, and sound application settings (Pulseaudio).
Startup Applications	Manage your session with startup programs and save options.
Time and Date Manager	Set the time, date, and time zone.
Windows	Enable window abilities like roll up on the title bar, movement key, window selection.

Table 10-9: The MATE Preferences

About Me: photo, name, and password

To set up personal information, including the icon to be used for your login screen, you use the About Me preferences tool. You can access it from the Preferences menu (Preferences | About Me) and from the Control Center. The About Me preferences dialog lets you change your password (see Figure 10-63) and the icon or image used to represent the user. Should you want to change your password, you can click on the Change Password button to open a change password dialog.

Clicking on the image icon opens a browser window where you can select a personal image. The **/usr/share/pixmaps/faces** folder is selected by default, which displays several images. The selected image displays at the right on the browser window. For a personal photograph, you can select the Picture folder. This is the Pictures folder on your home folder. Should you place a photograph or image there, you could then select if for your personal image. The image will be used in the login screen when showing your user entry.

Figure 10-63: About Me: Preferences | About Me

Appearance

Several appearance-related configuration tasks are combined into the Appearance Preferences dialog (Appearance entry in the Preferences menu or Appearance icon on the Control Center's Personal section). You can change your theme, background image, or configure your fonts. The Appearance dialog shows four tabs: Theme, Background, Fonts, and Interface (see Figure 10-64). On the Interface tab, you can choose to show icons in menus and on buttons.

Desktop Background

You use the Background tab on the Appearance Preferences dialog to select or customize your desktop background image (see Figure 10-64). You can also access the Background tab by right-clicking the desktop background and select Change Desktop Background from the desktop menu. Installed backgrounds are listed, with the current background selected. To add your own image, either drag-and-drop the image file to the Background tab or click on the Add button to locate and select the image file. To remove an image, select it and click the Remove button.

From the Style drop-down menu, you can choose display options such as Zoom, Centered, Scaled, Tiled, or Fill Screen. A centered or scaled image will preserve the image proportions. Fill screen may distort it. Any space not filled, such as with a centered or scaled images, will be filled in with the desktop color. From the Colors menu, you can set the desktop color to a solid color, horizontal gradient, or vertical gradient. Click on the color button next to the Colors menu to open a "Pick a Color" dialog where you can select a color from a selection of choices or add a new one from a graph or with the color number. For gradients, two color buttons are displayed for selecting a color at each end of the gradient.

Initially, the Ubuntu backgrounds are listed. Install the **gnome-backgrounds** package to add a collection of GNOME backgrounds. To download more backgrounds, click the "Get more backgrounds online" link.

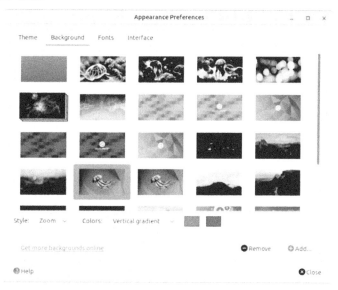

Figure 10-64: Choosing a desktop background, System | Preferences | Appearance

Desktop Themes

You use the Themes tab on the Appearance Preferences dialog to select or customize a theme. Themes control your desktop appearance. The Themes tab will list icons for currently installed themes (see Figure 10-65). It features an extensive list of Yaru based themes, each with a different accent color. Yaru is the official theme for Ubuntu. The icons show key aspects for each theme such as window, folder, and button images, in effect previewing the theme for you.

The Ubuntu MATE custom theme is initially selected. You can select a different theme if you wish. If you have downloaded additional themes from **https://www.gnome-look.org/**, you can click the install button to locate and install them. Once installed, the additional themes will also be displayed in the Theme tab. If you download and install a theme or icon set from the Ubuntu repository, it will be automatically installed for you.

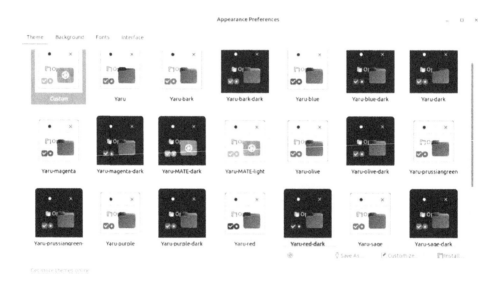

Figure 10-65: Appearance - Selecting GNOME themes

The true power of Themes is shown its ability to let users customize any given theme. Themes are organized into controls, window border, icons, and pointer. Controls covers the appearance of window and dialog controls like buttons and slider bars. Window border lets you choose title bars, borders, and window buttons sets. Icons lets you choose different icon sets. Pointers provides different pointer sets to use. You can even download and install separate components like specific icon sets, which you can then use in a customized theme.

Clicking the Customize button opens a Customize Theme dialog with tabs for different theme components. The components used for the current theme are selected by default. In the Controls, Window Border, Icons, and Pointer tabs you will see listings of the different themes. You can then mix and match different components from those themes, creating your own customized theme, using window borders from one theme and icons from another. Upon selecting a component, your desktop changes automatically showing you how it looks. If you have added a component, like a new icon set, it also is shown.

Once you have created a new customized theme, a Custom Theme icon appears in the list on the Theme tab. To save the customized theme, click the Save As button. This opens a dialog where you can enter the theme name, any notes, and specify whether you also want to keep the theme background.

Customized themes and themes installed directly by a user are placed in the **.themes** folder in the user's home folder. Should you want these themes made available for all users, you can move them from the **.themes** folder to the **/usr/share/themes** folder. In a terminal window run a **cp** command as shown here for the **mytheme** theme. The operation requires administrative access (**sudo**).

```
sudo cp -r .themes/mytheme  /usr/share/themes
```

You can do the same for icon sets you have downloaded. Such sets will be installed in the user's **.icons** folder. You can then copy them to the **/usr/share/icons** folder to make them available to all users.

Assistive Technologies

On MATE, the Assistive Technologies dialog is a simple set of buttons for accessing accessibility tabs for other tools (see Figure 10-66). In the Assistive Technologies section, use the "Enable assistive technologies" checkbox to turn assistive technologies on and off. The Preferred Applications button opens the Accessibility tab on the Preferred Applications dialog.

In the Preferences section, there are buttons to open the accessibility tabs for the keyboard and mouse preferences dialogs. On the keyboard accessibility tab, you can configure features such as sticky, slow, and bounce keys. The mouse button opens the mouse preferences dialog.

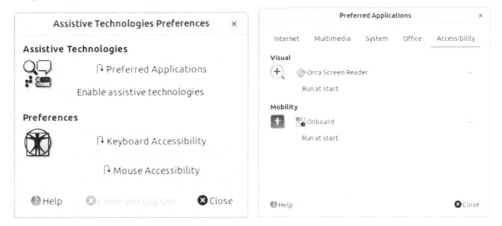

Figure 10-66: Assistive Technologies Preferences

Bluetooth Manager and Adapters

The Bluetooth Manager icon on the Control Center opens the Bluetooth Devices dialog where you can scan for and connect to Bluetooth devices (see Figure 10-67). Click the Search button to scan for and list available devices, and then click on the device you want to select it and click the plus button to connect to it.

The Bluetooth Adapters icon opens the Bluetooth Adapter dialog where you can set visibility settings (Hidden, Always visible, and Temporarily visible) and the name of the adapter. You can also access the Bluetooth Adapters dialog from the Adapter menu's Preferences entry on the Bluetooth Manager (Bluetooth Devices dialog).

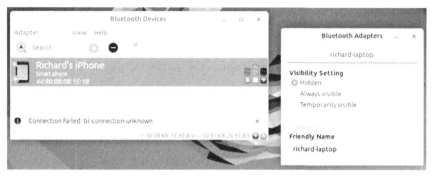

Figure 10-67: Bluetooth Manager and Adapters

You can quickly manage your Bluetooth devices from the Bluetooth Indicator menu on the right side of the top panel (see Figure 10-68). The Devices entry opens the Bluetooth Manager, and the Adapters entry opens Bluetooth Adapters. You can also turn Bluetooth off, list recently accessed devices (Recent Connections), and send files to a device.

Figure 10-68: Bluetooth Indicator Menu

You can also choose what plugins you want to user for your Bluetooth connections, as well as configure specific plugins (see Figure 10-69). You can access the Plugins dialog from the View menu on the Bluetooth Manager dialog (Bluetooth Devices) and from the Bluetooth indicator menu. Most plugins do not support configuration options. Those that do will be in bold type and their configuration button will be active (not faded type). For the Discovery Manager plugin you can set the Discoverable timeout. RecentConns lets you set the number of recent connections to display on the Recent Connections menu and the PowerManager lets you choose whether to power Bluetooth adapters automatically.

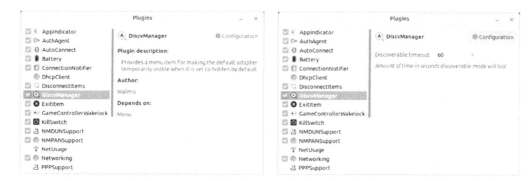

Figure 10-69: Bluetooth Plugins

Displays

Selecting the Displays icon on the Control Center or from the Preferences menu opens the Monitor Preferences dialog where you can set the resolution, refresh rate, and rotation of the monitor. Should you have multiple monitors, click the "Detect monitors" button to access them. Scaling can be set to auto, 100 percent, or 200 percent (see Figure 10-70). Click the Apply button to effect changes. The "Apply system-wide" button applies the changes for all users.

You can also choose to show monitors on the panel. From the monitor panel menu you can change the orientation, turn off a monitor, or open the Monitor Preferences dialog.

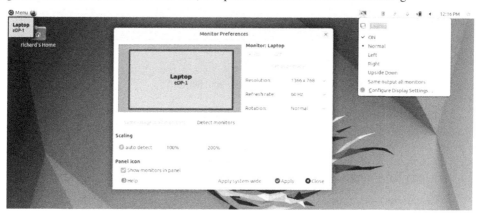

Figure 10-70:Monitor Preferences and panel menu.

Note: To scale a HiDPI monitor such as smaller 4k monitors, be sure to set the HiDIPI option in the MATE Tweak Windows tab. Auto-detect will scale when needed, Regular does no scaling, and HiDPI will always scale.

File Management: Default Applications for Media

Caja directly handles preferences for media operations. You set the preferences using the File Management Preferences dialog. It is accessible from the Edit | Preferences menu item on any

Caja file manager window, from the Preferences menu as File Management, or from the Control Center as File Management (in the Personal section).

The Media tab of the File Management Preferences dialog lists entries for CD Audio, DVD Video, Music Player, Photos, and Software. Menus let you select the application to use for the different media (see Figure 10-71). You also have options for Ask what to do, Do Nothing, and Open folder. The Open Folder options will just open a window displaying the files on the disc. A segment labeled "Other media" lets you set up an association for less used media like Blu-Ray discs. Initially, the "Ask what to do" option will be set for all entries. Possible options are listed on each menu, like Rhythmbox Music Player for CD Audio discs and Celluloid for DVD Video. Photos can be opened with the Shotwell Photo-manager. Once you select an option, when you insert removable media, like a CD Audio discs, its associated application is automatically started.

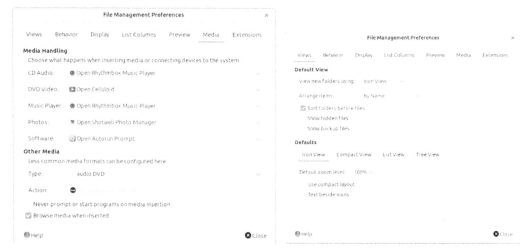

Figure 10-71: File Management Preferences for Media

If you just want to turn off the startup for a particular kind of media, you can select the Do Nothing entry from its application menu. If you want to be prompted for options, then set the "Ask what to do" entry. When you insert a disc, a dialog with a menu for possible actions is displayed. The default application is already selected. You can select another application or select the Do Nothing or Open Folder options.

You can turn the automatic startup off for all media by checking the box for "Never prompt or start programs on media insertion" at the bottom of the Media panel. You can also enable the option "Browse media when inserted" to just open a folder showing its files.

Fonts

On the Font tab, you can change font sizes, select fonts, and configure rendering options (see Figure 10-72). Fonts are listed for Applications, Documents, Desktop, Window title, and Fixed width. Click on a font button to open a "Pick a Font" dialog where you can select a font, choose its style (regular, italic, or bold), and change its size. You can further refine your font display by clicking the Details button to open a window where you can set features like the dots-per-inch, hinting, and smoothing.

Figure 10-72: Fonts

With very large monitors and their high resolutions becoming more common, one feature users find helpful is the ability to increase the desktop font sizes. On a large widescreen monitor, resolutions less than the native one tend not to scale well. A monitor always looks best in its native resolution. With a large native resolution text sizes become so small they are hard to read. You can overcome this issue by increasing the font size. The default size is 10; increasing it to 12 makes text in all desktop features like windows and menus much more readable.

Configuring Fonts

To refine your font display, you can use the font rendering features. Open the Fonts tab on the Appearance tool. In the Font Rendering section are basic font rendering features like Monochrome, Best contrast, Best shapes, and Subpixel smoothing. Choose the one that works best. For LCD monitors choose subpixel smoothing. For detailed configuration, click the Details button. Here you can set Smoothing, Hinting (anti-aliasing), and Subpixel color order features. The Subpixel color order is hardware dependent.

On MATE, clicking on a font button in the Appearance Fonts tab will open a "Pick a Font" dialog that lists all available fonts. You can also generate a listing by using the **fc-list** command. The list will be unsorted, so you should pipe it first to the sort command. You can use **fc-list** with any font name or name pattern to search for fonts, with options to search by language, family, or styles.

```
fc-list | sort
```

Adding Fonts

You can install a font from a font file you have downloaded or copied by clicking the "Add new font" button on the Appearance's Fonts tab. Numerous font packages are also available on the Linux repositories. When you install the font packages, the fonts are installed automatically on your system and ready for use. True type font packages begin with **ttf-** prefix. Microsoft true type fonts are available from the **ttf-mscorefonts-installer** package. Fonts are installed in the **/usr/share/fonts** folder. This folder will have subfolders for different font collections like **truetype** and **X11**. You can install fonts manually yourself by copying fonts to the **/user/share/fonts** folder (use the **sudo** command). For dual-boot systems, where Windows is installed as one of the operating systems, you can copy fonts directly from the Windows font folder on the Windows partition (which is mounted in **/media**) to **/usr/share/fonts**.

Mouse and Keyboard Preferences

The Mouse and Keyboard preferences are the primary tools for configuring your mouse and keyboard. Mouse preferences lets you choose speed, hand orientation, and double-click times. For laptops, you can configure your touchpad, enabling touchpad clicks and edge scrolling. Keyboard preferences shows several tabs for selecting your keyboard model (Layouts), configuring keys (Layouts tab, Options button), repeat delay (General tab), and enforcing breaks from power typing as a health precaution (Typing Break tab) (see Figure 10-73).

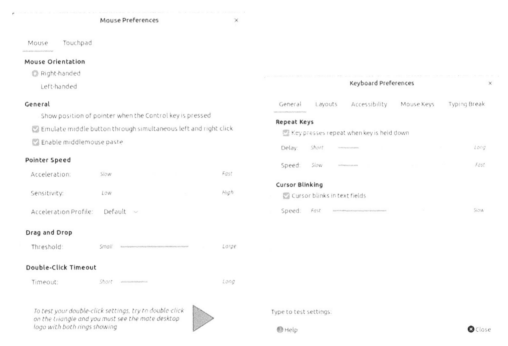

Figure 10-73: Mouse and Keyboard Preferences

To configure your sound devices you use the Sound Preferences tool (Sound). MATE uses sound themes to specify an entire set of sounds for different effects and alerts. On the Hardware tab you select a device to use. The Input tab configures input volume, and the Output tab configures output. The Applications tab lets you adjust the output of running applications.

MATE Power Management

For power management, MATE uses the MATE Power Manager, **mate-power-manager**, which makes use of Advanced Configuration and Power Interface (ACPI) support provided by a computer to manage power use. The MATE Power Manager can display an icon on the panel showing the current power source, a battery or plugin (lightning). Clicking on the battery icon displays a menu showing the power charge of your laptop and any wireless devices like a wireless mouse.

The MATE Power manager is configured with Power Management Preferences (**mate-power-preferences**), accessible from Preferences | Power Management, and by clicking on the MATE Power Management panel icon and selecting Power Settings from the pop-up menu (also on the GNOME Control Center | Hardware section). Power Manager preferences can be used to configure both a desktop and a laptop (see Figure 10-74).

For a desktop, two tabs appear on the Power Management Preferences window, On AC Power and General. The AC Power tab offers two sleep options, one for the computer and one for the display screen. You can put each to sleep after a specified interval of inactivity. On the General tab, you set actions to take when you press the power button or the suspend button.

Figure 10-74: MATE Power Manager - AC and Battery

A laptop will also have an On Battery Power tab where you can set additional options for the battery and display, such as shutting down if the battery is too low, or dimming the display when the system is idle. The laptop On AC Power tab will also have an Actions option for actions to take when the laptop lid is closed, like suspend, blank screen, and shutdown.

To see how your laptop or desktop is performing with power, you can use Power statistics. This is accessible from the System Tool menus as Power Statistics. The Power Statistics window will display a sidebar listing your different power devices. A right pane will show tabs with power use information for a selected device. The Laptop battery device will display three tabs: Details, History, and Statistics. The History tab will show your recent use, with graph options (Graph type menu) for Time to empty (time left), Time to full (recharging), Charge, and Rate. The Statistics tab can show charge and discharge graphs.

Popup Notifications

The Popup Notifications dialog lets you choose what position on the screen you want your notifications displayed, as well as what theme to use (see Figure 10-75). The themes available are Slider (the default), Nodoka, Coco, and Standard theme. Should you have multiple monitors you can choose the one on which to display notifications, or just use the active monitor. To turn off notification click the "Enable Do Not Disturb" option. To see a preview of your configuration changes, click the Preview button.

Notifications can be quickly accessed from the Popup Indicator button (bell icon) on the Indicator applet on the right side of the top menu. Clicking the Popup indicator button displays a list of current notification, with and close box for each (x). At the bottom of the list is a "Do not disturb" switch you can use the turn off notifications. To remove all notifications at once select the Clear entry. You can configure the Notifications indicator menu using the Ayatana Indicators Settings dialog's Notifications tab, accessible from the Control Center (System Settings) as Indicators in the Look and Feel section, and from the main menu's Preferences menu (see Indicator Applet Configuration at the beginning of this chapter).

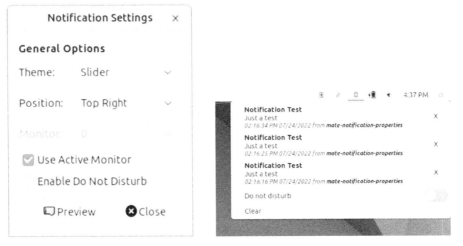

Figure 10-75: Pop-up Notifications

Preferred Applications for Web, Mail, Accessibility, and terminal windows

Certain types of files will have default applications already associated with them. For example, double-clicking a Web page file will open the file in the Firefox Web browser. If you prefer to set a different default application, you can use the Preferred Applications tool (see Figure 10-76) . You access the Preferred Applications tool from the Preferences menu (Preferences | Preferred Applications), and from the Control Center (Personal section). This tool will let you set default applications for Web pages, mail readers, accessibility tools, multimedia, office applications, and system-level tools. Available applications are listed in popup menus. The default mail reader is Evolution, and the default Web browser is Firefox. To make another application the default, click on the menu button to display a list of other possible installed applications. The Preferred applications tool has tabs for Internet, Multimedia, System, Office, and Accessibility. On the Multimedia tab, you can select default image viewer, video player, and multimedia player. On the Office tab, you can specify the default document viewer, word processor, and spreadsheet application. On the System tab, you can choose the default text editor, terminal window application, file manager, and calculator. The Accessibility panel has options for selecting visual and mobility support such as a screen reader and onboard keyboard.

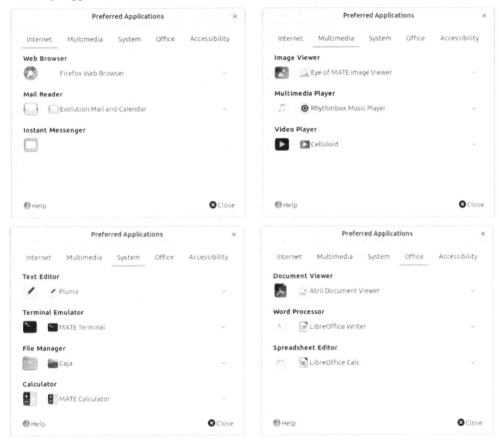

Figure 10-76: Preferred Applications tool

Screen Saver and Lock

With the Screensaver Preferences, you can control when the computer is considered idle and what screen saver to use if any (see Figure 10-77). You can access the Screensaver Preferences dialog from the Preferences menu as Screensaver, or from the Control Center in the Personal section. You can choose from various screen savers, using the scroll box to the left, with a preview displayed at the right. You can also control whether to lock the screen or not, when idle and for how long. You can turn off the Screensaver by unchecking the "Activate screensaver when computer is idle" box.

Figure 10-77: Screensaver Preferences

Sound

You configure sound devices and set the volume for sound effects, input and output, and applications using Sound dialog. Choose Sound on the Preferences menu or select Sound Settings from the panel sound indicator menu. This opens the Sound Preferences dialog, which has five tabs: Sound Effects, Output, Input, Sounds, and Applications (see Figure 10-78).

The Sound Effects tab lets you select the theme for an alert sound. A sliding bar lets you set the volume for your sound alerts, or turn them off by clicking the Mute option.

Volume Control is integrated into the Sound dialog. A sliding bar at the top of the dialog, above the tabs, lets you set the output volume.

The Hardware tab lets you choose a sound device to use, should you have several sound devices. You can then choose the sound format to configure the Profile menu such as Analog stereo output or Analog stereo input. Click the "Test Speakers" button to test the speakers.

On the Input tab, you set the input volume for an input device such as a microphone. A Mute option lets you disable it. When speaking or recording, the input level is displayed. If you have more than one input device, they will be listed in the Connector menu. Choose the one you want to configure.

On the Output tab, you can configure balance settings for a selected output device. If you have more than one device, it will be listed in the Connector menu. Choose the one you want to configure. The available settings will change according to the device selected. For a simple Analog Stereo Output, there is only a single balance setting

The Applications tab will show applications currently using sound devices. You can set the sound volume for each

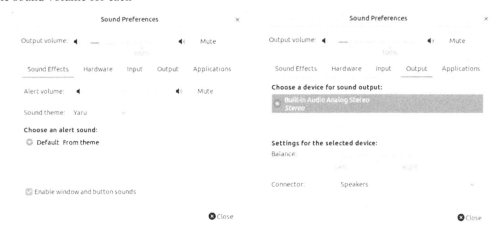

Figure 10-78: Sound Preferences - effects and output

Time and Date Manager

The Time and Date Manager dialog lets you set the time either from a Network Time Protocol server (the NTP sync switch), or to set it manually (see Figure 10-79). The Network Time Protocol server is the default. Turn off the NTP sync switch to enable manual settings or the time and date. Use the Calendar to set the date.

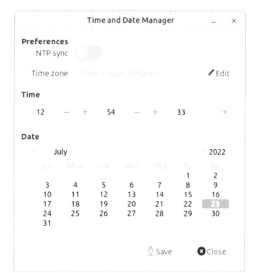

Figure 10-79: Time and Date Manager

You can also choose a time zone. Click the Edit button on the Time zone option to open a Time Zone Selection dialog where you can click on the time zone you want. You can use the search box to search for a time zone by city. A drop down menu will appear with city options as you enter the name.

The time and date are displayed on the Indicator applet on the right side of the top panel. You can configure the time and date Indicator menu using the Ayatana Inidcators Settings dialog's "Date and Time" tab, accessible from the Control Center (System Settings) as Indicators in the Look and Feel section, and from the main menu's Preferences menu (see Indicator Applet Configuration at the beginning of this chapter).

ubuntu

11. Ubuntu Flavors

Xubuntu (Xfce)
Lubuntu (LXQT)
Ubuntu Studio
Ubuntu Budgie

Ubuntu Flavors are based on the Ubuntu Linux distribution, but use different desktops and initial software collections. These are common desktops that are used for other Linux distribution, but have been adapted for Ubuntu and the Ubuntu software repositories, including Snap. These include Kubuntu based on the KDE Plasma desktop (see Chapter 9), Ubuntu MATE which uses the MATE desktop (see Chapter 10), Xubuntu which uses the Xfce desktop, Lubuntu adapts the LXDE desktop, Ubuntu Budgie uses the Budgie desktop, which is based on the Ubuntu GNOME desktop. Ubuntu Studio is a customized collection of multimedia production software from the Ubuntu repository and uses the Xubuntu desktop. Ubuntu Kylin is designed specifically for Chinese users.

The Ubuntu Flavors are available at:

```
https://ubuntu.com/download/flavours
```

They are also available at:

```
http://cdimage.ubuntu.com
```

Xubuntu (Xfce)

Xubuntu uses the Xfce desktop, with the Ubuntu repositories. The Xfce desktop is a lightweight desktop designed to run fast without the kind of overhead required for full featured desktops like KDE and GNOME. You can think of it as a window manager with desktop functionality. It includes its own file manager and panel, but the emphasis is on modularity and simplicity. Like GNOME, Xfce is based on GTK+ GUI tools. The desktop consists of a collection of modules like the thunar file manager, xfce4-panel panel, and the xfwm4 window manager. Keeping with its focus on simplicity, Xfce features only a few common applets on its panel. It small scale makes it appropriate for laptops or dedicated systems, that have no need for complex overhead found in other desktops. Xfce is useful for desktops designed for just a few tasks, like multimedia desktops.

Figure 11-1: Xubuntu (Xfce) Desktop

You can find out more about Xubuntu and download it from:

https://xubuntu.org

You can find out more about Xfce from:

https://xfce.org/

To install Xubuntu as an alternative desktop on a system, select the **xubuntu-desktop** package in the Synaptic Package Manager or use the **apt** command.

The desktop displays icons for your Home folder, file system, and trash (see Figure 11-1). The top panel holds a menu button on the left side for the main menu (Whisker menu). From the menu, you can access any applications along with administration tools. Next to the menu button are the window list buttons for open windows. The right side of the panel has buttons for the time and date (calendar), volume control, network connections, and power status. You can add more items by clicking on the panel and selecting Panel | Add new items. This opens a window with several applets like the clock and workspace switcher, as well as Applications menu and Indicator plugins applet. The Indicator plugins applet displays the Ubuntu Network Manager, sound volume, and messaging indicators. To move an applet, right-click on it and choose Move from the pop-up menu, and then move the mouse to the new insertion location and click.

Right-clicking anywhere on the desktop background displays the desktop menu with options such as create folders, open a terminal window, and arrange icons. The Applications entry displays the application categories and their submenus, as well as entries for the Settings Manager and Log Out.

Clicking the power button on the main menu or the Log Out entry in the desktop Applications menu, opens a dialog with buttons for logout, shut down, restart, suspend, and switch user. You can also choose to save your current session, restoring your open windows when you log back in.

Figure 11-2: Xubuntu (Xfce) Applications Menu

You can access applications from the Applications menu (left side of the top panel). Categories are shown to the left, and the items in the category are listed to the right (see Figure 11-2). You can use a search box at the top to find an application. The name of the current user is listed at the bottom of the menu. At the lower right are the Settings, Lock Screen, and Log Out buttons. Clicking the Log Out button displays a menu of log out, shut down, and restart buttons. You can also access applications by right-clicking on the desktop background to display the desktop menu and selecting the Applications entry to display application categories and submenus.

Xfce file manager is called Thunar. The file manager will open a side pane in the shortcuts view that lists entries for not just for the home folder, but also your file system, desktop, and trash folders (see Figure 11-1). The File menu lets you perform folder operations like creating new folders. From the Edit menu, you can perform tasks on a selected file like renaming the file or creating a link for it. You can change the side pane view to a tree view of your file system by selecting it from the menubar View | Side Pane | Tree, (Ctrl-e). The Shortcuts entry changes the view back (Ctrl-b).

To configure the Xubuntu desktop, you use the Settings Manager, accessible from the Applications menu by clicking the Settings button at the bottom right. This opens the Settings window, which shows icons for your desktop, display, panel, user interface, among others (see Figure 11-3). Use the Appearance tool to select themes, icons, fonts, and toolbar styles (Settings tab). The Panel tool lets you add new panels and control features like lock for freely movable and mode for horizontally or vertically positioned panels. You can also choose a background image and the items to include in the panel. You can also access the Settings Manager tools from the desktop menu and choosing Applications | Settings.

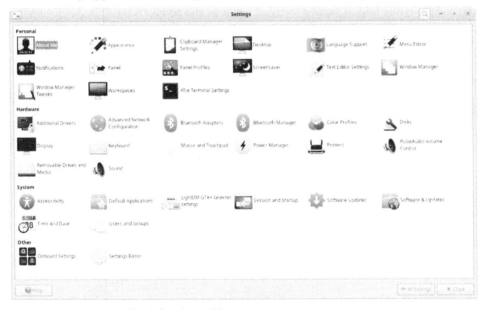

Figure 11-3: Xubuntu (Xfce) Settings Manager

To configure the desktop, select the Desktop icon on the Settings window or right-click on the desktop and select Desktop Settings from the desktop menu (you can also select Settings | Desktop). This opens the Desktop window where you can select the background image, control menu behavior, and set icon sizes (see Figure 11-4).

Figure 11-4: Xubuntu (Xfce) Desktop Configuration

Lubuntu (LXQT)

Lubuntu uses the LXQT desktop, the Lightweight QT Desktop Environment. The LXQT desktop provides a small desktop designed for use on minimal or low power systems like laptops, netbooks, or older computers.

You can find out more about Lubuntu and download it from:

https://lubuntu.me/

You can find out more about LXQT at:

https://lxqt.github.io/

To install Lubuntu as an alternative desktop on a system, select the **lubuntu-desktop** package on the Synaptic Package Manager or use the **apt** command.

The desktop displays a single panel at the bottom with the application menu to the left, followed by the windows taskbar, and system applets to the right (see Figure 11-5). From the panel applications menu, you can access any applications. Next to the menu is a workspace switcher, Quicklaunch widget, and a taskbar for open windows. You can drag any application entry in the menu to the Quicklauch widget to have its icon displayed on the panel.

Figure 11-5: Lubuntu (LXQT) desktop

The bottom panel shows widgets for the applications menu, the workspace switcher, the PC-Man file manager, Web browser, minimize windows, and the window list. On the right side of the panel are widgets for the removeable device manager, volume control, clipboard, power management, Network Manager, notifications, and the clock (see Figure 11-6).

Figure 11-6: Lubuntu (LXQT) panel

The Leave entry on the applications menu shows entries for logout, shutdown, suspend, hibernate, reboot, and leave. The leave entry opens a dialog with button for these options.

Lubuntu uses the PC-Man file manager as shown in Figure 11-5. The toolbar performs browser tasks like moving backward and forward to previously viewed folders, as well as new tabs and icon and list views. The side pane has a location (Places) and folder tree view. You can switch between the two using the menu at the top of the pane.

To configure your panel, right-click on the panel and select Configure Panel to open the Configure Panel dialog at the Panel tab (see Figure 11-7). You can set the position and size of the panel, the autohide feature, as well as the background and font color for the panel.

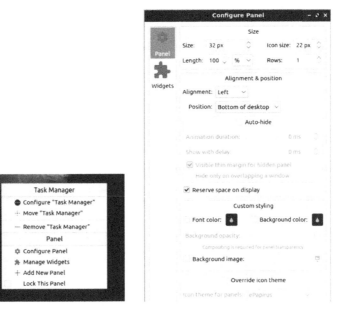

Figure 11-7: Lubuntu (LXQT) Configure Panel

To manage your widgets on the panel, right-click on the panel and select Manage Widgets from the menu to open the Configure Panel dialog at the Widgets tab (see Figure 11-8). Buttons to the right let you add, remove, and configure your widgets. Loaded widgets are listed. To remove a widget, select it and click the minus button. To configure a widget, click the configure button (gear symbol) to open the widget's configuration dialog. This will vary among applets. To set the time display format, select the world clock and click configure button to open the clock settings dialog. Widget settings can also be configured directly from the panel. Right-click on the widget and choose the Configure entry, like Configure "World Clock " for the world clock widget.

To add a new applet to the panel, Click the Plus button to open the Add Plugins window, which will list all available applets and panel features like spaces. Select the one you want and click the Add Widget button (see Figure 11-8).

To configure the desktop, right-click anywhere on the desktop and choose Desktop Preferences from the pop-up menu. This opens the Desktop Preferences window with tabs for General, Background, Slide Show, and Advanced (see Figure 11-9). The General tab lets you set the icon size, label text font and color, as well as the minimum item spacing. The Advanced tab lets you choose what icons to display on the desktop (home, trash, computer, and network). The Slide Show enables a wallpaper slideshow and lets you choose the folder for the slideshow images as well as the time intervals. The Background tab lets you select the background color, wallpaper mode, and wallpaper image file.

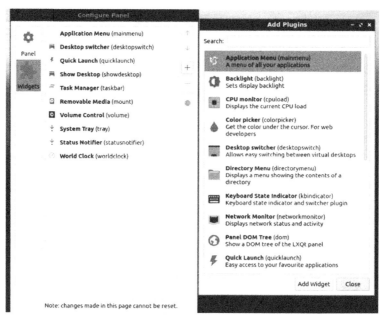

Figure 11-8: Lubuntu (LXQT) Configure Panel Widgets tab and Plugins

Figure 11-9: Lubuntu (LXQT) Desktop Preferences

Ubuntu Studio

Ubuntu Studio provides a collection of Linux-based multimedia software for graphic design, audio production, and video production (see Figure 11-10). Applications include Blender 3d modeling and the Audacity sound editor. Ubuntu Studio is based on Kubuntu and has the Kubuntu system tools such as the Dolphin file manager, the Discover software manager, and Kubuntu System Settings tools. The panel is at the top of the screen with button for popular applications such as Firefox, the Kdenlive video editor, and the Gimp image editor. The Studio Controls tool can be used to configure jacks and extra devices such as headphones. The task manager uses the KDE Icon-only task manager. Buttons for open applications are displayed on the panel. Passing your mouse over an application button display icons you can choose for all the windows currently open with that application.

You can download Ubuntu Studio from:

`https://ubuntustudio.org/`

The site also has documentation and support links for applications.

Figure 11-10: Ubuntu Studio

Ubuntu Budgie

Ubuntu Budgie uses the Budgie desktop, developed for the Solus Linux distribution (see Figure 11-11). It installs the full set of applications, though some of the default applications are different. The Web Browser is Chromium instead of Firefox, the media player is MPV instead of Videos, and the email application is Geary instead of Thunderbird. Ubuntu Budgie uses GNOME Software (Software) for managing software and GNOME Settings (Settings) to configure your system. Ubuntu Budgie features immediate updates, as they become available. This ensures a more secure system.

Figure 11-11: Ubuntu Budgie

You can download Ubuntu Budgie from:

```
https://ubuntubudgie.org/downloads
```

The Plank dock at the bottom has favorite applications. The top panel has applets on the right and the time and date in the center. When you open an application, an icon for it appears on the dock. You can right-click on it to have it shown permanently.

You can access applications from the menu at the top left of the panel. Buttons on the top left of the menu let you switch between an icon view of the menu and a list view with categories (see Figure 11-12)

Figure 11-12: Ubuntu Budgie menu

The Welcome dialog's Getting Started dialog has links for common tasks such as updates, drivers, and customization (see Figure 11-13).

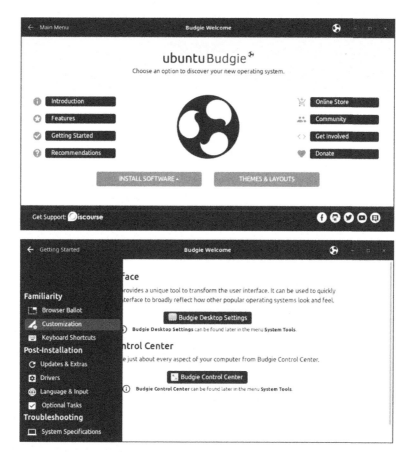

Figure 11-13: Ubuntu Budgie Welcome

For Budgie Applets you can use the Budgie Desktop Extras dialog accessible from the INSTALL SOFTWARE menu (see Figure 11-14). Budgie applets include Hotcorners that set up corners to activate features when you move your mouse to one, Clockworks which provides a world clock display, Weather and Forecast applet, and Window Shuffler for moving and arranging windows.

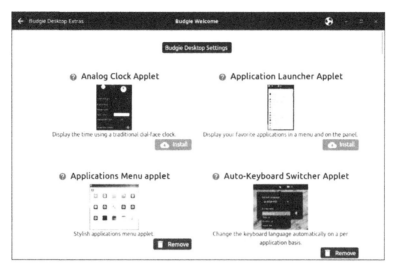

Figure 11-14: Budgie Applets

For Budgie themes you can use the Budgie Themes and dialog accessible from the THEMES & LAYOUTS button(see Figure 11-15).

Figure 11-15: Budgie Themes

12. Shells

The Command Line

History

Filename Expansion: *, ?, [ ]

Standard Input/Output and Redirection

Linux Files

The File Structure

Listing, Displaying, and Printing Files

Managing Directories: mkdir, rmdir, ls, cd, pwd

File and Directory Operations: find, cp, mv, rm, ln

The shell is a command interpreter that provides a line-oriented interactive and non-interactive interface between the user and the operating system. You enter commands on a command line and they are interpreted by the shell and then sent as instructions to the operating system (the command line interface is accessible from GNOME, KDE, and MATE through a Terminal windows). You can also place commands in a script file to be consecutively executed, much like a program. This interpretive capability of the shell provides for many sophisticated features. For example, the shell has a set of file expansion characters that can generate filenames. The shell can redirect input and output, as well as run operations in the background, freeing you to perform other tasks.

Shell	Web Site
www.gnu.org/software/bash	BASH website with online manual, FAQ, and current releases
www.gnu.org/software/bash/manual/bash.html	BASH online manual
www.zsh.org	Z shell website with referrals to FAQs and current downloads.
www.kornshell.com	Korn shell site with manual, FAQ, and references

Table 12-1: Linux Shells

Several different types of shells have been developed for Linux: the Bourne Again shell (BASH), the Korn shell, the TCSH shell, and the Z shell. All shells are available for your use, although the BASH shell is the default. You only need one type of shell to do your work. Ubuntu Linux includes all the major shells, although it installs and uses the BASH shell as the default. If you use the command line shell, you will be using the BASH shell unless you specify another. This chapter discusses the BASH shell, which shares many of the same features as other shells.

You can find out more about shells at their respective websites as listed in Table 12-1. In addition, a detailed online manual is available for each installed shell. Use the **man** command and the shell's keyword to access them, **bash** for the BASH shell, **ksh** for the Korn shell, **zsh** for the Z shell, and **tsch** for the TSCH shell. For example, the command **man bash** will access the BASH shell online manual.

Note: You can find out more about the BASH shell at www.gnu.org/software/bash. A detailed online manual is available on your Linux system using the man command with the bash keyword.

The Command Line

The Linux command line interface consists of a single line into which you enter commands with any of their options and arguments. From GNOME or KDE, you can access the command line interface by opening a terminal window (Applications Overview | Utilities | Terminal). Should you start Linux with the command line interface, you will be presented with a BASH shell command line when you log in.

By default, the BASH shell has a dollar sign ($) prompt, but Linux has several other types of shells, each with its own prompt (like % for the C shell). The root user will have a different prompt, the #. A shell *prompt,* such as the one shown here, marks the beginning of the command line:

```
$
```

You can enter a command along with options and arguments at the prompt. For example, with an **-l** option, the **ls** command will display a line of information about each file, listing such data as its size and the date and time it was last modified. In the next example, the user enters the **ls** command followed by a **-l** option. The dash before the **-l** option is required. Linux uses it to distinguish an option from an argument.

```
$ ls -l
```

If you wanted only the information displayed for a particular file, you could add that file's name as the argument, following the **-l** option:

```
$ ls -l mydata
-rw-r--r-- 1 chris weather 207 Feb 20 11:55 mydata
```

Tip: Some commands can be complex and take some time to execute. When you mistakenly execute the wrong command, you can interrupt and stop such commands with the interrupt key, CTRL-C.

You can enter a command on several lines by typing a backslash just before you press ENTER. The backslash "escapes" the ENTER key, effectively continuing the same command line to the next line. In the next example, the **cp** command is entered on three lines. The first two lines end in a backslash, effectively making all three lines one command line.

```
$ cp -i \
mydata \
/home/george/myproject/newdata
```

You can also enter several commands on the same line by separating them with a semicolon (;). In effect, the semicolon operates as an execute operation. Commands will be executed in the sequence in which they are entered. The following command executes an **ls** command followed by a **date** command.

```
$ ls ; date
```

You can also conditionally run several commands on the same line with the **&&** operator. A command is executed only if the previous command is true. This feature is useful for running several dependent scripts on the same line. In the next example, the **ls** command is run only if the **date** command is successfully executed.

```
$ date && ls
```

TIP: Commands can also be run as arguments on a command line, using their results for other commands. To run a command within a command line, you encase the command in back quotes.

Command Line Editing

The BASH shell, which is your default shell, has special command line editing capabilities (see Table 12-2). You can easily modify commands you have entered before executing them, moving anywhere on the command line and inserting or deleting characters. This is particularly helpful for complex commands.

Movement Commands	Operation
CTRL-F, RIGHT-ARROW	Move forward a character
CTRL-B, LEFT-ARROW	Move backward a character
CTRL-A or HOME	Move to beginning of line
CTRL-E or END	Move to end of line
ALT-F	Move forward a word
ALT-B	Move backward a word
CTRL-L	Clear screen and place line at top
Editing Commands	**Operation**
CTRL-D or DEL	Delete character cursor is on
CTRL-H or BACKSPACE	Delete character before the cursor
CTRL-K	Cut remainder of line from cursor position
CTRL-U	Cut from cursor position to beginning of line
CTRL-W	Cut the previous word
CTRL-C	Cut entire line
ALT-D	Cut the remainder of a word
ALT-DEL	Cut from the cursor to the beginning of a word
CTRL-Y	Paste previous cut text
ALT-Y	Paste from set of previously cut text
CTRL-Y	Paste previous cut text
CTRL-V	Insert quoted text, used for inserting control or meta (Alt) keys as text, such as CTRL-B for backspace or CTRL-T for tabs
ALT-T	Transpose current and previous word
ALT-L	Lowercase current word
ALT-U	Uppercase current word
ALT-C	Capitalize current word
CTRL-SHIFT-_	Undo previous change

Table 12-2: Command Line Editing Operations

You can press CTRL-F or the RIGHT ARROW key to move forward a character, or the CTRL-B or LEFT ARROW key to move back a character. CTRL-D or DEL deletes the character the cursor is on, and CTRL-H or BACKSPACE deletes the character preceding the cursor. To add text, you use the arrow keys to move the cursor to where you want to insert text and type the new characters.

You can even cut words with the CTRL-W or ALT-D key, and then press the CTRL-Y key to paste them back in at a different position, effectively moving the words. As a rule, the CTRL version of the command operates on characters, and the ALT version works on words, such as CTRL-T to transpose characters and ALT-T to transpose words. At any time, you can press ENTER to execute the command. For example, if you make a spelling mistake when entering a command, rather than re-entering the entire command, you can use the editing operations to correct the mistake. The actual associations of keys and their tasks, along with global settings, are specified in the **/etc/inputrc** file.

The editing capabilities of the BASH shell command line are provided by Readline. Readline supports numerous editing operations. You can even bind a key to a selected editing operation. Readline uses the **/etc/inputrc** file to configure key bindings. This file is read automatically by your **/etc/profile** shell configuration file when you log in. Users can customize their editing commands by creating an **.inputrc** file in their home directory (this is a dot file). It may be best to first copy the **/etc/inputrc** file as your **.inputrc** file and then edit it. **/etc/profile** will first check for a local **.inputrc** file before accessing the **/etc/inputrc** file. You can find out more about Readline in the BASH shell reference manual at **www.gnu.org/software/bash**.

Command and Filename Completion

The BASH command line has a built-in feature that performs command line and filename completion. Automatic completions can be displayed by pressing the TAB key. If you enter an incomplete pattern as a command or filename argument, you can press the TAB key to activate the command and filename completion feature, which completes the pattern. A directory will have a forward slash (/) attached to its name. If more than one command or file has the same prefix, the shell simply beeps and waits for you to press the TAB key again. It then displays a list of possible command completions and waits for you to add enough characters to select a unique command or filename. For situations where you know multiple possibilities are likely, you can just press the ESC key instead of two TABs. In the next example, the user issues a **cat** command with an incomplete filename. When the user presses the TAB key, the system searches for a match and, when it finds one, fills in the filename. The user can then press ENTER to execute the command.

```
$ cat pre <tab>
$ cat preface
```

The automatic completions also work with the names of variables, users, and hosts. In this case, the partial text needs to be preceded by a special character, indicating the type of name. A listing of possible automatic completions follows:

Filenames begin with any text or /.

Shell variable text begins with a $ sign.

Username text begins with a ~ sign.

Host name text begins with a @.

Commands, aliases, and text in files begin with normal text.

Variables begin with a **$** sign, so any text beginning with a dollar sign is treated as a variable to be completed. Variables are selected from previously defined variables, like system shell variables. Usernames begin with a tilde (~). Host names begin with a @ sign, with possible names taken from the **/etc/hosts** file. For example, to complete the variable HOME given just $HOM, simply press a tab key.

```
$ echo $HOM <tab>
$ echo $HOME
```

If you entered just an **H**, then you could press TAB twice to see all possible variables beginning with H. The command line is redisplayed, letting you complete the name.

```
$ echo $H <tab> <tab>
$HISTCMD $HISTFILE $HOME $HOSTTYPE HISTFILE $HISTSIZE $HISTNAME
$ echo $H
```

You can also specifically select the kind of text to complete, using corresponding command keys. In this case, it does not matter what kind of sign a name begins with.

Command (CTRL-R for listing possible completions)	Description
TAB	Automatic completion
TAB TAB or ESC	List possible completions
ALT-/, CTRL-R-/	Filename completion, normal text for automatic
ALT-$, CTRL-R-$	Shell variable completion, $ for automatic
ALT-~, CTRL-R-~	Username completion, ~ for automatic
ALT-@, CTRL-R-@	Host name completion, @ for automatic
ALT-!, CTRL-R-!	Command name completion, normal text for automatic

Table 12-3: Command Line Text Completion Commands

For example, the pressing ALT-~ will treat the current text as a username. Pressing ALT-@ will treat it as a hostname, and ALT-$, as a variable. Pressing ALT-! will treat it as a command. To display a list of possible completions, press the CTRL-X key with the appropriate completion key, as in CTRL-X-$ to list possible variable completions. See Table 12-3 for a complete listing.

History

The BASH shell keeps a *history list,* of your previously entered commands. You can display each command, in turn, on your command line by pressing the UP ARROW key. Press the DOWN ARROW key to move down the list. You can modify and execute any of these previous commands when you display them on the command line.

Tip: The ability to redisplay a command is helpful when you have already executed a command you had entered incorrectly. In this case, you would be presented with an error message and a new, empty command line. By pressing the UP ARROW key, you can redisplay the previous command, make corrections to it, and then execute it again. This way, you would not have to enter the whole command again.

History Events

In the BASH shell, the history utility keeps a record of the most recent commands you have executed. The commands are numbered starting at 1, and a limit exists to the number of commands remembered. The default is 500. The history utility is a kind of short-term memory, keeping track of the most recent commands you have executed. To see the set of your most recent commands, type **history** on the command line and press ENTER. A list of your most recent commands is then displayed, preceded by a number.

```
$ history
1 cp mydata today
2 vi mydata
3 mv mydata reports
4 cd reports
5 ls
```

History Commands	Description
CTRL-N or DOWN ARROW	Moves down to the next event in the history list
CTRL-P or UP ARROW	Moves up to the previous event in the history list
ALT-<	Moves to the beginning of the history event list
ALT->	Moves to the end of the history event list
ALT-N	Forward Search, next matching item
ALT-P	Backward Search, previous matching item
CTRL-S	Forward Search History, forward incremental search
CTRL-R	Reverse Search History, reverse incremental search
fc *event-reference*	Edits an event with the standard editor and then executes it **Options** **-l** List recent history events; same as **history** command **-e** *editor event-reference* Invokes a specified editor to edit a specific event
History Event References	
! *event num*	References an event with an event number
! !	References the previous command
! *characters*	References an event with beginning characters
! ?*pattern*?	References an event with a pattern in the event
! -*event num*	References an event with an offset from the first event
! *num-num*	References a range of events

Table 12-4: History Commands and History Event References

Each of these commands is technically referred to as an event. An event describes an action that has been taken, a command that has been executed. The events are numbered according to their sequence of execution. The most recent event has the highest number. Each of these events can be identified by its number or beginning characters in the command.

The history utility lets you reference a former event, placing it on your command line so you can execute it. The easiest way to do this is to use the UP ARROW and DOWN ARROW keys to place history events on the command line, one at a time. You need not display the list first with **history**. Pressing the UP ARROW key once places the last history event on the command line. Pressing it again places the next history event on the command line. Pressing the DOWN ARROW key places the previous event on the command line.

You can use certain control and meta keys to perform other history operations like searching the history list. A meta key is the Alt key, and the ESC key on keyboards that have no Alt key. The Alt key is used here. Pressing Alt-< will move you to the beginning of the history list. Alt-n will search it. Ctrl-s and Ctrl-r will perform incremental searches, displaying matching commands as you type in a search string. Table 12-4 lists the different commands for referencing the history list.

Tip: If more than one history event matches what you have entered, you will hear a beep, and you can then enter more characters to help uniquely identify the event.

You can also reference and execute history events using the ! history command. The ! is followed by a reference that identifies the command. The reference can be either the number of the event or a beginning set of characters in the event. In the next example, the third command in the history list is referenced first by number and then by the beginning characters:

```
$ !3
mv mydata reports
$ !mv my
mv mydata reports
```

You can also reference an event using an offset from the end of the list. A negative number will offset from the end of the list to that event, thereby referencing it. In the next example, the fourth command, **cd mydata**, is referenced using a negative offset, and then executed. Remember that you are offsetting from the end of the list, in this case event 5,up toward the beginning of the list, event 1. An offset of 4 beginning from event 5 places you at event 2.

```
$ !-4
vi mydata
```

To reference the last event, you use a following !, as in !!. In the next example, the command ! ! executes the last command the user executed—in this case, **ls**:

```
$ !!
ls
mydata today reports
```

Filename Expansion: *, ?, [ ]

Filenames are the most common arguments used in a command. Often you will know only part of the filename, or you will want to reference several filenames that have the same extension or begin with the same characters. The shell provides a set of special characters that search out, match, and generate a list of filenames. These are the asterisk, the question mark, and brackets (*****, **?**, **[]**). Given a partial filename, the shell uses these matching operators to search for files and expand to a list of filenames found. The shell replaces the partial filename argument with the expanded list of matched filenames. This list of filenames can then become the arguments for commands such as **ls**, which can operate on many files. Table 12-5 lists the shell's file expansion characters.

Common Shell Symbols	Execution
ENTER	Execute a command line.
;	Separate commands on the same command line.
`command`	Execute a command.
$ (command)	Execute a command.
[]	Match on a class of possible characters in filenames.
\	Quote the following character. Used to quote special characters.
|	Pipe the standard output of one command as input for another command.
&	Execute a command in the background.
!	Reference history command.
File Expansion Symbols	**Execution**
*	Match on any set of characters in filenames.
?	Match on any single character in filenames.
[]	Match on a class of characters in filenames.
Redirection Symbols	**Execution**
>	Redirect the standard output to a file or device, creating the file if it does not exist and overwriting the file if it does exist.
>!	The exclamation point forces the overwriting of a file if it already exists.
<	Redirect the standard input from a file or device to a program.
>>	Redirect the standard output to a file or device, appending the output to the end of the file.
Standard Error Redirection Symbols	**Execution**
2>	Redirect the standard error to a file or device.
2>>	Redirect and append the standard error to a file or device.
2>&1	Redirect the standard error to the standard output.

Table 12-5: Shell Symbols

Matching Multiple Characters

The asterisk (*) references files beginning or ending with a specific set of characters. You place the asterisk before or after a set of characters that form a pattern to be searched for in filenames.

If the asterisk is placed before the pattern, filenames that end in that pattern are searched for. If the asterisk is placed after the pattern, filenames that begin with that pattern are searched. Any matching filename is copied into a list of filenames generated by this operation.

In the next example, all filenames beginning with the pattern "doc" are searched for and a list generated. Then all filenames ending with the pattern "day" are searched for and a list is generated. The last example shows how the * can be used in any combination of characters.

```
$ ls
doc1 doc2 document docs mydoc monday tuesday
$ ls doc*
doc1 doc2 document docs
$ ls *day
monday tuesday
$ ls m*d*
monday
$
```

Filenames often include an extension specified with a period and followed by a string denoting the file type, such as **.c** for C files, **.cpp** for C++ files, or even **.jpg** for JPEG image files. The extension has no special status, and is only part of the characters making up the filename. Using the asterisk makes it easy to select files with a given extension. In the next example, the asterisk is used to list only those files with a **.c** extension. The asterisk placed before the **.c** constitutes the argument for **ls**.

```
$ ls *.c
calc.c main.c
```

You can use * with the **rm** command to erase several files at once. The asterisk first selects a list of files with a given extension, or beginning or ending with a given set of characters, and then it presents this list of files to the **rm** command to be erased. In the next example, the **rm** command erases all files beginning with the pattern "doc":

```
$ rm doc*
```

Caution: Use the * file expansion character carefully and sparingly with the **rm** command. The combination can be dangerous. A misplaced * in an **rm** command without the -i option could easily erase all the files in your current directory. The **-i** option will first prompt you to confirm whether the file should be deleted.

Matching Single Characters

The question mark (b) matches only a single incomplete character in filenames. Suppose you want to match the files **doc1** and **docA**, but not the file **document**. Whereas the asterisk will match filenames of any length, the question mark limits the match to one extra character. The next example matches files that begin with the word "doc" followed by a single differing letter:

```
$ ls
doc1 docA document
$ ls doc?
doc1 docA
```

Matching a Range of Characters

Whereas the * and ? file expansion characters specify incomplete portions of a filename, the brackets ([]) enable you to specify a set of valid characters to search for. Any character placed within the brackets will be matched in the filename. Suppose you want to list files beginning with "doc", but only ending in *1* or *A*. You are not interested in filenames ending in *2* or *B*, or any other character. This is how it is done.

```
$ ls
doc1 doc2 doc3 docA docB docD document
$ ls doc[1A]
doc1 docA
```

You can also specify a set of characters as a range, rather than listing them one by one. A dash placed between the upper and lower bounds of a range of characters selects all characters within that range. The range is usually determined by the character set in use. In an ASCII character set, the range "a-g" will select all lowercase alphabetic characters from *a* through *g*, inclusive. In the next example, files beginning with the pattern "doc" and ending in characters *1* through *3* are selected. Then, those ending in characters *B* through *E* are matched.

```
$ ls doc[1-3]
doc1 doc2 doc3
$ ls doc[B-E]
docB docD
```

You can combine the brackets with other file expansion characters to form flexible matching operators. Suppose you want to list only filenames ending in either a **.c** or **.o** extension, but no other extension. You can use a combination of the asterisk and brackets: * **[co]**. The asterisk matches all filenames, and the brackets match only filenames with extension **.c** or **.o**.

```
$ ls *.[co]
main.c  main.o  calc.c
```

Matching Shell Symbols

At times, a file expansion character is actually part of a filename. In these cases, you need to quote the character by preceding it with a backslash (\) to reference the file. In the next example, the user needs to reference a file that ends with the **?** character, called **answers?**. The **?** is, however, a file expansion character and would match any filename beginning with "answers" that has one or more characters. In this case, the user quotes the **?** with a preceding backslash to reference the filename.

```
$ ls answers\?
answers?
```

Placing the filename in double quotes will also quote the character.

```
$ ls "answers?"
answers?
```

This is also true for filenames or directories that have white space characters like the space character. In this case, you could either use the backslash to quote the space character in the file or directory name, or place the entire name in double quotes.

```
$ ls My\ Documents
My Documents
$ ls "My Documents"
My Documents
```

Generating Patterns

Though not a file expansion operation, {} is often useful for generating names that you can use to create or modify files and directories. The braces operation only generates a list of names. It does not match on existing filenames. Patterns are placed within the braces and separated with commas. Any pattern placed within the braces will be used to generate a version of the pattern, using either the preceding or following pattern, or both. Suppose you want to generate a list of names beginning with "doc", but ending only in the patterns "ument", "final", and "draft". This is how it is done.

```
$ echo doc{ument,final,draft}
document docfinal docdraft
```

Since the names generated do not have to exist, you could use the {} operation in a command to create directories, as shown here:

```
$ mkdir {fall,winter,spring}report
$ ls
fallreport springreport winterreport
```

Standard Input/Output and Redirection

The data in input and output operations is organized like a file. Data input at the keyboard is placed in a data stream arranged as a continuous set of bytes. Data output from a command or program is also placed in a data stream and arranged as a continuous set of bytes. This input data stream is referred to in Linux as the standard input, while the output data stream is called the standard output. A separate output data stream reserved solely for error messages is called the standard error.

Because the standard input and standard output have the same organization as that of a file, they can easily interact with files. Linux has a redirection capability that lets you easily move data in and out of files. You can redirect the standard output so that, instead of displaying the output on a screen, you can save it in a file. You can also redirect the standard input away from the keyboard to a file, so that input is read from a file instead of from your keyboard.

When a Linux command is executed that produces output, this output is placed in the standard output data stream. The default destination for the standard output data stream is a device, usually the screen. Devices, such as the keyboard and screen, are treated as files. They receive and send out streams of bytes with the same organization as that of a byte-stream file. The screen is a device that displays a continuous stream of bytes. By default, the standard output will send its data to the screen device, which will then display the data.

For example, the **ls** command generates a list of all filenames and outputs this list to the standard output. Next, this stream of bytes in the standard output is directed to the screen device.

The list of filenames is then printed on the screen. The **cat** command also sends output to the standard output. The contents of a file are copied to the standard output, whose default destination is the screen. The contents of the file are then displayed on the screen.

Command	Execution
ENTER	Execute a command line.
;	Separate commands on the same command line.
command *opts args*	Enter backslash before carriage return to continue entering a command on the next line.
`` `command` ``	Execute a command.
Special Characters for Filename Expansion	**Execution**
*	Match on any set of characters.
?	Match on any single characters.
[]	Match on a class of possible characters.
\	Quote the following character. Used to quote special characters.
Redirection	**Execution**
command > *filename*	Redirect the standard output to a file or device, creating the file if it does not exist and overwriting the file if it does exist.
command < *filename*	Redirect the standard input from a file or device to a program.
command >> *filename*	Redirect the standard output to a file or device, appending the output to the end of the file.
command **2>** *filename*	Redirect the standard error to a file or device
command **2>>** *filename*	Redirect and append the standard error to a file or device
command **2>&1**	Redirect the standard error to the standard output in the Bourne shell.
command **>&** *filename*	Redirect the standard error to a file or device in the C shell.
Pipes	**Execution**
command | *command*	Pipe the standard output of one command as input for another command.

Table 12-6: The Shell Operations

Redirecting the Standard Output: > and >>

Suppose that instead of displaying a list of files on the screen, you would like to save this list in a file. In other words, you would like to direct the standard output to a file rather than the screen. To do this, you place the output redirection operator, the greater-than sign (>), followed by the name of a file on the command line after the Linux command. Table 12-6 lists the different ways you can use the redirection operators. In the next example, the output of the **ls** command is redirected from the screen device to a file:

```
$ ls -l *.c > programlist
```

The redirection operation creates the new destination file. If the file already exists, it will be overwritten with the data in the standard output. You can set the **noclobber** feature to prevent overwriting an existing file with the redirection operation. In this case, the redirection operation on an existing file will fail. You can overcome the **noclobber** feature by placing an exclamation point after the redirection operator. You can place the **noclobber** command in a shell configuration file to make it an automatic default operation. The next example sets the **noclobber** feature for the BASH shell and then forces the overwriting of the **oldarticle** file if it already exists:

```
$ set -o noclobber
$ cat myarticle >! oldarticle
```

Although the redirection operator and the filename are placed after the command, the redirection operation is not executed after the command. In fact, it is executed before the command. The redirection operation creates the file and sets up the redirection before it receives any data from the standard output. If the file already exists, it will be destroyed and replaced by a file of the same name. In effect, the command generating the output is executed only after the redirected file has been created.

In the next example, the output of the **ls** command is redirected from the screen device to a file. First, the **ls** command lists files, and in the next command, **ls** redirects its file list to the **listf** file. Then the **cat** command displays the list of files saved in **listf**. Notice the list of files in **listf** includes the **listf** filename. The list of filenames generated by the **ls** command includes the name of the file created by the redirection operation—in this case, **listf**. The **listf** file is first created by the redirection operation, and then the **ls** command lists it along with other files. This file list output by **ls** is then redirected to the **listf** file, instead of being printed on the screen.

```
$ ls
mydata intro preface
$ ls > listf
$ cat listf
mydata intro listf preface
```

Tip: Errors occur when you try to use the same filename for both an input file for the command and the redirected destination file. In this case, because the redirection operation is executed first, the input file, because it exists, is destroyed and replaced by a file of the same name. When the command is executed, it finds an input file that is empty.

You can also append the standard output to an existing file using the >> redirection operator. Instead of overwriting the file, the data in the standard output is added at the end of the file. In the next example, the **myarticle** and **oldarticle** files are appended to the **allarticles** file. The **allarticles** file will then contain the contents of both **myarticle** and **oldarticle**.

```
$ cat myarticle >> allarticles
$ cat oldarticle >> allarticles
```

The Standard Input

Many Linux commands can receive data from the standard input. The standard input itself receives data from a device or a file. The default device for the standard input is the keyboard. Characters typed on the keyboard are placed in the standard input, which is then directed to the

Linux command. Just as with the standard output, you can also redirect the standard input, receiving input from a file rather than the keyboard. The operator for redirecting the standard input is the less-than sign (<). In the next example, the standard input is redirected to receive input from the **myarticle** file, rather than the keyboard device. The contents of **myarticle** are read into the standard input by the redirection operation. Then the **cat** command reads the standard input and displays the contents of **myarticle**.

```
$ cat < myarticle
hello Christopher
How are you today
$
```

You can combine the redirection operations for both standard input and standard output. In the next example, the **cat** command has no filename arguments. Without filename arguments, the **cat** command receives input from the standard input and sends output to the standard output. However, the standard input has been redirected to receive its data from a file, while the standard output has been redirected to place its data in a file.

```
$ cat < myarticle > newarticle
```

Redirecting the Standard Error: >&, 2>, |&

When you execute commands, it is possible for an error to occur. You may give the wrong number of arguments or some kind of system error could take place. When an error occurs, the system will issue an error message. Usually, such error messages are displayed on the screen along with the standard output. Error messages are placed in another standard byte stream called the standard error. In the next example, the cat command is given as its argument the name of a file that does not exist, **myintro**. In this case, the **cat** command will simply issue an error. Redirection operators are listed in Table 12-6.

```
$ cat myintro
cat : myintro not found
```

Because error messages are in a separate data stream from the standard output, this means that if you have redirected the standard output to a file, error messages will still appear on the screen for you to see. Though the standard output may be redirected to a file, the standard error is still directed to the screen. In the next example, the standard output of the **cat** command is redirected to the file **mydata**. The standard error, containing the error messages, is still directed toward the screen

```
$ cat myintro > mydata
cat : myintro not found
```

Like the standard output, you can also redirect the standard error. This means that you can save your error messages in a file for future reference. This is helpful if you need to save a record of the error messages. Like the standard output, the standard error's default destination is the display. Using special redirection operators, you can redirect the standard error to any file or device that you choose. If you redirect the standard error, the error messages will not be displayed on the screen. You can examine them later by viewing the contents of the file in which you saved them.

All the standard byte streams can be referenced in redirection operations with certain numbers. The numbers 0, 1, and 2 reference the standard input, standard output, and standard error respectively. By default an output redirection, >, operates on the standard output, 1. You can modify the output redirection to operate on the standard error by preceding the output redirection operator with the number 2, **2>**. In the next example, the **cat** command again will generate an error. The error message is redirected to the standard byte stream represented by number 2, the standard error.

```
$ cat nodata 2> myerrors
$ cat myerrors
cat : nodata not found
```

You can also append the standard error to a file by using the number 2 and the redirection append operator, **>>**. In the next example, the user appends the standard error to the **myerrors** file, which then functions as a log of errors.

```
$ cat nodata 2>> myerrors
$ cat compls 2>> myerrors
$ cat myerrors
cat : nodata not found
cat : compls not found
$
```

To redirect both the standard output as well as the standard error, you would need a separate redirection operation and file for each. In the next example, the standard output is redirected to the file **mydata**, and the standard error is redirected to **myerrors**. If nodata were to exist, then **mydata** would hold a copy of its contents.

```
$ cat nodata 1> mydata 2> myerrors
cat myerrors
cat : nodata not found
```

If you want to save a record of your errors in the same file as that used for the redirected standard output, you need to redirect the standard error into the standard output. You can reference a standard byte stream by preceding its number with an ampersand. **&1** references the standard output. You can use such a reference in a redirection operation to make a standard byte stream a destination file. The redirection operation **2>&1** redirects the standard error into the standard output. In effect, the standard output becomes the destination file for the standard error. Conversely, the redirection operation **1>&2** would redirect the standard input into the standard error.

Pipes: |

You may encounter situations in which you need to send data from one command to another. In other words, you may want to send the standard output of a command to another command, rather than to a destination file. Suppose you want to send a list of your filenames to the printer to be printed. You need two commands to do this: the **ls** command to generate a list of filenames and the **lpr** command to send the list to the printer. In effect, you need to take the output of the **ls** command and use it as input for the **lpr** command. You can think of the data as flowing from one command to another. To form such a connection in Linux, you use what is called a pipe. The pipe operator (|, the vertical bar character) placed between two commands forms a connection between them. The standard output of one command becomes the standard input for the other. The pipe operation receives output from the command placed before the pipe and sends this data as input to the command placed after the pipe. As shown in the next example, you can connect the **ls** command and the **lpr** command with a pipe. The list of filenames output by the **ls** command is piped into the **lpr** command.

```
$ ls | lpr
```

You can combine the pipe operation with other shell features, such as file expansion characters, to perform specialized operations. The next example prints only files with a **.c** extension. The **ls** command is used with the asterisk and ".c" to generate a list of filenames with the **.c** extension. Then this list is piped to the **lpr** command.

```
$ ls *.c | lpr
```

In the preceding example, a list of filenames was used as input. What is important to note is that pipes operate on the standard output of a command, whatever that might be. The contents of whole files, or even several files, can be piped from one command to another. In the next example, the **cat** command reads and outputs the contents of the **mydata** file, which are then piped to the **lpr** command:

```
$ cat mydata | lpr
```

Linux has many commands that generate modified output. For example, the **sort** command takes the contents of a file and generates a version with each line sorted in alphabetic order. The **sort** command works best with files that are lists of items. Commands such as **sort** that output a modified version of its input are referred to as filters. Filters are often used with pipes. In the next example, a sorted version of **mylist** is generated and piped into the **more** command for display on the screen. The original file, **mylist**, has not been changed and is not sorted. Only the output of **sort** in the standard output is sorted.

```
$ sort mylist | more
```

The standard input piped into a command can be more carefully controlled with the standard input argument (**-**). When you use the dash as an argument for a command, it represents the standard input.

Linux Files

You can name a file using any letters, underscores, and numbers. You can also include periods and commas. Except in certain special cases, you should never begin a filename with a period. Other characters, such as slashes, question marks, or asterisks, are reserved for use as special characters by the system and should not be part of a filename. Filenames can be as long as 256 characters. Filenames can also include spaces, though to reference such filenames from the command line, be sure to encase them in quotes. On a desktop like GNOME or KDE, you do not need to use quotes.

You can include an extension as part of a filename. A period is used to distinguish the filename proper from the extension. Extensions can be useful for categorizing your files. You are probably familiar with certain standard extensions that have been adopted by convention. For example, C source code files always have a **.c** extension. Files that contain compiled object code have an **.o** extension. You can make up your own file extensions. The following examples are all valid Linux filenames. Keep in mind that to reference the name with spaces on the command line, you would have to encase it in quotes as "New book review":

```
preface
chapter2
9700info
New_Revisions
calc.c
intro.bk1
New book review
```

Special initialization files are also used to hold shell configuration commands. These are the hidden, or dot, files, which begin with a period. Dot files used by commands and applications have predetermined names, such as the **.mozilla** directory used to hold your Mozilla data and configuration files. When you use **ls** to display your filenames, the dot files will not be displayed. To include the dot files, you need to use **ls** with the **-a** option.

The **ls -l** command displays detailed information about a file. First, the permissions are displayed, followed by the number of links, the owner of the file, the name of the group to which the user belongs, the file size in bytes, the date and time the file was last modified, and the name of the file. Permissions indicate who can access the file: the user, members of a group, or all other users. The group name indicates the group permitted to access the file object. The file type for **mydata** is that of an ordinary file. Only one link exists, indicating the file has no other names and no other links. The owner's name is **chris**, the same as the login name, and the group name is **weather**. Other users probably also belong to the **weather** group. The size of the file is 207 bytes, and it was last modified on February 20 at 11:55 A.M. The name of the file is **mydata**.

If you want to display this detailed information for all the files in a directory, simply use the **ls -l** command without an argument.

```
$ ls -l
-rw-r--r-- 1 chris weather 207 Feb 20 11:55 mydata
-rw-rw-r-- 1 chris weather 568 Feb 14 10:30 today
-rw-rw-r-- 1 chris weather 308 Feb 17 12:40 monday
```

All files in Linux have one physical format, a byte stream, which is simply a sequence of bytes. This allows Linux to apply the file concept to every data component in the system. Directories are classified as files, as are devices. Treating everything as a file allows Linux to organize and exchange data more easily. The data in a file can be sent directly to a device such as a screen because a device interfaces with the system using the same byte-stream file format used by regular files.

This same file format is used to implement other operating system components. The interface to a device, such as the screen or keyboard, is designated as a file. Other components, such as directories, are themselves byte-stream files, but they have a special internal organization. A directory file contains information about a directory, organized in a special directory format. Because these different components are treated as files, they can be said to constitute different file types. A character device is one file type. A directory is another file type. The number of these file types may vary according to your specific implementation of Linux. Five common types of files exist: ordinary files, directory files, first-in first-out (FIFO) pipes, character device files, and block device files. Although you may rarely reference a file's type, it can be useful when searching for directories or devices.

Although all ordinary files have a byte-stream format, they may be used in different ways. The most significant difference is between binary and text files. Compiled programs are examples of binary files. However, even text files can be classified according to their different uses. You can have files that contain C programming source code or shell commands, or even a file that is empty. The file could be an executable program or a directory file. The Linux **file** command helps you determine what a file is used for. It examines the first few lines of a file and tries to determine a classification for it. The **file** command looks for special keywords or special numbers in those first few lines, but it is not always accurate. In the next example, the **file** command examines the contents of two files and determines a classification for them:

```
$ file monday reports
monday: text
reports: directory
```

If you need to examine the entire file byte by byte, you can do so with the **od** (octal dump) command, which performs a dump of a file. By default, it prints every byte in its octal representation. You can also specify a character, decimal, or hexadecimal representation. The **od** command is helpful when you need to detect any special character in your file or if you want to display a binary file.

The File Structure

Linux organizes files into a hierarchically connected set of directories. Each directory may contain either files or other directories. In this respect, directories perform two important functions. A directory holds files, much like files held in a file drawer, and a directory connects to other directories, much as a branch in a tree is connected to other branches. Because of the similarities to a tree, such a structure is often referred to as a *tree structure*.

The Linux file structure branches into several directories beginning with a root directory, /. Within the root directory, several system directories contain files and programs that are features of the Linux system. The root directory also contains a directory called **home** that contains the home directories of all the users in the system. Each user's home directory, in turn, contains the directories the user has made for their own use. Each of these can also contain directories. Such nested directories branch out from the user's home directory.

Note: The user's home directory can be any directory, though it is usually the directory that bears the user's login name. This directory is located in the directory named /home on your Linux system. For example, a user named dylan will have a home directory called dylan located in the system's /home directory. The user's home directory is a subdirectory of the directory called /home on the system.

Home Directories

When you log in to the system, you are placed within your home directory. The name given to this directory by the system is the same as your login name. Any files you create when you first log in are organized within your home directory. Within your home directory, you can create more directories. You can then change to these directories and store files in them. The same is true for other users on the system. Each user has a home directory, identified by the appropriate login name. Users, in turn, can create their own directories.

You can access a directory either through its name or by making it your working directory. Each directory is given a name when it is created. You can use this name in file operations to access files in that directory. You can also make the directory your working directory. If you do not use any directory names in a file operation, the working directory will be accessed. The working directory is the one from which you are currently working. When you log in, the working directory is your home directory, which usually has the same name as your login name. You can change the working directory by using the **cd** command to move to another directory.

Directory	Function
/	Begins the file system structure, called the *root*.
/home	Contains users' home directories.
/bin	Holds all the standard commands and utility programs.
/usr	Holds those files and commands used by the system; this directory breaks down into several subdirectories.
/usr/bin	Holds user-oriented commands and utility programs.
/usr/sbin	Holds system administration commands.
/usr/lib	Holds libraries for programming languages.
/usr/share/doc	Holds Linux documentation.
/usr/share/man	Holds the online Man files.
/var/spool	Holds spooled files, such as those generated for printing jobs and network transfers.
/sbin	Holds system administration commands for booting the system.
/var	Holds files that vary, such as mailbox files.
/dev	Holds file interfaces for devices such as the terminals and printers (dynamically generated by udev, do not edit).
/etc	Holds system configuration files and any other system files.

Table 12-7: Standard System Directories in Linux

Pathnames

The name you give to a directory or file when you create it is not its full name. The full name of a directory is its *pathname*. The hierarchically nested relationship among directories forms paths, and these paths can be used to identify and reference any directory or file uniquely or absolutely. Each directory in the file structure can be said to have its own unique path. The actual name by which the system identifies a directory always begins with the root directory and consists of all directories nested below that directory.

In Linux, you write a pathname by listing each directory in the path separated from the last by a forward slash. A slash preceding the first directory in the path represents the root. The pathname for the **chris** directory is **/home/chris**. If the **chris** directory has a subdirectory called **reports**, then the full the pathname for the **reports** directory would be **/home/chris/reports**. Pathnames also apply to files. When you create a file within a directory, you give the file a name. The actual name by which the system identifies the file is the filename combined with the path of directories from the root to the file's directory. As an example, the pathname for **monday** is **/home/chris/reports/monday** (the root directory is represented by the first slash). The path for the **monday** file consists of the root, **home**, **chris**, and **reports** directories and the filename **monday**.

Pathnames may be absolute or relative. An *absolute pathname* is the complete pathname of a file or directory beginning with the root directory. A *relative pathname* begins from your working directory; it is the path of a file relative to your working directory. The working directory is the one you are currently operating in. Using the previous example, if **chris** is your working directory, the relative pathname for the file **monday** is **reports/monday**. The absolute pathname for **monday** is **/home/chris/reports/monday**.

The absolute pathname from the root to your home directory can be especially complex and, at times, even subject to change by the system administrator. To make it easier to reference, you can use the tilde (**~**) character, which represents the absolute pathname of your home directory. You must specify the rest of the path from your home directory. In the next example, the user references the **monday** file in the **reports** directory. The tilde represents the path to the user's home directory, **/home/chris**, and then the rest of the path to the **monday** file is specified.

```
$ cat ~/reports/monday
```

System Directories

The root directory that begins the Linux file structure contains several system directories that contain files and programs used to run and maintain the system. Many also contain other subdirectories with programs for executing specific features of Linux. For example, the directory **/usr/bin** contains the various Linux commands that users execute, such as **lpr**. The directory **/bin** holds system level commands. Table 12-7 lists the basic system directories.

Listing, Displaying, and Printing Files: ls, cat, more, less, and lpr

One of the primary functions of an operating system is the management of files. You may need to perform certain basic output operations on your files, such as displaying them on your screen or printing them. The Linux system provides a set of commands that perform basic file-management operations, such as listing, displaying, and printing files, as well as copying, renaming, and erasing files. These commands are usually made up of abbreviated versions of words. For example, the **ls** command is a shortened form of "list" and lists the files in your directory. The **lpr** command is an abbreviated form of "line print" and will print a file. The **cat**, **less**, and **more** commands display the contents of a file on the screen. Table 12-8 lists these commands with their different options. When you log in to your Linux system, you may want a list of the files in your home directory. The **ls** command, which outputs a list of your file and directory names, is useful for this. The **ls** command has many possible options for displaying filenames according to specific features.

Displaying Files: cat, less, and more

You may also need to look at the contents of a file. The **cat** and **more** commands display the contents of a file on the screen. The name **cat** stands for concatenate.

```
$ cat mydata
computers
```

The **cat** command outputs the entire text of a file to the screen at once. This presents a problem when the file is large because its text quickly speeds past on the screen. The **more** and **less** commands are designed to overcome this limitation by displaying one screen of text at a time. You can then move forward or backward in the text at your leisure. You invoke the **more** or **less** command by entering the command name followed by the name of the file you want to view (**less** is a more powerful and configurable display utility).

```
$ less mydata
```

When **more** or **less** invoke a file, the first screen of text is displayed. To continue to the next screen, you press the F key or the SPACEBAR. To move back in the text, you press the B key. You can quit at any time by pressing the Q key.

Command or Option	Execution
`ls`	This command lists file and directory names.
`cat` *filenames*	This filter can be used to display a file. It can take filenames for its arguments. It outputs the contents of those files directly to the standard output, which, by default, is directed to the screen.
`more` *filenames*	This utility displays a file screen by screen. Press the SPACEBAR to continue to the next screen and **q** to quit.
`less` *filenames*	This utility also displays a file screen by screen. Press the SPACEBAR to continue to the next screen and **q** to quit.
`lpr` *filenames*	Sends a file to the line printer to be printed; a list of files may be used as arguments. Use the **-P** option to specify a printer.
`lpq`	Lists the print queue for printing jobs.
`lprm`	Removes a printing job from the print queue.

Table 12-8: Listing, Displaying, and Printing Files

Printing Files: lpr, lpq, and lprm

With the printer commands such as **lpr** and **lprm**, you can perform printing operations such as printing files or canceling print jobs (see Table 12-8). When you need to print files, use the **lpr** command to send files to the printer connected to your system. In the next example, the user prints the **mydata** file:

```
$ lpr mydata
```

If you want to print several files at once, you can specify more than one file on the command line after the **lpr** command. In the next example, the user prints out both the **mydata** and **preface** files:

```
$ lpr mydata preface
```

Printing jobs are placed in a queue and printed one at a time in the background. You can continue with other work as your files print. You can see the position of a particular printing job at any given time with the **lpq** command, which gives the owner of the printing job (the login name of the user who sent the job), the print job ID, the size in bytes, and the temporary file in which it is currently held.

If you need to cancel an unwanted printing job, you can do so with the **lprm** command, which takes as its argument either the ID number of the printing job or the owner's name. It then removes the print job from the print queue. For this task, **lpq** is helpful, for it provides you with the ID number and owner of the printing job you need to use with **lprm**.

Managing Directories: mkdir, rmdir, ls, cd, pwd

You can create and remove your own directories, as well as change your working directory, with the **mkdir**, **rmdir**, and **cd** commands. Each of these commands can take as its argument the pathname for a directory. The **pwd** command displays the absolute pathname of your working directory. In addition to these commands, the special characters represented by a single dot, a double dot, and a tilde can be used to reference the working directory, the parent of the working directory, and the home directory, respectively. Taken together, these commands enable you to manage your directories. You can create nested directories, move from one directory to another, and use pathnames to reference any of your directories. Those commands commonly used to manage directories are listed in Table 12-9.

Creating and Deleting Directories

You create and remove directories with the **mkdir** and **rmdir** commands. In either case, you can also use pathnames for the directories. In the next example, the user creates the directory **reports**. Then the user creates the directory **articles** using a pathname.

```
$ mkdir reports
$ mkdir /home/chris/articles
```

You can remove a directory with the **rmdir** command followed by the directory name. In the next example, the user removes the directory **reports** with the **rmdir** command.

```
$ rmdir reports
```

To remove a directory and all its subdirectories, you use the **rm** command with the **-r** option. This is a very powerful command and could be used to erase all your files. You will be prompted for each file. To remove all files and subdirectories without prompts, add the **-f** option. The following example deletes the **reports** directory and all its subdirectories.

```
rm -rf reports
```

Displaying Directory Contents

To distinguish between file and directory names, you need to use the **ls** command with the **-F** option. A slash is then displayed after each directory name in the list.

```
$ ls
weather reports articles
$ ls -F
weather reports/ articles/
```

The **ls** command also takes as an argument any directory name or directory pathname. This enables you to list the files in any directory without first having to change to that directory. In the next example, the **ls** command takes as its argument the name of a directory, **reports**. Then the **ls** command is executed again, only this time the absolute pathname of **reports** is used.

```
$ ls reports
monday tuesday
$ ls /home/chris/reports
```

```
monday tuesday
$
```

Command	Execution
mkdir *directory*	Creates a directory.
rmdir *directory*	Erases a directory.
ls -F	Lists directory name with a preceding slash.
ls -R	Lists working directory as well as all subdirectories.
cd *directory name*	Changes to the specified directory, making it the working directory. **cd** without a directory name changes back to the home directory: **$ cd reports**
pwd	Displays the pathname of the working directory.
directory name / *filename*	A slash is used in pathnames to separate each directory name. In the case of pathnames for files, a slash separates the preceding directory names from the filename.
..	References the parent directory. You can use it as an argument or as part of a pathname: **$ cd ..** **$ mv ../larisa oldarticles**
.	References the working directory. You can use it as an argument or as part of a pathname: **$ ls .**
~ / *pathname*	The tilde is a special character that represents the pathname for the home directory. It is useful when you need to use an absolute pathname for a file or directory: **$ cp monday ~/today**

Table 12-9: Directory Commands

Moving Through Directories

The **cd** command takes as its argument the name of the directory to which you want to move. The name of the directory can be the name of a subdirectory in your working directory or the full pathname of any directory on the system. If you want to change back to your home directory, you need to enter only the **cd** command by itself, without a filename argument.

```
$ cd reports
$ pwd
/home/chris/reports
```

Referencing the Parent Directory

A directory always has a parent (except, of course, for the root). For example, in the preceding listing, the parent for **reports** is the **chris** directory. When a directory is created, two entries are made: one represented with a dot (**.**), and the other with double dots (**..**). The dot represents the pathname of the directory, and the double dots represent the pathname of its parent directory. Double dots, used as an argument in a command, references the parent directory. The single dot references the directory itself.

You can use the single dot to reference your working directory, instead of using its pathname. For example, to copy a file to the working directory retaining the same name, the dot can be used in place of the working directory's pathname. In this sense, the dot is another name for the working directory. In the next example, the user copies the **weather** file from the **chris** directory to the **reports** directory. The **reports** directory is the working directory and can be represented with the single dot.

```
$ cd reports
$ cp /home/chris/weather .
```

The .. symbol is used to reference files in the parent directory. In the next example, the **cat** command displays the **weather** file in the parent directory. The pathname for the file is the .. symbol (for the parent directory) followed by a slash and the filename.

```
$ cat ../weather
raining and warm
```

Tip: You can use the cd command with the .. symbol to step back through successive parent directories of the directory tree from a lower directory.

File and Directory Operations: find, cp, mv, rm, ln

As you create more and more files, you may want to back them up, change their names, erase some of them, or even give them added names. Linux provides several file commands that you can use to search for files, copy files, rename files, or remove files (see Table 12-5). If you have a large number of files, you can also search them to locate a specific one. The commands are shortened forms of full words, consisting of only two characters. The **cp** command stands for "copy" and copies a file, **mv** stands for "move" and renames or moves a file, **rm** stands for "remove" and erases a file, and **ln** stands for "link" and adds another name for a file, often used as a shortcut to the original. One exception to the two-character rule is the **find** command, which performs searches of your filenames to find a file. All these operations can be handled by desktops, such as GNOME and KDE.

Searching Directories: find

Once a large number of files have been stored in many different directories, you may need to search them to locate a specific file, or files, of a certain type. The **find** command enables you to perform such a search from the command line. The **find** command takes as its arguments directory names followed by several possible options that specify the type of search and the criteria for the search; it then searches within the directories listed and their subdirectories for files that meet these criteria. The **find** command can search for a file by name, type, owner, and even the time of the last update.

```
$ find directory-list -option criteria
```

The **-name** option has as its criteria a pattern and instructs **find** to search for the filename that matches that pattern. To search for a file by name, you use the **find** command with the directory name followed by the **-name** option and the name of the file.

```
$ find directory-list -name filename
```

Command or Option	Execution
`find`	Searches directories for files according to search criteria. This command has several options that specify the type of criteria and actions to be taken.
`-name` *pattern*	Searches for files with the *pattern* in the name.
`-lname` *pattern*	Searches for symbolic link files.
`-group` *name*	Searches for files belonging to the group *name.*
`-gid` *name*	Searches for files belonging to a group according to group ID.
`-user` *name*	Searches for files belonging to a user.
`-uid` *name*	Searches for files belonging to a user according to user ID.
`-mtime` *num*	Searches for files last modified *num* days ago.
`-context` *scontext*	Searches for files according to security context (SE Linux).
`-print`	Outputs the result of the search to the standard output. The result is usually a list of filenames, including their full pathnames.
`-type` *filetype*	Searches for files with the specified file type. File type can be **b** for block device, **c** for character device, **d** for directory, **f** for file, or **l** for symbolic link.
`-perm` *permission*	Searches for files with certain permissions set. Use octal or symbolic format for permissions.
`-ls`	Provides a detailed listing of each file, with owner, permission, size, and date information.
`-exec` *command*	Executes command when files found.

Table 12-10: The find Command

The **find** command also has options that merely perform actions, such as outputting the results of a search. If you want **find** to display the filenames it has located, you simply include the **-print** option on the command line along with any other options. The **-print** option is an action that instructs **find** to write to the standard output the names of all the files it locates (you can also use the **-ls** option instead to list files in the long format). In the next example, the user searches for all the files in the **reports** directory with the name **monday**. Once located, the file, with its relative pathname, is printed.

```
$ find reports -name monday -print
reports/monday
```

The **find** command prints out the filenames using the directory name specified in the directory list. If you specify an absolute pathname, the absolute path of the found directories will be output. If you specify a relative pathname, only the relative pathname is output. In the preceding example, the user specified a relative pathname, **reports**, in the directory list. Located filenames were output beginning with this relative pathname. In the next example, the user specifies an absolute pathname in the directory list. Located filenames are then output using this absolute pathname.

```
$ find /home/chris -name monday -print
/home/chris/reports/monday
```

Tip: Should you need to find the location of a specific program or configuration file, you could use **find** to search for the file from the root directory. Log in as the root user and use / as the directory. This command searched for the location of the **more** command and files on the entire file system: **find / -name more -print**.

Searching the Working Directory

If you want to search your working directory, you can use the dot in the directory pathname to represent your working directory. The double dots would represent the parent directory. The next example searches all files and subdirectories in the working directory, using the dot to represent the working directory. If your working directory is your home directory, this is a convenient way to search through all your own directories. Notice that the located filenames that are output begin with a dot.

```
$ find . -name weather -print
./weather
```

You can use shell wildcard characters as part of the pattern criteria for searching files. The special character must be quoted, however, to avoid evaluation by the shell. In the next example, all files (indicated by the asterisk, *) with the **.c** extension in the **programs** directory are searched for and then displayed in the long format using the **-ls** action:

```
$ find programs -name '*.c' -ls
```

Locating Directories

You can also use the **find** command to locate other directories. In Linux, a directory is officially classified as a special type of file. Although all files have a byte-stream format, some files, such as directories, are used in special ways. In this sense, a file can be said to have a file type. The **find** command has an option called **-type** that searches for a file of a given type. The **-type** option takes a one-character modifier that represents the file type. The modifier that represents a directory is a **d**. In the next example, both the directory name and the directory file type are used to search for the directory called **travel**:

```
$ find /home/chris -name travel -type d -print
/home/chris/articles/travel
```

File types are not so much different types of files, as they are the file format applied to other components of the operating system, such as devices. In this sense, a device is treated as a type of file, and you can use **find** to search for devices and directories, as well as ordinary files. Table 12-10 lists the different types available for the **find** command's **-type** option.

You can also use the find operation to search for files by ownership or security criteria, like those belonging to a specific user or those with a certain security context. The **-user** option lets to locate all files belonging to a certain user. The following example lists all files that the user **chris** has created or owns on the entire system. To list those just in the users' home directories, you would use /**home** for the starting search directory. This would find all those in a user's home directory as well as any owned by that user in other user directories.

```
$ find /home -user chris -print
```

Copying Files

To make a copy of a file, you give the **cp** command two filenames as its arguments (see Table 12-11) . The first filename is the name of the file to be copied, the one that already exists. This is often referred to as the source file. The second filename is the name you want for the copy. This will be a new file containing a copy of all the data in the source file. This second argument is referred to as the destination file. The syntax for the **cp** command follows:

```
$ cp source-file destination-file
```

Command	Execution
cp *filename filename*	Copies a file. **cp** takes two arguments: the original file and the name of the new copy. You can use pathnames for the files to copy across directories:
cp -r *dirname dirname*	Copies a subdirectory from one directory to another. The copied directory includes all its own subdirectories:
mv *filename filename*	Moves (renames) a file. The **mv** command takes two arguments: the first is the file to be moved. The second argument can be the new filename or the pathname of a directory. If it is the name of a directory, then the file is moved to that directory, changing the file's pathname:
mv *dirname dirname*	Moves directories. In this case, the first and last arguments are directories:
ln *filename filename*	Creates added names for files referred to as links. A link can be created in one directory that references a file in another directory:
rm *filenames*	Removes (erases) a file. Can take any number of filenames as its arguments. Literally removes links to a file.

Table 12-11: File Operations

In the next example, the user copies a file called **proposal** to a new file called **oldprop**:

```
$ cp proposal oldprop
```

You could unintentionally destroy another file with the **cp** command. The **cp** command generates a copy by first creating a file and then copying data into it. If another file has the same name as the destination file, that file is destroyed and a new file with that name is created. By default, Ubuntu configures your system to check for an existing copy by the same name (**cp** is aliased with the **-i** option). To copy a file from your working directory to another directory, you need to use that directory name as the second argument in the **cp** command. In the next example, the **proposal** file is overwritten by the **newprop** file. The **proposal** file already exists.

```
$ cp newprop proposal
```

You can use any of the wildcard characters to generate a list of filenames to use with **cp** or **mv**. For example, suppose you need to copy all your C source code files to a given directory. Instead of listing each one individually on the command line, you could use an * character with the **.c** extension to match on and generate a list of C source code files (all files with a **.c** extension). In the next example, the user copies all source code files in the current directory to the **sourcebks** directory:

```
$ cp *.c sourcebks
```

If you want to copy all the files in a given directory to another directory, you could use *
to match on and generate a list of all those files in a **cp** command. In the next example, the user
copies all the files in the **props** directory to the **oldprop** directory. Notice the use of a **props**
pathname preceding the * special characters. In this context, **props** is a pathname that will be
appended before each file in the list that * generates.

```
$ cp props/* oldprop
```

You can, of course, use any of the other special characters, such as **.**, **?**, or **[]**. In the next
example, the user copies both source code and object code files (**.c** and **.o**) to the **projbk** directory:

```
$ cp *.[oc] projbk
```

When you copy a file, you can give the copy a name that is different from the original. To
do so, place the new filename after the directory name, separated by a slash.

```
$ cp filename directory-name/new-filename
```

Moving Files

You can use the **mv** command to either rename a file or to move a file from one directory
to another. When using **mv** to rename a file, you use the new filename as the second argument. The
first argument is the current name of the file you are renaming. If you want to rename a file when
you move it, you can specify the new name of the file after the directory name. In the next example,
the **proposal** file is renamed with the name **version1**:

```
$ mv proposal version1
```

As with **cp**, it is easy for **mv** to erase a file accidentally. When renaming a file, you might
accidentally choose a filename already used by another file. In this case, that other file will be
erased. The **mv** command also has an **-i** option that checks first to see if a file by that name already
exists.

You can also use any of the special characters to generate a list of filenames to use with
mv. In the next example, the user moves all source code files in the current directory to the
newproj directory:

```
$ mv *.c newproj
```

If you want to move all the files in a given directory to another directory, you can use * to
match on and generate a list of all those files. In the next example, the user moves all the files in the
reports directory to the **repbks** directory:

```
$ mv reports/* repbks
```

Note: The easiest way to copy files to a CD-R/RW or DVD-R/RW disc is to use the built-in
   GNOME Files burning capability. Just insert a blank disk, open it as a folder, and
   drag-and-drop files on to it.

Copying and Moving Directories

You can also copy or move whole directories at once. Both **cp** and **mv** can take as their
first argument a directory name, enabling you to copy or move subdirectories from one directory

into another (see Table 12-11). The first argument is the name of the directory to be moved or copied, and the second argument is the name of the directory within which it is to be placed. The same pathname structure used for files applies to moving or copying directories.

You can just as easily copy subdirectories from one directory to another. To copy a directory, the **cp** command requires you to use the **-r** option, which stands for "recursive." It directs the **cp** command to copy a directory, as well as any subdirectories it may contain. In other words, the entire directory subtree, from that directory on, will be copied. In the next example, the **travel** directory is copied to the **oldarticles** directory. Now two **travel** subdirectories exist, one in **articles** and one in **oldarticles**.

```
$ cp -r articles/travel oldarticles
$ ls -F articles
/travel
$ ls -F oldarticles
/travel
```

Erasing Files and Directories: the rm Command

As you use Linux, you will find the number of files you use increases rapidly. Generating files in Linux is easy. Applications such as editors, and commands such as **cp**, can easily be used to create files. Eventually, many of these files may become outdated and useless. You can then remove them with the **rm** command. The **rm** command can take any number of arguments, enabling you to list several filenames and erase them all at the same time. In the next example, the file **oldprop** is erased:

```
$ rm oldprop
```

Be careful when using the **rm** command, because it is irrevocable. Once a file is removed, it cannot be restored (there is no undo). With the **-i** option, you are prompted separately for each file and asked whether you really want to remove it. If you enter **y**, the file will be removed. If you enter anything else, the file is not removed. In the next example, the **rm** command is instructed to erase the files **proposal** and **oldprop**. The **rm** command then asks for confirmation for each file. The user decides to remove **oldprop,** but not **proposal**.

```
$ rm -i proposal oldprop
Remove proposal? n
Remove oldprop? y
$
```

Links: the ln Command

You can give a file more than one name using the **ln** command. You might do this because you want to reference a file using different filenames to access it from different directories. The added names are often referred to as *links.* Linux supports two different types of links, hard and symbolic. Hard links are literally another name for the same file, whereas symbolic links function like shortcuts referencing another file. Symbolic links are much more flexible and can work over many different file systems, while hard links are limited to your local file system. Furthermore, hard links introduce security concerns, as they allow direct access from a link that may have public access to an original file that you may want protected. Links are usually implemented as symbolic links.

Symbolic Links

To set up a symbolic link, you use the **ln** command with the **-s** option and two arguments: the name of the original file and the new, added filename. The **ls** operation lists both filenames, but only one physical file will exist.

```
$ ln -s original-file-name added-file-name
```

In the next example, the **today** file is given the additional name **weather**. It is just another name for the **today** file.

```
$ ls
today
$ ln -s today weather
$ ls
today weather
```

You can give the same file several names by using the **ln** command on the same file many times. In the next example, the file **today** is assigned the names **weather** and **weekend**:

```
$ ln -s today weather
$ ln -s today weekend
$ ls
today weather weekend
```

If you list the full information about a symbolic link and its file, you will find the information displayed is different. In the next example, the user lists the full information for both **lunch** and **/home/george/veglist** using the **ls** command with the **-l** option. The first character in the line specifies the file type. Symbolic links have their own file type, represented by an **l**. The file type for **lunch** is **l**, indicating it is a symbolic link, not an ordinary file. The number after the term "group" is the size of the file. Notice the sizes differ. The size of the **lunch** file is only 4 bytes. This is because **lunch** is only a symbolic link, a file that holds the pathname of another file and a pathname takes up only a few bytes. It is not a direct hard link to the **veglist** file.

```
$ ls -l lunch /home/george/veglist
lrw-rw-r-- 1 chris group 4 Feb 14 10:30 lunch
-rw-rw-r-- 1 george group 793 Feb 14 10:30 veglist
```

To erase a file, you need to remove only its original name (and any hard links to it). If any symbolic links are left over, they will be unable to access the file. In this case, a symbolic link would hold the pathname of a file that no longer exists.

Hard Links

You can give the same file several names by using the **ln** command on the same file many times. To set up a hard link, you use the **ln** command with no **-s** option and two arguments: the name of the original file and the new, added filename. The **ls** operation lists both filenames, but only one physical file will exist.

```
$ ln original-file-name added-file-name
```

In the next example, the **monday** file is given the additional name **storm**. It is just another name for the **monday** file.

```
$ ls
today
```

```
$ ln monday storm
$ ls
monday storm
```

To erase a file that has hard links, you need to remove all its hard links. The name of a file is actually considered a link to that file. Hence the command **rm** removes the link to the file. If you have several links to the file and remove only one of them, the others stay in place and you can reference the file through them. The same is true even if you remove the original link, the original name of the file.

Part 4: Administration

System Tools
System Administration
Network Connections

13. System Tools

GNOME System Monitor

Scheduling Tasks

System Log

Disk Usage Analyzer

Virus Protection

Hardware Sensors

Disk Utility

Plymouth

Logical Volume Management

OpenZFS

Useful system tools, as well as user specific configuration tools, can be found in the Applications overview and its Utilities application folder (see Table 13-1). The Utilities application folder lists specialized tools like the Disk Utility, System Monitor, and the Disk Usage Analyzer.

Ubuntu System Tools	Name	Description
gnome-system-monitor	System Monitor	GNOME System Monitor
gnome-logs	Logs	GNOME Logs
gnome-terminal	Terminal	GNOME Terminal Window
baobab	Disk Usage Analyzer	Disk usage analyzer with graphic representation
gnome-nettool	Network Tools	Network analysis
KDE task scheduler	Task Scheduler	KDE schedule manager (KDE desktop only)
ClamTK	Virus Scanner	Clam Virus scanner
Disk Utility	Disk Utility	Udisks utility for managing hard disks and removable drives

Table 13-1: Ubuntu System Tools

GNOME System Monitor

Ubuntu provides the GNOME System Monitor for displaying system information and monitoring system processes, accessible from the Applications overview. There are three tabs: Processes, Resources, and File Systems (see Figure 13-1).

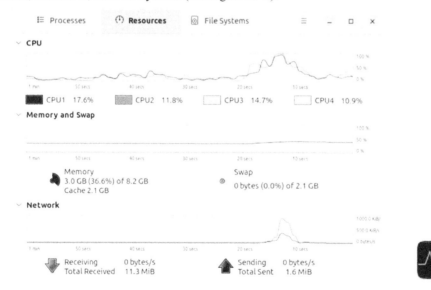

Figure 13-1: GNOME System Monitor: Resources

The Resources tab displays graphs for CPU History, Memory and Swap History, and Network History. If your system has a multi-core CPU, the CPU History graph shows the usage for each CPU. The Memory and Swap Memory graph shows the amount of memory in use. The Network History graph displays both the amount of sent and received data, along with totals for the current session. The File Systems tab lists your file systems, where they are mounted, and their type, as well as the amount of disk space used and how much is free. Double clicking on a file system entry will open that file system in a file manager window.

The Processes tab lists your processes, letting you sort and search processes. You can use field buttons to sort by name (Process Name), process ID (ID), percentage of use (%CPU), and memory used (Memory), among others. The menu (right side of the menu bar) lets you select all processes, just your own (My Processes), or active processes. You can stop any process by selecting it and then clicking the End Process button (lower-right corner) or by right-clicking on it and choosing End. You can right-click a process entry to display a menu with actions you can take on the selected process, such as stopping (Stop), ending (End), killing (Kill), and continuing a process (Continue), as well as changing the priority of the process (Change Priority). The Open Files entry opens a dialog listing all the files, sockets, and pipes the process is using. The Properties entry displays a dialog showing all the details for a process, such as the name, user, status, memory use, CPU use, and priority. The Memory Maps display, selected from the Memory Maps entry, shows information on virtual memory, inodes, and flags for a selected process.

Display features such as the colors used for CPU graphs can be set using the dconf editor's gnome-system-monitor keys at org | gnome | gnome-system-monitor.

Managing Processes

Should you have to force a process or application to quit, you can use the Gnome System Monitor Processes tab to find, select, and stop the process. You should be sure of the process you want to stop. Ending a critical process could cripple your system. Application processes will bear the name of the application, and you can use those to force an application to quit. Ending processes manually is usually performed for open-ended operations that you are unable to stop normally. In Figure 13-2, the Firefox application has been selected. Clicking the End Process button on the lower left will then force the Firefox Web browser to end.

firefox (PID 10483)   ×

Process Name	firefox
User	richard (1000)
Status	Running
Memory	149.3 MiB
Virtual Memory	3.0 GiB
Resident Memory	294.6 MiB
Writable Memory	N/A
Shared Memory	145.3 MiB
CPU	0.08%
CPU Time	0:18.56
Started	Today 11:28 AM
Nice	0
Priority	Normal
ID	10483
Security Context	snap.firefox.firefox (enforce)
Command Line	/snap/firefox/1232/usr/lib/firefox/firefox
Waiting Channel	do_poll.constprop.0
Control Group	/user.slice/user-1000.slice/user@1000.service/app.sli

Figure 13-2: GNOME System Monitor: Processes

The pop-up menu for a process (right-click) provides several other options for managing a selected process: stop, continue, end, kill, and change priority. There are corresponding keyboard keys for most options. The stop and continue operations work together. You can stop (Stop) a process, and then later start it again with the Continue option. The End option stops a process safely, whereas a Kill option forces an immediate end to the process. The End option is preferred, but if it does not work, you can use the Kill option. Change Priority can give a process a lower or higher priority, letting it run faster or slower. The Properties option opens a dialog listing process details such as the name, user, status, different types of memory used, CPU usage, start time, process id, and priority. The Open Files option lists all the files, sockets, and pipes the process is using.

You can also use the **pkill** command with a process name or a process ID to end a process. To use a process name, enter the process name with the **-n** option for the most recent process for that name.

```
pkill -n firefox
```

You can use the **kill** command in a terminal window to end a process. The **kill** command takes as its argument a process number. Be sure you obtain the correct one. Use the **ps** command to display a process id. Entering in the incorrect process number could cripple your system. The **ps** command with the **-C** option searches for a particular application name. The **-o pid=** option will display only the process id, instead of the process id, time, application name, and tty. Once you have the process id, you can use the **kill** command with the process id as its argument to end the process.

```
$ ps -C firefox -o pid=
5555
$ kill 5555
```

One way to ensure the correct number is to use the **ps** command to return the process number directly as an argument to a **kill** command. In the following example, an open-ended process was started with the **mycmd** command. An open-ended process is one that will continue until you stop it manually.

```
mycmd > my.ts
```

The process is then ended by first executing the **ps** command to obtain the process id for the **mycmd** process (back quotes), and then using that process id in the **kill** command to end the process. The **-o pid=** option displays only the process id.

```
kill `ps -C mycmd -o pid=`
```

Glances

Glances is a comprehensive system monitoring tool run from the command line in a terminal window with the **glances** command. Install with Ubuntu Software, the Synaptic Package Manager, or the **apt** command (**glances** and **glances-doc** packages). If you install with Ubuntu Software, be sure to set the permissions to allow access to logs, hardware information, and the other options (click the Permissions button on the Ubuntu Software Glances page). Glances shows detailed resource use for the system, network, disk, file system, sensors, and processes. (see Figure 13-3). It also warns you of any critical alerts. The system section covers detailed memory, CPU, swap and load usage. The network section shows the activity on each network device. The Disk I/O section lists your storage devices and their read/write usage. The File Sys section shows all your partitions and how much memory is used. The Sensors section shows the temperature detected by your sensors such as those for CPU, GPU, and the ambient temperature. The Tasks section lists your active processes by CPU usage, showing memory used, pid, user and the command. Press **q** to end your glances session.

Glances is organized into modules which you can disable to show only a limited set of reports. For example, if you are not interested in the disk I/O reports, you can disable the diskio module with the **--disable-diskio** option. See the **glances** man page for a complete list of module options you can use.

```
glances --disable-diskio.
```

There are also several runtime commands you can use to show and hide modules, such as **f** to toggle the file system reports on an off, **d** to toggle disk I/O, **n** for network stats, **s** for showing sensors, and **p** to sort processes by name.

Figure 13-3: Glances System Monitor

Scheduling Tasks

Scheduling regular maintenance tasks, such as backups, can be managed either by using the systemd timers or by the cron service. The systemd timers are systemd files that run service files. Check the man page for **systemd.timer** for a detailed description of timers. They have the extension **.timer**. A timer file will automatically run a corresponding service file that has the same name. For example, the **dnf-automatic.timer** will run the **dnf-automatic.service** file. The timer file only contains scheduling information. Its filename determines which service file to run. It is possible to designate a different service file with the Unit directive in the timer file. If you want to run a command line operation for which there is no service file, you can create your own with an ExecStart entry for that command.

The timer files have a timer section in which you define when the service file is run. There are options that are relative to certain starting points like when system booted up, and the **OnCalendar** option that that reference calendar dates. The **OnCalendar** option uses calendar event expressions as defined on the **systemd.time** man page. A calendar event expression consists of a weekday, year, month, and time. The time is specified in hour, minute, and second, separated by colons. A range of weekdays is separated by two periods, and specific weekdays by commas. Leaving out the year or month selects any year or month. The following references weekdays in May at 2 pm.

```
OnCalendar=Mon..Fri 05 14:00
```

You can create timer files and place them in the **/etc/systemd/system** folder. If you also have to set up a service file for it, you can place it in the same folder. To activate a timer be sure to enable it with **systemctl**. If you created a service file, be sure to enable that also.

You can still use the older cron service to schedule tasks. The cron service is implemented by the cron daemon that constantly checks for certain actions to take. These tasks are listed in the **crontab** file. The **cron** daemon constantly checks the user's **crontab** file to see if it is time to take these actions. Any user can set up a **crontab** file. An administrative user can set up a **crontab** file to take system administrative actions, such as backing up files at a certain time each week or month.

Creating cron entries can be a complicated task, using the **crontab** command to make changes to crontab files in the **/etc/crontab** folder. Instead, you can use desktop cron scheduler tools to set up cron actions.

KDE Task Scheduler

On KDE you can use the KDE Task Scheduler to set up user and system-level scheduled tasks (install the **kde-config-cron** package). You access the Task Scheduler on the KDE System Settings window in the System Administration section as Task Scheduler. The Task Scheduler window will list your scheduled tasks. Task can be either personal or system-wide. Click the New Task button to open a New Task window where you can enter the command to run, add comments, and then specify the time in months, days, hours, and minutes from simple arranged buttons. On the Task Scheduler window, you can select a task and use the side buttons to modify it, delete the task, run it now, or print a copy of it. For tasks using the same complex commands or arguments, you can create a variable, and then use that variable in a command. Variables are listed in the Environment Variables section. To use a variable in a scheduled task, precede its name with the **$**

character when you enter the command. Entering just the **$** symbol in the Command text box will display a drop-down list of pre-defined system variables you can use like **$PATH** and **$USER**.

Logs

Various system logs for tasks performed on your system are stored in the **/var/log** folder. Here you can find logs for mail, news, and all other system operations, such as Web server logs (see Figure 8-4). This usually includes startup tasks, such as loading drivers and mounting file systems. If a driver for a device failed to load at startup, you will find an error message for it here. Logins are also recorded in this file, showing you who attempted to log into what account. The **/var/log/mail.log** file logs mail message transmissions and news transfers.

Figure 13-4: System Log

To view logs, you can use Gnome Logs accessible as Logs on the Applications overview (see Figure 13-4). A side panel lists different log categories. Selecting one displays the log messages to the right. Critical messages are listed under the Important category. The "Logs" label on the title bar is a button you can click to display a list of recent boot sessions. You can select one to refine the messages displayed. By default, the most recent one is chosen. A search button on the top right opens a search box where you can search for messages in the selected log. Search has options (menu to the right) for refining the search by fields and by time.

Disk Usage Analyzer

The disk usage analyzer lets you see how much disk space is used and available on all your mounted hard disk partitions (see Figure 13-5) . It will also check all LVM and RAID arrays. You can access it from the Applications overview Utilities application folder.

Figure 13-5: Disk Usage Analyzer

Usage is shown in a simple graph, letting you see how much overall space is available and where it is. On the scan dialog, you can choose to scan your home folder (Home Folder, your entire file system (disk drive icon), an attached device like a floppy or USB drive, or a specific or remote folder (see Figure 13-6). To scan a folder click the gear button (top right) to open a menu with the option "Scan Folder." When you scan a folder or a file system, disk usage for your folder is analyzed and displayed. Each file system is shown with a graph for its usage, as well as its size and the number of top-level folders and files. Then the folders are shown, along with their size and contents (files and folders).

A representational graph for disk usage on is displayed on the right pane. The graph can be either a Ring Chart or a Treemap. The Ring Chart is the default. Choose the one you want from the buttons on the lower right. For the Ring Chart, folders are shown, starting with the top level folders at the center and moving out to the subfolders. Passing your mouse over a section in the graph displays its folder name and disk usage, as well as all its subfolders. The Treemap chart shows a box representation, with greater disk usage in larger boxes, and subfolders encased within folder boxes.

Figure 13-6: Disk Usage Analyzer: Scan dialog

Virus Protection

For virus protection, you can use the Linux version of ClamAV, which uses a GNOME front-end called ClamTk, **https://www.clamav.net**. This Virus scanner is included on the Ubuntu main repository. You can install ClamTk from Ubuntu Software. The supporting ClamAV packages will also be selected and installed for you (clamav-base and clamav-freshclam). You can also install ClamAV using the Synaptic Package Manager, choose the clamav, clamav-base, clamav-freshclam (online virus definitions), and ClamTK packages (Klamav for KDE). Selecting just ClamTk will automatically select the other clamav packages for installation. The **clamav-freshclam** package retrieves current virus definitions from the ClamAV servers. For ClamAV to check your mail messages automatically, you need to install the ClamAV scanner daemon (**clamav-daemon** and **clamdscan** packages).

You can access ClamTk from the Applications overview as ClamTk. With ClamTk, you can scan specific files and folders, as well as your home folder (see Figure 13-7). Searches can be recursive, including subfolders (Settings). You have the option to check configuration files (scan files with a dot). You can also perform quick or recursive scans of your home folder. Infected files are quarantined.

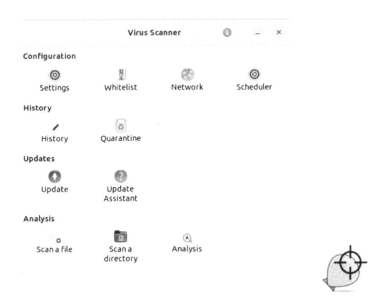

Figure 13-7: The ClamTK tool for ClamAV virus protection

Your virus definitions will be updated automatically. If you want to check manually for virus definitions, you need to click Update Assistant and choose to update the signatures yourself and click the Apply button and then the Back button. Then click the Updates icon and click the Yes button next to "Check for updates."

Hardware Sensors

A concern for many users is the temperatures and usage of computer components. You can install different software packages to enable certain sensors (see Table 13-2) .

Sensor application	Description
lm-sensors	Detects and accesses computer (motherboard) sensors like CPU and fan speed. Run **sensors-detect** once to configure.
hddtemp	Detects hard drive temperatures (also detected by Disk Utility)
Disk Utility	Disk Utility provides SMART information for hard disks showing current hard disk temperatures as well as detailed disk health information and checks.
Psensor	Application to detect and display system and hard drive temperatures.
Xsensors	Application to detect and display system temperatures and fans.
Sensors Utility	Application to detect and display system temperatures and fans.
auto-cpufreq	Automatic CPU speed and power optimizer.

Table 13-2: Sensor packages and applications

For CPU, system, fan speeds, and any other motherboard supported sensors, you can use Psensor, Xsensors, Sensors Utility, or the **lm-sensors** tools. Psensors installs the hddtemp hard drive temperature server and displays your CPU, graphics card, and hard drive temperatures. You can set temperature thresholds for alerts. Sensors Utility and Xsensors display your CPU temperatures, fan speeds, and voltages. Install with Ubuntu Software. For Sensors Utility set permissions to allow access to hardware information.

If not already installed, install the **lm-sensors** package. Then you have to configure your sensor detection. In a terminal window enter the following command and press ENTER to answer yes to the prompts.

```
sudo sensors-detect
```

Disk Utility lets you know your hard disk temperature. Disk Utility uses Udisks to access SMART information about the disk drive, including the temperature and overall health. Open Disk Utility, select the hard disk to check, and then, on the right pane, click on the "SMART Data" link located middle right. A hard disk dialog opens showing the disk temperature along with other details.

The **auto-cpufreq** tool automatically switches between performance and powersave CPU optimization depending on the state of your battery. Use the --**monitor** options to see its status, the --**live** option to temporarily engage it, and the --**install** option to run it and --**remove** to stop it.

```
sudo auto-cpufreq --monitor
```

Disk Utility and Udisks

Disk Utility is a Udisks supported user configuration interface for your storage media, such as hard disks, USB drives, and DVD/CD drives (**gnome-disk-utility** package, installed by default). Tasks supported include disk labeling, mounting disks, disk checks, and encryption. You can also perform more advanced tasks, like managing RAID and LVM storage devices, as well as partitions. Disk Utility is accessible on GNOME from the Applications overview Utility folder. Users can use Disk Utility to format removable media like USB drives. Disk Utility is also integrated into GNOME Files, letting you format removable media directly.

Figure 13-8: Disk Utility

The Disk Utility window shows a sidebar with entries for your storage media (see Figure 13-8). Clicking on an entry displays information for the media on the right pane. Removable devices such as USB drives display power and eject buttons on the title bar, along with a task menu with an entry to format the disk. If you are formatting a partition, like that on removable media, you can specify the file system type to use.

Warning: Disk Utility will list your fixed hard drives and their partitions, including the partitions on which your Ubuntu Linux system is installed. Be careful not to delete or erase these partitions.

If you select a hard disk device, information about the hard disk is displayed on the right pane at the top, such as the model name, serial number, size, partition table type, and SMART status (Assessment) (see Figure 13-9). Click the menu button to display a menu on the upper right with tasks you can perform on the hard drive: Format, Benchmark, and SMART Data.

Figure 13-9: Disk Utility, hard drive

The Volumes section on the hard disk pane shows the partitions set up on the hard drive (see Figure 13-10). Partitions are displayed in a graphical icon bar, which displays each partition's size and location on the drive. Clicking on a partition entry on the graphical icon bar displays information about that partition such as the file system type, device name, partition label, and partition size. The "Contents" entry tells if a partition is mounted. If in use, it displays a "Mounted at:" entry with a link consisting of the path name where the file system is mounted. You can click on this path name to open a folder with which you can access the file system. The button bar below the Volumes images provides additional tasks you can perform, such as unmounting a file system (square button) and deleting a partition (minus button). From the more tasks menu (gear button), you can choose entries to check and repair the file system, resize or format it, and change the partition label (Edit Filesystem), partition type (Edit partition), and mount options (Edit Mount Options). Certain partitions, like extended partitions, display limited information and have few allowable tasks.

Figure 13-10: Disk Utility, Volumes

For more detailed hardware information about a hard drive, you can click on the "SMART Data and Tests" entry from the task menu in the upper right. This opens a SMART data dialog with hardware information about the hard disk (see Figure 13-11) including temperature, power cycles, bad sectors, and the overall health of the disk. The Attributes section lists SMART details such as the Read Error Rate, Spinup time, temperature, and write error rate. Click the switch on to enable the self-tests, and off to disable testing. Click the "Refresh" button to manually run the tests. Click the "Start Self-test" button to open a menu with options for short, extended, and conveyance tests.

SMART Data & Self-Tests   ×

Updated 6 minutes ago   Self-test Result Last self-test completed successfully
Temperature 34° C / 93° F   Self-assessment Threshold not exceeded
Powered On 3 months and 6 days   Overall Assessment Disk is OK

SMART Attributes

ID	Attribute	Value	Normalized	Threshold	Worst	Type	Updates	Assessment
1	Read Error Rate	0	200	51	200	Pre-Fail	Online	OK
3	Spinup Time	1 second	148	21	142	Pre-Fail	Online	OK
4	Start/Stop Count	2069	98	0	98	Old-Age	Online	OK
5	Reallocated Sector Count	0 sectors	200	140	200	Pre-Fail	Online	OK
7	Seek Error Rate	0	200	0	200	Old-Age	Online	OK
9	Power-On Hours	3 months and 6 days	97	0	97	Old-Age	Online	OK
10	Spinup Retry Count	0	100	0	100	Old-Age	Online	OK
11	Calibration Retry Count	0	100	0	100	Old-Age	Online	OK
Short	cle Count	2050	98	0	98	Old-Age	Online	OK
Extended	rror Rate	17	83	0	83	Old-Age	Online	OK
Conveyance	Retract Count	158	200	0	200	Old-Age	Online	OK
	oad Cycle Count	80631	174	0	174	Old-Age	Online	OK

Start Self-test   Refresh   Close

Figure 13-11: Disk Utility: Hard Disk hardware SMART data

Plymouth

Plymouth provides a streamlined, efficient, and faster graphical boot that does not require X server support. It relies on the kernel's Kernel Modesettings (KMS) feature that provides direct support for basic graphics. With the Direct Rendering Manager driver, Plymouth can make use of different graphical plugins. KMS support is currently provided for AMD, Nvidia, and Intel graphics cards.

The Plymouth Ubuntu text theme is installed by default. You can install others like ubuntu-logo, breeze, or kubuntu-logo. The theme packages begin with the prefix **plymouth-theme**. You can search for them on the Synaptic Package Manager or with the **apt** command. The default is theme is **plymouth-theme-ubuntu-text**.

Choosing to use a Plymouth theme involves using the Debian alternatives system, which is designed to designate an application to use when there are several alternative versions to select. A link is set up for the application to use in the **/etc/alternatives** folder. For Plymouth, this link is named **default.plymouth**. You can choose a Plymouth theme by entering the **update-alternatives** command with the **--config** option, the **default.plymouth** link, and the **sudo** command in a terminal window as shown here.

```
sudo update-alternatives --config default.plymouth
```

This displays a numbered menu listing your installed themes. An asterisk indicates the current theme. Enter the number of the theme you want to use. The **default.plymouth** link is then set to the theme you choose. When your system starts up again, it will use that Plymouth theme.

Some of the non-Ubuntu themes may hang on start up. In that case, you can edit the boot kernel line to remove the **splash** option and then boot to your system (see Chapter 3). Then use **update-alternatives** to change your Plymouth theme.

Managing keys with Seahorse

For GPG and SSH encryption, signing, and decryption of files and text, GNOME provides Seahorse. With Seahorse you can manage your encryption keys stored in keyrings as well as SSH keys and passphrases. You can import keys, sign keys, search for remote keys, and create your own keyrings, as well as specify keyservers to search and publish to. All these operations can also be performed using the **gpg** command. Seahorse is installed by default.

Passwords and Keys

To import, sign, and locate keys you use the Password and Keys application, accessible from the Utilities application folder on the applications overview (Utilities | Passwords and Keys). The Passwords and Keys window displays a sidebar with three sections: Passwords, Keys, and Certificates (see Figure 13-12). The Seahorse menu on the right side of the Seahorse header bar shows options for viewing keys (personal, trusted, and any) and the "Password and Keys" folder menu (left side) shows options for finding remote keys, syncing and publishing keys, preferences, and help.

Figure 13-12: Seahorse Passwords and Keys (version 3.3)

Keyrings

The Passwords section lists your keyrings. Keyrings store network and application passwords. A login keyring is set up for you. You can create new keyrings by clicking the plus button on the left of the "Passwords and Keys" title bar and select Password keyring. An "Add password keyring" dialog prompts you for the name of the keyring, and then a "New keyring password" dialog prompts you to enter the keyring password. The strength of the password is indicated. The new keyring is listed in the Passwords section.

To manage keys in your keyring, right-click on the key entry and choose Properties from the menu (see Figure 13-13). Here you can change the description, password for accessing the key, and delete the key. Information about the key's use, type, login, and additional details. A key used to access a network would have the server accessed, protocol used, domain, and the user needed.

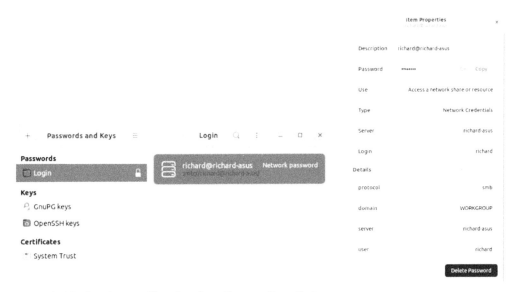

Figure 13-13: Seahorse Keyring key Properties dialog

Creating a new GPG key

Your personal encryption keys are displayed on the PGP Keys section. The entry "GnuPG keys" in the sidebar displays your GPG keys. To create your own private/public click the plus button (+) on the left side of the title bar. You can choose whether to set up a GPG, Private, or Secure Shell key. Choose the "GPG key" entry and click Continue (see Figure 13-14). Keep in mind that before you can perform any encryption, you first have to set up your own GPG key pair, private and public.

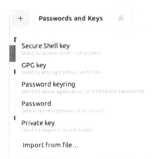

Figure 13-14: Choose Encryption key type

This opens a New PGP Key window where you enter your name and email address. In the "Advanced key options" section you can set Encryption type (DSA, RSA, or the signature only for each), Key strength, and Expiration Date (see Figure 13-15). You can also choose to never have it expire. Then click the Create button.

Cancel   **New PGP key**   Create

A PGP key allows you to encrypt email or files to other people.

Full Name   Richard Petersen

Email Address   richard@laptop

Advanced key options

Comment

Encryption Type   RSA

Key Strength (bits)   2048 — +

Expiration Date   ☑ Never Expires

Figure 13-15: Create Encryption key

You are then asked to enter a passphrase (password) for the encryption key (see Figure 13-16). This passphrase will allow you to decrypt any data encrypted by your key.

Passphrase for New PGP Key   ×

Enter the passphrase for your new key twice.

Password: ••••••••

Confirm: ••••••••

Cancel   OK

Figure 13-16: Passphrase for encryption key

The key is then generated. This can take a few moments.

Once you key is created, it will appear in the "GnuPG keys" tab of the Passwords and Keys dialog (see Figure 13-17).

+   Passwords and Keys   ≡   GnuPG keys   🔍   ⋮   – □ ×

Passwords

🗂 Login   ■

Keys

GnuPG keys   Richard Petersen   Personal PGP key
                    richard@laptop
🔑 OpenSSH keys

Certificates

System Trust

Figure 13-17: My Personal Keys

Right-clicking on the key and selecting Properties, displays a dialog titled with the name of the key and showing three sections: User IDs, Subkeys, and Trust. The Owner section shows the key type and ID, as well as a photo for the key and a button to allow you to change the passphrasse for the key (see Figure 13-18). Click the plus button to select a new image file for the photo. Clicking on the calendar button on the Expires entry opens a calendar where you can set an expiration date. The menu on the top left side of the titlebar lists entries for changing the passphrase for the key and exporting the key to a file as a public or secret key.

Any subkeys are also listed, which you can expire, revoke, or delete. You can add new subkeys, specifying a key type, length, and expiration date. Expanding a subkey shows the key's fingerprint, type, and creation date. Buttons allow you to change the expiration date, revoke the key, and delete it..

Figure 13-18: GnuPGP key dialog: Owner tab

In the User IDs section, you can expand the key to show its signatures. The entry for the key shows a menu to the right with entries for "Make primary", Sign, and Delete. Selecting the Sign entry opens the Sign Key dialog where you can sign the key (see Figure 13-19), choose how much you trust the key, and whether others can see it and if you want to be able to revoke it. Then click the Sign button to sign the key.

Figure 13-19: GnuPGP key dialog: Details tab

Keyservers

When you created your own private key, you also generated a corresponding public key that others can use to encrypt data they send to you and decrypt signatures of messages you send to them. Many applications will publish public keys that you can download and import to your system with Seahorse. The keys are available on keyservers. To manage your keyservers, choose Preferences from the Seahorse folder menu to open the Preferences dialog (see Figure 13-20). Here you can specify the keyservers to access. Two default servers are listed: **hkp://keyserver.ubuntu.com:11371** and **ldap://keyserver.pgp.com**. To add a keyserver, click the

Add button to open a dialog where you enter the keyserver address and port. You will see the keyserver added to the list.

Figure 13-20: Seahorse Preferences - Keyservers

Importing Public Keys

In the "Passwords and Keys" dialog, press **Ctrl-i** to import a public key from a file you have already downloaded to your system. Alternatively, if you know the name of the key, you can try searching the keyservers for it. Choose "Find remote keys" from the "Passwords and Keys" folder menu on the left side of the title bar to open the Find Remote Keys dialog where you can enter a search string for the key (see Figure 13-21). The search term is treated as a prefix, matching on all possible completions. The keyservers to search are listed in the "Where to search" section, with checkboxes to choose those you want searched.

Results are listed in a new window labeled "Remote keys containing" (see Figure 13-22). Select the one you want, and then click the download/import button to the right of the key entry to import the key. To see information about a key, double click the entry (see Figure 13-23). Information about the owner (Owner tab), the trust level (Trust tab), and details about the key such as type and strength are displayed (Details tab).

Figure 13-21: Searching for keys

Figure 13-22: Importing keys

Sendmail Signing Key/2022 — Public key   ×

Sendmail Signing Key/2022
sendmail@Sendmail.ORG

Key ID   FD79DC0C81D9210A
Fingerprint   6327 DDCB 5E7E 80E4 987E
               A3B7 FD79 DC0C 81D9 210A
Expires   Never

User IDs

Sendmail Signing Key/2022
sendmail@sendmail.org

Subkeys

FD79DC0C81D9210A
Never expires

F05EDBEE03142938
Never expires

Trust

Signature trust

Sign key   Sign key

Owner trust   Unknown

Figure 13-23: Key information

Once you have imported the key, it will appear in the "GnuPG keys" tab in the Passwords And Keys window (see Figure 13-24). The Seahorse menu on the right side of the title bar lists the types of keys to display: Show personal, Show trusted, and Show any. For newly imported keys, be sure to choose the "Show any" option otherwise the new entry will not be displayed.

+ Passwords and Keys ≡	GnuPG keys Q ⋮ — ☐ ×
Passwords	Filter
🗔 Login	
Keys	Richard Petersen Personal PGP key
GnuPG keys	richard@laptop
🖭 OpenSSH keys	Sendmail Signing Key/2022 PGP key
Certificates	sendmail@Sendmail.ORG
⁎ System Trust	

Figure 13-24: Imported keys

If you know that you can trust the key, you can sign it, making it a valid key. Double click on its entry, or right-click and select Properties, to open its Properties dialog, and in the Trust section (see Figure 13-25), click the "Signature trust" switch. Then click the "Sign Key" button to open the Sign key dialog (see Figure 13-26). You are asked how carefully you have checked the key: Not at all, Casually, or Very Carefully. You also choose whether others can see your signature and if you can revoke it later. Then click the Sign button. A dialog appears prompting you to enter your GPG passphrase. On the Properties dialog, the Sign entry is replaced by a "Revoke key signature" entry, and the User ID section lists the key signatures (see Figure 13-27). The key is then listed as a trusted key when you choose the "Show trusted" option in the Seahorse menu (see Figure 13-28).

Figure 13-25: Imported key Trust tab for an unsigned key

Figure 13-26: Signing a key

Figure 13-27: Signed key

Figure 13-28: Trusted keys

Sharing Keys

To make your public key available to others, you can export it to a file to send directly to other users, automatically share it with other users on your system, or publish on a keyserver. You export your public key to a **.pgp** binary file by right-clicking on it and choosing Export from the pop-up menu. Alternatively, you can export the public key to an ASCII-armored coded **.asc** text file by opening the key's Properties dialog, selecting the Details tab, and then clicking the "Export" button and selecting "Export public key." You can do this for your private (secret) key also.

You can also share your key by publishing it on a public keyserver for anyone to download and import. On the Seahorse Preferences dialog (folder menu), from the "Publish Keys to:" menu you can choose the keyserver to publish to or choose not to publish (the default) (see Figure 13-29). You also have the options to automatically retrieve keys and synchronize modified keys. To then publish a key choose "Sync and publish keys" from the Seahorse folder menu to open the Sync Keys dialog and click the Sync button. The Key Servers button opens the Preferences dialog showing the keyservers, letting you choose the one you want to publish to ("Publish keys to" menu).

Figure 13-29: Seahorse Preferences

Seahorse integrates support for GPG. Should you import a key with the **gpg** command, it will appear in the GnuPG keys tab. Also, you can sign a key using the **gpg** command with the **--sign-key** option and the key is validated.

Logical Volume Manager

For easier hard disk storage management, you can set up your system to use the Logical Volume Manager (LVM), creating LVM partitions that are organized into logical volumes, to which free space is automatically allocated. Logical volumes provide a more flexible and powerful way of dealing with disk storage, organizing physical partitions into logical volumes in which you can easily manage disk space. Disk storage for a logical volume is treated as one pool of memory, though the volume may, in fact, contain several hard disk partitions spread across different hard disks. Adding a new LVM partition merely increases the pool of storage accessible to the entire system. Check the LVM HOWTO at **www.tldp.org** for detailed examples.

LVM Structure

In an LVM structure, LVM physical partitions, also known as extents, are organized into logical groups, which are, in turn, used by logical volumes. In effect, you are dealing with three different levels of organization. At the lowest level, you have physical volumes. These are physical hard disk partitions that you create with partition creation tools such as **Gparted** or **fdisk**. The partition type will be a Linux LVM partition, **fdisk** code **8e**. These physical volumes are organized into logical groups, known as volume groups, that operate much like logical hard disks. You assign collections of physical volumes to different logical groups.

Once you have your logical groups, you can then create logical volumes. Logical volumes function much like hard disk partitions on a standard setup. For example, on the **turtle** group volume, you could create a **/var** logical volume, and on the **rabbit** logical group, you could create **/home** and **/projects** logical volumes. You can have several logical volumes on one logical group, just as you can have several partitions on one hard disk.

You treat the logical volumes as you would any ordinary hard disk partition. Create a file system on it with the **mkfs** command, and then you can mount the file system to use it with the mount command. For Ubuntu, the file system type would be **ext4**.

Storage on logical volumes is managed using what are known as extents. A logical group defines a standard size for an extent, say 4MB, and then divides each physical volume in its group into extents of that size. Logical volumes are, in turn, divided into extents of the same size, which are then mapped to those on the physical volumes.

Logical volumes can be linear, striped, or mirrored. The mirror option will create a mirror copy of a logical volume, providing a restore capability. The striped option lets you automatically distribute your Logical volume across several partitions, as you would a RAID device. This adds better efficiency for very large files but is complicated to implement. Like a RAID device, stripe sizes have to be consistent across partitions. As LVM partitions can be of any size, the stripes sizes have to be carefully calculated. The simplest approach is just to use a linear implementation, much like a RAID 0 device, just treating the storage as one large ordinary drive, with storage accessed sequentially.

There is one restriction and recommendation for logical volumes. The boot partition cannot be part of a logical volume. You still have to create a separate hard disk partition as your boot partition with the **/boot** mountpoint in which your kernel and all needed boot files are installed. This is why a default partition configuration set up during Ubuntu installation for LVM will include a separate **/boot** partition of type **ext4**, whereas the root partition will be installed on Logical volumes. There will be two partitions, one for the logical group (LVM physical volume,

pv) holding the root volume, and another for the boot partition (**ext4**). The logical volumes will in turn both be **ext4** file systems.

LVM Tools: using the LVM commands

To use LVM be sure that the **lmv2** package is installed (Ubuntu repository). Use the Synaptic Package Manager or the **apt** command. You can then use a collection of LVM tools to manage your LVM volumes, adding new LVM physical partitions and removing current ones. For the LVM tools, you can either use LVM tools directly or use the **lvm** command to generate an interactive shell from which you can run LVM commands. There are Man pages for all the LVM commands. LVM maintains configuration information in the **/etc/lvm/lvm.conf** file, where you can configure LVM options such as the log file, the configuration backup folder, or the folder for LVM devices (see the **lvm.conf** Man page for more details).

You can use the **pvdisplay**, **vgdisplay**, and **lvdisplay** commands to show detailed information about a physical partition, volume groups, and logical volumes. The **pvscan**, **vgscan**, and **lvscan** commands list your physical, group, and logical volumes.

Managing LVM Physical Volumes with the LVM commands

A physical volume can be any hard disk partition or RAID device. A RAID device is seen as a single physical volume. You can create physical volumes either from a single hard disk or from partitions on a hard disk. On very large systems with many hard disks, you would more likely use an entire hard disk for each physical volume.

You would first use a partition utility like **fdisk**, **parted**, or **gparted** to create a partition of the LVM partition type (**8e**). Then, you can initialize the partition as a physical volume using the **pvcreate** command.

To initialize a physical volume on an entire hard disk, you use the hard disk device name, as shown here:

```
pvcreate /dev/sdc
```

This will initialize one physical partition, **pv**, called **sdc1** on the **sdc** hard drive (the third Serial ATA drive, c).

If you are using a particular partition on a drive, you create a new physical volume using the partition's device name, as shown here:

```
pvcreate /dev/sda3
```

To initialize several drives, just list them. The following create two physical partitions, sdc1 and sdd1.

```
pvcreate /dev/sdc /dev/sdd
```

You could also use several partitions on different hard drives. This is a situation in which your hard drives each hold several partitions. This condition occurs often when you are using some partitions on your hard drive for different purposes like different operating systems, or if you want to distribute your Logical group across several hard drives. To initialize these partitions at once, you simply list them.

```
pvcreate /dev/sda3 /dev/sdb1 /dev/sdb2
```

Once you have initialized your partitions, you have to create LVM groups on them.

Managing LVM Groups

Physical LVM partitions are used to make up a volume group. You can manually create a volume group using the **vgcreate** command and the name of the group along with a list of physical partitions you want in the group.

If you are then creating a new volume group to place these in, you can include them in the group when you create the volume group with the **vgcreate** command. The volume group can use one or more physical partitions. The configuration described in the following example used only one physical partition for the **VolGroup00**. In the following example, a volume group called **mymedia** that is made up two physical volumes, **sdc** and **sdd**.

```
vgcreate mymedia  /dev/sdc /dev/sdd
```

The previous example sets up a logical group on two serial ATA hard drives, each with its own single partition. Alternatively, you can set up a volume group to span partitions on several hard drives. If you are using partitions for different functions, this approach gives you the flexibility for using all the space available across multiple hard drives. The following example creates a group called **mygroup** consisting of three physical partitions, **/dev/sda3**, **/dev/sdb4**, and **/dev/sdb4**:

```
vgcreate mygroup  /dev/sda3 /dev/sdb2 /dev/sdb4
```

If you later want to add a physical volume to a volume group you would use the **vgextend** command. The **vgextend** command adds a new partition to a logical group. In the following example, the partition **/dev/sda4** is added to the volume group **mygroup**. In effect, you are extending the size of the logical group by adding a new physical partition.

```
vgextend mygroup  /dev/sda4
```

To add an entire new drive to a volume group, you would follow a similar procedure. The following example adds a fifth serial ATA hard drive, **sde**, first creating a physical volume on it and then adding that volume, **sde**, to the **mymedia** volume group.

```
pvcreate /dev/sde
vgextend mymedia /dev/sde
```

To remove a physical partition, first, remove it from its logical group. You may have to use the **pmove** command to move any data off the physical partition. Then use the **vgreduce** command to remove it from its logical group.

You can remove an entire volume group by first deactivating it with **vgchange -a n** and then using the **vgremove** command.

Activating Volume Groups

Whereas in a standard file system structure you mount and unmount hard disk partitions, with an LVM structure, you activate and deactivate entire volume groups. The group volumes are accessible until you activate them with the **vgchange** command with the **-a** option. To activate a group, first, reboot your system, and then enter the **vgchange** command with the **-a** option and the y argument to activate the logical group (an **n** argument will deactivate the group).

```
vgchange -a  y  mygroup
```

Managing LVM Logical Volumes

To create logical volumes, you use the **lvcreate** command and then format your logical volume using the standard formatting command like **mkfs.ext4**. With the **-n** option you specify the volume's name, which functions like a hard disk partition's label. You use the **-L** or **--size** options to specify the size of the volume. Use a size suffix for the measure, **G** for Gigabyte, **M** for megabyte, and **K** for kilobytes. There are other options for implementing features like whether to implement a linear, striped, or mirrored volume, or to specify the size of the extents to use. Usually, the defaults work well. The following example creates a logical volume named **projects** on the **mygroup** logical group with a size of 20GB.

```
lvcreate -n projects  -L 20GB mygroup
```

The following example sets up a logical volume on the **mymedia** volume group that is 540GB in size. The **mymedia** volume group is made up of two physical volumes, each on 320GB hard drives. In effect, the two hard drives are logically seen as one.

```
lvcreate -n myvideos  -L 540GB mymedia
```

Once you have created your logical volume, you then need to create a file system to use on it. The following creates an **ext4** file system on the **myvideos** logical volume.

```
mkfs.ext4 myvideos
```

You could also use:

```
mkfs -t ext4 myvideos
```

With **lvextend**, you can increase the size of the logical volume if there is unallocated space available in the volume group.

Should you want to reduce the size of a logical volume, you use the **lvreduce** command, indicating the new size. Be sure to reduce the size of any file systems (**ext4**) on the logical volume, using the **resize2fs** command.

To rename a logical volume use the **lvrename** command. If you want to completely remove a logical volume, you can use the **lvremove** command.

Steps to create a new LVM group and volume

Physical Partition   First create a physical partition on your hard drive. You can use GParted or fdisk with the disk device name to create the partition. For example, to use fdisk to create a new partition on a new hard drive, whose device name is **/etc/sde**, you would enter:

```
fdisk /etc/sde
```

Then, in the fdisk shell, use the **fdisk n** command to create a new partition, set it as a primary partition (**p**), and make it the first partition. If you plan to use the entire hard drive for your LVM, you would need only one partition that would cover the entire drive.

Then use the **t** command to set the partition type to 8E. The 8E type is the LVM partition type. To make your changes, enter **w** to write changes to the disk.

Physical Volume   Next create a physical volume (pv) on the new and empty LVM partition, using the **pvcreate** command and the device name.

```
pvcreate /dev/sde
```

Volume Group   Then, create your volume group with **vgcreate** command, with the volume group name and the hard disk device name.

```
vgcreate mynewgroup  /dev/sde
```

Be sure the volume group is activated. Use the **vgs** command to list it. If not listed, use the following command to activate it.

```
vgchange -a  y  mynewgroup
```

Logical Volume   Then, create a logical volume, or volumes, for the volume group, using the **lvcreate** command. The **--size** or **-L** options determines the size and the **--name** option specifies the name. To find out the available free space, use the **vgs** command. You can have more than one logical volume in a volume group, or just one if you prefer. A logical volume is conceptually similar to logical volumes in an extended partition on Windows systems.

```
lvcreate --size --name mynewvol1
```

Format the Logical volume. You then use the **mkfs** command with the **-t** option to format the logical volume. The logical volume will be listed in a folder for the LVM group, within the **/dev** folder, **/dev/mynewgroup/mynewvol1**.

```
mkfs -t ext4 /dev/mynewgroup/mynewgroup-mynewvol1
```

Steps to add a new drive to an LVM group and volume

Physical Partition   First create a physical partition on your hard drive. You can use GParted or **fdisk** with the disk device name to create the partition. For the type specify LVM (**8E**).

Physical Volume   Next, create a physical volume (pv) on the new and empty LVM partition, using the **pvcreate** command and the device name.

```
pvcreate /dev/sdf
```

Add to Logical Group   Use the **vgextend** command to add the new physical volume to your existing logical group (LG).

```
vgextend  mynewgroup  /dev/sdf
```

Add to Logical Volume   Then, you can create new logical volumes in the new space, or expand the size of a current logical volume. To expand the size of a logical volume to the new space, first, unmount the logical volume. Then use the **lvextend** command to expand to the space on the new hard drive that is now part the same logical group. With no size specified, the entire space on the new hard drive will be added.

```
umount /dev/mynewgroup/mynewvol1
lvextend /dev/mynewgroup/mynewvol  /dev/sdf
```

Use the **-L** option to specify a particular size, **-L +250G** . Be sure to add the + sign to have the size added to the current logical volume size. To find out the available free space, use the **vgs** command.

Add to file system Use the **resize2fs** command to extend the linux file system (ext4) on to logical volume to include the new space, formatting it. Unless you specify a size (second parameter), all the available unformatted space is used.

```
resize2fs /dev/mynewgroup/mynewvol1
```

LVM Device Names: /dev/mapper

The **device-mapper** driver is used by LVM to set up tables for mapping logical devices to hard disk. The device name for a logical volume is kept in the **/dev/mapper** folder and has the format *logical group –logical volume*. The default LVM setup for Ubuntu has the name **ubuntu-root**. The **mypics** logical volume in the **mymedia** logical group would have the device name, **/dev/mapper/mymedia-mypics**. In addition, there will be a corresponding device folder for the logical group, which will contain logical volume names. For the **ubuntu** logical group, there is a device folder called **/dev/ubuntu**.

Note: You can backup volume group metadata (configuration) using the **vgcfgbackup** command. This does not backup your logical volumes (no content). Metadata backups are stored in **/etc/lvm/backup**, and can be restored using **vgcfgrestore**.

Using LVM to replace drives

LVM can be very useful when you need to replace an older hard drive with a new one. Hard drives are expected to last about six years on the average. You could want to replace the older drive with a larger one (hard drive storage sizes double every year or so). Replacing additional hard drives is easy. To replace a boot drive is much more complicated.

To replace the drive, simply incorporate the new drive to your logical volume (see Steps to add a new drive to an LVM group and volume). The size of your logical volume will increase accordingly. You can use the **pmove** command to move data from the old drive to the new one. Then, issue commands to remove the old drive (**vgreduce**) from the volume group. From the user and system point of view, no changes are made. Files from your old drive will still be stored in the same folders, though the actual storage will be implemented on the new drive.

Replacement with LVM become more complicated if you want to replace your boot drive, the hard drive from which your system starts up and which holds your linux kernel. The boot drive contains a special boot partition and the master boot record. The boot partition cannot be part of any LVM volume. You would first have to create a boot partition on the new drive using a partition tool such as Parted or fdisk, labeling it as boot (the boot drive is usually very small, about 200 MB). Then mount the partition on your system, and copy the contents of your **/boot** folder to it. Then add the remainder of the disk to your logical volume and logically remove the old disk, copying the contents of the old disk to the new one. You would still have to boot with the install USB/DVD and issue the **grub-install** command to install the master boot record on your new drive. You can then boot from the new drive.

LVM Snapshots

A snapshot records and defines the state of the logical volume at a designated time. It does not create a full copy of data on the volume, but only just changes since the last snapshot. A snapshot defines the state of the data at a given time. This allows you to back up the data in a consistent way. Should you need to restore a file to its previous version, you can use the snapshot of it. Snapshots are treated as a logical volume and can be mounted, copied, or deleted.

To create a snapshot, use the **lvcreate** command with the **-s** option. In this example, the snapshot is given the name mypics-snap1 (**-n** option). You need to specify the full device name for the logical group you want to create the snapshot for. Be sure there is enough free space available in the logical group for the snapshot. In this example, the snapshot logical volume is created in the **/dev/mymedia** logical group. It could just as easily be created in any other logical group. Though a snapshot normally uses very little space, you have to guard against overflows. If the snapshot is allocated the same size as the original, it will never overflow For systems where little of the original data changes, the snapshot can be very small. The following example allocates one-third the size of the original (60GB).

```
sudo lvcreate -s -n mypics-snap1 -l 20GB /dev/mymedia
```

You can then mount the snapshot as you would any other file system.

```
sudo mount /dev/mymedia/mypic-snap1 /mysnaps
```

To delete a snapshot you use the **lvremove** command, removing it like you would any logical volume.

```
sudo lvremove -f /dev/mymedia/mypics-nap1
```

Snapshots are very useful for making backups while a system is still active. You can use tar or dump to back up the mounted snapshot to a disk or tape. All the data from the original logical volume will be included, along with the changes noted by the snapshot.

Snapshots also allow you to perform effective undo operations. You can create a snapshot of a logical volume, then unmount the original and mount the snapshot in its place. Any changes you make will be performed on the snapshot, not the original. Should problems occur, unmount the snapshot and then mount the original. This restores the original state of your data. You could also do this using several snapshots, restoring to a previous snapshot. With this procedure, you could test new software on a snapshot, without endangering your original data. The software would be operating on the snapshot, not the original logical volume.

You can also use them as alternative versions of a logical volume. You can read and write to a snapshot. A write will change only the snapshot volume, not the original, creating, in effect, an alternate version.

OpenZFS

The ZFS file system incorporates the features of a logical volume manager (LVM), RAID systems, and file systems. It is now an experimental option in the install process ("Advanced features" button on the "Installation type" screen). ZFS abstracts a file system, much like LVM, setting up a pool of storage from which a file system can be generated. Checksums for data blocks are saved outside the data blocks and are checked for any corruption within the blocks. This makes ZFS effective in protecting against silent data corruption from problems such as write interrupts, driver bugs, and access failures. If RAID-Z support has been set up, corrupted blocks can be recovered. RAID-Z implements a data-oriented RAID-like support with automatic mirroring of your data within the file system. In addition, the LVM-like abstraction of ZFS allows for large files.

Writes are performed with a copy-on-write transaction method, where data is not overwritten directly, but added.

ZFS was developed by SUN, which is now controlled by Oracle. Since 2010, OpenZFS provides an open source version of ZFS for Linux systems. Ubuntu now supports the ZFS file system, using the OpenZFS kernel module. Tools to manage ZFS file systems can be installed with the **zfsutils-linux** package (Ubuntu main repository, Synaptic Package Manager or **apt** command). See the following for more information:

```
https://wiki.ubuntu.com/Kernel/Reference/ZFS
```

Much like an LVM system, you have the physical devices (called virtual devices, VDEVs) that are combined and striped into a data pool (**zpool** command), which can then be used to create the ZFS file system. At the pool level, you can implement RAIDZ options. With the **zfs** command, you can then create file systems in your pool, as well as create snapshots (read-only copy) of a ZFS file system, or a clone (writeable copy). To perform an integrity check of the pool, use the **zpool** command's **scrub** option.

Use **zfs-auto-snapshots** to have ZFS automatically generate snapshots as you update your system.

```
sudo apt install zfs-auto-snapshot
```

To restore your system to one of these snapshots, you would access the History entry in the Grub boot menu when you start your system. This opens a list of previous snapshots. Choose the one you want to open options for restoring the system with or without user data, or to a recovery state.

Ubuntu also provides the ZSys system tool (**zsys** package) for easily managing your ZFS file systems. It is still under development. ZSys implements the **zsysctl** command that interfaces with ZFS through the **zsysd** daemon. You can use the **zsysctl** command to perform operations on your ZFS file systems. The **list** command lists your file systems and the **show** command shows their status.

```
zsysctl list
```

```
zsysctl show
```

If you choose the ZFS install option during installation, both the **zfsutils-linux** and **zsys** packages are installed for you. You can find out more about ZSys at:

```
https://github.com/ubuntu/zsys
```

14. System Administration

Ubuntu Administrative Tools

Controlled Administrative Access

Users and Groups

Bluetooth

File System Access

Shared Folders and Samba

GRUB Bootloader

Editing Configuration Files Directly

Backup Management

Most administrative configurations tasks are performed for you automatically. Devices like printers, hard drive partitions, and graphics cards are detected and set up for you. There are cases where you may need to perform tasks manually like adding new users and installing software. Such administrative operations can be performed with user-friendly system tools. Most administration tools are located in GNOME Settings or listed on the Applications overview and its Utilities application folder.

Ubuntu Administration Tools	Description
Ubuntu Software	Software management using online repositories (GNOME Software)
Software Updater	Update tool using Ubuntu repositories
Synaptic Package Manager	Software management using online repositories (no longer supported by Ubuntu, available on the Universe repository)
Network Manager	Detects, connects, and configures your network interfaces
clock	GNOME Time & Date tool (see Chapter 3)
Users	GNOME User configuration tool
users-admin	Older User and Group configuration tool, install gnome-system-tools.
system-config-printer	Printer configuration tool used for additional printer configuration
Gufw and FirewallD	Configures your network firewall
Deja-dup	Backup tool using rsync

Table 14-1: Ubuntu Administration Tools

Ubuntu Administrative Tools

On Ubuntu, administration is handled by a set of specialized administrative tools, such as those for user management and printer configuration (see Table 14-1). To access the desktop-based administrative tools, you need to log in as a user who has administrative access. You created such a user when you first installed Ubuntu. On the Ubuntu desktop, system administrative tools are accessed from the Applications overview and from GNOME Settings. Here you will find tools to set the time and date, manage users, configure printers, and install software. Settings Users lets you create and modify users. Setting Printers lets you install and reconfigure printers. All tools provide easy-to-use and intuitive desktop interfaces. Tools are identified by simple descriptive terms.

TIP: If you have difficulties with your system configuration, check the **https://ubuntuforums.org** and the **https://askubuntu.com/** sites for possible solutions. The site offers helpful forums ranging from desktop and installation problems to games, browsers, and multimedia solutions. Also, check the Community tab at **https://ubuntu.com** for documentation and tutorials.

Ubuntu uses the GNOME administrative tools and independent tools developed by open source projects. PolicyKit is used for device authorizations, and Ubuntu Software, the Synaptic Package Manager, and the **apt** command provide software management. In addition, Virus protection is handled by the third party application ClamAV. The older GNOME administrative tools such as Users and Groups are also available, but not installed by default (**gnome-system-tools** package).

Note: Many configuration tasks can also be handled on the command line, invoking programs directly. To use the command line, select the Terminal entry in the Applications overview in the Utilities application folder to open a terminal window with a command line prompt. You will need administrative authorization, so precede the application name with the **sudo** command.

Controlled Administrative Access

To access administrative tools, you have to log in as a user who has administrative permissions. The user that you created during installation is given administrative permissions automatically. Log in as that user. When you attempt to use an administrative tool, a dialog opens prompting you to enter your user password. As an administrative user, this is the password you logged in with. Some tools will open without authorization but remain locked, preventing any modifications. These tools, like GNOME Settings Users have an Unlock button you can press to gain access. You can use the Settings Users tool to grant or deny particular users administrative access.

To perform system administration operations, you must first have the access rights enabling you to perform administrative tasks. There are several ways to gain such access: login as a **sudo** supported user, unlocking an administrative tool for access with PolicyKit, using **pkexec** from a terminal window (PolicyKit authorization), or logging in as the root user. PolicyKit is the preferred access method and is used on many administrative tools. The **sudo** granted access method was used in previous Ubuntu releases, and is still used for many tasks including software upgrade and installation. The **root** user access is still discouraged but provides complete control over the entire system.

PolicyKit: Provides access only to specific applications and only to users with administrative access for that application. It requires that the specific application be configured for use by PolicyKit. Ubuntu 22.04 LTS uses the policykit-1 version of PolicyKit (Ubuntu repository). It is installed by default and fully supported.

sudo and **pkexec**: Provides access to any application with full administrative authorization. It imposes a time limit to reduce risk. The **pkexec** command is used for graphical administrative tools like the Synaptic Package Manager. You will still need to use **sudo** to perform any command-line Linux commands at the root level, like moving files to an administrative folder or running the **systemctl** command to start or stop servers.

root user access, **su**: Provides complete direct control over the entire system. This is the traditional method for accessing administrative tools. It is disabled by default on Ubuntu, but can be enabled. The **su** command will allow any user to log in as the root user if they know the root user password.

PolicyKit

PolicyKit controls access to certain applications and devices. It is one of the safest ways to grant a user direct access. PolicyKit configuration and support is already set up for you. The PolicyKit-1version of PolicyKit is used for PolicyKit operations. Configuration files for these operations are held in **/usr/share/polkit-1**. There is, as yet, no desktop tool you can use to configure these settings.

Difficulties occur if you want to change the authorization setting for certain actions, like mounting internal hard drives. Currently, you can change the settings by manually editing the configuration files in the **/usr/share/polkit-1/actions** folder. To make changes, you first have to know the action to change and the permission to set. The man page for **polkit** will list possible authorizations. The default authorizations are **allow_any** for anyone, **allow_inactive** for a console, and **allow_active** for an active console only (user logged in). These authorizations can be set to the following specific values.

auth_admin	Administrative user only, authorization required always
auth_admin_keep	Administrative user only, authorization kept for a brief period
auth_self	User authorization required
auth_self_keep	User authorization required, authorization kept for a brief period
yes	Always allow access
no	Never allow access

You will need to know the PolicyKit action to modify and the file to edit. The action is listed in the PolicyKit dialog that prompts you to enter the password (expand the Details arrow) when you try to use an application. The filename will be the first segments of the action name with the suffix "policy" attached. For example, the action for mounting drives is:

```
org.freedesktop.udisks2.filesystem-mount-system
```

Its file is:

```
org.freedesktop.UDisks2.policy
```

The file is located in the **/usr/share/polkit-1/actions** folder. It's full path name is:

```
/usr/share/polkit-1/actions/org.freedesktop.UDisks2.policy
```

Users with administrative access, like your primary user, can mount partitions on your hard drives automatically. However, users without administrative access require authorization using an administrative password before they can mount a partition (see Figure 14-13). Should you want to allow non-administrative users to mount partitions without an authorization request, the **org.freedesktop.UDisks2.policy** file in the **/usr/share/polkit-1** folder has to be modified to change the **allow_active** default for **filesystem-mount-system** action from **auth_admin_keep** to **yes**. The **auth_admin_keep** option requires administrative authorization.

Enter the following to edit the **org.freedesktop.UDisks2.policy** file in the **/usr/share/polkit-1/actions** folder:

```
sudo gedit /usr/share/polkit-1/actions/org.freedesktop.UDisks2.policy
```

Locate the **action id** labeled as:

```
<action id ="org.feedesktop.udisks2.filesystem-mount-system">
  <description>Mount a filesystem on a system device</description>
```

This is usually the second action id. At the end of that action section, you will find the following entry. It will be located within a defaults subsection, <defaults>.

```
<allow_active>auth_admin_keep</allow_active>
```

Replace **auth_admin_keep** with **yes**.

```
<allow_active>yes</allow_active>
```

Save the file. Non-administrative users will no longer have to enter a password to mount partitions.

sudo

The sudo service provides administrative access to specific users. You have to be a user on the system with a valid username and password that has been authorized by the sudo service for administrative access. This allows other users to perform specific super user operations without having full administrative level control such as **root** user access. You can find more about sudo at **https://www.sudo.ws**.

sudo command

Some administrative operations require access from the command line in the terminal window. For such operations, you would use the **sudo** command. You can open a terminal window from the Applications overview. For easier access, you can pin the Terminal icon to the dock (right-click and choose "Add to Favorites").

To use **sudo** to run an administrative command, you would precede the command with the **sudo** command. You are then prompted to enter your password. You will be issued a time-restricted ticket to allow access. The following example sets the system date using the **date** command.

```
sudo date 0406165908
password:
```

You can also use the **sudo** command to run an application with administrative access. From the terminal window, you would enter the **sudo** command with the application name as an argument. For example, to use the **nano** editor to edit a system configuration file, you would start **nano** using the **sudo** command in a terminal window, with the **nano** command and the filename as its arguments. This starts up **nano** editor with administrator privileges. The following example will allow you to edit the **/etc/fstab** file to add or edit file system entries. You will be prompted for your user password.

```
sudo nano /etc/fstab
```

sudo configuration

Access for **sudo** is controlled by the **/etc/sudoers** file. This file lists users and the commands they can run, along with the password for access. If the NOPASSWD option is set, then users will not need a password. The ALL option, depending on the context, can refer to all hosts on your network, all root-level commands, or all users. See the Man page for **sudoers** for detailed information on all options.

```
man sudoers
```

To make changes or add entries, you have to edit the file with the special sudo editing command **visudo**. This invokes the **nano** editor (see Chapter 5) to edit the **/etc/sudoers** file. Unlike a standard editor, **visudo** will lock the **/etc/sudoers** file and check the syntax of your entries. You are not allowed to save changes unless the syntax is correct. If you want to use a different editor, you can assign it to the EDITOR shell variable. Use Ctrl-x to exit and Ctrl-o to save. Be sure to invoke **visudo** with the **sudo** command to gain authorized access.

```
sudo visudo
```

A **sudoers** entry has the following syntax.

```
user    host=command
```

The *host* is a host on your network. You can specify all hosts with the ALL term. The *command* can be a list of commands, some or all qualified by options such as whether a password is required. To specify all commands, you can also use the ALL term. The following gives the user **george** full root-level access to all commands on all hosts.

```
george  ALL = ALL
```

In addition, you can let a user run as another user on a given host. Such alternate users are placed within parentheses before the commands. For example, if you want to give **george** access to the **beach** host as the user **mydns**, you use the following.

```
george beach = (mydns) ALL
```

To specify a group name, you prefix the group with a **%** sign, as in **%mygroup**. This way, you can give the same access to a group of users. By default, **sudo** will grant access to all users in the **admin** group. These are user granted administrative access. The ALL=(ALL) ALL entry allows access by the administrative group users to all hosts as all users to all commands.

```
%admin   ALL=(ALL)    ALL
```

With the NOPASSWD option, you can allow members of a certain group access without a password. A commented **sudo** group is provided in the **/etc/sudoers** file.

```
%sudo   ALL=NOPASSWD:    ALL
```

Though on Ubuntu, sudo is configured to allow **root** user access, Ubuntu does not create a **root** user password. This prevents you from logging in as the **root** user, rendering the sudo root permission useless. The default **/etc/sudoers** file does configure full access for the root user to all commands. The ALL=(ALL:ALL) ALL entry allows access by the root user to all hosts as all users to all commands. If you were to set up a password for the root user, the root user could then log in and have full administrative access.

```
root   ALL=(ALL:ALL)    ALL
```

The sudo group also has the same permissions, allow execution of any commands.

```
sudo   ALL=(ALL:ALL)    ALL
```

If you want to see what commands you can run, you use the **sudo** command with the **-l** option. The **-U** option to specify a particular user. In the following example, the user richard has full administrative access.

```
$ sudo -U richard -l
User richard may run the following commands on this host:
    (ALL : ALL) All
```

The **/etc/sudoers.d** folder holds configuration files for **sudo** that are included in the sudoers file. They usually hold permissions for applications to have **sudo** access such as the Snap server.

pkexec

You can use the **pkexec** command in place of **sudo** to run graphical applications with administrative access. The **pkexec** tool is a policykit alternative to **sudo**, and requires that your application has a corresponding policykit action file. Applications like user accounts, Udisks, and NetworkManager already have action files. Others, like Gedit, do not. To use **pkexec** with Gedit, you have to create a policykit action file for it. This is a simple process, copying most of the entries from the example in the **pkexec** man page. The askubuntu site (**http://askubuntu.com**) also has a detailed explanation on how to do this (search on "pkexec" and open the "How to configure pkexec" entry). Whenever you use the **pkexec** tool, it will prompt you to enter your password (See Figure 14-1).

Authentication Required

Authentication is needed to run `/usr/bin/gedit`
as the super user

Richard Petersen

Password

Cancel   Authenticate

Figure 14-1: pkexec prompt for secure access

You can enter the **pkexec** command in a terminal window with the application as an argument, or set up an application launcher with **pkexec** as the command. The following example will start up the Gedit editor with administrative access, allowing you to edit system configuration files directly (see Figure 14-2).

```
pkexec gedit
```

One way to set up a policy file for an application such as Gedit is to copy the example in the **pkexec** man page. Change the example entries to gedit. For the message entry, you only need a simple message. Be sure to add an annotate line at the end for desktop access, setting the **exec.allow_gui** option to true.

```
<annotate key="org.freedesktop.policykit.exec.allow_gui">true</annotate>
```

Alternatively, you could simply copy a simple policy file, change the name, and edit it to replace the program names and the message (for example, making a copy of

com.ubuntu.pkexec.synaptic.policy located in the **/usr/share/polkit-1/actions** folder). Be sure to use the **sudo** command with **cp** command in a terminal window to perform the copy.

A sample policy file for Gedit follows.

org.freedesktop.policykit.pkexec.gedit.policy

```
<?xml version="1.0" encoding="UTF-8"?>
   <!DOCTYPE policyconfig PUBLIC
      "-//freedesktop//DTD PolicyKit Policy Configuration 1.0//EN"
      "http://www.freedesktop.org/standards/PolicyKit/1/policyconfig.dtd">
 <policyconfig>

  <action id="org.freedesktop.policykit.pkexec.gedit">
    <description>Run the Gedit program</description>
    <message>Authentication is required to run gedit</message>
    <icon_name>gedit</icon_name>
    <defaults>
       <allow_any>auth_admin</allow_any>
       <allow_inactive>auth_admin</allow_inactive>
       <allow_active>auth_self_keep</allow_active>
    </defaults>
    <annotate key="org.freedesktop.policykit.exec.path">/usr/bin/gedit</annotate>
    <annotate key="org.freedesktop.policykit.exec.allow_gui">true</annotate>
  </action>

</policyconfig>
```

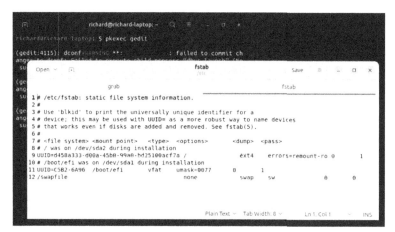

Figure 14-2: Invoking Gedit with pkexec command

Root User Access: root and su

You can access the root user from any normal terminal window using the **sudo** command on the **su** command. The **su** command is the superuser command. Superuser is another name for the **root** user. A user granted administrative access by **sudo** could then become the **root** user. The following logs into the root user.

```
sudo su
```

Ubuntu is designed never to let anyone directly log in as the root user. The **root** user would have total control over the entire system. Instead, certain users are given administrative access with which they can separately access administrative tools, performing specific tasks. Even though a **root** user exists, a password for the root user is not defined, never allowing access to it.

You can activate the root user by using the **passwd** command to create a root user password. Enter the **passwd** command with the **root** username in a **sudo** operation.

```
sudo passwd root
```

You are prompted for your administrative password, and then prompted by the **passwd** command to enter a password for the **root** user. You are then prompted to repeat the password.

```
Enter new UNIX password:
Retype new UNIX password:
passwd: password updated successfully
```

You can then log in with the **su** command as the root user, making you the superuser (you still cannot login as the root user from the display manager login screen). Because a superuser has the power to change almost anything on the system, such a password is usually carefully guarded, changed very frequently, and given only to those whose job it is to manage the system. With the correct password, you can log in to the system as a system administrator and configure the system any way you want.

```
su root
```

The **su** command alone will assume the root username.

```
su
```

The **su** command can be used to login to any user, provided you have that user's password.

To exit from an **su** login operation, just enter **exit**.

```
exit
```

/etc/hostname and hostnamectl

The **/etc/hostname** file contains your hostname. You can use the **hostnamectl** command in a terminal window to display your current hostname and all information pertaining to it such as the machine ID, the kernel used, the architecture, chassis (type of computer), and the operating system (you can add the **status** option if you want). Three different kinds of hostnames are supported: static, pretty, and transient. You can set each with the **hostnamectl**'s **set-hostname** command with the corresponding type. The static hostname is used to identify your computer on the network (usually a fully qualified host name). You can use the **--static** option to set it. The pretty hostname is a descriptive hostname made available to users on the computer. This can be set by **set-hostname** with the **--pretty** option. The transient hostname is one allocated by a network service such as DHCP, and can be managed with the **--transient** option. Without options, the **set-hostname** command will apply the name to all the host name types.

```
hostnamectl set-hostname --pretty "my computer"
```

The **set-chassis** command sets the computer type, which can be desktop, laptop, server, tablet, handset, and vm (virtual system). Without a type specified it reverts to the default for the system. The **set-icon-name** command sets the name used by the graphical applications for the host.

User (GNOME Settings | Users)

You can configure and create user accounts using the GNOME Users tool accessible from GNOME Settings as Users. Users does not provide any way to control groups. If you want group control and more configuration options, you can use the GNOME Users and Groups application (**gnome-system-tools** package).

You can access GNOME Users from the Users tab on GNOME Settings,. The Users tab displays an icon bar at the top showing a list of configured users with arrow buttons to the right and left to move through the list. Below the list is information about a selected user (see Figure 14-3). Initially, at the top of the Users tab is an Unlock button. Click on this button to open an authentication dialog, prompting for your password. Once active, you can then change the password, account type, icon, or name for the currently selected user. To remove a user, click its Remove User button on the lower right.

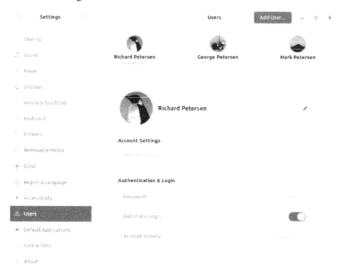

Figure 14-3: GNOME Users

Once authentication is accepted, the Unlock button changes to an Add User button, which you click to add a new user. When you add a new account, the Add User dialog opens, allowing you to set the account type (standard or administrator), the full name of the user, and the username (see Figure 14-4). For the username, you can enter a name or choose from a recommended list of options. You can also choose to set the password at this time. Click the Add button on the upper right to create the user. The new account appears in the icon list of users at the top of the Users tab, showing the name and icon. Selecting the user shows its account type, language, password, an automatic login option, and the Account activity showing if the user is logged in or when they last logged out. You can change the account type, language, password, and icon by clicking on their entries. Clicking on the Account Activity link open and Account Activity dialog showing when a user previously logged in and logged out.

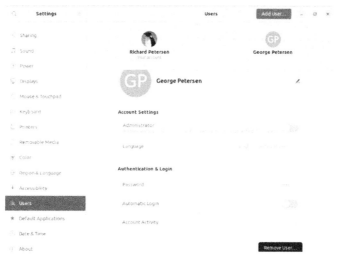

Figure 14-4: Add a new user

The account remains inactive until you specify a password (see Figure 14-5). You can do this when you add the account or later. You can also change the password for an account. Click the password entry to open the "Change Password" dialog in which you can enter the new password (see Figure 14-6). On the right side of an empty Password text box a password generator button is displayed that will generate a password for you when clicked. Once clicked, a generated password is entered in the text box and the button disappears, replaced by a checkmark. Deleting the password to show an empty box, once again displays the password generator button. Once the password is selected, the account becomes enabled.

Figure 14-5: Users, inactive user

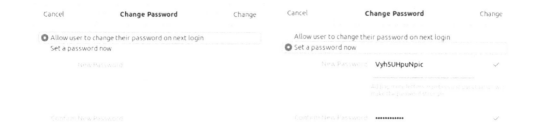

Figure 14-6: Users, password dialog

To change the user icon, click the icon image to display a pop-up dialog showing available images you can use (see Figure 14-7). You can also take a photo from your web cam (Take a Picture entry) or select a picture from a folder (Select a File). The Select a File button opens to your Pictures folder, but you can navigate to other folders. Many of the photos used in previous releases are at **/usr/share/pixmaps/faces**.

Currently, group configuration is not supported.

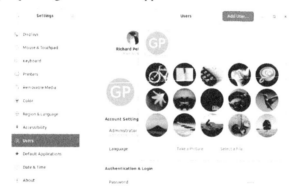

Figure 14-7: **Accounts dialog, User Icon**

Users and Groups

Alternatively, you can install (**gnome-system-tools**) and then use the older "Users and Groups" application (users-admin), accessible from "User and Groups" on the Applications overview (The **gnome-system-tools** package is no longer supported by Ubuntu). This opens a User Settings window, which displays two panes, a left scrollable pane for a list of users, showing their icon and login name, and a right pane showing information about a selected user. Below the left pane are buttons for adding and deleting users, as well as Managing Groups.

When you start up the users-admin application, only read access is allowed, letting you scroll through the list of users, but not make any changes or add new ones (see Figure 14-8). Read-only access is provided to all users. Users will be able to see the list of users on your system, but they cannot modify their entries, add new ones, or delete current users. Administrative access is required to perform these operations.

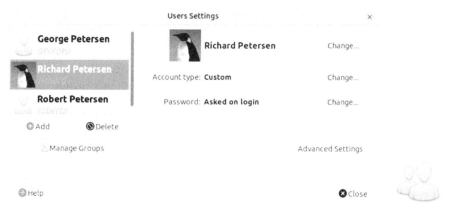

Figure 14-8: Users and Groups

When you first click a task button, such as Add, Delete, or Advanced Settings, an Authenticate dialog will open and prompt you to enter your user password. You will also be prompted to authenticate if you click a Change link to change a user password, account type, or name.

To change settings for a user, select the user in the User Settings window. On the left pane the username, account type and password access are listed with a Change link to the right of each. Clicking on a Change link lets you change that property. When you click a Change link, an authentication dialog will prompt you to enter an administrative user password. To change a username, click the Change link to the right of the username to open the "Change User Name" dialog with a text box for entering the new name.

To change a user password, you would click the Change link to the right of the Password entry to open the "Change User Password" dialog with entries for the current password and the new password (see Figure 14-9). You can also choose to generate a random password.

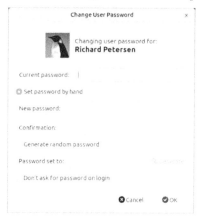

Figure 14-9: User Settings: Change User Password dialog

An account type can be Administrator, Desktop User, or Custom. When you click the Change link for the Account type, the "Change User Account Type" dialog opens with options for each.

For more detailed configuration, you click the Advanced Settings button to open the "Change Advanced User Settings" dialog, which has tabs for Contact Information, User Privileges, and Advanced (see Figure 14-10). On the Contact tab, you can add basic contact information if you wish, for an office address, as well as work and home phones.

On the User Privileges tab you can control device access and administrative access (see Figure 14-10). You can restrict or allow access to CD-ROMs, scanners, and external storage like USB drives. For a Desktop user to create a share, they have to have permission to do so (administrative users already have this permission). On the Users and Groups's Advanced dialog's Privileges tab set the "Share files with the local network" option.

The Advanced tab lets you select a home folder, the shell to use, a main group, and a user ID. Defaults are already chosen for you. A home folder in the name of the new user is specified and the shell used is the BASH shell. Normally you would not want to change these settings, though you might prefer to use a different shell, like the C-Shell. For the group, the user has a group with its own username (same as the short name).

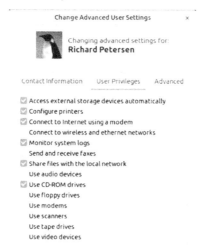

Figure 14-10: Users and Groups: Change User Privileges

Should to you decide to delete a user, you are prompted to keep or delete the user's home folder along with the user's files.

New Users (Users and Groups)

To create a new user, click the Add button in the Users Settings window to open a "Create New User" dialog, where you can enter the username. You enter the full name of the User in the Name textbox. Select a possible user name from the menu by the Username label. The user name is also the name of the new user's main group (see Figure 14-11). The new user is then added to the User Settings window.

The "Change User Password" dialog is then displayed, with entries for the new password and confirmation. You can also choose to use a randomly generated password instead (see Figure 14-12). Click the Generate button generate a password.

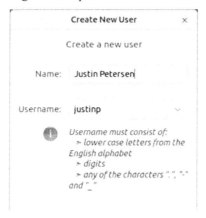

Figure 14-11: Users and Groups: Create New User

Figure 14-12: Users and Groups: new user password

If you decide not to enter a password (click Cancel), the account will remain disabled. To enable it later, click on the Enable Account button to open the "Change User Password" dialog where you can add the password.

The Account type is set initially to Desktop user, restricting access by the new user. Should you want to enable administrative access for this user, click the Change link to the right of the Account type entry to open the "Change User Account Type" dialog, where you can change the account type to Administrator. To set more specific privileges and for key user configuration settings such as the home folder and user id, click the Advanced Settings button to open the "Change Advanced User Settings" dialog with Contact Information, User Privileges, and Advanced tabs.

The icon used for a user is chosen by the user from their Preference's About dialog.

Alternatively, you can use the **useradd** command in a terminal window or command line to add user accounts and the **userdel** command to remove them. The following example adds the user **dylan** to the system:

```
$ useradd dylan
```

Groups (Users and Groups)

To manage groups, click the Manage Groups button in the Users Settings window. This opens a Group Settings window that lists all groups (see Figure 14-13). To add or remove users to or from a group, click the group name in the Group Settings window and click Properties. You can then check or uncheck users from the Group Members listing.

To add a new group, click the Add Group button in the Group Settings window to open a New Group dialog, where you can specify the group name, its id, and select the users to add to the group (see Figure 14-14). If you want to remove a group, just select its entry in the Groups Settings window and click the Delete button.

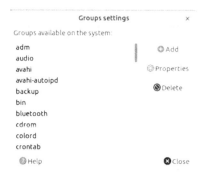

Figure 14-13: Users and Groups: Groups settings

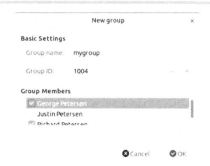

Figure 14-14: Group Properties: Group Users panel

Passwords

The easiest way to change your password is to use the Users dialog available from GNOME Settings as User. Select your username, then click the Password entry to open the Change User Password dialog (see Figure 14-7).

Alternatively, you can use the **passwd** command. In a terminal window enter the **passwd** command. The command prompts you for your current password. After entering your current password and pressing ENTER, you are then prompted for your new password. After entering the new password, you are asked to re-enter it. This makes sure you have actually entered the password you intended to enter.

```
$ passwd
Changing password for richard.
(current) UNIX password:
Enter new UNIX password:
Retype new UNIX password:
passwd: password updated successfully
$
```

Managing Services

Many administrative functions operate as services that need to be turned on. They are daemons, constantly running and checking for requests for their services. When you install a service, its daemon is normally turned on automatically. You can start, stop, and restart a service from a terminal window using the **systemctl** command with the service name and the commands: **start**, **stop**, **restart**, and **status**. The **status** command tells you if a service is already running. To restart the Samba file sharing server (**smdb**) you would use the following command. Use the status command to see if it is enabled.

```
sudo systemctl restart smbd
```

To disable a service so that it is not turned on automatically, you would use the **disable** command. To have it turned on you use the **enable** command. The **enable** command starts up the service when you system starts. If you enable before a restart and want to run the service, you would use the **start** command.

```
sudo systemctl disable smbd
sudo systemctl enable smbd
sudo systemctl start smbd
```

Ubuntu uses systemd to manage services. The systemd services are managed using **.service** configuration files in the **/lib/systemd/system** and **/etc/systemd/system** folders.

File System Access

Various file systems can be accessed on Ubuntu easily. Any additional internal hard drive partitions on your system, both Linux and Windows NTFS, will be detected automatically, but not mounted. In addition, you can access remote Windows shared folders and make your shared folders accessible to other hosts on your network.

Access to Internal Linux File Systems

Ubuntu will automatically detect other Linux file systems (partitions) on all your internal hard drives. Entries for these partitions are displayed on a file manager Other Locations folder. Initially, they are not mounted. Administrative users can mount internal partitions by clicking on its entry or icon, which mounts the file system and displays an icon for it on the Ubuntu dock. A file manager window opens displaying the top-level contents of the file system. The file system is mounted under the /**media** folder, in a sub-folder with the username, and then in a folder named with the file system (partition) label, or, if unlabeled, with the device UUID name.

Non-administrative users (users you create and do not specify as administrators), cannot mount internal partitions unless the task is authenticated using an administrative user's password. An authorization window will appear, similar to that shown in Figure 14-15. You will be asked to choose a user who has administrative access from a drop-down menu, and then enter that user's password. If there is only one administrative user, that user is selected automatically and you are prompted to enter that user's password. Whenever you start up your system again, you will still have to mount the file system, again providing authorization.

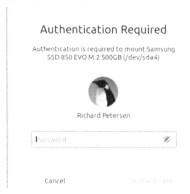

Figure 14-15: Mount authorization request for non-administrative users

Access to Windows NTFS File Systems on Local Drives

If you have installed Ubuntu on a dual-boot system with Windows, Linux NTFS file system support is installed automatically. Your NTFS partitions are mounted using Filesystem in Userspace (FUSE). The same authentication control used for Linux file systems applies to NTFS file systems. Entries for the NTFS partitions are listed on the Other Locations folder of any file manager window in the On This Computer section following the Computer entry. Click on an NTFS partition to mount it. If you are a user with administrative access, the file system is mounted automatically. If you are a user without administrative access, you will be asked to choose a user that has administrative access from a drop-down menu, and then enter that user's password, providing authorization. The NTFS file system is then mounted with an Eject button displayed at the right side of its entry on the Other Locations folder and an icon for it is displayed on the Ubuntu dock with an umount option. You can access the file system by clicking on its entry in a file manager Other Locations folder or by clicking on its icon on the Ubuntu dock. The partitions will be mounted under the /**media** folder with their UUID numbers or labels used as folder names. The NTFS partitions are mounted using **ntfs-3g** drivers.

Zero Configuration Networking: Avahi and Link Local Addressing

Zero Configuration Networking (Zeroconf) allows the setup of non-routable private networks without the need of a DHCP server or static IP addresses. A Zeroconf configuration lets users automatically connect to a network and access all network resources, such as printers, without having to perform any configuration. On Linux, Zeroconf networking is implemented by Avahi (**http://avahi.org**), which includes multicast DNS (mDNS) and DNS service discovery (DNS-SD) support that automatically detects services on a network. IP addresses are determined using either IPv6 or IPv4 Link Local (IPv4LL) addressing. IPv4 Link Local addresses are assigned from the 168.254.0.0 network pool. Derived from Apple's Bonjour Zeroconf implementation, it is a free and open source version currently used by desktop tools, such as the GNOME virtual file system. Ubuntu implements full Zeroconf network support with the Avahi daemon that implements multicast DNS discover, and **avahi-autoipd** that provides dynamic configuration of local IPv4 addresses. Both are installed as part of the desktop configuration. Avahi support tools like **avahi-browse** and **avahi-publish** are located in the **avahi-utils** package. Access to Linux Local Network Shared File Systems with Avahi

Permissions for Shared Folders in User Home Folders

New and fresh installations of Ubuntu 22.04 implement an added security measure for protecting users home folders. In previous releases the permissions for user home folders was set to allow any user read access to anyone's home folder. This has been changed to restrict access to the user only. The permissions for user home folders in prior releases in octal format was 755, with the last 5 allowing read and execute permission to anyone (other). This has been changed to 750, removing any permissions for other users. In symbolic format the permissions would be **u+rwx** and **g+rx**, with no entries for **o**, the other users.

```
$ ls -ld /home/richard
drwxr-x---  16 richard richard 4096 Sep 25 10:23  /home/richard
```

This restriction means that you can no longer share folders in your home folder. The mDNS (Avahi) operation is denied access and will not work on any shared folder in a user's home folder.

One way around this restriction is to the change the permission of the user's home folder. For users that want to share a folder in their home folder, you can simply change their home folder permission to 755, allowing access (read and execute) to any users. These are the less secure permissions used in previous releases. You can use the **chmod** command in a terminal window to change the permission.

```
sudo chmod 755 /home/richard
```

or

```
sudo chmod o+rx /home/richard
```

Reverting back to the original permissions loses the protections for user folders provided with the new permissions (750). There is a way to keep these protections and still allow shared folders in a user's home folder. You can set up a share definition for the shared folder in the Samba **/etc/smb.conf** file. You will have to add **force** commands to the configuration to allow other user to access the shared folder, as if they were you. You will need a **force** command for the create, directory, and user options, setting the mode to 0666 (read and write for all users) for the create, and 0777 (read, write, and execute for all users) for the shared folder (directory). For the user, specify the user's user name.

```
force create mode = 0666
force directory mode = 0777
force user = richard
```

The following example sets up the Documents folder in the user richard's home folder as a shared folder open to other users. The configuration allows read and write access (writable = yes).

```
[Documents]
path = /home/richard/Documents
guest ok = yes
browsable = yes
writable = yes
read only = no
force create mode = 0666
force directory mode = 0777
force user richard
```

Be sure that Samba is installed. You can use the "Open as root" entry in the desktop menu to open the file manager as an administrator and then navigate to the the **/etc/samba/** folder. Double click on the file **smb.conf** file to edit it and add the share entry at the end. Then save the file. In a terminal window you can then use **systemctl** command to restart the samba server, **smbd**.

```
sudo systemctl restart smbd
```

Other users can now use mDNS (Avahi) and Samba to access the shared folder in that user's home folder. Other local Linux users can use nDNS Avahi to access the share folder, and Windows systems can use Samba to access it.

Access to Linux Local Network Shared File Systems with mDNS

Once configured, shared Windows folders and printers on any of the computers connected to your local network are accessible from any file manager window sidebar. The multicast DNS discovery service, mDNS (called Avahi in Linux), automatically detects hosts on your home or local network. Supporting Samba libraries are already installed and will let you directly access any shared folders.

Figure 14-16: Accessing shared folders using multicast DNS discovery (Avahi)

You can use the multicast DNS discovery service (Avahi) to access any shared Linux folders on Linux systems that are running a Samba server. For such Linux system network browsing is enabled. You can open the Other Locations folder on the file manager to see the other Linux systems on your network (see Figure 14-16). Double click on the one you want to access to open a listing of the shared folders on that system. The shared folders are then displayed. Double click on the folder you want to open it. You are first asked to login using the remote systems user name and password. It is mounted on your system, with and entry for it on the file manager sidebar and on the Other Locations folder. When finished, you can eject the folder using either the sidebar entry (eject button) or the folder's entry on the Other Locations folder.

If you are using a firewall, be sure that it is configured for access to allow multicast DNS discovery. For the UFW firewall installed with Ubuntu, access for multicast DNS discovery service can be configured with Gufw by selecting the Multicast DNS application when adding a rule from the Preconfigured tab (UDP port 5353). For FirewallD, on firewall-config (Administration | Firewall), be sure that the **mdns** service is enabled, both runtime and permanent (Zones | Services tab) (see Figure 14-17) .

Figure 14-17: Gufw and FirewallD configuration for multicast DNS discovery (Avahi), mdns service

Problems can occur if the discovery process is not able to resolve the names of the hosts on your network. The multicast DNS discovery (mdns) service will append a **.local** to your host name for use by mdns, such as **richard-laptop.local**. If your host has the **.local** extension added irregularly or if it is missing, you will not be detected on your network. The way to ensure that your host is referenced is to create a **/etc/mdns.allow** file with entries for the **.local** and **.local.** which will remove the strict mdns requirement for the **.local** part of the host name. In the **/mdns.allow** file place the two lines as shown here.

/etc/mdns.allow
```
.local
.local.
```

In addition, you have to use **mdns4** instead of **mdns4_minimal** in the **/etc/nsswitch.conf** file. **mdns4_minimal** does not check the **/etc/mdns.allow** file, whereas **mdns4** does check it. In the **/etc/nsswitch.conf** file, modify the current hosts line:

```
hosts     files mdsn4_minimal [NOTFOUND=return] dns myhostname
```

to the following:

```
hosts    files mdsn4 [NOTFOUND=return] dns myhostname
```

Discovery is handled by the **nss-mdns** tool. For more information check:

```
https://github.com/lathiat/nss-mdns
```

Access to Windows Local Network Shared File Systems

Currently, both Linux and Windows are in the process of transitioning from the older SMBv1 protocol (Secure Message Block) to the more secure SMBv3 protocol. As a result, network browsing through the Linux file manager does not work currently. Instead, you can access Windows shares directly using the Connect to Server entry on the GNOME file manager's Other Locations window. Enter in the **smb://** protocol and the name of the shared folder or that of the remote Windows system you want to access. A dialog opens prompting you to enter the network domain and your Samba username and password (see Figure 14-18). Click the Connect button and then the particular shared folder or the shared folders on that host will be displayed. You can then access the shared folder and is mounted automatically on your desktop. The file manager sidebar will show an entry for the folder with an eject button for un-mounting it. Figure 14-19 shows the **myshared-data** shared folder on a Windows system mounted with an eject button on the sidebar.

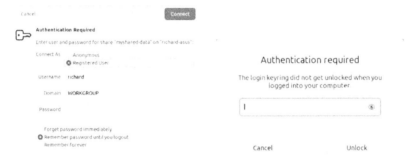

Figure 14-18: Network authorization

Figure 14-19: Other Locations - Network

You have the option to forget the password, in which case you will have to re-enter it each time you want to access the shared folder. The "Remember password" option remembers the username and password during your current session, and the "Remember forever" option lets you add the username and password to your password keyring. Whenever you try to access the shared folder again for the first time during a new session, you are simply asked for your Ubuntu user password (see Figure 14-20).

Figure 14-20: Mount remote Windows shares

Other local computers cannot access the shared folders on your Linux system until you install a sharing server, Samba for Windows systems and NFS for Linux/Unix systems. Should you attempt to share a folder, a notice is displayed prompting you to install the sharing service (Samba and NFS). Be sure also to allow firewall access for Samba and desktop browsing (see Chapter 15, Firewalls).

Shared Folders for your network

To share a folder on your Ubuntu system, right-click on it and select Local Network Share. This opens a window where you can allow sharing, and choose whether to permit modifying, adding, or deleting files in the folder. You can also use the Share tab on the file's properties dialog (see Figure 14-21). You can also allow access to anyone who does not also have an account on your system (guest). Once you have made your selections, click the Create Share button. You can later change the sharing options if you want.

Figure 14-21: Folder Sharing Options

Permissions on the user home folder no longer allow folders in their home folder to be shared. If you try to do so, a warning message is displayed telling you that access is prevented (see Figure 9-32).

```
The permissions for /home/richard
prevent other users from accessing this share
```

To allow access, you can either change the permission of the user home folder to allow access by other users to the entire user home folder (755), or add a Samba share definition for the share folder in the **/etc/samba/smb.conf** file using the **force** commands with **create**, **directory**, and **user** options. The Samba share definition method preserves the permissions of the user home folder, making it more secure. See the previous section "Permissions for Share Folders in User Home Folders" for more details.

To allow access by other users, permissions on the folder will have to be changed. You will be prompted to allow the file manager to make these changes for you. Just click the "Add the permissions automatically" button (see Figure 14-22).

Figure 14-22: Folder Sharing permissions prompt

Note: If you are running a firewall, be sure to configure access for the NFS and Samba services, including browsing support. Otherwise, access to your shared folders by other computers may be blocked (see Chapter 15).

Folders that are shared display a sharing emblem next to their icon on a file manager window.

Documents

To allow other computers to access your folders be sure the sharing servers are installed, Samba for Windows systems and NFS (**nfs-kernelserver**) for Linux/Unix systems. The servers are configured automatically for you and run. You will not be able to share folders until these servers are installed. If your sharing servers are not installed, you will be prompted to install them the first time you try to share a folder (see Figure 14-23). Click the Install service button. The Samba servers will be downloaded and installed. You are then prompted to restart your desktop session. Click the Restart session button. You are placed in the GDM login screen. Log in again and then open the folder sharing dialog for the folder you want to share (Sharing Options).

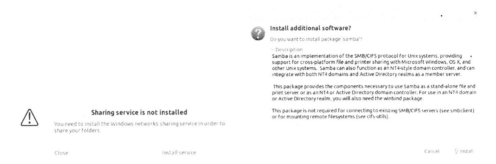

Figure 14-23: Prompt to install sharing service (Samba and NFS)

You can also install the Samba server directly with the Synaptic Package Manager or the **apt** command (**samba** package). Two servers are installed and run using the **smbd** and **nmbd** systemd service scripts. The **smbd** server is the Samba server, and the **nmbd** server is the network discovery server.

Should the Samba server fail to start, you can start it manually in a terminal window with the commands:

```
sudo systemctl start nmbd
sudo systemctl start smbd
```

You can check the current status with the **status** option and restart with the **restart** option:

```
systemctl status nmbd
systemctl status smbd
```

When first installed, Samba imports the user accounts already configured on your Ubuntu system. Corresponding Windows users with the same username and password as an Ubuntu account on your Ubuntu system are connected automatically to the Ubuntu shared folders. Should the Windows user have a different password, that user is prompted on Windows to enter a username and password. This is an Ubuntu username and password. In the case of a Windows user with the same username but different password, the user would enter the same username with an Ubuntu user password, not the Windows password.

To change the sharing permissions for a folder later, open the folder's Properties window and then select the Share tab. When you make a change, a Modify Share button is displayed. Click it to make the changes. In Figure 14-24 share access is added to the Pictures folder.

Figure 14-24: Folder Share panel

If you are using a firewall, be sure that it is configured for access by Samba to allow multicast DNS discovery. For Gufw (Preferences | Firewall Configuration), be sure that the rules are added for Samba. For FirewallD, on firewall-config (Sundry | Firewall), be sure that the mdns, samba, and samba-client services are enabled (Zones | Services tab) (see Figure 14-25) .

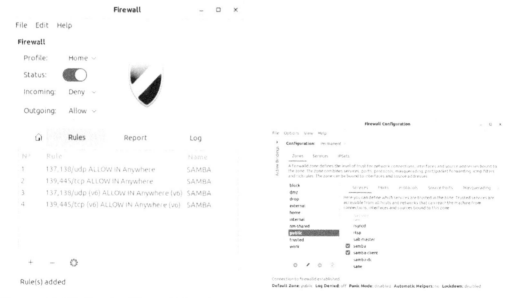

Figure 14-25: Samba Firewall Configuration, Gufw (UFW) and firewall-config (FirewallD)

Accessing Samba Shares from Windows

Accessing Samba shares from Windows is an issue for Windows 10. Upgrades to Windows 10 has disabled the SMBv1 network browsing capabilities of Windows, as it transitions to SMBv3 from SMBv1. You could try to manually re-enable SMBv1 browsing, but SMBv1 is being disabled due to security issues. It is not advisable to re-enable it. This means you cannot simply browse a Linux host currently, but you can still easily set up access to each Samba shared folder on that Linux host. It is still easy to access your Samba Linux shares from Windows 10. You can add a new network location for it, that will be accessible from a shortcut you can set up for it on your Windows file manager "This PC" folder. To set up the shortcut, open the Windows file manager to any folder and right-click on the "This PC" entry in the sidebar to display a menu. Click on the "Add a network location" entry to open the "Add Network Location Wizard" and click Next. Click on the "Choose a custom network location" entry and click Next. In the text box labeled "Internet or network address:" enter the host name of your Linux system that holds the shares you want to access, beginning with the two backward slashes and followed by a backward slash (you may have to also enter the name of one of the shared folders on that system).

```
\\richard-laptop\
```

You can then click the Browse button to open a dialog showing a tree of all the shared folders on that host. You can choose a share, or any of a share's subfolders. Their file pathname is automatically added to the address textbox. Alternatively, you could enter the folder path name in the text box directly with the subfolders separated by single backward slashes. If you are sharing your Linux home folders, then the shared folder is the name of the user's Home folder, the user name. Samples are shown here.

```
\\richard-laptop\richard
```

```
\\richard-laptop\richard\Pictures
```

```
\\richard-laptop\mydocs
```

Once the locations for your shared folders are set up in Windows, you can access them again quickly from their shortcuts in the "This PC" folder.

File and Folder Permissions

On the desktop, you can set a folder or file permission using the Permissions tab in its Properties window (see Figure 14-26). For Files, right-click the icon (icon view) or entry (list view) for the file or folder in the file manager window and select Properties to open the Properties dialog. Then select the Permissions tab. Here you will find pop-up menus for read and write permissions, along with rows for Owner, Group, and Others. You can set owner permissions as Read Only or Read And Write. For the group and others, you can also set the None option, denying access. The group name expands to a menu listing different groups; select one to change the file's group. If you want to execute this file as an application (say, a shell script) check the "Allow executing file as program" checkbox. This has the effect of setting the execute permission

Figure 14-26: File Permissions

The Permissions tab for folders (folders) operates much the same way, with Access menus for Owner, Group, and Others (see Figure 14-27). For subfolders, right-click on the folder and choose Properties from the menu. For the current open folder, choose Properties from the folder's menus on the location bar. The Access menu controls access to the folder with options for List Files Only, Access Files, and Create And Delete Files. These correspond to the read, read and execute, and read-write-execute permissions given to folders. To set the permissions for all the files and folders in the folder accordingly (not just the folder), click the "Change Permissions for Enclosed Files" button to open a dialog where you can specify the owner, group, and others permissions for files and folders in the folder (see Figure 14-27). The access options are the same as for files: for the owner, there are Read or Read and Write permissions. The group and others access menus add a None option to deny access.

Figure 14-27: Folder Permissions

Automatic file system mounts with /etc/fstab

Though most file systems are automatically mounted for you, there may be instances where you need to have a file system mounted manually. Using the mount command you can do this directly, or you can specify the mount operation in the **/etc/fstab** file to have it mounted automatically. Ubuntu file systems are uniquely identified with their UUID (Universally Unique IDentifier). These are listed in the **/dev/disk/by-uuid** folder (or with the **sudo blkid** command). In the **/etc/fstab** file, the file system disk partitions are listed as a comment, and then followed by the actual file system mount operation using the UUID. The following example mounts the file system on partition **/dev/sda3** to the **/media/sda3** folder as an **ext4** file system with default options (**defaults**). The UUID for device **/dev/sda3** is b8c526db-cb60-43f6-b0a3-5c0054f6a64a.

```
# /dev/sda3
UUID=b8c526db-cb60-43f6-b0a3-5c0054f6a64a /media/sda3 ext4 defaults 0 2
```

You can also identify your file system by giving it a label. You can use the **ext2label** command to label a file system. In the following **/etc/fstab** file example, the Linux file system labeled **mydata1** is mounted to the **/mydata1** folder as an **ext4** file system type.

To find out the UUID of any device you use the **blkid** command.

```
blkid
```

/etc/fstab

```
# /etc/fstab: static file system information.
#
# <file system> <mount point>   <type>  <options>       <dump>  <pass>
# / was on /dev/sda2 during installation
UUID=a179d6e6-b90c-4cc4-982d-a4cfcedea7df / ext4 errors=remount-ro 0 1
# /boot/efi was on /dev/sda1 during installation
UUID=7982-2520 /boot/efi vfat umask=0077 0 1
# /dev/sda3
UUID=b8c526db-cb60-43f6-b0a3-5c0054f6a64a /media/sda3 ext4 defaults 0 2
/swapfile          none  swap  sw      0 0
LABEL=mydata1 /newdata        ext4        defaults              1 1
```

Should you have to edit your **/etc/fstab** file, you can use the **sudo** command with the **gedit** editor on your desktop. In a terminal window enter the following command. You will first be prompted to enter your password.

```
sudo gedit /etc/fstab
```

To mount a partition manually, use the **mount** command and specify the type with the **-t** option. Use the **-L** option to mount by label. List the file system first, and then the folder name to which it will be mounted. For an NTFS partition, you would use the type **ntfs**. For partitions with the Ext4 file system you would use **ext4**, and for older Linux partitions you would use **ext3**. The mount option has the format:

```
mount -t type  file-system  folder
```

The following example mounts the **mydata1** file system to the **/newdata** folder

```
mount -t ext4  -L mydata1  /newdata
```

Bluetooth

Bluetooth is a wireless connection method for locally connected devices such as keyboards, mice, printers, and Bluetooth-capable cell phones. BlueZ is the official Linux Bluetooth protocol and is integrated into the Linux kernel. The BlueZ protocol was developed originally by Qualcomm and is now an open source project, located at **http://www.bluez.org/**. It is included in the bluez and bluez-libs packages, among others. Check the BlueZ site for a complete list of supported hardware.

If you have Bluetooth devices attached to your system, a Bluetooth entry is displayed on the system status area menu on the top panel (see Figure 14-28). It will display a message showing the number of connected devices if there are any. Click the entry to display items to turn off Bluetooth and for Bluetooth Settings. Should you turn off Bluetooth, Bluetooth will be disabled and its entry removed from the system status area menu. Use the Bluetooth Settings dialog, accessible from the Settings dialog, to turn it on again.

Figure 14-28: Bluetooth Settings (GNOME Settings)

The Bluetooth Settings item opens Settings to the Bluetooth tab (see Figure 14-29). You can also access Bluetooth tab on GNOME Settings directly. On the Bluetooth settings tab, a Bluetooth switch at the top right lets you turn Bluetooth on or off. Clicking the menu button at the top left displays entries that let you set the name of your system's Bluetooth service and set switches to show the Bluetooth icon on the panel and whether to receive files from Bluetooth connected devices.

Detected devices are listed in the Devices section at the center. Initially, devices are disconnected. Click on a device entry to connect it. A dialog opens with a detected pin number, which you confirm. Then the device configuration dialog is displayed, with a switch to connect or disconnect the device (see Figure 14-30). Pair, type, and address information are also displayed. If the device supports sound, a Sound Setting button is shown, which opens the Sound tab in Settings which displays that device (see Figure 14-31). To remove the device configuration, click the Remove Device button.

Figure 14-29: Bluetooth Settings (GNOME Settings)

Figure 14-30: Bluetooth Device Configuration

Figure 14-31: Bluetooth Sound

When connecting to a phone (see Figure 14-32), a pin number is detected and displayed. On the configuration dialog, you can choose to connect or disconnect. If you enable a phone to operate as a mobile phone network device (PAN/NAP), then a new entry appears for the device in the system status area menu, which you can expand to list the entries: Use as Internet connection" and "Mobile Broadband Setting." When you click the "Use as Internet connection" entry, it will change to a Turn Off entry, once you have connected.

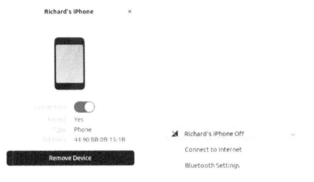

Figure 14-32: Bluetooth for phones

DKMS

DKMS is the Dynamic Kernel Module Support originally developed by DELL. DKMS enabled device drivers can be generated automatically whenever your kernel is updated. This is helpful for proprietary drivers like the Nvidia and AMD proprietary graphics drivers (the X11 open source drivers, Xorg, are automatically included with the kernel package). In the past, whenever you updated your kernel, you also had to download and install a separate proprietary kernel module compiled just for that new kernel. If the module was not ready, then you could not use a proprietary driver. To avoid this problem, DKMS was developed, which uses the original proprietary source code to create new kernel modules as they are needed. When you install a new kernel, DKMS detects the new configuration and compiles a compatible proprietary kernel module for your new kernel. This action is fully automatic and entirely hidden from the user.

On Ubuntu both the Nvidia and AMD proprietary graphics drivers are DKMS enabled packages that are managed and generated by the DKMS service. The generated kernel modules are placed in the **/lib/modules/**/*kernel-version*/**kernel/updates** folder. When you install either graphics proprietary package, their source code is downloaded and used to create a graphics driver for use by your kernel. The source code is placed in the **/usr/src** folder. The DKMS configuration files and build locations for different DKMS-enabled software are located in subfolders in the **/var/lib/dkms** folder.

DKMS is not installed by default. Use the Synaptic Package Manager or the **apt** command to install it. DKMS configuration files are located in the **/etc/dkms** folder. The **/etc/dkms/framework.conf** file holds DKMS variable definitions for folders that DKMS uses, like the source code and kernel module folders. The **/etc/init.d/dkms_autoinstaller** is a script the runs the DKMS operations to generate and install a kernel module. DKMS removal and install directives for kernel updates are maintained in the **/etc/kernel** folder.

Should DKMS fail to install and update automatically, you can perform the update manually using the **dkms** command. The **dkms** command with the **build** action creates the kernel module, and then the **dkms** command with the **install** action installs the module to the appropriate kernel module folder. The **-m** option specifies the module you want to build and the **-k** option is the kernel version (use **uname -r** to display your current kernel version). Drivers like Nvidia and AMD release new versions regularly. You use the **-v** option to specify the driver version you want. See the man page for **dkms** for full details.

Editing Configuration Files Directly

Though the administrative tools will handle all configuration settings for you, there may be times when you will need to make changes by editing configuration files directly. Most system configuration files are text files located in the **/etc** folder. To change any of these files, you will need administrative access, requiring you use the **pkexec** or **sudo** commands.

You can use any standard editor, such as nano or Vi, to edit these files, though one of the easiest ways to edit them is to use the Gedit editor on the GNOME desktop. In a terminal window, enter the **sudo** command with the **gedit** command. You will be prompted for the root user password. The Gedit window then opens (see Figures 14-2 and 14-3 near the beginning of this chapter). Click Open to open a file browser where you can move through the file system to locate the file you want to edit.

```
sudo gedit
```

Caution: Be careful when editing your configuration files. Editing mistakes can corrupt your configurations. It is advisable to make a backup of any configuration files you are working on first, before making major changes to the original.

Gedit will let you edit several files at once, opening a tab for each. You can use Gedit to edit any text file, including ones you create yourself. Two commonly edited configuration files are **/etc/default/grub** and **/etc/fstab**. The **/etc/fstab** file lists all your file systems and how they are mounted, and **/etc/default/grub** file is the configuration file for your Grub 2 boot loader.

You also can specify the file to edit when you first start up gedit (the Gedit editor).

```
sudo gedit /etc/default/grub
```

User configuration files, dot files, can be changed by individual users directly without administrative access. An example of a user configuration file is the **.profile** file, which configures your login shell. Dot files like **.profile** have to be chosen from the file manager window, not from the Gedit open operation. First configure the file manager to display dot files by selecting the Show Hidden Files entry in the tools menu of any file manager window. This displays the dot files in your file manager window. Double-click the file to open it in Gedit.

GRUB 2

The Grand Unified Bootloader (GRUB) is a multiboot boot loader used for most Linux distributions. Linux and Unix operating systems are known as multiboot operating systems and take arguments passed to them at boot time. With GRUB, users can select operating systems to run from a menu interface displayed when a system boots up. Use arrow keys to move to an entry and press ENTER. If instead, you need to edit an entry, press **e**, letting you change kernel arguments or specify a different kernel. The **c** command places you in a command line interface. Provided your system BIOS supports very large drives, GRUB can boot from anywhere on them. For detailed information and instructions on Grub2 on Ubuntu, check the Ubuntu Grub2 Wiki at:

`https://help.ubuntu.com/community/Grub2`

Check the GRUB Man page for GRUB options. GRUB is a GNU project with its home page at **https://www.gnu.org/software/grub/**, the manual at **https://www.gnu.org/software/grub/manual/grub/**. The Ubuntu forums have several helpful threads on using Grub2 on Ubuntu, **https://ubuntuforums.org** and on **https://help.ubuntu.com**. Search on Grub2.

Grub2 detects and generates a menu for you automatically. You do not have to worry about keeping a menu file updated. All your operating systems and Ubuntu kernels are detected when the system starts up, and a menu to display them as boot options is generated at that time.

With Grub2, configuration is placed in user-modifiable configuration files held in the **/etc/default/grub** file and in the **/etc/grub.d** folder. There is a Grub2 configuration file called **/boot/grub/grub.cfg**, but this file is generated by Grub each time the system starts up, and should never be edited by a user. Instead, you would edit the **/etc/default/grub** file to set parameters like the default operating system to boot. To create your own menu entries, you create entries for them in the **/etc/grub.d/40_custom** file.

Grub options are set by assigning values to Grub options in the **/etc/default/grub** file. You can edit the file directly to change these options (see Figure 14-33). To edit the file with the Gedit editor, open a terminal window and enter the following command. You will be prompted to enter your password. If **sudo** is not already installed, you will have to install it.

`sudo gedit /etc/default/grub`

You can then edit the file carefully. The **grub** file used on Ubuntu 22.04 LTS is shown here:

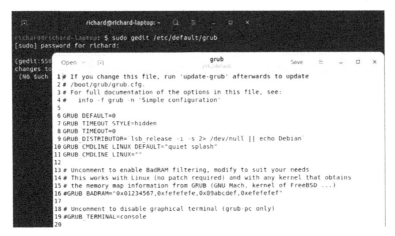

Figure 14-33: Editing the /etc/default/grub file

/etc/default/grub

```
# If you change this file, run 'update-grub' afterwards to update
# /boot/grub/grub.cfg.

GRUB_DEFAULT=0
GRUB_TIMEOUT_STYLE=hidden
GRUB_TIMEOUT="0"
GRUB_DISTRIBUTOR=`lsb_release -i -s 2> /dev/null || echo Debian`
GRUB_CMDLINE_LINUX_DEFAULT="quiet splash"
GRUB_CMDLINE_LINUX=""

# Uncomment to enable BadRAM filtering, modify to suit your needs
# This works with Linux (no patch required) and with any kernel that obtains
# the memory map information from GRUB (GNU Mach, kernel of FreeBSD ...)
#GRUB_BADRAM="0x01234567,0xfefefefe,0x89abcdef,0xefefefef"

# Uncomment to disable graphical terminal (grub-pc only)
#GRUB_TERMINAL=console

# The resolution used on graphical terminal
# note that you can use only modes which your graphic card supports via VBE
# you can see them in real GRUB with the command `vbeinfo'
#GRUB_GFXMODE=640x480

# Uncomment if you don't want GRUB to pass "root=UUID=xxx" parameter to Linux
#GRUB_DISABLE_LINUX_UUID=true

# Uncomment to disable generation of recovery mode menu entrys
#GRUB_DISABLE_RECOVERY="true"

# Uncomment to get a beep at grub start
#GRUB_INIT_TUNE="480 440 1"
```

For dual boot systems (those with both Ubuntu and Windows or Mac), the option that users are likely to change is GRUB_DEFAULT, which sets the operating system or kernel to boot automatically if one is not chosen. The option uses a line number to indicate an entry in the Grub boot menu, with numbering starting from 0 (not 1). First, check your Grub menu when you boot up (press the ESC key on boot to display the Grub menu), and then count to where the entry of the operating system you want to make the default is listed. If the Windows entry is at 4th, which would be line 3 (counting from 0), to make it the default you would set the GRUB_DEAULT option to 3.

```
GRUB_DEFAULT=3
```

Should you want to change the default frequently, you would have to edit the **/etc/default/grub** file each time to change it. A safer way to set the default is to configure GRUB to use the **grub-set-default** command. First, edit the **/etc/default/grub** file and change the option for GRUB_DEFAULT to **save**.

```
GRUB_DEFAULT=saved
```

Then update GRUB.

```
sudo update-grub
```

The **grub-set-default** command takes as its option the number of the default you want to set (numbering from 0) or the name of the kernel or operating system. The following sets the default to 0, the first kernel entry.

```
sudo grub-set-default 0
```

For a kernel name or operating system, you can use the name as it appears on the GRUB menu (enclosing the name in quotes), such as:

```
sudo grub-set-default  'Windows (loader) (on /dev/sda1)'
```

The GRUB_TIMEOUT option sets the number of seconds Grub will wait to allow a user to access the menu, before booting the default operating system. The default options used for Ubuntu kernels are listed by the GRUB_CMDLINE_LINUX_DEFAULT option. Currently, these include the **splash** and **quiet** options to display the Ubuntu emblem on startup (**splash**), but not the list of startup tasks being performed (**quiet**).

The GRUB_TIMEOUT_STYLE option sets whether the menu is displayed or not during the timeout period. Options can be **menu**, which displays the Grub menu, **countdown**, which only displays a countdown timer for the timeout period, and **hidden**, which does not display the menu unless the user presses the ESC key. On Ubuntu this option is set to **hidden** by default.

```
GRUB_TIMEOUT_STYLE=hidden
```

The following would always display the Grub menu.

```
GRUB_TIMEOUT_STYLE=menu
```

Should you have other operating systems on your computer such as Windows, and GRUB fails to detect them, it could be that the **os-prober** application has been disabled. You can enable it with the following option added to the **/etc/default/grub** file.

```
GRUB_DISABLE_OS_PROBER=false
```

Once you have made your changes, you have to run the **update-grub** command with **sudo**, as noted in the first line of the **/etc/default/grub** file. Otherwise, your changes will not take effect. This command will generate a new **/etc/grub/grub.cfg** file, which determines the actual Grub 2 configuration.

```
sudo update-grub
```

You can add your own Grub2 boot entries by placing them in the **/etc/grub.d/40_custom** file. The file is nearly empty except for an initial **exec tail** command that you must take care not to change. Samples of added entries are shown on the Ubuntu Grub2 Wiki, **https://help.ubuntu.com/community/Grub2**. After you make your additions to the **40_custom** file, you have to run **sudo update-grub** to have the changes take effect.

When the GRUB package is updated by Ubuntu, you will be given the choice to keep your current local version or use the maintainer's version. Keeping the local version is selected by default. However, unless you have extensively customized your configuration, it is always advisable to select the maintainer's version. The maintainer's version is the most up-to-date. If you had made any changes previously to the **/etc/default/grub** file, you will have to edit that file and make the same changes again, such as setting the default operating system to load. Be sure to run **sudo update-grub** to make the changes take effect.

Backup Management: Deja Dup, rsync, BackupPC, and Amanda

Backup operations have become an important part of administrative duties. Several backup tools are provided on Linux systems, including Amanda and the traditional dump/restore tools, as well as the **rsync** command used for making individual copies. Deja Dup is a front end for the duplicity backup tool, which uses **rsync** to generate backup archives. Deja Dup is the recommended default backup tool, available from the Applications overview as Backup. Amanda provides server-based backups, letting different systems on a network backup to a central server. BackupPC provides network and local backup using configured **rsync** and **tar** tools. The dump tools let you refine your backup process, detecting data changed since the last backup. Table 14-2 lists websites for Linux backup tools.

Website	Tools
`https://rsync.samba.org`	rsync remote copy backup
`https://launchpad.net/deja-dup` `http://www.nongnu.org/duplicity`	Deja Dup frontend for duplicity which uses rsync to perform basic backups
`http://www.amanda.org`	Amanda network backup
`https://sourceforge.net/projects/dump/`	dump and restore tools
`https://backuppc.github.io/backuppc/`	BackupPC network or local backup using configured rsync and tar tools.

Table 14-2: Backup Resources

Deja Dup (Backups)

Deja Dup is a front end for the duplicity backup tool, which uses rsync to generate backup archives (**http://www.nongnu.org/duplicity/**). Once installed, you can access Deja Dup on the Applications overview in the Utilities application folder as Backups.

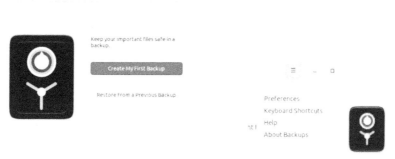

Figure 14-34: Deja Dup settings - overview

The default backup setting for Deja Dup is to store your backups on Google Drive. However, you can change this setting to a local folder or a network share (Storage location tab). Should you want to use Google Drive, you will also have to install the **python3-pydrive** package, which will manage access to your Google drive account.

The deja-dup dialog shows buttons for backing up and restoring backups (see Figure 14-34). A menu on the upper right of the titlebar has entries for Preferences, Help, and Keyboard shortcuts. Select the Help entry on the titlebar menu to display the Deja Dup manual.

The deja-dup Preferences dialog shows tabs for General and Folders (see Figure 14-35). A switch in the Schedule section of the dialog allows you to turn automatic backups on and off. The General tab provides storage and scheduling settings with buttons to automatically perform a backup and a menu for selecting the the time interval for your backups.

Figure 14-35: Deja Dup Preferences

The Storage section lets you specify the location and how long you want to keep backups (see Figure 14-36). You can choose different locations, such as an FTP account, a cloud account, SSH server, Samba (Windows) share, or a local folder. Choose the one you want from the "Storage Location" menu. With each choice, you are prompted for the appropriate configuration information.

Figure 14-36: Deja Dup settings - storage for Windows share and Local folder

In the Storage section, the Keep Backups menu lets you specify the frequency of your backups and how long to keep them (see Figure 14-37). First turn on Automatic backup. Backups can be performed daily, weekly, every two weeks, or monthly. They can be kept for a week, month, several months, a year, or forever.

Storage

Location

Keep Backups   Forever ⌄

The oldest backups will still be deleted eas At least three months
space or kept up to three months longer to
backups
                                                    At least six months
Schedule

                                                    At least a year
Back Up Automatically

                                                    Forever ✓

Figure 14-37: Deja Dup settings - backup times

The Folders tab has sections for "Folders to Back Up" and "Folders to Ignore" (see Figure 14-38). Click the plus button (+) at the bottom of the folders list to add a new folder for backup. Do the same to specify folders to ignore. The minus button at the right of each entry removes selected folders from the list. Your home folder has been added already. The "Folders to ignore" section specifies folders you do not want to back up. The Downloads and Trash folders are already specified.

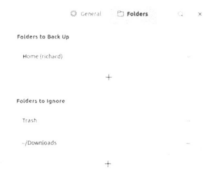

Figure 14-38: Deja Dup settings - Folders to save and ignore

When you perform a backup, you first choose the folders to backup and to ignore. Click the Forward button to continue. Next you choose a storage location. You are then are prompted to backup with or without encryption. For encrypted backups, you are prompted to enter a password, which you will need to restore the files (see Figure 14-39). You are then asked to select the date of the backup to use, the most recent being the default.

To restore a backup, click on the Restore tab on the Deja-dup window. This displays all the folders in your current backup (see Figure 14-40). Click on the ones you want to restore. The Restore button on the lower left becomes active. Click it to the start the restore process. You can choose what backup to use from the Date menu on the lower right. To automatically choose all the folders and files either press Ctrl-a or click on the check-mark button on the right side of the Deja-dup window header bar. Click on the "Click on items to select them" button on the center of the header to display a menu with "Select All" and "Select None" options. You can also search for files and folders by clicking the Search button (looking glass) on the right side of the Deja-dup header bar.

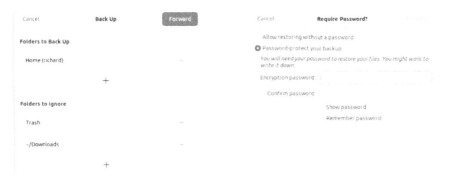

Figure 14-39: Deja Dup backup: encryption

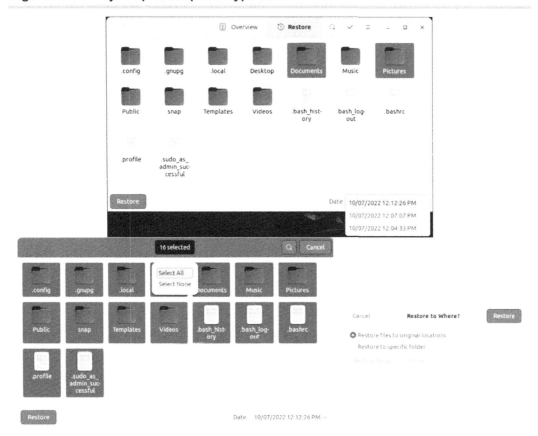

Figure 14-40: Deja Dup restore

Once you have selected the files to restore and have clicked the Restore button, you can choose whether to restore to the original location or a specific folder. The backup restore operation is then performed. When restoring, you are prompted to specify the location you are backing up from, the backup date to restore from, and whether to restore to the original location or a specific folder.

Individual Backups: archive and rsync

You can backup and restore particular files and folders with archive tools like **tar**, restoring the archives later. For backups, **tar** is used usually with a tape device. To schedule automatic backups, you can schedule appropriate **tar** commands with the **cron** utility. The archives can be also compressed for storage savings. You can then copy the compressed archives to any medium, such as a DVD disc, USB drive, external hard drive, or tape. On GNOME you can use File Roller (Archive Manager) to create archives easily.

File Roller also supports LZMA compression, a more efficient and faster compression method. On Archive Manager, when creating a new archive, select "Tar compressed with lzma (.tar.lzma)" for the Archive type. When choosing Create Archive from GNOME Files file manager window on selected files, on the Create Archive dialog, choose the **.lzma** file type for just compression, and the **.tar.lzma** type for a compressed archive.

If you want to remote-copy a folder or files from one host to another, making a particular backup, you can use **rsync**, which is designed for network backups of particular folders or files, intelligently copying only those files that have been changed, rather than the contents of an entire folder. In archive mode, it can preserve the original ownership and permissions, providing corresponding users exist on the host system. The following example copies the **/home/george/myproject** folder to the **/backup** folder on the host **rabbit**, creating a corresponding **myproject** subfolder. The **-t** specifies that this is a transfer. The remote host is referenced with an attached colon, **rabbit:**

```
rsync -t /home/george/myproject   rabbit:/backup
```

If instead, you wanted to preserve the ownership and permissions of the files, you would use the **-a** (archive) option. Adding a **-z** option will compress the file. The **-v** option provides a verbose mode.

```
rsync -avz  /home/george/myproject   rabbit:/backup
```

A trailing slash on the source will copy the contents of the folder, rather than generating a subfolder of that name. Here the contents of the **myproject** folder are copied to the **george-project** folder.

```
rsync -avz  /home/george/myproject/   rabbit:/backup/george-project
```

The **rsync** command is configured to use Secure Shell (SSH) remote shell by default. You can specify it or an alternate remote shell to use with the **-e** option. For secure transmission, you can encrypt the copy operation with SSH. Either use the **-e ssh** option or set the **RSYNC_RSH** variable to ssh.

```
rsync -avz -e ssh  /home/george/myproject   rabbit:/backup/myproject
```

You can copy from a remote host to the host you are on.

```
rsync -avz  lizard:/home/mark/mypics/  /pic-archive/markpics
```

You can also run **rsync** as a server daemon. This will allow remote users to synchronize copies of files on your system with versions on their own, transferring only changed files rather than entire folders. Many mirror and software FTP sites operate as **rsync** servers, letting you update files without have to download the full versions again. Configuration information for rsync as a server is kept in the **/etc/rsyncd.conf** file.

Tip: Though it is designed for copying between hosts, you can also use **rsync** to make copies within your own system, usually to a folder in another partition or hard drive. Check the **rsync** Man page for detailed descriptions of each.

BackupPC

BackupPC provides an easily managed local or network backup of your system or hosts, on a system using configured rsync or tar tools. There is no client application to install, just configuration files. BackupPC can backup hosts on a network, including servers, or just a single system. Data can be backed up to local hard disks or to network storage such as shared partitions or storage servers. You can configure BackupPC using your Web page configuration interface. This is the host name of your computer with the **/backuppc** name attached, like **http://richard1/backuppc**. Detailed documentation is installed at **/usr/share/doc/BackupPC**. You can find out more about BackupPC at **https://backuppc.github.io/backuppc/**. You can install BackupPC using the Synaptic Package Manager and with the **apt** command. Canonical provides critical updates. Configuration files are located at **/etc/BackupPC**. The **config.pl** file holds BackupPC configuration options and the **hosts** file lists hosts to be backed up.

BackupPC uses both compression and detection of identical files to reduce the size of the backup, allowing several hosts to be backed up in limited space. Once an initial backup is performed, BackupPC will only backup changed files, reducing the time of the backup significantly.

Amanda

To back up hosts connected to a network, you can use the Advanced Maryland Automatic Network Disk Archiver (Amanda) to archive hosts. Amanda uses **tar** tools to back up all hosts to a single host operating as a backup server. Backup data is sent by each host to the host operating as the Amanda server, where they are written out to a backup medium such as tape. With an Amanda server, the backup operations for all hosts become centralized in one server, instead of each host having to perform its backup. Any host that needs to restore data simply requests it from the Amanda server, specifying the file system, date, and filenames. Backup data is copied to the server's holding disk and from there, to tapes. Detailed documentation and updates are provided at **http://www.amanda.org**. For the server, be sure to install the amanda-server package, and for clients you use the amanda-clients package. You can install Amanda using the Synaptic Package Manager, Utilities (universe) section, and from Ubuntu Software. Canonical does not provide critical updates.

Printing

This section covers the printing-configuration tools: the GNOME Printers tool (GNOME Settings Printers) and the older **system-config-printer** tool. Most printers are detected for you automatically. You can use the GNOME Settings Printers tab to turn them on or off and access their print queues. As an alternative, you can still use the older **system-config-printer**, also available on the GNOME Settings Printers tab as "Additional Printer Settings". Both are front ends for the Common UNIX Printing System (CUPS), which provides printing services (**www.cups.org**).

When you attach a local printer to your system for the first time, the GNOME Printers tool automatically detects the printer and installs the appropriate driver. A message appears briefly in the notifications dialog, indicating that a new printer has been detected. The printer is then listed in both the GNOME Settings Printers tool and in the older **system-config-printer**. If the detection fails, you can use the GNOME Settings Printers tool, accessible from GNOME Settings, to set up your printer.

Most newer printer models support driverless printing. Instead of installing a driver, the printer supports a driverless driver. You can print to any of these printers without first downloading and installing a driver for them. The printers are automatically detected through DNS Service Discovery (DNS-SD). The CUPS Web configuration interface, system-config-printer, GNOME printers, and **lpadmin** already support driverless printing.

CUPS uses the driverless utility to detect available driverless printers and to generate PPD configuration files for them. The drivers may not be as complete in features as their official drivers, but will print. Currently printers compatible with IPP Anywhere and Apple Raster supported printers can make use of driverless drivers, usually newer printers. GNOME Printer, system-config-printer, and the CUP Web interface all use the driverless tool to detect and configure driverless printers. See the man page for **driverless** for more information.

KDE provides support for adding and configuring CUPS printers through the KDE System Settings Printer Configuration dialog. Select the Printer Configuration icon under Hardware. USB printers that are automatically detected will be listed in the KDE Printer Configuration dialog.

Printers can be local or remote. Both are referenced using Universal Resource Identifiers (URI). URIs support both network protocols used to communicate with remote printers and device connections used to reference local printers.

Remote printers are referenced by the protocol used to communicate with them, including **ipp** for the Internet Printing Protocol used for UNIX network printers, **smb** for the Samba protocol used for Windows network printers, and **lpd** for the older LPRng UNIX print servers. Their URIs are similar to a web URL, indicating the network addresses of the system the printer is connected to.

```
ipp://mytsuff.com/printers/queue1
smb://guest@lizard/myhp
```

For attached local printers, the URI will use the device connection and the device name. The usb: prefix is used for USB printers; **parallel:** is used for older printers connected to a parallel port; **serial:** is used for printers connected to a serial port; **scsi:** is used for SCSI-connected printers. For a locally attached USB printer, the URI would be something like the following:

```
usb://Canon/S330
```

GNOME Printers: GNOME Settings

The GNOME Printers tool is accessible from the GNOME Settings Printers tab. It lists installed printers, letting you configure them and access their job queues (see Figure 14-41) . If no printers are detected, an Add button is displayed on the tab, which you can use to detect your printer. To detect additional printers, you can click the Add button. The Printers tab will list entries for detected and configured printers. A printer entry displays the printer name, model, status, a jobs button with the number of jobs, and a configuration button (gear icon). Click the jobs button to open a dialog listing active jobs for this printer (see Figure 14-42). For each job entry there are buttons to the right to pause or remove the job.

Figure 14-41: GNOME Settings Printers tab

Figure 14-42: GNOME Printers - Jobs

To configure a printer, click the configure button (gear icon) to display a menu with entries for the printer's options, details, default, and removal (see Figure 14-43). Choosing the "Use Printer by Default", makes it your default printer. The "Remove Printer" entry remove the printer configuration from your system. The "Printer Details" entry opens a dialog with printer's details, such as the name, location, address, and driver. There are buttons for selecting a driver from a search, database, or a PPD file. Clicking on the "Printing Options" entry open the printer's options dialog (see Figure 14-43). You can configure printer features, such as page setup, image quality, and color. The Advanced tab lets you set specialized options, such as contrast, ink type, and saturation.

Figure 14-43: GNOME Printers - Details and Options

On the Settings Printers tab, you can click the Add button to open the Add Printer dialog, which lists printers attached to your system (see Figure 14-44). They are detected automatically. If you know the address of a printer on your network, you can enter it in the search box at the bottom to have it detected and displayed.

Figure 14-44: GNOME Printers - add printer

Remote Printers

Most newer printers support driverless printing. Available remote printers are detected automatically, and driverless configurations generated by CUPS. To manually search for a remote printer remote printer that is attached to a Windows system or another Linux system running CUPS, you specify its location, using special URL protocols. For another CUPS printer on a remote host, the protocol used is **ipp**, for Internet Printing Protocol, whereas for a Windows printer, it would be **smb**. Older Unix or Linux systems using LPRng would use the **lpd** protocol. Be sure your firewall is configured to allow access to remote printers.

Shared Windows printers on any of the computers connected to your local network are automatically accessible once configured. Be sure the Samba server is installed to let you access directly any of shared Windows printers.

Should you want to share a printer on your Ubuntu computer with users on other computers, you need to install the Samba server (Samba package) and have the Server Message Block services enabled using the **smbd** and **nmbd** daemons. You would then configure the printer as a shared device. You can use the **systemctl** command to restart, stop, and start the services.

```
sudo systemctl restart smbd
sudo systemctl restart nmbd
```

Also, be sure that the **smbclient** package is installed. Ubuntu does not install it by default.

```
sudo apt install smbclient
```

On the GNOME Settings Printers tab, click the Add button to open the Add Printer dialog listing Printers attached to your system. Remote printers will be automatically detected and listed. To manually add a remote printer and you know the address of the printer on your network, you can enter it in the search box at the bottom to have it detected and displayed.

Additional Printer Settings: system-config-printer

You can also use the older **system-config-printer** tool to edit a printer configuration or to add a remote printer. You can start **system-config-printer** by clicking the "Additional Printer Settings" button on the Settings Printers tab. A printer configuration window is displayed, showing icons for installed printers. As you add printers, icons for them are displayed in the Printer configuration window (see Figure 14-45).

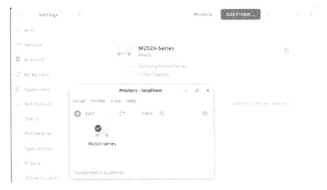

Figure 14-45: system-config-printer

To see the printer settings, such as printer and job options, access controls, and policies, double-click the printer icon or right-click and select Properties. The Printer Properties window opens with six tabs: Settings, Policies, Access Control, Printer Options, Job Options, and Ink/Toner Levels (see Figure 14-46).

Printer Properties - 'M2020-Series' on localhost

Settings	**Settings**
Policies	
Access Control	Description: Samsung M2020 Series
Printer Options	
Job Options	Location: richard-laptop
Ink/Toner Levels	
	Device URI: usb://Samsung/M2020%20Series?serial=070MB8GFAA00ZWD Change...
	Make and Model: Samsung M2020 Series Change...
	Printer State: Idle
	Tests and Maintenance
	Print Test Page

Cancel   OK

Figure 14-46: Printer Properties window

The Printer configuration window Printer menu lets you rename the printer, enable or disable it, and make it a shared printer. Select the printer icon and then click the Printer menu. The Delete entry will remove a printer configuration. Use the Set As Default entry to make the printer a system-wide or personal default printer. There are also entries for accessing the printer properties and viewing the print queue.

The Printer icon menu is accessed by right-clicking the printer icon. If the printer is already a default, there is no Set As Default entry. The Properties entry opens the printer properties window for that printer.

The View Print Queue entry opens the Document Print Status window, which lists the jobs for that printer. You can change the queue position as well as stop or delete jobs. From the toolbar, you can choose to display printed jobs and reprint them. You will be notified if a job should fail.

To check the server settings, select Settings from the Server menu. This opens a new window showing the CUPS printer server settings. The Common UNIX Printing System (CUPS) is the server that provides printing services (**www.cups.org**).

To select a particular CUPS server, select the Connect entry in the Server menu. This opens a Connect to CUPS Server window with a drop-down menu listing all current CUPS servers from which to choose.

To add, edit, or remove printers requires root-level access. You have to enter your root user password (set up initially during installation) to edit a printer configuration, add a new printer, or remove an old one. For example, when you try to access the printer server settings, you will be prompted to enter the administrative user password.

Again, when you edit any printer's configuration settings, you will be prompted for authorization. Whenever you try to change a printer setting, such as its driver or URI, you are prompted to enter the administrative password for device authorization.

To make a printer the default, either right-click the printer icon and select Set As Default or single-click the printer icon and then, from the Printer configuration window's Printer menu, select the Set As Default entry. A Set Default Printer dialog opens with options for setting the system-wide default or setting the personal default. The system-wide default printer is the default for your entire network served by your CUPS server, not just your local system. The system-wide default printer will have a green check mark emblem on its printer icon in the Printer configuration window (see Figure 14-47).

Figure 14-47: Default Printer

Should you wish to use a different printer as your default, you can designate it as your personal default. To make a printer your personal default, select the entry Set as My Personal Default Printer in the Set Default Printer dialog. A personal emblem, a heart, will appear on the printer's icon in the Printer configuration window.

If you have more than one printer on your system, you can make one the default by clicking the Make Default Printer button in the printer's properties Settings pane.

The Class entry in the New menu lets you create a printer class. You can access the New menu from the Server menu or from the New button. This feature lets you select a group of printers to print a job, instead of selecting just one. That way, if one printer is busy or down, another printer can be automatically selected to perform the job. Installed printers can be assigned to different classes.

To edit an installed printer, double-click its icon in the Printer configuration window or right-click and select the Properties entry. This opens a Printer Properties window for that printer. A sidebar lists the configuration tabs. Click one to display that tab. There are configuration entries for Settings, Policies, Access Control, Printer Options, Job Options, and Ink/Toner Levels.

To install a new printer, choose the Server | New | Printer menu entry or click the Add button on the toolbar (see Figure 14-48). A New Printer window opens and displays a series of dialog boxes from which you select the connection, model, drivers, and printer name with location.

Figure 14-48: system-config-printer - New Printer

The location is specified using special URI protocols. For another CUPS printer on a remote host, the protocol used is **ipp**, for Internet Printing Protocol, whereas for a Windows printer, it is **smb**. Older UNIX and Linux systems using LPRng use the **lpd** protocol.

You can also use system-config-printer to set up a remote printer on Linux, UNIX, or Windows networks. When you add a new printer or edit one, the New Printer dialog will list possible remote connection types under the Network entry. When you select a remote connection entry, a pane will be displayed to the right where you can enter configuration information.

First, you need to install the **smbclient** package along with **python3-smbc**, using the Synaptic Package Manager. This package is currently not installed by default.

To find any connected printers on your network automatically, click the Find Network Printer

Figure 14-49: Finding a network printer

entry. Enter the hostname of the system the remote printer is connected to, then click the Find button. The host is searched and the detected printers are displayed as entries under the Network Printer heading (see Figure 14-49). Because of the changes from SMB1 to SMB3 in Samba, the Find operation does not work for Windows printers.

To configure a specific type of printer, choose from the available entries. For a remote Linux or UNIX printer, select either Internet Printing Protocol (ipp), which is used for newer systems, or LPD/LPR Host or Printer, which is used for older systems. Both panes display entries for the Host name and the queue. For the Host name, enter the hostname of the system that controls the printer. For an Apple or HP jet direct printer on your network, select the AppSocket/HP jetDirect entry.

A "Windows printer via Samba" printer is one located on a Windows network. You need to specify the Windows server (hostname or IP address), the name of the share, the name of the printer's workgroup, and the username and password. The format of the printer SMB URL is shown on the SMP Printer pane. The share is the hostname and printer name in the **smb** URI format *//workgroup/hostname/printername*. The workgroup is the windows network workgroup that the printer belongs to. On small networks, there is usually only one. The hostname is the computer where the printer is located. The username and password can be for the printer resource itself, or for access by a particular user. The pane will display a box at the top where you can enter the share host and printer name as an **smb** URI.

Because of the changes from SMB1 to SMB3, the Browse operation accessed by the Browse button does not work. Because of this, you have to enter the exact name of the printer, including special characters such as spaces and parenthesis (see Figure 14-50). These special characters are referenced with a preceding percent sign, **%**, followed by the ASCII hexadecimal value for the character. A space is referenced as **%20**, an open parenthesis as **%28**, and a close parenthesis as **%29**. In these examples, the Windows name of the Samsung M2020 printer is:

```
Samsung M2020 Series (USB001)
```

This would be:

```
Samsung%20M2020%20Series%20%28USB001%29
```

Figure 14-50: Selecting a Windows printer with full name and authentication

Be sure to also include your host name. If you have multiple workgroups on your network, include the workgroup name also. The full entry for the previous example, with the host 'richard-asus" would be:

```
richard-asus/Samsung%20M2020%20Series%20%28USB001%29
```

With the workgroup name "workgroup" it would be:

```
workgroup/richard-asus/Samsung%20M2020%20Series%20%28USB001%29
```

You also can enter in any needed Samba authentication, if required, like username or password. Check "Authentication required" to allow you to enter the Samba Username and Password. The Connections section to the lower right will list "Windows Printer via Samba" as the connection. With the current version of Samba, if you do not enter it now though, it will prompt you for a user name and password when you try to use the printer. This may not work. To be sure of access you should enter the user and password on this dialog now.

You then continue with install screens for the printer model, driver, and name. Once installed, you can then access the printer properties just as you would any printer (see Figure 14-51).

Figure 14-51: Remote Windows printer Settings

The configured remote printer is then listed in the system-config-printer window, along with other printers (see Figure 14-52). When you choose to print from an application, the remote printer will be listed along with your local printers.

Figure 14-52: Remote Windows Printers

15. Network Connections

Ubuntu will automatically detect and configure your network connections with Network Manager. Should the automatic configuration either fail or be incomplete for some reason, you can perform a manual configuration using the GNOME Settings Wi-Fi and Network tabs. If you want to make a simple dial-up modem connection, you can use WvDial. Your network will also need a firewall. UFW (with the Gufw interface) or FirewallD is recommended. Table 15-1 lists several network configuration tools.

Network Connections: Dynamic and Static

If you are on a network, you may need to obtain certain information to configure your connection interface. Most networks now support dynamic configuration using either the older Dynamic Host Configuration Protocol (DHCP) or the IPv6 Protocol and its automatic address configuration. In this case, you need only check the DHCP entry in most network configuration tools. If your network does not support DHCP or IPv6 automatic addressing, or you are using a static connection (DCHP and IPv6 connections are dynamic), you will have to provide detailed information about your connection. For a static connection, you would enter your connection information manually such as your IP address and DNS servers, whereas in a dynamic connection this information is provided automatically to your system by a DHCP server or generated by IPv6 when you connect to the network. For DHCP, a DHCP client on each host will obtain the information from a DHCP server serving that network. IPv6 generates its addresses directly from the device and router information such as the device hardware MAC address.

Network Configuration Tool	Description
Network Manager	Used for all network connections including wired, wireless, mobile broadband, VPN, and DSL. **nmcli** is the command line interface version of Network Manager.
Network (Settings)	GNOME Network connection preferences, allowing quick connection to wired networks and proxies.
Wi-Fi (Settings)	GNOME Wi-Fi connection preferences, allowing quick connection to wireless networks.
ufw	Sets up a network firewall.
Gufw	GNOME interface for UFW firewall
FirewallD	Sets up a network firewall.
wvdial	PPP dial-up modem connection
systemd-networkd	systemd-based network configuration

Table 15-1: Ubuntu Network Configuration Tools

In addition, if you are using a dynamic DSL, ISDN, or a modem connection, you will also have to supply provider, login, and password information, and specify whether your system is dynamic or static. You may also need to supply specialized information such as DSL or modem compression methods or dialup number.

You can obtain most of your static network information from your network administrator, or from your ISP (Internet Service Provider). You would need the following information:

The device name for your network interface   For LAN and wireless connections, this is network device name, which you can find using the **ifconfig** or **ip l** commands. For a modem, DSL, or ISDN connection, this is a PPP device named **ppp0** (**ippp0** for ISDN). Virtual private network (VPN) connections are also supported.

Hostname   Your computer will be identified by this name on the Internet. Do not use localhost; that name is reserved for special use by your system. The name of the host should be a simple word, which can include numbers, but not punctuation such as periods and backslashes. On a small network, the hostname is often a single name. On a large network that could have several domains, the hostname includes both the name of the host and its domain.

Domain name   This is the name of your network.

The Internet Protocol (IP) address assigned to your machine   This is needed only for static Internet connections. Dynamic connections use the DHCP protocol to assign an IP address for you automatically. Every host on the Internet is assigned an IP address. Small and older network addresses might still use the older IPv4 format consisting of a set of four numbers, separated by periods. The IP protocol version 6, IPv6, uses a new format with a complex numbering sequence that is much more automatic.

Your network IP address   Static connections only. This address is similar to the IP address but lacks any reference to a particular host.

The netmask   IPv4 Static connections only. This is usually 255.255.255.0 for most networks. If, however, you are part of a large network, check with your network administrator or ISP.

The broadcast address for your network, if available (optional)   IPv4 Static connections only. Usually, your broadcast address is the same as your IP address with the number 255 added at the end.

The IP address of your network's gateway computer   Static connections only. This is the computer that connects your local network to a larger one like the Internet.

Name servers   The IP address of the name servers your network uses. These enable the use of URLs.

NIS domain and IP address for an NIS server   Necessary if your network uses an NIS server (optional).

User login and password information   Needed for dynamic DSL, ISDN, and modem connections.

Network Manager

Network Manager detects your network connections automatically, both wired and wireless. It uses the automatic device detection capabilities of udev to configure your connections. Should you instead need to configure your network connections manually, you can also use Network Manager to enter the required network connection information. Network Manager operates as a daemon with the name NetworkManager. It will automatically scan for both wired and wireless connections. Information provided by Network Manager is made available to other applications.

Network Manager is designed to work in the background, providing status information for your connection and switching from one configured connection to another as needed. For an initial configuration, it detects as much information as possible about a new connection.

Network Manager is also user specific. When a user logs in, wireless connections the user prefers will start up (wired connections are started automatically).

User and System-Wide Network Configuration: Network Manager

Network Manager will automatically detect your network connections, both wired and wireless. It is the default method for managing your network connections. Network Manager makes use of the automatic device detection capabilities of udev to configure your connections. Should you instead have to configure your network connections manually, you would use the GNOME Settings Wi-Fi and Network tabs.

Network Manager is user specific. When a user logs in, it selects the network connection preferred by that user. For wireless connections, the user can choose from a list of current possible connections. For wired connections, a connection can be started automatically, when the system starts up. Initial settings will be supplied from the system-wide configuration.

Configurations can also be applied system-wide to all users. When editing or adding a network connection, the edit or add dialog displays an Available to All Users check box in the lower-left corner. Click this check box and then click the Apply button to make the connection configuration system-wide. A PolicyKit authentication dialog will first prompt you to enter your administrative password.

Network Manager can configure any network connection. This includes wired, wireless, and all manual connections. Network Interface Connection (NIC cards) hardware is detected using udev. Information provided by Network Manager is made available to other applications over D-Bus.

With multiple wireless access points for Internet connections, a system could have several different network connections to choose from, instead of a single-line connection such as DSL or fiber. This is particularly true for notebook computers that access different wireless connections at different locations. Instead of manually configuring a new connection each time one is encountered, the Network Manager tool can automatically configure and select a connection to use.

By default, an Ethernet connection will be preferred, if available. For wireless connections, you will have to choose the one you want.

Network Manager is designed to work in the background, providing status information for your connection and switching from one configured connection to another, as needed. For initial configuration, it detects as much information as possible about the new connection.

Network Manager operates as a daemon with the name **NetworkManager**. If no Ethernet connection is available, Network Manager will scan for wireless connections, checking for Extended Service Set Identifiers (ESSIDs). If an ESSID identifies a previously used connection, then it is automatically selected. If several are found, then the most recently used one is chosen. If only a new connection is available, the Network Manager waits for the user to choose one. A connection is selected only if the user is logged in. If an Ethernet connection is later made, the Network Manager will switch to it from wireless.

The NetworkManager daemon can be turned on or off, using the **systemctl** command as the root user.

```
sudo systemctl start NetworkManager
sudo systemctl stop NetworkManager
```

Network Manager Manual Configuration using GNOME Settings

The GNOME Network configuration is available on GNOME Settings, can be used to configure all your network connections manually. Automatic wireless and wired connections were covered in Chapter 3. On the GNOME Settings dialog there is a Wi-Fi tab for wireless configuration and a Network tab for wired, VPN, and proxy configurations (see Figure 15-1). On the Wi-Fi tab, an Airplane Mode switch and a list of visible wireless connections are listed to the right. The currently active connection will have a checkmark next to its name. On the top right bar is a switch for turning wireless on and off. A menu to the right of the switch list entries for connections to hidden networks, turning on your computer's Wi-Fi hotspot capability, and listing previously accessed Wi-Fi Networks.

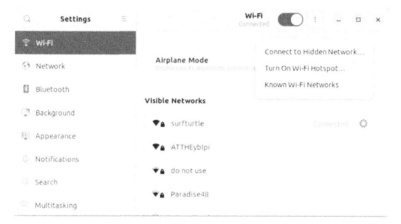

Figure 15-1: Wi-Fi (GNOME Settings)

Selecting an entry in the Visible Networks list will create a gear button for it, which you can click to open the network configuration dialog with tabs for Details, Security, Identity, IPv4, IPv6, and Reset. The Details tab show strength, speed, security methods, IP and hardware addresses, routes, and the DNS server IP address (see Figure 15-2). You can choose to connect automatically and whether to make the connection system-wide. You can also choose to impose data limits. It also has a "Forget Connection" button for removing this Wi-Fi connection information.

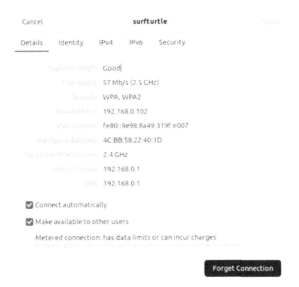

Figure 15-2: Wi-Fi (GNOME Settings) - Details tab

To edit the connection manually, you use the Security, Identity, and IP tabs. The Security tab displays a menu from which you can choose a security method and a password (see Figure 15-3).

Figure 15-3: Wi-Fi (GNOME Settings) - Security tab

On the Identity tab, you can specify the SSID name and MAC Address (see Figure 15-4).

Figure 15-4: Wi-Fi (GNOME Settings) - Identity tab

On the IPv4 and IPv6 Settings tabs, there are sections for Method, Addresses, the DNS servers, and Routes. In the Method section you can choose the type connection you want. By default, it is set to Automatic. If you change it to Manual, the Address section appears for the address, netmask, and gateway (see Figure 15-5). On the IPv6 tab, the netmask in the Address section is replaced by prefix. The disable option turns off the connection. You can turn off Automatic switches for the DNS and Routes sections to make them manual. Separate multiple DNS IP addresses with a comma.

Figure 15-5: Wi-Fi (GNOME Settings) - IPv4 tab, Manual

For a wired connection, click the Network tab on GNOME Settings to display lists for Wired, VPN, and Network Proxy. The Wired list shows your current wired connections with on and off switched for each. A plus button at the top right of the Wired list lets you add more wired connections. Next to a connection's switch a gear button is displayed (see Figure 15-6). Clicking the gear button opens a configuration dialog with tabs for Details, Identity, IPv4, IPv6, and Security (see Figure 15-7).

Figure 15-6: Network (GNOME Settings)

The Details tab list the connection information such as the speed IP addresses, hardware addresses, route, and DNS server. You can choose to connect automatically and whether to make the connection system-wide. You can also choose to impose data limits.

Figure 15-7: Wired Configuration -Details tab

You can use the Security, Identity, and IP tabs to manually configure the connection. The Security tab lets you turn on 802.1x security and choose an authentication method, as well as provide a username and password (see Figure 15-8).

Figure 15-8: Wired Configuration - Security tab

On the Identity tab, you can set the name, choose the hardware address and set the MTU blocks (see Figure 15-9).

Figure 15-9: Wired Configuration - Identity tab

The IPv4 and IPv6 Settings tabs have sections for Method, Addresses, DNS servers, and Routes. From the Method set of options at the top, you can also choose to make the connection automatic, manual, link-local, or to disable it. If you choose manual, The Addresses section appears, which lets you enter the address, netmask, and gateway (see Figure 15-10). On the IPv6 tab, the netmask entry is replaced by a prefix entry. DNS and Routes have a switch for automatic. Turning the switch off allows you to manually enter a DNS server address or routing information.

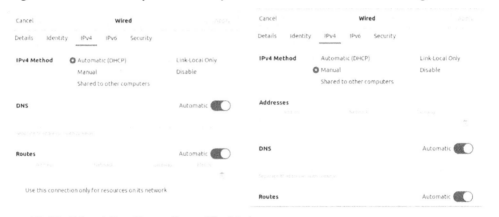

Figure 15-10: Wired Configuration - IPv4 tab

For VPN connections, click the plus button at the top right of the VPN list in the Settings Network tab to open an Add VPN dialog. The dialog lists supported VPN connection types, such as Point-to-Point or OpenVPN (see Figure 15-11). The Bond, Bridge, and VLAN entries open the Network Connections dialogs for those connections.

Figure 15-11: Network (GNOME Settings), new connections and VPN connections

You can then configure the VPN connections in the "Add VPN" dialog, which shows three tabs: Identity, IPv4, and IPv6 (see Figure 15-12). The IP tabs are the same as for wireless and wired configuration dialogs. On the Identity tab, you can enter the name, gateway, and authentication information. Click the Advanced button for detailed connection configuration.

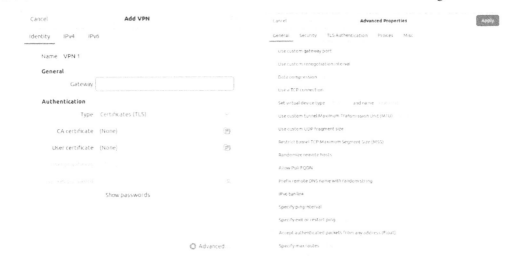

Figure 15-12: Network (GNOME Settings) OpenVPN connection

Several VPN services are available from the Universe repository (not Snap). You can install them with either the Synaptic Package Manager (search on network-manager) or the **apt** command. The PPTP service for Microsoft VPN connections and OpenVPN are installed by default. Other popular VPN services include Fortinet (SSL), OpenConnect (SSL), Layer 2 Tunneling Protocol (IPSec encryption), Cisco Concentrator, Iodine (DNS tunneling), and Openswan (IPSec). Network Manager support is installed using the corresponding Network Manager plugin for these services. The plugin packages begin with the name **network-manager**. OpenVPN, which uses the **openvpn** software along with the **network-manager-openvpn** plugin, is install be default. For the Layer 2 Tunneling Protocol VPN install the **network-manager-l2tp** plugin. For the Fortinet SSL VPN install the **network-manager-fortisslvpn** plugin. For the OpenConnect VPN (Juniper SSL client) install the **network-manager-openconnect** plugin. For Cisco Concentrator based VPN, install the **network-manager-vpnc** plugin. Strongswan uses the

network-manager-strongswan plugin. For the Iodine VPN (DNS tunneling) install the **network-manager-iodine** plugin.

Wireguard VPN

Ubuntu supports the new Wireguard virtual network manager, which provides better encryption and efficiency than the older IPsec and OpenVPN tools. Wireguard works by setting up dedicated network interfaces (**wg**), which are then used for the VPN connections. There is no NetworkManager support for Wireguard as yet. Check the Wireguard Web site for instructions on how to configure and manage a Wireguard connection (**https://www.wireguard.com**). You can install Wireguard with Ubuntu Software (Snap repository), the **apt** command (Universe repository), or with the Synaptic Package Manager (Universe repository).

```
sudo apt install wireguard
```

Network Manager Manual Configuration Using Network Connections: nm-connection-editor

You can also use the older Network Connections utility (**nm-connection-editor**) to edit any network connection. It is part of the **network-manager-gnome** package, which is installed by default. You can run it from a terminal window with the following command.

```
sudo nm-connection-editor
```

Established connections are listed, with at toolbar at the bottom for adding, removing, and editing network connections (see Figure 15-13). Your current network connections should already be listed.

Figure 15-13: Network configuration (nm-connection-editor)

When you add a connection, you can choose its type from a drop-down menu. The menu organizes connection types into three categories: Hardware, Virtual, and VPN. Hardware connections cover both wired (Ethernet, DSL, and InfiniBand) and wireless (Wi-Fi, WiMAX, and Mobile Broadband) connections. VPN lists the supported VPN types, such as OpenVPN, PPTP, and Cisco. You can also import a previously configured connection. Virtual supports VLAN and Bond virtual connections.

Configuration editing dialogs display a General tab from which you can make your configuration available to all users and automatically connect when the network connection is available. You can also choose to use a VPN connection and specify a firewall zone.

Editing an Ethernet connection opens an Editing window. The Create button on the "Choose a Connection Type" dialog is used to add a new connection and opens a similar window, with no settings. The Ethernet tab lists the MAC hardware address and the MTU. The MTU is usually set to automatic. The standard default configuration for a wired Ethernet connection uses DHCP. Connect automatically will set up the connection when the system starts up. There are seven tabs, General, Ethernet, 8.02.1x Security, DCB, Proxy, IPv4 Settings, and IPv6 Settings. The IPv4 Settings tab lets you select the kind of wired connection you have. The manual configuration entries for an IPv4 connection are shown in Figure 15-14. Click the Add button to enter the IP address, network mask, and gateway address. Then enter the address for the DNS servers and your network search domains. The Routes button will open a window in which you can manually enter any network routes.

Figure 15-14: IPv4 wired configuration (nm-connection-editor)

For a wireless connection, you enter wireless configuration data, such as your ESSID, password, and encryption method. For wireless connections, you choose Wi-Fi or WiMAX as the connection type. The Editing Wi-Fi connection window opens with tabs for general configuration, your wireless information, security, proxy, and IP settings (see Figure 15-15). On the Wi-Fi tab, you specify your SSID, along with your mode and MAC address.

On the Wi-Fi Security tab, you enter your wireless connection security method. The commonly used method, WEP, is supported, along with WPA personal. The WPA personal method only requires a password. More secure connections, such as Dynamic WEP and Enterprise WPA, are also supported. These will require much more configuration information, such as authentication methods, certificates, and keys.

For a new broadband connection, choose the Mobile Broadband entry in the connection type menu. A 3G wizard starts up to help you set up the appropriate configuration for your particular 3G service. Configuration steps are listed on the left pane. If your device is connected, you can select it from the drop-down menu on the right pane.

Figure 15-15: Wireless configuration (nm-connection-editor)

Once a service is selected, you can further edit the configuration by clicking its entry in the Mobile Broadband tab and clicking the Edit button. The Editing window opens with tabs for Mobile Broadband, PPP, IPv4, and IPv6 settings. On the Mobile Broadband tab, you can enter your number, username, and password. Advanced options include the APN, Network, and PIN. The APN should already be entered.

On the Network Manager panel applet menu, the VPN Connection entry submenu will list configured VPN connections for easy access. The Configure VPN entry will open the Network Connections window to the VPN section, from which you can then add, edit, or delete VPN connections. The Disconnect VPN entry will end the current active VPN connection. To add a VPN connection, choose a VPN connection type from the connection type menu.

The Editing VPN Connection dialog opens with two tabs: VPN and IPv4 Settings. On the VPN tab, you enter VPN connection information, such as the gateway address and any additional VPN information that may be required. For an OpenVPN connection, you will have to provide the authentication type, certificates, and keys. Clicking the Advanced button opens the Advanced Options dialog. An OpenVPN connection will have tabs for General, Security, and TLS Authentication. On the Security tab, you can specify the cipher to use.

Note: If your system detects a cellular network modem (Wireless WAN Cellular device), you can use the System Settings Mobile Network tab to configure it.

Network Manager wireless router, using your wireless connection as a Hotspot and for a Hidden Network.

You can set up your wireless connection as a wireless router for your own wireless network. The "Turn On Wi-Fi Hotspot" entry in the Wi-Fi menu of the Wi-Fi dialog in Settings, opens a dialog letting you set up your computer as a wireless router that other computers can connect to (see Figure 15-16) .

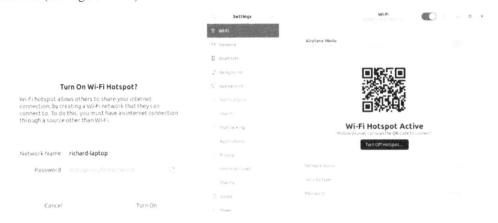

Figure 15-16: Turn on Wi-Fi Hotspot

The wireless network you created will not perform any SSID broadcasting. You access it through the "Connect to Hidden Network" entry on the network menu. This opens the "Connect to Hidden Wi-Fi Network" window (see Figure 15-17).

Figure 15-17: Connect to a Hidden Wi-Fi Network

Managing Network Connections with nmcli

The **nmcli** command is NetworkManager Command Line Interface command. Most network configuration tasks can be performed by **nmcli**. The **nmcli** command manages NetworkManager through a set of objects: general (**g**), networking (**n**), radio (**r**), connection (**c**), device (**d**), and agent (**a**). Each can be referenced using the full name or a unique prefix, such as **con** for connection or **dev** for device. The unique prefix can be as short as a single character, such as **g** for general, **c** for connections, or **d** for device. See Table 15-2 for a list of the objects and commonly used options. The **nmcli** man page provides a complete listing with examples.

Object	Description
`general`	NetworkManager status and enabled devices. Use the terse (**-t**) and field (**-f**) option to limit the information displayed.
`networking`	Manage networking, use `on` and `off` to turn networking on or off, and `connectivity` for the connection state.
`radio`	Turns on or off the wireless networking (on or off). Can turn on or off specific kinds of wireless: `wifi`, `wwan` (mobile broadband), and `wimax`. The `all` option turns on or off all wireless.
`connection`	Manage network connections.
	`show` List connection profiles. With `--active` show only active connections.
	`up` Activate a connection
	`down` Deactivate a connection
	`add` Add a new connection, specifying `type`, `ifname`, `con-name` (profile).
	`modify` Edit an existing connection, use + and – to add new values to properties
	`edit` Add a new connection or edit an existing one using the interactive editor
	`delete` Delete a configured connection (profile)
	`reload` Reload all connection profiles
	`load` Reload or load a specific
`device`	Manage network interfaces (devices).
	`status` Display device status
	`show` Display device information
	`connect` Connect the device
	`disconnect` Disconnect the device
	`delete` Delete a software device, such as a bridge.
	`wifi` Display a list of available wifi access points
	`wifi rescan` Rescan for and display access points
	`wifi connect` Connect to a wifi network; specify `password`, `wep-key-type`, `ifname`, `bssid`, and `name` (profile name)
	`wimax` List available WiMAX networks
`agent`	Run as a Network Manager secret agent or polkit agent.
	`secret` As a secret agent, nmcli listens for secret requests.
	`polkit` As a polkit agent it listens for all authorization requests.

Table 15-2: The nmcli objects

The general object shows the current status of NetworkManager and what kind of devices are enabled. You can limit the information displayed using the **-t** (terse) and **-f** (field) options. The STATE field show the connection status, and the CONNECTIVITY field the connection.

```
$ nmcli general
STATE        CONNECTIVITY  WIFI-HW  WIFI      WWAN-HW   WWAN
connected    full          enabled  enabled   enabled   enabled

$ nmcli -t -f STATE general
connected
```

The **connection** object references the network connection and the **show** option displays that information. The following example displays your current connection.

nmcli connection showYou can use **c** instead of **connection** and **s** instead of show.

```
$ nmcli c s
NAME        UUID                                            TYPE             DEVICE
enp7s0      f7202f6d-fc66-4b81-8962-69b71202efc0  802-3-ethernet   enp7s0
AT&T LTE 1  65913b39-789a-488c-9559-28ea6341d9e1  gsm              --
```

As with the general object, you can limit the fields displayed using the **-f** option. The following only list the name and type fields.

```
$ nmcli -f name,type c s
NAME        TYPE
enp7s0      802-3-ethernet
AT&T LTE 1  gsm
```

Adding the **--active** option will only show active connections.

```
nmcli c s --active
```

To start and stop a connection (like **ifconfig** does), use the **up** and **down** options.

```
nmcli con up enp7s0.
```

Use the **device** object to manage your network devices. The **show** and **status** options provide information about your devices. To check the status of all your network devices use the **device** object and **status** options:

```
nmcli device status
DEVICE   TYPE      STATE          CONNECTION
enp7s0   ethernet  connected      enp7s0
wlp6s0   wifi      disconnected   --
lo       loopback  unmanaged      --
```

You can abbreviate **device** and **status** to **d** and **s**.

```
nmcli d s
```

You also use the **device** object to connect and disconnect devices. Use the **connect** or **disconnect** options with the interface name (ifname) of the device, in this example, **enp7s0**. With the **delete** option, you can remove a device.

```
nmcli device disconnect enp7s0
nmcli device connect enp7s0
```

To turn networking on or off you use the **networking** object and the **on** and **off** options. Use the **connectivity** option to check network connectivity. The networking object alone tells you if it is enabled or not.

```
$ nmcli networking
enabled
```

```
$ nmcli networking on
```

```
$ nmcli networking connectivity
full
```

Should you want to just turn on or off the Wifi connection, you would use the **radio** object. Use **wifi**, **wwan**, and **wimax** for a specific type of wifi connection and the **all** option for all of them. The radio object alone shows wifi status of all your wifi connection types.

```
$ nmcli radio
WIFI-HW   WIFI WWAN-HW   WWAN
enabled  enabled  enabled  enabled
```

```
$ nmcli radio wifi on
```

```
$ nmcli radio all off
```

nmcli Wired Connections

You can use **nmcli** to add connections, just as you can with the desktop NetworkManager tool. To add a new static connection use the connection object with the **add** option. Specify the connection's profile name with the **con-name** option, the interface name with the **ifname** option, the **type**, such as ethernet. For a static connection you would add the IP address (**ipv4** or **ipv6**), and the gateway address (**gw4** or **gw6**). For a DHCP connection simply do not list the IP address and gateway options. The profile name can be any name. You could have several profile names for the same network device. For example, for your wireless device, you could have several wireless connection profiles, depending on the different networks you want to connect to. Should you connect your Ethernet device to a different network, you would simply use a different connection profile that you have already set up, instead of manually reconfiguring the connection. If you do not specify a connection name, one is generated and assigned for you. The connection name can be the same as the device name as shown here, but keep in mind that the connection name refers to the profile and the device name refers to the actual device.

```
$ nmcli c s
NAME        UUID                                     TYPE          DEVICE
enp7s0      f7202f6d-fc66-4b81-8962-69b71202efc0  802-3-ethernet  enp7s0
```

For a DHCP connection, specify the profile name, connection type, and ifname. The following example creates an Ethernet connection with the profile name "my-wired."

```
nmcli con add con-name my-wired type ethernet ifname enp7s0
```

For a static connection add the IP (**ip4** or **ip6**) and gateway (**gw4** or **gw6**) options with their addresses.

```
nmcli con add con-name my-wired-static ifname enp7s0 type ethernet ip4
192.168.1.0/24 gw4 192.168.1.1
```

In most cases, the type is Ethernet (wired) or wifi (wireless). Check the **nmcli** man page for a list of other types, such as gsm, infiniband, vpn, vlan, wimax, and bridge.

You can also add a connection using the interactive editor. Use the **edit** instead of the **add** option, and specify the **con-name** (profile) and connection type.

```
nmcli con edit type ethernet con-name my-wired
```

To modify an existing connection, use the **modify** option. For an IP connection, the property that is changed is referenced as part of the IP settings, in this example, **ip4**. The IP properties include addresses, gateway, and method (ip4.addresses, ip4.gateway, and ip4.method).

```
nmcli con mod my-wired ip4.gateway 192.168.1.2
```

To add or remove a value for a property use the + and - signs as a prefix. To add a DNS server address you would use **+ip4.dns**. To remove one use **-ip4.dns**.

```
nmcli con mod my-wired +ip4.dns 192.168.1.5
```

You can also modify a connection using the interactive editor. Use the edit instead of the modify option with the connection name.

```
nmcli con edit enp7s0
```

You are then placed in the interactive editor with an **nmcli>** prompt and the settings you can change are listed. The **help** command lists available commands. Use the **describe** command to show property descriptions.

Use **print** to show the current value of a property and **set** to change its value. To see all the properties for a setting, use the **print** command and the setting name. Once you have made changes, use the **save** command to effect the changes.

```
print ipv4
print ipv4.dns
print connection
set ipv4.address 192.168.0.1
```

The connection edit command can also reference a profile using the **id** option. The Name field in the connection profile information is the same as the ID. Also, each profile is given a unique system UUID, which can also be used to reference the profile.

Once you are finished editing the connection, enter the **quit** command to leave the editor.

nmcli Wireless Connections

To see a list of all the available wifi connections in your area, you use the **wifi** option with the **device** object. You can further qualify it by interface (if you have more than one) by adding the **ifname** option, and by BSSID adding the **bssid** option.

```
nmcli device wifi
```

To connect to a new Wifi network, use the **wifi connect** option and the SSID. You can further specify a password, wep-key-type, key, ifname, bssid, name (profile name), and if it is private. If you do not provide a name (profile name), nmcli will generate one for you.

```
nmcli dev wifi connect surfturtle password mypass wep-key-type wpa ifname wlp6s0
name my-wireless1
```

To reconnect to a Wifi network for which you have previously set up a connection, use the **connection** object with the **up** command and the **id** option to specify the profile name.

```
nmcli connection up id my-wireless1
```

You can also add a new wireless connection using the **connection** object and the **wifi** type with the **ssid** option.

```
nmcli con add con-name my-wireless2 ifname wlp6s0 type wifi ssid ssidname
```

Then, to set the encryption type use the **modify** command to set the **sec.key-mgmt** property, and for the passphrase set the **wifi-sec.psk** property.

```
nmcli con mod my-wirless2 wifi-sec.key-mgmt wpa-psk
nmcli con modify my-wireless2 wifi-sec.psk mypassword
```

Variable	Description
Inherits	Explicitly inherits from the specified section. By default, sections inherit from the [Dialer Defaults] section.
Modem	The device wvdial should use as your modem. The default is **/dev/modem**.
Baud	The speed at which wvdial communicates with your modem. The default is 57,600 baud.
Init1...Init9	Specifies the initialization strings to be used by your modem; wvdial can use up to 9. The default is "ATZ" for Init1.
Phone	The phone number you want wvdial to dial.
Area Code	Specifies the area code, if any.
Dial Prefix	Specifies any needed dialing prefix—for example, 70 to disable call waiting or 9 for an outside line.
Dial Command	Specifies the dial operation. The default is "ATDT".
Login	Specifies the username you use at your ISP.
Login Prompt	If your ISP has an unusual login prompt, you can specify it here.
Password	Specifies the password you use at your ISP.
Password Prompt	If your ISP has an unusual password prompt, you can specify it here.
Force Address	Specifies a static IP address to use (for ISPs that provide static IP addresses to users).
Auto Reconnect	If enabled, wvdial attempts to reestablish a connection automatically if you are randomly disconnected by the other side. This option is on by default.

Table 15-3: Variables for wvdial

Dial-up PPP Modem Access: wvdial

For direct dial-up PPP modem connections, you can use the wvdial dialer, an intelligent dialer that, not only dials up an ISP service but also performs login operations, supplying your username and password. The wvdial tool runs on the command line using the wvdial command, and on the desktop with the GNOME PPP application. The wvdial program first loads its configuration from the **/etc/wvdial.conf** file. In this file, you can place modem and account information, including modem speed, ISP phone number, username, and password.

The **wvdial.conf** file is organized into sections, beginning with a section label enclosed in brackets. A section holds variables for different parameters that are assigned values, such as **username = chris**. The default section holds default values inherited by other sections, so you need not repeat them. Table 15-3 lists the wvdial variables.

You can use the **wvdialconf** utility to create a default **wvdial.conf** file, detecting your modem and setting default values for basic features automatically. You can then edit the **wvdial.conf** file and modify the Phone, Username, and Password entries entering your dial-up information. Remove the preceding semicolon (**;**) to unquote the entry. Any line beginning with a semicolon is ignored as a comment.

You can also create a named dialer. This is helpful if you have different location or services you log in to.

To start wvdial, enter the command **wvdial** in a terminal window, which then reads the connection configuration information from the **/etc/wvdial.conf** file; wvdial dials the location and initiates the PPP connection, providing your username and password when requested.

You can set up connection configurations for any number of connections in the **/etc/wvdial.conf** file. To select one, enter its label as an argument to the **wvdial** command, as shown here:

```
wvdial mylocation
```

Netplan

Netplan is used to configure and set up your network connections. The **/etc/netplan** folder holds network service and interface information for configuring your network device. The actual configuration file is generated when the system starts up and, for NetworkManager, is placed in the **/run/NetworkManager/system-connections** folder (for systemd-networkd it is placed in the **/var/run/systemd/network** folder). There is no fixed configuration file in the **/etc** folder. Instead a simple Netplan configuration file in the **/etc/netplan** folder is used to generate the network configuration file. The **/etc/netplan** files are written using YAML (YAML Ain't Markup Language) and have the extension **.yaml**. This method provides a level of abstraction that make configuration of different available network devices much more flexible. The default network service for the Ubuntu desktop is NetworkManager and for the Ubuntu server it is **networkd**. You can use networkd on the Ubuntu desktop, instead of NetworkManager if you want. You can find out more about Netplan at:

```
https://netplan.io
```

Use the **networkctl status** command to check on the status of your network connections.

```
networkctl status
```

For information about a specific device add the device name to the status command.

```
networkctl status enp7s0
```

Detailed examples of Netplan configurations files can be found at:

```
/usr/share/doc/netplan/examples
```

These include examples for static, wireless, NetworkManager, dhcp, bridge, bonding, and vlans.

Netplan configuration file

The Netplan configuration files are located in the **/etc/netplan** folder. The Ubuntu Desktop version generates a Netplan configuration file for NetworkManager, **01-network-manager-all.yaml**. NetworkManager is the default for the Ubuntu desktop. You can edit this file to add configuration for more devices, or you can add more configuration files, each of which will be read by Netplan and a corresponding runtime configuration file generated in the **/run/NetworkManager/system-connections** folder. As NetworkManager is designed to configure multiple devices, you only need the one Netplan configuration file. But for other network managers such as **systemd-network**, you could have files for different types of network devices such as ethernet and Wi-Fi, or a different file for each device. Configuration file names usually begin with a number, starting with **1-** for the default, though they can be any name. An easy way to create a new file is to copy the default or an example file from **/usr/share/doc/netplan/examples** and then edit it.

A Netplan configuration file is organized into keys consisting of upper level configuration definitions that apply to different types of devices such as ethernets, and lower level IDs that are used to configure devices. The file begins with the top-level **network:** key followed by the Netplan version, in this case, version 2. The **renderer:** ID specifies the network service to use. For the Ubuntu desktop this is **NetworkManager**. Ubuntu uses NetworkManager by default instead of systemd-networkd, which simplifies the default Netplan configuration file. The file holds only the renderer information, as NetworkManager handles all the details. You would use the Settings Network or Network Connections to configure your network.

/etc/netplan/01-network-manager-all.yaml

```
# Let NetworkManager manage all devices on this system
network:
  version: 2
  renderer: NetworkManager
```

For other types of connections such as systemd-networkd, there are additional keys you can use. For a wired connection, the configuration type is **ethernets:** Under **ethernets:** the keys for the available network devices are listed. Under each device are the IDs used to configure it. In the case of a DHCP connection you usually only need one, **dhcp:** Other IDs such as **address:** for a static connection or **gateway:** for a gateway address could also be listed. An sample configuration is shown here.

The run time configuration files for NetworkManager are in the **/run/NetworkManager/system-connections** folder and have the NetworkManager name of the connection, such as **'Wired connection-1'.nmconnections**.

Configure a network with systemd-networkd

The systemd based network manager called **systemd-networkd** can currently be used for basic operations. You would use it as a small, fast, and simple alternative to a larger manager such as NetworkManager. The service, target, and socket files for systemd-networkd are located in the

/lib/systemd/system: **systemd-networkd.service** and **systemd-networkd.socket.** Network resolvconf operations are handled with **systemd-resolved.service**. User configuration files for **systemd-networkd** are located in **/etc/systemd/network**.

In the **systemd-networkd.service** file several security features are enabled. A capability bounding set (CapabilityBoundingSet) lets you limit kernel capabilities to those specified. The man page for **capabilities** list the available capabilities. The CAP_NET capabilities limit the networkd service to network operations such as interface configuration, firewall administration, multicasting, sockets, broadcasting, and proxies. The CAP_SET capabilities allow for file and process GID and UIDs. The CAP_CHOWN, CAP_DAC_OVERRIDE, and CAP_FOWNER capabilities deal with bypassing permission checks for files. The CAP_SYS capabilities that provide system administrative capabilities are not included. In addition, the ProtectSystem option (**systemd.exec**) prevents the service from making any changes to the system (**/usr**, **/boot**, and **/etc** folders are read only for this service). The ProtectHome option makes the **/home**, **/root**, and **/run/user** folders inaccessible. WatchdogSec sets the watchdog timeout for the service. Check the **systemd.directives** man page for a list of all systemd directives.

```
ExecStart=/lib/systemd/systemd-networkd
CapabilityBoundingSet=CAP_NET_ADMIN CAP_NET_BIND_SERVICE CAP_NET_BROADCAST
CAP_NET_RAW CAP_SETUID CAP_SETGID CAP_SETPCAP CAP_CHOWN CAP_DAC_OVERRIDE
CAP_FOWNER
ProtectSystem=strict
ProtectHome=yes
WatchdogSec=3min
```

The **systemd-networkd.socket** file sets **systemd.socket** options for buffer size (ReceiveBuffer), network link (ListenNetlink), passing credentials (PassCredentials). As a condition for starting the service, the CAP_NET_ADMIN capability needs to be set in the capability bounding set (ConditionCapability).

systemd-networkd.socket

```
[Unit]
Description=Network Service Netlink Socket
Documentation=man:systemd-networkd.service(8) man:rtnetlink(7)
ConditionCapability=CAP_NET_ADMIN
DefaultDependencies=no
Before=sockets.target

[Socket]
ReceiveBuffer=8M
ListenNetlink=route 1361
PassCredentials=yes

[Install]
WantedBy=sockets.target
```

The **systemd-resolved.service** provides for the resolvconf operations (DNS server information). It has the same capabilities as **systemd-neworkd.service**, except for the network capabilities.

In addition, the **systemd-networkd-resolvconf-update.service** updates the DNS information. The **systemd-networkd-wait-online.service** delays activation of other services, until **systemd-networkd** service comes online.

The systemd-networkd Netplan configuration file

You have to create a Netplan configuration file for the systemd-networkd service. You could have files for different types of network devices such as ethernet and Wi-Fi, or a different file for each device. Configuration file names usually begin with a number, starting with **1-** for the default, though they can be any name.

You would then have to know how networking on your system is configured. For many systems, especially those using DHCP, this is a simple configuration, but for others, such as a static connection, it can be complex. For a system using a standard DHCP connection, as shown in this chapter, you can simply copy the **dhcp.yaml** file from the **/usr/share/doc/netplan/examples** folder to the **/etc/netplan** folder. Prefix the file name with a number, such as **2-**. You can leave the **01-network-manager-all.yaml** file in **/etc/netplan** in case you should want to switch back to using NetworkManager

```
cd /usr/share/doc/netplan/examples
sudo cp dhcp.yaml /etc/netplan/02-dhcp.yaml
```

If you do not know it already, find out the name of your Ethernet device with **ip link** command. Then use a text editor like **nano** to edit the **02-dhcp.yaml** and replace the name of ethernet device, **enp3s0**, with the name of the one on your system. You can use the **ifconfig** command to find the name or your device. Be sure to use the **sudo** command to start the editor.

```
cd /etc/netplan
sudo nano 02-dhcp.yaml
```

A Netplan configuration file is organized into keys consisting of upper level configuration definitions that apply to different types of devices such as ethernets, and lower level IDs that are used to configure devices. The file begins with the top-level **network:** key followed by the Netplan version, in this case, version 2. The **renderer:** ID specifies the network service to use. For the Ubuntu server this is the netplan default, **networkd**. For a wired connection, the configuration type is **ethernets:**, as shown in this example. Under **ethernets:** the keys for the available network devices are listed. Under each device are the IDs used to configure it. In the case of a DHCP connection you usually only need one, **dhcp:** Other IDs such as **address:** for a static connection or **gateway:** for a gateway address could also be listed. The final would look something like the following.

/etc/netplan/02-dhcp.yaml

```
network:
  version: 2
  renderer: networkd
  ethernets:
    enp7s0:
      dhcp4: true
```

The runtime file generated by Netplan for network configuration will be located in **/var/run/systemd/network** and will have a name that includes "netplan" and the network device name, such as **10-netplan-enp7s0.network**. This file is generated automatically at startup. If you have edited the Netplan configuration file or added a new one, and do not wish to restart your system, you can use the Netplan **generate** command to create the run time configuration file directly, and then use the **apply** command to have Netplan apply that configuration to your network connections.

```
sudo netplan generate
sudo netplan apply
```

You then have to shut down and disable NetworkManager. The service script for managing NetworkManager is **network-manager**.

```
sudo systemctl stop network-manager
sudo systemctl disable network-manager
```

Then enable and start systemd-networkd.

```
sudo systemctl enable systemd-networkd
sudo systemctl start systemd-networkd
```

You can check the status of your network device configuration and activation with the **networkctl** command.

```
networkctl
```

Netplan wireless configuration for systemd-networkd

For systemd-networkd wireless devices you have to edit your Netplan configuration file to add your wireless device name, the wireless network you want to access, and the password for that network. Instead of editing the default file directly, you can copy the **02-dhcp.yaml** file with the 2 changed to 3 and give it a name such as **03-wireless.yaml**. Netplan will read any **yaml** file in the **/etc/netplan** folder. You can find an example of a wireless configuration file at **/usr/share/doc/netplan/examples**, but it is for the network that does not support dhcp and is more complicated.

```
cd /etc/netplan
sudo cp 2-dhcp.yaml 03-wireless.yaml
```

Then edit the file to add keys for Wi-Fi, accesspoints, the SSID, and the password.

```
sudo nano 3-wireless.yaml
```

An example of a wireless Netplan configuration is shown below. Instead of the **ethernets:** definition you use the **wifis:** definition. This is followed by a key consisting of the wireless device name, such as **wlp6s0:**. Below that key is the **dhcp4:** ID and the **accesspoints:** ID, used to configure the Wi-Fi device. Under the accesspoints: ID you add an ID consisting of the SSID of the wireless network you want to connect to (the wireless network's name). The SSID must be within quotes. Under this ID you add the **password:** ID and the password for accessing that wireless network. The password must be within quotes.

/etc/netplan/03-wireless.yaml

```
network:
  version: 2
  renderer: networkd
  wifis:
    wlp6s0:
      dhcp4: true
       accesspoints:
           "SSID":
                password: "password"
```

Netplan generates a wireless configuration file at startup in **/run/netplan**. A wireless file will have the name of the device added along with the name of wireless network (SSID), such as **netplan-wlp6s0-surfturtle**.

This file is then used the by **netplan-wpa@service** to submit the SSID and password to **wpa_supplicant**, which then accesses the wireless network. The **netplan-wpa@.service** file is shown here.

netplan-wpa@.service

```
[Unit]
Description=WPA supplicant for netplan %I
Requires=sys-subsystem-net-devices-%i.device
After=sys-subsystem-net-devices-%i.device
Before=network.target
Wants=network.target

[Service]
Type=simple
ExecStart=/sbin/wpa_supplicant -c /run/netplan/wpa-%I.conf -i%I
```

If you reboot, the wireless netplan file will be read and your wireless device configured. To configure your device without rebooting, you can use the Netplan **generate** command to create the run time configuration file directly (**/var/run/systemd/network**), and then use the **apply** command to have Netplan apply that configuration to your network connection.

```
sudo netplan generate
sudo netplan apply
```

Then restart systemd-networkd.

```
sudo systemctl restart systemd-networkd
```

You can use the **networkctl** command to see if your wireless device has been properly configured and is connected. The **networkctl** command works only for systemd-networkd..

$ networkctl

```
IDX LINK            TYPE             OPERATIONAL SETUP
  1 lo              loopback         carrier     unmanaged
  2 enp7s0          ether            routable    configured
  3 wlp6s0          wlan             routable    configured

3 links listed.
```

Switching between systemd-networkd and network-manager

Your original Netplan configuration file for NetworkManager, **01-network-manager-all.yaml**, should still be in your **/etc/netplan** folder.

To change from systemd-networkd back to NetworkManager, first stop and disable systemd-networkd with the **systemctl** command.

```
sudo systemctl stop systemd-networkd
sudo systemctl disable systemd-networkd
```

Then enable and start NetworkManager. Use the service name for NetworkManager, **network-manager**. Also, remove or move the systemd-networkd netplan file in the **/etc/netplan** folder so that it is not read. You could also just rename the extension.

```
sudo systemctl enable network-manager
sudo systemctl start network-manager
sudo mv /etc/netplan/netplan/02-dhcp.yaml /home
```

You can use the **status** command for **systemctl** to see if your network device is active or inactive.

```
systemctl status systemd-networkd
systemctl status network-manager
```

To change back to systemd-networkd, disable NetworkManager and enable systemd-networkd. Also add your systemd-networkd netplan file back to the **/etc/netplan** folder.

```
sudo systemctl stop network-manager
sudo systemctl disable network-manager
sudo systemctl enable systemd-networkd
sudo systemctl start systemd-networkd
```

If your NetworkManager file is, for some reason, missing from the **/etc/netplan** folder, you can just copy the **network_manager.yaml** file from the **netplan.io** doc folder, **/usr/share/doc/netplan/examples**.

```
cd /usr/share/doc/netplan/examples
sudo cp network_manager.yaml  /etc/netplan/1-network-manager-all.yaml
```

Then use the **netplan** command with the **apply** option to generate a new network configuration file.

```
sudo netplan generate
sudo netplan apply
```

Firewalls

You can choose from several different popular firewall management tools. Ubuntu provides a firewall management tool called the Uncomplicated Firewall (ufw), which is a frontend for IPtables. You can also choose to use other popular management tools like FirewallD or Fwbuilder. Both ufw and FirewallD are covered in this chapter. Search Synaptic Package Manager for "firewall" to see a complete listing.

IPtables has been replaced by nftables. Whereas IPtables works like an interpreter, processing each individual rule one at a time, nftables operates more like a programming language, able to handle many rules at once on incoming packets. On Linux Mint 21 and on Ubuntu 22.04, the **/sbin/iptables** command is a link to the **/etc/alternatives/iptables** command, which, in turn, is a link to the **/usr/sbin/iptables-nft-multi**, which is one of the **iptables-nft** commands such as **iptables-nft-save** and **iptables-nft-restore**. The **iptables-nft** commands read IPtables rules and convert them to nftables format using the **nft_compat** module. Though the ufw frontend manages IPtables rules, these rules are converted and used by nftables. FirewallD, on the other hand, operates as a frontend for nftables directly. Also, if you have to add rules directly to your firewall and need to covert from IPtables to nftables, you can use the **iptables-translate** command. The **iptables-translate** command takes as its argument an IPtables rule and generates the nftables equivalent. You can find out more about nftables at: **https://wiki.nftables.org/**.

Important Firewall Ports

Commonly used services like Linux and Windows file sharing, FTP servers, BitTorrent, and Secure SHell remote access, use certain network connection ports on your system (see Table 15-4). A default firewall configuration will block these ports. You have to configure your firewall to allow access to the ports these services use before the services will work.

For example, to access a Windows share, you not only have to have the Samba service running, but also have to configure your firewall to allow access on ports 135, 137, 138, and 445 (the ports Samba services use to connect to Windows systems), and port 5353 used for multicast DNS discovery (Avahi). Most can be selected easily as preconfigured items in firewall configuration tools, like Gufw and FirewallD. Some, though, may not be listed.

Port number	Service
135,137,138,and 445	Samba ports 135 and 445 use the TCP Protocol, and 137 and 138 use the UDP protocol.
139	Netbios-ssn
22	Secure SHell, ssh
2049	NFS, Linux and Unix shares
631	IPP, Internet Printing Protocol, access to remote Linux/Unix printers
21	FTP
25	SMTP, forward mail
110	POP3, receive mail
143	IMAP, receive mail
5353	multicast DNS discovery service (mdns), Zeroconf

Table 15-4: Service ports

Setting up a firewall with ufw

The Uncomplicated Firewall, ufw, is the supported firewall application for Ubuntu. It provides a simple firewall that can be managed with the Gufw desktop interface or with **ufw** commands. ufw uses the IPtables format to define rules and run the firewall. The ufw application is just a management interface for IPtables rules. The IPtables rule files are held in the **/etc/ufw** directory. Default IPtables rules are kept in **before** and **after** files, with added rules in user files.

Firewall configuration for certain packages will be placed in the **/usr/share/ufw.d** directory. Keep in mind, that these IPtable rules are automatically converted for use by nftables. nftables is the actual firewall backend for Ubuntu 22.04. You can find out more about ufw at the Ubuntu Firewall site at **https://wiki.ubuntu.com/UncomplicatedFirewall** and at the Ubuntu firewall section in the Ubuntu Server Guide at **https://ubuntu.com/server/docs**. The Server Guide also shows information on how to implement IP Masquerading on ufw.

Gufw

Gufw provides an easy to use GNOME interface for managing your ufw firewall. A simple interface lets you add rules, both custom and standard. You can install Gufw from Ubuntu Software as Firewall Configuration (Snap repository) or from the Synaptic Package Manager (Universe repository, **gufw** package). On the Applications overview, search on firewall and choose Firewall Configuration. If Gufw does not start, you may also have to install the **python-gobject** package.

```
sudo apt-get install python-gobject
```

Gufw will initially open with the firewall disabled, with no ports configured. The application is locked initially. The Status button is set to off, and the shield image will be gray. To enable the firewall, click the left side of the Status button, setting the status to on. The shield image will be colored and the firewall rules will be listed. Figure 15-18 shows the firewall enabled and several rules listed. Rules for both IPv4 and IPv6 (**v6**) network protocols are listed.

Figure 15-18: Gufw

The Gufw dialog has a Firewall section and three tabs: Rules, Report, and Log. The Firewall section has a Status button for turning the firewall on or off. There is a Profile menu for Home, Office, and Public configurations. The Incoming and Outgoing drop down menus are for setting the default firewall rules. Available options are Deny, Reject, or Allow, and are applied to incoming and outgoing traffic, respectively. By default, incoming traffic is denied (Deny), and outgoing traffic is allowed (Allow). Rules you specified in the Rules tab will make exceptions, allowing only certain traffic in or out. Should you select the Allow option, the firewall accepts all incoming traffic. In this case you should set up rules to deny access to some traffic, otherwise, the firewall becomes ineffective, allowing access to all traffic. The Report tab lists active services and ports such as the Samba server on port 139. The Log tab list firewall notices. You can copy notices, as well as delete a log. The Home tab provides basic help on how to use Gufw.

To add a rule, click the Rules tab, and then click the plus button (+) on the lower left corner of the Rules tab to open the "Add a Firewall Rule" dialog, which has three tabs for managing rules: Preconfigured, Simple, and Advanced. The Preconfigured tab provides five menus: the first for the policy (Allow, Deny, Reject, and Limit), the second for the traffic direction (In or Out), the third for the category of the application and the fourth for a subcategory, and the fifth for the particular application or service for the rule. The list of possible applications is extensive. You can narrow the list down by using the Category and Subcategory menus. The main categories are Audio video, Games, Network, Office, and System. The Network category with the Services subcategory lists most network services like SSH, Samba, and FTP. You could also simply use the search box (Application Filter) to search for a service.

If there is a security issue with the rule, a warning is displayed. Should you need to modify the default rule for an application, you can click on the arrow button to the right of the search box to open the Advanced tab for that rule.

Click the Add button to add the rule. Once added a port entry for the rule appears in the Rules section. In Figure 15-19 the Samba service has been selected and then added, showing up in the Rules section as "137,138/udp ALLOW IN Anywhere."

Figure 15-19: Gufw Preconfigured rules

Applications and services can also be blocked. To prevent access by the FTP service, you would first select Deny, then Service, and then the FTP entry.

Besides Allow and Deny, you can also choose a Limit option. The Limit option will enable connection rate limiting, restricting connections to no more than 6 every 30 seconds for a given port. This is meant to protect against brute force attacks.

Figure 15-20: Gufw Simple rules

Should there be no preconfigured entry, you can use the Simple tab to allow access to a port (see Figure 15-20). The first menu is for the rule (Allow, Deny, Reject, and Limit), and the second for the protocol (TCP, UDP, or both). In the Port text box, you enter the port number.

On the Advanced tab, you can enter more complex rules. You can set up allow or deny rules for tcp or udp protocols, and specify the incoming and outgoing host (ip) and port (see Figure 15-21).

Figure 15-21: Gufw Advanced rules

If you decide to remove a rule, select it in the Rules section and then click the minus button on the lower left corner (-). To remove several rules, click and press Shift-click or use Ctrl-click to select a collection of rules, and then click the minus button.

You can edit any rule by selecting it and clicking the edit button (gear image) to open an "Update a Firewall Rule" dialog (see Figure 15-22). For a default or simple rule, you can only change a few options, but you can turn on logging.

Figure 15-22: Gufw edit a rule

You can also create rules for detected active ports. Click the Report tab and then select a port and click on the plus button at the bottom of the tab. An "Add a Firewall Rule" dialog opens to the Advanced tab with the name of the service active on that port and the port number (see Figure 15-23). You can change any of the options. The port number is already entered.

Should you want to you can pause any activity on a port by selecting it and clicking the pause button at the bottom of the tab. The button will change to a play button. Select the port and click the play button to activate the port.

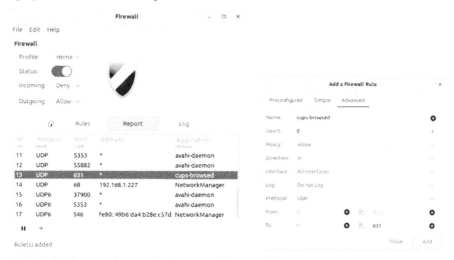

Figure 15-23: Gufw create a rule for an active port

ufw commands

You can also manage your ufw firewall using **ufw** commands entered on a command line in a Terminal window. A **ufw** command requires administrative access and must be run with the **sudo** command. To check the current firewall status, listing those services allowed or blocked, use the **status** command.

```
sudo ufw status
```

If the firewall is not enabled, you first will have to enable it with the **enable** command.

```
sudo ufw enable
```

You can restart the firewall, reloading your rules, using the **systemctl** command with the **restart** option.

```
sudo systemctl restart ufw
```

You can add rules using allow and deny rules and their options as listed in Table 15-5. To allow a service, specify the allow rule and the service name. This is the name for the service listed in the **/etc/services** file. For connection rate limiting, use the **limit** option in place of **allow**. The following allows the ftp service.

```
sudo ufw allow ftp
```

Commands	Description
enable | disable	Turn the firewall on or off
status	Display status along with services allowed or denied.
logging on | off	Turn logging on or off
default allow | deny	Set the default policy, allow is open, whereas deny is restrictive
allow *service*	Allow access by a service. Services are defined in **/etc/services**, which specify the ports for that service.
allow *port /protocol*	Allow access on a particular port using specified protocol.
deny *service*	Deny access by a service
delete *rule*	Delete an installed rule, use allow, deny, or limit and include rule specifics.
proto *protocol*	Specify protocol in allow, deny, or limit rule
from *address*	Specify source address in allow, deny, or limit rule
to *address*	Specify destination address in allow, deny, or limit rule
port *port*	Specify port in allow, deny, or limit rule for from and to address

Table 15-5: UFW firewall operations

If the service you want is not listed in **/etc/services**, and you know the port and protocol it uses, you can specify the port and protocol directly. For example, the Samba service uses port 445 and protocol tcp (among others, see Table 15-4).

```
sudo ufw allow 445/tcp
```

The status operation shows what services the firewall rules allow.

```
sudo ufw status
To                  Action        From
21:tcp              ALLOW         Anywhere
21:udp              ALLOW         Anywhere
139,445:tcp           ALLOW            Anywhere
```

To remove a rule, prefix it with the **delete** command.

```
sudo ufw delete allow 445/tcp
```

More detailed rules can be specified using address, port, and protocol commands. These are very similar to the actual IPtables commands. Packets to and from particular networks, hosts, and ports can be controlled. The following denies ssh access (port 22) from host 192.168.03.

```
sudo ufw deny proto tcp from 192.168.03 to any port 22
```

ufw rule files

The rules you add are placed in the **/etc/ufw/user.rules** file as IPtables rules. The ufw program is just a front end for **iptables-restore**, which will read this file and set up the firewall using **iptables** commands. **ufw** will also have **iptables-restore** read the **before.rules** and **after.rules** files in the **/etc/ufw** folder. These files are considered administrative files that include needed supporting rules for your IPtables firewall. Administrators can add their own IPtables rules to these files for system specific features like IP Masquerading. The **before.rules** file will specify a table with the * symbol, as in ***filter** for the netfilter table. For the NAT table, you would use ***nat**. At the end of each table segment, a COMMIT command is needed to instruct ufw to apply the rules. Rules use **-A** for allow and **-D** for deny, assuming the **iptables** command.

Default settings for ufw are placed in **/etc/default/ufw**. Here you will find the default INPUT, OUTPUT, and FORWARD policies specified by setting associated variables, like DEFAULT_INPUT_POLICY for INPUT and DEFAULT_OUTPUT_POLICY for OUTPUT. The DEFAULT_INPUT_POLICY variable is set to DROP, making DROP the default policy for the INPUT rule. The DEFAULT_OUTPUT_POLICY variable is set to ACCEPT, and the DEFAULT_FORWARD_POLICY variable is set to DROP. To allow IP Masquerading, DEFAULT_FORWARD_POLICY would have to be set to ACCEPT. These entries set default policies only. Any user rules you have set up would take precedence.

FirewallD and firewall-config

Though not supported by Ubuntu directly, you can use the FirewallD dynamic firewall daemon to set up a firewall. FirewallD operates as a frontend for nftables, directly. To configure FirewallD you use the **firewalld-config** desktop interface. You can also use **firewalld-cmd** command from the command line. You can install firewalld-config as Firewall on Ubuntu Software. Both the FirewallD daemon and the firewalld-config packages are installed. To set up your firewall, run **firewall-config** (the Firewall icon in the Applications overview) (see Figure 15-24).

You can also start and stop the FirewallD daemon in a terminal window with the following command.

```
sudo systemctl start firewalld
sudo systemctl stop firewalld
```

With **firewall-config,** you can configure either a Runtime or Permanent configuration. Select one from the Configuration menu. The Runtime configuration shows your current runtime set up, whereas a Permanent configuration does not take effect until you reload or restart. If you wish to edit your zones and services, you need to choose the Permanent Configuration (see Figure 15-25). This view displays a zone toolbar for editing zone at the bottom of the zone scroll box, and an Edit Services button on the Services tab for editing service protocols, ports, and destination addresses.

Figure 15-24: firewall-config: Runtime Configuration

Additional tabs can be displayed from the View menu for configuring ICMP types, and for adding firewall rules directly (Direct Configuration).

From the Options menu, you can reload your saved firewall.

Figure 15-25: firewall-config: Permanent Configuration

A firewall configuration is set up for a given zone, such as a home, work, internal, external, or public zone. Zones provide an added level of protection by the firewall. They divide the network protected by the Firewall into separate segments, which can only communicate as permitted by the firewall. In effect, zones separate one part of your network from another. Each zone has its own configuration. Zones are listed in the Zone scroll box on the left side of the firewall-config window. Select the one you want to configure. The firewall-config window opens to the default, Public. You can choose the default zone from the System Default Zone dialog (see Figure 15-26), which you open from the Options menu as "Change Default Zone."

To the left of the Zones tab is the Active Bindings section, which list the network connections, interfaces, and sources on your system. For each active connection the zone bound to it is listed, such as the public zone bound to the wired connection in Figure 15-26. To change the zone bound to a connection you select the entry and click the Change Zone button at the bottom of the Active Binding section. This open a Select zone dialog where you can choose a different zone to be bound to a connection. You can choose from any of the zones in the zones tab. You can also change a connection binding from the Options menu by choosing "Change Zones of Connections."

Default Zone   ×

Please select default zone from the list below.

block
dmz
drop
external
home
internal
nm-shared
public
trusted
work

Cancel   OK

Figure 15-26: Default Zone

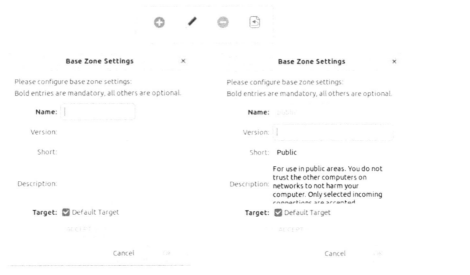

Figure 15-27: Base Zone Settings

If you choose Permanent Configuration from the Current View Menu, a toolbar for zones is displayed below the Zone scroll box. The plus button lets you add a zone and the minus button removes a zone. The pencil button lets you edit a zone. The add and edit buttons open the Base Zone Settings dialog, where you enter or edit the zone name, version, description, and the target (see Figure 15-27). The default target is ACCEPT. Other options are REJECT and DROP. The Load Zone Defaults button (yellow arrow) loads default settings, removing any you have made.

Each zone, in turn, can have one or more network connections. From the Options menu choose "Change Zones of Connections" to select a network connection for the zone.

For a given zone you can configure services, ports, masquerading, port forwarding, and ICMP filter. A Linux system is often used to run servers for a network. If you are creating a strong firewall but still want to run a service such as a Web server, an FTP server, Samba desktop browsing, or SSH encrypted connections, you must specify them in the Services tab. Samba desktop browsing lets you access your Samba shares, like remote Windows file systems, from your GNOME desktop.

For a selected service, you can specify service settings such as ports and protocols it uses, any modules, and specific network addresses. Default settings are already set up for you such as port 139 for Samba, using the TCP protocol. To modify the settings for a service, click the Services tab on the Firewall Configuration window to list your services (see Figure 15-28). Choose the service you want to edit from the Service scroll box at the left. For a given service you can then use the Ports, Protocols, Source Port, Modules, and Destination tabs to specify ports, protocols, modules, and addresses. On the Ports tab, click the Add button to open the Port and Protocol dialog where you can add a port or port range, and choose a protocol from the Protocol menu (see Figure 15-29). On the Destination tab, you can enter an IPv4 or IPv6 destination address for the service.

Figure 15-28: Service Settings

Figure 15-29: Service Protocols and Ports

On the Zones tab, the Ports tab lets you specify ports that you may want opened for certain services, like BitTorrent. Click the Add button to open a dialog where you can select the port number along with the protocol to control (tcp or udp), or enter a specific port number or range.

If your system is being used as a gateway to the Internet for your local network, you can implement masquerading to hide your local hosts from outside access from the Internet. This, though, also requires IP forwarding which is automatically enabled when you choose masquerading. Local hosts will still be able to access the Internet, but they will masquerade as your gateway system. You would select for masquerading the interface that is connected to the Internet. Masquerading is available only for IPv4 networks, not IPv6 networks.

The Port Forwarding tab lets you set up port forwarding, channeling transmissions from one port to another, or to a different port on another system. Click the Add button to add a port, specifying its protocol and destination (see Figure 15-30).

Figure 15-30: Port Forwarding

Figure 15-31: ICMP Filters

The ICMP Filters tab allows you to block ICMP messages. By default, all ICMP messages are allowed. Blocking ICMP messages makes for a more secure system. Certain types of ICMP messages are often blocked as they can be used to infiltrate or overload a system, such as the ping and pong ICMP messages (see Figure 15-31).

If you have specific firewall rules to add, use the Direct Configuration tab (displayed from the View | Direct Configuration menu).

GNOME Nettool

The GNOME Nettool utility (**gnome-nettool**) provides a GNOME interface for network information tools like the ping and traceroute operations as well as Finger, Whois, and Lookup for querying users and hosts on the network (see Figure 15-32). You can install it from the Ubuntu Software Center as Network Tools. Nettool is then accessible from the Applications overview as Network Tools. The first tab, Devices, describes your connected network devices, including configuration and transmission information about each device, such as the hardware address and bytes transmitted. Both IPv4 and IPv6 host IP addresses are listed.

You can use the ping, finger, lookup, whois, and traceroute operations to find out status information about systems and users on your network. The ping operation is used to check if a remote system is up and running. You use finger to find out information about other users on your network, seeing if they are logged in or if they have received mail. The traceroute tool can be used to track the sequence of computer networks and systems your message passed through on its way to you. Whois will provide domain name information about a particular domain, and Lookup will provide both domain name and IP addresses. Netstat shows your network routing (addresses used) and active service (open ports and the protocols they use). Port Scan lists the ports and services they use on a given connection (address).

Figure 15-32: Gnome network tool

Predictable and unpredictable network device names

Network devices now use a predictable naming method that differs from the older naming method. Names are generated based on the specific device referencing the network device type, its hardware connection and slot, and even its function. The traditional network device names used the **eth** prefix with the number of the device for an Ethernet network device. The name **eth0** referred to the first Ethernet connection on your computer. This naming method was considered unpredictable as it did not accurately reference the actual Ethernet device. The old system relied on probing the network driver at boot, and if you're your system had several Ethernet connections, the names could end up being switched, depending you how the startup proceeded. With systemd udev version 197, the naming changed to a predictable method that specifies a particular device. The predictable method references the actual hardware connection on your system.

Name	Description
sen	Ethernet
sl	serial line IP (slip)
wl	wlan, wireless local area network
ww	wwan, wireless wide area network (mobile broadband)
p	pci geographical location (pci-e slot)
s	hotplug slot index number
o	onboard cards
f	function (used for cards with more than one port)
u	USB port
i	USB port interface

Table 15-6: Network Interface Device Naming

The name used to reference predictable device names connection has a prefix for the type of device followed by several qualifiers such as the type of hardware, the slot used, and the function number. Instead of the older unpredictable name like **eth0**, the first Ethernet device is referenced by a name like **enp7s0**. The interface name **enp7s0** references an Ethernet (en) connection, at pci slot 7 (p7) with the hotplug slot index number 0 (s0). **wlp6s0** is a wireless (wl) connection, at pci slot 6 (p6) with the hotplug slot index number 0 (s0). **virvb0** is a virtual (vir) bridge network (vb) interface. Table 15-6 lists predictable naming prefixes. Unlike the older unpredictable name, the predictable name will most likely be different for each computer. Predictable network names, along with alternatives, are discussed at:

```
https://www.freedesktop.org/wiki/Software/systemd/PredictableNetworkInterfaceName
s/
```

The naming is carried out by the kernel and is describe in the comment section of the kernel source's **systemd/src/udev/udev-bultin-net_id.c** file.

Network device path names

The folder **/sys/devices** lists all your devices in subfolders, including your network devices. The path to the devices progresses through subfolders named for the busses connecting the device. To quickly find the full path name, you can us the **/sys/class** folder instead. For network devices use **/sys/class/net**. Then use the **ls -l** command to list the network devices with their links to the full pathname in the **/sys/devices** folder (the **../..** path references a cd change up two folders (class/net) to the **/sys** folder).

```
$ cd /sys/class/net
$ ls
enp7s0  lo  wlp6s0
$ ls -l
total 0
lrwxrwxrwx 1 root root 0 Feb 19 12:27 enp7s0 ->
../../devices/pci0000:00/0000:00:1c.3/0000:07:00.0/net/enp7s0
lrwxrwxrwx 1 root root 0 Feb 19 12:27 lo -> ../../devices/virtual/net/lo
lrwxrwxrwx 1 root root 0 Feb 19 12:28 wlp6s0 ->
../../devices/pci0000:00/0000:00:1c.2/0000:06:00.0/net/wlp6s0
```

So the full path name in the **/sys/devices** folder for **enp7s0** is:

```
/sys/devices/pci0000:00/0000:00:1c.3/0000:07:00.0/net/enp7s0
```

You can find the pci bus slot used with the **lspci** command. This command lists all your pci connected devices. In this example, the pci bus slot used 7, which is why the pci part of the name **enp7s0** is **p7**. The **s** part refers to a hotplug slot, in this example **s0**.

```
$ lspci
06:00.0 Network controller: Qualcomm Atheros QCA9565 / AR9565 Wireless Network
Adapter (rev 01)
07:00.0 Ethernet controller: Realtek Semiconductor Co., Ltd. RTL8101/2/6E PCI
Express Fast/Gigabit Ethernet controller (rev 07)
```

Devices have certain properties defined by udev, which manages all devices. Some operations, such as systemd link files, make use these properties. The ID_PATH, ID_NET_NAME_MAC, and INTERFACE properties can be used to identify a device to udev. To display these properties, you use the **udevadm** command to query the udev database. With the **info** and **-e** options, properties of all active devices are displayed. You can pipe (|) this output to a **grep** command to display only those properties for a given device. In the following example, the properties for the **enp7s0** device are listed. Preceding the properties for a given device is a line, beginning (^) with a "P" and ending with the device name. The **.*** matching characters match all other intervening characters on that line, **^P.*enp7s0**. The **-A** option displays the specified number of additional lines after that match, **-A 22**.

```
$ udevadm info -e | grep -A 22 ^P.*enp7s0
P: /devices/pci0000:00/0000:00:1c.3/0000:07:00.0/net/enp7s0
E: DEVPATH=/devices/pci0000:00/0000:00:1c.3/0000:07:00.0/net/enp7s0
E: ID_BUS=pci
E: ID_MM_CANDIDATE=1
E: ID_MODEL_FROM_DATABASE=RTL8101/2/6E PCI Express Fast/Gigabit Ethernet
controller
E: ID_MODEL_ID=0x8136
E: ID_NET_DRIVER=r8169
E: ID_NET_LINK_FILE=/lib/systemd/network/99-default.link
E: ID_NET_NAME_MAC=enx74e6e20ec729
E: ID_NET_NAME_PATH=enp7s0
E: ID_OUI_FROM_DATABASE=Dell Inc.
E: ID_PATH=pci-0000:07:00.0
E: ID_PATH_TAG=pci-0000_07_00_0
E: ID_PCI_CLASS_FROM_DATABASE=Network controller
E: ID_PCI_SUBCLASS_FROM_DATABASE=Ethernet controller
E: ID_VENDOR_FROM_DATABASE=Realtek Semiconductor Co., Ltd.
E: ID_VENDOR_ID=0x10ec
E: IFINDEX=2
E: INTERFACE=enp7s0
E: SUBSYSTEM=net
E: SYSTEMD_ALIAS=/sys/subsystem/net/devices/enp7s0
E: TAGS=:systemd:
E: USEC_INITIALIZED=1080179
```

For certain tasks, such as renaming, you many need to know the MAC address. You can find this with the **ip link** command, which you can abbreviate to **ip l**. The MAC address is before the brd string. In this example, the MAC address for **enp7s0** is 74:e6:e2:0e:c7:29. The **ip link** command also provides the MTU (Maximum Transmission Unit) and the current state of the connection.

```
$ ip link
1: lo: <LOOPBACK,UP,LOWER_UP> mtu 65536 qdisc noqueue state UNKNOWN mode DEFAULT
group default qlen 1 link/loopback 00:00:00:00:00:00 brd 00:00:00:00:00:00
2: enp7s0: <BROADCAST,MULTICAST,UP,LOWER_UP> mtu 1500 qdisc fq_codel state UP
mode DEFAULT group default qlen 1000 link/ether 74:e6:e2:0e:c7:29 brd
ff:ff:ff:ff:ff:ff
3: wlp6s0: <BROADCAST,MULTICAST> mtu 1500 qdisc noop state DOWN mode DEFAULT
group default qlen 1000 link/ether 4c:bb:58:22:40:1d brd ff:ff:ff:ff:ff:ff
```

Renaming network device names with udev rules

If you should change your hardware, like your motherboard with its Ethernet connection, or, if you use an Ethernet card and simply change the slot it is connected to, then the name will change. For firewall rules referencing a particular Ethernet connection, this could be a problem.

606	*Part 4: Administration*

You can, if you wish, change the name to one of your own choosing, even using the older unpredictable names. This way you would only have to update the name change, rather than all your rules and any other code that reference the network device by name.

You can change device name by adding a user udev rule for network device names. Changes made with udev rules work for both NetworkManager and systemd-networkd. In the **/etc/udev/rules.d** folder, create a file with the **.rules** extension and prefixed by a number less than 80, such as **70-my-net-names.rules**.The .rules files in **/etc/udev/rules.d** take precedence over those in the udev system folder, **/lib/udev/rules.d**.

In the udev rule, identify the subsystem as net (SUBSYSTEM=="net"), the action to take as add (ACTION=="add")), then the MAC address (ATTR[address}, the address attribute). Use **ip link** to obtain the mac address. The MAC address is also listed as the ID_NET_NAME_MAC entry in the **udevadm info** output (be sure to remove the prefix and add intervening colons). Use the NAME field to specify the new name for the device. Use the single = operator to make the name assignment.

/etc/udev/rules.d/70-my-net-names.rules

```
SUBSYSTEM=="net", ACTION=="add", ATTR{address}=="74:e6:e2:0e:c7:29", NAME="eth0"
```

To further specify the device you can add the kernel name (KERNEL) of the device. The kernel name is the INTERFACE entry.

```
SUBSYSTEM=="net", ACTION=="add", ATTR{address}=="74:e6:e2:0e:c7:29",
KERNEL=="enp7s0", NAME="eth0"
```

Renaming network device names for systemd-networkd with systemd.link

The systemd-networkd manager provides an alternate way to change network device names (keep in mind that an udev rule will also work for systemd-networkd). To change the name you would set up a systemd link file in the **/etc/systemd/network** folder. The **systemd.link** man page shows how to do this. A systemd link file consists of Match and Link sections. In the Match section you specify the network device, and in the Link section specify the name you want to give it. The network device can be referenced by its predictable name (Path) or MAC address (MACAddress).

The default systemd link file is **/lib/systemd/network/99-default.link**. The file has a Link section which lists policies to use in determining the name. The NamePolicy key lists the policies to be checked, starting with the kernel, then the udev database, udev firmware onboard information, udev hot-plug slot information, and the device path. In most cases, the slot policy is used. The MACAddressPolicy is set to persistent, for devices that have or need fixed MAC addresses.

99-default.link

```
[Link]
NamePolicy=keep kernel database onboard slot path
MACAddressPolicy=persistent
```

To rename a device, you would set up a systemd link file in the **/etc/systemd/network** folder. The **/etc/systemd** folder takes precedence over the **/lib/systemd** folder. A link file consists of a priority number, any name, and the **.link** extension. Lower numbers have a higher priority. In this example, the network device **enp7s0** has its named changed to **eth0**. The Match section uses the Path key to match on the device path, using the ID_PATH property for the device provided by udev.

You can query the udev database for information on your network device using the **udevadm info** command and match on the device. An added **grep** operation for ID_PATH= will display only the ID_PATH property.

```
$ udevadm info -e | grep -A 22 ^P.*enp7s0 | grep ID_PATH=
E: ID_PATH=pci-0000:07:00.0
```

For the Path key, use the udev ID_PATH value and a * glob matching character for the rest of the path. The Link section uses the Name key to specify the new name. The MacAddressPolicy should be set to persistent, indicating a fixed connection. Start the name of the link file with a number less than 99, so as to take precedence over the **99-default.link** file.

10-my-netname.link

```
[Match]
Path=pci-0000:07:00.0-*

[Link]
Name=eth0
MacAddressPolicy=persistent
```

Instead of the Path key, you could use the MACAddress key to match on the hardware address of the network device. The MAC address is udev ID_NET_NAME_MAC property without the prefix and with colons separation. The MAC address in this example is 74:e6:e2:0e:c7:29. You can also use **ip link** to find the MAC address (the numbers before **brd**).

10-my-netname.link

```
[Match]
MACAddress=74:e6:e2:0e:c7:29

[Link]
Name=eth0
MacAddressPolicy=persistent
```

Alternatively, you could use the OriginalName key in the Match section instead of the Path. The original name is the udev INTERFACE property, which also the name of the device as displayed by **ifconfig**.

10-my-netname.link

```
[Match]
OriginalName=enp7s0*

[Link]
Name=eth0
MacAddressPolicy=persistent
```

Table Listing

Figure Listing

Index

BASH

Made in the USA
Las Vegas, NV
04 April 2024

88263104R00361